CW00404457

INTERPRETING TRIPS

Protection of intellectual property rights (IPRs) has become a global issue. The Trade-Related Aspects of Intellectual Property (TRIPS) Agreement outlines the minimum standards for IPR protection for WTO members and offers a global regime for IPR protection. However, the benefits of TRIPS are more questionable in poorer countries where national infrastructure for research and development (R&D) and social protection are inadequate, whereas the cost of innovation is high. Today, after more than a decade of intense debate over global IPR protection, the problems remain acute, although there is also evidence of progress and cooperation.

This book examines various views of the role of IPRs as incentives for innovation against the backdrop of development and the transfer of technology between globalised, knowledge-based, high technology economies. The book retraces the origins, content and interpretations of the TRIPS Agreement, including its interpretations by WTO dispute settlement organs. It also analyses sources of controversy over IPRs, examining pharmaceutical industry strategies of emerging countries with different IPR policies.

The continuing international debate over IPRs is examined in depth, as are TRIPS rules and the controversy about implementing the 'flexibilities' of the Agreement in the light of national policy objectives. The author concludes that for governments in developing countries, as well as for their business and scientific communities, a great deal depends on domestic policy objectives and their implementation. IPR protection should be supporting domestic policies for innovation and investment. This, in turn requires a re-casting of the debate about TRIPS, to place cooperation in global and efficient R&D at the heart of concerns over IPR protection.

Interpreting TRIPS

Globalisation of Intellectual Property Rights and Access to Medicines

Hiroko Yamane

·HART·
PUBLISHING
OXFORD AND PORTLAND, OREGON
2011

Published in the United Kingdom by Hart Publishing Ltd
16C Worcester Place, Oxford, OX1 2JW
Telephone: +44 (0)1865 517530
Fax: +44 (0)1865 510710
E-mail: mail@hartpub.co.uk
Website: http://www.hartpub.co.uk

Published in North America (US and Canada) by
Hart Publishing
c/o International Specialized Book Services
920 NE 58th Avenue, Suite 300
Portland, OR 97213-3786
USA
Tel: +1 503 287 3093 or toll-free: (1) 800 944 6190
Fax: +1 503 280 8832
E-mail: orders@isbs.com
Website: http://www.isbs.com

© Hiroko Yamane 2011

Hiroko Yamane has asserted her right under the Copyright, Designs and Patents Act
1988, to be identified as the author of this work.

All rights reserved. No part of this publication may be reproduced, stored in a retrieval
system, or transmitted, in any form or by any means, without the prior permission of
Hart Publishing, or as expressly permitted by law or under the terms agreed with the
appropriate reprographic rights organisation. Enquiries concerning reproduction which
may not be covered by the above should be addressed to Hart Publishing Ltd at the address above.

British Library Cataloguing in Publication Data
Data Available

ISBN: 978-1-84113-953-1

Typeset by Hope Services, Abingdon
Printed and bound in Great Britain by
TJ International Ltd, Padstow, Cornwall

To Lélia

Foreword

The Agreement on Trade-Related Aspects of Intellectual Property Rights (the TRIPS Agreement) of the World Trade Organization (WTO) marks a watershed in the formation of international rules relating to the protection and enforcement of intellectual property rights. Along with the multilateral trade agreements on Agriculture, Textiles and Clothing, Services, and Dispute Settlement Mechanism, the TRIPS Agreement constitutes one of the new and most significant products of the Uruguay Round of Multilateral Trade Negotiations.

Although international conventions like the Paris Convention and the Berne Convention administered by the World Intellectual Property Organization (WIPO) did exist for the protection of certain intellectual property rights, the industrialized countries were keen to bring the subject of intellectual property rights within the ambit of the new multilateral trade rules mainly for two reasons. First, technology, especially in new and emerging fields, was increasingly becoming an important asset for them for maintaining competitiveness in world markets and for preservation and penetration of those markets. Protection of intellectual property and prevention of piracy in products such as films, computer software and medicines were seen to be critical for this purpose. Second, the conventions administered by WIPO, especially the Paris Convention relating to patents, were seen to be lacking not only with respect to their scope and substantive standards of protection, but more so with respect to effective enforcement of the intellectual property rights. The Single Undertaking concept and the Dispute Settlement Mechanism contemplated under the new multilateral trade rules would provide for effective enforcement of those rights and for cross-retaliation in the event of infringement of the intellectual property rights. On their part, the developing countries, although deeply apprehensive about the inclusion of substantive norms and standards for the protection of intellectual property rights in multilateral trade rules, felt that this would at least put an end to unilateral and arbitrary action being taken by some industrialized countries for presumed violation of those rights, besides ensuring the inclusion of Agriculture and Textiles and Clothing within the ambit of the new trade rules. Scholars generally agree that the nomenclature 'trade-related aspects' has been included in the title of the agreement only to confer legitimacy on the inclusion of the subject in the multilateral trade rules.

Stated simply, the term 'intellectual property' connotes a product arising from the creativity of the human mind and that has literary, artistic, industrial or commercial value or utility. The TRIPS Agreement encompasses the following categories of intellectual property: Copyright and Related Rights, Trademarks, Geographical Indications, Industrial Designs, Patents for living and non-living matter, Patents for micro-organisms and microbiological processes, Patents and/or Plant Breeders Rights for plant varieties, Layout-designs of Integrated Circuits, and Trade Secrets (Undisclosed Information). Besides ensuring the applicability of 'National Treatment', 'Most-Favoured Nation Treatment' and the Dispute Settlement Understanding (DSU) of the WTO, the Agreement prescribes substantive norms and standards for the availability and adequate and effective protection of those intellectual property rights. The Agreement makes it clear that these standards are in addition to those prescribed under the Paris Convention, the Berne Convention, the Rome Convention and the Washington Treaty on Integrated Circuits.

The TRIPS Agreement has received some general criticism from scholars such as that the subject of intellectual property rights belongs more properly to the jurisdiction of the WIPO, that it sets standards of protection which are too stringent and which are not suitable for developing countries, that it is a rent-seeking agreement skewed wholly in favour of the industrialized world, and that it will constrain the economic and technological development of the developing world. But the more specific and pointed criticism of the Agreement is in relation to three areas, namely, patents, especially for drugs, patenting of life forms, and protection of plant varieties. The protection given for other categories of intellectual property has not generated much criticism or controversy.

With respect to patents for drugs, the chief criticism is that product patents for drugs for as long as twenty years and the stringent conditions imposed for compulsory licensing would push up the drug prices to unaffordable levels in developing countries and that it would also stifle their indigenous capability for production of such drugs at affordable prices. This could have a severe effect particularly for maintaining the public health system for poor people and for making available drugs at cheaper prices for diseases like AIDS or cancer. This criticism may be valid to a certain extent, but the extent to which drug prices might generally rise because of patent protection, would depend on several factors, including mainly the nature of the drug and disease in question, the alternative drugs available for treatment, and the purchasing power in the market. The TRIPS Agreement does permit compulsory licensing based on the 'individual merits' of each case. What the Agreement prohibits is automatic or across-the-board licences as of right without hearing the rights holder. It would appear that if compulsory licensing is used selectively and judiciously in a clear case of public interest or need, with a view to increasing the availability of the drug and enhancing the competition in the domestic market, it would meet the requirements of the TRIPS Agreement. However, the question of compulsory licensing would arise for consideration only if there is an alternative manufacturer with the technological and financial capacity to manufacture the drug, and who finds it commercially viable to manufacture the drug for the domestic market and compete with the rights holder. This may not be the realistic situation in most developing countries but has become increasingly realistic for leading emerging economies like India and China.

The patenting of life forms raises a different set of concerns, including moral, ethical and environmental issues that go far beyond the realm of intellectual property protection per se. Patents are given not for discoveries, but for inventions that satisfy the criteria of novelty, inventive step and utility. In the case of inventions in the field of biotechnology, the dividing line between where discovery ends and invention begins is becoming increasingly blurred, as all such inventions build on pre-existing biological matter. The TRIPS Agreement does not define the term 'micro-organism', but it seems that any living matter that replicates by itself or via a host cell, including sub-cellular matter, would be covered by the term. Naturally occurring micro-organisms, that is, micro-organisms as they are found in their original or natural state, may not be patentable, but genetically altered or modified micro-organisms, that is, micro-organisms whose naturally occurring genetic make-up has been altered or modified to some extent, may qualify for patent if the criteria for patentability are satisfied. Thus, the nature and extent of human intervention as well as the nature and extent of the utility created by that intervention would determine whether the resulting product is a 'product of man' or 'product of nature' and whether it would qualify for patentability. Judicial pronouncements and patent office practices in the industrial countries, rather than clear cut legal provisions, are presently determining these questions applying what may be called the doctrine of 'man-made-ness', with varying degrees of consistency and clarity.

Bio-technology, including the mapping of the complete genome, identification of the genes responsible for the desired traits, and genetic manipulation, is the technology of the future for agriculture, medicine, industry and environment. Rather than being overly concerned with patents for non-living matter, developing countries would do well to devote increasing attention and resources to enhancing their knowledge and skills in understanding, assimilating and adopting bio-technology. This would also suit them well because of their biological wealth and because of the fact that bio-technology is less capital intensive and more skill and human resource intensive. This would also help them in curbing piracy or uncompensated use of their biological resources as well as in the preservation of their biodiversity.

As regards protection of plant varieties, the TRIPS Agreement requires that plant varieties must be protected by patents or by an effective *sui generis* system or by any combination of both. It is not, therefore, compulsory for any country to provide for patents in this area so long as they have an effective system for the protection of new plant varieties, typically called Plant Breeders Rights (PBR). The Agreement does not stipulate that any of the UPOV Conventions on PBRs would be the benchmark for judging the effectiveness of a *sui generis* system. Under the PBR system, the breeder of a new variety of a plant, that is, variety of a plant that satisfies the four basic criteria of 'novelty', 'distinctness', 'uniformity' and 'stability', is entitled to certain exclusive marketing rights for that variety for a specified duration. As with biotechnological inventions, developing countries would need to see the positive side of establishing a PBR system that would put to use their biological resources and traditional human skills in order to build a seed industry that could serve their needs as well as tap external markets. Such a system can take care of two main concerns in this area, namely, 'farmer's privilege' to use farm saved seed for replanting and 'researcher's privilege' to use a new plant variety in research for developing other new plant varieties. The system could also require the breeder to disclose the identity and source of the genetic material on which a new plant variety is based and to provide for appropriate remuneration for the use of such material. A good PBR system can also help in bringing in private investment and newer technology to the seed industry.

At the time of the Uruguay Round negotiations, the two agreements that were raising utmost apprehensions in the minds of developing countries were those on services (now GATS) and intellectual property (now TRIPS). Developing countries then felt that GATT (now WTO) should continue to deal with only merchandise trade and that new subjects like services, intellectual property or investment (now TRIMS) do not properly fall under its jurisdiction. The WTO has now been in existence for nearly fifteen years. It may be fair to say that the apprehensions over these agreements in most developing countries have considerably waned or, at any rate, their current apprehensions or demands are of a different nature. Several factors may be at play for this change in their outlook. Liberalization in their economic policies, rapid pace of globalization, faster economic growth and the utility of agreed-upon multilateral rules to curb unilateralism may be among these factors. Globalization has clearly shown that as long as markets are reasonably open for imports and exports, production of goods and services can be located at any place that offers the most competitive advantage. This in turn has set the pace for flows of foreign direct investment and technology and the need for policies that encourage such flows.

The key issue in intellectual property protection is not whether such property should be protected or whether the standards of protection are excessive, but how such protection is balanced or tempered with genuine public interest needs, when the protection given comes in to conflict with such needs. It is naïve to think that investment of capital and human skills and resources will take place on a tangible scale in innovation, creativity and research and development without adequate protection and enforcement of intellectual property rights, be they copyright, trademarks, trade secrets, patents or any other form of intellectual property. In particular, developing countries with large or lucrative domestic markets and a sufficient pool of technological skills and human resources can become the base for production of goods and services as well as for research and development activities in a globalizing world. The protection and enforcement of intellectual property in accordance with multilaterally agreed rules can play a vital role in attracting investment, especially technology-oriented investment, for production of goods and services both for the domestic and overseas markets. A positive attitude towards intellectual property protection can, over time, broaden and deepen the technological base of such countries, including the technological strength of their domestic firms. At the same time, selective and judicious intervention on the part of the governments may be necessary in circumstances where genuine public interest is hurt or where the right is abused by the rights holder. The flexibilities provided in the TRIPS Agreement must be used to deal with such exceptional cases keeping intact the basic framework of protecting and enforcing intellectual property rights.

Professor Hiroko Yamane has addressed these and other complex issues in her book with great erudition and scholarship. She has traced in detail the negotiating history of the TRIPS Agreement and the different viewpoints of developing and industrialized countries during the course of the Uruguay Round negotiations. She has also examined the nature and character of different categories of intellectual property, the views of scholars on the value of intellectual property protection as an incentive for innovation, and the legal implications and ambiguities in the protection of certain types of intellectual property, particularly the patenting of biotech inventions. She has also questioned the efficacy of certain hortatory provisions of the TRIPS Agreement in safeguarding the public interest needs of developing countries, noting that the Appellate Body of the WTO has not yet pronounced on them. She is skeptical about whether 'flexibilities' provided under the TRIPS Agreement would always benefit developing countries but she has advocated a balanced approach towards protection of intellectual property, with a futuristic outlook on emerging technologies, and that is characterized by objectivity and not dogmatism. I am certain that her book will be a valuable contribution to the growing literature on this subject.

Chennai, India
25 September 2010

A.V. Ganesan
Former Commerce Secretary
to the Government of India
and Former Member,
Appellate Body of the WTO

Acknowledgements

My parents took me to remote countries in Africa, Asia and Latin America when I was a young student. Undertaking research on globalisation of intellectual property rights in developing countries in the 1990s was for me a kind of homecoming. More recently, I am learning that the 'knowledge economy' is bringing remote peoples together and enabling them to discuss common challenges, of which the subject of this book is one.

For my understanding of the complexities of the subject, I owe a great deal to those people whom I met in different countries and in various organisations, dealing with the difficult tasks that lie beyond the polarising debate. It is my wish that the 'knowledge economy' will benefit those people who have always been dissociated from progress.

I wish to express my gratitude to AV Ganesan, the Indian negotiator during the Uruguay Round, former Secretary of Commerce to the Indian Government and former member of the WTO Appellate Body, who reminded me of the important balance to be struck between scientific/technological progress and public interest. His clarity of thinking, far-sighted vision and courage to face and analyse global questions from all angles will always be a source of my understanding of the subject of this book.

I would like to thank those specialists who read and commented on my manuscript. Jost Pauwelyn, Professor of International Law, Université de Neuchatel, made superb comments on chapters 6 and 7. Hannu Wager, Counsellor, Intellectual Property Division of the WTO, had the kindness to read chapter 5 and advised me on very important points. Shigeo Takakura, Professor at the Meiji University, read the entire manuscript and made precious comments. Sadao Nagaoka, Professor at Hitotsubashi University, Kensuke Kubo at the International Institute of Developing Economics and Dr Francesco Rosati, RBB Economics, Brussels, commented on chapter 1.

I am particularly thankful to Ruth Dreifuss, the Chair, the Secretariat and member colleagues of the Commission on Intellectual Property, Innovation and Public Health (CIPIH, 2003–06)[1] of the World Health Organization (WHO) for the stimulating and fruitful discussions, which nourished my further research.

I also benefited from the knowledge, insight and suggestions of Dr Heinz Redwood, health policy consultant, about the history of medicines, the pharmaceutical industry and healthcare services. I owe my understanding of AIDS treatment to the knowledge and experience of Dr Yasuhiro Nakatani,

---

[1] Members of the CIPIH were R Dreifuss (Chairperson), RA Mashelkar (Vice-Chair), C Correa, M Fathalla, M Freire, T Jones, T Matona, F Pammolli, P Pothisiri and the author.

Chief of Infectious Diseases, Maricopa Medical Center and Clinical Assistant Professor of Medicine, University of Arizona College of Medicine, Phoenix.

Dilip Shah, Secretary General of the Indian Pharmaceutical Association and Professor Sudip Chaudhuri, Indian Institute of Management, helped my understanding of the Indian Pharmaceutical Industry. Satoshi Nakajima and Isshin Shirasu, both attorneys, provided helpful insights into the Chinese Patent Law and its evolution.

I benefited also from discussions with Pedro Roffe, Senior Fellow at the International Centre for Trade and Sustainable Development (ICTSD) with his 30 years of experience with the United Nations Conference on Trade and Development (UNCTAD), on the nature of developing countries' policies towards intellectual property rights. Pedro and Kiyoshi Adachi, Chief, Intellectual Property Unit, Investment Capacity-Building Branch Division, UNCTAD, kindly read and commented on the parts of this book relating to the UNCTAD. Professor Felix Addor, University of Bern, and his colleagues at the Swiss Federal Institute of Intellectual Property kindly organised meetings for me to discuss different aspects of recent changes in European intellectual property laws and their implications for various industries, such as the biotechnology industry.

I would like to thank my colleagues at the National Graduate Institute for Policy Studies, Professors Koichi Sumikura and Donna Amoroso who provided me constant support. I am thankful also to the team of editors and producers at Hart Publishing and Richard Hart, with whom I have had the pleasure of having discussions on a wide spectrum of issues for many years.

However, the views expressed in this book remain solely the responsibility of the author.

10 December 2010

Hiroko Yamane
Professor, National Graduate Institute for Policy Studies
Tokyo

Contents

Table of Cases

NATIONAL

*Court of Justice of the European Union (formerly Court of Justice of the
    European Communities)*

General Court of the European Union (formerly Court of First Instance)

Table of Legislation

OTHER INTERNATIONAL INSTRUMENTS

EUROPEAN UNION LEGISLATION

Treaties

Directives

Introduction

IN 1995, THE Agreement on Trade-related Aspects of Intellectual Property Rights (TRIPS Agreement) entered into force for Members of the World Trade Organization (WTO). This Agreement outlines the minimum standards for intellectual property rights (IPRs) protection for WTO Members. It was presumed that the TRIPS Agreement would increase, on a global scale, incentives to invest in the research and development of new ideas and technologies.

In developing countries, however, resources for R&D are inadequate, and the cost of innovation is high; therefore, the long-term benefits to these countries of IPR protection may not be tangible, while losing the possibility of copying or of importing copies may have immediate social costs.

Since the adoption of the TRIPS Agreement, the fear of losing the supply of locally produced or imported generic drugs has naturally arisen. Local production or importation of new medicines without the consent of the right holder could encounter obstacles if product patent protection is introduced and the patent in question is actually registered in that country. Many essential medicines are off-patent and the existence of patents normally increases the availability of new medicines in developed countries.[1] However, without appropriate public policy measures, patented medicines could be too expensive to be accessible for those who lack purchasing power. Thus, health policy issues are often discussed in the context of local supply of medicines, sometimes intertwined with discussions of pharmaceutical industry policies.

Lack of access to medicines is an increasingly important issue in developing countries. In a 2003 report, the World Health Organization (WHO) estimated that 30 per cent of the world's population lacked access to essential medicines in 1999.[2] The improvements as of 2008 did not seem to be adequate. The United Nations reported that essential medicines were available for only 34.9 per cent

---

[1] Among the WHO list of essential medicines, the drugs that are still under patents that would effectively prevent generic entry are limited mostly to AIDS drugs and a few others. Among the products listed on the 16th WHO list of essential medicines, updated in March 2010 those medicines still under such patents in developed countries are treatment drugs for HIV/AIDS a combination malaria drug, and oseltamivir (antiviral for the treatment of avian flu) www.who.int/medicines/publications/essentialmedicines/en/index.html. See ch 8.

[2] WHO, *The World Medicines Situation* (Geneva, WHO, 2004), WHO/EDM/PAR/2004.5, 61–74: www.searo.who.int/LinkFiles/Reports_World_Medicines_Situation.pdf.

of public health services in 27 developing countries.[3] In developing countries, significantly, the cost of medicines accounts for 20–60 per cent[4] of health spending, and up to 90 per cent of the population pay out-of-pocket for medicines. In the Organisation for Economic Co-operation and Development (OECD) countries, by contrast, the cost of medicines accounts for only 18 per cent of the total healthcare bill, and remains stable.

Today, opinion is polarised as to what causes these difficulties in developing countries, as is reflected in the commentaries attached to the Final Report of the WHO Commission on Intellectual Property, Innovation and Public Health (CIPIH, 2003–06).[5] A growing number of developing countries assume the causes of these difficulties to be IPRs, whereas developed countries attribute the cause to the inadequacy of distribution, healthcare and insurance systems. The nature of the controversies over the effects of a domestic patent system on invention and innovation in developing countries may not be so different from what E Penrose observed in the 1970s. According to this pioneer economist, '. . . we have only the same type of evidence both for and against the arguments outlined as we have with regard to the effect of a domestic patent system on invention and innovation generally.'[6] Inherent difficulties are found in assessing the global, dynamic innovation effects of IPR protection, as they vary over time and depend on multiple factors other than IPRs.[7]

---

[3] United Nations, *Delivering on the Global Partnership for Achieving the Millennium Development Goals: MDG Gap Task Force Report 2008* (New York, United Nations, 2008) 36–43.

[4] A Cameron, M Ewen, D Ross-Degnan, D Ball, R Laing, 'Medicine prices, availability, and affordability in 36 developing and middle-income countries: a secondary analysis', www.thelancet.com, published online December 2008. Here, 'developing countries' include 'transition economies'.

[5] The CIPIH (www.who.int/intellectualproperty/) was established in May 2003 at the 56th World Health Assembly (WHA) by Resolution WHA56.27. The terms of reference for the work of CIPIH were to summarise the existing evidence on the prevalence and the social and economic impact of diseases of public health importance with an emphasis on those that particularly affect poor people; review the volume and distribution of existing research, development and innovation efforts directed at these diseases; consider the importance and effectiveness of intellectual property regimes and other incentive and funding mechanisms in stimulating research and the creation of new medicines and other products against these diseases; analyse proposals for improvements to the current incentive and funding regimes, including intellectual property rights, designed to stimulate the creation of new medicines and other products, and facilitate access to them; and produce concrete proposals for action by national and international stakeholders. The Final Report of this Commission was examined at the 59th WHA in May 2006 (www.who.int/intellectualproperty/documents/thereport/ENPublicHealthReport.pdf). The Commentaries Section of this Report is found at 201–18. The same WHA established the Intergovernmental Working Group on Intellectual Property, Innovation and Public Health (IGWG) with a view to adopting a global action plan based on the recommendations of the CIPIH. In May 2008, the 61st WHA adopted the Global Strategy and Plan of Action on public health, innovation and intellectual property, designed to promote innovation, build capacity, improve access and mobilise resources (WHA 61.21).

[6] ET Penrose, 'International Patenting and the Less-Developed Countries' (1973) 83 *The Economic Journal* 772.

[7] On the differing effects of IPR protection on different timeframes in various countries, see, for example, P McCalman, 'Who Enjoys TRIPs Abroad? An Empirical Analysis of Intellectual Property Rights in the Uruguay Round' (2005) 38(2) *Canadian Journal of Economics* chs 2 and 11 of this book. As for the pharmaceutical sector, see S Schweitzer, *Pharmaceutical Economics and Policy*, (Oxford University Press, 2007) ch 5.

Since the adoption of the TRIPS Agreement, the focus has shifted from socio-economic and political reasons to IPRs as a main factor preventing access to medicines.[8] A less hostile stance to IPR protection would have emerged, if, following the TRIPS Agreement, technologically skilful developing countries had quickly brought to market new pharmaceutical products that originated in inventions resulting from their own R&D. This, however, does not seem to be happening.[9]

Patents are usually filed in large markets where competitors or potential competitors exist, ie, in developed countries and, more recently, among emerging economies such as China and India in particular. As for medicines patents, the number of patients and the existence of wealthy segments of the population are also factors for patenting; the pricing behaviour of originator and generic companies differs significantly.[10]

Particularly in those developing countries where the technological level is relatively sophisticated, opinions on industrial policy and IPR protection may conflict, and the balance between the IP holder's rights and the public interest is particularly uncertain. This author observed this during study visits to different countries as a member of the CIPIH. Interestingly, in the controversy over IPR protection in these countries, both the arguments in favour of and the criticisms against the patent system drew examples mainly from US literature[11] and cases,[12] as well as from European political debate, rather than from developing country data.

In seeking ways to meet the rising demand for access to medicines in developing countries, the idea of promoting dynamic welfare through innovation has been subordinated to arguments that patents only hinder access to medicines by raising prices. Today, there is a widely held view that, for all developing countries, the weaker IPR protection is, the better access to medicines will be.

---

[8] See ch 2. In the 1980s, the fight against multinationals was at the forefront of political struggles in developing countries, much more than the fight against the patent system. See for example, G Velasquez, *L'Industrie du médicament et le tiers monde* (Paris, Edition l'Harmattan, 1983).

[9] See, for example, S Chaudhuri, 'Ranbaxy Sell-out: Reversal of Fortunes, *Economic & Political Weekly*, 19 July 2008; 'Death of a Dream', *Businessworld*, 30 January 2010 (www.businessworld.in/bw/2010_01_30_Death_Of_A_Dream.html); S Chaudhuri, 'Indian Pharmaceutical Industry after TRIPS', Paper presented at the technical consultation held on 11 December 2009 in New Delhi, as part of the United Nations Development Programme (UNDP) project on '5 years into Product Patent Regime: India's response', to be published by the UNDP (file with author).

[10] K Kubo and H Yamane, 'Determinants of HIV/AIDS Drug Prices for Developing Countries: Analysis of Global Fund Procurement Data' in H Uchimura (ed) *Making Health Services More Accessible in Developing Countries: Finance and Health Resources for Functioning Health Systems* (Palgrave MacMillan, 2009) 137–72. For the earlier version of this article, see www.ide.go.jp/English/Publish/Download/Jrp/pdf/142_05.pdf. For details on various determinants of ARV procurement prices, see ch 9 of this book.

[11] A widely recommended work in these countries seems to be AB Jaffe and J Lerner, *Innovation and Its Discontents: How Our Broken Patent System is Endangering Innovation and Progress and What to Do About It* (Princeton University Press, 2004).

[12] Later, the US Supreme Court decisions in *KSR International Co v Teleflex Inc* 550 US 398 (2007) and *eBay v MercExchange* 547 US 338 (2006) were often quoted in the courts of these countries, as we will see in chs 10 and 12.

During the Uruguay Round of trade negotiations (1986–94), the concept of 'constructive ambiguities' was key in reconciling negotiating parties who held conflicting opinions and who defended different industrial and commercial interests concerning the scope of IP protection. Today, the concept of 'flexibilities' has replaced this expression, and is used by almost all parties to achieve a vague political truce.

The TRIPS Agreement certainly provides a degree of 'flexibility' that allows countries to formulate a variety of national IPR and industrial or public policies, and to accommodate TRIPS rights and obligations within diverging national legal, institutional and procedural frameworks. Flexibility is therefore necessary and commendable, particularly because the impact of IPRs differs among countries in different technological or economic situations.

However, the interpretative rules concerning the boundaries of 'flexibilities' that are consistent with the rights and obligations under TRIPS have not been defined with precision, and the extent of permissible national discretion remains controversial. For example, specific practices such as compulsory licensing or exceptions are sometimes treated as matters of national discretion when in fact they are regulated by the TRIPS Agreement. Such 'flexibilities' seem to differ from the way the WTO dispute settlement organs interpret the margin of flexibility accorded by TRIPS provisions.[13]

The concept of 'flexibilities' is often supported by the expectation that they would *ipso facto* solve socio-economic problems allegedly created by IPRs, such as the lack of development, access to medicines, or environmental protection. The extent to which these 'flexibilities' have provided solutions to these problems has not been assessed and remains uncertain. In the meantime, a considerable amount of legal uncertainty in implementing and interpreting the TRIPS Agreement has been observed. In this context, further blurring of rules and boundaries of legal rights would not necessarily be helpful. Clarification of TRIPS rules is also needed so that they become effective as rules, providing legal security and predictability for viable international cooperation.

Rather than throwing unilaterally interpreted flexibilities of the TRIPS Agreement at each other and holding IPRs solely responsible for all kinds of situations, fruitful grounds for cooperation should be sought for creating dynamic processes whereby new knowledge, technologies and products are created and brought to market, to be used widely. This, in turn, requires objective understanding of facts, including the realities of R&D markets and details of technological evolution and its characteristics.

This book examines various views about IPRs as incentives for innovation against the backdrop of development and the transfer of technology between globalised, knowledge-based, high-technology economies, and it explores the controversial areas of patentable subject matter and patentability requirements in new technological fields. It also looks into the rationale for global protection

---

[13] See ch 7 of this book.

of IPRs and retraces the reactions in developing countries against such protection (chapters 1 to 3). It then recounts the negotiating history of the TRIPS Agreement (chapter 4). It describes the Agreement as it stands (chapter 5) and as it has been interpreted by the WTO dispute organs in accordance with the customary rules of treaty interpretation (chapters 6 and 7). The book then examines the origins, content and impact of the Doha Declaration on the TRIPS Agreement and Public Health[14] adopted by the Fourth WTO Ministerial Conference in November 2001. It attempts to analyse this highly important Declaration particularly in light of the overall TRIPS provisions (chapters 8 and 9). The differing IPR policies and pharmaceutical industry strategies of emerging countries are examined, with a view to understanding how and in what social and economic contexts the TRIPS Agreement has been implemented in these countries (chapters 10 and 11). TRIPS flexibilities as they are understood by national legislators, administration and courts in developing countries are then analysed, with a view to exploring how these practices may impact the quality of patents and the functioning of the patent systems or regulatory control in these countries (chapters 12 and 13). The book analyses the text of the US Free Trade Agreements, to explore what is attempted in these IPR provisions which also use TRIPS flexibilities (chapter 14). Finally, the book explores what perspectives and facts must be examined in approaching IPRs as innovation incentives. The TRIPS Agreement would merely be an object of interminable lobbying from all sides without the clarity of rules based on the balance of considerations (chapter 15).

The urgency of improving access to medicines and certain technologies in developing countries is indisputable. To do this, governments and industry need to increase cooperation to solve access problems and to preserve market incentives for innovation. IPR protection should be placed in its own context as a supporting institution where substantial efforts are made by individuals, governments, universities and companies towards increased scientific and research efforts.

Local innovations always occur whenever technologies are used locally. Instead of negating the possibilities of local innovations, governments could encourage them by building local scientific and technological capacity and infrastructure and by eliminating inefficiencies in domestic industrial organisation and its regulations. This would require coordinated implementation of domestic policies on investment, R&D and dissemination of knowledge and technological skills, with IPR protection incorporated into the overall policy perspective.

International efforts should respond to the diverse local situations in developing countries and strike a rational balance between poorer countries' need for access and the global need for innovation. Recasting the debate over TRIPS is necessary to place global cooperation and efficient R&D for innovation at the heart of concerns over IPR protection.

In emerging economies, disease patterns and pharmaceutical demands are increasingly following the patterns of developed countries. Governments of

---

[14] Adopted on 14 November 2001 in Doha, Qatar. WT/MIN(01)/DEC/2 (20 November 2001).

these countries have realised the scale of the problems relating to access to medicines, but are hesitant or unwilling to acknowledge the conditions under which the necessary increases of the scope of innovation can be achieved. Developed country governments[15] and companies should respond effectively but differentially to diverging situations among developing countries, not only to improve access to medicines but also to encourage long-term scientific and research interest. In this context, interpreting TRIPS requires clarification based on customary rules of interpretation, which should be supported by more factual understanding and analyses of the realities and challenges to future innovation. Otherwise, wider interest in IPR protection and sustained efforts for R&D will lose out.

---

[15] There are today only a few developed country governments with their own research-based pharmaceutical industries (US, Japan, UK, France, Switzerland and Germany) which are overall supporting pharmaceutical R&D backed by their patent systems, in comparison to those countries that have no research-based pharmaceutical industry, ie the majority.

Part I

Background

1

Innovation Incentives

THIS CHAPTER DISCUSSES the role of intellectual property rights (IPRs) as one type of incentive to promote creative research and development (R&D), taking into consideration such factors as competition, products, markets and industrial characteristics. These factors determine the environment in which incentives for creative R&D operate. Discussing the role of IPRs alone and in the abstract, as though they produced the same effects in different market conditions and for different industries, may risk defining the problem poorly, and retarding its solutions. Analyses undertaken by economists show how and in what varying degrees intellectual property protection needs differ with different industrial sectors. The cumulative (sequential) nature of innovation also requires consideration of the scope of patent protection and licensing policies to enable innovation to occur continuously. Many analyses have also been made of market structure and patent race. These analyses indicate why controversies over IPRs are likely to occur, particularly in the pharmaceutical and biotechnological sectors. By the same token, the analyses suggest that IPR protection should be integrated into R&D policies, to improve efficiencies of investment and increase possibilities for innovation. This means that coordinating and implementing various policies is a prerequisite to a balanced approach to IPRs.

I VARIETIES OF INCENTIVES

Innovation generally refers to new ideas which contribute to the creation of new technologies and products, improvements in product quality or the reduction of production costs. Innovation can be the result of the industrial application of new scientific knowledge and information, but the processes by which innovation occurs are not completely known, and attempts to innovate can be risky.

Mansfield in 1986 found among 100 randomly sampled US manufacturing firms that the patent system had a very small effect on innovation in most industries (primary metals, electrical equipment, motor vehicles, etc), but had substantial effects in a few industries, particularly pharmaceuticals and chemicals.[1] According to Burk and Lemley, patent protection must have leverage (mostly

---

[1] E Mansfield, 'Patents and Innovation: An Empirical Study' (1986) 32(2) *Management Science* 173–81.

achieved in the courts) to meet the needs of all new and existing technologies, to be applied with sensitivity to the industry-specific nature of innovation.[2] Within industries, firm size, incumbency, corporate culture and financing have been considered to be some of the factors influencing innovation. However, no theory seems to be definitive.[3] The ways in which large companies innovate are probably very different from the ways that small start-ups or mid-size companies do. Lemley, observing these findings, remarks that 'part of the problem is that we may never be able to know exactly what sparks a thought or a creative idea in somebody's mind'.[4]

Thus the causes of innovation are circumstantial, but industries have often used IPRs to ensure that their investments in R&D are recouped.

IPRs comprise such rights as copyrights, trademarks, patents, industrial design rights and trade secrets. IPR protection is considered to be a system of awards to intellectual creators such as artists and inventors. This approach is reflected in the US Constitution, which stipulates that: 'to promote the progress of science and useful arts, by securing for limited times to authors and inventors the exclusive right to their respective writings and discoveries'.[5] According to Ladas, literary and artistic property is based on the right created by the law for authors of all forms of literary and artistic creation, whereas trademarks, patents, industrial design rights, utility models and trade secrets constitute industrial property,[6] which is an aggregate of rights referring to the industrial or commercial activity of a person. Patents, utility models and industrial design rights are granted to inventors or creators to exclusively use or to exploit their respective creations (or to allow those to whom the creators have given consent to use or exploit their inventions) for a limited period of time.

Trademarks, trade names, appellations of origin, by contrast, are 'vehicles of advantageous business relations . . . used to protect, maintain, and extend their

---

[2] DL Burk and MA Lemley, 'Policy Levers in Patent Law' (2003) University of California at Berkeley Law School Public Law & Legal Theory Research Paper Series, Research Paper No 135.

[3] For example, small companies with venture financing are better suited for biomedical discoveries than megacompanies funded by shareholders and investment bankers who know little about pharmaceutical innovation. P Cuatrecasas, 'Drug discovery in jeopardy' (2006) 116 (11) *Journal of Clinical Investigation* 2837–42. However, biotech ventures rarely arrive at innovating final products, for which large, sustainable sources of capital may be indispensable.

[4] MA Lemley, 'Reconceiving Patents in the Age of Venture Capital' (2000) 4 *Journal of Small and Emerging Business Law* (Northwestern School of Law of Lewis & Clark College) 137, 139.

[5] Art I s 1(8) of the US Federal Constitution.

[6] According to Art 1(3) of the Paris Convention, industrial property is understood in the broadest sense to cover not only industry and commerce proper but also 'agricultural and extractive industries and all manufactured or natural products, for example, wines, grain, tobacco leaf, fruit, cattle, minerals, mineral waters, beer, flowers, and flour'. Ladas, in analysing the meaning and origins of the term 'industrial property' (which is used in many countries), states that the term is ambiguous, in that 'industry' may be taken in a strict sense, as opposed to trade, agriculture, and extractive work, or in a broad sense, embracing all sorts of human labour. Equally, according to Ladas, the term 'property' includes dissimilar kinds of interests and rights and could designate tangibles, whereas industrial property concerns only intangibles: S Ladas, *Patents, Trademarks & Related Rights: National & International Protection* (Cambridge, Harvard University Press, 1975) vol I. 1–16.

activities and their association with the public'.[7] A trademark is a sign which appropriately distinguishes goods or services provided by a company from those of other companies. It also serves to maintain business confidence of persons using the goods or service. It thus contributes to the development of industry and to the protection of consumer interests.

These industrial property rights over different intangible assets have historical origins which date back to very different times in history: the origin of trademarks can be traced back to the Middle Ages and even ancient Greece, and the first patent law to fifteenth-century Venice,[8] but others, such as industrial designs and utility models, date only from the nineteenth century.[9] Protection of trade secrets dates back to old times when there was no patent protection, but know-how is a notion that is a relatively recent development.[10] Trade secrets ('undisclosed information', in the TRIPS Agreement) include a broad range of confidential information relating to business, production or marketing operations or processes that provide competitive advantage to the right holder. Know-how is confidential, technical information necessary for designing, manufacturing the product or information needed for any other technical or commercial operations. Under domestic laws, normally, trade secrets and know-how are defined as secret information that gives economic advantage, which the company takes reasonable measures to protect[11] through secrecy of documents and contracts with employees, for example (see chapters 3, 4, 5, 13 and 14).

A patent is a legal title granting its holder the right to prevent third parties from commercially exploiting an invention without authorisation.[12] The use of patents evolved over time, responding to changing technologies and different industries in various national and international contexts. Patent protection supported the marketing of new technologies and products and helped industries grow through innovation. However, filing and maintaining a patent may have multiple purposes, and, increasingly, patenting has become a business in itself.

Today, the idea that IPR protection is an incentive for innovation is disputed in various contexts. Lessig argues that new technologies make copyright protection unnecessary, and that the protection also burdens creativity.[13] Jaffe and Lerner[14] described situations where patent rights retarded the improvement of technology, despite licensing agreements. In a similar vein, the advent of biotechnology

---

[7] Ladas, ibid 3.

[8] The Law of 19 March 1474, which encouraged and reward inventors. The translation of the law is found in Ladas (n 6) 6–7.

[9] On historical developments of different national laws, see Ladas, (n 6) vol I 2-11.

[10] Ladas (n 6), vol III 1616.

[11] In the US, 'trade secret' is defined under 18 USC § 1839(3) (A), (B) (1996) as information which derives independent economic value from not being publicly known and which is protected by reasonable measures.

[12] European Patent Office (EPO), 'About Patents', www.epo.org/patents/Grant-procedure/About-patents.html.

[13] L Lessig, *Free Culture: The Nature and Future of Creativity* (New York, Penguin Press, 2004).

[14] AB Jaffe and J Lerner, *Innovation and Its Discontents: How Our Broken Patent System is Endangering Innovation and Progress, and What to Do About It* (Princeton University Press, 2004).

inventions and their patenting has reinforced the argument that patent protection of basic life-science information raises the cost of life-saving research. Concerns have been expressed by many developing countries that IPR protection hinders transfer of technology and economic development (see chapters 2, 4, 10 and 12).

In what follows, we will describe some typical incentives for undertaking R&D to innovate, with a view to exploring the potential sources of controversies over international rules relating to IPRs.

A Patents

A patent is granted by the state to an inventor, to an invention (and under certain conditions identical to those for inventions, to a discovery, in some countries) which fulfils the criteria of novelty, inventive step (non-obviousness in the US) and industrial applicability (utility in the US).

One of the important factors making up an invention (the subject matter specified by claims) is that it has not been publicly known. The novelty is tested by assessing the prior art, the state of knowledge and technology, of the country where the patent application is made, or anywhere in the world (absolute novelty).[15] In this context, the medium (such as exhibitions,[16] publications or goods which incorporate said 'technical solutions', etc) and the date of past disclosures are examined. In some countries such as the US, a period of grace is permitted between disclosure and the filing for patents. The criteria for judging 'novelty', therefore, are not harmonised internationally.

An invention must have achieved an 'inventive step', which is normally tested by the standard of knowledge of a person having an ordinary skill and knowledge in the art working in the relevant field (average expert). Patent offices and courts in the world have applied criteria with varying levels of stringency in examining the existence of 'inventive step'. Additionally, an invention is not an abstract, theoretical construct, but must be capable of being carried out in practice. Whether or not an invention fulfils this requirement is closely related to the

[15] Each country has its own method and timing for determining novelty. Currently many countries have absolute novelty standards. Section 102 of the US Patent Act, like the Patent Law in Japan, provides conditions for novelty and loss of the right to receive a patent. Art 54 of the EPC, which concerns 'novelty', provides that 'an invention shall be considered to be new if it does not form part of the state of the art', and it provides that the state of the art is 'held to comprise everything made available to the public by means of a written or oral description, by use, or in any other way, before the date of filing of the European patent application'.

[16] The immediate reason for the adoption of the 1883 Paris Convention for Protection of Industrial Property (Paris Convention) was to ensure that countries could present their technologies at international expositions. Thus, Art 11 of the Paris Convention provides that: '(1) The countries of the Union shall, in conformity with their domestic legislation, grant temporary protection to patentable inventions, utility models, industrial designs, and trademarks, in respect of goods exhibited at official or officially recognized international exhibitions held in the territory of any of them; (2) Such temporary protection shall not extend the periods provided by Article 4. If, later, the right of priority is invoked, the authorities of any country may provide that the period shall start from the date of introduction of the goods into the exhibition . . .'

test of enablement, ie whether the specification sufficiently discloses the mode of manufacturing the invention in the patent specification.

Patent protection benefits the public, as the invention is disclosed, instead of being hidden. An invention must, therefore, be sufficiently disclosed in the 'abstract' (ie a brief abstract for the Patent Office and the public generally to determine quickly the nature and gist of the technical disclosure) and in the claims specification (a written description of the invention), as a matter of contract in exchange with the legal exclusivity. In return for the protection bestowed by the patent, the holder has to disclose the details of the invention. The disclosure of the invention in exchange for patent protection is also known as the 'patent bargain'.[17]

Patents confer exclusive rights over the claimed invention, granted for a certain period of time in return for disclosure of the invention in a patent specification. The description of the invention in the specification should therefore be sufficient to allow others skilled in the art to read the specification and work on the invention after the patent expires. The disclosure of patented invention increases the likelihood that the invention will be used without restriction after the patent expires.

The scope of exclusive rights is defined in the part of the patent application known as the 'claims'. During the period of protection, the right holder has the exclusive right to use or licence the invention and to prohibit third parties from using it without his or her authorisation. Third parties carrying out activities which fall within the claims are deemed to infringe the patent.[18]

Claims constitute the core of an invention and are set out as the scope of patent claims in a specification, the primary document for a patent application. A specification of an invention must be sufficiently accurate for such an invention to be carried out repeatedly by a person skilled in the art (an average expert in the same field). An inventive step means a remarkable technical level which a person skilled in the art could not have conceived easily based on prior art. The interpretation of industrial applicability includes whether the invention can be used repeatedly in production, or whether the invention relates to value creation in a market.

Markets in which new technologies are protected encourage firms to invest in R&D and, sooner or later, reduce production costs and product prices (known as dynamic effects of innovation). Patents normally encourage investment before a product is marketed, but market exclusivity does not always generate welfare. (Exclusivity could diminish the use of technology in the short run, because of the difficulties of obtaining licences or the high licensing fees thereof.) This, of course, depends on the licensing policies of individual firms, as well as the field of technology in question. If the term of patent protection is too long, or the scope of exclusivity too wide, the lost production due to the existence of a

---

[17] EPO, 'About Patents' (n 12).

[18] The ways in which the claims are interpreted have evolved within countries, and differ depending on the jurisdiction.

monopoly – often referred to as deadweight loss – causes a loss of social welfare, ie consumers lose more than the monopoly gains) It may give rise also to an inefficient allocation of resources (to the extent that resources are shifted to the monopolist from its customers). Much of the debate about patent policy has focused on this trade-off between the dynamic benefits of innovation and the static costs of market exclusivity.

The exclusive ownership of information in early research processes has become controversial, as it could impede knowledge diffusion. In such circumstances, various other incentives are sought to move towards better collaboration. However, each incentive has its own inefficiencies, and the respective pros and cons of each type of incentive should be weighted for the attainment of efficiency and welfare gains.

B Open Source

Today, the sharing of information as an incentive for innovation is considered to be a possible alternative to the exclusivity model in certain fields of technology. In the early stages of scientific research or software development, there are competing incentive systems. There are systems that use copyright protection, trade secrets or know-how protection or secrecy, and those that use more or less open-source methods.

For software, open source generally refers to a licence (e.g. terms and conditions of a software licence) which protects the rights of the software copyright holder and also allows the source code of the software to be publicly disclosed, distributed under the same terms as the licensing of the original software and modified under certain conditions. It is generally considered to be an incentive for innovation which is the antithesis of exclusivity. Although this is not unrelated to 'freeware', ie software which can be freely improved, open source is a corporate strategy which does not deny software developer copyrights. Open source software (OSS) is a method elaborated on for the purpose of developing software, and requires compliance with prescribed conditions such as the Open Source Initiative (OSI). [19]

'Open source' could be an efficient incentive for innovation, particularly when technological innovation is assured by the network effects of the efforts made by individuals participating in an innovation scheme, and is therefore adopted by certain businesses. There have been variations of business models relying partly on the 'open source' model of innovation. For example, hardware manu-

---

[19] Open Source Initiative (2006), *Open Source Definition*, available at http://opensource.org/docs/osd. According to Chesbrough et al, open innovation processes combine and utilise internal and external ideas into architectures and systems, defining internal mechanisms to claim some portion of that value which is taken to market through external channels, to generate additional value. HW Chesbrough et al (eds), *Open Innovation: Researching a New Paradigm* (Oxford, Oxford University Press, 2006) 1.

facturers such as IBM and SONY are presently forming the Open Invention Network (OIN) [20] to enhance Linux. This system is said to be efficiently increasing the number of users by using network effects, resulting in increased sales of hardware manufactured by these developers at reduced cost to consumers. Companies can earn income from 'open source' innovation by selling complementary goods or services. For example, by offering consulting services relating to open source software (IBM), selling hardware incorporating the open source software (Hewlett-Packard), or offering free access to e-mail software (Microsoft).

Liebowitz and Watt find, however, that the staying power of open source is as yet unknown, and its underlying business model is not fully understood.[21] According to these authors, a new business model in software (the open source software movement) has achieved a great deal of attention 'far in excess of its current market share'. They also find that such a model may not be considered generally as an alternative to copyright protection, because '[e]ven the claim that creators of open source do it for reasons contrary to normal markets is questionable since many of the individuals providing the lion's share of the work are apparently paid to do so by large corporations'.[22] Whatever incentive schemes are used, what is important for all firms is to maximise profits, and at least to recoup R&D and other costs.

In the biological and life sciences, certain 'open source' models have been pursued, borrowing from the software model. Some scientists and researchers have advocated free sharing of genetic information, a 'science common' for society's free use for interpreting and developing new products. For them, the current patent system orients scientists and universities to focus on patenting technologies that might otherwise have been placed in the public domain, and slows down the scientific understanding of the role of genetic variations in human disease and other traits.[23] The relative success of freely sharing genetic information is expected in agricultural biotechnology, where the number of potential licensees is numerous and the reduction of transaction cost could therefore be a factor for consideration. Furthermore, innovation lifecycles in agricultural biotechnology are relatively short without involving costly clinical trials.[24] Biological

[20] Open Invention Network (OIN) is a limited liability company created in 2005 to promote the development of the Linux system. For this purpose, OIN acquires patents and makes them available royalty-free to any company, institution or individual that agrees not to assert its patents against Linux's operating system and related application systems (http://www.openinventionnetwork.com). Currently, IBM, Novell, Philips, Red Hat, Sony and NEC are participating in the OIN, and Google is the first end user licensee.

[21] SJ Liebowitz and R Watt, 'How to Best Ensure Remuneration for Creators in the Market For Music? Copyright and its Alternatives' (2006) 20(4) *Journal of Economic Surveys* 528.

[22] ibid 529.

[23] J Stiglitz and J Sulston, 'The Case Against Gene Patents' *The Wall Street Journal* (New York, 16 April 2010).

[24] For seeds, the costs of establishing contracts between hundreds or thousands of farmers and breeders, as well as among breeders, often outweigh the cost of limiting the scope of breeders' intellectual property rights. Art 12.3(d) of The International Treaty on Plant Genetic Resources for Food and Agriculture (ITPGRFA), which entered into force in 2004, is a comprehensive treaty whose

Innovation for Open Society (BiOS), for example, has shared information on the beta-glucuronidase gene (GUS) and the know-how to use it with hundreds of laboratories around the world, including Monsanto, [25] to develop products. The interesting focus of BiOS is sharing patents to generate continuous innovation for the next generation of technology which, according to BiOS, would seldom occur if multinationals were the owners of lucrative patents. The BiOS-compatible licensing agreement model for patented technologies and know-how provides, *inter alia*, that those who use royalty-free BiOS technologies, derivatives and know-how must agree not to assert any IPRs,[26] including patents, pending patent claims, or bailments against any others that have agreed to these conditions.[27]

In the life sciences, however, the value and cost of inventions are generally greater than in other fields of technology, and innovation cycles take longer than in software development. There is no network effect in the life science development processes. The cost of copying production of the resulting products, on the other hand, is not high. In these conditions, it may require much time and ingenuity for an open source scheme in this field to generate income to recoup investment and to become economically viable. Patent protection, which obliges the right holder to disclose information but assures them of recouping the investments already sunk at the time of patenting, may be more realistic in these circumstances.

C Subsidies to R&D

According to Scotchmer, given that the length and breadth of patent protection cannot depend on the expected costs of an R&D project, the only way to ensure that firms undertake every research project that is efficient is to let the firms collect as revenue all the social value they create. If an innovation leads to a reduction in the cost of producing a good, then the social value is the saved

---

objectives are the conservation and sustainable use of plant genetic resources for food and agriculture. ITPGRFA provides that recipients shall not claim any intellectual property or other rights that limit the facilitated access to the plant genetic resources for food and agriculture, or their genetic parts or components, in the form received from the multilateral system (Art 12.3(d)). The case of golden rice, a variety of rice that was engineered to provide Vitamin A, the free use of which was successful in promoting research, encountered obstacles in the translation of the research results into deliverable plants. On the ITPGRFA, see also ch 12 nn 28 and 31.

[25] Monsanto used it and developed Roundup Ready soya beans, www.monsanto.com/monsanto/ag_products/input_traits/products/roundup_ready_soybeans.asp.

[26] Non-assertion clauses in licensing contracts typically stipulate that a contracting party will not assert patents or other IP rights against the other contracting party, even if that party infringes the IPRs. These clauses allow firms to avoid litigation, which reduces transaction costs, but may, under certain conditions, discourage innovation by limiting the ability of licensees to collect rents on their own IP.

[27] www.patentlens.net/daisy/bios/3541/version/default/part/AttachmentData/data/CAMBIA%20PMET%20BiOS%20agreement.pdf.

cost. If the innovation is an improvement to a product, the social value is the difference in consumers' willingness to pay for the improved and unimproved products. When research firms collect all the social value as profit, shareholders rather than consumers benefit.[28] However, there are situations where neither exclusivity nor open source incentives work well enough to ensure companies can earn money to invest in R&D for subsequent innovations.

Some projects which are socially desirable may not be undertaken under patent protection if the potential market is too small, because it is a decentralised, market-based economic incentive for R&D, under which the innovator's incentive to invest in research is likely to be the economic rewards he may earn by taking risks.

When the scale of the market for a particular technology or product is not large enough to provide returns on R&D investments,[29] government assistance or incentive awards may be useful. In this case, taxpayers, instead of the market and consumers, will bear specific R&D expenses in advance. Under certain circumstances, direct, public intervention in the form of contracts for research services or prizes may be more welfare-enhancing, even in market economies.

Wright assumed that patent revenues incur a higher deadweight loss than an equivalent amount of public funds financed by government contracts, and analysed the advantages of public intervention for research, such as research contracts or prizes, if administered by a social welfare maximising administrator in a competitive economy.[30] His study paid explicit attention to differences in the informational roles of these alternative incentives. The system of patent protection is advantageous because it incorporates researchers' information about the value of best inventions in the allocative processes. Both patents and prizes utilise private information about research costs and the probability of success, whereas a public administrator may not. Wright concludes that the allocative advantages of contractual research and of prizes may be undervalued if researchers are highly responsive to incentives. He indicates, however, that the choice of incentives depends on the nature of the information search process, and he suggests that further studies should take into account researcher attributes.

Market size is insufficient when either (i) potential beneficiaries are few, or (ii) each beneficiary (or his insurer/government) has a low willingness to pay. In either case, the value of the innovation (relative to other R&D projects) could actually be low, in which case government intervention may not necessarily be justified. At least from an economic point of view, if the cost of R&D (plus the cost of production) is greater than the utility that consumers derive from

---

[28] S Scotchmer, 'Standing on the Shoulders of Giants: Cumulative Research and the Patent Law' (1991) 5(1) *Journal of Economic Perspectives* 30.

[29] For example, developing or improving drugs for neglected diseases for which the demand is not sufficient for companies to expect returns, and which therefore remain undeveloped.

[30] BD Wright, 'The Economics of Invention Incentives: Patents, Prizes, and Research Contracts' (1983) 73(4) *The American Economic Review* 691–707.

product, then innovation is socially wasteful. Government R&D subsidies should therefore be awarded with care: only when a specific market failure would prevent efficient innovation, or if they are necessary to achieve specific policy objectives. R&D on new medicines for neglected diseases is an example of a socially desirable policy objective which might require government subsidy.

II R&D INVESTMENTS INCENTIVES IN DIFFERENT INDUSTRIAL SECTORS

A The Role of Complementary Intellectual Assets (Trade Secrets and Know-How)

The ease and speed with which innovative products or processes can be imitated by a third party vary in different industrial sectors, depending on the ways in which the invention is technically or commercially exploited. This in turn depends in part on how easily know-how necessary for designing, manufacturing and distributing the patented products can be learned.

There is a subtle relationship between patent protection and know-how. For technologies to be patented, the inventor must disclose his or her invention in a manner that is sufficiently clear and complete so that a person skilled in the art will be able to make and use the invention defined in the claim. Although they are protected from copying, patented technologies are therefore disclosed. In order to prevent inventors from only disclosing what they know to be a 'second-best' embodiment of the invention so that others cannot imitate it, some domestic laws require the inventor to disclose the 'best mode' he or she knows at the time of patent filing (see chapter 5). This requirement could sometimes delicately conflict with the protection of 'trade secrets' or 'know-how'.

Innovative technologies can be protected not only by patents but also by trade secrets (in the TRIPS Agreement, 'undisclosed information').[31]

In 1995 Arora analysed licensor/licensee behaviour and suggested that the marginal value of know-how is higher for the licensee when it is used together with the patented part of codified technology, and that a major benefit of broader patents would be that complementary know-how, critical to the utilisation of technologies, could be bought and sold more efficiently, even when important components of the technology are not protected by patents.[32] He suggested that the second-stage supplies of know-how depend on sequential opportunistic behaviour and that the joint surplus maximising the amount of tacit know-how is contracted for and provided, if a sufficiently broad scope of patent protection

---

[31] Computer software can be protected not only by patents and trade secrets, but also by copyright. For undisclosed information, see chs 4, 5 and 13.

[32] A Arora, 'Licensing Tacit Knowledge: Intellectual Property Rights and the Market for Know-how' (1995) 4 *Economics of Innovation and New Technology* 41–59. See also JI Bulow, JD Geanakoplos and PD Klemperer, 'Multimarket Oligopoly: Strategic Substitute and Complements' (1985) *Journal of Political Economy* (https://faculty-gsb.stanford.edu/bulow/articles/Multimarket%20Oligopoly. pdf).

exists. Arora et al further investigated whether patents enable the transfer of know-how in the case of technology transfer agreements, and found that patents facilitate know-how licensing.[33] Their studies showed that know-how transmission, such as setting up an R&D-unit, quality control and training, tends to be promoted together with patent licensing.

There are significant differences in the protective value of trade secrets and know-how, depending on the industry. Genuinely 'secret' know-how (ie, know-how that is difficult or impossible to copy) is uncommon, but there are greater tendencies to keep inventions secret in capital-intensive industries than in organic chemistry. In such fields as aeronautics, automobiles and other highly engineering-based industries, for example, knowledge and coordination of different fields of technologies, safety devices and test methods and other products that form part of the final product could constitute trade secrets.

However, in organic chemistry, as long as the person who imitates has a level of technological competency to design and manufacture a given product, active ingredients of small-molecule medicines can often only be produced with patented data. For commercialisation of these chemical products as medicines, quality, safety and efficacy requirements are regulated by national pharmaceutical laws, and therefore a varying degree of clinical data is necessary, depending on the national regulatory standards.

In organic chemistry, by contrast, skills in chemical synthesis can be developed and used in-house. In pharmaceuticals, the patented invention concerns a substance that forms the core of technological know-how (data and production techniques and experience about the chemical substances). Only a small range of engineering devices or installations are necessary in order to manufacture and commercialise active ingredients for small-molecule pharmaceuticals. For tabletting, for example, only certain technological installations are necessary, and these may be patented. In administering medicines, specific know-how for stabilising a given product and delivering it through the human body is necessary, and these also may be protected by patents.[34] Aspects of the production process that could be protected as trade secrets are limited in this sector.

Manufacturing small-molecule chemical medicines could require less know-how than biotechnology medicines (such as genetically modified biotech medicines based on a large number of proteins). Examples of such know-how include cell culture[35] and isolation/purification technologies.[36] In biotech

---

[33] A Arora, A Fosfuri and A Gambardella, *Markets for Technology* (Cambridge, MIT Press, 2001); Arora, 'Licensing Tacit Knowledge' (n 33); profiting from licensing: A Arora and M Ceccagnoli, 'The role of patent protection and commercialization capabilities' (2006) 52(2) *Management Science* 293–308.

[34] Today, new methods of administering drugs, such as controlled-release formulation, deposit formulation and sustained-release have become a necessary part of innovation for drug efficacy.

[35] Cell culture know-how includes creating conditions in which factors such as CO_2 concentration, temperature levels, pH levels, mixing blend times, shear sensitivity and oxygen supply are controlled to scale up the culture.

[36] Isolation/purification technologies include: filtration for unprocessed cell culture harvest clarification and cell removal; protein A affinity chromatography for antibody capture from the clarified

medicines, copies do not exactly reflect the glycosylation of proteins of the original products and could be commercialised as biogenerics, depending on the regulatory requirements of each country. Finding suitable methods of administrating biotech medicines is a further hurdle for those who copy them. However, in pharmaceutical or biotechnological industries, trade secrets and know-how afford little protection for the reasons indicated above, in comparison to other engineering industries where production costs are high and where many different components industries may be involved in producing the final product.

B Profitability of Imitation

In 1986, Mansfield, Schwartz and Wagner published their empirical study, which found that the cost and time for imitating new products have an important effect on the incentives for innovation in a market economy.[37] In this study, 'imitation cost' was defined as 'all costs of developing and introducing the imitative product, including applied research, product specification, pilot plant or prototype construction, investment in plant and equipment, and manufacturing and marketing startup', and the 48 sample products were chosen randomly from four industries in the north east of the United States.[38] The study revealed that:

- Imitation cost was no smaller than innovation cost in about one-seventh of the samples, due mainly to the technological edge of the originator products, often in the form of superior 'know-how', or barriers to entry such as powerful brand names.
- Patent protection does not make entry impossible: 60 per cent of the samples were imitated within four years of the originator product's entry into the market.
- A new product is more likely to be imitated if the imitation cost is small. About 50 per cent of the patented innovations among the samples would not have been introduced without patent protection, and the bulk of these innovations occurred in the drug industry. In less than 25 per cent of the samples, the lack of patent protection would have affected business decisions in other industries.[39]

Since it is possible to manufacture similar chemical entities at a low cost with nothing more than the requisite knowledge, there would be no economic incentive to invest in R&D, had the benefits of exclusivity not been there. Other surveys show that the time and capital required for a patent application for a chemical compound that is a potential pharmaceutical to be approved as a

---

harvest; and viral filtration for virus removal.

[37] E Mansfield et al, 'Imitation Costs and Patents: An Empirical Study' (1981) 91 *The Economic Journal* 907–18.

[38] ibid 907.

[39] Mansfield et al, 'Imitation Costs and Patents: An Empirical Study' (n 37) 909–17.

pharmaceutical that can be marketed, is longer (presently from 8 to 15 years)[40] and more costly than for other industries (see chapter 3).[41]

A company that invests in R&D aimed at innovation must be able to expect that it will at least recoup its costs. In some industries, such as certain areas of the sophisticated engineering sector, imitation is difficult, costly and slow, and the cost of manufacturing is high. The accumulation of know-how may be much more important in these fields. In certain electronics sectors, companies may rely more on 'time to market' (lead time) advantage, rather than IPR, to benefit from innovation. When the cost of production by a third party using that technology without the company's authorisation is very low, recouping R&D costs is difficult without IPR protection. Despite the evolution from strong IPR protection to less exclusive approaches to innovation in some industrial fields, certain industries still trust firmly in IP protection, patents in particular.

The pharmaceutical industry's interest in and dependence on patent protection seems to reside in the ease and speed of imitation of unprotected drugs. For small molecule drugs, the main invention is a chemical substance. It forms only part of the technical know-how involved, which includes test data, information on the structure and function of the substance, duration period of the substance for pharmaceutical use and other experience with it. If know-how is common to various chemical manufacturing processes, this know-how will end up in the possession of a third party, and if it is specific to the compound in question, it will often form part of the patent claim, so copying will be discouraged by the risk of patent infringement. Furthermore, many of the trade secrets that pharmaceutical companies would like to protect are made public when the drug is approved.[42] Drug approval packages often reveal information on chemical and clinical pharmacology, biopharmaceutical and statistical data review, as well as administrative documents and correspondence. Research-based pharmaceutical companies therefore tend not to rely on know-how protection and depend almost entirely on patent protection and clinical data exclusivity to avoid copied products being marketed during the term of their protection.

[40] An average of 24 years were spent from the discovery of the candidate compound to marketing of the drug, for the 21 pharmaceutical compounds that are believed to have contributed the most to treatments from 1965 to 1992 in the US (Cyclosporine, Flucanozole, Foscarnet, Gemfibrozil, Ketoconazole, Nifedipine, Tamoxifen, AZT, Captopril, Cimetidine, Finasteride, Fluozetine, Lovastatin, Omeprazole, Ondansetron, Propranolol, Sumatriptan, Acyclovir, Cisplatin, Erythropoietin, Interferon β): Cockburn and Henderson, 'Public Private Interaction and the Productivity of Pharmaceutical Research' (1999) NBER Working Paper 6018 39, Table (1).

[41] According to the Japanese Pharmaceutical Manufacturers' Association (JPMA) survey between 2004 and 2008, average costs for JPMA companies to develop a drug was 55.2 billion yen (JPMA News Letter No 136 (2010/03) 35). Average costs for Pharmaceutical Research and Manufacturers of America (PhRMA) companies to develop a drug in 2005 was $1.3 billion (in 2001, $802 million, 1987 $318 million and 1975 $138 million); cost to develop a biologic in 2005 was $1.2 billion (PhRMA, *Profile Pharmaceutical Industry 2010*, 2).

[42] The list of the US Drug Approval Package is found at www.accessdata.fda.gov/scripts/cder/drugsatfda/index.cfm. That of the European Medicines Agency (EMEA, a decentralised regulatory body of the European Union) is at. www.ema.europa.eu/home.htm. The drug approval package of the Japanese Pharmaceuticals and Medical Devices Agency (PMDA) is found at www.info.pmda.go.jp/shinyaku/shinyaku_hanbaimei_index.html.

Could we say that the higher the ratio of R&D to the cost of manufacturing, the greater the incentive to short-cut the process through unauthorised copying? First, defining the cost of manufacturing is not easy. Production costs are typically a mix of sunk costs (such as the investment to build a new plant), fixed costs, and variable costs. The variable cost of manufacturing depends on the number of units produced, but what is the right volume to use for the purpose of comparing production costs to the costs of R&D? Second, the incentive to copy rather than invest in R&D depends on the difference between the profits that can be made in each scenario. That depends on manufacturing costs (sunk, fixed and variable), as well as on the prices, on the volume of sales, and on the cost of R&D. In general, all else being equal, the higher the cost of R&D, the greater the incentive to short-cut the process through unauthorised copying.

III ECONOMISTS' IDEAS ABOUT OPTIMUM PROTECTION

Ideally, the patent protection system should benefit companies only to an extent comparable to the investment needed for R&D, to minimise social welfare losses from the granting of exclusive rights. There has been a diversity of arguments as to the optimal term (length) and scope (width) of patent protection.[43]

Economists have developed ideas concerning the optimal scope (width, breadth) and term (length) of patent protection for providing incentives for R&D efforts which would minimise the loss of welfare. While Nordhaus (1969)[44] and Scherer (1972)[45] examined the optimal length, Klemperer (1990)[46] analysed the optimal width[47] to design the shape of patent protection that would allocate a given profit reward to the innovator at the least social cost. He argued that broad, short-lived patents can be optimal, if broader patents discourage substitution away from the patented product by making the non-infringing alternatives less attractive to buyers. While Klemperer's analysis focused on the optimal scope of patent protection in a model of spatial product differentiation, Gilbert and Shapiro (1990) analysed the extent to which a patentee may exploit the patent monopoly for a given coverage of the patent grant, and identified the 'breadth' of a patent with the flow rate of profit available to the patentee while the patent is in force.[48] According to these authors, if the current level of reward for inno-

---

[43] There has been a series of discussions as reflected in: NT Gallini, 'Patent Policy and Costly Imitation' (1992) 23(1) *RAND Journal of Economics* (RJE); L DeBrock, 'Market Structure, Innovation, and Optimal Patent Life' (1985) 28(1) *Journal of Law and Economics*; Scotchmer, 'Standing on the Shoulders of Giants: Cumulative Research and the Patent Law' (n 28).

[44] W Nordhaus, 'The Optimum Life of a Patent: Reply' (1969) 62(3) *American Economic Review*.

[45] FM Scherer, 'Nordhaus Theory of Optimal Patent Life: A Geometric Reinterpretation' (1972) 62(3) *American Economic Review*.

[46] P Klemperer, 'How Broad should the Scope of Patent Protection Be?' (1990) 21 RJE 113–30.

[47] For example, if a company invents a new drug to alleviate a heart condition, how similar a drug should a competitor be allowed to sell? If a computer software firm markets a new program, how different should any rival product be required to be? ibid 113.

[48] Klemperer, 'How Broad should the Scope of Patent Protection Be?' (n 46) 106.

vators is viewed to be inadequate, limiting the scope and increasing the term of patent protection is the optimum patent arrangement, as long as this is combined with carefully designed antitrust law application to patent practices such as licensing contracts.[49] Alternatively, if technology becomes obsolete quickly, the patentowner will not receive sufficient rent even if the patent is protected for a longer term (the optimal length may easily be infinite). They therefore recommended extension of the term of protection to provide R&D incentives.

According to Shapiro, most patents turn out to have little or no commercial significance and, therefore, little litigation is attempted against them, leaving the boundaries of rights uncertain. Shapiro finds that only 1.5 per cent of patents are litigated, and only 0.1 per cent of patents are litigated to trial.[50] Lemley and Shapiro consider that a patent confers upon its owner not the right to exclude, but rather a right to try to exclude by asserting the patent in court. Patents are therefore rather uncertain and probabilistic and, therefore, measures should be taken to increase the efficacy of litigation.[51]

Different economists have defined patent 'width' or 'breadth' differently. Green and Scotchmer understand the concept of patent breadth to include not only legal provisions concerning patentability criteria (ie, novelty, inventive step and industrial applicability), but also judicial decisions relating to infringement.[52] O'Donahue[53] explains that for designing patent breadth, it is necessary to take into account not only patentability requirements but also a set of products that the courts would find to infringe the patent, ie, those products that no other firm can produce without permission from the patent-holder (ie, a licensing agreement),[54] and assess the trade-off between the incentives for innovation and the extent of static monopoly deadweight loss.

Green and Scotchmer (1995) suggested that patent breadth should be broad enough to protect the R&D incentives of original patent-holders if technological innovation is cumulative (as opposed to stand-alone innovations). Because there will be competition between the prior patent and follow-on innovations, if the breadth of patent protection is limited, the original innovator's profit will be insufficient to encourage continuing innovative R&D.[55] According to these

---

[49] R Gilbert and C Shapiro, 'Optimal Patent Length and Breadth' (1990) 1 RJE106–12.

[50] C Shapiro, 'Antitrust Limits to Patent Settlements' (2003) 34(2) RJE 391–411. Various proposals have been made to remedy the situation.

[51] MA Lemley and C Shapiro, 'Probabilistic Patents' (2005) 19(2) *The Journal of Economic Perspectives* 75–95.

[52] S Scotchmer, 'Standing on the Shoulders of Giants: Cumulative Research and the Patent Law' (n 28) 29–41; JR Green and S Scotchmer, 'On the Division of Profit in Sequential Innovation' (1995) 26(1) RJE 20–33. See also V Denicolo, 'Two-Stage Patent Races and Patent Policy' (2000) 31(3) RJE 488–501.

[53] E O'Donoghue, 'A Patentability Requirement for Sequential Innovation' (1998) 29(4) RJE 657.

[54] Including such policies as the doctrine of equivalents, which is a method of claim interpretation whereby an invention described in the claims of a patent and an equivalent invention are considered as falling within the same technological scope. On the doctrine of equivalents, see ch 3 n 157.

[55] The division of profit in each period depends on whether the second product infringes the first patent. If a second product infringes, the second innovator must license, which transfers profit from the second innovator to the first. Because the breadth of the first patent determines whether a

authors, patent law would provide no protection at all if it did not protect against trivial changes, such as derivative products. The breadth determines how profit is divided among licensor and licensees which are actually potential competitors in each period of the patent, and the length determines the total profit that is collected by all the firms involved. Without protection against minor changes, patents may prevent the original patent holder from obtaining sufficient profit.[56] In designing the patent protection when innovation is cumulative, therefore, the criteria used in judging 'inventive step' should encourage original innovators to be ambitious about investing in subsequent innovation. According to these authors, however, patent breadth that is too broad may prevent cumulative technological innovation, depending on the licensing terms.

Patent breadth designing could be an industrial policy instrument in developing economies. For example, in Japan, after the introduction of product patent protection in 1976, the patentability requirements were the same as in other developed countries, but patent breadth was designed and interpreted narrowly to encompass only the extent supported by working examples described in the claims. This allowed domestic incremental inventions to compete on the Japanese market with the original, dominant foreign patents. In India, by contrast, patent breadth is designed not to allow certain minor inventions to be easily patented, leaving relative margins for copying products that are patented abroad (see chapters 10 and 12).

Patent protection is designed to provide financial reward for continued R&D efforts and to provide conditions for further innovation. This alone, however, is far from adequate for encouraging innovative R&D. Other factors, such as education and training, appropriate regulations in the sector, favourable conditions for market entry and a commitment by the industry to stay up-to-date on the relevant science and technology are also necessary. Market structures have been considered to be one of the main factors influencing the R&D behaviour of firms that leads to innovation, with causality probably trending both ways (ie, there are opposing views about whether certain market structures such as monopolistic or oligopolistic markets cause benefit or harm to innovative R&D).

Schumpeter in 1942 referred to 'creative destruction',[57] the endogenous process whereby the old ways of doing things are replaced by new ones through competition from new technologies and sources of supplies. According to Schumpeter, the

---

product infringes, it thus determines the division of profit. Scotchmer, 'Standing on the Shoulders of Giants: Cumulative Research and the Patent Law' (n 28) 21.

[56] If a licensing contract has an exclusive grant-back clause (a licensee agrees to extend to the licensor of intellectual property the right to use the licensee's improvements of the licensed technology), a licensee's incentive to invest in R&D may be reduced. Inversely, if a licensing contract provides that the licensor pays a high price for the improvements of the licensed technology (assign-backs), this may mitigate the licensing relationship in favour of the licensor's profits (which is important for his incentive to innovate). How incentives to innovate shift from the licensor to the licensee or vice versa depends on further details of contractual conditions, as well as sequential stages of cumulative innovation where the licensor-licensee relationship may change.

[57] JA Schumpeter, *Capitalism, Socialism and Democracy* (London, Routledge, 1994; originally published by Allen & Unwin, 1942).

expectation that a company can earn profits from its new technology encourages innovation, whereas tough competition discourages innovation and inhibits productivity growth by reducing the expected rents from innovation. Schumpeter's ideas that a certain degree of monopolistic power would be more suitable for realising innovation than perfect competition provoke much discussion still today.

Forty years later, in 1962, Arrow criticised Schumpeter and argued that there is less incentive to invent under monopolistic than under competitive conditions.[58] Until the 1980s, the predominant thinking was that product markets should be competitive and entry should be easy, to promote innovation. According to this school of thought, actual and potential new entrants play a crucial role in stimulating technical progress. In the 1980s, there were studies on the impact on innovation of patent races between the incumbent and potential entrants. If patenting were made to block the entry of actual or potential competitors in the market pre-emptively, what would happen to the R&D efforts of the incumbent companies and entrants?

Gilbert and Newbery[59] focused their analysis on the threats of potential entrants as a spur to the incumbent's R&D, whereas Reinganum[60] analysed the effect of a current monopoly profit upon an incumbent firm's incentives to invest in R&D. Reinganum showed, for example, that the incumbent firm invests less in a given project than does the potential entrant when the first successful innovator captures a sufficiently high share of the post-innovation market. In this case, the incumbent is less likely to be the innovator than is the challenger. According to Caves and Porter, if inefficient incumbent firms are sufficiently innovating, they can deter more innovative products by offsetting the pay-offs for the innovative efforts.[61]

On the other hand, innovation might also be affected if market entry is too easy. Salop's theory of entry[62] suggests that intense product market competition discourages entry by reducing the rents of those firms which successfully enter the market. Competition may also work to reduce the current profit rate, which would drive companies to actively work towards innovation. By re-examining the contrary scenarios and evidence used by various scholars, Aghion and Griffith argue that the degree to which competition encourages innovation depends on the difference of profit rates, before and after the innovation, in a given product market. Graphically, this difference forms a reverse U-shape.[63] In other words, where the level of competition is low, promoting

[58] K Arrow, 'Economic Welfare and the Allocation of Resources for Invention', in RR Nelson (ed), *The Role and Direction of Inventive Activity* (Princeton NJ, Princeton University Press, 1962).

[59] J Gilbert and DMG Newbery, 'Preemptive patenting and the persistence of monopoly' (1982) 72 *American Economic Review* 514–26.

[60] J Reiganum, 'Uncertain innovation and the persistence of monopoly' (1983) 73 *American Economic Review* 741–48.

[61] RE Caves and ME Porter, 'From Entry Barriers to Mobility Barriers: Conjectural Decisions and Contrived Deterrence to New Competition' (1977) 91(2) *The Quarterly Journal of Economics* 241–61.

[62] S Salop 'The Noisy Monopolist: Imperfect Information, Price Dispersion, and Price Discrimination' (1977) 44 *Review of Economic Studies* 393.

[63] P Aghion and R Griffith, *Competition and Growth: Reconciling Theory and Evidence* (Cambridge MA, MIT Press, 2005).

competition promotes innovation, but if competition is already strong, innovation is discouraged.

It is possible that the size of individual companies or the structure of the market as a whole are interrelated with innovation, with causality probably trending both ways. Until the 1980s, the predominant thinking was that product markets should be competitive and entry should be easy in order for innovation to occur.

IV LEGAL VERSUS ECONOMIC MONOPOLIES

A patent confers on the right holder the legal right to exclude, for a limited time, competitors in the technology market of the right holder's claimed invention. During the term of protection, it would be possible for a right holder to raise the price of his or her technology above the competitive level (ie market power) if no similar technology or products are available in the market. Market power is the ability profitably to maintain prices above, or output below, competitive levels[64] for a significant period of time.[65] In many cases, however, there are substitute technologies available in the same product market, which means that the market power of a patented product depends on the strength (in scope and validity) of the patent in relation to competitor products.[66] A patent does 'not necessarily confer market power upon the patentee'[67] or automatically raise the price of the patented products.

[64] Prices at a competitive level means prices at or near marginal cost (additional costs required to produce the next unit). Fixed cost does not directly affect the pricing decision. In the Cournot oligopoly model, quantity is set so that marginal revenue equals marginal cost. 'Cournot competition' is a model which describes an industry structure in which firms compete based on the amount of output they will produce independently of each other and simultaneously. In the absence of fixed costs of production, as the number of firms in the market increases, market output will reach a competitive level and prices will converge to a marginal cost level. Fixed cost does not affect the quantity-setting decision, and hence does not affect prices. In the Bertrand model likewise, fixed cost does not affect the pricing decision. The Bertrand model is a model in which prices are set by competition among firms, and their customers choose quantities at those prices. On the other hand, fixed cost (including sunk cost) affects entry conditions. Hence, fixed cost indirectly affects prices through changes in the market structure.

[65] US Department of Justice and Federal Trade Commission, 'Antitrust Guidelines for the Licensing of Intellectual Property' (1995 DOJ-FTC Licensing Guidelines) para 2.2. In its footnote 10 the Guidelines add that: 'Market power can be exercised in other economic dimensions, such as quality, service, and the development of new or improved goods and processes. It is assumed in this definition that all competitive dimensions are held constant except the ones in which market power is being exercised; that a seller is able to charge higher prices for a higher-quality product does not alone indicate market power. The definition in the text is stated in terms of a seller with market power. A buyer could also exercise market power (e.g., by maintaining the price below the competitive level, thereby depressing output).' www.justice.gov/atr/public/guidelines/0558.htm#t22.

[66] According to the 1995 DOJ-FTC Licensing Guidelines, ibid para 2.2, 'market power does not by itself offend the antitrust laws. As with any other tangible or intangible asset that enables its owner to obtain significant supracompetitive profits, market power (or even a monopoly) that is solely a consequence of a superior product, business acumen, or historic accident does not violate the antitrust laws.' .

[67] In order to establish certain types of conduct as violating competition law, there are further conditions to be met. *Illinois Tool Works Inc et al v Independent Ink* [2006] US LEXIS 2024 (S Ct, March 1, 2006); US Dept of Justice and FTC, Antitrust Guidelines for the Licensing of Intellectual Property

For this reason, a legal monopoly permitted by a patent cannot be equated with an economic monopoly.[68] IPRs are often viewed as monopoly power, but on the product markets, substitutes may be readily available. The relationship between the patent and price depends on the competition among those products that constitute a relevant market[69]. Normally, several substitute products or technologies of the same class compete and, therefore, the width of patent protection is relevant.[70]

IPRs and competition share the goal of innovation but approach it through different means.[71] IP protection is intended to reward the efforts made in developing new or improved products and processes to encourage further investment in R&D. Competition law aims to bring about better allocation of resources to (increased productivity), better distribution of goods and services to (increased consumer welfare) and better products and services (as a result of innovation).[72] Competition authorities generally agree today that competition and IPRs should strike a 'proper balance'.[73] There is no easy answer to the question of how competition and IPR protection work for innovation in reality and where the right balance lies.

To what extent and how efficiently can patent designs be an instrument of social policy? An interesting question which may be addressed is: which is the most effective way to lower prices in a given market: (i) by price regulations, (ii) by strengthening patent protection to encourage cost-reducing innovations, or (iii) market competition among close substitutes? Some degree of competition is normally essential to give firms the incentive to innovate, including cost-reducing innovation. In that sense, innovation and competition are not mutually exclusive. However, too much competition, as well as excessive regulation, may lead to reduced innovation. Excessive price regulation of drugs (which exists in most countries except the US), for example, may hinder efforts for R&D.[74]

§2.2 (6 Apr 1995); European Commission, 'DG Competition Discussion Paper on the Application of Article 82 [102]of the Treaty to Exclusionary Abuses', (December 2005) para 40; Opinion.,Case C-53/03, *Syfait and Others v Glaxosmithkline AEVE* [2005] ECR I-4609 [100] ((28 October 2004)).

[68] The US Circuit Courts are divided on this issue. According to the 11th Circuit Court, patents by nature exclude and cripple competition so that an anticompetitive effect is already present (*Valley Drug* 344F 3d 2003).

[69] The market where close substitutes exist and compete create a 'relevant market' for the purpose of competition analysis.

[70] See for example, Klemperer, 'How Broad should the Scope of Patent Protection Be?' (n 46) .

[71] 'Goals not at odds' in H Hovenkamp, M D Janis, M A Lemley, IP and antitrust: an analysis of antitrust principles applied to intellectual property law (Aspen Law & Business, 2002) I-9.

[72] O Williamson, *Allocative Efficiency and the Limits of Antitrust* (1969) May *American Economic Review Papers & Proceedings* 105–118; H Hovenkamp, *Antitrust Policy After Chicago*, (1985) <div align=center>84 *Michigan Law Review* 213; </div>H-D Ehlermann and L Laudati (eds), European Competition Law Annual *1997:* Objectives of Competition Policy (Oxford, Hart Publishing, 1998).

[73] See, for example, 'To Promote Innovation: The Proper Balance of Competition and Patent Law and Policy: A Report by the Federal Trade Commission' (FTC), October 2003.

[74] For example, in Japan, for reasons of political acceptability, price regulation sets such low average medicine prices that R&D investment cannot be recouped by sales in the Japanese market. The top 10 research-based Japanese pharmaceutical companies undertake their research primarily in Japan and in the US, which offers a considerably large market (more than 50% of the world pharmaceutical market in value), where they invest twice as much as in Japan. The five next largest companies have research activities in Japan and license the research results in the US and Europe.

All of these discussions concerning the effectiveness of IPR protection for innovation, not surprisingly, are based only on developed country experiences and data. The basic principles advanced by economists concerning IPR protection may probably be common to both developed and developing countries, but the realities of such protection in developing countries are not sufficiently known. Patent designing presupposes well-functioning administration and courts, without which any theoretical exercise remains futile.

2

International IP Cooperation and Developing Country Perspectives

BECAUSE IPRS ARE protected only within a particular territorial jurisdiction, authors and inventors cannot exercise their rights outside the country where they are recognised. International cooperation to facilitate protection abroad for foreign inventions and artistic works started in the second half of the nineteenth century. The Paris Convention for Protection of Industrial Property (Paris Convention), signed in 1883, was one of the first global treaties covering 'industrial property' such as patents and trademarks.[1] The Berne Convention for the Protection of Literary and Artistic Works (Berne Convention) was signed in 1886 to enhance international cooperation in protecting tangible manifestations of creative efforts, such as literature and paintings.

Patent protection rewards inventors for their scientific and technological endeavours, but the national economies of the Contracting Parties of the Paris Convention are heterogeneous and competitive in different industrial areas. Revision conferences of the Paris Convention became not only a focus of international cooperation but also a battleground of competing industrial and commercial policies and opposing ideas as to what form international patent protection rules should take. A new dimension was added to such conflicts in the 1950s, with increased membership of the Convention comprising newly independent states with even more diverse economies.

This chapter examines the origins of the controversies over the provisions concerning several substantive standards in the Paris Convention, particularly compulsory licensing provisions. It then looks at how developing countries gradually joined the discussions over these questions and summarises the history of the debate on 'the global patent system' and its consequences for the economies of developing countries since the 1950s.

[1] According to Art 1(3) of the Paris Convention, industrial property is understood in the broadest sense to cover not only industry and commerce proper, but also 'agricultural and extractive industries and all manufactured or natural products, for example, wines, grain, tobacco leaf, fruit, cattle, minerals, mineral waters, beer, flowers, and flour'. Ladas, in analysing the meaning and origins of the term 'industrial property' (which is used in many countries), states that the term is ambiguous in that 'industry' may be taken in a strict sense, as opposed to trade, agriculture, and extractive work, or in a broad sense, embracing all sorts of human labour. Equally, according to Ladas, the term 'property' includes dissimilar kinds of interests and rights, and could designate tangibles whereas industrial property concerns only intangibles. S Ladas, *Patents, Trademarks & Related Rights: National & International Protection* (Cambridge MA, Harvard University Press, 1975) 1–16 (see also ch 1 (n 6)).

Additionally, this chapter retraces the 'the global patent system' discussions at the United Nations (UN) and the United Nations Conference on Trade and Development (UNCTAD)[2] during the decades prior to the Uruguay Round negotiations which started within the framework of the General Agreement on Tariffs and Trade (GATT)[3] in 1986. As today, those discussions centred around the costs of patent protection in developing countries and the negative role of IPRs in technology transfer. Finally, the chapter examines economists' analyses of international transfer of technology, with a focus on its impact on developing countries.

I THE BEGINNING OF GLOBAL INTELLECTUAL PROPERTY TREATIES

A Paris Convention for Protection of Industrial Property

The Paris Convention, which entered into force in 1884 with 14 Member States,[4] establishes principles and procedures of cooperation among contracting parties of the Paris Union in relation to industrial property, such as patents, trademarks, trade names, well-known marks,[5] industrial designs and indications of source or

---

[2] The first UNCTAD was held in Geneva in 1964. Subsequently, UNCTAD has met every four years, with intergovernmental bodies meeting between sessions and a permanent secretariat presiding located in Geneva. UNCTAD is a subsidiary organ of the UN. It provides an intergovernmental forum to discuss the place of developing countries in international trade, and it has contributed to launching the Generalized System of Preferences in 1968 and to adopting a series of international instruments such as the International Commodities Agreements, the Convention on a Code of Conduct for Liner Conferences and the Set of Multilaterally Agreed Equitable Principles and Rules for the Control of Restrictive Business Practices. 193 countries are Members of UNCTAD (as of 15 October 2010).

[3] The GATT was signed on 30 October 1947 and the tariff concessions came into effect by 30 June 1948 through a 'Protocol of Provisional Application' for 23 original Members. As the International Trade Organization (ITO) (signed on 21 November 1947) did not enter into force, the GATT became the only multilateral instrument governing international trade from 1948 until the World Trade Organization (WTO) was established in 1995 after the Uruguay Round negotiations. Within the framework of the GATT, efforts to reduce tariffs were made through a series of multilateral negotiations known as 'trade rounds' (five major trade rounds were organised from 1948 to 1994): www.wto.org/english/thewto_e/whatis_e/tif_e/fact4_e.htm. 153 countries are Members of WTO (as of 15 October 2010).

[4] The immediate reason for the adoption of the Paris Convention in 1883 was to ensure that countries could present their technologies at international expositions. Belgium, Brazil, Ecuador, France, Guatemala, Italy, the Netherlands, Portugal, El Salvador, Serbia, Spain, Switzerland and Tunisia were original members (Ecuador, Guatemala and El Salvador withdrew in 1886, 1887 and 1895, respectively). The US acceded in 1887, and Japan in 1889. The Paris Convention was revised in 1900, 1911, 1925, 1934, 1958, 1967 and 1979. 173 countries are Members of the Paris Convention as of 15 October 2010.

[5] Generally, those marks with respect to goods and services which have gained a reputation, irrespective of whether they are registered or not. According to the 1999 WIPO Joint Recommendation concerning Provisions on the Protection of Well-Known Marks (adopted by the Assembly of the Paris Union for the Protection of Industrial Property and the General Assembly of the WIPO www.wipo.int/sme/en/ip_business/marks/well_known_marks.htm, the determination of well-known marks is made by such factors as at least: reputation, recognition, duration, extent, geographical area and value associated with the mark. 184 countries are WIPO Members as of 15 October 2010.

appellations of origin ('geographical indications' in the TRIPS Agreement), as well as the prevention of unfair trade practices. The Convention was designed to facilitate the ability of inventors of one Union member country to obtain protection in other member countries for their intellectual creations, in the form of industrial property rights.

Article 2 of the Convention, which concerns national treatment for nationals of countries of the Union, provides in its paragraph 1 that:

> Nationals of any country of the Union shall, as regards the protection of industrial property, enjoy in all the other countries of the Union the advantages that their respective laws now grant, or may hereafter grant, to nationals; all without prejudice to the rights specially provided for by this Convention. Consequently, they shall have the same protection as the latter, and the same legal remedy against any infringement of their rights, provided that the conditions and formalities imposed upon nationals are complied with.

Article 3 also stipulates that: 'nationals of countries outside the Union who are domiciled or who have real and effective industrial or commercial establishments in the territory of one of the countries of the Union shall be treated in the same manner as nationals of the countries of the Union.'

One of the principles of the Paris Convention is the right of priority, whereby the filing date in one Paris Union member must not be invalidated before the expiration of the periods referred by reason of any acts accomplished in the interval, in particular, another filing in another member, the publication or exploitation of the invention. In other words, it establishes that an applicant from one contracting party is able to use its first filing date (in one of the members) as the effective filing date in another member, provided that he or she files another application within six months (for industrial designs and trade marks) or 12 months (for patents and utility models) from the first filing.

The independence of patents, as affirmed in Article 4 *bis,* is another principle of the Paris Convention. According to Article 4 *bis*(1), patents applied for in the various countries of the Union by nationals of countries of the Union are independent of patents obtained for the same invention in other countries, whether Members of the Union or not. Article 4 *bis*(2) of the Convention specifically provides that 'patents applied for during the period of priority are independent, both as regards the grounds for nullity and forfeiture, and as regards their normal duration'. However, in contrast to patents, Article 6 *quinquies* A provides that protection of marks registered in one country of the Union 'shall be accepted for filing and protected as is [*telle quelle*[6]] in the other countries of the Union, subject to the reservations indicated in this Article'. At the same time, Article 6 *quinquies* B enumerates exceptions for accepting *telle quelle* the registration of marks protected in foreign countries. Most Paris Union members use Article 6 *quinquies* B provisions as conditions for not accepting '*telle quelle*' marks (see also Chapter 6).

---

[6] Inserted by author.

If disputes relating to interpretation or application of the Convention are not settled by negotiation (Article 28), the Paris Convention provides only the procedures of the International Court of Justice, which are onerous.

B Berne Convention for the Protection of Literary and Artistic Works

The Berne Convention for the Protection of Literary and Artistic Works was signed in 1886.[7] There were and have been wide national differences in the ways literary and artistic works are protected and, therefore, the principles whereby certain rights held by the nationals of one country can be asserted in another have been important. The purpose of the Berne Convention was to facilitate the ability of nationals of its contracting State to obtain protection of their creative literary and artistic works and to exercise their rights in other Union member countries.

There are three basic principles underlying the Berne Convention. The first is the principle of national treatment. According to Article 5, when the works originate in one of the Union countries (ie, when the author of the work is a national of a Union country or when works were first published in such a country),[8] foreign authors are given the same rights and privileges to copyrighted material as domestic authors in any other Union countries (Article 5(1)). However, there are exceptions to the principle of national treatment, such as the provisions concerning the term of protection (Article 7(8)). Unless otherwise provided in the legislation of the country where protection is claimed, the term of copyright protection cannot exceed the term fixed in the country of origin of the work (reciprocity). The second principle is that copyrights for creative works are, in principle, automatically recognised in each member State of the Convention without being asserted or declared (Article 5(2)).[9] The third principle is, like the Paris Convention, the independence of rights in different countries (Article 5(3)).

The Berne Convention was influenced heavily by the French concept of the moral rights of the author (*droit d'auteur*), which contrasts with the American

---

[7] As of 15 October 2010, 164 countries are Parties to the Berne Convention.

[8] The 'country of origin' for published and unpublished works is defined in Art 5(4) for the following circumstances: (a) in the case of works first published in a country of the Union, that country; in the case of works published simultaneously in several countries of the Union which grant different terms of protection, the country whose legislation grants the shortest term of protection; (b) in the case of works published simultaneously in a country outside the Union and in a country of the Union, the latter country; (c) in the case of unpublished works or of works first published in a country outside the Union, without simultaneous publication in a country of the Union, the country of the Union of which the author is a national, with, however, specific rules for cinematographic works and works of architecture concerning business headquarters or residence.

[9] An author does not need to 'register' or 'apply for' a copyright, for his or her rights to be recognised. However, in the US, statutory damages and attorney's fees are available only for registered works. This exception has remained after the US joined the Convention in 1989 (17 USC § 101). The US assumes that the registration requirement is compatible with and not an 'exception' to the non-formality principle. Committee on the Judiciary, *The House Report on the Berne Convention Implementation Act of 1988* (1988) ch 5.

concept of 'copyright', which deals solely with economic aspects. In the US, the concept of 'neighbouring rights' does not exist and phonograms[10] are protected by copyright (producers of phonograms are treated as authors), while performers and broadcasting organisations are protected under the common law rather than a copyright statute. The US was not a party to the Berne Convention until 1989. This was because the country would not accept significant changes to its copyright law, particularly with regard to moral rights, general requirements for the registration of copyright works and mandatory copyright notices. The Universal Copyright Convention was introduced in 1952 to accommodate these differences until the Berne Convention Implementation Act of 1988[11] came into force in the US in March 1988.

The original (1886) text of the Berne Convention did not state any standard or minimum term of copyright protection, variations in which are still a cause of international friction among countries. The US became a party to the Berne Convention in 1989. A minimum term of protection became obligatory in the Brussels Act of 1948 and was maintained in the current Paris Act of 1971. The revised Berne Convention sets out a minimum term of protection, and parties are free to provide longer terms (Article 7(6)). Generally, except for photographic, cinematographic and anonymous or pseudonymous works, the term of protection is 50 years after the author's death (Article 7(1)). For cinematographic works, the term is 50 years after the work has been made available to the public with the consent of the author, or, failing such an event within 50 years from the making of such a work, 50 years after the making (Article 7(2)), and for anonymous or pseudonymous works, 50 years after the work has been lawfully made available to the public (Article 7(3)). For photographic works and works of applied art, in so far as they are protected as artistic works, the minimum term is until the end of a period of 25 years from the making of such a work (Article 7(4)).

C National, Regional and International Cooperation and the Establishment of WIPO

In 1893, the International Bureaux for the protection of intellectual property (*Bureaux Internationaux Réunis pour la Protection de la Propriété Intellectuelle*, BIRPI) was established to administer the Paris and Berne Conventions, as well as the Madrid Agreement concerning the International Registration of Marks (1891). The 'Madrid system' functions under the latter Agreement and the Madrid Protocol, adopted in 1989, and offers a trademark owner the possibility

---

[10] In the WIPO Performances and Phonograms Treaty (WPPT, adopted in Geneva on 20 December 1996), 'phonogram' is defined as the fixation of the sounds of a performance or of other sounds, or of a representation of sounds, other than in the form of a fixation incorporated in a cinematographic or other audiovisual work (Art 2 (b)). The WPPT entered into force on 20 May 2002 and, as of 15 October 2010, has 86 contracting parties.

[11] 17 USC § 101.

of having his trademark protected in several countries by filing one application with his own national or regional trademark office.

Based on the Convention Establishing the World Intellectual Property Organization (WIPO Convention), signed in Stockholm on 14 July 1967 (which entered into force in April 1970 and was amended on 28 September 1979), WIPO was created to take over the work of BIRPI, with a view to promoting and protecting intellectual property throughout the world (Article 3, WIPO Convention).[12] The agreement that was concluded between the United Nations and WIPO in 1974 recognised WIPO as a specialised agency of the United Nations.[13] Today, WIPO administers 24 international treaties.[14]

Certain aspects of IPRs which had not been dealt with in the Paris and Berne Conventions or Madrid Agreement gradually became the subject of international agreements.

In 1970, the Patent Cooperation Treaty (PCT) was adopted and entered into force on 1 April 2002.[15] Any international application made under the PCT is given the same treatment as if the applicant had made simultaneous applications in each PCT contracting party.[16] After filing a PCT application, an international examination will be conducted to confirm whether there has been any application in the past (which is publicly known) for an invention which is similar to the invention in the application in question. An examiner will prepare an opinion on whether the invention has the elements required for obtaining a patent, such as novelty, an inventive step and industrial applicability. If an applicant wishes, he or she can receive a preliminary examination of the elements necessary to obtain a patent (international preliminary examination) and can continue the patent application procedures in only selected countries based on his or her chances of obtaining a patent. Each country decides whether to grant a patent based on an actual examination by that country. The Patent Law Treaty (PLT), which attempts certain harmonisation of patent procedures, was adopted in June 2000 and came into effect in April 2005.[17]

---

[12] WIPO's mission is to promote the protection of intellectual property internationally, based on IP protection treaties, and to establish treaties for the purpose of harmonising the IP systems of each country. WIPO also carries out the administration and management of international registration services for IPRs and is currently involved in resolving disputes concerning Internet domain names.On 20 December 1996, the WIPO Copyright Treaties (WCT), which attempt to address the development of digital information technology (IT) and communications over the Internet, and the WIPO Performances and Phonograms Treaty (WPPT (n 10)), an international framework of rights concerning audio performances and phonograms, were adopted and introduced in WIPO, at roughly the same time as the TRIPS Agreement came into force. The WCT entered into force on 6 March 2002 and, as of 15 October 2010, has 88 contracting parties. As of 1 December 2006, WIPO had jurisdiction over 11 treaties concerning international rules for IP protection, eight treaties concerning international registration systems and services, and four treaties concerning the classification of industrial property rights.

[13] As of 15 October 2010, the number of WIPO contracting parties is 184.

[14] www.wipo.int/treaties/en/index.jsp.

[15] Adopted in Washington DC on 19 June 1970, amended on 28 September 1979 and modified on 3 February 1984 and 3 October 2001.

[16] 142 contracting parties as of 15 October 2010.

[17] 27 contracting parties as of 15 October 2010.

The Budapest Treaty on the International Recognition of the Deposit of Microorganisms for the Purposes of Patent Procedure (Budapest Treaty; see chapters 3 and 12) was signed on 28 April 1977[18] to be administered by the WIPO. For inventions relating to microorganisms, a deposit of biological material must be made to meet the disclosure requirement for enabling third parties to carry out the invention. The Budapest Treaty allows international recognition of the deposit of microorganisms to be made at a recognised institution for the purposes of patent procedure. This measure thus allows inventors to avoid the need to depositing microorganisms in all the countries where they wish to apply for patents. Today, the WIPO administers 24 international treaties.[19]

There have also been attempts at promoting regional cooperation relating to IPRs. Since the end of World War II, Europe has been working towards regional integration, but European countries have opted for keeping fundamental powers with respect to the protection of IPRs and only partially accepted regional agreements.[20] The Convention on the Grant of European Patents, commonly known as the European Patent Convention (EPC), was signed on 5 October 1973.[21] The EPC provides a legal framework and procedure for the granting of European patents. These are essentially nationally enforceable, nationally revocable patents, subject to central revocation or narrowing pursuant to unified, post-grant procedures.[22] European patents, once granted, become a bundle of nationally enforceable patents in the designated states, but enforcement must be carried out through national courts in individual countries.[23]

[18] Entered into force on 9 August 1980 and was amended on 26 September 1980. 73 contracting parties as of 15 October 2010.

[19] www.wipo.int/treaties/en/index.jsp.

[20] Following the European Convention on the International Classification of Patents for Invention (1954), the Convention on the Unification of Certain Points of Substantive Law on Patents for Invention (Strasbourg Convention), was signed by several Member States of the Council of Europe on 27 November 1963 and entered into force on 1 August 1980. The Strasbourg Convention established patentability criteria and led to certain harmonisation of patent laws across European countries.

[21] The number of contracting parties of the EPC was 38 as of 1 October 2010: the EU Member States individually and Albania, Switzerland, Liechtenstein, Turkey, Monaco, Iceland, Norway, Croatia, the Former Yugoslav Republic of Macedonia and San Marino and Serbia. Bosnia and Herzegovina and Montenegro are extension states which can request protection under the EPC. In November 2000, the Diplomatic Conference agreed to introduce revisions to the Convention and to add a level of judicial review through Boards of Appeal decisions. The revised EPC, called EPC 2000, entered into force on 13 December 2007. On 1 May 2008, the London Agreement was adopted to limit the number of translations required, so reducing the cost of translation. For the protection of European Community trademarks, the Office for Harmonization in the Internal Market (OHIM) was established in 1996. The OHIM has carried out the procedures also for the registered Community design (RCD) since 2003.

[22] Up to nine months after publication of the mention that a European patent has been granted, any person (other than the patent proprietor) may file a notice of opposition to the patent with the European Patent Office (EPO). Limitation and revocation procedures can be initiated by the patent proprietor only.

[23] The Convention for the European Patent for the Common Market (Luxembourg Convention) Community Patent Convention was signed on 15 December 1975 by nine Member States of the European Economic Community but did not enter into force. Many initiatives have been taken to establish Community patents for the European Community. On 8 December 2009, the Council of

As the membership to and the scope of international treaties relating to intellectual property rights increased, decision-making among contracting parties became complex and difficult. In 1973, the membership of the Paris Convention increased to 80 states, of which 44 were developing countries. In the same year, the number of developing countries with national patent legislation increased to 84 countries, up from 10 in 1873. Among the BIRPI Members, the number of developing country members was 15 in 1960. However, in 1967, this number increased to 42, of which 10 were Asian, 8 Latin American, and 24 African nations.[24]

Attempts at harmonising national patent law had been made among developed countries, but they stalled in the 1970s for a variety of reasons, including problems relating to the first-to-invent principle,[25] which is characteristic of the US patent system, as opposed to the first-to-file principle used in most countries. As these efforts for international cooperation were being made, the international community became more diverse. WIPO Member states came to be divided into three groups: developed, developing and socialist countries. The countries in each of these groups developed widely different views with respect to the protection of IPRs, making it nearly impossible to reach a unanimous decision within WIPO.

II PARIS CONVENTION AND ITS CONTROVERSIES: INDUSTRIAL POLICY ASPECTS OF PATENT PROTECTION

Since the inception of international cooperation, patent protection has been designed differently in national laws. According to GHC Bodenhausen, Director-General of BIRPI from 1963 to 1973:

> the Paris Convention leaves the Member States entirely free to establish the criteria of patentability, to decide whether patent applications should or should not be examined in order to determine, before a patent is granted, whether these criteria have been met, whether the patent should be granted to the first inventor or to the first applicant for a patent, or whether patents should be granted for products only, for processes only, or for both, and in which fields of industry and for what terms.[26]

the European Union Council agreed on steps to be taken regarding the EU patent. According to the agreed plan, the EU will accede to the EPC as a contracting State, and the European patents granted by the EPO will, when validated for the EU, have unitary effect in the territory of the EU.

[24] ET Penrose, 'International Patenting and the Less-Developed Countries' (1973) 83 *The Economic Journal* 768.

[25] To determine who has the right to the grant of a patent for the same invention, most countries use the first-to-file principle, according to which the first person to file a patent application for protection of that invention, regardless of the date of actual invention, is entitled to the patent. The US, on the other hand, operates on the first-to-invent principle that the first person to invent an invention will be awarded a patent. According to 35 US Code § 102(a), 'a person shall be entitled to a patent unless the invention was known or used by others in this country, or . . .'. The first applicant to file has the prima facie right to the grant of a patent. If a second patent application is filed for the same invention, the second applicant can institute interference proceedings to determine who was the first inventor and thereby who is entitled to the grant of a patent, which is a very costly procedure.

[26] GHC Bodenhausen, *Guide to the Application of the Paris Convention for the Protection of Industrial Property as revised at Stockholm in 1967* (Geneva, BIRPI, 1968) (reprinted in 2007).

Later, this passage from Bodenhausen was quoted in the Joint Report by the UN, UNCTAD and WIPO of 1974 (published in 1975 – hereafter the 1975 UN/UNCTAD/WIPO report)[27] on the Role of the Patent System in the Transfer of Technology to Developing Countries, where it explains the 'flexibility' of international standards at that time.

Although the main purpose of the Paris Convention is to delineate the principles of international cooperation to ensure protection of industrial property, it contains several substantive provisions, the main examples of which are:

Article 5A: patents: importation of articles; failure to work or insufficient working; compulsory licences.

Article 5B: industrial designs: failure to work; importation of articles.

Article 5B: industrial designs: failure to work; importation of articles.

Article 5C: marks: failure to use; different forms; use by co-proprietors.

Article 5D: patents, utility models, marks, industrial designs: marking.

-Article 5 ter: patents: patented devices forming part of vessels, aircraft, or land vehicles.

Article 5 quater: patents: importation of products manufactured by a process patented in the importing country.

Article 6 bis: protection of well-known marks.

Article 6 ter: marks: prohibitions concerning state emblems, official hallmarks, and emblems of intergovernmental organisations.

Article 6 quinquies: marks: protection of marks registered in one country of the union in the other countries of the union.

Article 6 sexies: protection of service marks.

Article 6 septies; marks: registration in the name of the agent or representative of the proprietor without the latter's authorisation.

Article 7 bis: protection of collective marks.

Article 8: protection of trade names.

Article 9: seizure, on importation, etc, of goods unlawfully bearing a mark or trade name.

Article 10: false indications: seizure, on importation, etc, of goods bearing false indications as to their source or the identity of the producer.

Article 10 bis: protection against unfair competition.

Article 10 ter: marks, trade names, false indications, unfair competition: remedies, right to sue.

---

[27] This report was prepared jointly by the UN Department of Economic and Social Affairs, the UNCTAD Secretariat and the International Bureau of the WIPO, TD/B/AC.11/19/Rev 1, 23 April 1974, 96–7. The same document was published by the UN in NY in 1975 (1975 UN/UNCTAD/WIPO Report).

A Compulsory Licensing

i Compulsory Licences for Failure to Work

In the discussions concerning international substantive rules of patent protection, compulsory licensing and patentability questions have been continuously contentious issues. The original Paris Convention of 1883 contained a substantive rule concerning forfeiture of patents. Article 5A of the Convention stipulated that:

> The introduction by the patentee into the country where the patent has been granted of objects manufactured in any of the States of the Union shall not entail forfeiture of the patent.

This provision was agreed upon in reaction to the prevalent industrial policy practices of countries at that time, including France, by which patents were invalidated if the patented products were imported but not manufactured locally in the country where the patent was protected. Paragraph (2) of Article 5A of the 1883 text stipulated, however, that: 'Nevertheless, the patentee shall remain bound to work his patent in conformity with the laws of the country into which he introduces the patented objects'. This meant that, if the right holder did not 'work' his patent, it could be revoked, depending on how the local law defined 'working'. The Paris Convention leaves to Members' discretion the question of whether or not to consider importation (either by the patentee or by his licensee) as 'working of patents'.[28]

The 'working' obligation of patented inventions was originally based on the idea that an invention to which the privilege of enjoying exclusivity is granted should be implemented, so that society also benefits from it. Incidentally, the statute of the City State of Venice, where the patent institution originated, enumerated four motives for the grant of a patent: the utility to society; the encouragement of inventive activity; the refund of costs incurred by the inventor; and the inventor's rights to the fruits of his mind.[29] This law provided explicitly that it was within the power and discretion of the government of Venice to use any patented invention, subject to the provision that the patentee should be a person who had the right to work the patent on behalf of the government.

In 1925, at the Revision Conference in The Hague, Article 5A was modified. The new Article 5A introduced the concept of compulsory licensing as a means 'to prevent the abuses, which might result from the exclusive rights conferred by the patent, for example, failure to work'. When the above provision was instituted in Article 5A(2) in 1925, two conditions were attached. First, patents were not subject to forfeiture unless the grant of compulsory licenses was insufficient

---

[28]   In the Revision Conference in Washington (1911), a condition was added to Art 5A(2) that the patent may not be forfeited for non-working until after a period of three years from the date of filing the application in that country, and only in case the patentee cannot justify his inaction.

[29]   1975 UN/UNCTAD/WIPO Report (n 26) 97.

to prevent such abuses (Article 5A(3)). Second, compulsory licenses were not to be issued before at least three years from the date of grant or if the patentee proved the existence of 'legitimate excuses' (Article 5A(4)). Bodenhausen explains that 'legitimate excuses' may be based on the existence of legal, economic or technical obstacles to exploitation, or more intensive exploitation, of the patent in the country.[30]

The new rule was that Paris Union Members were allowed to forfeit patents only when the grant of compulsory licenses was insufficient to prevent such abuses. The rule remains in force today in the Paris Convention, as amended in Stockholm in 1967.

So that an industrial policy of one country would not override the rights of inventors beyond the scope that exceptions to the rights conferred would possibly justify, various proposals were made regarding Article 5A of the Paris Convention. At the Revision Conferences in London (1934) and Lisbon (1958), further conditions were added to Articles 5A(3) and (4).[31] Thus, Article 5A(3) of the Paris Convention 1967 provides that 'Forfeiture of the patent shall not be provided for except in cases where the grant of compulsory licenses would not have been sufficient to prevent the said abuses. No proceedings for the forfeiture or revocation of a patent may be instituted before the expiration of two years from the grant of the first compulsory license.' Article 5A(4) reads:

> A compulsory license may not be applied for on the ground of failure to work or insufficient working before the expiration of a period of four years from the date of filing of the patent application or three years from the date of the grant of the patent, whichever period expires last; it shall be refused if the patentee justifies his inaction by legitimate reasons. Such a compulsory license shall be non-exclusive and shall not be transferable, even in the form of the grant of a sub-license, except with that part of the enterprise or goodwill which exploits such license.

Proposals made at the Lisbon Revision Conference requiring compulsory licences for patents to be subject to a royalty payment by the licensee were not adopted. This was due to the US insistence on exceptions for antitrust violations.[32] At the London Revision Conference, the application of the provisions in Article 5A to utility models was inserted. Article 5B was added at The Hague Revision Conference and stipulates that the protection of industrial designs shall not be subject to any forfeiture, either by reason of failure to work or importation of Articles corresponding to those which are protected in the importing country.

Article 5A of the Paris Convention has been one of the most discussed provisions. For developing countries which promote local manufacture of patented goods, employment and training, the 'working of patents' in the sense of domestic manufacturing has been considered as important, as reflected in their laws (see chapter 10).

---

[30] Bodenhausen (n 26) 73.
[31] ibid 67–79.
[32] Ladas (n 1) 87.

India, which was not a contracting party to the Paris Convention before December 1998, asserted in a government report by Justice Ayyangar (the Ayyangar Report)[33] that securing priority rights for Indian inventors would be the sole advantage of the Convention. He argued that this was not worth sacrificing India's economic and industrial interest[34] and jeopardising India's system of ensuring local working of foreign patents by 'licences of right',[35] compulsory licensing and revocation of patents to protect against the growing demands of developed countries to strengthen patent rights (see chapter 10).[36] The Ayyangar Report warned against the former Patents Enquiry Committee recommendation that India join the Paris Convention for the Protection of Industrial Property.

In an interdependent economy, global efficiency may benefit a national economy more than reliance on domestic industrial production at any cost. The obligation to manufacture domestically in a country with patent protection may, in many cases, have little rationale. Those countries with technological competitiveness that consider importation in addition to local manufacturing to be part of the working of patents struggled for over a hundred years to make this conception an international rule.

On the other hand, those countries that view patent protection as a means of domestic industrial development (including those which protect inefficient domestic industry) continue to emphasise the importance of domestic manufacturing as the only acceptable form of 'working'. Significantly, the Convention leaves each country to define the meaning of 'working' a patent. For more than one hundred years, the complexities of Article 5A were to entertain an inter-

---

[33] R. Ayyangar, *Report on the Revision of the Patent Law* (New Delhi, 1959). See ch 10 for further analyses.

[34] ibid 117–19.

[35] The system of 'licences of right' has generally existed in British legal tradition countries such as Great Britain, Ireland, India, New Zealand and South Africa, as well as Germany and Greece, to safeguard patents from a compulsory licence or revocation for non-working by the grant of the patent endorsed, for any person to obtain a licence under the patent as a right. The patent applicant declares his readiness to license out his patent and voluntarily accepts the restriction of the exclusive monopoly. The annuities for such patents are reduced to one half (Ladas (n 1) 429). The Indian Patents Act 1970, ss 86–8 under c XIV (Working of Patents, Compulsory Licences and Revocation) provided for its system of licences of right. According to s 86(2), if the reasonable requirements of the public with respect to the patented invention have not been satisfied or the patented invention is not available to the public at a reasonable price, the Controller may make an order that the patent be endorsed with the words 'licences of right'. Under this system, process patents pertaining to substances capable of being used as medicines or foods, as well as process patents for making chemical substances (such as alloys), were automatically deemed to be endorsed as 'licences of right' and were available for compulsory licensing by all applicants. In *Imperial Chemical Industries Ltd v Controller General of Patents* 1987 AIR 77 (Kolkata), the Kolkata High Court affirmed the Controller's order deeming ICI's patent, claiming a catalyst useful in hydrocarbon reforming as well as a process for making the catalyst, to be subject to licensing of right. Cited in J Mueller, 'The Tiger Awakens: The Tumultuous Transformation of India's Patent System and the Rise of Indian Pharmaceutical Innovation' (2007) 68(3) *University of Pittsburgh Law Review* 576 (n 501). By s 39 of the Patents (Amendment) Act 2002, c XVI (ss 82–98) of the Patents Act was substituted by a new c XVI (ss 82–94) and the words 'licences of right' are no longer used.

[36] Ayyangar Report (n 33) 118–19.

minable debate, notably over the question of whether merely importing the patented objects fulfils the requirement of 'working', which the TRIPS Agreement did not entirely resolve (see chapters 4, 5, 7 and 10).

A compulsory licence is an authorisation given by an authority (usually a competent administrative body or a court) to a person, other than the patentee, to undertake certain acts (such as manufacturing), without authorisation by the patentee, which would have otherwise been excluded by the patent.[37] Other government-use authorisations can be given to permit use of patented technology for public non-commercial purposes or emergencies.

Most countries came to include in their patent laws, in one form or another, forms of non-voluntary use of inventions, for example, on the grounds of 'public interest', which includes emergency situations, or certain abuses such as certain anti-competitive behaviour. However, non-voluntary use of inventions could be resorted to by governments or companies in the name of public interest, for reasons closely related to their own economic interests, such as industrial progress, local manufacturing of patented goods and prices thereof, employment or training.

The Paris Convention deals with compulsory licences only from the point of view of abuses of exclusive rights, of which failure to work and insufficient working are considered examples. The criteria for determining whether there has been an abuse of rights contrary to the purposes of the patent system have changed. At present, there is still an extremely wide range of opinions about what constitutes an abuse, and there is no sign of any agreement being reached in the near future.

ii Compulsory Licences on the Grounds of Public Interest

The Paris Convention does not deal with public policy issues and does not refer to compulsory licensing on these grounds. Many countries provided for exceptions to patentability in certain technological fields and developed a compulsory licensing system for situations that could be subsumed under the term 'public interest' or public policy, particularly in medicines and food, as in the UK and Canada. The industrial policy objectives in these cases overlap with what the law enshrines as 'public interest'.

The UK Patents Act 1949 also provided special rules for compulsory licensing of inventions capable of being used as food, drink, medicine or germicide or methods of manufacturing any such substances, or as a surgical or therapeutic

---

[37] According to the 1979 WIPO Model Law for Developing Countries on Inventions, 'non-voluntary licence' refers to the authorisation to perform in a country without the agreement of the owner of the patent, in respect of the patented invention, any of the acts referred to in s 135(2) (concerning the effects of grant of patent; definition of 'exploitation'), with the exception of importation, granted by a government to a third party to use the invention without the consent of the patent holder. WIPO, *WIPO Model Law for Developing Countries on Inventions* (1979) vol I, Patents 33.

device or any part thereof, with payment of reasonable royalties to the right holder, presumably for public interest.[38] This provision was repealed in 1977.

For many years, the country that most often granted compulsory licences was Canada.[39] From 1923 Canada had strong compulsory licensing provisions which allowed the granting of compulsory licenses for the manufacture of drugs and food products protected in Canada by patents. In 1969 the law was amended in accordance with compulsory licence policies, particularly for the pharmaceutical industry to provide compulsory licensing even for imports of bulk pharmaceutical ingredients. A provision was made under Canada's Patent Act under which the Commissioner of the Canadian Intellectual Property Office was given the power to grant licences for substances or manufacturing processes for pharmaceuticals or foods, unless there were justifiable grounds to refuse the application. At that time it became possible to import under a compulsory licence not only pharmaceutical products manufactured by manufacturing process patented in Canada, but also active pharmaceutical ingredients (API).[40] This system, together with the sufficient size of its pharmaceutical markets and its efficient regulatory organisations assuring the quality, efficacy and safety of the products, made it possible to build up an efficient generic drugs industry in Canada. The system was extensively utilised until 1992, when it was modified in conformity with the free trade agreement concluded between Canada and the US (Canada-United States Free Trade Agreement – see chapter 14).

With a succession of formerly colonised countries achieving their independence, there was growing criticism that patent protection only benefited multinationals, and this developed into a political issue in many developing countries.

In 1965, the Expert Committee of BIRPI adopted the Model Law for Developing Countries on Inventions.[41] This Model Law stipulated the procedures for: granting of compulsory licences for important technology relating to economic development or public health; technology necessary for the exploitation of another patent; and the failure to work a patent (ie, to exploit the patented invention by, for example, manufacturing, making or selling). In order to prevent the abuse of compulsory licences for the purpose of protecting domestic industry, the Model Law emphasised the principle of national treatment and strict procedural rules, as well

---

[38] According to Scherer, 20 compulsory licences were issued in response to 54 applications between 1953 and 1971, including Chloromycetin, Librium and Valium. FM Scherer, 'The Economic Effects of Compulsory Licences' (New York, University Monograph Series in Finance and Economics 1977–2 (1977)) 40–5.

[39] In Canada, from 1935 to 1970, 192 applications for compulsory licences were filed, 79 licences were granted, 14 applications were dismissed and 72 applications were waived. It is said that 613 compulsory licences were granted between when the Patents Act was reformed in 1969, and 1992. S Chaudhuri, 'TRIPS and Changes in Pharmaceutical Patent Regime in India' (2005) www.who.int/intellectualproperty/documents.

[40] This term which refers to (bulk) drug substances was used during the International Conference on Harmonization (ICH). On the ICH, see ch 8, n 132 and ch 11, n 24.

[41] BIRPI, *Model Law for Developing Countries on Inventions*, Publication No 801(E) (Geneva, 1965). The content was renewed and published in 1979 (n37).

as the date from which compulsory licences can be granted (four years from the application or three years from the granting of the patent, whichever is sooner).

The US and other developed countries oriented the discussion to strengthen the Paris Convention so that importation would be considered to be the working of patents.[42] Developing countries opposed this view and criticised these restrictions on compulsory licences as being contrary to the benefits they are intended to deliver to developing countries. No agreement was reached on this issue at the 1981 Nairobi Diplomatic Conference for the revisions of the Paris Convention. In July 1985, WIPO began discussions to harmonise the different patent systems among its Members. A diplomatic conference was held in June 1991 for this purpose, but it failed for multiple reasons, including the US refusal to give up its 'first-to-invent' principle (note 26).

B Patentable Subject Matter

The Convention left largely to national discretion substantive issues of patentability (ie patentable subject matter and patentability requirements). The survey on the role of the patent system in the transfer of technology to developing countries, conducted by the UN/WIPO/UNCTAD and published in 1975,[43] revealed that any invention was patentable in 14 UN Member states, eight of which were developing countries. In contrast, Ghana, Iraq and Peru generally excluded all matters considered to be against the public interest from being patentable.[44] Medicine was excluded from patentability in 43 countries including six developed countries, six socialist countries and 13 countries of the African and Malagasy Industrial Property Office (OAMPI). Many of those countries granted patents for manufacturing processes, but did not provide protection for products. Medicines and nutritional supplement substances and manufacturing processes were not patentable in Italy or Brazil. In Brazil, not only products, but also processes for manufacturing chemical formulas were unpatentable (chapter 10). Those developed countries not at the cutting edge of the chemical industry also avoided product patent protection and sought different processes for manufacturing new chemical compounds whose pharmaceutical value was discovered and invented in more advanced countries (on patent protection of chemical and pharmaceutical substances in European countries, see chapter 10). In these countries it was possible to file patent applications for derivatives (such as salts, crystals and isomers), thereby circumventing existing patents.

Although Japan was a latecomer in chemical and pharmaceutical R&D, by the 1970s, it had a relatively strong chemical industry with good processing

---

[42] The Paris Convention does not say whether or not importation is considered exploitation of patents.

[43] 1975 UN/UNCTAD/WIPO Report (n 27) 139.

[44] ibid 156.

technology.[45] In Japan, between 1959 and 1976, pharmaceuticals, chemicals, food and beverages could be protected only by process patents.[46] Product patent protection was introduced by the 1975 Law of Adoption of a Patent System for Substances, which came into force on 1 January 1976.

Redwood cites a Japanese commentator, who wrote that:

> . . . the reason why the 1959 law and patent law prior to that did not adopt a patent system for substances was based on the viewpoint of national life . . . that such things as pharmaceuticals and foods and beverages were indispensable to the daily life of the people; and with regard to chemical substances it was based on industrial policy, attempting to protect the chemical industry which was weak in technical development, from patent monopoly of foreign business.[47]

Various technical studies on product and process patent protection and their implications for the Japanese industry were undertaken throughout the post-World War II era.[48]With the overall improvement in technical levels through the 1960s and 1970s, the absence of product patent protection came to be viewed negatively as impeding development efforts for original new substances. Multiple processes had to be patented to build fences around the new processes in order to pre-empt both foreign and domestic competitors. Many of the processes developed at the time were inferior to existing ones, which resulted in low social returns to R&D. The aggregate number of process patents dropped dramatically after 1976. As process R&D decreased, scientific resources were redirected to other areas, including new chemical entities (NCE) research. At that time, because the patent scope was narrow, firms that were accustomed to process-related R&D found it relatively easy to shift into product R&D. A shift in the direction of R&D from new processes to new products may raise or lower social welfare, depending on the existing technological opportunities. Studies suggest that technological opportunities in products became greater than those in processes in 1970s Japan.[49] Before the introduction of product patent protection, the number of medicinal products developed in Japan and marketed in more than 20 countries was two in the 1960s and four in the 1970s. After the introduction of product patent protection, this number increased to 18 in the 1980s and 14 in the 1990s.

---

[45] H Iwata et al, *Busshitsu no Chishiki* ('Knowledge about Product Patents') (*Tusho-Sangyo Chosakai*, 1975) 83–91; H Redwood, *New Horizons in India: the Consequences of Pharmaceutical Patent Protection* (Felixstowe, Oldwicks Press, 1994) 91–7.

[46] In the first Patent Law of 1885, pharmaceuticals were non-patentable, but there was no prohibition of patent protection of chemicals, foods or beverages. Under the Patent Laws of 1888, 1900 and 1910, chemicals were patentable but pharmaceuticals, foods and beverages were not patentable; under the Patent Laws of 1922 and 1959, pharmaceuticals, chemicals, foods and beverages were not patentable. Japan became a member of the Paris Convention in 1899.

[47] Redwood, *New Horizons in India* (n 45) 91 (translation from K Yoshifuji, *Commentary on Patent Law*, 9th edn, 1991).

[48] Iwata et al account for numerous studies undertaken on patent protection abroad. (n 45) 39–86.

[49] K Murayama, '*Nihon ni okeru busshitsu iyakutokkyoseido donyu no keiken ni tshuite*' ('On the Experience of Product and Pharmaceutical Patent Introduction in Japan') (1983) 33(10) *Tokkyo Kanri* 1261–71.

With the expanded industrial use of frontier scientific discoveries and bio-technology, patent protection of substances became all the more important. It was in the context of the advancement of modern biotechnology in the 1980s that industries in developed countries started to seek a global system of IPR protection.

III UNCTAD DISCUSSIONS IN THE 1970S ON THE TRANSFER OF TECHNOLOGY

A 1964 UN Report

Brazil, one of the 11 original Members of the Paris Convention (see chapters 1 and 10), proposed at the UN General Assembly in 1961[50] that the UN Secretary General undertake a study of the effects of patents on developing country economies, survey national patent legislations with special emphasis on the treatment given to foreign patents, and advise on holding an international conference to examine the special needs of developing countries regarding existing provisions of international conventions.[51] Following this resolution, a report by the Secretary-General, entitled *The Role of Patents in the Transfer of Technology to Developing Countries* was published in 1964 (the 1964 UN Report).[52] The relevant provisions of the patent laws in some 29 countries were compared and the views of these countries on the importance of patents, and especially of foreign patents, for their industrial development were summarised. Most of these countries, including 12 'less-developed countries',[53] believed that patents were a valuable aid to their development, assisted the spread of technology through publication and promoted manufacturing and investment.

Exceptions were India, Lebanon and Cuba; these three countries responded that they did not benefit from international patenting. Cuba complained about import monopoly by foreign right holders, India complained about the predominance of foreign-owned patents and Lebanon complained about the nonworking of these patents.[54]

Based on the analysis of national patent legislations, government regulations and their relevance to transfer of technology in both developed and developing countries, the 1964 UN Report pointed out, inter alia, that:

[50] Resolution 2091(XX) calling for examination of the adequacy of existing national and international practices for transfer of patented and unpatented technologies to developing countries.

[51] UN GA Res 1713(XVI) (adopted 19 December 1961) 16 UN GAOR Supp (No 17) 20.

[52] United Nations, *The Role of Patents in the Transfer of Technology to Developing Countries: Report of the Secretary-General*, UN Publication Sales No 65.II.B.1 (New York, 1964) (1964 UN Report).

[53] This was a term of art used before GA decided to use the Least Developed Country (LDC) classification in 1977. For LDCs, see ch 4 n 153 and ch 5 n 87.

[54] Annex C of the report lists governments' evaluation of the manner in which access to inventions and know-how had been helped or hindered through the existence or non-existence of a national patent system. 1964 UN Report (n53) 56–60.

- The establishment of patent systems in developing countries raised no specific problems, subject to the possible need for technical assistance or regional arrangements in administering such systems, and the general importance of conserving the scarce scientific human power for directly productive tasks.
- The real issues revolved around the position of foreign patentees. Developing countries may suffer from high prices if a patent granted to a foreign national is not worked, although high prices may be the result of factors other than the exclusionary monopoly given to the patentee. It would be exceptional if patented products or processes were advantageously introduced into the economy of developing countries without the cooperation of the foreign patentee or any other resources outside the developing country. Both developed and developing countries should operate the patent system in a context of general legislation which reduces possible misuses of the system. Fairly and effectively administered compulsory licences would deal with situations of abuse, if, exceptionally, no patentee cooperation were needed. Screening and control of licence agreements could deal with unduly restrictive practices.
- The governments of developing countries have a legitimate interest in preventing excessive exploitation of their one-sided technological and financial dependence. However, one of the chief drawbacks of the patent system in developed countries, ie, the limitation of competition accompanying the protection given to the pioneer, may not be particularly serious in those countries at an early stage of development, due to the smaller size of markets and resources (as only one manufacturing plant in various economic sectors may be present in the developing country).[55]

The 1964 UN Report concluded that: '. . . the question of patents must be seen – and dealt with – in the broader context of facilitating the transfer of patented and unpatented technology to the developing countries, and enhancing the ability of the latter to adopt and use such foreign technology in the implementation of their development programmes.'[56] According to this report, 'since the problems connected with transfer of technology go much beyond the operation of patent systems, more could be done through action at the national level than by calling a conference'.[57]

B UNCTAD and Transfer of Technology

Notably, it was UNCTAD that provided a forum for developing countries to discuss this issue. In June 1971, the Intergovernmental Group on Transfer of Technology adopted its programme of work.[58] At the Third UNCTAD Conference, in May

[55] The 1964 UN Report (n 52) 49–50.

[56] ibid 50.

[57] The 1964 UN Report (n 52) 7.

[58] On the work of UNCTAD on transfer of technology, see 'An International Code of Conduct on Transfer of Technology', report by the UNCTAD Secretariat, TD/B/C.6/AC.1/2/Supp.1/Rev.1(1975);

1972, a resolution was adopted calling for a study for possible bases for new international legislation regulating the transfer from developed to developing countries of patented and non-patented technology.[59] Within this framework, UNCTAD subsequently launched a series of studies on the role of patents and technology transfer which went in parallel with the elaboration of the UNCTAD Multilaterally Agreed Equitable Principles and Rules for the Control of Restrictive Business Practices.[60] In 1975, the Group of Governmental Experts on the Role of the Patent System in the Transfer of Technology of the Trade and Development Board of UNCTAD started its discussions to draft a code of conduct on the transfer of technology (TOT Code). Between 1978 and 1985, several sessions were held but failed to adopt the TOT Code.[61]

UNCTAD discussions on the transfer of technology covered a wide range of subjects such as national scientific and economic development, institutional infrastructure, competition, but the Group of Governmental Experts focused on the international patent system and included the following issues: (1) the impacts of the international patent system practices on developing countries, particularly concerning the transfer of technology; and (2) a future revision of the patent system.

The WIPO, for its part, was initiating in 1974 discussions for a possible Revision Conference of the Paris Convention[62] In December 1977, the WIPO Ad Hoc Group of Government Experts adopted a Declaration which enumerated the objectives to guide the Diplomatic Conference. This Declaration of Objectives stated that the revision of the Paris Convention should aim to contribute to the establishment of a new economic order[63] in which social justice prevails and economic inequalities between nations are reduced and that considerations for the revision should include 'the question of equality of treatment for all existing forms of protection of industrial property', implying the principle of national treatment and possible preferential treatment for development countries. [64] The Sixth Revision Conference of the Paris Convention met first in 1981 and finally in 1983, without results.

S J Patel, P Roffe and A Yusuf, *International Technology Transfer – The Origins and Aftermath of the United Nations Negotiations on a Draft Code of Conduct*, Kluwer Law International (The Hague, 2001) 3 et seq 259 et seq; P Roffe, 'Transfer of Technology: UNCTAD's Draft International Code of Conduct', (1985) 19 *The International Lawyer* 689.

[59] UNCTAD Proceedings, UNCTAD Doc. TD/108 (1972).

[60] The UN General Assembly, at its thirty-fifth session in its resolution 35/63 of 5 December 1980, adopted the Set of Multilaterally Agreed Equitable Principles and Rules for the Control of Restrictive Business Practices approved by the United Nations Conference on Restrictive Business Practices. This UNCTAD work later evolved into what today is known as 'Trade and Competition Policies'.

[61] The draft International Code of Conduct on the Transfer of Technology can be found at http://stdev.UNCTAD.org/compendium/documents/totcode%20.html.

[62] In June 1974, the Director General of WIPO called for the creation of an Ad Hoc Group of Governmental Experts with the idea of possible revision of the Paris Convention.

[63] See 'Programme of Action on the Establishment of New International Economic Order' (adopted 9 May 1974) (A/9556) UNGA Res 3201 (S-VI) IV.

[64] On the WIPO process leading up to the aborted Sixth Revision Conference, see P Roffe and G Vea, 'The WIPO Development Agenda in an Historical and Political Context', in NW Netanel (ed.) *The Development Agenda: Global Intellectual Property and Developing Countries* (Oxford, Oxford University Press, 2009) 99–109.

Various UNCTAD papers prepared for the Group of Governmental Experts recommended a series of revisions for the Paris Convention in this historical context. The UNCTAD Group of Governmental Experts discussed such questions as the principle of national treatment, patentability criteria, independence of patents, terms of protection, and provisions to prevent and correct the abuses resulting from the exercise of the rights conferred by the patent, with a view to possible modifications of the Paris Convention.

In the UNCTAD discussions in the 1970s through 1985, the primary concern was that the majority of the patents in developing countries were owned by foreign companies, and they were not 'worked' (chapters 4, 7 and 10). Since the 1950s, economic, statistical, or other studies relating to IPR protection in developing countries have been undertaken in the United States and Europe. Some of these studies influenced the literature on the subject in Latin America.[65] Grundmann's 1976 study, based on his statistical data on patenting in 17 African states, enquired into the role of patents in technology transfer in these countries. It found that most patents were held by foreign companies and were intended to protect their imports against imitators, or to license the use of the equipment they imported. These patents had the effect of enforcing monopolies in the use of their advanced technology. However, these studies also disclosed factors other than the international patent system that hindered technology transfer in developing countries. Grundmann's study also showed that insufficient capacity to absorb modern industrial technology led to inadequate transfer of technology to these countries.[66] Vernon in 1971[67] analysed investor behaviour and policies and suggested that, in one way or another, patent protection factors are considered by investors as part of the investment environment.

Vaitsos, who advised and represented the ANDEAN Community[68] in the series of UNCTAD discussions on the role of the patent system in the transfer of technology to developing countries, criticised the international system of patent protection for its alleged negative effects on developing country economies.[69] Based on rough investment accounts from Chile in 1970, India in 1959 and Argentina in 1970, which showed that local patent-holders were individual inventors and not companies, Vaitsos argued that, if the number of patents were weighted by

[65] E Penrose, *The Economics of the International Patent System* (Baltimore MD, The Johns Hopkins University Press, 1951); HE Grundmann, 'Patent Laws in New African States' (1968) 50(7) *Journal of the Patent Office Society* 486–503; RE Baldwin and JD Richardson, 'Other Issues: North-South Trade, IPRs, and Subsidies' (1986) *Issues in the Uruguay Round*, NBER Conference Report; A Jaffe, 'Technological Opportunity and Spillovers of R&D' (1988) 76 *American Economic Review* 984–1001.

[66] HE Grundmann, 'Foreign patent monopolies in developing countries: An empirical analysis' (1976) 12(2) *Journal of Development Studies* 186–96.

[67] R Vernon, *Sovereignty at Bay: The Multinational Spread of US Enterprises* (New York, Basic Books, 1971) 107.

[68] The ANDEAN Community was established on 25 May 1969 and comprises Chile, Peru, Bolivia, Ecuador, Colombia and Venezuela.

[69] CV Vaitsos, 'Patents Revisited: Their Function in Developing Countries' (1972) 9 *Journal of Development Studies*. In this analysis, patents are assumed to have an immediate impact on the economy.

their economic or technological worth (sales and value added), weighted patents belonging to national citizens would amount to only 1 per cent of total patents granted by these countries.

According to Vaitsos, patents create monopoly privileges with forward linkages which, in turn: (1) limit import possibilities of related products other than by the choice of the right holder, thus restricting competition in the local markets and the entry of local technologies; (2) help only multinational companies to control international markets and allow excessive profits by eliminating competitors; and (3) hinder the flow of technology from industrialised to developing countries.[70] Vaitsos asserted, therefore, that the patent system affects developing country economies only negatively, unlike other economic policies such as tariffs or taxation, which have some benefits. The UNCTAD Group of Governmental Expert discussions[71] suggested that strong patent protection allowed the right holder to raise the price of imported technology, hindering access by local manufacturers not only to the technologies of right holders but also to other technologies developed in the developing countries. According to this argument, IPR protection in the technology-recipient country increases the cost of filling in the gap between foreign and local technologies.

The UNCTAD Group of Governmental Experts also discussed patentability criteria[72] with a particular focus on the patentability of pharmaceuticals. During the Second World War in Europe and in the 1970s in developing countries, policies of import substitution were strengthened by mitigating patent protection (see Chapter 10). Processes for the manufacture of medicines were excluded from patentability in Italy.[73] In Brazil, similarly, patentability of processes for obtaining nutritive and chemical substances was abolished.[74] In Mexico, pharmaceutical processes were protected only by a *certificado de invencion* (certificate of invention). Concomitant to such policies, patent protection of chemicals for agricultural and pharmaceutical products was criticised as contributing only to strengthening multinational corporations. In this context, the behaviour of multinational companies has often been bracketed with the conduct of the international patent system in developing countries, for its alleged negative effects on

---

[70]   ibid.

[71]   See, for example, 'The international patent system as an instrument of policy for national development', report by the UNCTAD Secretariat, July 1975, TD/B/C.6/AC.2/3; 'Systems, including industrial property systems, for improving national scientific and technological infrastructures of the developing countries', report by the UNCTAD Secretariat, August 1975, TD/B/C.6/AC.2/4; 'Promotion of national scientific and technological capabilities and revision of the patent system', report by the UNCTAD Secretariat, July 1975, TD/B/C.6/AC.2/2; 'The international patent system: The revision of the Paris Convention for the Protection of Industrial Property', report by the UNCTAD Secretariat, 28 June 1977, TD/B/C.6/AC.3/2; 'The Role of the Patent System in the Transfer of Technology to Developing Countries', note by the UNCTAD Secretariat transmitting a study by INTAL, 'Industrial Property in Latin America and its Role in Development and Economic Integration', TD/B/C.6/16 and Corr.l.

[72]   'Promotion of national scientific and technological capabilities and revision of the patent system' (n 71) 11–15.

[73]   Royal Decree No 1127, 1939.

[74]   Industrial Property Code, Law 5772, 1971.

their economies. Vaitsos put forward an analysis that claimed patent protection dramatically increased the price of imported pharmaceutical products in developing countries by as much as 5,647 per cent.[75]

During the UNCTAD discussions, the following provisions of the Paris Convention were criticised for their failure to contribute to the national economies of developing countries[76]:

- Article 5 *quater*[77] allows that if a patent is granted only for a process, not only the application of the process but also, and independently, the sale and use of its products constitute patent infringement. This provision allows patent owners in developed countries to hold import monopolies in the markets of developing countries,[78] which, in turn, discourages investment and the transfer of technology.[79]
- Time limits and conditions imposed on the issuance of compulsory licensing and forfeiture (Article 5A(3) and 5A(4)).[80]
- Novelty criteria which oblige developing countries to rely on the expertise and exogenous knowledge of developed countries, discouraging local innovation.[81]

ET Penrose, who was a pioneering researcher on the role of patent systems in developing countries in the 1970s and one of the experts at the UNCTAD discussions, recognised that, if patents were protected in developing countries, it would mainly result in foreign companies being granted patents. She also stated that certain forms of abusive behaviour of multinationals appeared to exist in developing countries.[82] Penrose, admitting that the patent system in developing countries might not be assisting local inventors' inventions or industrial innovation, and that multinational companies' motives for patenting in developing

---

[75] Vaitsos explained that prices of imported pharmaceutical product in countries such as Colombia, Chile and Peru increased from a minimum of 40% to a maximum of 5647%, due to the introduction of the patent system. Apparently, Vaitsos did not examine factors other than patents affecting prices. Vaitsos (n 69) 85–7.

[76] 'The International Patent System: the Revision of the Paris Convention for the protection of Industrial Property', report by the UNCTAD Secretariat', 28 June 1977, TD/B/C.6/AC.3/2; 'Systems, including industrial property systems, for improving national scientific and technological infrastructures of the developing countries' (n 71).

[77] Art 5 *quater* provides that: 'When a product is imported into a country of the Union where there exists a patent protecting a process of manufacture of the said product, the patentee shall have all the rights with regard to the imported product, that are accorded to him by the legislation of the country of importation, on the basis of the process patent, with respect of products manufactured in that country.' Art 5 *quater* of the Paris Convention was introduced into the Convention at the Revision Conference of Lisbon in 1958. Before the amendment, the Convention left complete freedom to the Member States to define in their national legislation the acts of third parties by which a patent would be infringed. Bodenhausen (n 26) 85 (on Art 5 *quater*).

[78] 'The International Patent System' (n 71) 17.

[79] ibid 19.

[80] See above at p 38.

[81] Vaitsos argued that due to the high cost and the expertise required to efficiently run patent offices, the evaluation of patents in developing countries depends on foreign knowledge. Countries such as Brazil, which carried out 'prior [art] examinations', had immense backlogs for evaluation. Brazil was thought to have had nearly 400,000 pending patent applications in 1970. Vaitsos (n 69) 89.

[82] Penrose, 'International Patenting and the Less-Developed Countries' (n 24) 768–70.

countries may differ from those in relation to developed countries, said, first of all, that:

> So much for the arguments and counter-arguments; what is the evidence?
>
> Unfortunately, we have only the same type of evidence both for and against the arguments outlined as we have with regard to the effect of a domestic patent system on invention and innovation generally.[83]

Penrose went on to explain that in Vaitsos' arguments, for example, a number of considerations other than patents could produce similar results, especially in the pharmaceutical industry, such as 'brand-name protection, transfer pricing to subsidiaries which would continue regardless of patents, subsidised or loss-making exports which would not be available on a continuing basis.'[84] According to Penrose, such overpricing could be attributed also to the passing on of development costs, and there is no evidence that high prices would be attributable solely to patents. Penrose further pointed out that when a foreign firm grants a patent licence, with illegal restrictions, 'these abuses can be dealt with under the ordinary law. One should not hold the patent law, and in particular the international patent convention, responsible for illegal restrictive activities which are otherwise'.[85] Comparing the UN 1964 Report and other economists' analyses and the criticisms that came out of UNCTAD discussions, Penrose said that there was no evidence on the question of benefits and costs associated with patent protection. She also pointed out the significant differences in the economic situations of developing countries and concluded, in relying on the wisdom of individual countries' assessment, that:

> The bargaining power of the less-developed countries is not negligible and they can and should use it to ensure that their interests are adequately safeguarded. Different countries will, of course, place different weights on the various considerations involved; ... There is no doubt that foreign investment and foreign technology can increase the rate of growth, but it can also be so costly as to retard it in the longer run unless care is taken to control the terms on which it is obtained, for there is a cost, and sometimes a high cost. We know ways of reducing this cost, but we cannot say with any confidence for any economy at what point the cost exceeds the benefits. Hence, the final decision must, for each economy, rest on informed judgment, and this will inevitably be strongly influenced by the political orientation of the government.[86]

IV INTELLECTUAL PROPERTY PROTECTION AND TRANSFER OF TECHNOLOGY: ECONOMISTS' VIEWS

Since these discussions in the 1970s and 1980s, various regulations relating to investment, patents and import/export and licensing controls in develop-

---

[83] ibid 772.
[84] Penrose, 'International Patenting and the Less-Developed Countries' (n 24) 777.
[85] Ibid 785.
[86] Penrose, 'International Patenting and the Less-Developed Countries' (n 24) 778.

ing countries have been established. Economists have continued to engage in analyses of licensing and technology transfer and have elucidated certain, albeit limited, aspects of international technology transfer.

Technologies can be transferred by formal, contractual means such as patent licensing, joint-ventures, R&D cooperation, technology servicing, direct foreign investment, technology-sharing agreements and training. They can also be transferred informally, through reverse engineering or imitation. Research on the relationship between patent protection and transfer of technology has been undertaken from different perspectives and using varying definitions. There is no well-established definition of 'transfer of technology', either in law or in economics, although it can generally be characterised as a process of absorption, by enterprises, of knowledge and technology through various channels of learning.

Around that time and since then, much has been written about the role played by patents in technology transfer. On the one hand, patents enable dissemination of knowledge, first from the disclosure of inventions and through export, sales and licensing, allowing the entry and market expansion of innovator technologies and products. The cost of technology diffusion is usually lower than that of its production, but by reducing imitation through the use of patents, the proprietor firm may ensure a return on its R&D investment. On the other hand, patents may allow right holders to have market power by excluding competitor technologies or constraining the quantity supplied, depending on the market situation.

Earlier literature in the 1970s on licensing behaviour in different industrial sectors showed the relevance of the existence of competitors in the domestic market where a right holder operates, as well as the importance of economies of scale. Tayler and Silbertson (1973)[87] showed that half of the firms licensed their patented technologies only when the *quid pro quo* offer was significant, and to foreign firms when there were many competitors in the domestic market. When there were only a small number of competitors on the domestic market, the product patent-right holder tended not to license but used the patent only as a bargaining chip in order to find an owner of suitable formulation patents.[88] After conducting surveys in Germany, Grefermann and Rothlingshofer[89] found that chemical industry firms do not license to foreign firms even when domestic competitors are numerous. German firms, according to this study, tended to license when the size of the firm was small and when an infringement suit was staged. Scherer[90] found contrary tendencies in the US, and argued that clear refusal to license was rare in the US.

Technology transfer has often been discussed in the context of two countries, ie, with respect to international transfer of technology. The controversial role of

[87] CT Tayler and ZA Silbertson, *The Economic Impact of the Patent System* (Cambridge, Cambridge University Press, 1973).

[88] ibid 57.

[89] K Grefermann and KC Rothlingshofer, *Patentwesen und technischer Fortschritt* (Gottingen, Verlag Otto Schwarz & Co, 1974) vol II.

[90] FM Scherer, *The Economic Effects of Compulsory Patent Licensing* (New York, New York University, 1977) 58–9.

patents has mostly been discussed in the context of technology transfer involving two countries at different levels of development. There has been research from the viewpoint of right holders' incentive to invest, export or license. It is often argued that weak protection of IPRs in foreign countries would make a licensor unwilling to undertake investments. Such a conventional view has been refined or detailed by a series of studies, some of which are empirical.

The survey undertaken by Mansfield et al (1996)[91] found that weak protection of IPRs in technology recipient countries negatively affects the quality of technology transferred, depending on the extent of ownership control. However, Mansfield explained that lines of causation can be notoriously difficult to establish unambiguously in a basically non-experimental field such as economics. Although interviews with a wide variety of firms, together with the record of their behaviour, provide convincing evidence that weak intellectual property protection influences the volume and composition of foreign direct investment, any estimate of the size of these effects must be treated with caution because of data limitations and possible specification errors. Also, countries with weak protection may have other characteristics of their legal, social, and economic systems that tend to discourage foreign direct investment, and these effects may be confounded with those of weak protection. Mansfield et al found, for example, that newly introduced IPR protection in Taiwan did not change the perception of the firms there that it would not be enforced. The lesson was that developing countries are likely to accomplish little if they merely go through the motions of enacting a patent or copyright law and if they do not convince firms that these laws will be fairly and effectively enforced. In reality, companies would look at the market size, education and training potential, consider IPR protection, evaluate the overall research/business environment for investment, and provide technologies that are adapted to the overall environment thus evaluated. In some parts of the world, such as in Africa, IP factors do not seem to be as important as in Asia for direct investment.

Smith[92] examined the 'relative effects' of foreign patent rights, because the means of imitation tend to differ across exports (reverse engineering), affiliate sales (movement of employees from affiliate to local firms) and licences. Smith then considered the fact that the impact of stronger patent protection on trade depends on the importing country's capacity to imitate.[93] According to Smith, in countries with a weak capacity to imitate, there is a de facto protection of knowledge and, therefore, firms would not actually need IPRs to appropriate the returns on their innovation. In such circumstances, stronger patent rights provide greater market power, which could outweigh any market expansion effects.

---

[91] JY Lee and E Mansfield 'Intellectual Property Protection and US Foreign Direct Investment' (1996) 78(2) *The Review of Economics and Statistics* 181–6.

[92] PJ Smith, 'How do foreign patent rights affect U.S. exports, affiliate sales, and licenses?' (2001) 55 *Journal of International Economics* (J Int Econ) 411–39.

[93] US export data on 92 countries for 1992 were used. R&D/GDP ratios were used as an indicator of the capacity to imitate.

Smith confirms from her 1999 empirical analysis that where the capacity for imitation is high, strengthening IPRs increases the flow of trade.

She further argued that stronger patent protection was associated with larger licences, particularly across countries with strong imitative abilities. Further, strengthening patent protection in foreign countries had larger effects on knowledge transferred outside the country and a given firm, relative to knowledge located inside the country and internalised inside a given firm. Patent protection therefore functions as an exogenous factor, influencing the structures of licensing-out contracts. Strengthening patent protection facilitates the transition from intra-firm transfer of technology licensing to inter-firm arms' length transaction. However, a broader socio-economic analysis with data would be necessary to understand better the processes relating to the transfer of technology.

IPR protection in developing countries would be meaningful when well-functioning markets and public institutions are capable of preventing the abuses of IPRs by dominant companies, as the 1964 UN Report (n 52) suggested. What kinds of public institutions are needed is another complex question. Lee and Mansfield observed in 1996 that:

> . . . a country's system of intellectual property protection is inextricably bound up with its entire legal and social system and its attitudes toward private property; it involves much more than the mere passage of a patent or copyright law.[94]

This was not what certain developing countries considered to be the core problem of the patent system. For them, avoiding negative effects of foreign patents was the focus of attention. From this perspective, flexibilities of international rules, particularly relating to compulsory licences and patentability requirements were necessary. It was also assumed that public health and food policies required developing domestic industry.

Today, old patterns of investment have certainly changed, and globalisation of economic activities has accelerated. However, the opposing approaches to the international system of patent protection may not have changed significantly, particularly those expressed within the international fora for debate. For example, a recent OECD working paper (2008)[95] found that a 1 per cent increase in patent protection is said to be associated with a 0.5 per cent increase in foreign direct investment (FDI), and asserted that strengthening IP protection has positive effects on inward FDI in all countries and at different stages of development, and that the increase is stronger for Least Developed Countries (LDCs).[96] The

---

[94] JY Lee and E Mansfield, 'Intellectual Property Protection and US Foreign Direct Investment' (1996) 78(2) *The Review of Economics and Statistics* 181–6.

[95] WG Park and DC Lippoldt, 'Technology Transfer and the Economic Implications of the Strengthening of Intellectual Property Rights in Developing Countries' (2008) OECD Trade Policy Working Paper No 62.

[96] The impact of IPR strength, according to this research, varies according to industry sector: it has a stronger influence in sectors like petroleum, finance, information, computer-related services and telecommunications equipment, and it influences the nature of R&D in sectors such as the pharmaceutical and biopharmaceutical industries which rely heavily on R&D. On LDCs, see ch 4, n 153.

working paper also found that stronger levels of patent protection are positively and significantly associated with patent applications, particularly by multinational companies. They have an impact also on R&D expenditure, measured as a percentage of GDP. In this study, however, little attention was paid to the impact of strengthened IPR protection on local capacity to innovate, patent local technology and produce product, and therefore the study provides no convincing replies to developing country concerns.

On the other side, the views expressed during the UNCTAD meetings in the 1970s and 80s seem to persist among some developing countries. According to India, strengthened IPR protection is worsening conditions for technology transfer for developing countries. In preparation for the Cancun WTO Ministerial Conference in September 2003, India pointed out Members' concerns on intellectual property rights, namely that:[97]

> A recent analysis of the mode of technology transfers suggests a reversal of the growing popularity of arm's length licensing in the 1970s and mid-1980s to intra-firm transfers since the mid-1980s. For example, 80 per cent of transfers by US corporations and 95 per cent by German corporations in 1995 were made on internal basis compared to 69 per cent and 92 per cent respectively in 1985. This is only one example of the changing pattern of technology transfers, provided here to highlight the need to address in the WTO issues such as transfer, dissemination and innovation.

The above statistics about licensing conditions (intra- or inter-firm licensing) of US and German companies are not accompanied by any further information or reference and, therefore, are difficult to evaluate.

V INTELLECTUAL PROPERTY PROTECTION IN DEVELOPING COUNTRIES: ECONOMISTS' ANALYSES

How should patent systems of developing countries be designed so as to lead to increased investment, innovation and consumer welfare in these countries? Relatively little is known about the effects of intellectual property on prices, technology transfer and competition in developing country markets, despite the fact that many arguments have been made about these concepts. Since the 1970s, when globalisation had not reached the extent that it has today, research using economic models was conducted on the effect that science and innovation incentives in developed countries have on developing countries. Hypotheses have been tested in relation to the global level of innovation, whether patents were not protected in developing countries or whether patent protection existed in both developing and developed countries.

In 1988, Chin and Grossman found that the protection of IPRs enhances global efficiency when R&D productivity is significant, but not when innovations are

---

[97] Communication from India: Proposals on IPR Issues, Preparations for the 1999 WTO Ministerial Conference WT/GC/W/147(18 February 1999) para 3.

small. According to the authors, patent protection in developing countries and developed countries is interrelated and impacts upon innovation in developed countries.[98] This model was based on an equilibrium analysis in the context of competition between a single developed country producer and a single developing country producer selling goods to a globalised market.[99] Based on this analysis, they urged governments of developed countries to argue against copying in developing countries, not as a matter of moral principle or self-interest, but rather as a matter of conflicting national interests.

Alternatively, in 1991 Diwan and Rodrik analysed a continuum of potential technologies with different distributions of preference in developed and developing countries. Their analysis suggested that patent protection in these two classes of countries affects not only the quantity of innovation, but also its quality. They found different results depending on whether these two types of countries have differing or identical technological needs and preferences.

Like the software market, if the needs and preferences of developed countries and developing countries are similar, developing countries will have a strong incentive to free-ride on the technological innovations of developed countries. This could lead to consumer welfare through the production of copies in the short-run. By contrast, if the needs and preferences of developed and developing countries are different, patent protection must be strengthened and innovation must be encouraged not only in developed countries, but in developing countries as well. Some examples include agricultural technology and diseases specific to developing countries.[100]

Of course, other factors, such as scientific and technological level and the institutional strength of courts and administration, also play a role in the economic effect of patent protection in developing countries. It is difficult to foresee the long-term consequences of introducing IPR protection, taking into account both societal and external factors that may intervene. In many countries, imitation products may satisfy consumer tastes and interests, at least in the short run.

Products such as DVDs and computer programs require considerable development costs, but the costs to produce copies of these are minimal. Thus, consumers in those countries where copyright in these products is not protected may enjoy low prices due to the availability of imitations. Similarly, other pirated or counterfeit goods [101] and trade marks and designs can receive greater

---

[98] JC Chin and GM Grossman,'IPRs and North-South Trade' (1988) NBER Working Paper Series, Working Paper No 2769.

[99] ibid.

[100] I Diwan and D Rodrik, 'Patents, appropriate technology, and North-South trade' (1991) 30 *Journal of International Economics* 27–47,

[101] Before the TRIPS Agreement, there was no international definition concerning types of illicit goods (copies which have been produced to resemble an authentic product without the authorisation of the right holder), be they counterfeit products, illegal copies of copyrighted works or any other form of piracy. Often, the term 'pirated goods' was used to denote products which infringe copyrights (such as musical albums, films, broadcast programmes and video games). Products

support from consumers, even if they are of inferior quality. This can also lead to a vicious circle where dependence on unauthorised copying discourages innovative efforts, which can be an obstacle to the country shifting to a more sustainable, technology-based economy and thus stifling economic development. This state of the economy could lead to increased price competition and low profitability, which discourages investment in R&D. If, as a result, companies are unable to benefit from the economies of scale and entering the export market, relative product quality may fall and the development of R&D infrastructure and skilled human resources may not easily occur.

One of the reasons for this is that, in developing countries, investment of public funds into administrative and judicial institutions to ensure that IPR regimes function is often ineffective, in addition to R&D investment being insufficient. Well-functioning IP protection systems contribute to attracting R&D activities and investment by foreign companies, but these do not happen in isolation. Overall conditions, and most importantly such factors as market size, general business environment and infrastructure, are more important in terms of influencing investment decisions. Companies often supply a level of technology that is adapted to the level of IPR protection in a given country. What ultimately determines companies' investment decisions seems to be the potential market size. Arora and Gambardella, in their research on the size, technical competencies and learning effects as determining factors of entry, found that larger markets tend to have more efficient firms and select more efficient leaders; although the advantages of market size diminish generally with size because an increase in market size increases the intensity of competition, the advantages remain important when performance is based on narrow, product-specific competencies, rather than on broad-based, generic competencies.[102] This implies that a country does not reap the benefits of innovation unless there are markets sufficiently large for innovative products. Government therefore should encourage not only the entry of new products, services and technologies into the domestic market, but also promote measures for domestic companies to find overseas markets through cooperative ventures with foreign companies.

More recently, Grossman and Lai (2004)[103] found that, in a non-cooperative equilibrium, governments' incentives for patent protection are stronger with a larger market for innovative products and a greater human endowment for

which infringe patent rights, utility model rights, design rights or trade mark rights are often called 'counterfeit goods'. On occasion, imitations of inventions contain improvements or elements which are related to particular industrial policy. The manufacture of counterfeit and pirated goods often constitutes infringement of IPRs, but the criteria and procedures used to determine whether or not infringement has occurred are based on the laws of each country. Footnote 14 (Art 51) of the TRIPS Agreement defines counterfeit trade mark goods and pirated copyright goods (see ch 5).

[102] A Arora and A Gambardella, 'Domestic Markets and International Competitiveness: Generic and Product-specific Competencies in the Engineering Sector' (1997) 18 *Strategic Management Journal* 53–74. Their theory implies that large markets are beneficial, even if factors such as economies of scale or leaning effects are absent.

[103] GM Grossman and ELC Lai, 'International Protection of Intellectual Property' (2004) 94(5) *The American Economic Review* 1635–53.

R&D. It is clear from examples such as the Indian film and software industries[104] that governments of developing countries will take a more active approach to protecting intellectual property if industries in their own countries develop. Outsourcing seems to contribute to reducing the cost of innovation in developing countries. This means that the marginal cost of strengthening IPR protection varies around the globe. For those countries with smaller markets for innovative products and capacity for R&D, the IPR protection may have less effect. More efficient IPR protection can direct the efforts of these countries to strengthen scientific and technological human resources as well as market size, and also to guide development efforts, with IPR protection as a component thereof.

McCalman analysed, in 2005, the possible long-term impact of the TRIPS Agreement, using three factors (patents, innovation and income) and a model of semi-endogenous growth with intermediate inputs, subject to constant returns to scale.[105] With a static model, the costs of raising the standards of patent protection are captured by the transfers of income between countries. The United States would be by far the major beneficiary from this model. With a dynamic model, however, these transfers are offset by the greater incentives that exist to innovate. The short-run effect of IPR enforcement is to stifle the possibilities of imitation, which allows foreign owners of technology to increase their ability to appropriate rents.[106] This is the reason why the losers from a global, substantive rule of IPR protection would be those countries with relatively high levels of technical skills. However, there are other factors to be taken into account. Countries with scientific and technological skills and infrastructure may offset short-run losses with long-run gains from intensified R&D activities, by taking advantage of a superior set of technologies licensed globally, thus increasing income from subsequently developed technologies. According to McCalman's model, the country that offsets the losses with higher income in the subsequent phase is Switzerland;[107] developing countries such as Brazil and Mexico can benefit from the strengthened IP protection in the long run, even though the benefits are skewed towards developed countries. However, this may not happen in all countries. McCalman finds that India has little incentive to abide by the terms of the TRIPS Agreement. In reality, however, there are many other factors besides these three that will influence the level of innovation and income for formulating a variety of dynamic models. At the time of McCalman's research, few predicted the significant increase in outsourcing and merger activities in India.

---

[104] United Nations Conference on Trade and Development (UNCTAD), 'Changing Dynamics of Global Computer Software and Service Industry: Implications for Developing Countries' (2002) 12, Technology for Development Series, www.unctad.org/en/docs/psitetebd12.en.pdf.

[105] ibid 577–80.

[106] P McCalman, 'Who Enjoys TRIPs Abroad? An Empirical Analysis of Intellectual Property Rights in the Uruguay Round' (2005) 38(2) *Canadian Journal of Economics* 574–603.

[107] ibid 14–23.

3

Biotech Inventions and Patentable Subject Matter

INFORMATION IS CRUCIAL in a knowledge economy based mainly on computer science, electronics, nuclear energy and biomedical technology. Biotechnology has brought about new types of drugs and agricultural technology. This chapter retraces the evolution of biotech industry and patent protection in developed countries. In comparing the US and European approaches to patentability of biotechnological inventions, the chapter attempts to explain possible ethical, economic and political concerns arising from their patent protection. The granting of overly broad patents that could potentially block further research has been one such concern. Raw sequence data, for example, should therefore be treated as 'pre-competitive information kept in the public domain'.[1] Licensing policies are another aspect for consideration. Later, in developing countries, there emerged a widespread fear that biotechnology patents would be extended to animals and plants found in nature, or traditional knowledge taken as such.[2] Obviously, patents are given not to living organisms found in nature or traditionally applied knowledge as such, but to man-made inventions which fulfil the criteria of novelty, inventive step and industrial applicability.

For these complex reasons, patenting in the area of genomics requires patent owners, the law makers and enforcers to have particular responsibilities in 'balancing the system in a way so as to strictly commensurate the scope of patent protection to the actual contribution to the art by the inventors and to deny patents whenever purely speculative "inventions" are at stake'.[3] Some scholars later argued that where there is no biotech research or industry, patent protection of genes is not useful.[4] However, there will be few societies which do not need any form of biotech research. For promoting international scientific or research cooperation or for encouraging new businesses in developing countries, such protection may be useful, as ownership in trade in technology encourages responsibility and cooperation.

---

[1] J Straus, 'Biotechnology and Patents' (2000) 54 *Chimia* 298.

[2] J Watal, 'Intellectual property and biotechnology: trade interests of developing countries' (2000) 2(1/2/3) *International Journal of Biotechnology* 51.

[3] Straus, 'Biotechnology and Patents' (n 1) 298.

[4] CM Correa, 'Patenting Human DNA: What Flexibilities Does the TRIPS Agreement Allow?' (2007) 10 *Journal of World Intellectual Property* 419.

This chapter explores various approaches to the patentability of biotechnology inventions. Biotechnology and its controversies developed prior to and in parallel with the Uruguay Round negotiations. This subject was important in the making of the TRIPS Agreement and has become even more important and controversial today.

I BIOMEDICAL RESEARCH AND GENE PATENTING

A A New Generation of Biotechnology

Biotechnology medicines utilising enzymes and protein which are produced by the human body have existed for centuries. However, in 1953 publication in the journal *Nature* of the discovery by JD Watson and F Crick of the DNA[5] double helix structure represented the beginning of a new era of genetic engineering based on life science. In the 1970s, S Cohen[6] and H Boyer[7] invented a recombinant DNA (rDNA) technology. This technology allowed the coding of heterogeneous DNA, to be introduced into host organisms (such as microorganisms or cell lines) by appropriate vectors (such as plasmids and viruses). If genes to be transformed come from different biological species, the resulting genetically modified organisms (GMOs) are transgenic, while GMOs without DNA from other species are cisgenic. Modified or novel DNA is expressed in transformed host organisms and translated into a protein. For biotechnology to be useful for health purposes, gene expression and protein formation in the human body, and their extraction, purification and manufacturing are necessary. This, in turn, requires further scientific knowledge and biotechnology such as cell culture, genetic modification and gene cloning.

---

[5] DNA (deoxyribonucleic acid) and RNA (ribonucleic acid) contain genetic codes, placing amino acids to form proteins, and translating the transcript into proteins. Proteins are made in cells (ribosomes) responding to special codes called codons – three base pairs inform the ribosome which amino acid to add to the protein. In most living organisms, DNA transmits genetic information. DNA is a nucleic acid in the cytoplasm, separated from the rest of the cell by a membrane or wall. DNA is shaped like a double helix, or a ladder in a spiral shape. Each leg of the ladder is a line of nucleotides. A nucleotide is a molecule made up of deoxy-ribose (a kind of sugar with five carbon atoms), a phosphate group (which is made of phosphorus and oxygen), and a nitrogen base. DNA has four nitrogen bases – Adenine (A), Guanine (G), Cytosine (C) and Thymine (T) – and encodes 20 types of amino acids with combinations of three (there are 64 combinations). These bases are connected by hydrogen bonds (A connects only with T, and C connects only with G). A chain of multiple amino acids form a stereoscopic structure constituting a protein, which carries a living structure and functions. RNA is transcribed from DNA by an enzyme called RNA polymerase and is further processed by other enzymes. RNA is physically different from DNA, which contains two intercoiled strands. RNA only contains one single strand and contains: Adenine (A), Guanine (G), Cytosine (C) and Uracil (U). The first three bases are also found in DNA, but U replaces T as a complement to A. RNA also contains ribose, as opposed to deoxyribose found in DNA. RNA is the carrier of genetic material in different types of RNA viruses (retroviruses) such as HIV (human immunodeficiency virus).

[6] Professors at Stanford University.

[7] Professors at University of California, San Francisco.

In 1975, C Milstein and G Köhler[8] discovered monoclonal antibodies (mAb) which recognise only specific antigen, which is a substance that directs the generation of antibodies.[9] They are made of two large chains and two small ones to form a Y-shaped structure which binds to a specific antigen. Antibodies are used by the immune system to identify and neutralise foreign objects such as bacteria and viruses. This discovery became the basis of antibody technology. Monoclonal antibody therapy uses mAb to target cells to stimulate the immune system, or to block specific receptors on the cell surfaces of a patient.

In 1985, polymerase chain reaction (PCR) technology was invented by K Mullis and was patented by his employer company Cetus, later Chiron, and sold to Hoffman-la-Roche.[10] PCR enzymatically amplifies short segments of DNA and nucleotides by using single-stranded DNA as a template, and DNA oligo-nucleotides (also called DNA primers) which are required to initiate DNA synthesis. PCR and its improved technologies (such as those using Taq thermo-stable DNA polymerase) were created to perform a wide range of genetic manipulations and contributed not only to the advancement of genomics and molecular biology, but also to the establishment of new methods of drug, diagnostic and therapeutic discoveries.

In 1989, President Bush proposed the idea of discovering each of the estimated 20–25,000 human genes and making them accessible for biological study. The following year the Human Genome Project, a US-led international team of 350 scientific institutions, was established. The Department of Energy's Human Genome Program and the National Institute of Health (NIH) and National Human Genome Research Institute (NHGRI) jointly sponsored the Human Genome Project. Known as the HGP, this became an international effort which continued for 13 years from the time it formally began in October 1990 until it was completed in 2003. Another goal of this project was to determine the complete sequence of the 3 billion DNA subunits (based on the human genome). As part of the HGP, parallel studies were carried out on selected model organisms, such as *E coli* bacteria[11] and mice, to help develop technology and interpret human gene functions.

Ten years later, on 26 June 2000, the international consortium declared that the HGP was almost complete. R&D investments in genomics and gene technology have led to the discovery of new genes, screening of drug targets and lead-compounds, and subsequent clinical studies. Patent protection created a scheme to recover these costs and help the US lead genome-based drug discoveries.

Increased knowledge of genes, together with recombinant DNA (rDNA) technology, came to be used in a wide spectrum of agricultural, biological and

[8] Researchers at the Sanger Institute in the UK.

[9] Antibodies are gamma globulin produced by plasma cells, a kind of white blood cell, found in blood and other bodily fluids.

[10] See ch 1, n 19. Chiron merged with Novartis in 2006. PCR-related patents remained with Roche Molecular Diagnosis, http://molecular.roche.com/roche_pcr/pcr_timeline.html.

[11] In 1885, T Escherich described *E coli* as *Bacterium coli commune*, a diverse group of bacteria which are found widely.

medical research and production, and for the discovery of pharmaceutical drug targets and exploring gene therapy. Drug development which once relied mainly on chemistry has since shifted to controlling biological systems using biological material (such as genes, protein, antibodies, cells, and genetically modified animals and plants) and biotechnology.

B   Spread of New Technologies

The advent of genomics, genetics, and proteomics has created massive opportunities but also poses challenges to university researchers, pharmaceutical companies and regulators alike. For drug discovery and development, the paradigm change in the late 1990s was radical. A wide range of new in-vitro technologies and techniques for animals and humans replaced traditional chemical manipulation, requiring not only more sophisticated, massive investments, but also further education in science, basic research, and biotechnology. For companies, increased regulatory requirements in both the pre- and post-launch periods resulted in significant changes in risks and benefits. For regulators, the need to ensure non-toxic, safe and effective drugs has led to significant delays in developing new criteria for judging whether medical inventions submitted for examination are indeed safe and effective.[12]

Medicinal compounds can be therapeutically effective when they inhibit or change the behaviour of pathogens (such as bacteria and viruses which cause diseases) or by blocking the metabolism of pathogens. They can also be effective by selectively targeting disease-causing organisms such as receptors or cells. When conducting biomedical research, receptors, enzymes and proteins became important targets of screening to discover possible drug candidates. Pharmacogenomics, a new field of drug designing, discovery and development, was made possible by using information on the human genome. This, in turn, gave rise to a new therapeutic method which dealt with the genetic causes of diseases and tailor-made therapy by taking into account individual variations.

Recombinant DNA technology also became indispensable in inventing research tools for life science such as agricultural, biological research and drug discovery. Regardless of whether it is a commercial product or not, a research tool is any instrument, information or technology which can be used by laboratory researchers in the fields of life science or drug discovery. In addition to genetic information such as receptors, analytical methods (such as PCR methods, screening methods, rDNA technology) and devices (such as PCR devices, DNA chips, and DNA sequencers), and biotechnology-related informatics (such as gene sequence databases, protein bioinformatics, gene libraries, and combinatorial chemistry) also became necessary research tools for R&D. Laboratory

---

[12]   K Kawakami and H Yamane, 'Clinical Research in Japan: Ways to Alleviate Unnecessary Regulatory Burdens' (2007) 1(1) *RECIIS* 57–61, http://www.reciis.cict.fiocruz.br/index.php/reciis/.

animals such as transgenic animals, with insertion or deletion of genes for specific diseases, came to be frequently used.

For the spread of rDNA technology and innovation of technology, licence terms became vital. Licensing conditions differ considerably among different biomedical research tools. Cohen-Boyer rDNA technology[13] and the polymerase chain reaction (PCR) technology[14] are often contrasted, iconic illustrations.[15] The question of whether any licence terms promote R&D and technological innovation depends on the scope of patentable subject matter, the technical fields concerned and the structure of the R&D market (such as the number of competitors). Cohen-Boyer cloning technology as well as the PCR became indispensable for the further advancement of life science, but the ways in which these technologies were licensed differed considerably. Cohen-Boyer cloning patents were granted to Stanford University and the University of California, both of which granted non-exclusive licences for low royalties to Genentech (founded by Boyer) and hundreds of other companies.[16] These universities used this type of licence revenue as a source of income for their basic research, which contributed to the spread of technology and to R&D. Kohler and Milstein were the first to obtain patents for murine monoclonal antibodies.[17] However, they did not claim for rights to each individual antibody with respect to each individual antigen which resulted from their research. Just like the Cohen-Boyer patents, these research tools were licensed at reasonable prices, which led to significant achievements. The Keller and Milstein licence terms contributed also to the successful commercialisation and widespread use by researchers of their technologies, and are said to be the most successful examples of university technology transfer, generating revenue and leading to a range of new products.

The use of PCR technology, by contrast, was conditioned on the payment of reach-through royalties, even on PCR products and the purchase of Roche reagents. A reach-through agreement is an agreement which requires the payment of royalties as a fixed percentage of sales of the licensee products, which

---

[13] Cohen-Boyer recombinant technology was licensed non-exclusively to a wide range of firms and institutions on flexible conditions. See, for example, MP Feldman et al, 'Lessons from the Commercialization of the Cohen-Boyer Patents: The Stanford University Licensing Program, 2007 http://www.iphandbook.org/handbook/chPDFs/ch17/ipHandbook-Ch%2017%2022%20Feldman-Colaianni0Liu%20Cohen-Boyer%20Patents%20and%20Licenses.pdf.

[14] The PCR technique was patented by K Mullis and assigned to Cetus, where Mullis worked when he invented the technique in 1983. When Cetus was bought by Chiron in 1992, related patents were sold to Hoffmann-La Roche.

[15] On the 'basics' of different types of biotech patent licensing, see for example Secretary's Advisory Committee on Genetics, Health, and Society (SACGHS), 'Report on Gene Patents and Licensing Practices and their Impact on Patient Access to Genetic Tests' (5 February 2010) 24–6.

See also BIO presentation on the 2009 Member Survey, Technology Transfer and the Biotechnology Industry, available at http://bio.org/ip/techtransfer/PDF.TECH.TRANSFER.PRESENTATION.10.25.pdf.

[16] MP Feldman et al, 'Lessons from the Commercialization of the Cohen-Boyer Patents' (n 13).

[17] These applications were filed in 1974 and on 2 December 1980 a manufacturing method patent (US Patent 4,237,224 (process for making rDNA)) was granted and product patents were granted for recombinant prokaryotic cells and eukaryotic cells based on divisional applications (US Patent 4,468,464 (recombinant plasmids) and US Patent 4,740,470 (method for replicating rDNA)).

are developed using the licenced technology. Research tools without substitute technology, combined with network effects, became a controversial R&D issue.

In the process of analysing the human genome, researchers and venture companies have continued to apply for patents for genes using the Patent Cooperation Treaty (PCT) route (see chapter 2). Not only are DNAs chemical substances, they have specific characteristics of carrying information. For example, receptors conveying information regarding intruding entities (which could play the role of a doorkeeper for the cell entry of viruses, etc). As there was often no prior art for this type of chemical substance, patents could be granted relatively easily. In the early stages of drug discovery, it is possible to determine whether specific genes would become screening materials as drug targets. When gene patents with broad claims were granted, there were possible problems in relation to whether this would have any effect on pharmaceutical research and development and future industrial structures. Gradually, debate has grown on how substitutable this type of information is and whether the protection of such information by patents will have any effect on pharmaceutical R&D.

II PATENT PROTECTION OF BIOTECH INVENTIONS

A Expansion of Patentable Subject Matter

With the advent of biotechnology, the discussion arose as to whether and how products of nature could be patented. In the 1980s a groundbreaking decision that expanded patentable subject matter was handed down. In *Diamond v Chakrabarty*,[18] the US Supreme Court decided that genetically engineered plasmids,[19] capable of decomposing crude oil into multiple components, are patentable, and found that such microorganisms could be patentable.[20] Section 101 of the US Patent Act defines patentable inventions and stipulates that: 'whoever invents or discovers any new and useful (a) process, (b) machine, (c) manufacture, (d) composition of matter, or (e) any new and useful improvement thereof, may obtain a patent, subject to the conditions and requirements in the

---

[18] *Diamond, Commissioner of Patents and Trademarks v Chakrabarty* 447 US 303 (1980). Chakrabarty filed a patent application for his genetically engineered bacterium from the genus *Pseudomonas* containing two stable energy-generating plasmids, each of which provided a separate hydrocarbon degradative pathway. The USPTO allowed Chakrabarty's process claims for the method of producing the bacteria and claims for an inoculum comprised of a carrier material floating on water, but not for the bacteria themselves. It ruled that these were products of nature and that as living things they are not patentable subject matter under 35 USC 101. Chakrabarty lost the case both at the Patent Office Board of Appeals and the Court of Appeals for the Federal Circuit (CAFC) but appealed to the Supreme Court. The Supreme Court justices were split 5 to 4.

[19] Plasmids are asexually reproduced, hereditary units in a form of circular DNA, which are physically separate from the chromosomes of the cell (some of them are incorporated in chromosomal DNA and constitute part of a chromosome.) and which are important tools for genetic engineering.

[20] In his carefully worded dissent, Justice Brennan stated that it is the role of the legislature, not the judiciary, to broaden or narrow the scope covered by patent laws, and the granting of patents for living matter in particular should be determined by guidance from the legislature.

law'.[21] Items (b) to (d) are products, as opposed to (a) which is a process. Sections 102 and 103 set out those conditions for patentability, which are novelty, and for loss of right to patent, and non-obvious subject matter. The inclusion of the word 'useful' in section 101 shows that there is no pre-emption from a public perspective. The Supreme Court has found limits to section 101, expressed as 'abstract ideas', 'laws of nature'[22] and 'natural phenomena'. The Court later stated that not all discoveries are patentable, independently of the question of whether they are products or processes.[23]

In *Chakrabarty*, the Supreme Court interpreted section 101 to mean that the decision of whether to grant patents depended not on whether the subject matter was a living thing (a product found in nature) or not, but whether or not the subject matter of the claims were human-made inventions, in the form of process, machine, manufacture, or composition of matter. According to the Court, 'anything under the sun that is made by man' that is not an abstract idea, law of nature, or natural phenomenon which fulfils the conditions delineated in sections 102 and 103, as well as other requirements under the US Patent Act, is patentable. The patent claims in *Chakrabarty* covered: (i) a method of producing bacteria; (ii) an inoculum comprised of a carrier material floating on water; and, (iii) the genetically modified bacteria itself. According to the Supreme Court, the microorganism in *Chakrabarty* was 'a product of human ingenuity "having a distinctive name, character [and] use" and research'.[24]

The petitioner in *Chakrabarty* argued that the legislature should determine the patentability of genetic technology, which was unknown when Congress enacted section 101. The Court, however, held that these provisions were written in broad terms to fulfil the constitutional and statutory intention of promoting 'the progress of science and the useful arts', which encompassed all possible meanings for social and economic benefits, and a legislative or judicial fiat as to patentability would not hinder scientific probing into the unknown. This judgment recognised that patents could be granted not only for microorganisms but also for certain living things under specific conditions, and worked to promote biotechnology and subsequent breakthroughs in the US.

---

[21] 35 USC §§ 1 et seq, entitled 'inventions patentable'. *Funk Brothers Seed Co v Kalo Inoculant Co*, (333 US 127 (1948))

[22] The earlier case law included *Le Roy v Tatham* (55 US 156 (1852)), *O'Reilly v Morse* (56 US 62 (1853)), *Corning v Burden* (56 US 2528 (1854)). In 1948, the Supreme Court in *Funk Brothers Seed Co v Kalo Inoculant Co*, (333 US 127 (1948)) held that the newly discovered natural principle that was applied to the problem of packaging inoculants was not an invention or discovery within the meaning of the patent laws because the qualities of inhibition or of non-inhibition in bacteria are the work of nature. The Court added that: 'The qualities of these bacteria, like the heat of the sun, electricity, or the qualities of metals, are part of the storehouse of knowledge of all men. They are manifestations of laws of nature, free to all men and reserved exclusively to none. He who discovers a hitherto unknown phenomenon of nature has no claim to a monopoly of it which the law recognizes. If there is to be invention from such a discovery, it must come from the application of the law of nature to a new and useful end . . .'. (US 130, 333).

[23] *Parker v Flook* 437 US 584 (1978).

[24] *Diamond v Chakrabarty* (n 18), IV(A) and (B).

The US Supreme Court in 1978 suggested in *Parker v Flook*[25] that a new 'mathematical formula' would ill serve the principles underlying the prohibition against patents for 'ideas' or phenomena of nature and said that these were not 'the kind of discoveries' that the statute was enacted to protect. The Supreme Court in *Chakrabarty* quoted the *Parker v Flook* judgment, which said:

> the rule that the discovery of a law of nature cannot be patented rests not on the notion that natural phenomena are not processes, but rather on the more fundamental understanding that they are not the kind of 'discoveries' that the statute was enacted to protect. The obligation to determine what type of discovery is sought to be patented must precede the determination of whether that discovery is, in fact, new or obvious.[26]

The *Chakrabarty* judgment by the US Supreme Court gave a decisive signal for venture capitalists to pour money into the scientific efforts of predominantly academic researchers and led to the rise of a new branch of industry – the biotechnology industry.[27]

B Genetically-engineered Animals and Plants

Since the 1970s, biotechnology has been one of the factors leading to innovations in the agricultural and pharmaceutical R&D. Inventions relating to recombinant DNA technologies on plants, animals and microorganisms began to be protected in different countries under patent or plant varieties protection laws. In the late 1980s, it was still only in the US, Switzerland, Japan and a few European countries that biotechnology was used for industrial purposes. Yet the globalising market made it necessary to harmonise the conditions in which patents are granted to promote biotechnology inventions. Patent protection efficiently expands the market beyond the domestic market to make global competition possible.

To grant a patent, an invention must be disclosed through a written description. If an invention involves a microorganism[28] or the use thereof, disclosure may be made only by providing a sample. For this reason, the Budapest Treaty on the International Recognition of the Deposit of Microorganisms for the Purposes of Patent Procedure was adopted in 1977 (amended in 1980). The Contracting Parties[29] are required to recognise, for the purposes of patent applications, the deposit of microorganisms with any 'international depositary authority'. This description refers to any scientific institution capable of 'culture collection' of

---

[25] *Parker v Flook* (n 23).

[26] ibid 593.

[27] Straus, 'Biotechnology and Patents' (n 1) 293.

[28] 'Microorganism' is interpreted in a broad sense to refer to biological material, the deposit of which is necessary for the purposes of disclosure, in particular regarding inventions relating to the food and pharmaceutical fields.

[29] See ch 2 n 8, ch 10 n 96, ch 12 n 32.

samples of microorganisms, irrespective of whether such authority[30] is within or outside the territory of that state (on the TRIPS Agreement and microorganisms see chapters 5, 10 and 12).

In the US, biotechnology inventions relating to animals were recognised as patentable, and since *Ex parte Hibberd*[31] in 1985, patentability of those inventions concerning plants was also recognised. In Japan in the 1980s, a number of administrative and court decisions confirmed that gene-engineered animals and plants (microorganisms in 1981, plants in 1985, and animals and living organisms in 1991), as well as the processes to produce them, and new varieties of plants could be protected by patents, under the Plant Variety Protection and Seed Act. In Europe, harmonising patent protection of biotechnology inventions encountered more resistance.

C EPC Statutory Exceptions and Biotechnology Inventions

i Before the European Patent Convention

In Europe, the path to establishing a system for protecting biotech inventions has been long and not linear. Since the late 1960s, Member States of the European Community started to grant patents to protect biotechnology inventions. In 1969, the German Federal Supreme Court (BGH) in its *Red Dove* (*Rote Taube*) decision,[32] recognised in principle the eligibility of inventions relating to animals and breeding methods for patent protection, provided that the technique could be reproduced with sufficient prospects of success. The Court however did not confirm the patent in question, due to the lack of repeatability in this case. Eighteen years after the German Federal Supreme Court decision on *Red Dove*, the same Court, in the 'Rabies Virus' decision,[33] accepted that deposits of biological material (microorganisms) were a complement to the written description and as an enabling disclosure.

In the meantime, the European Patent Convention (EPC) was adopted in 1973. Its Article 53(b) excludes from patent protection essentially biological processes for the production of animals and plants. Thus, a breeding method, such as crossing and selection, which existed in the *Red Dove* decision, became ineligible for patentability. On the other hand, non-essentially biological methods for the production of animals and plants remain patentable, as do inventions related to

---

[30] As of 15 October 2010, there are 37 such authorities: seven in the UK, three in the Russian Federation and South Korea respectively, two each in China, Italy, Japan, Poland, Spain and the US, and one each in Australia, Belgium, Bulgaria, Canada, the Czech Republic, France, Germany, Hungary, Latvia, India, the Netherlands and Slovakia.

[31] *Ex parte Hibberd* (1985) 227 USPQ 443.

[32] In June 1969, in the *Rote Taube* case (Bundesgerichtshof, 1 IIC136), the Federal Supreme Court of the former West Germany affirmed the decision of the patent office that rejected the grant of patent of a breeding technique to produce red doves through breeding and selection, but held that, in general terms, livings things are patentable subject matter under these conditions.

[33] *Toll-wutvirus*, IIC 1987, 396; H-R Jaenichen, *Biotechnology Law Report* (1996) 15(6) 883–91.

animals and plants, if their feasibility is not limited to a plant variety or animal race.[34]

ii EPC and Patentability

Chapter I of the EPC concerns 'patentability', under which Article 52 EPC defines patentable inventions. According to Article 52(1), 'European patents shall be granted for any inventions, in all fields of technology,[35] provided that they are new, involve an inventive step and are susceptible of industrial application. Article 52(2) however notes that the following shall not be regarded as inventions within the meaning of Article 52(1): (a) discoveries, scientific theories and mathematical methods; (b) aesthetic creations; (c) schemes, rules and methods for performing mental acts, playing games or doing business, and computer programs. According to Article 52(4) EPC 1973, 'methods for treatment of the human or animal body by surgery or therapy and diagnostic methods practiced on the human or animal body shall not be regarded as inventions which are susceptible of industrial application within the meaning of paragraph 1. This provision shall not apply to products, in particular substances or compositions, for use in any of these methods.' This provision was deleted by the EPC 2000 and its content transferred to Article 53 (c) of the EPC 2000 as one of the matters in respect of which European patents shall not be granted.

Notable for comparative purposes is that the EPO generally applies the problem-solution approach in assessing the requirement of inventive step.[36] The problem-solution approach was developed during the 1980s by the Technical Board of Appeals (TBA) and generally applied today by the Examining Divisions, the Opposition Divisions, and the TBA of the EPO. This approach consists of defining the technical problem to be solved by the proposed invention, identifying the closest prior art in view of which the technical results of the proposed invention is assessed for determining whether a person skilled in the art would have suggested the claimed technical features for the solution provided by that invention.

Whereas the US patent law does not pre-empt patentability on the public or morality grounds or specifically for agricultural concerns, the EPC 1973 and 2000 (and the subsequent EU Biotech Directive) provide for exceptions to patentability in Article 53.[37] According to Article 53 of the EPC, European patents

---

[34] This idea also underlies Art 4 of Directive 98/44/EC of the European Parliament and of the Council of 6 July 1998 on the legal protection of biotechnological inventions (Biotech Directive) [1998] OJ L213/13–21.

[35] Inserted by the EPC 2000 in order to bring the wording into line with the first sentence of Art 27(1) of the TRIPS Agreement.

[36] Examination Guidelines, C-IV 9.4.

[37] Art 52(4) EPC was deleted and its contents transferred to Art 53(c) EPC. Prior to the amendment, 'methods for treatment of the human or animal body by surgery or therapy and diagnostic methods practiced on the human or animal body' were excluded from patentability on the basis that these were not industrially applicable.

shall not be granted in respect of: (a) inventions the commercial exploitation[38] of which would be contrary to *ordre public* or morality; (b) plant or animal varieties or essentially biological processes for the production of plants or animals; this provision shall not apply to microbiological processes or the products thereof; (and (c) 'methods for treatment of the human or animal body by surgery or therapy and diagnostic methods practiced on the human or animal body' was added in the EPC 2000, as described above[39]).

These exceptions can be traced back to the circumstances of the time when the EPC was adopted in 1973. Article 53(b) of the EPC excludes 'plant or animal varieties or essentially biological processes for the production of plants or animals', whereas microbiological processes and the products thereof are patentable under this provision. The main reason at this time for these EPC exclusions was the existence of other international treaties. As for the protection of plant varieties, the International Convention for the Protection of New Varieties of Plants (UPOV Convention)[10] was adopted in 1961 in Paris (see chapter 2). This Convention regarded the protection of new varieties of plants solely as an 'agricultural issue', and prohibited dual protection by providing that a contracting party may provide only one form of protection for one variety. This provision was lifted when the Convention was revised on 19 March 1991, but Article 53(b) of the EPC, which was signed in 1973, continued to exclude plant varieties from the patentable subject matter.

Later, the Technical Board of Appeal (TBA) of the European Patent Office (EPO), in *Ciba-Geigy*[41] and *Lubrizol*,[42] held that plants themselves taken as a genus claim, as opposed to a 'variety',[43] were patentable. Subsequently, dozens of

---

[38] The words 'publication or exploitation' as the backdrop against which to assess whether an invention is contrary to *ordre public* or morality were amended by the EPC 2000 to 'commercial exploitation'.

[39] Case law on medical methods is found in the Case Law of the Boards of Appeal of the European Patent Office, Section I-A.2, 20–37.

[40] The UPOV (l'Union internationale pour la Protection des Obtentions Végétales – UPOV) was established by the Convention for the Protection of New Varieties of Plants (UPOV Convention), adopted in Paris in 1961, and revised in 1972, 1978, 1991 and more recently, in 2008. The objective of the Convention is to provide a *sui generis* form of intellectual property protection, specifically adapted for the process for plant breeding and developed with the aim of encouraging breeders to develop new varieties of plants. Contracting parties should provide, inter alia, (i) protection of more than 24 varieties of plants, (ii) requirements for protection including novelty, and (iii) protection which reaches at least the commercialisation stage for new varieties.

[41] T 49/83 *Ciba-Geigy* [1984] OJ EPO 112.

[42] T 320/87 *Lubrizol Genetics Inc* [1990] OJ EPO 71.

[43] Art I(vi)of the UPOV Convention defines 'variety' as: a plant grouping within a single botanical taxon of the lowest known rank, which grouping, irrespective of whether the conditions for the grant of a breeder's right are fully met, can be: defined by the expression of the characteristics resulting from a given genotype or combination of genotypes; distinguished from any other plant grouping by the expression of at least one of the said characteristics; and considered as a unit with regard to its suitability for being propagated unchanged: Council Regulation (EC) 2100/94 on Community plant variety rights, which covers varieties of all botanical genera and species, including, inter alia, hybrids between genera or species. Art 1 uses the same definition of 'variety' (Art 2), and Art 2(3) of the later EC Directive refers to this definition.

patents were granted on plants. However, the TBA Decision in *PGS*[44] in 1995 held that plants and plant varieties including the genus claim were not patentable, in accordance with the provisions of Article 53(b) of the EPC 1973. These decisions took into account the European Community Plant Varieties Regulation,[45] which came into force in 1994.

Following this, in 1999, the Enlarged Board of Appeal of the EPO decided in a case relating to *Transgenic Plant/Novartis II*[46] that plants which are products of rDNA technology avoid the prohibition on patent grant under Article 53(b), if specific plant varieties are not individually claimed. This decision indicated that, even if plant varieties themselves are not patentable, patent granted to a certain invention might cover a plant variety as well. The Board was probably conscious of the draft Biotechnology Directive of the European Community (EC), which proposed that a concept of genetic engineering applicable to more than one variety was an invention.[47]

Patentability of animal varieties was discussed during the negotiations for the Strasbourg Convention on the Unification of Certain Points of Substantive Law on Patents for Invention (Law on International Patent Treaties) which was adopted in 1963, two years after the UPOV Convention[48]. Participating countries debated fiercely the ethical implications of patenting animal varieties, and no agreement was reached. Article II of the Strasbourg Convention, therefore, allows Contracting Parties not to protect plant or animal varieties or essentially biological processes for the production of plants or animals, except for microbiological processes or the products thereof. The EPC exclusion of plant and animal varieties derives from this provision of the Strasbourg Convention.

In general, the exclusions from patentability in Article 53 of the EPC 1973 have been construed narrowly. In Europe, patent protection of biotechnological inventions relating to animals was resisted from various perspectives, such as ethical, religious, traditional values, animal protection and farmers' rights perspectives.[49] In the *Harvard OncoMouse* case of 1990, the Examination Division of the EPO initially rejected the patent application in 1989, on the grounds of above-mentioned Article 53(b) EPC. The OncoMouse is a laboratory mouse, genetically modified and designed to carry a specific gene which increases the mouse's susceptibility to cancer.[50] The applicant appealed against this decision

---

[44]   T 356/93 *Plant Genetic Systems* [1995] EPOR 357; [1995] OJ EPO 545.

[45]   Council Regulation (EC) 2100/94 on community plant variety rights.

[46]   Decision G1/98 concerning the invention of anti-pathogenically effective compositions comprising lytic peptides and hydrolytic enzymes.

[47]   Page 5 of the above Decision.

[48]   The Strasbourg Patent Convention was adopted in 1963 by the Council of Europe and entered into force in 1980 with 13 ratifications. This Convention deals with the granting of patents. This treaty had a profound influence on the formation of the EPC, but because of the EPC, the Treaty of Strasbourg has lost its relevance.

[49]   T 19/90 *Oncomouse/Harvard* [1990] OJ EPO 476.

[50]   On 24 June 1985, Harvard College applied to patent a process for producing a transgenic non-human mammalian animal having an increased probability of developing neoplasms, and transgenic animals produced by said method. The application was refused by the Examining Division on

(T 19/90) and the Board of Appeal of the EPO held that the exception to patentability under Article 53(b) EPC applied to certain categories of animals, but not to animals as such; and that, in the absence of serious doubts substantiated by evidence, there was no reason to reject the application on the ground that it involved an extrapolation from mice to mammals in general.[51] According to the Board, the exception to patentability under Article 53(b) EPC should be construed narrowly, and a test should have to be performed on a case-by-case basis. In terms of *ordre public* or morality under Article 53(a) EPC, the Board stated that the suffering of animals and possible risks to the environment on the one hand, and the invention's usefulness to mankind, on the other, must be weighed up. The decision to grant a patent was dated 3 April 1992 and took effect on 13 May 1992, the day it was mentioned in the *European Patent Bulletin*. In this case, 'animal varieties', '*races animales*' and '*Tierarten*', whose scientific meanings differ, were used in the three authentic languages of the EPC and remained undefined.

A patent was finally granted,[52] but 17 oppositions were filed against it based, in particular, on Article 53(a) and (b) EPC. On 7 November 2001, the Board of Appeal limited the claims to rodents (T 315/03)[53] under which animal variety is only a subunit.[54] While science is evolving and uncertain, and technology is rapidly moving, patent protection of biotechnological inventions has remained controversial in Europe. In the years leading to the adoption of European Community Directive 98/44/EC of 6 July 1998 on the legal protection of biotechnological inventions (EU Biotech Directive)[55], particularly, questions relating to patent protection of biotech inventions were intensely discussed.[56]

---

14 July 1989 on the grounds that the EPC did not permit the patenting of animals per se. On appeal, the case was remitted to the Examining Division by Technical Board of Appeal 3 3.2 (T 19/90), which found that the EPC ruled out patents only for certain categories of animals, not for animals as such. The USPTO had granted a patent to Harvard University on 12 April 1988 (US Patent 4,736,866, filed on 22 June 1984, issued on 12 April 1988, and expired on 12 April 2005), whose main claim was: 'A transgenic non-human mammalian animal whose germ cells and somatic cells contain an activated oncogene sequence introduced into said animal, or an ancestor of said animal, at an embryonic stage, said oncogene optionally being further defined according to any one of claims 3 to 10.'

[51] *Oncomouse/Harvard* (n 49) 589.

[52] EP 169.672B1.

[53] OJ EPO 2006,15.

[54] T-0315/03–3.3.8, 6 July 2004 OJ EPO 1991, 589.

[55] Biotech Directive (n 34).

[56] Certain issues relating to biotechnological inventions were clarified within the framework of the EPC, notably through EPC Rules 26, 27, 28 and 29. These define biotechnological inventions and provide that they are patentable if they involve either the isolation of biological material from its natural environment or biological material produced by means of a technical process even if it previously occurred in nature (EPC R 27(a)). Certain biotechnological inventions are expressly excluded from patentability, including processes for cloning human beings or modifying human germ lines, inventions involving human embryos and inventions that cause suffering to animals without there being any substantial medical benefits to man or animal (EPC R 28). Parts of the human body are also excluded from patentability (EPC R 29(1)), as is the patenting of human gene sequences where an industrial application of the sequence is not also disclosed (EPC R 29(3)).

D EU Biotech Directive

Each European country had its own approach to patentability, reflecting in part the agricultural or industrial focus of their individual economies and particular values. These countries also employed different legal formulations, concepts and interpretations in order to conceptualise biotechnology inventions and when to grant patent protection. Where biotechnology based on life science was concerned, different religious and ethical values also made the issue more complex. Among Member States of the EU (European Community (EC) at that time), legislation, implementation and interpretation of domestic laws concerning the patentability of genetic manipulation or parts of the human body varied and lacked legal predictability and certainty. This was the aim of the draft Directive proposed in 1988 by the European Commission. This was proposed with a view to harmonising[57] national laws, promoting commercialisation of biotech R&D results, and clarifying the scope of patent protection of biotechnology inventions, across EC Member States. Biotechnology inventions were becoming socially useful, but raised issues not only for legal harmonisation, but also relating to ethical norms which some felt could be infringed.

Inventions of a technical character which are new, having inventive step and industrial applicability, are patentable in the EC Member States, and genes which fulfil these requirements and which are found in nature may be patentable, provided that they are isolated from the human body or produced by means of a technical process.[58] The US Supreme Court in *Chakrabarty* noted that the patentee, by his inventive activity, produced a new and useful bacterium with markedly different characteristics from any found in nature.[59] Under the EU Biotech Directive, genes found in nature are patentable, if isolated, purified and

[57] Later, in Case C-377/98 *The Netherlands v European Parliament and Council of the European Union*, the Netherlands argued that differences in the laws and practices of the Member States, and the likelihood of their becoming greater, to which the fifth and sixth recitals of the preamble to the Directive allude, stating that they could create barriers to trade, do not exist, or only concern secondary issues which do not justify harmonisation. The Court responded that the examples given by the Parliament and the Council suffice to establish that the differing interpretations to which EPC provisions are open as regards the patentability of biotechnological inventions are liable to give rise to divergences of practice and case law prejudicial to the proper operation of the internal market and that significant consequences were already apparent between certain national laws on specific points such as the patentability of plant varieties and that of the human body. It concluded therefore that approximation of the legislation of the Member States based on Art 100a of the EC Treaty is not inappropriate. It follows that the Directive was correctly adopted.

[58] Preamble (20) says: 'whereas, therefore, it should be made clear that an invention based on an element isolated from the human body or otherwise produced by means of a technical process, which is susceptible of industrial application, is not excluded from patentability, even where the structure of that element is identical to that of a natural element, given that the rights conferred by the patent do not extend to the human body and its elements in their natural environment'. AG Jacobs in his Opinion on Case C-377/98 *Netherlands v European Parliament* added the word 'synthesised'.

[59] The interesting question concerns the meaning of 'human intervention'. National laws may provide different answers to this question. N Pires de Carvalho, 'The Problem of Gene Patents' (2004) 3 *Washington University Global Studies Law Review* 701–23; *The TRIPS Regime of Patent Rights*, 3rd edn (Alphen aan den Rijn, Kluwer Law International, 2010) 252–65.

classified, and reproduced outside the human body, even if the product found in nature has identical functions.[60] A mere genomic DNA sequence is not considered to be an invention, unless it is isolated from nature and sequenced. The inventor must also indicate the method for its repeatable production, in fulfilment of the general rule for patentability.

In the EU Biotech Directive, respect for dignity and integrity of the person is the basic ethical rule wherever such a rule is relevant to biotechnology inventions, as Recital 16 of the Directive states:

> ... patent law must be applied so as to respect the fundamental principles safeguarding the dignity and integrity of the person; whereas it is important to assert the principle that the human body, at any stage in its formation or development, including germ cells, and the simple discovery of one of its elements or one of its products, including the sequence or partial sequence of a human gene, cannot be patented; whereas these principles are in line with the criteria of patentability proper to patent law, whereby a mere discovery cannot be patented.[61]

For ethical considerations, Article 6 of the EU Directive notes possible exceptions to patentability of those inventions whose commercial exploitation would be contrary to *ordre public* or morality, in particular: (a) processes for cloning human beings; (b) processes for modifying the germ line genetic identity of human beings; (c) uses of human embryos[62] for industrial or commercial purposes; and (d) processes for modifying the genetic identity of animals which are likely to cause them suffering without any substantial medical benefit to man or animal, and also animals resulting from such processes. Article 6 separates the granting of patents for the results of research and development, and the commercial exploitation of that technology. This is the reason why this provision states that exploitation shall not be deemed to be contrary to *ordre public* or morality 'merely because it is prohibited by law or regulation'.

The ways in which the EU Biotech Directive is construed differ significantly from the US Code. The Directive not only provides statutory exceptions such as Article 4, but also states explicitly that only 'inventions' are patentable. In the US, exceptions to patentability are decided judicially.

According to Article 1 of the Biotech Directive, EU Member States shall protect under national patent law biotechnological 'inventions'. Article 3(1) stipulates the principle that 'inventions which are new, which involve an inventive step and which are susceptible to industrial application shall be patentable, 'even if

---

[60] Preamble (21).

[61] EU Biotech Directive (n 34).

[62] On 25 November 2008, referring to the earlier decision of the Technical Board of Appeal in T 1374/04 *Stem Cells/WARF* (OJ EPO 2007, 313), the EPO Enlarged Board of Appeal decided (in G 2/06) that Art 53(a) EPC forbids patenting of claims directed to products which, at the filing date, could only be prepared by a method that necessarily involved destruction of human embryos from which the products were derived, even if this method was not part of the claims; it was not relevant whether, after the filing date, the same products could be obtained by other means that did not involve the destruction of human embryos.

they concern a product consisting of or containing biological material[63] or a process by means of which biological material is produced, processed or used'. Article 3(2), which clarified the specific conditions in which natural products could be patented, provides that 'biological material which is isolated from its natural environment, or produced by means of a technical process, may be the subject of an invention even if it previously occurred in nature'. This condition is also required for biological material which previously occurred in nature.[64] Thus, the EU Biotech Directive confirms the patentability of naturally occurring biological material defined in Article 2(1).[65]

Articles 4 to 6 provide statutory exceptions to patentability. Article 4(1), like Article 53(b) of the EPC, excludes from patentability: (a) plant and animal varieties, and (b) essentially biological processes for the production of plants or animals. However, Article 4(2) of the Directive explicitly provides what is not found in the EPC; namely: 'inventions which concern plants or animals shall be patentable if the technical feasibility of the invention is not confined to a particular plant or animal variety'. Article 4(2), confirming the *Transgenic/ Novartis II* decision,[66] makes patent protection possible for a plant or animal variety, unless specific varieties are individually claimed. This was already the case in many EC Member States, which Article 4(2) made explicit. However, it created a certain discrepancy with regard to the text of Article 53(b) of the EPC, even though the case law suggests such an interpretation. On 16 June 1999, the EPO Administrative Council adopted the Regulation,[67] so that the content of the EU Biotech Directive would be reflected on the EPC. Article 4(3) mentions

---

[63] Art 2 of the Biotech Directive explains that, in this Directive, 'biological material' refers to 'any material containing genetic information which is capable of reproducing itself or being reproduced in a biological system' and 'microbiological process' refers to 'any process involving or performed upon or resulting in microbiological material'.

[64] EPC R 23c(a).

[65] EPC R 23b(3).

[66] Enlarged Board of Appeal, G1/98 (n 46).

[67] OJ EPO 1999, 101. Rule 23b concerning general matters and definitions relating to Arts 52 and 53 EPC, according to which: (1) for European patent applications and patents concerning biotechnological inventions, the relevant provisions of the Convention shall be applied and interpreted in accordance with the provisions of this chapter. Directive 98/44/EC on the legal protection of biotechnological inventions shall be used as a supplementary means of interpretation; (2) 'biotechnological inventions' are inventions which concern a product consisting of or containing biological material or a process by means of which biological material is produced, processed or used; (3) 'biological material' means any material containing genetic information and capable of reproducing itself or being reproduced in a biological system; (4) 'plant variety' means any plant grouping within a single botanical taxon of the lowest known rank, which grouping, irrespective of whether the conditions for the grant of a plant variety right are fully met, can be: (a) defined by the expression of the characteristics that results from a given genotype or combination of genotypes, (b) distinguished from any other plant grouping by the expression of at least one of the said characteristics, and (c) considered as a unit with regard to its suitability for being propagated unchanged. This Rule refers to decision G1/98 of the Enlarged Board of Appeal (n 46); (5) a process for the production of plants or animals is essentially biological if it consists entirely of natural phenomena such as crossing or selection; (6) 'microbiological process' means any process involving or performed upon or resulting in microbiological material.

For amendment of the EPC, a decision of the diplomatic conference is necessary (Art 172, EPC).

the patentability of inventions which concern a microbiological or other technical process or a product obtained by means of such a process.

The EU Biotech Directive in Article 5(1) distinguishes a 'simple discovery' from a 'patentable invention' with respect to elements of the human body,[68] including the sequence or partial sequence of a gene. According to Article 5(2), an element isolated from the human body or otherwise produced by means of a technical process, including the sequence or partial sequence of a gene, may constitute a 'patentable invention', even if the structure of that element is 'identical to that of a natural element'. Article 5(3) stipulates disclosure obligations, at the time of patent application, in relation to the industrial application of a sequence or a partial sequence of a gene.[69]

Articles 8 and 9 of the Directive concern the extent to which patent protection is given to biological materials possessing specific characteristics. Such protection is extended to any biological material derived through propagation or multiplication in an identical or divergent form and possessing those same characteristics. However, Article 11 derogates from this extended protection in cases where plant propagating material has been sold (or commercialised in other ways) to a farmer by the holder of the patent with his consent for agricultural use. In this case, the farmer is authorised to use the product of his harvest for propagation or multiplication by his own farm, to the extent provided for under Article 14 of Regulation (EC) 2100/94 on Community plant variety rights.[70]

E Examination Guidelines for DNA Sequences

Although the differences between the US and Europe resided mostly in the formulation of laws, there were also delicate differences in the criteria by which to consider to what extent biotech inventions are patentable, where human creativity is found, how repeatability of the invention (utility) is shown, in what cases separated DNA and protein structures can be said to constitute an inventive step (non-obviousness), and whether a patent right covers proliferation of gene-engineered animals and plants.

Even today, Europe, the US, and Japan seem to have slightly different views in determining novelty, inventive step, and industrial applicability (utility). Most differences reside in the timing of patent examination and thoroughness with which examiners investigate prior art inventions, according to the JPO study on

---

[68] Art 5(1) stipulates that the human body, at the various stages of its formation and development, and the simple discovery of one of its elements, including the sequence or partial sequence of a gene, cannot constitute patentable inventions. 'Human' is not defined, and EU Member States have different views on when a foetus is considered to be a human.

[69] Preamble (24): 'whereas, in order to comply with the industrial application criterion it is necessary in cases where a sequence or partial sequence of a gene is used to produce a protein or part of a protein, to specify which protein or part of a protein is produced or what function it performs.'

[70] Reg (EC) 2100/94 on Community plant variety rights [1994] OJ L227/1-30.

the differences of inventive step.[71] However, there remain also certain minimum substantive differences in the criteria of measuring inventive step, such as the example below.

In the US, in the early period of DNA-related inventions, the CAFC recognised non-obviousness (inventive step) with respect to a DNA invention specified by a DNA sequence (*Re Deuel*[72]). The *Deuel* case relates to an invention of DNA molecules encoding 'human and bovine heparin-binding growth factors' (HBGFs). A USPTO examiner rejected the non-obviousness of some claims in the patent application in *Deuel*, citing prior art literature.[73] The USPTO Board of Patent Appeals and Interferences also determined that the cloning method[74] (to facilitate the handling through the amplification of the subject gene sequences in experiments to produce gene clones) used in this invention was ordinary, and that if a specified protein sequence is public knowledge, so are its genes.

In the appeal against this judgment, the CAFC held that even if an applied cloning method is obvious, DNA with a specific sequence of encoding proteins which have actually been obtained is not obvious (ie, there is an inventive step). In this case, the CAFC based its judgment on the idea that even if an amino acid sequence for a protein is known, the number of types of DNA sequences corresponding to that protein is high. Therefore, prior art implying an amino acid sequence for a certain protein will not necessarily make DNA molecules encoding that protein obvious. The genetic code between protein and DNA does not overcome the deficiencies of cited references, and a partial HBGF amino acid sequence already disclosed by the EPO is not a sufficient description. Unless there is prior art which suggests that such amino acid can lead to a particular DNA and be prepared, such a DNA cannot be considered obvious.

This ruling of the CAFC led to many criticisms that the US had established lax standards for non-obviousness with respect to biotechnology inventions. In Japan and EPO jurisdictions, where cloning methods are known, it is considered that if the amino acid sequence of an encoded protein is known, no inventive step is present, because a person skilled in the art could easily clone the subject gene. Thus, there have been some noticeable differences in applying the criteria of patentability between the US on the one hand, and the EPO and JPO, on the other, although the differences have been minimised by cooperation among these agencies. In *Re Kubin*,[75] however, the CAFC re-examined its own approach to 'obvious-to-try' tests in view of the of the Supreme Court criticism in KSR[76] and its own understanding of these tests in *Re O'Farrell*.[77] It concluded that the claimed invention (isolation and sequencing of the gene for natural killer cell

---

[71] JPO Appeals Division, 'Report on the Study of Inventive Steps' (2007) (in Japanese).

[72] *Re Deuel* 51 F 3d 1552, 1559 (CA Fed 1995).

[73] A handbook published by the EPO concerning partial amino acid sequences of HBGF and genetic cloning.

[74] The polymerase chain reaction (PCR) technology (n 10), is one such method.

[75] *Re Kubin* 561 F 3d 1351 (Fed Cir 2009).

[76] *KSR International Co v Teleflex Inc* 550 US 398 (2007).

[77] *Re O'Farrell* 853 F 2d 894, 903 (Fed Cir 1988).

activation-inducing ligand (NAIL) and the corresponding protein) was obvious. According to the CAFC, the prior art in this case teaches a protein of interest, a motivation to isolate the gene coding for that protein, and illustrative instructions to use a monoclonal antibody specific to the protein for cloning this gene, which is a well-known and reliable cloning and sequencing technique. The claimed invention, therefore, was judged as a product 'not of innovation but of ordinary skill and common sense'. The *Kubin* judgment has brought the US biotechnology patentability criteria closer to those of Europe and Japan, although the US 'obviousness' standards still seem somewhat lower than those of the European and Japanese Patent Offices.

III COMMERCIALISATION OF BIOTECH MEDICINES

A First-Generation Biotech Medicines

Early examples of biotech medicines developed mostly in biotechnology allowing for extraction, cloning and mass-production of bioactive substances (proteins) in the body, such as human insulin – by bacillus Interferon α (which has therapeutic effects for cancer and hepatitis C, and belongs to a cytokine). Cytokines are a large and diverse family of polypeptide regulators produced throughout the body by cells of diverse embryological origin and encompassing proteins, peptides and glycoproteins. They are signalling molecules like hormones and neurotransmitters and are used for communication and interaction among cells. They regulate reactive adjustments such as immune or allergic reactions. In contrast to small-molecule chemical medicines, biotech medicines are large, complex and unstable protein molecules containing polysaccharide or oligosaccharide, and are capable of replacing or supplementing, and respond to therapeutic needs unmet by small-molecule medicines.

Erythropoietin is another example of a first generation biomedicine. It is also a cytokine, a glycoprotein hormone produced mainly by the renal cortex which controls red blood cell production and was discovered by French scientists in the early 1900s. Renal failure causes abnormal haemoglobin levels which can provoke anaemia. Later, in the 1980s, through a series of clinical trials and cloning technique inventions[78] developed in the US, Amgen (α-EPO) and the Genetics

---

[78] Erythropoietin genes are cloned by determining amino-acid sequences of erythropoietin which are isolated and purified from patients' urine. A base sequences (DNA fragments) which correspond to those amino-acid sequences are chemically synthesised using DNA synthesiser, in order that the base sequences work as probes to find erythropoietin genes. To find genes, gene libraries (materials that include all types of genes that are necessary to extract genes) produced from human embryonal cells are searched. Cloned genes are introduced into suitable host cells and use the function of those cells to produce protein. In order to produce large volumes of cloned genes, necessary genes are introduced into expression vectors (vectors are vehicles for transferring target DNA fragment as a passenger into cells) and the vectors are transfected into cells, and after the cells have been cultured, erythropoietin is secreted from the cells. Human erythropoietins which have been mass produced using recombinant DNA technologies received approval after non-clinical and clinical trials, and have become a leading biomedical product.

Institute (GI) (β-EPO) began producing this hormone. In 1989, the US Food and Drug Administration approved the hormone, which was called Epogen. More recently, a novel protein (an erythropoiesis-stimulating protein, NESP), with anti-anaemic capabilities and a longer terminal half-life than erythropoietin, has been produced.

Biotechnology has been a fast growing sector of both science and industry. According to the European Commission Report in 2004,[79] the worldwide bio-technology-based products market had grown at an annual average rate of 15% to reach approximately € 30 bn in 2000 of which biopharmaceuticals made up € 20 bn. Biotech medicines in 2000 accounted for less than 5% of the total phar-maceuticals market but were growing at 2.5 times its overall growth rate.

Table 3.1: Reported worldwide indications and sales of the top 15 biotechnology medicines (2000)

Originator	Brand	Active ingredient	Indication	Sales ($ million)
Amgen	Procrit	Erythropoietin alfa (J&J)	Dialysis-dependent anaemia	2,709
Amgen	Epogen	Erythropoietin alfa (J&J)	Dialysis-dependent anaemia	1,960
Biogen	Intron-A*	Interferon alpha-2b (Sch-P)	Hepatitis, cancers	1,360
Amgen	Neupogen	Filgrastim (Amgen)	Neutropenia	1,220
Genentech	Humulin	-insulin (Eli Lilly)	Diabetes	1,137
Biogen	Avonex	Interferon beta-la (Biogen)	Multiple sclerosis	761
Genentech	Engerix-B	Hepatitis-B vaccine (GSK)	Hepatitis B	700
Immunex	Enbrel	Etanercept (AmHomeProds)	Rheumatoid arthritis	652
Chiron	Betaseron	Interferonbeta-lb (ScheringAG)	Multiple sclerosis	548
Genzyme	Ceredase	Alglucerase (Genzyme)	Gaucher's Disease	537
IDEC/Genentech	Rituxan	Rituximab (Roche**)	Non-Hodgkin's lymphoma	533

---

[79] S J R Bostyn, 'Patenting DNA sequences (polynucleotides) and scope of protection in the European Union: an evaluation' (European Commission; Directorate-General for Research Food Quality and Safety, 2004) 6.

Kabi (Pharmacia)	Genotrpin	Somatropin (Pharmacia)	Growth hormone	467
Genentech	Kogenate	Octacog-alpha (Bayer)	Haemophilia	453
Protein Design	Synagis	Palivizumab (Medimmune)	Respiratory antiviral	427
Centocor	Reo-Pro	Abciximab (Centocor/J&J)	Coronary angioplasty	419

Source: H Redwood, *Where is the Pharma Industry Going? Insights for the New Millennium* (Felixstowe, Oldwicks Press, 2002) 75.

Today, the basic gene patents for the early biotech medicines have expired or will soon end, and generic versions of the original medicines (called 'biosimilars' in the EU; 'follow-on biologics' in Japan[80] and the US) have started to receive market authorisation in the EU. In the EU, the European Medicines Agency (EMEA) adopted the first positive opinion for a similar biological medicinal products in early 2006, and as of February 2009, 11 products were approved.[81]

A few developing countries, such as India, China and Cuba, are producing follow-on biotechnology medicines.[82] The Indian regulator has approved production and marketing of 20 biogeneric medicines.[83] India's exports of healthcare biotech medicine during 2007 amounted to 15.95 billion Rs and were estimated

[80] Guidelines adopted on 6 March 2009. Biosimilarity and bioequivalence are to be established through clinical trials.

[81] The products (Somatropin (2), Filgrastim (4), Epoetin (5)) were authorised to market by January 2009 and a further four (Interferon-alfa (1), Insulin (3)) received positive opinions. The basic principles for examination (biological, biotech (rDNA), immunological & blood/plasma-derived products) are based on the Guideline on Similar Biological Medicinal Products (CHMP/437/04). To show the products are essentially similar ('generics', according to Art 10(1)(a)(iii) Dir 2001/83/EC) would not allow the demonstration of the similar nature of two biological medicinal products, and, therefore, additional data, in particular the toxicological and clinical profile, must be provided (Art 10(4) Dir 2001/83/EC). If there there are differences (particularly) in raw materials or manufacturing processes of biosimilar and reference product, then results of appropriate pre-clinical tests or clinical trials relating to these conditions must be provided. See P Richardson, 'EMEA Regulatory Approaches to Biosimilars and Guidelines' Graduate Institute for Policy Studies (GRIPS) International Conference on 'Biotech Medicines Innovations in Developing Countries: Intellectual Property Protection and Regulations for Safety and Efficacy', 19 February 2009 www.grips.ac.jp/docs/richardson.pdf.

[82] www.grips.ac.jp/docs/090219.html.

[83] Human insulin, erythropoietin, hepatitis B vaccine, human growth hormone, interleukin 2, interleukin 11 (treatment of thrombocytopenia), granulocyte colony stimulating factor (treatment of chemotherapy-induced neutropenia), granulocyte macrophage (colony stimulating factor for chemotherapy-induced neutropenia), interferon 2 alpha (treatment of chronic myeloid leukemia), interferon 2 Beta (treatment of chronic myeloid leukemia), hepatitis B and C, interferon gamma (chronic granulomatous disease and severe malignant osteopetrosis), streptokinase (acute myocardial infarction), tissue plasminogen activator (acute myocardial infarction), blood factor VIII (haemophilia type A), follicle stimulating hormone (reproductive disorders), teriparatide ((Forteo) osteoporosis), drerecogin (Xigris), alpha (severe sepsis), platelet-derived growth factor (PDGF) (prophylaxis for bone marrow induction and osteoblasts proliferation), epidermal growth factor (EGF) (mitogenesis and organ morphogenesis), eptacogalpha (r-F VIIa), r-coagulation factor haemorrhages (congenital or acquired haemophilia), Nimotuzumab (treatment of breast cancer), and Rituximab (non-Hodgkin's nymphoma and arthritis). http://igmoris.nic.in/commercial_release.asp

to grow to 47 billion Rs by 2012.[84] Most of these products are said to be sold abroad.

As of May 2009, more than 3,000 medicines were approved as natural product-based medicines by China's regulatory agency, the State Food and Drug Administration (SFDA).[85] By what criteria these medicines are designated as natural product-based medicines is not clear.

Cuba's product portfolio combines off-patent products (Hepatitis B vaccine, interferons, EGF) and innovative compounds (streptokinase, synthetic Hib vaccine, Heberprot P), and registered in 111 countries in total: HB vaccine 40, Interferon 34, Streptokinase 28, GAVAC 4, Hebertrans 3, EGF 2 (see chapter 11).[86]

B Patenting Biotech Medicines Inventions and Enforcement

In addition to patent offices, courts have adopted different policies for patentability criteria of biotechnology inventions. For example, there had been much debate in the area of biotechnology over whether it was possible to claim that something which goes beyond a natural product (for instance, a protein altered or modified to add, insert, delete or substitute amino acid residue). For example, tissue Plasminogen activator (tPA) catalyses the conversion of plasminogen to plasmin, which is the major enzyme responsible for clot breakdown. TPA can be produced by rDNA technology to be used to block this conversion process and thus to treat fibrinolysis (the physiological breakdown of blood clots) and acute myocardial infarctions (AMI or heart attacks). In Japan, the *245-Met-tPA* case tested whether it is possible to expand the scope of rights beyond genetically modified tPA. The case involved a dispute between Sumitomo Pharmaceuticals, which produced Met-tPA, and Genentech, which produced tPA.[87] Of the 459 amino acids in these two activators, only one amino acid was different. If the language in the claims was given a strict interpretation, Sumitomo's Met-tPA would have been considered an improvement. The Osaka District Court gave the scope of the patent a literal interpretation and ruled that the Sumitomo patent did not infringe the Genentech patent. However, the Osaka High Court overturned this decision by applying the doctrine of equivalents, and ruled that the Sumitomo patent did infringe the Genentech patent.[88]

[84] PK Ghosh, 'Indian Efforts for Developing Biotechnology' (2008) 11(1) *Asian Biotechnology and Development Review*, 41.

[85] http://app1.sfda.gov.cn/datasearch/face3/dir.html.

[86] 'Biotechnology in Cuba', presentation by R de Silva Rodriguez, International Conference on 'Biotech Medicines Innovations in Developing Countries: Intellectual Property Protection and Regulations for Safety and Efficacy', National Graduate Institute for Policy Studies (GRIPS), Tokyo, 19 February 2009 www.grips.ac.jp/docs/silva.pdf.

[87] Activase is approved for treating acute ischemic strokes and acute massive pulmonary embolisms and has been shown to have the ability to manage strokes.

[88] *Appeal Seeking Injunction (Preventing Patent Infringement)*, Osaka High Court, 1994 (*ne*) No 3292.

In the UK, in *Kirin-Amgen, Inc v Hoechst Marion Roussel Ltd*,[89] the House of Lords examined two remarkably similar technologies used to produce the hormone erythropoietin. The issue in this case was whether the claims of a European patent granted to Kirin-Amgen, Inc were infringed by Transkaryotic Therapies Inc (TKT) and Hoechst Marion Roussel Ltd.

In 1987, Amgen brought an action for alleged infringement by Genetics Institute (GI) and its licensee, Chugai Pharmaceutical Company. Amgen argued its case in the US federal district court and the ITC (for an injunction against exportation from Japan to the US), and the GI side made a counterclaim in the federal court. However, in 1991 the CAFC affirmed the federal district court's judgment on the infringement of Amgen's patent '008 and ruled that GI's patent '95 was invalid.[90] Amgen has taken a large share of the EPO market in the US. In 1992 in Japan, Kirin and Chugai opted for a settlement with Amgen.

Later, TKT developed a process for making erythropoietin involving gene activation (GA-EPO) by introducing a promoter DNA inside human cells (according to TKT, GA-EPO is manufactured by the expression of GA-EPO using DNA sequences inside human cells. Amgen asserted that GA-EPO infringed the claims of its patents (production of erythropoietin by recombinant DNA technology) in several countries. The central question was whether the TKT technology was included in the claims by Amgen, ie, GA-EPO is exogenous to the cell and therefore switching on the endogenous EPO gene does not constitute infringement.

In the US, the federal district court of Massachusetts applied the doctrine of equivalents and decided that TKT had infringed five Amgen patents. The CAFC upheld this claim construction and said the fact of being 'uniquely characterized' by the expression of exogenous DNA sequences did not impel the court to accept TKT's position when the asserted claims did not contain such an express limitation. However, it remanded the federal district court on several other points.[91] In its reversal of the federal district court judgment,[92] the CAFC ruled that Amgen's '422 patent was not invalid and it applied the *Cybor* rule,[93] which requires a de novo review by the appellate court of the claim construction of the lower court. Based on its independent review, the CAFC found that the claim construction regarding a 'therapeutically effective amount' by the district court was too narrow, and it therefore returned the case to the district court's decision. Amgen's petition for a rehearing was dismissed, but the dissenting judges highlighted problems with the *Cybor* rule. On 22 March 2007, Amgen appealed to the Federal Supreme Court.

The House of Lords in the UK, by contrast, decided that there was no infringement. Amgen brought an action against TKT and Hoechst Marion Roussel,

[89] *Kirin-Amgen, Inc v Hoechst Marion Roussel Ltd* [2004] UKHL 46.
[90] *Amgen v Chugai Pharmaceutical Co* 927 F 2d 1200, 1206; *Genetics Institute v Amgen* 502 US 856 (1991).
[91] *Amgen v Hoechst Marion Roussel* 314 F 3d 1313, 65 USPQ 2d 1385 (Fed Cir 2003).
[92] 339 F Supp 2d 202 (D Mass 2004).
[93] *Cybor Corp v FAS Techs Inc* 138 F 3d 1448, 46 USPQ 2d 1169 (Fed. Cir 1998).

which imported GA-EPO into the UK. Amgen asserted that GA-EPO infringed claims of European Patent 0,148,605. According to Amgen, EPO and GA-EPO were chemical equivalents and the importation of GA-EPO into the UK (by a subsidiary of Hoechst) constituted infringement. TKT requested a declaration of non-infringement and revocation of Amgen's patent.

The main question here was whether the construction of the claims regarding the 'host cell' by Amgen covered only those exogenous to the cell, or alternatively, those endogenous to the cell including the TKT process. This contention focused on Amgen's patent claim 1 (DNA sequence for securing expression in a prokaryotic or eukaryotic host cell of EPO), claim 19 (recombinant polypeptide characterised as being the product of eukaryotic expression of an exogenous DNA sequence and which has a higher molecular weight by SDS-Page than EPO isolated from urinary sources), and claim 26 (polypeptide production of the expression in a eukaryotic host cell of a DNA sequence according to claims 1, 2, 3, 5, 6, and 7). The House of Lords interpreted the claims by Amgen narrowly and dismissed its appeal. Claim 19 was interpreted literally and it was held to be invalid (insufficient). Claim 26 was also held to be invalid (anticipated by prior art), even though Amgen invented the process in reality. The two cases show the contrast that could result from whether and how the doctrine of equivalents is applied.

C Inventions, Discoveries and Patentable Subject Matter

In the US, under the Federal Constitution (see chapter 1) as well as under the patent code, inventions and discoveries can be patentable, subject to the conditions and requirements of the law. Section 100 (definitions) of the US Code states that the term 'invention' means invention or discovery; and Section 101 (inventions patentable) states that 'whoever invents or discovers' any new and useful process, machine . . . may obtain a patent therefore. Thus, the conditions and requirements for granting patents imply what inventions and patentable discoveries are, and whose criteria are clarified by case law.

The European Patent Convention (EPC) defines what are not considered as inventions, as well as inventions which are not patentable. The European Patent Office (EPO) generally applies the technical problem-solution approach in assessing the requirement of inventive step. The EU Biotech Directive, as we have seen, elaborated a definition of invention adapted to biotechnology, faced with certain resistance in expanding patentability.

It was in the US that courts recognised patentability for a wide range of inventions in biotechnology. However, even the scope of patentable subject matter in the US has limits. Not all discoveries or inventions are patentable, and the laws of nature, physical phenomena or abstract ideas, in particular, are excluded from patentability by case law and hence, the Supreme Court still today is interested in patentable subject matter. In 1972 in *Gottschalk v Benson*, the US

Supreme Court held that, in addition to the laws of nature, natural phenomena and mere abstract ideas, the steps to implement mathematical algorithms do not constitute patentable subject matter.[94] This was based on the reasoning that the mathematical formula in question had no substantial practical application except in connection with a digital computer. A method for converting binary-coded decimal numerals into pure binary numerals was not considered sufficient transformation.

In *Parker v Flook,* the Supreme Court indicated that there are kinds of 'discoveries' that the statute was enacted to protect and those which are not.[95] In the year following *Chakrabarty*, the US Supreme Court ruled in *Diamond v Diehr* that a method of manufacturing synthetic rubber using a computer program was patentable.[96] This decision did not consider the descriptive material itself patentable, but recognised that functional descriptive material, which is recorded on recording media, such as a data structure or computer program which functions as a computer component, was patentable. However, this applied only to technically practical inventions, not abstract concepts.

The issue essentially focused on the meaning of 'abstract' and how much transformation was involved in the invention. The CAFC decided later in *Re Alappat* that concrete algorithms were patentable.[97] The idea of whether a useful and non-abstract algorithm could be patentable was also raised in the judgment of *State Street Bank.*[98] With the advent of the digital economy, certain inventions concerning financial services, electronic sales and advertising methods and business methods started to be patented, particularly in the US. In *State Street Bank*, the CAFC found that business methods, if they were useful, concrete, and had a tangible result, were not excluded from patentability simply because they were business methods. Despite the fact that patentability of business methods was unsettled in this judgment, filings of business method patent applications increased from 7,400 in 2002 to 9,027 in 2005 and 12,779 in 2008.[99] Certain business methods consisting of processes to be performed on the Internet, and telephone exchange and billing methods, were also granted patents.[100]

In 1996, the US Patent and Trademark Office (USPTO) published the Examination Guidelines for computer-related inventions. They stated that

---

[94] *Gottschalk v Benson* 409 U.S. 63 (1972).

[95] In *Parker v Flook* (n 23), the Supreme Court citing Newton's formulation of the law of universal gravitation as a scientific principle, stated that 'this relationship always existed – even before Newton announced his celebrated law. Such 'mere' recognition of a theretofore existing phenomenon or relationship carries with it no rights to exclude others from its enjoyment. . . . Patentable subject matter must be new (novel), not merely heretofore unknown. There is a very compelling reason for this rule. The reason is founded upon the proposition that, in granting patent rights, the public must not be deprived of any rights that it theretofore freely enjoyed.'

[96] *Diamond v Diehr* 450 US 175 (1981).

[97] *Re Alappat* 33 F 3d 1526, 31 USPQ 2d 1545 (Fed Cir 1994).

[98] *State Street Bank & Trust v Signature Financial Group* 149 F 3d 1368, 47 USPQ 2d 1596 (Fed Cir 1998).

[99] USPTO www.uspto.gov/web/menu/busmethp/class705.htm#top.

[100] WIPO Report, 'Intellectual Property on the Internet: A Survey of Issues' (2002), www.wipo.int/copyright/en/ecommerce/ip_survey/chap3.html#_ftnref356.

patentable subject matter must have a technical and practical application and affirmed that the mere laws of nature, abstract ideas, natural phenomena, or programmes which operate mathematical algorithms were not patentable. However, under these Guidelines, it was possible for these descriptive materials to be considered inventions of a process claim, and for data structures, which are considered non-statutory subject matter, to constitute inventions recorded on a medium.

There has been further evolution on the question since that time. Nearly 20 years after *Gottschalk v Benson*, and 10 years since the adoption of these Guidelines, the Supreme Court, in *Lab Corps v Metabolite Labs* took renewed interest in substantial patentability questions.[101] In this case, three Supreme Court judges dissented from the withdrawal of *certiorari* on the grounds that the patent claim was nothing more than a natural phenomenon. Subsequently, the CAFC discussed the eligibility of process and system claims in *Re Bilski* and overturned the *State Street Bank* test for patent eligibility of business methods.[102] According to the CAFC, the mere fact that a business method is 'useful, concrete, and [has a] tangible result' does not confer patentability. The CAFC affirmed that the invention in question was an abstract idea and that a claimed process would have been patentable under 35 USC § 101 if it is tied to a particular machine or apparatus, or if it 'transforms a particular Article into a different state of thing[s]'. In other words, the CAFC found that claims directed to hedging risks during commodities trading are not patentable, implying that the existing patents may be invalid under this judgment. On 28 June 2010, upon Bilski's petition, the Supreme Court affirmed the decision of the CAFC invalidating the Bilski method for the following reaons: Bilski had attempted to patent abstract ideas, just like the algorithms at issue in *Benson* and *Parker v Flook*, then instructed the use of well-known random analysis techniques to help establish some of the inputs into the equation, adding even less to the underlying abstract principle than the claimed invention that was held patent ineligible in *Parker v Flook*. However, the Court held that business methods are, under certain circumstances, 'methods' within the meaning of 35 USC § 273, and patentable under § 101, as Congress 'plainly contemplated that the patent laws would be given wide scope', in order to ensure that 'ingenuity should receive a liberal encouragement.'[103] The Court also held that the machine-or-transformation test is not the sole test for determining the patentability of a process and that business methods are not categorically excluded from protection under the Patent Act.[104]

[101] *Laboratory Corporation of America Holdings, DBA Labcorp, Petitioner v Metabolite Laboratories, Inc et al, on Writ of Certiorari to the US Court of Appeals for the Federal Circuit* 548 US 124 (2006).

[102] *Re Bilski* 499F 3d 1365, 1371 (Fed Cir 2008).

[103] *Diamond v Chakrabarty* (n 18) 308–9 is cited.

[104] *Bilski et al v Kappos, Under Secretary of Commerce for Intellectual Property and Director, PTO* (No 08–964), 545 F 3d 943.

Recently also, in a case concerning Myriad Genetics' gene patents over BRCA1 and 2,[105] the New York District Court ruled that these patents, even though they are isolated from their natural state, are invalid. Myriad identified the components of genes BRCA1 and BRCA2 and used them to assess mutations in women for the purpose of determining whether they have a higher risk of developing breast cancer. The Court said that Myriad simply identified something that occurred in the body, and that the comparisons of DNA sequences are 'abstract mental processes'. The identification of the gene sequencing, according to the judge, is a valuable scientific achievement but is not eligible for patent protection. In June 2010, Myriad Genetics appealed to the US Court of Appeals for the Federal Circuit against this decision. Further court discussions would clarify and refine whether isolated but otherwise unmodified genomic DNA is patent-eligible under section 101.

The New York District Court judgment spurred criticisms that basic knowledge on genes should not be patented. These critics recognise, however, that knowledge cannot be produced without cost, and, therefore, governments and foundations should financially support research in universities and laboratories.[106] The US Department of Justice (DOJ) filed an amicus brief with the CAFC for this case on 29 October 2010. The brief states that section 101 embraces only 'human-made inventions' and not the products and processes of nature itself. According to the DOJ, the NY District Court erred in invalidating the challenged compositions that are man-made transformation or manipulation of the raw materials of the genome, such as cDNAs. However, the DOJ states that the Court was correct in holding that genomic DNA that has merely been isolated from the human body, without further alteration or manipulation, is not patent-eligible. Thus, the criteria that the DOJ uses seem to differ slightly from the case law and USPTO practices relating to section 101.[107]

D Research Tool Patents

Another evolution has taken place on the difficult question of research tool patents. Gene patenting has caused concern that it imposes difficulties on bio-medical R&D[108] since basic, genomic information started being patented in great numbers (patent thickets) in the US. The increased university patenting following the Bayh-Dole policy of encouraging commercialisation through

---

[105] Brief for the United States as Amicus Curiae in Support of Neither Party, No 2010-1406.

[106] J Stiglitz and J Sulston 'The Case Against Gene Patents' *The Wall Street Journal* (New York, 16 April 2010).

[107] 'USDOJ Files Brief Opposing Gene Patents', (1 November 2010) *GenomeWeb News* (New York).

[108] MA Heller and RS Eisenberg, 'Can Patents Deter Innovation? The Anticommons in Biomedical Research' (1998) 280(5364) *Science* 698–701.

patenting of the results of scientific research raised doubts about its contribution to scientific research.[109]

Research tools can be a matter (product) or a process for laboratory use for drug, diagnostic or other inventions. They are multifunctional and may comprise various protein and gene coding for marker protein, human receptor protein (to examine interaction with a drug candidate or for gene coding), genes for diagnosis, genes for studying a treatment method, vectors, transformant or cell lines, transgenic animals, knock-out animals and antibodies, for example. The use of research tools is circumscribed in various ways, and, depending on the kind of research tools, the nature of problems differs. For example, proteins which are coded as targets can be used only for those genes unique to a person and there is no economy of scale. Another limitation may arise from the fact that gene patents often cover an extended scope, including modified genes, which increases the chance of the user infringing the patents. Rights holders may impose high royalties, or require royalties extended over to the product, instead of asking courts for injunction. Screening assay or biotechnological procedures such as PCR, combinatorial libraries, bioinformatics technology such as genomics databases or DNA chips are also research tools.

Access to patented research tools is particularly difficult in broad therapeutic areas and rival-in-use (tools that are primarily used to develop innovations that will compete with one another in the marketplace). Under normal circumstances, information sharing schemes do not seem attractive to companies and institutes, because such cooperation undermines competition, both in the research and product markets. Cross-licensing (or patent pooling) is more difficult in biomedical research than in other industries such as information technology. The widely diverging values of biotechnology patents, heterogeneous interests of patent owners in upstream research (universities, companies, other institutions), the difficulties in objectively evaluating the value of patents at the early stage of research and the importance of proper bargaining for an individual invention due to its possibly high value (in comparison to electronics patents, for example) make it difficult for collectively framed licensing. Financially powerful companies can buy out the necessary tools or the biotech companies possessing such tools. However, for smaller companies, finding a viable solution is much more onerous.

Late disclosure of patented technology and national differences in disclosure systems have also caused costly duplication of research by many institutions and firms, particularly in the search for antibodies and antigens. Furthermore, certain research tools may rapidly become obsolete or meaningless. Insufficient

---

[109] DC Mowery, RR Nelson, BN Sampat and AA Ziedonis, 'The growth of patenting and licensing by US universities: An assessment of the effects of the Bayh-Dole Act of 1980' (2001) 30 *Research Policy* 99–119; RR Nelson 'The market economy, and the scientific commons' (2004) 33(3) *Research Policy* 455–71; PA David, 'Can "Open Science" be Protected from the Evolving Regime of IPR Protections?' (2004) 160(1) *Journal of Institutional and Theoretical Economics* 9–34.

information and forecasting concerning the viability of tools can be detrimental and costly.

Discussions over research tool patents as obstacles to genomic research developed as gene patenting progressed in the early 1990s. The NIH is said to have filed more than 7000 expressed sequence tags (ESTs) for patents. The US Patent and Trademark Office (USPTO) in October 1998 granted to INCYTE the first patent covering ESTs which encode 44 novel protein kinases.[110] In February 2000, Human Genome Science was granted a patent on the chemokine receptor type 5 (CCR5).[111] Amidst international concerns, the CAFC in 2004 tightened the disciplines in expanding the scope of claims (particularly by adding new medicinal functions in this case, for example).[112] Enablement requirements were also reinforced so that from antagonist functions discovered of particular genes, a large scope of resulting drug target compounds would not be claimed. More stringent patent examination procedures have been put in place in the US and various guidelines were adopted which encourage licensing.[113] Parallel and gradual processes by which the factual situations relating to research tools became clearer and different kinds of solutions and palliatives have been provided by laws, case law and guidelines.

Reflecting the idea that ESTs are research tools that should be made available for research to advance the public good,[114] in June 1998 the USPTO published its Interim Written Description Guidelines. Various studies showed that the actual extent to which research is hindered by gene patents seems more limited than originally feared.[115] Gradually, in many countries, the scope of research exemptions

---

[110] USP 5,817,479.

[111] USP 6,025,154. CCR5 is a protein that in humans is encoded by the CCR5 gene and can function as viral co-receptors. Later, US researchers found that the Human Immunodeficiency Virus (HIV) uses CCR5 or another protein, CXCR4, as a co-receptor to enter its target cells and, based on this discovery, several HIV drugs (entry inhibitors) which interfere with the interaction between CCR5 and HIV have been developed. See also ch 8.

[112] *University of Rochester v GD Searle & Co Inc, Monsanto Company, Pharmacia Corporation, and Pfizer Inc* 375 F 3d 1303; CAFC, 2 July 2004. The CAFC referenced the written description requirement in the patent law which is independent of the need to enable one skilled in the relevant art to make and use the invention, and invalidated claims 1, 5 and 6 of the patent '850 held by the University of Rochester due to the lack of written description in its specification concerning the chemical structure of the non-steroidal compound which selectively blocks prostaglandin H synthase (PGHS)-2 (COX-2).(on written description and enablement requirements, see ch 5)

[113] 'Principles and Guidelines for Recipients of NIH Research Grants and Contracts' (1999) 64(246) *Federal Register*. The NIH adopted a best-practice guideline for the licensing of government-funded genomic inventions that encourages limiting patent protection when significant further research and development investment is not required. Subsequently, many other national and international organisations have compiled reports on the situation. For example, OECD Guidelines for the Licensing of Genetic Inventions, 2006.

[114] 64 Fed Reg, 21 December 1999. JM Mueller, 'No "Dilettante Affair": Rethinking the Experimental Use Exception to Patent Infringement for Biomedical Research Tools' (2001) 76 *Washington Law Review*. 1, 52, fn 255.

[115] W Cohen and J Walsh 'Research Tool Patent and Licensing and Biomedical Innovation,' in Cohen and Merrill (eds), *Patents in the Knowledge-based Economy* (Washington DC, National Academies Press, 2003) 285–340; SA Merrill and AM Mazza, *Reaping the Benefits of Genomic and Proteomic Research: Intellectual Property Rights, Innovation, and Public Health* (Washington DC, National Academies Press, 2006). In the second publication, the surveys on academic researchers

has been clarified or legislated. In the US, the scope of the 'FDA safe harbour'[116] experimental exemption was recognised but limited to those activities 'reasonably related to the development and submission of information' to the FDA.[117] According to the US Supreme Court, basic scientific research on a particular compound, performed without the intent to develop a particular drug or a reasonable belief that the compound will cause the sort of physiological effect the researcher intends to induce, is not exempted from infringement. The Court however stated: '[We] . . . need not – and do not – express a view about whether, or to what extent, § 271(e)(1) exempts from infringement the use of "research tools" in the development of information for the regulatory process.'[118]

In Europe, in the early 2000s, there was growing criticism that biotechnology patents were increasing the number of research tool patents, creating patent thickets which, in turn, were blocking the use of patented inventions. Myriad Genetics' aggressive commercial policy for its BRCA1 and 2 genes for diagnosis of predisposition to breast and ovarian cancer raised international concerns over the access to diagnostic use of genes.[119]

E DNA sequences-related patents

In response, several countries introduced legislation limiting the scope of protection of human DNA sequences-related patents only to those functions which are disclosed.

For example, in France, Article L611-18 of the Industrial Property Code, as amended in 2004, restricts the protection of inventions relating to an element of the human body to the extent necessary for the realisation and exploitation of the particular use disclosed in the patent application 'in a concrete and precise manner'.[120] Furthermore, the first paragraph of article L 613-2-1 of the same Code limits the scope of a claim covering a genetic sequence only to the sequence directly linked to the 'specific function concretely disclosed in the description'.

(including university, non-profits and government labs) and industry researchers showed that patenting does not seem to limit research activity significantly, particularly among those who conduct basic research. Access to tangible research from others is somewhat more problematic, although factors other than patents, scientific competition, transaction costs and commercial interests limit access to material research input. Material transfers, particularly for research related to proteomics with high scientific and commercial interest (researchers on signalling proteins, CTLA-4, EGF and NF-kB were surveyed), seem to be even more difficult for industry researchers. The survey concludes that policy makers should devote their attention to maintaining the institutional environment as a free space for academic research and alleviating those factors that cause friction in the flow of needed research materials.

[116] USC 271(e)(1).

[117] *Merck KGaA v Integra Lifesciences I* 545 US 193 (2005).

[118] ibid para 7.

[119] A Odell-West, 'The Legacy of Myriad for gene-based diagnostics: a new policy and regulatory option' 2009 4(4) *Journal of Intellectual Property Law & Practice* 267–77.

[120] Intellectual Property Code as amended by Act No 2006-236 of 1 March 2006 www.jpo.go.jp/shiryou_e/s_sonota_e/fips_e/pdf/france_e/e_chiteki_zaisan.pdf.

In Germany, section 1a(4) of the amended Patent Act limits the scope of patent protection for an invention relating to a sequence or partial sequence of a gene, the structure of which corresponds to the structure of a natural sequence or partial sequence of a human/primate gene sequences, to their disclosed purpose.[121]

In Switzerland, the amended federal law on patents for inventions, which came into force on 1 July 2008, introduced certain limitations on the scope of DNA-related inventions, and it also clarified the effects of biotechnology patents. Article 1b of the amended law provides that 'naturally occurring sequence or partial sequence of a gene is not patentable as such' (1b-1) but that 'sequences that are derived from naturally occurring genes or partial sequence of a gene' (cDNA, expressed sequence tags (ESTs) etc) may be patented if they are produced by a technical process; their function is specifically indicated; and they fulfil related requirements in the law (1b-2).

Article 8c specifically deals with claims on a nucleotide sequence derived from a naturally occurring sequence or partial sequence of a gene and limits the protection to the parts performing the function concretely disclosed in the patent.[122] By the same amendment, the Swiss Patents Act clarified and extended the scope of experimental exemption.[123] Clarification of the scope of experimental exemption such as this is helpful for researchers and companies operating in the biotechnology fields.

The Swiss amendments also provided, in Article 40b, that '[w]hoever intends to use a patented biotechnological invention as an instrument or means in research, is entitled to a non-exclusive licence'.

In response to the alleged difficulties that gene biotechnology patents create for researchers, the Belgian Patent Law, by amending the Act of 28 April 2005, introduced Article 28.1(b) which states that the rights conferred by the patent do not extend to scientific purposes 'on and/or with' the subject of patented invention. This provision enlarged considerably the scope of research exemption.

How has the above series of legislative measures, limiting the scope of patent protection of DNA sequences and making available patented biotechnologies

---

[121] Patent Act as amended by the Act on Improvement of Enforcement of Intellectual Property Rights of 31 July 2009 www.jpo.go.jp/shiryou_e/s_sonota_e/fips_e/pdf/germany_e/e_tokkyo.pdf.

[122] Art 49 provides that patent applications must contain a description of the invention and, for a claim to a sequence derived from a sequence or partial sequence of a gene, a specific description of the function it performs.

[123] Art 9(1) of the Swiss Patent Law states that: 'The effects of a patent do not extend:

  a) to acts undertaken in the private sphere for non-commercial purposes
  b) to acts undertaken for experimental and research purposes in order to obtain knowledge about the object of the invention, including its possible utilities; in particular all scientific research concerning the object of the invention is permitted
  c) to acts necessary to obtain a marketing authorisation for a medicament according to the provisions of the law of 15 December 2000 on therapeutic products
  d) to the use of the invention for the purpose of teaching in teaching establishments
  e) to the use of biological material for the purposes of selection or the discovery and development of a plant variety
  f) to biological material obtained in the field of agriculture which was due to chance or which was technically unavoidable.'

for a wide range of research, improved the much-discussed problems of biotech 'anti-commons'? There have been few infringement cases concerning biotech patents recently in Europe.[124]

It is probably too early to evaluate with facts the effects on biotechnological R&D of this legislation. Opposing views however have been expressed by a wide spectrum of observers. The Second Report on the EU Biotech Directive in 2005[125] examined various views on gene-related patent protection which limits its effect to what is specifically disclosed (so-called 'purpose-bound' protection). For a majority of the experts, there were 'no objective reasons to create a specific regime of purpose-bound protection in this area differing from the classic patent protection'.[126] These experts felt there were no differences between DNA sequences and chemical substances which would justify different treatment regarding the scope of patent protection. The Report further stated that 'it may be questionable whether attempting to further refine the scope of protection of gene sequence patents in the light of divergences between national legislations will have any significant effect on actors in the field'.[127] According to Pyrmont,[128] 'purpose-bound' protection amounts to restricting the scope of gene patents only to the protection conferred by use or method patents, unlike the principle of absolute product patent protection in other technical fields.[129] This may have some bearing on the non-discrimination principle across different technologies provided for in Article 27 of the TRIPS Agreement, which will be examined in chapter 7 of this book.

---

[124] On 6 July 2010, the Court of Justice of the European Union, in its decision in *Monsanto v Cefetra* (Case C-428/08) concerning the EU Biotech Directive 98/44, limited protection of DNA sequences to its performing functions. According to the Court, Art 9 of Directive 98/44 does not confer protection on a patented DNA sequence when it is contained in soya meal, where it does not perform the function for which it was patented. This is regardless of the fact that it did perform that function previously in the soya plant, of which the meal is a processed product, and that the DNA could again perform its function after extraction from the soya meal and insertion into the cell of a living organism. Art 9 of the Directive stipulates that: 'The protection conferred by a patent on a product containing or consisting of genetic information shall extend to all material, save as provided in Article 5(1), in which the product is incorporated and in which the genetic information is contained and performs its function.'

[125] Commission (EC) 'Development and implications of patent law in the field of biotechnology and genetic engineering, Report from the Commission to the Council and the European Parliament' COM(2005) 312, 14 July 2005. This report is called the '16c Report', because it is based on the provision in Art 16c of the Biotech Directive, which reads: '(c) annually as from the date specified in Article 15(1), a report on the development and implications of patent law in the field of biotechnology and genetic engineering.'

[126] ibid 4.

[127] Commission (EC) 'Development and implications of patent law in the field of biotechnology and genetic engineering' (n 125) 4–5.

[128] 'Special Legislation for Genetic Inventions – A Violation of Article 27(1) TRIPS?' in WPW Pyrmont et al (eds), *Patents and Technological Progress in a Globalized World: Liber Amicorum Joseph Straus* (MPI Studies on Intellectual Property, Competition and Tax Law, Berlin and Heidelberg, Springer, 2007) 293.

[129] In *Monsanto v Cefetra* (Case C 428/08, 6 July 2010) paras 71–7, the Court of Justice held that Arts 27 and 30 of the TRIPS Agreement do not affect the interpretation given of Art 9 of the Directive (see ch 7).

Amidst the polarising discussions on the European legislations above, the Court of Justice of the European Union (Court of Justice, formerly the Court of Justice of the European Communities), rendered its judgment on the scope of 'purpose-bound' claims in *Monsanto v Cefetra*, leaving its impact primarily in the field of genetically engineered agricultural products. Monsanto is the holder of the European Patent EP 0 546 090 B1 ('090 patent) issued on 19 June 1996 for a DNA sequence which, when introduced into the DNA of a soya plant, makes that plant resistant to Glyphosate (Roundup). Monsanto sued in different European countries the Argentine company Cefetra BV for infringing its 090 patent. In Argentina, RR soya is cultivated on a vast scale and is an important export product. Monsanto does not hold a patent in Argentina for the DNA sequence characteristic of the RR soya plant, due to the circumstances of Argentina's law. [130] The Dutch court found that the production process leaves some DNA sequences in the soya meal intact and asked the ECJ for a preliminary judgment on a series of questions, including the interpretation of Article 9 of EU Directive 98/44 entitled 'scope of protection', which provides:

> The protection conferred by a patent on a product containing or consisting of genetic information shall extend to all material . . . in which the product is incorporated and in which the genetic information is contained and performs its function.

Following the opinion of the Advocate General, the Court of Justice held that the protection for a patent relating to a DNA sequence is limited to situations in which the genetic information is currently performing the functions described in the patent.[131]

This judgment may impact not only on patent protection of DNA sequences which are translated into proteins but also on the viability of patents claiming isolated DNA or RNA sequences used as reagents – including reagents used in diagnostic methods such as gene tests and DNA chips.[132] At any rate, unlike the French, German and other European legislations limiting the scope of human DNA sequence patents to the functions disclosed in the specification, the judgment affects the existing patent rights. On the other hand, Monsanto could have

---

[130] Due to Argentina's Supreme Court ruling (*Unilever*, 24 October 2000) that denied with retroactive effect so-called revalidation patents (ie a patent in another country, 'revalidated' in Argentina), the Argentine Patent Office (INPI) refused all applications for such patents. M Kock, 'Purpose-bound protection for DNA sequences: in through the back door?' (2010) 5(7) *Journal of Intellectual Property Law & Practice* 496–7.

[131] According to the Court of Justice, Art 9 of the Directive must be interpreted as 'not conferring patent right protection in circumstances such as those of the case in the main proceedings, in which the patented product is contained in the soy meal, where it does not perform the function for which it is patented, but did perform that function previously in the soy plant, of which the meal is a processed product, or would possibly again be able to perform that function after it had been extracted from the soy meal and inserted into the cell of a living organism.' *Monsanto v Cefetra* (n 129).

[132] R Peet et al, 'The Potential Impact of *Monsanto Technology LLC v Cefetra et al* on Patent Infringement', (2010) *IP Watch*, 17 August. Moreover, the authors of this article think that Art 9 of the Directive was intended to define what constitutes patentable subject matter when the claims in question cover living and replicating organisms, and not to define the scope of enforceable rights in the context of alleged patent infringement.

won its case, if it had included claims covering the GM soy. The relevance of the above European legislative measures to the TRIPS Agreement will be discussed later in chapter 7.

F Japan's Experiences with Research Tool Patents

In Japan, in the early years of the 2000s, various means were sought to resolve problems relating to research tool patents, for example applying competition law, amending the Patent Law to clarify research exemption and instituting compulsory licensing, and adopting Guidelines on lifescience research.[133] Some of these proposed measures turned out to be unrealistic or irrelevant. For example, high royalties would not be considered a competition problem in most cases.[134] Possible infringement cases would arise at the stage of commercialising the molecules obtained, not at the pure research stage. Overall, the lack of competitiveness of the Japanese industry in this field was identified as one of the basic problems.

The most feared situation, infringement suits, did happen, but the court judgment was a victory for the defendant as the patented invention in question was invalidated as lacking novelty and obviousness in comparison to the prior art.[135] In this case involving Euroscreen's patent concerning chemokine receptor 88C (CCR5), the Osaka District Court dismissed its demand for the following main reasons. First, the scope and definition of the invention by Euroscreen relating to chemokine receptor CCR5 could not be clarified in the written description of the basic application 1. In other words, neither the CCR5 receptor ligand nor the function of CCR5 were described in the basic application 1. Thus, the basic application 1 did not satisfy the enablement requirement. Therefore, the application did not satisfy the requirements of a priority date of the basic application

---

[133] To facilitate the use of research tools, two guidelines were adopted by the Ministry of the Economy, Trade and Industry and the Japan Biotechnology Association and by the Ministry of Education, Science and Technology. Website information on research tools was made available, although this does not seem to be often used.

[134] See chs 2, 4 and 9.

[135] *Euroscreen v Ono Pharmaceutical Co*, Osaka District Court, Heisei 18(wa) 7760, 6 October 2008. The plaintiff, Euroscreen, which is a bioventure company based in Brussels, complained that the defendant violated the plaintiff's patent concerning chemokine receptor 88C (CCR5) by screening drug targets. The plaintiff requested payment of damages and demanded a preliminary injunction of production, use, and the transfer of CCR5 receptor DNA, DNA vectors, the transfected cell, the polypeptide, and ONO4128. The Osaka District Court dismissed the plaintiff's demand for the following main reasons. First, the scope and definition of the invention by Euroscreen relating to chemokine receptor CCR5 could not be clarified in the written description of the basic application 1. In other words, neither the CCR5 receptor ligand nor the function of CCR5 were described in the basic application 1. Thus, the basic application 1 did not satisfy the enablement requirement. Therefore, the application did not satisfy the requirements of a priority date of the basic application 1. Second, the basic application 2 disclosed specific CCR5 ligands, RANTES, MIP-1α and MIP-1β. However, on 7 June 1996, the prior art had already disclosed RANTES, MIP-1α and MIP-1β, before the filing date of the basic application 2. Therefore, the Euroscreen invention of the present application lacked novelty and was 'obvious' in comparison to the prior art. The Court thus invalidated Euroscreen's patent and rejected its claims.

1. Second, the basic application 2 disclosed specific CCR5 ligands, RANTES, MIP-1α and MIP-1β. However, on 7 June 1996, the prior art had already disclosed RANTES, MIP-1α and MIP-1β, before the filing date of the basic application 2. Therefore, the Euroscreen invention of the present application lacked novelty and was 'obvious' in comparison to the prior art. The Court thus invalidated Euroscreen's patent and rejected its claims.

Ten years of discussions seem to have produced a reasonable and predictable situation. On balance, the Japanese Pharmaceutical Industry concluded that the proper functioning of the patent system helps research activities, in the sense that the disclosure of relevant scientific and technological information outweigh disadvantages of the system. This may also depend on the field (and subfield) of technology (see chapters 1 and 12).

IV ROAD TO THE URUGUAY ROUND NEGOTIATIONS

A IP-Reliant US Industries and International Protection

During the 1980s, there was a sense of frustration in the United States with respect to its trade deficit, which was running at over \$100 billion every year. American manufacturing industry was losing ground to rising economies in Asia and elsewhere in the 1970s. Efforts were necessary to ensure its high tech sector would not follow the same path as its manufacturing sector. The President's Commission on Industrial Competitiveness, established to address the situation, issued a Report[136] which showed that, although the US had the world's most advanced technology, this was not reflected in its trade account. The Report indicated that one of the reasons for this was that the intellectual property rights of US companies across the world were not sufficiently protected. The US began to focus on IPR protection policies not only within its own borders, but overseas as well, through enforcement efforts with US trade partners.

Preceding this government report, certain US companies began to adopt IPR protection policies towards countries in Asia and South America. The motion picture and sound recording industries were united in taking measures against piracy. Industry groups traditionally involved with copyright and rights of performers, producers and broadcasting organisations,[137] such as the Motion Picture Association of America (MPAA) and the Recording Industry Association of America (RIAA), were joined by high-tech companies such as Pfizer, Dupont and IBM, similarly concerned about patent protection in Latin America and Asia. During this decade, companies such as Monsanto and Dupont demanded that Hungary strengthen patent protection for chemical and agricultural chemical

---

[136] President's Commission on Industrial Competitiveness, *Global Competition: The New Reality* (Washington DC, US Government Printing Office, 1985).

[137] In Europe, they are called 'neighbouring rights', which later in the TRIPS Agreement came to be called 'related rights'.

products.[138] The Republic of Korea, Mexico, Singapore and Taiwan were also requested to reinforce their patent protection policies. The MPAA sent personnel to Latin America to assist those countries in controlling pirated copies. In 1990, the Pharmaceutical Manufacturers of America (now the Pharmaceutical Research and Manufacturers of America (PhRMA)) demanded that the Chilean Government introduce product patent protection for pharmaceuticals. Product patent protection with a term of 15 years was introduced in Chile in 1991.[139]

Their concern was that, with increasingly widespread copying of their technology resulting in the rapid rise in piracy and counterfeit products in the world markets, the licensing incomes of US companies would inevitably decrease. Although there was a wide variety of intellectual property involved, including copyrights, patents and trademarks, companies with an interest in IPR protection set common goals, joined together to push for the establishment of a single external policy, and promoted IPR protection through the domestic laws of countries with which the US traded. These companies insisted that the protection of America's IPR by its trading partners would help the US regain its competitiveness.

It was industry that warned the US Government about the danger of America's reduced competitiveness in the manufacturing sector, suggesting that there was a connection between IPR protection and trade balance. This external IPR policy came to be implemented mainly by the Office of the United States Trade Representative (USTR).[140] The ideas of a multilateral intellectual property treaty within the General Agreement on Tariffs and Trade (GATT) and IPR arrangements within bilateral commercial treaties or free trade agreements (FTA) derive from cooperation between the USTR and the industrial sector. In this context, section 301 of the US Trade Act of 1974[141] played an important role in the US negotiations that lead to these agreements.[142]

---

[138]   SK Sell, *Private Power, Public Law* (Cambridge University Press, 2003); MP Ryan, *Knowledge Diplomacy: Global Competition and the Politics of Intellectual Property* (Washington DC, Brookings Institution Press, 1998) 78–9.

[139]   Ryan, *Knowledge Diplomacy* (n 138).

[140]   The USTR is a government body which assists the President with trade negotiations and issues, and aims to unify the position of the US on external trade policy.

[141]   Presently, under ss 301 (19 USC § 2411), 304 (19 USC § 2414) and 306 (19 USC § 2416) http://uscode.house.gov/usc.htm.

[142]   Title II, s 201 of the US Trade Act of 1974 gives the President authority to take actions to protect US businesses from injury caused by increased imports, and Title III, s 301 allows retaliatory measures to be taken against imports from countries that injure US economic interests by using unfair trade practices. With the revisions to the Trade Act in 1984, it became possible to also impose sanctions under s 301 of the Trade Act against countries that fail to sufficiently protect intellectual property rights. If any trading partner of the US does not have an effective intellectual property protection system, a US company can request that the USTR conduct an investigation on that country. Based on 'Special 301' (which was introduced as s 1303 of the Omnibus Trade and Competitiveness Act of 1988), the USTR, on 30 April of each year, identifies foreign countries that deny 'adequate and effective' protection of intellectual property rights (or 'fair and equitable market access') to US persons relying upon IPR protection. Normally, the USTR must self-initiate s 301 investigations of priority foreign countries within 30 days of the identification date, unless it determines that the initiation of an investigation would be detrimental to US economic interests.

In 1994, s 301 was amended with a view to ensuring consistency with the Understanding on Rules and Procedures Governing the Settlement of Disputes (DSU) of the WTO, adopted as a result of

The Paris Convention does not require patent protection of pharmaceuticals. Similarly, the Berne Convention does not contain provisions relating to the protection of computer programs by copyright. During the 1980s, there was a sharp increase in complaints by originator firms in the US about software piracy (the term software is often used to mean computer programs, but it can include other digital data) and copy medicines. The US then started to negotiate bilateral treaties backed by the implementation of the mechanisms in Section 301 of the US Trade Act. In August 1986, the US concluded a bilateral agreement with Korea relating to pipeline protection. Pipeline protection generally refers to an agreement whereby administrative protection is provided in a trading partner country to the pharmaceuticals or agrochemical products which are patented but which have not received marketing approval in the original country, without the consent of the right holder in the original country. The US–Korea bilateral agreement provided protection (but only to US companies) through administrative guidance issued by Korea's Ministry for Health, Welfare and Family Affairs, from sales and export of pharmaceuticals copies in Korea. Following the US Agreement, the European Community settled for a similar arrangement with Korea. Japan, being left out of these bilateral arrangements, later insisted during the Uruguay Round on application of the most-favoured nation principle in negotiating the TRIPS Agreement.[143]

B Border Measures

Parallel to US demands for its trade partners to protect IPRs held by US firms, border measures against products and technologies infringing such IPRs were

the Uruguay Round negotiations within the GATT. Subsequently, the EU complained to the WTO Dispute Settlement Body (DSB) that, in particular, ss 306 and 305 of the Trade Act do not allow the US to comply with the rules of the DSU in situations where a prior multilateral ruling under the DSU on the conformity of measures taken pursuant to implementation of DSB recommendations has not been adopted by the DSB. According to the EU, the amended version of Title III, c 1 (ss 301–10) of the Trade Act of 1974 and, in particular, ss 306 and 305 of the Act, were inconsistent with arts 3, 21, 22 and 23 of the DSU, Art XVI: 4 of the WTO Agreement, and Arts I, II, III, VIII and XI of GATT 1994 (*U.S. Sections 301–310 of the Trade Act of 1974*, Panel Report (adopted 27 January 2000) WT/DS152/R). Art 23(2)(a) of the DSU prohibits any determination to the effect that a violation has occurred whose benefits have been nullified or impaired, or where the attainment of any objective of the covered agreements has been impeded, except through recourse through dispute settlement in accordance with the DSU. The Panel found that it was important that the US Administrative Statements 'explicitly, officially, repeatedly and unconditionally confirmed' its commitment that the USTR would base a s 301 or 304 decision only on adopted DSB findings (para 7.114), and that various facts support the reliance of these statements. The Panel found that ss 304(a)(2)(A), 305(a) and 306(b) of the above Act were not inconsistent with Art 23.2(a) or (c) of the DSU or with any of the GATT 1994 provisions referred to. This is because, even if domestic law grants the executive branch the authority to take measures that are inconsistent with WTO Agreements, 'this does not mean that the administration is necessarily in violation of these agreements unless it exercises that authority'. The Panel found that ss 304(a)(2)(A), 305(a) and 306(b) of the above Act are not inconsistent with Art 23.2(a) or (c) of the DSU or with any of the GATT 1994 provisions referred to.

[143] S Takakura, *Recent Development of Multilateral Agreements on Intellectual Property Rights* (Tokyo, Yuhikaku, 2001) 153.

gradually strengthened under the US Tariff Act of 1930. Section 337 of this Act[144] provides that infringement of specific US statutory intellectual property rights, and other forms of unfair competition in import trade, are unlawful practices. Unfair use and copies of know-how and trade secrets are not dealt with under Special section 301, but protection against these practices is possible under section 337.[145]

If the ITC determines under the proper procedures[146] that section 337 has been violated, it can issue an exclusion order barring the products at issue from entry into the US, as well as a cease and desist order directing the violating party to stop certain actions. Appeals to Commission orders entered under section 337 investigations are heard by the US Court of Appeals for the Federal Circuit (CAFC) within 60 days of the decision. The right to appeal, however, initially was available only to US nationals.

With revisions to the Tariff Act in 1988, the requirements for providing evidence of damage to US industry became less onerous. Prior to the revisions, legal action could only be taken if it could be proved that there was injury to an industry efficiently and economically operated in the United States. Judicial precedents were established[147] that when manufacturing methods are protected by patents in the US, the importation into the US of products manufactured by those methods may also constitute infringement. In 1988 the European Community sought recourse through GATT dispute settlement procedures, complaining that the appeals procedures under section 337 were inconsistent with the principle of national treatment under the GATT III.4.[148] In 1994, section 337 was amended and the right to appeal was assured to foreign nationals also.[149]

---

[144]   19 USC § 1337.

[145]   Under 19 USC, the following acts are unlawful: (a) unfair methods of competition and unfair acts in the importation of articles into the United States whose effect is (i) to destroy or substantially injure an industry in the United States (ii) to prevent the establishment of such an industry or (iii) to restrain or monopolise trade and commerce in the United States; (b) the importation into the United States of products which (i) are made, produced, processed, or mined under, or by means of, a process covered by the claims of a valid and enforceable United States patent and (ii) infringe a valid and enforceable United States patent or trade mark, copyright registered under title 17 or mask work; and, (c) the misappropriation of trade secrets, passing off and false advertising, and antitrust claims relating to imported goods.

[146]   Section 337 investigations must be initiated by an International Trade Commission (ITC) decision within 30 days of the receipt of a properly filed complaint. When an investigation is initiated, the ITC assigns an Administrative Law Judge to preside over the proceedings and to render an initial decision based on 19 USC § 1337 and the Administrative Procedure Act. If the Commission determines that section 337 has been violated, the ITC may issue an exclusion order barring the products at issue from entry into the US, as well as a cease and desist order directing the violating parties to cease certain actions. Appeals against Commission orders entered in section 337 investigations are heard by the US Court of Appeals for the Federal Circuit.

[147]   *Bio-Technology Gen. Corp v Genentech, Inc* 80 F 3d 1553 (Fed Cir 1996).

[148]   *US–Section 337 of the Tariff Act of 1930*, Panel Report (adopted 7 November 1989), BISD 36S/345 (see also ch 4).

[149]   This also led to restrictions such as the elimination of investigation time limits, the possibility of counterclaims, adjustments to overlapping ITC and court procedures, reimbursement of guarantee money to respondents, and a limited application of general cease and desist orders

C 'Pro-Patent' Policies within the US

US policy was not limited to a defensive strategy that protects asset prices and licensing fees through measures against counterfeit goods, it also aimed at encouraging science and technology domestically by gathering and nurturing competitive talent from around the globe. The competitiveness of the US in such fields as biotech and pharmaceutical research, software and space technology achieved remarkable success, in stark contrast to America's faltering manufacturing industry. Following a shift in the structure of US markets which was occurring at this time, emphasis was gradually placed on the merits of 'economies of scale', due to significant improvements in distribution and technological innovation. There were also changes in approaches to business efficiency and behaviour,[150] from which a number of policy changes were attempted. Further, there were changes in economic policy taking into account technological innovation and international competition.

As part of this, there were calls for better commercialisation of inventions by scientists and researchers through licensing to companies. The Bayh-Dole Act of 1980, which granted US universities and small- and medium-size enterprises (SMEs) the right to patent inventions made through federal government-funded research,[151] was part of this policy. Researchers at universities and scientific institutions were encouraged to obtain patents and rights for the results of their joint research with private companies and other bodies. In 1983, in addition to non-profit organisations and SMEs, large corporations were entitled to the system established under the Bayh-Dole Act, and the scope for using public funds for R&D became wider.[152]

These policy shifts also reached the judicial system with the creation in 1982 of a new Court of Appeals for the Federal Circuit (CAFC),[153] which assumed exclusive jurisdiction over all appeals involving patents and trademarks from US federal district courts. The CAFC became one of 13 federal appellate courts in the US (the others were the 11 Courts of Appeals for the Federal Circuit and the Court of Appeals of the District of Columbia). This was an attempt to reduce forum shopping by litigants[154] and ensure more consistent and stable case law.

---

[150] In response to those changes, analyses of market competition came to value economic analyses and technological capabilities, and Judges Posner and Easterbrook have focused their analysis on market entry conditions rather than market share, on the assumption that the high market share of specific companies is the result of greater competitiveness (in other words, effort) and that monopolistic profit promotes new market entry and has led to the dissolution of monopolies.

[151] USC § 200–12.

[152] See 35 USC § 202(c)(4) and § 203 for the requirements for R&D agreements.

[153] The new CAFC took over the functions of the Court of Customs and Patent Appeals and some of the functions of the Court of Claims, and assumed the jurisdiction previously held by the 12 regional courts of appeals to hear appeals on patent matters from the Federal District Courts. In 1984, several changes, such as the relaxation of the rules on joint inventorship, the formation of a new Board of Appeals and Interferences, and provision for 'Statutory Invention Registration' were introduced.

[154] Forum shopping is a litigation strategy whereby the plaintiff chooses a court that is likely to rule in its favour. In the US, in addition to factors such as the adoption of the jury system and the

Up to that point, there were few judges with detailed knowledge of patents or technology, and juries were prone to show sympathy towards the generally held view that patents represent monopolies. It appears that the rate of success of plaintiffs, whose patents were held to be valid, increased for a while following the creation of the CAFC,[155] although there are no definite statistics. The amount of damages claimed in patent cases has increased[156]and, generally, claim constructions that anticipate a broad scope of equivalents[157] have come to be expected.[158]

The scope of patent rights depends on the elements claimed in the patent. The doctrine of equivalents is an approach where an invention described in the claims of a patent and an equivalent invention fall within the same technological

maintenance of the discovery system, fluctuations in the level of damages, and state laws pertaining to international (interstate) jurisdiction, called long arm statutes, have also led to the adoption of this type of strategy.

[155] Statistics on the rate that patents are held to be valid in appellate courts vary. According to R Mazzoleni and RR Nelson, 'The benefits and costs of strong patent protection: a contribution to the current debate' (1998) 27(3) *Research Policy*, 30% of judgments held patents to be valid before the creation of the CAFC; this rose to 89% during a five-year period following the creation of the CAFC. AB Jaffe, 'The US patent system in transition: policy innovation and the innovation process' (2000) 29(4–5) *Research Policy* 531 pointed out there is more to an increase in success rate of plaintiffs in infringement cases than just the creation of the CAFC, because if there is a high rate of judgments that find patents to be valid and those patents have been infringed, even if there are questions concerning the validity of the patent, any party who is subject to a judgment for infringement would prefer to settle.

[156] In *Polaroid Co v Eastman Kodak Co* 17 USPQ 2d 1711 (D Mass 1991), the District Court of Massachusetts entered a judgment for the then record-high damages.

[157] The doctrine of equivalents is founded on the theory that if two devices do the same work in substantially the same way and accomplish substantially the same result, they are the same, even though they differ in name, form or shape (US Supreme Court in *Graver Tank & Manufacturing Co v Linde Air Products Co* 339 US 605 (1950) 608–9). Otherwise, it would 'encourage . . . the unscrupulous copyist to make unimportant and insubstantial changes and substitutions in the patent which, though adding nothing, would be enough to take the copied matter outside the claim' (ibid). In determining equivalents, however, consideration must be given to the purpose for which an ingredient is used in a patent, the qualities it has when combined with other ingredients, the functions which it is intended to perform, and whether persons reasonably skilled in the art would have known of the inter-changeability of an ingredient not contained in the patent with one that was. Like any other issue of fact, final determination requires a balancing of credibility, persuasiveness, and weight of evidence. In *Warner-Jenkinson Co v Hilton Davis Chem Co* (1997)) equivalence was established if there was only an 'insubstantial change' between each of the elements of the accused device or process and each of the elements of the patent claim, on the condition that there was no prosecution history *estoppel* by the patentee.It is unclear whether there was already recognition of the doctrine of equivalents in the field of biotechnology when attitudes in the US became more pro-patent. Koda has suggested that with an increasingly pro-patent sentiment in the US, the extensive use of the doctrine of equivalents, the strengthening of patent rights validity and the rise in the amount of damages were important. He explained that he believes that intellectual property rights gradually became stronger and this definitely led to the rejuvenation of research, development, and production activities in the US (H Koda, *Commentary of the US Patent Act*, 4th edn (in Japanese) (Tokyo, Hatsumei Kyoukai, 2001) 298).

[158] Currently, by comparing examples of the application of the doctrine of equivalents in the US in infringement suits involving biotechnology, it is more common to see the application of this doctrine restricted by prosecution history estoppel than in other fields. In other respects, however, biotechnology is the same as other fields. RA Schwartsman 'Assertion of the Doctrine of Equivalents in Biotechnology Litigation: About as Successful as in Other Arts' (2005) 17(12) *Intellectual Property & Technology Law Journal*.

scope. Even if elements of a claim are not included in the strict language of the claim of the original patent, both inventions are deemed to fall under the scope of rights as equivalents if any essential parts are the same and there are only minor differences. If the doctrine of equivalents is applied,[159] a broader scope of rights than the scope shown in the language of the patent claims could be recognised. Therefore, manufacturing, selling or otherwise exploiting an invention that is considered an equivalent would constitute an infringement of patent rights. The court determines whether an invention is an equivalent at the time of the claim of patent infringement by the plaintiff, but not at the time of the application.

Parallel to the development of biotechnology, and in a context where only a few countries were expanding commercialisation of the original products which resulted from their biotech inventions, negotiations over a new trading system began in 1986 in Uruguay, within the GATT framework. The majority of the participating countries in the Uruguay Round supported the discussions on the TRIPS Agreement which coincided with new discoveries and rapid technological advancement in biotechnology, with a concomitant controversy over patentability criteria and exclusions which we have seen above.[160]

The percentage of R&D expenditure relative to sales revenues of US industries evolved variably depending on the type of industrial sector, as Figure 3.1 shows.

Figure 3.1: Research and Development Spending as a Percentage of Sales Revenue for Various US Industries

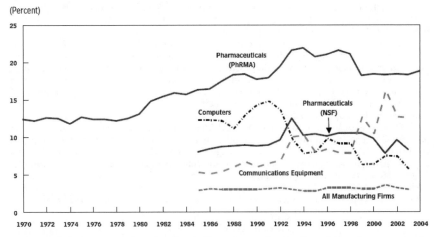

Source: US Congressional Budgetary Office (CBO), *Research and Development in the Pharmaceutical Industry*, October 2006 at 10. (NSF = National Science Foundation, PhRMA = Pharmaceutical Research and Manufacturers of America)

---

[159] See below, n 157.
[160] See chs 4 and 12.

Later, the accuracy of industry information came to be contested and debated by NGOs, scholars and political leaders.[161]

According to the US Congressional Budgetary Office (CBO), between 1980 and 2005, the percentage spending of domestic company-financed R&D to US sales and exports was high in comparison to others, and increased during the 1980s.[162] Sell and Prakash refer to Standard & Poor's data in 2002[163] which says that the ratio was 11.9 per cent in 1980 and reached 17.7 per cent in 2001. Increases in drug R&D by and large were matched by rising revenues of drug sales.[164] The CBO Report in 2006 accounts that this ratio reached 19 per cent in 2005.[165] In the pharmaceutical development process in the US, public R&D is important. The economic stakes of R&D are high in pharmaceuticals, as the chances of failure are high.[166] According to Cockburn and Henderson, only five

[161]   Sell and Prakash mention the critiques by scholars of the statistics used by companies and US government agencies. For example, Gadbaw and Richards (N Gadbaw and T Richards, *Intellectual Property Rights: Global Consensus, Global Conflict?* (Boulder CO, Westview Press, 1988) 379–83) estimated the figure of $3.4 billion lost in revenues for US companies by 'piracy' counterfeiting, in comparison to the range of $43 billion to $61 billion which had been reported in the 1988 Report of the US International Trade Commission, 'Foreign Protection of IPR and the Effects on the US Industry and Trade' (ITC, 1988, US ITC Pub.2065 Inv. No.332-245). SK Sell and S Prakash, 'Using Ideas Strategically: The Contest Between Business and NGO Networks in Intellectual Property Rights' (2004) 8(1) *International Studies Quarterly* 143–75. Later in 2006, Rep H Waxman criticised the R&D figures advanced by the industry as a 'myth' among 'many of the pharmaceutical industry's myths about drug development', when the Government Accountability Office (GAO) Report 'New Drug Development: Science, Business, Regulatory and Intellectual Property Issues Cited as Hampering Drug Development Effort' (GAO-07-49, November 2006) was published. 'US report on declining R&D productivity stokes criticism of drug industry' (2007) *SCRIP World Pharmaceutical News* 1 February.

[162]   CBO, 'Research and Development in the Pharmaceutical Industry', October 2006, 9.

[163]   Standard & Poor's (2002) 'Industry Surveys: Healthcare: Pharmaceuticals', June 27, 2002 cited in Sell and Prakash, 'Using Ideas Strategically' (n 160) 148.

[164]   See ch 1 on the question of the degree to which competition encourages innovation. According to Aghion and Griffith, this depends on the difference in profit rates before and after the innovation in a given product market. According to the CBO, a relatively close relationship exists between drug firms' R&D spending and sales revenue because: (i) successful new drugs generate cash flows that can be invested in R&D (their manufacturing costs are usually very low relative to their price); (ii) alternative sources of investment capital are not perfect substitutes for cash flow financing. CBO, 'Research and Development in the Pharmaceutical Industry' (n 161) 9–11.

[165]   The EU Pharmaceutical Sector Inquiry Final Report (July 2009) later stated, based on the data on 219 INNs (pharmaceutically active molecules) and the behaviour of 43 research-based global companies between 2000 and 2007, that, on average, approximately 30% of the turnover is reported as profit (para 68) and the respondent originator companies spent on average 17% of their turnover generated at global level with prescription medicines on R&D for new or improved prescription medicines (para 72).

In 2007, the costs in clinical and pre-clinical phases were distributed as follows at global level:

Cost	% R&D
Pre-clinical trial	8%
Phase I	12%
Phase II	20%
Phase III	60%

Source: Commission (EU), 'EU Pharmaceutical Sector Inquiry, Final Report', 8 July 2009. http://ec.europa.eu/competition/sectors/pharmaceuticals/inquiry/staff_working_paper_part1.pdf

[166]   According to the JPMA study over 2003–07, the cumulative success rate is one out of 21,677 molecules.

among the 21 pharmaceutical compounds of most therapeutic significance from 1965 to 1992 did not receive funding from public institutes such as the NIH or National Science Foundation. Public institutions discover more than 80 per cent of compounds, while private companies conduct more than 90 per cent of clinical trials leading to a compound reaching the market as a pharmaceutical. It is generally reported that clinical trial costs double research costs. The efficacy and safety (toxicity) of the drug candidate compounds are assessed through different stages of clinical trials. The pre-clinical testing is undertaken mainly on animals; Phase I tests are undertaken to determine safety and side-effects on a small number (30-100) of healthy human beings; Phase II tests determine the efficacy of the new medicine for the given indication with parallel tests with placebo (medicines without the active pharmaceutical ingredients) on a control group (100–300); Phase III tests are undertaken on large patient groups (1000–10,000) involves long-term trials. Figure 3.2 shows that development cost by private companies rose in comparison to the public sector R&D, due probably to the continuously increasing cost of clinical studies.[167]

Annual Spending on Research and Development by Drug Companies and the National Institutes of Health

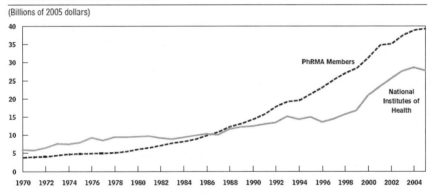

Figure 3.2: Annual Spending on R&D by Drug Companies and the National Institutes of Health

Source: CBO, 'Research and Development in the Pharmaceutical Industry' (n 162) 28.

---

[167] Commission (EU), 'EU Pharmaceutical Sector Inquiry, Final Report' (n 164) 56.

Part II

The TRIPS Agreement

4

Uruguay Round Negotiations and the Adoption of TRIPS

D URING A PERIOD when the non-market economies were declining, in the
late 1980s, the Uruguay Round of trade negotiations (1986–94) started. The
negotiating parties held widely opposing views on the scope and standard of
protection of intellectual property (IP), to be introduced within the framework
of the General Agreement on Tariffs and Trade (GATT) as a common text, and
later adopted as the Agreement on Trade-Related Intellectual Property Rights
(TRIPS).[1] This chapter describes the positions held by different countries on
the controversial questions that divided the Uruguay Round negotiators, and
retraces how diplomatic compromises were arrived at, thanks to the 'constructive ambiguities' of the text which was agreed upon.

In fact, TRIPS negotiators opted for preserving (with some updating)
the level of protection provided in the existing IPR conventions, such as the
Paris Convention for the Protection of Industrial Property (1967), the Berne
Convention (1971), the Rome Convention and the Treaty on Intellectual Property
in Respect of Integrated Circuits (1967). Novel aspects of the GATT IP agreement under negotiation included provisions on enforcement, and the improvement of dispute settlements among governments, both of which were lacking
under these preceding conventions. A few new principles were also being proposed, such as transparency and most-favoured-nation treatment (MFN), which
had not existed in the previous intellectual property conventions, but which are
important for counteracting unilateral actions, such as the US retaliation under
section 301 of its Trade Act.

The introduction within the GATT of substantive rules concerning IPR encountered opposition from Brazil, India and some other developing countries. Unclear
and precarious compromise was achieved on the objectives and principles of IPR
protection (Articles 7 and 8), and on certain provisions important for research-
based pharmaceutical and biotechnology industries (notably Articles 27.3, 39.3,
70.8 and 70.9). The underlying opposing views concerning the role of IPRs in
the economic development of developing countries remained a strong source
of discord. In the historical hiatus in the early 1990s, created by the situation
in which leading developing countries confronted difficulties in re-negotiating

---

[1] Annex 1C of the Marrakesh Agreement Establishing the WTO, signed on 15 April 1994 which
entered into force on 1 January 1995.

conditionality with the International Monetary Fund (IMF), and with the dissolution of the Soviet Union, which had often supported the positions of developing countries, the demands of the US and European countries were probably relatively less difficult to accept than either before or after this particular period.

I DEVELOPING COUNTRIES AND IPRs IN THE URUGUAY ROUND NEGOTIATIONS

A Mandate to Negotiate Trade-Related Aspects of IPRs

T Cottier pointed out in 1991 that 'linking intellectual property to the GATT' probably came about due to 'the gradual changes in fundamental perceptions of the function and role of IPRs in many quarters of the world',[2] explaining that 'the absence of adequate protection [contributed] considerably to an unfair competitive environment for many industries operating on highly competitive foreign markets'. The importance of the protection of intellectual property rights in international competition and cooperation in various areas of economic relations was growing, and benefits of holders of intellectual property rights should be able to enjoy the benefits of their creativity and inventiveness.

Others have explained the genesis of the TRIPS Agreement in terms of rising R&D spending, accompanied by the profitability of imitation (see chapter 1): the higher the ratio of R&D to the cost of manufacturing, the greater the incentive to short-cut the process through unauthorised copying.[3] On the other hand, Cooper-Dreyfuss has argued that, 'to the extent that the United States was a prime mover in the Uruguay Round, its intent was to ease US trade deficits by creating broader exclusive markets for intellectual products, a goal with rather a scant role for user right'.[4] Some others have simply attributed the origin of the TRIPS Agreement to the rent-seeking activities of large US corporations.

Whatever the motives may have been, the TRIPS Agreement resulted from the last multilateral trade negotiations in the GATT where reciprocity and the exchange of mutual advantage in different economic sectors were important.

While the positions of the Members of the Paris Convention remained polarised, initiatives for establishing a global system of IP disciplines and standards came from a different forum – the Preparatory Committee of the Uruguay Round[5] negotiations within the GATT. The United States and Japan requested

[2] T Cottier, 'The Prospects for Intellectual Property in GATT' (1991) 28 *Common Market Law Review* 385.

[3] GE Evans, *Lawmaking under the Trade Constitution: A Study in Legislating by the World Trade Organization* (The Hague London, Boston, Kluwer Law International, 2000) 108–10.

[4] R Cooper Dreyfuss, 'TRIPS Round II: Should Users Strike Back?' (2004) 71(1) *The University of Chicago Law Review* 21.

[5] Since its establishment in 1948, the GATT has promoted reduction of tariffs and other restraints on trade through multilateral negotiations. Comprehensive trade negotiations have been called 'Rounds' ever since the Fifth Round.

that protection of IPRs be inscribed as the subject matter of the trade negotiations, but Argentina and Brazil opposed this.[6]

Under the GATT, provisions relating to IPRs were limited only to those on marks of origin[7] and their relationship to restrictive effects on international trade and to discriminatory treatment.[8] The general thrust of the GATT had been the liberalisation of international trade, where protection of IPRs could be considered merely as part of the regulations restricting free trade, as referred to in Article XX(d) of the GATT 1947.[9]

Article XX GATT stipulates rules for general exceptions to GATT provisions. Paragraph (d) of the Article refers to 'the protection of patents, trademarks and copyrights, and the prevention of deceptive practices', considered as measures not contrary to the GATT, in so far as it is 'necessary to secure compliance with laws or regulations which are consistent with the GATT' and 'provided that such measures are not applied in a manner which would constitute a means of arbitrary or unjustifiable discrimination between countries where the same conditions prevail, or a disguised restriction on international trade', as provided by the *chapeau* (introductory phrase) of Article XX.

---

[6] PREP.COM(86)W/47/Rev.1 (30 July 1986) and PREP.COM(86)W/49 (29 July 1986), as cited by D Gervais, *The TRIPS Agreement: Drafting History and Analysis* (London, Sweet & Maxwell, 1998) 10.

[7] GATT IX concerns marks of origin in their relationship to international trade, as exemplified by para 2, which provides: 'The contracting parties recognize that, in adopting and enforcing laws and regulations relating to marks of origin, the difficulties and inconveniences which such measures may cause to the commerce and industry of exporting countries should be reduced to a minimum, due regard being had to the necessity of protecting consumers against fraudulent or misleading indications.'

[8] Work Undertaken in GATT Concerning Trade-Related Aspects of Intellectual Property Rights, including Trade in Counterfeit Goods, note by the Secretariat MTN.GNG/NG11/W/4 (6 May 1987).

[9] *US–Section 337 of the Tariff Act of 1930*, Panel Report (adopted 7 November 1989) BISD 30S/149. In this case, the EC complained that the US had failed to carry out its obligations under Art III.4 GATT by applying procedures under s 337 which subjected imported goods to a treatment which was less favourable than the treatment accorded by US federal district courts to goods of national origin, in patent infringement suits. The US argued that: (i) application of s 337 was consistent with the requirements of Art XX(d), and that s 337 fell under the general exception to GATT obligations provided by that Article; (ii) the procedural differences between s 337 and federal district court litigation did not result in less favourable treatment for importers and manufacturers of imported products; and, (iii) s 337 on balance accorded manufacturers and sellers of imported products more favourable treatment than that accorded to domestic producers of products challenged under US patent law. The US argued that s 337 was 'necessary', within the meaning of Art XX(d), to secure compliance with US patent law and that it met the other conditions in that Article, ie, it was not applied in a manner which would constitute a means of 'arbitrary or unjustifiable discrimination between countries where the same conditions prevail, or a disguised restriction on international trade'. On the basis of the findings set out in the Report, the Panel stated that a contracting party cannot justify a measure inconsistent with another GATT provision as 'necessary', in terms of Art XX(d), if an alternative measure which it could reasonably be expected to employ and which is not inconsistent with other GATT provisions, is available to it. The Panel concluded that s 337 of the US Tariff Act of 1930 was inconsistent with Art III:4, in that it accorded, to imported products challenged as infringing US patents, treatment less favourable than the treatment accorded to products of US origin similarly challenged. The Panel also stressed that neither Art III:4 nor Art XX(d) puts obligations on contracting parties specifying the level of protection that they should accord to patents or the effectiveness of procedures to enforce such protection.

Although of a limited scope, rules for international trade in counterfeit goods had been discussed during the Tokyo Round (1973–79), and the decisions concerning measures against the import of counterfeit goods which infringe trade mark rights were included in the Ministerial Declaration of 29 November 1982.[10]

The Preparatory Committee, co-chaired by Colombia and Switzerland, attempted to reconcile opposing views. Based on the Swiss-Colombian majority text, which was not a consensus text of the Round Preparatory Committee, the Ministerial Conference at Punta del Este in Uruguay on 20 September 1986[11] inscribed the following items to be discussed as 'trade-related aspects of IPRs' with a view to elaborating rules, principles and disciplines, within the framework of the GATT Round Negotiations:

- to reduce the distortions and impediments to international trade, taking into account the need to promote effective and adequate protection of IPRs, and to ensure that measures and procedures to enforce IPRs do not themselves become barriers to legitimate trade; and
- to develop a multilateral framework dealing with international trade in counterfeit goods.[12]

A 'Negotiating Group on Trade-Related Aspects of IPRs, including Trade in Counterfeit Goods' (TRIPS Negotiating Group), which was one among a total of 14 negotiating groups, was set up under the 'Group of Negotiation on Goods' (GNG) to deal with the forthcoming GATT rule on the above subjects relating to IPRs. The GNG, as well as the Group of Negotiations on Services (GNS), in turn, reported to the Trade Negotiations Committee (TNC). India explained, through a statement at the concluding session of the Punta del Este Ministerial, that it understood the agenda on IPRs to include border measures only, and did not agree to discuss substantive norms and standards.

From the first meetings in February 1987 until 1989, discussions at the Negotiating Group centred around the 'mandate' of the Group, namely, what should be the objective, coverage and the jurisdiction of the future GATT intellectual property agreement.[13] During this period, the Chairman of the Negotiating Group, Lars ER Anell from Sweden, invited expert information, including from WIPO, and suggestions from participants.[14]

The US considered that the objective of IPR protection within the GATT would be to 'reduce distortions of and impediments to legitimate trade in goods and services caused by deficient levels of protection and enforcement of IPRs'

[10] D Hartridge and A Subramanian, 'Intellectual Property Rights: The Issues in GATT' (1989) 22 *Vanderbilt Journal of Transnational Law* 893–910.

[11] Ministerial Declaration on the Uruguay Round: Declaration of 20 Sept1986, in GATT, Basic Instruments and Selected Documents (BISD), 33d Supp.19, 25–26 (1987).

[12] MIN.DEC of 20 September 1986, 7–8. The Declaration added that 'these negotiations shall be without prejudice to other complementary initiatives that may be taken in the World Intellectual Property Organization (WIPO) and elsewhere to deal with these matters.'

[13] Note by the Secretariat MTN.GNG/NG11/14 (12 September 1989); MTN.GNG/NG11/20 (24 April 1990).

[14] Gervais (n 6) 12–16.

and in response submitted a proposal[15] to the Negotiating Group. It urged the participants to:

- create an effective economic deterrent to international trade in goods and services which infringe IPRs through implementation of border measures;
- recognise and implement standards and norms that provide adequate means of obtaining and maintaining IPRs and provide a basis for effective enforcement of those rights;
- ensure that such measures to protect IPRs do not create barriers to legitimate trade;
- extend international notification, consultation, surveillance and dispute settlement procedures to protection of IP and enforcement of IPRs;
- encourage non-signatory governments to achieve, adopt and enforce the recognised standards for protection of IP and join the agreement.

B Communications from Brazil and India: The Place and Meaning of Public Policy

In discussing 'standards and principles concerning the availability, scope and use of trade-related intellectual property rights' within the Negotiating Group, India and Brazil, in particular, expressed their concern about the economic and social consequences of IPR protection. Brazil prided itself upon having long-standing experience in sophisticated IP laws, as 'the only original Member among developing countries to the Paris Convention'.[16] It raised an important question about what should be the trade and developmental aspects of IPR protection within the GATT, as distinct from more legalistic discussions in other fora such as WIPO.[17] India was not yet a party to the Paris Convention. [18]

Both India and Brazil asserted that IPRs are essentially monopolistic and impede trade and, therefore, the objective of IP protection should be to ensure 'public interest' by preventing and deterring[19] possible abusive behaviour and to ensure greater access to technological innovation for users.[20] India said at that

---

[15] Suggestion by the United States for Achieving the Negotiating Objective: Revision, MTN. GNG/NG11/W/14/Rev.1 (17 October 1988).

[16] Communication from Brazil, MTN.GNG/NG11/W/30 (31 October 1988) para 10. On the original members of the Paris Union, see ch 2, n 4.

[17] 'Attentive consideration should be given to the cases where IPR protection and enforcement become a barrier or harassment to legitimate trade.' Communication from Brazil (n 16) para 29.

[18] On 7 December 1998, Botswana, Cambodia, Grenada, Guatemala, India, the Lao People's Democratic Republic, Mozambique, and Sao Tome and Principe joined the Paris Convention, and Croatia, Cyprus, Grenada, India, South Africa and the United Arab Emirates adhered to the Patent Cooperation Treaty (PCT), www.wipo.int/edocs/prdocs/en/1999/wipo_upd_1999_47.html.

[19] Communication from India MTN.GNG/NG11/W/37 (10 July 1989) paras 11 and 13, referring to compulsory licences.

[20] ibid para 6: 'a patent system is not essential as an incentive to encourage inventions and investments in R&D for the following reasons: (1) it provides R&D incentives only in limited sectors and even in their case, the motivation for obtaining a patent is often the apprehension that someone else would come upon the same discovery or invention; (2) investment in R&D and technological

time, 'it is only the restrictive and anti-competitive practices of the owners of intellectual property rights that can be considered to be trade-related because they alone distort or impede international trade'. [21] Both countries advocated the necessity to exclude certain areas from IP protection and to maintain the 'flexibility' of the international IP system for developing countries in need of new technologies. In 1989, Brazil submitted to the Negotiating Group its second detailed document, which stated that patents should be granted 'in a way conducive to or consistent with national development, technological objectives and public interest', [22] with exceptions made for 'inventions that are contrary to morality, religion, public order, public health and bearing in mind public interest and technological and economic development considerations'.[23]

India proposed in July 1989 that:

- there should be no attempt to harmonise the patent laws of industrialised and developing countries, nor should there be any imposition on developing countries of standards and principles that may be relevant to industrialised countries, but which are inappropriate for developing countries; [24]
- international conventions on this subject should incorporate, as a central philosophy, the freedom of the member states to attune their IP protection system to their own economic needs and social conditions;[25]
- the patent system can hamper domestic research and development and technological capabilities[26] and, therefore, steps should be taken to prevent and deter[27] the possible abuse of monopoly rights, be it by compulsory licence for public interest, licence of right,[28] exceptions from patentability, or government use of patents in the public interest.

India wished to exclude from patentable subject matter a broad range of technical fields, particularly where the 'public interest' would be involved, including 'national security, food production, poverty alleviation, nutrition, health care or the development of other vital sectors of the national economy'. For inven-

breakthroughs are taking place in a wide variety of industries where the patent system is not considered to be important; (3) investments in R&D are made by firms for maintaining their technological leadership and market position and they would do so regardless of the availability of patent protection; (4) the underlying know-how to operate the patent is kept secret in order to prevent others from operating the patent on the basis of the patent disclosure.'

[21] Communication from India (n 19) para 2: 'India is of the view that it is only the restrictive and anti-competitive practices of the owners of intellectual property rights that can be considered to be trade-related because they alone distort or impede international trade'.

[22] Communication from Brazil, MTN.GNG/NG11/W/57 (11 December 1989) para 17.

[23] ibid para 19.

[24] Communication from India (n 19) para. 5 says: '. . . In the crucial phase of their industrial development, many of the industrialized countries of today had either "no-patent"or "weak patent" standards in vital sectors in order to strengthen their own industrial and technological capabilities.'

[25] ibid para.4, where India states: '. . . [the] experience of developing countries clearly shows that a patent system can have serious adverse effects in sectors of critical importance to them, such as food production, poverty alleviation, nutrition, health care and disease prevention.'

[26] Communication from India (n 19) para 7.

[27] ibid para 11.

[28] See ch 2 n 36.

tions in these fields, India argued that the host country government or any third person designated by it should be 'free to work and use the patented invention in the country, including the importation of the patented product if necessary, without the consent of the patent owner on such terms and conditions as the host country government may decide.'[29]

Later in September 1989, India submitted another paper on enforcement[30] to emphasise that enforcement only at the border (as opposed to internal enforcement) should be treated within the General Agreement on Tariffs and Trade (GATT). India argued that:

- border measures can easily become arbitrary or unjustifiable barriers to legitimate trade;
- each country's laws differ, which makes it difficult to establish a common procedure for identifying counterfeit goods under an international trade regime;
- enforcement is possible only through normal administrative and judicial systems, and international agreements should stay at the level of general principles; and
- developing countries should not allocate additional resources establishing separate machinery for this purpose.

Other developing countries also submitted written statements. Mexico, for example, strongly supported measures within the GATT rules to strengthen action against trade in counterfeit goods, but expressed its concern that the improved IP protection should not become a barrier to access by developing countries to technologies produced in developed countries.[31] Thailand opposed the establishment of international norms and standards of IPR protection and proposed that the negotiations be confined to issues relating to the enforcement of IPRs at the border, on the condition that they lead to further liberalisation, so that IPRs do not 'become barriers of harassment to legitimate trade or lead to excessive protection that obstructs technology transfer'.[32]

At this time, the issue of access to medicines was not prominent in these written submissions. India, however, warned about the possible increase in the cost of healthcare systems as a result of IP protection.[33]

[29] Communication from India (n 19) para 28.
[30] Enforcement of Trade-Related Intellectual Property Rights, Communication from India MTN. GNG/NG11/W/40 (5 September 1989).
[31] Statement made by the Delegation of Mexico at the Meeting of 17, 18 and 21 October 1988, MTN.GNG/NG11/W/28 (19 October 1988) .
[32] Statement by Thailand at the meeting of 12–14 September 1988, MTN.GNG/NG11/W27 (21 September 1988).
[33] Communication from India (n 19) para 18: 'There is ample evidence to show that the prices of essential drugs have ruled at abnormally high levels in industrialized as well as developing countries, and the public health care systems has had to pay excessively high cost, when those drugs were under the patent monopoly of a few transnational corporations. There is also enough documentary evidence to show that transfer pricing has been particularly rampant in the pharmaceutical sector leading to excessive prices being paid for bulk drugs and intermediates. A similar situation has also prevailed in the case of patent monopoly in agro-chemicals that are crucial to enhancing the agricultural production of developing countries.'

In April 1989, Ministers adopted a Mid-Term Review[34]of the Uruguay Round negotiations. Concerning the 'Trade-Related Aspects of Intellectual Property Rights (TRIPS), Including Trade in Counterfeit Goods', they urged negotiations to encompass the following issues:

(a) the applicability of the basic principles of the GATT and of relevant international intellectual property agreements or conventions;
(b) the provision of adequate standards and principles concerning the availability, scope and use of trade-related intellectual property rights;
(c) the provision of effective and appropriate means for the enforcement of trade-related intellectual property rights, taking into account differences in national legal systems;
(d) the provision of effective and expeditious procedures for the multilateral prevention and settlement of disputes between governments, including the applicability of GATT procedures;
(e) transitional arrangements aiming at the fullest participation in the results of the negotiations.

Ministers also agreed that consideration would be given to concerns related to the underlying public policy objectives of their national systems for the protection of intellectual property, including 'developmental and technological objectives'.[35] They particularly emphasised the importance of reducing tensions through multilateral resolution of disputes in this area and through multilateral procedures, which the European Communities and Japan expected would counter unilateral actions.[36]

Despite its scepticism and its opposition to the creation of substantive norms and standards concerning IPR protection within the GATT context, India agreed, at the mid-term meeting in 1989, to include IP issues in the Uruguay Round negotiations.[37]

In attempting to explain this change, some attributed Indian interest in copyright protection for its film industry. AV Ganesan, India's negotiator during the

---

[34]   MTN.TNC/11 (21 April 1989). Ministers had mid-term meetings in Montreal on 5–6 December 1988 and in Geneva on 5–8 April 1989.

[35]   ibid para 5.

[36]   Trade-Related Aspects of Intellectual Property Rights – Submission from the EC, MTN.GNG/ NG11/W/49 (14 November 1989), B(d)(i); Japan proposed an international mechanism of dispute settlement where (i) any unilateral action is prohibited, and (ii) IP experts participate (Suggestion by Japan for Achieving the Negotiating Objective MTN.GNG/NG11/W/17 (23 November 1987).

[37]   'India accepts principle of policing trade-related intellectual property' (1989) 3 *World Intellectual Property Report* 244–5. This report quotes from the Communication from India (n 19) inter alia, para 4(c), which says: 'Provisional remedies by way of injunctions should be provided. Compensation should be provided to persons suffering damage from provisional orders based on the assumption that they were infringing IPRs, if the assumption is subsequently found to be wrong' and comments: 'in other words, there should be provision for compensation for persons wrongly accused of infringing those rights'. This report refers also to the position of Canada, which 'called for international enforcement of rules on TRIPS but said that it should not be too heavy-handed, lest it hurt companies wanting to export to other markets and thus negate the free-trade objective of the Uruguay Round.'

Uruguay Round Negotiations, explained that the shift of fora from the WIPO to the GATT changed the focus of attention and negotiating perspectives of developing countries. Furthermore, during the early 1990s, many developing countries adopted new IPR legislation under US pressure. China introduced product patent protection in 1993, as did Malaysia and Thailand. In light of changes in national laws, there were no longer substantial reasons to oppose a certain degree of harmonisation of IP protection rules, provided that the level of protection was the same as under the Paris or the Berne Conventions. For Ganesan, one of the advantages of introducing provisions concerning the dispute settlement procedures of the WTO into the IP agreement was that it would limit the scope and effect of the unilateral measures based on section 301 of the US Trade Act.[38] For developing countries in particular, US retaliation in sectors not related to IPRs, such as agriculture or textiles, for IPR infringements by developing countries, was a matter of concern that had to be dealt with seriously. [39]

C Earlier Drafts (Anell and Brussels Texts)

In 1990, Chairman Anell elaborated upon a synthesis of various proposals,[40] which was distributed in June of that year, and which, in July, became a formal document called the 'Chairman's report to the GNG on the status of work in the TRIPS Negotiating Group' (the Anell text).[41] Conflicting opinions arose not only between developed and developing countries, but probably more intensely among developed countries, on such questions as the first-to-file and the first-to-invent systems,[42] the protection of neighbouring rights and rental rights on sound recordings. [43]

Opposing views and proposals from participants were consolidated under the articles numbered with a letter A from developed countries, and with a letter B from developing countries. Options within an approach, A or B, were indicated by the use of square brackets. The Chairman's introductory note explains

---

[38] ibid.

[39] Interview with AV Ganesan, 20 December 2009 in Chennai. AV Ganesan was India's negotiator during the Uruguay Round Negotiations. He later served as a member of the WTO Appellate Body between 2000 and 2008.

[40] The Anell Report in Annex explains that the report was prepared on the basis of the draft legal texts submitted by the European Communities (NG11/W/68), the US (NG11/W/70), Argentina, Brazil, Chile, China, Colombia, Cuba, Egypt, India, Nigeria, Peru, Tanzania and Uruguay, and subsequently also sponsored by Pakistan and Zimbabwe (NG11/W/71), Switzerland (NG11/W/73), Japan (NG11/W/74) and Australia (NG11/W/75). In July 1986 China filed its application to rejoin GATT and participated in the Uruguay Round negotiations.

[41] MTN.GNG/NG11/W/76 (23 July 1990).

[42] The US insisted on maintaining its 'first-to-invent' system, as opposed to the 'first-to-file' system which is the position of most countries in the world. The first-to-invent system grants patents to the person who actually invented the innovation first, on the condition that the patentability and other procedural requirements are met.

[43] Gervais (n 6) 23, Cottier, (n 2) 396, S Takakura, *Chiteki Zaisan Housei to Kokusai Seisaku* (IP Laws and International Policy, in Japanese) (Tokyo, Yuhikaku, 2001) 147.

that Approach A envisaged a single TRIPS agreement encompassing all the areas of negotiation, covering seven categories of intellectual property; whereas Approach B provided two parts, one on trade in counterfeit and pirated goods, and the other on standards and principles concerning the availability, scope and use of IPRs. In the Annex to the Anell text, those proposals on preambular provisions and objectives, dispute prevention and settlement, transitional arrangements, institutional arrangements and final provisions, which had not been the subject of detailed consultations, were attached.

In the Anell text, proposals made earlier by India and Brazil concerning the principles of IP protection are found in Article 8B, 1-3 of Part II concerning 'General Provisions, Basic Principles', as follows:

8. Principles

8B.1 PARTIES recognize that IPRs are granted not only in acknowledgement of the contributions of inventors and creators, but also to assist in the diffusion of technological knowledge and its dissemination to those who could benefit from it in a manner conducive to social and economic welfare and agree that this balance of rights and obligations inherent in all systems of IPRs should be observed.

8B.2 In formulating or amending their national laws and regulations on IPRs, PARTIES have the right to adopt appropriate measures to protect public morality, national security, public health and nutrition, or to promote public interest in sectors of vital importance to their socio-economic and technological development.

8B.3 PARTIES agree that the protection and enforcement of IPRs should contribute to the promotion of technological innovation and enhance the international transfer of technology to the mutual advantage of producers and users of technological knowledge.

In the Annex to the Anell text, the following proposals from participating countries were noted as part of 'Notes on the composite text':

'1.4 Recognizing that adequate protection of IPRs is an essential condition to foster international investment and transfer of technology;

1.5 Recognizing the importance of protection of IRPs for promoting innovation and creativity;'

The Anell text was subsequently updated[44] and made into one composite text (instead of A and B), called 'Trade-Related Aspects of Intellectual Property Rights, including Trade in Counterfeit Goods' (this title was in brackets), for the Ministerial Conference in Brussels in 1990.[45] The Brussels text[46] already resembled the future TRIPS Agreement, including substantive regulations concerning the availability, scope and use of IPRs, enforcement, dispute prevention and settlement and transitional arrangements.

---

[44] Gervais (n 6) 21.
[45] Trade Negotiations Committee, Draft Final Act Embodying the Results of the Uruguay Round of Multilateral Trade Negotiations, Part 2 Revision MTN.TNC/W/35/Rev 1 (3 December 1990)
[46] ibid.

The preamble to the TRIPS part of the Brussels text incorporated what was decided at the 1986 Ministerial Conference at Punta del Este, as well as the Mid-Term Review Decision[47] of TNC in April 1989 and all important points advanced by developing countries in the negotiations (chapter 5). While calling for the effective and adequate protection of IPRs, the preamble recognised that protection of IPRs that was either insufficient or excessive would lead to distortions of trade, and that differences in national legal systems should be taken into account. It also drew attention to public policy objectives of national systems for IP protection, including developmental and technological objectives.

The important proposal from Brazil and India concerning the objectives and principles of IP protection, drafted as Article 8B above, was rearranged in Articles 7 and 8 of the Brussels text, taking into account not only the user's rights, dissemination and transfer of technology, but also the creator's and inventor's rights, as well as the promotion of technological innovation.

It seems that the legal status of Articles 7 and 8 was not explicitly discussed in the elaboration of the Brussels text. Gorlin's commentary on the TRIPS Agreement from the pharmaceutical industry's point of view states:

> The issue of whether Article 7 has any operational significance was not raised in the course of the negotiations out of fear that the LDCs would insist on changing the language to explicitly make it operational. As a result, and EC efforts, during the course of the negotiations on the Article, which were described by one negotiator as more UNCTAD[48] than GATT-like, were aimed at making the language sound 'preambular' while letting 'sleeping dogs lie'. Adrian Otten of the WTO agrees that the language is hortatory. He, however, referred to the 1969 Vienna Convention on the Law of Treaties in pointing out that, as a matter of practice, the legal effect of these Articles is only relevant when the literal interpretation of the other TRIPS provisions is inadequate. He thought that Article 7 (as well as Article 8) might only have relevance in a 'nullification and impairment' case. . . . In addition, he cited the reliance by India on Articles 7 and 8 in its submissions to the WTO Committee on Trade and Environment as an indication of the future direction that some countries may want the WTO to take with respect to IP protection.[49]

On points of substance, the Brussels text indicated that the following major outstanding issues remained unresolved:[50]

> Part I: Article 4 concerning the exemption to the Most-Favoured-Nation Treatment, in particular regarding 'TRIPS-plus obligations';[51] Part II: Protection of computer

---

[47] MTN.TNC/11 (n 34) 19–21.

[48] United Nations Conference on Trade and Development; see ch 2.

[49] JJ Gorlin, *An analysis of the Pharmaceutical-related Provisions of the WTO TRIPS (IP) Agreement* (Washington DC, IP Institute, 1999) 17–18.

[50] Brussels text (n 45) 1–2.

[51] Art 4 of the Brussels text exempts from MFN those countries: '(d) exceeding the requirements of this Agreement and provided in an international agreement to which the PARTY belongs, provided that such agreement is open for accession by all PARTIES to this Agreement, or provided that such PARTY shall be ready to extend such advantage, favour, privilege or immunity, on terms equivalent to those under the agreement, to the nationals of any other PARTY so requesting and to enter into good faith negotiations to this end.'

programs (Articles 10.1 and 12), rental rights (Articles 11 and 16.4), the rights of performers and broadcasters (Article 16), the term of protection of phonograms (Article 16.5), moral rights (Article 9), limitations and exemptions (Article 13.2) and the definition of 'public' (Article 14), geographical indications (Articles 25, 26 and 27), criteria for industrial design protection (Article 28.1), the complex issues concerning patentable subject matter and exclusions therefrom (Article 30), the term of protection (Article 36) and non-voluntary licensing and government use (sub-paragraphs (g), (k), (h), (n) and (o) of Article 34 and related provisions of Article 32), non-discrimination as to the place of invention (Article 30.1), rights conferred by process patents (Article 31) and reversal of the burden of proof (Article 37), the appropriateness of so-called 'plus elements' concerning layout-designs of integrated circuits, protection of undisclosed information, the control of abusive or anti-competitive practices in contractual licences; Part VI: the length of transition periods and on the extent of obligations to be assumed during that period and details of a dispute prevention system in respect of the transfer of technologies.

Interestingly, bracketed draft Article 14 of the Brussels text referred to the definition of 'public' that regulated exceptions of copyright in domestic laws. The draft Article 14 provided that: 'The term "public" shall not be defined in the domestic law of PARTIES in a manner that conflicts with a normal commercial exploitation of a work and unreasonably prejudices the legitimate interests of right holders.'

Thus, for one group of countries, public interest is a matter outside of IPR protection which should be pursued by policy instruments such as social security, education and welfare measures. For another, IPR protection should be 'balanced' by public interest objectives. India's conception of 'public interest objectives', as Ganesan explains, includes: the goal of medicines being available in sufficient quantities at affordable prices; technological objectives realised by the working of patents, for example through compulsory licensing; and developmental objectives.[52]

As a corollary to what would later become Article 8 of the TRIPS Agreement, some developing countries insisted that abuse of intellectual property or anti-competitive abuse be dealt with in the future Agreement as a matter of public interest.[53] The provision was to be included in Article 40 of section 8 concerning control of anti-competitive practices in contractual licences. Throughout the drafting process, not much discussion seems to have been undertaken as to the meaning of such terms as 'abuse' of IPRs, 'anticompetitive practices' or 'restrictions' in licensing contracts.[54] Both India and Brazil asserted that IPRs are essentially monopolistic and impede trade and, therefore, the objectives of IP protection should be to ensure 'public interest' by preventing and deterring

---

[52] Interview with AV Ganesan (n 39).

[53] The following documents dealt with anticompetitive abuse of IPRs. Communication from Peru, MTN.GNG/NG11/W/45 (27 October 1989); Communication from India (n 19); Communication from Brazil (n25); Communication from Argentina, Brazil, Chile China, Colombia, Cuba, Egypt, India, Nigeria, Peru, Tanzania and Uruguay, MTN.GNG/NG11/W/71(14 May 1990).

[54] On the negotiating history of Article 40, see N Pires de Carvalho, *The TRIPS Regime of Antitrust and Undisclosed Information*, ((The Hague, London, Boston, Kluwer Law International, 2008) 161–187; Gervais, (n6) 191–192.

possible abusive behaviour and to ensure greater access to technological innovation for users.[55] Peru stated in its proposal that '[i]n order to limit the impact of restrictive business practices on trade, a patent or trademark owner should be prohibited from imposing conditions on the licensee.'[56]

Gervais[57] explains that, when attempts were made to define the scope of contractual practices to be dealt with during the Uruguay Round negotiations, there was a possibility of separating the following practices: (a) those which constitute an abuse of IPRs, and/or (b) those which have an adverse effect on competition. Abuses of intellectual property rights do not cover the same types of conduct as anti-competitive abuse. In the end, both were retained, leaving vast ambiguities in the scope of Article 40. The criteria for judging (b) differs from those for judging (a), which should be based on general competition law principles, while (a) may be only one of the means for achieving anti-competitive objectives. For example, fraudulent patent procurement or the litigation to enforce those patents which are known to be invalid could constitute patent abuse under the Patent Law. However, in order to establish these types of conduct as violating competition law, there are further conditions to be met. For example, under section 2 of the Sherman Act[58] in the US, the moving party must show that: the patentee knowingly and wilfully misrepresented facts to the patent office; the patent would not have been issued 'but for' the patentee's fraud; and the patentee has monopoly power or the dangerous probability of achieving it, depending on the nature of the claim.[59]

Draft Article 8B.4 under Part II (General Provisions and Basic Principles) of the Anell text recognised that: '. . . appropriate measures [. . .] may be needed to prevent the abuse of intellectual property rights by right holders or the resort to practices which unreasonably restrain trade or affect the international transfer of technology'. Part III (Standards Concerning the Availability, Scope and Use of Intellectual Property Rights), section 9, entitled 'Control of Abusive or Anti-Competitive Practices in Contractual Licences', referred to appropriate national legislative measures to prevent or control abusive or anti-competitive practices

[55] Communication from India (n 19) paras 11 and 13 referring to compulsory licences; Brazil (n 16).

[56] Peru proposed that: 'The following cases are among those that should be considered: that the supply of technology or trademark licence should be accompanied by the obligation for the host country or undertaking to acquire goods or services from a specified source; that the owner should reserve the right to fix the sales price of the products manufactured using the technology in question or the right to use the trademark; the imposition of restrictions on the volume or structure of output and the prohibition or limitation of exports to specific countries of the products manufactured using the patent or trademark; the prohibition of the use of competing technologies; the payment of royalties for unused patents or trademarks; the imposition of a purchase option for the supplier of the technology and/or trademark; or the requirement that any inventions or improvements obtained as a result of the use of the technology in question should be transferred to the supplier of the patent.'.

[57] Gervais (n 6) 191–92.

[58] s 2 of the Sherman Act (US Code Title 15-2) prohibits persons to 'monopolize, or attempt to monopolize, or combine or conspire with any other person or persons, to monopolise any part of the trade or commerce' among several States, or with foreign nations. See also ch 9.

[59] E Gellhorn et al. *Antitrust Law and Economics in a Nutshell* (fifth edn) (St Paul, MN, West Publishing, 2004) 502–503. It cites C R Bard, Inc. v M3 Systems, Inc. (Fed, Cir.1998).

in licensing contracts deemed to constitute an abuse of intellectual property rights or to have an adverse effect on competition in the relevant market. On the other hand, the fear that abuse of IPRs might restrain international trade was expressed in draft Article 6B (Control of Anti-competitive and Trade-distorting Practices) in Part IX (Trade in Counterfeit and Pirated Goods), under section 2 (Guiding Principles and Norms), which said that 'PARTIES shall co-operate with each other to ensure the free flow of goods and prevent that intellectual property rights are used, through arrangements among enterprises, to create restrictions or distortions to international trade or to engage in anti-competitive practices having adverse effects on their trade . . .'

Draft Article 8.2 in Part I (General Provisions and Basic Principles) of the Brussels text added to the previous text the phrase, 'provided that they do not derogate from the obligations arising under this Agreement'. It was in the Brussels text that control of abusive or anti-competitive practices in contractual licences was placed in the context of section 8, Part II (Standards Concerning the Availability, Scope and Use of Intellectual Property Rights). Its Article 43.1 stated that ' PARTIES agree that some licensing practices or conditions pertaining to intellectual property rights which restrain competition may have adverse effects on trade and may impede the transfer and dissemination of technology.' Article 43.2B added that: 'PARTIES may specify in their national legislation licensing practices or conditions that may be deemed to constitute an abuse of intellectual property rights or to have an adverse 'effect on competition in the relevant market', and may adopt appropriate measures to prevent or control such practices and conditions, including non-voluntary licensing in accordance with the provisions of Article 34 and the annulment of the contract or of those clauses of the contract deemed contrary to the laws and regulations governing competition and/or transfer of technology.' This text enumerated the following 'practices and conditions [which] may be subject to such measures where they are deemed to be abusive or anti-competitive: (i) grant-back provisions; (ii) challenges to validity; (iii) exclusive dealing; (iv) restrictions on research; (v) restrictions on use of personnel; (vi) price fixing; (vii) restrictions on adaptations; (viii) exclusive sales or representation agreements; (ix) tying arrangements; (x) export restrictions; (xi) patent pooling or cross-licensing agreements and other arrangements; (xii) restrictions on publicity; (xiii) payments and other obligations after expiration of industrial property rights; (xiv) restrictions after expiration of an arrangement.' No explanation is given in any of the Uruguay Round documents as to why, among the above 14 practices which have radically different competitive/anticompetitive effects, 'challenges to exclusive grantback conditions', 'conditions preventing challenges to validity' and 'coercive package licensing' were retained as examples of abuses or anticompetitive practices in Article 40 of the TRIPS Agreement. The Dunkel text of 20 December 1991[60] reiterated the phrase

---

[60] Draft Final Act Embodying the Results of the Uruguay Round of Multilateral Trade Negotiations MTN.TNC/W/FA (20 December 1991).

'consistently with the other provisions of this Agreement', which made the draft close to Article 40 of the TRIPS Agreement (see chapters 5 and 9).

Some of the outstanding issues during the Uruguay Round were later resolved, while others developed into controversies and eventually found a precarious compromise. Some other issues were simply left out. Definition(s) of 'public' and the relationship of 'public policies' to IPR protection were not discussed further during the Uruguay Round negotiations.

D Controversies

The TRIPS draft was submitted to the Brussels Ministerial Conference, and would have been adopted, 'had other parts of the Round package been sufficiently advanced.'[61] However, negotiations on agriculture, services and other problematic issues stalled.[62] On the IPR agreement, the GNG continued its progress at the Brussels meeting. Gervais explains that it was at this occasion that the following difficult substantive issues split the participants: 'the protection of pharmaceutical products by patents; dispute settlement; the nature and duration of transitional arrangements for developing nations; and finally, the protection of geographical indications'. In addition, there were divisions in relation to the following copyright fields: exclusion of 'moral rights', protection of computer programs, data bases and sound recordings, and protection of the rights of music performers and broadcasters (neighbouring rights).[63]

The Uruguay Round negotiations collapsed over the issue of agricultural subsidies at the Brussels meeting in December 1990. During this time, the then Director-General of the GATT, A Dunkel, established an informal working group to review draft texts. The Round negotiations resumed in September 1991. In December 1991, Dunkel, in an attempt to reconcile opposing interests by making fields such as agriculture and textiles more attractive to developing countries, proposed a comprehensive draft in a single package for all negotiated fields (the Dunkel Text).[64] The negotiations proceeded on the following four tracks: 1) market access (tariffs and non-tariff measures, natural resource-based products, tropical products, and textiles); 2) new areas of services, trade-related IPRs, and trade-related investment measures; 3) agriculture; and 4) GATT rules (dispute settlement, safeguards, balance-of-payments reform, and the non-tariff

---

[61] Gervais (n 6) 21.

[62] According to Watal, 'Interestingly, while the Argentine delegation was angry and disappointed at this outcome, the Indian delegation was relieved that there was no agreement on TRIPS, which was politically most sensitive aspect of the Uruguay Round negotiation for India. This shows the differing perceptions on the trade-offs for TRIPS within the Uruguay Round among developing countries.' J Watal, *Intellectual Property Rights in the WTO and Developing Countries* (The Hague, London, Boston, Kluwer Law International, 2001) 35.

[63] Gervais (n 6) 23–5.

[64] Draft Final Act Embodying the Results of the Uruguay Round of Multilateral Trade Negotiations (n 60).

measure codes, including subsidies and anti-dumping). The Dunkel text (which would later become the TRIPS Agreement) did not go through substantial changes at the last stage of negotiations,[65] although important changes were made on the provisions concerning the following controversial subjects of discussion during the final stages.

i *Patentable Subject Matter*

Scope and standards of patentability (Article 27 TRIPS)

When the Uruguay Round negotiations started in 1986, of the 82 Member States of the Paris Convention for the Protection of Industrial Property, 49 excluded pharmaceutical products from the scope of patentable subject matter. Ten Members excluded pharmaceutical processes; 35, foods; 42, animal and plant varieties; 32, computer programs and 9 excluded microorganisms.[66] Legislative formulations and examination guidelines of patentability criteria (novelty, inventive step (non-obviousness in the US) and industrial applicability (utility in the US)) differed considerably, particularly in the new technological fields (see chapter 3). The question of patentable subject matter constituted one of the most controversial subjects of negotiation during the Uruguay Round.

Article 5.1 of Chairman Anell's composite text of 23 July 1990 dealt with 'patentable subject matter'. Following the suggestions by Canada and developing countries,[67] Article 5.1.1 proposed non-agreed proposals in brackets that 'patents shall be [available] [granted] for [any inventions, whether products or processes, in all fields of technology,] [all products and processes] which are new, which are unobvious or involve an inventive step and which are useful or industrially applicable.'

The reference to 'whether products or processes', was significant for the US, Switzerland, the EU and Japan. For these countries, one of the important objectives in negotiating TRIPS during the Uruguay Round was to not have 'medicines' excluded from patentable subject matter. If, however, the term 'medicines' was used in the text of the Agreement, then agricultural chemicals and foods would be left out of patentability.[68] Instead of singling out 'medicines', therefore, the term 'in all fields of technology' was suggested.[69] By contrast, Article 5,1, paragraph 1B, proposed by developing countries, stated that ' PARTIES may exclude from patentability certain kinds of products, or processes for the manufacture of those products on grounds of public interest, national security, public

[65] Gervais (n 6) 22–7.
[66] J Straus, 'TRIPS Agreement and Access to Medicines', Annual Meeting of the Japanese Intellectual Property Association, Tokyo, 14 February 2003.
[67] Gorlin (n 49) 21.
[68] Takakura (n 43) 163–5.
[69] Gorlin (n 49) 21.

health or nutrition.' Article 5.1.4 also proposed a long list of exclusions from patentability.[70]

These exclusions opposed patentability of a wide range of biotechnological inventions. It excluded discoveries and substances found in nature ('1.4.2 scientific theories, mathematical methods, discoveries and materials or substances [already existing] [in the same form found] in nature'), and allowed the ineligibility of genetically modified animal and plant varieties ('1.4.4 [Any] plant or animal [including microorganisms] [varieties] or [essentially biological] processes for the production of plants or animals').[71] From the Brussels Draft, paragraph 1.4.2 of the Anell text regarding the exclusion of 'scientific theories, mathematical methods, discoveries and materials or substances [already existing] [in the same form found] in nature' was eliminated.

Proposed Article 30 of the Brussels text (Article 27 of the TRIPS Agreement) used a structure and content similar to that of the current Article 27 TRIPS concerning 'patentable subject matter'. Article 30.1 of the Brussels text stated the general principle of patentability for all inventions, whether products or processes, in all fields of technology, provided that they were new, involved an inventive step and were capable of industrial application.[72] The bracketed phrase 'patents shall be available without discrimination as to where the inventions were made' was inserted into Article 30.1 of the Brussels text. Article 30.2 allowed the conditions of exclusion concerning individual cases, namely, 'to protect public morality or order, including to secure compliance with laws or regulations which are not inconsistent with the provisions of this Agreement, or to protect human, animal or plant life or health'. Article 30.3 allowed for the exclusion from patentability of certain categories of inventions: (a) diagnostic, therapeutic and surgical methods for the treatment of humans or animals; and (b) animal or plant-related biotechnology inventions[73], subject to a review after the entry into force of the Agreement.

---

[70] 5. 1.4 The following [shall] [may] be excluded from patentability:

1.4.1 Inventions, [the publication or use of which would be], contrary to public order, [law,] [generally accepted standards of] morality, [public health,] [or the basic principle of human dignity] [or human values].1.4.2 Scientific theories, mathematical methods, discoveries and materials or substances [already existing] [in the same form found] in nature. 1.4.3 Methods of [medical] treatment for humans [or animals];1.4.4 [Any] plant or animal [including micro-organisms] [varieties] or [essentially biological] processes for the production of plants or animals; [this does not apply to microbiological processes or the products thereof]. [As regards biotechnological inventions, further limitations should be allowed under national law]; 1.4.5, '[Production, application and use of] nuclear and fissionable material, [and substances manufactured through nuclear transformation]

[71] The following bracketed sentences were added: [this does not apply to microbiological processes or the products thereof]. [As regards biotechnological inventions, further limitations should be allowed under national law].

[72] Footnote 1 attached to Article 30.1 of the Brussels text stated that: 'For the purposes of this Article, the terms "inventive step" and "capable of industrial application" may be deemed by a PARTY to be synonymous with the terms "non-obvious" and "useful" respectively.'

[73] Article 30.3(b) of the Brussels text allowed the exclusion of 'Animal varieties [and other animal inventions] and essentially biological processes for the production of animals, other than microbiological processes or the products thereof' and stated that: 'PARTIES shall provide for the protection of plant varieties either by patents or by an effective sui generis system or by any combination thereof.'

Non-Discrimination (Article 27.1)

According to Gervais, the principles of non-discrimination in the drafting of paragraph 1 of the Brussels draft Article 30 (Article 27.1 TRIPS) were made against the background of: (i) conflicting applications arising from the differences between the first-to-invent system and the first-to-file system; (ii) the controversial question of whether the invention is locally produced or imported (with concomitant issues of working requirements, the failure of which could possibly justify compulsory licensing); and, (iii) the issues of compulsory licences which, in certain countries, specifically target pharmaceutical patents.[74] The prohibition of discrimination 'as to the place of invention' originated from those countries critical of the discriminatory practices of the US, based on section 104 of its Patent Law. Section 104 of the US Patent Act 35 USC § 104 prohibited proof of knowledge, use or other activity in any country outside the US for the purpose of establishing a date of invention. This was one of the practices deriving from the 'first-to-invent' system in the US, as opposed to the 'first-to-file' system.[75] This provision was amended to permit an applicant for a patent to establish a date of invention in any WTO country.

The Brussels text merely mentioned that 'patents shall be available' without discrimination as to 'the place of invention'. The sentence concerning the 'enjoyment' of patents was added in the Dunkel text,[76] as was the phrase 'without discrimination as to the field of technology and whether products are imported or locally produced'. This was because many countries at that time had special provisions relating to medicines, such as shorter terms of patent protection or less stringent rules for the granting of compulsory licensing than in other technological fields. The clause, 'whether products are imported or locally produced' was a compromise between the long-standing demand of developed countries that imports be regarded as the 'working' of patents, and developing countries which insisted on limiting the meaning of 'working' to local manufacturing (on compulsory licensing and local working, see below p 127).

Public Morality or Order (Article 27.2 TRIPS)

The Anell text referred to the exclusion of inventions, 'the publication or use of which' would be contrary to public order, law, generally accepted standards of morality' [77] to permit Members to prohibit the patenting of certain inventions to protect public morality or order. Thus the patentability of inventions may not be prevented merely because their exploitation is prohibited by domestic law. To

---

[74] Gervais (n 6) 147.

[75] See ch 2, n 26.

[76] Dunkel text Section 5 PATENTS, Article 27 Patentable Subject Matter para 1: '. . . Subject to paragraph 4 of Article 65 and paragraph 3 of this Article, patents shall be available and patent rights enjoyable without discrimination as to the place of invention, the field of technology and whether products are imported or locally produced.' MTN.TNC/W/FA (n 60).

[77] These words existed in Art 53(a) of the EPC, before its amendment in 2000.

'protect public morality or order', the Brussels text added 'including to secure compliance with laws or regulations which are not inconsistent with the provisions of this Agreement; or to protect human, animal or plant life or health.'

Toward the end of the 1991 negotiations, the reference to 'environment' was added, making this provision unique among TRIPS provisions.[78] The Dunkel text provided the following for Article 27.2:

> PARTIES may exclude from patentability inventions, the prevention within their territory of the commercial exploitation of which is necessary to protect *ordre public* or morality, including to protect human, animal or plant life or health or to avoid serious prejudice to the environment, provided that such exclusion is not made merely because the exploitation is prohibited by domestic law.

Gervais explains that the concept in French civil law of '*ordre public*' is typically applied to mean that the freedom of private persons to contract in or out of their obligation is limited by *ordre public,* ie the interest of society, or 'public policy'.[79] Article 53(a) of the EPC also employs the French term,[80] but the European Patent Office (EPO) Guidelines for Examination on this provision do not infer any specifically French civil law issue: 'the purpose of this is to deny protection to inventions likely to induce riot or public disorder, or to lead to criminal or other generally offensive behaviour. Anti-personnel mines are an obvious example.'[81] In Europe, patenting of certain biotechnology inventions gave rise to heated discussions on morality and ethical standards. In examining the patentability of Harvard's 'OncoMouse', the EPO Board, in 1991, carefully weighed the suffering of animals and possible risks to the environment on the one hand and the invention's usefulness to mankind on the other. Ethical questions arose in Europe, particularly when patent claims came to include technologies relating to germ lines or the use of stem cells relating to humans. The scope to be given to patents related to sequences or partial sequences of genes isolated from the human body. In this regard, patenting human stem cells and cell lines obtained from them became the subject of public discussion.[82] Later, in 2000, the European patent covering the 'isolation, selection and propagation

---

[78] Gorlin (n 49) 24.

[79] Gervais (n 6) 149.

[80] Art 53(a) of the EPC: 'Any invention the commercial exploitation of which would be contrary to "*ordre public*" or morality is specifically excluded from patentability'.

[81] In Japan, the standard textbook for training, published by the National Center for Industrial Property Information and Training (INPIT), gives the examples of machines to smuggle gold or to forge money, as instances of inventions which are against the interest of society, although such machines need not be prohibited for use.

[82] For example, stem cell research and xenotransplantation offer possibilities of replacement tissues and organs to treat degenerative diseases and injury resulting from stroke, Alzheimer's and Parkinson's diseases, burns and spinal-cord injuries cited in SJR Bostyn, Patenting DNA sequences (polynucleotides) and scope of protection in the European Union: an evaluation (European Commission; Directorate-General for Research Food Quality and Safety, 2004) 5. Induced pluripotent stem cells (iPS cells) potentially have transplantational uses without transplant rejection. They may also allow researchers to obtain pluripotent stem cells, which are important in research, without the controversial use of embryos. IPS cells are artificially derived from a non-pluripotent cell, typically an adult somatic cell, by inducing a 'forced' expression of certain genes.

of animal transgenic stem cells'[83] for generating transgenic animals from stem cells provoked controversy.[84] This patent was considered to violate common standards of ethics, because the claims did not explicitly exclude the application of these techniques to humans. The interpretation of one granted claim could extend to a method for genetically altering humans and the claims were subsequently modified.

Later, in *US–Gambling*,[85] the WTO dispute case involving the General Agreement on Trade in Services (GATS), the US as a defendant invoked the clause of protecting 'public morals and to maintain public order' provided for in Article XIV(a) GATS[86] to justify the prohibition of internet gambling. In this services industry case, the Panel Report stated that the term 'public order' refers to the familiar civil-law concept denoted in French by the expression *'ordre public'* and its functional counterpart in common-law systems, the concept of 'public policy' (although the latter term is also used in other contexts with a broader meaning).[87] The Report mentions that 'public morals' refers to standards of right and wrong that can be described as 'belonging to, affecting, or concerning the community or nation', and 'moral' means 'of or pertaining to human character or behavior considered as good or bad; of or pertaining to the distinction between right and wrong . . .'

Probably underlying the mention of morality and *ordre public*, is the idea that no branch of law should defeat the fundamental purpose of a legal order. This seems to be the reason why an invention may not be patentable, if its commercialisation goes against what is commonly believed to be morality or public order, even though not granting a patent will not prevent its commercial exploitation.[88]

---

[83]   EP 0695351 B1 filed in 1994 by the Centre for Genome Research of the University of Edinburgh.

[84]   Q Schiermeier, 'Germany challenges human stem cell patent awarded "by mistake"' (2000) 404 *Nature* 3–4.

[85]   *US–Measures Affecting the Cross-Border Supply of Gambling and Betting Services* Panel Report (circulated 10 November 2004) WT/DS285/R, Appellate Body Report (circulated 7 April 2005) WT/DS285/AB/R.

[86]   Art XIV(a) of the GATS provides that: 'Subject to the requirement that such measures are not applied in a manner which would constitute a means of arbitrary or unjustifiable discrimination between countries where like conditions prevail, or a disguised restriction on trade in services, nothing in this Agreement shall be construed to prevent the adoption or enforcement by any Member of measures: (a) necessary to protect public morals or to maintain public order . . .'. Fn 6 to Art XIV (a) of the GATS states that: 'The public order exception may be invoked only where a genuine and sufficiently serious threat is posed to one of the fundamental interests of society.'

[87]   Panel Report, *US–Gambling* (n 85) para 358, where a case concerning the application of the Convention of 1902 Governing the Guardianship of Infants (*Netherlands v Sweden*) 1958 ICJ 55, 90 is cited. The Report explores *New Shorter Oxford English Dictionary*, cited at fn 475, to find that the term 'public morals' denotes 'standards of right and wrong conduct maintained by or on behalf of a community or nation'. The Panel further found that the definition of the term 'order', read in conjunction with fn 6 of the GATS, suggests that 'public order' refers to the preservation of the fundamental interests of a society, as reflected in public policy and law.

[88]   According to the WIPO Secretariat in 2009, 'Excluding certain categories of subject matter from patentability can neither stop inventors from inventing in the area of such subject matter, nor can it prohibit the commercial exploitation of such inventions. Indeed, where no patent exists, nobody is required to obtain the consent from the inventor to use the invention. It is sometimes

Obviously, the notion of morals is based on the values of a person or a society. In the TRIPS negotiations, according to Watal,

> . . . the concern was clearly directed at exclusions of biotechnological inventions on grounds of morality or public order. Developing countries and others can only exclude such an invention from patent grant if they also disallow the commercial exploitation of these harmful inventions by others. This is a guiding principle for patent examiners and courts. However, few countries have added such a caveat in the post-TRIPS period to their laws, a notable exception being Argentina.[89]

In the TRIPS negotiations, the consideration may also derive from industrial policy grounds as some developing countries are today important suppliers of biotechnology products (see chapters 3, 10 and 11).

This provision is likely to be invoked only in rare and extreme cases. A fair test to apply is to consider whether it is probable that the public in general would regard the invention as so abhorrent that the grant of patent rights would be inconceivable. If it is clear that this is the case, objection should be raised under Article 53(a); otherwise they should not be raised.[90] Gorlin explains the meaning of 'commercial exploitation' as excluding research, marketing of the product by government, and free marketing.[91]

The wording, 'necessary to' in this paragraph is also found in Articles XX(a) and (d) of the GATT 1947 and 1994, and in Article XIV(a), (b), (c) of the GATS, both concerning general exceptions. Traditionally, GATT Panels have generally interpreted this expression as meaning that a measure is justified only when there is no alternative GATT-inconsistent or less inconsistent measure, which a country could reasonably be expected to take.[92] Later in the WTO dispute cases, however, in *US–Gambling*[93] and *Brazil–Retreaded Tyres*, for example, these

---

argued that the control of commercial activities based on, for example, ethical, health and environmental grounds should rather be regulated by other laws than the patent law. On the other hand, some argue that the patent system does not exist in a vacuum, and that the State should not grant exclusive rights to inventions that obviously harm public interests and consequently do not deserve to generate any economic return thanks to patent protection.' Standing Committee on the Law of Patents, 'Exclusions from Patentable Subject Matter and Exceptions and Limitations to the Rights', 13th Session, Geneva, 23–7 March 2009 para 4.

[89] Watal (n 62) 97.

[90] www.epo.org/patents/law/legal-texts/html/guiex/e/c_iv_4_1.htm.

[91] Gorlin (n 49) 24.

[92] Panel Report, *Thailand–Restrictions on Importation of and Internal Taxes on Cigarettes*, adopted 7 November 1990, BISD 37S/200.

[93] The 'weighing and balancing process' approach was taken earlier in the context of *US–Gambling* (n 77). The Panel held that three US laws were qualified to fall under the exception 'public order and morals', but did not satisfy the necessity test because the US had not explored the possibility of consultation with Antigua to find 'alternative less trade restrictive means of satisfying these values'. The Appellate Body (AB) corrected the Panel by saying that public order and good morals should be 'weighed and balanced' with other factors, such as the contribution of the measures to the end pursued. On the necessity test, the AB reversed the Panel's ruling and stated that the consultation with Antigua which the Panel required was a process and not an alternative. On the burden of proof, the AB held that the respondent did not have to enumerate every alternative in 'the universe of alternatives' to prove the ineffectiveness of each alternative. According to the AB, the respondent

restrictive conditions were loosened. The Appellate Body in *Brazil–Retreaded Tyres* case stated that:[94]

- 'necessary' is not limited to that which is 'indispensable'; whether or not the measure is 'necessary' involves a 'weighing and balancing process' which begins with an assessment of the 'relative importance' of the interests or values furthered by the challenged measure (such as 'human, animal or plant life or health' in Article XX(b)) and other factors contributing to the realisation of the ends pursued and 'the restrictive impact of the measure on international commerce';
- a qualitative analysis (instead of quantitative analysis) is within the bounds of the methodology for the analysis of the contribution of the measure in question to its objectives;
- when the measure is accepted as necessary, it does not have to show, in the first instance, that there are no 'reasonably available alternatives' to achieve its objectives.

'Animals and Plants other than Microorganisms . . .'(Article 27.3 (b)TRIPS)

Canada and some developing countries were proposing a broad range of exclusions, in opposition to the US, Japan and Switzerland, to which biotechnological and pharmaceutical product patent protections mattered. As a result of a compromise, draft Article 30, paragraphs 2 and 3 of the Brussels text came to resemble articles 53(a) and 53(b) of the European Patent Convention (EPC) (see chapter 3).[95]

Paragraph 3 of the Brussels draft Article 30 (later adopted as TRIPS 27.3)[96] allows specific categories of inventions to be excluded from patentability. Paragraph 3(a) followed Article 53(b) of the EPC, to which the US had been objecting.[97] Paragraph 3(b) (later adopted as TRIPS 27.3(b)),[98] often called the

only has to prove the usefulness of the measure it takes and, when a claimant comes forward with alternatives, the burden is on the respondent to disprove their effectiveness.

[94] *Brazil–Measures Affecting Imports of Retreaded Tyres* Appellate Body Report WT/DS332/ AB/R (adopted 17 December 2007) paras 139–56. In examining whether the import ban on retreaded tyres could be justified, reference was made to Art XX(b) of the GATT 1994, which refers to 'measures necessary to protect human, animal or plant life or health' (Appellate Body in para 141 identified the term 'necessary' also in Art XX(a) and (d) GATT, Art XIV(a), (b), (c) of the GATS but not TRIPS provisions).

[95] Art 53 of the EPC concerns 'exceptions to patentability' and in (b) refers to 'plant or animal varieties or essentially biological processes for the production of plants or animals; this provision shall not apply to microbiological processes or the products thereof'. However, Art 52.2(a) of the EPC explicitly provides that 'discoveries, scientific theories and mathematical methods shall not be regarded as inventions within the meaning of Art 52.1, the equivalent provision of which does not exist in the Brussels text or in the TRIPS Agreement' (see ch 3).

[96] Brussels draft Art 30.3(a): 'PARTIES may also exclude from patentability: (a) [Diagnostic, therapeutic and] surgical methods for the treatment of humans or animals'.

[97] Gorlin (n 49) 25.

[98] Brussels draft Art 30.3: '[PARTIES may also exclude from patentability: (b): Animal varieties [and other animal inventions] and essentially biological processes for the production of animals, other than microbiological processes or the products thereof. PARTIES shall provide for the protection of plant varieties either by patents or by an effective sui generis system or by any combination thereof. This provision shall be reviewed . . . years after the entry into force of this Agreement.]'.

'biotech clause', was even more controversial, because the US opposed any exclusion, whereas developing countries and Canada pressed for a broader scope of life forms to be excluded from patentability. As we have seen in chapter 3, the EPO granted a patent to plant varieties and to the Harvard OncoMouse in mid-1991. Canada, however, persisted in proposing that all life forms be excluded from patentability for three years during which the TRIPS Council should study the issue. Gorlin reports that in the Quad meetings (US, Japan, EC and Canada) during the last months of 1991, 'Japan was hesitant, [the] EC hesitant and Switzerland a non-member' and, as a result, the US was isolated.[99]

On Article 27.3(b), Ganesan explains that, during the Uruguay Round, negotiators were fully aware of rapidly changing biotechnology and its increasing importance. This was perceived as an example of where technological changes might necessitate certain adaptations of rules.[100] According to him, this was the reason why Article 27.3(b) of the TRIPS Agreement was written with deliberate ambiguities: in today's language, 'flexibilities', permitting Member States to exclude plants and animals from patentability (other than microorganisms and essentially biological processes for the production of plants or animals other than non-biological and microbiological processes).

The EU was proposing that there should be a review mechanism regularly to renew and readapt IP protection to technological evolution.[101] Drafting of Article 27.3(b) reflected the large uncertainty that existed in the field of biotechnology at the time of the Uruguay Round negotiations.[102]

ii Compulsory licensing

During the Uruguay Round negotiations, in 1987, the US proposed, in a series of suggestions for negotiating objectives, limiting compulsory licences.[103] In its October communication in 1988, the US suggested that a compulsory license may be given solely to address 'a declared national emergency or to remedy an adjudicated violation of antitrust laws'[104] (this policy later materialised in the US's post-TRIPS era Free Trade Agreements).

[99] Gorlin (n 49) 25.

[100] Interview with AV Ganesan (n 39).

[101] The EC, in its submission to the Negotiating Group on 14 November 1989 (MTN.GNG/NG11/W/49), proposed the following review clause: 'The TRIPS agreement should contain a review clause allowing for the possibility of amendment to take account of, *inter alia*, technological developments.'

[102] N Pires de Carvalho *The TRIPS Regime of Patent Rights: With an Introduction on the History and the Economic Function of Patents* 2nd edn (The Hague, London, Boston, Kluwer Law International, 2005)216.

[103] 'Suggestion by the US for achieving the negotiating objective' MTN.GNG/NG11/W/14 (20 October 1987) para 4, stated that 'Governments should generally not grant compulsory licences to patents and shall not grant a compulsory licence where there is a legitimate reason for not practising the invention, such as governmental regulatory review. If a government does grant a compulsory licence, it should do so only on a case-by-case basis, subject to agreed narrowly defined circumstances.' MTN.GNG/NG11/W/14/Rev 1 (17 October 1988) para 4.

[104] Communication from the United States MTN.GNG/NG11/W/70(11 May 1990) on Art 27 states that: 'Contracting parties may limit the patent owner's exclusive rights solely through

In July 1988, the EC included, in its proposals for the TRIPS negotiations, that compulsory licences, for the lack or insufficiency of exploitation, in respect of dependent patents, official licences, and any right to use patented inventions in the public interest shall, in particular in respect of compensation, be subject to review by a court of law.[105]

The idea of compulsory licensing had been recognised and reserved in the patent laws of many countries, either explicitly or implicitly, whatever the terminology is used. In the US, statutory compulsory licences are not provided in the Patent Act, but specific procedures for the Federal government to use IP for a particular public interest are provided under special laws.[106] In the US, licensing can be ordered for the purposes of bringing remedies to the violation of anti-trust laws.[107] However, most oft-quoted recent examples of US compulsory licensing[108] are licensing arrangements in the process of pre-merger notification, which are rather voluntary.[109]

India argued that compulsory licence was a deterrent against abuse or misuse by the right holder.[110] The system of 'licence of rights' was instituted in India,

compulsory licenses and only to remedy an adjudicated violation of competition laws or to address, only during its existence, a declared national emergency. Where the law of a contracting party allows for the grant of compulsory licenses, such licenses shall be granted in a manner which minimizes distortions of trade, and the following provisions shall be respected: . . .'

[105] 'Guidelines and objectives proposed by the European Community for the negotiations on trade-related aspects of substantive standards of intellectual property rights' MTN.GNG/NG11/W/26 (7 July 1988) para 3(a)(iv).

[106] 28 USC § 1498 allows the US Federal Government to use or manufacture US-patented inventions without the licence of the owner and stipulates that the owner's remedy shall be by action in the US Court of Federal Claims for the recovery of his reasonable and entire compensation; Under 35 USC § 203 (march-in rights), when the invention is made under the Federal funding agreement, the Federal agency can require the subject invention to be licensed upon terms that are reasonable under the circumstances: (1) when the contractor or assignee has not taken, or is not expected to take within a reasonable time, effective steps to achieve practical application of the subject invention; (2) action is necessary to alleviate health or safety needs which are not reasonably satisfied by the contractor, assignee, or their licensees; (3) action is necessary to meet requirements for public use specified by Federal regulations and such requirements are not reasonably satisfied by the contractor, assignee, or licensees. The following laws contain procedures for the Federal government to use a subject invention without authorisation of the inventor: the Atomic Energy Act (42 USC § 2183), the Clean Air Act 1990 (42 USC § 7608) Sec 308 'mandatory licensing', Plant Variety (7 USC § 2404) 'public interest in wide usage', Integrated Circuit 17 USC § 907) 'Limitation on exclusive rights: innocent infringement'.

[107] The Department of Justice (DOJ) enforces anti-trust laws by bringing an antitrust action to district courts, based on s 1 or s 2 of the Sherman Act (1890). The Federal Trade Commission (FTC) is empowered to enforce s 5 of the FTC Act (1914, 15 USC §§ 41–58, as amended) empowers the FTC, among other things, to prevent unfair methods of competition, and unfair or deceptive acts or practices affecting commerce. S 5 of the FTC Act prohibits unfair methods of competition etc, which, by case law, is considered to include monopolisation and attempts to monopolise in the sense of s 1, Sherman Act.

[108] FM Scherer, *Competition Policy, Domestic and International* (Cheltenham, Edward Elgar, 2000) 327–42. Most of the cases of 'compulsory licences' listed at www.cptech.org/ip/health/cl/us-at. html concerned merger cases in which remedies were proposed by merging parties and approved by antitrust authorities during the pre-merger control processes.

[109] Hart-Scott-Rodino Antitrust Improvements Act of 1976 (s 7A Clayton Act).

[110] Communication from India (n 19) paras 11–15.

to provide for cases of the failure of a patent owner to work a patent sufficiently and on reasonable terms (chapter 2). Section 90 of the Indian Patents Act, 1970, offered an explanation as to when 'the reasonable requirements of the public' were not considered to have been satisfied, for the purposes of compulsory licensing.[111] India, pursuant to its adhesion to the Paris Convention, on 7 December 1998, amended the system of licences of rights in the Amendment of 2003, to be consistent with the conditions provided in the Paris Convention and the TRIPS Agreement.

Article 5A(2) of the Paris Convention refers to 'failure to work' as an example of the abuses which might result from the exercise of the exclusive rights conferred by the patent. The same Article recognised the right of each Union member to take legislative measures providing for the grant of compulsory licenses to prevent, for example, failure to work. Article 5A(4) provides that a compulsory licence on the ground of 'failure to work or insufficient working' may not be applied:

- before the expiration of a period of four years from the date of filing of the patent application or three years from the date of the grant of the patent, whichever period expires last;
- if the patentee justifies his inaction by legitimate reasons; and
- if the licence is not non-exclusive and transferable, even in the form of the grant of a sub-licence, except with that part of the enterprise or goodwill which exploits such licence.

In elaborating the TRIPS Agreement during the Uruguay Round, negotiating parties advanced widely different arguments concerning the question of whether importation could be regarded as 'working'.

The EC argued along the procedural provisions of Article 5A(4) of the Paris Convention 1967, but no clarification was made regarding the question of whether importation was considered as 'working' the patent. According to the EC:

> ... where the law of a contracting party allows for the grant of compulsory licences, such licences shall not be granted in a manner which distorts trade, and the following provisions shall be respected: ... (4) Compulsory licences may not be issued for non-working or insufficiency of working on the territory of the granting authority if the right holder can show that the lack or insufficiency of local working is justified by the existence of legal, technical or commercial reasons.[112]

Developing countries considered local working to be a mandatory patentee obligation. These countries argued that compulsory licences are 'remedies for non-fulfilment of obligations' and proposed that they read as follows:

[111] Art 5A (4) of the Paris Convention imposes the following conditions for compulsory licensing: that a period of four years has expired from the date of filing of the patent application or three years from the date of the grant of the patent, whichever period expires last, and that the request for licensing be refused if the patentee justifies his inaction by legitimate reasons (see ch 2).

[112] Communication from the European Communities MTN.GNG/NG11/W/68 (29 March 1990) on Art 26,

Parties may adopt appropriate measures to remedy the non-fulfilment of obligations arising from the protection provided for intellectual property rights under the provisions of this agreement or in accordance with national legislation. Such measures may include:(i) in respect of non-working or insufficient working of patents, the granting of a compulsory licence; (ii) compulsory licence may also be granted wherever necessary in public interest to secure free competition and to prevent abuses by the holder of the right; (iii) where the effective use of a trademark is required by national legislation to maintain trademark rights, the cancellation of the registration of such a trademark after a reasonable period, unless valid reasons based on the existence of obstacles to such use are shown by the trademark owner; (iv) in respect of abusive or anti-competitive practices in licensing contracts, the annulment of the contract or of those clauses of the contract deemed contrary to the laws and regulations governing competition and/or transfer of technology.[113]

The Anell Draft, reflected both arguments in 'A'[114] and 'B'.[115] According to the Note by the Secretariat on the meeting of the Negotiating Group in May 1990, some participants preferred the EC approach to focus on the conditions attached to the grant of a compulsory licence and that the grounds for the granting of compulsory licences had been too narrowly defined and failed to take into account the circumstances of developing countries which emphasise 'national defence, public interest and non-working'.[116]

Thus, the Brussels text of December 1990 retained the developing countries' proposal to make local working an obligation on the part of patentees:

PARTIES may provide that a patent owner shall have the following obligations:

(a) To ensure the [working] [exploitation] of the patented invention in order to satisfy the reasonable requirements of the public. [For the purposes of the Agreement the term 'working' may be deemed by PARTIES normally to mean manufacture of a patented product or industrial application of a patented process and to exclude importation.][117]

---

[113] Communication from Argentina, Brazil, Chile, China, Colombia, Cuba, Egypt, India, Nigeria, Peru, Tanzania, Uruguay, and Pakistan MTN.GNG/NG11/W/71 (14 May 1990) on Art 13.

[114] The Anell Draft (2.2.2) 'A' text which proposed an introductory note saying that 'PARTIES shall minimise the grant of compulsory licences', listed specific and limited grounds on which licences might be granted (the public interest concerning national security, or critical peril to life of the general public or body thereof) and stated that 'compulsory licences for non-working or insufficiency of working on the territory of the granting authority shall not be granted if the right holder can show that the lack or insufficiency of local working is justified by the existence of legal, technical or commercial reasons'. The issue of judicial review was in brackets. For drafting processes relating to this question, see A Attaran and P Champ, 'Patent Rights and Local Working under the WTO TRIPS Agreement: An Analysis of the U.S.-Brazil Patent Dispute' 27 *Yale Journal of International Law* 365–80.

[115] para 13 of the Anell Draft stated that: '. . . Taking into account its own needs and conditions, each country must be free to specify the grounds on which compulsory licences can be granted under its law and the conditions for such grant. The grant of compulsory licences may, however, be subject to judicial review in accordance with the host country's legal system.'

[116] Meeting of Negotiating Group of 14–16 May 1990: Note by the Secretariat Negotiations on Goods – Negotiating Group on Trade-Related Aspects of Intellectual Property Rights, including Trade in Counterfeit Goods MTN.GNG/NG11/21(22 June1990) para13 on Art 27.

[117] Brussels Text (n 45) Art 13. The words in brackets are non-agreed proposals.

India was advocating, as was the US, broad government use provisions. According to Watal, India proposed in November 1990 that both 'government use' and 'compulsory licensing' be subject to the same set of conditions, as a negotiating tactic to isolate the US.[118]

With the acceptance of the EC, Japan and Canada, the phrasing 'other use without the authorisation of the right holder', instead of 'compulsory licence', came to be used. Then, the US and other countries accepted the 'conditions approach' as opposed to the 'grounds approach'. The conditions approach meant that the specific conditions for the grant of compulsory licences are regulated by the TRIPS Agreement, but not the grounds on which such licences are given. The US proposed that unauthorised use shall be: considered on its individual merits; preceded by prior negotiation with the right holder for a voluntary licence on reasonable commercial terms and conditions within a reasonable period of time; non-exclusive licence; of a duration of use limited to the purpose for which it was authorised and proportional to the scope of the problem; and authorised predominantly for the supply of a domestic market.[119] The legality of any decision relating to the authorisation of such use shall be subject to judicial review or other independent review by a distinct higher authority in that party, and any decision relating to the remuneration provided in respect of such use shall be subject to judicial review or other independent review by a distinct higher authority in that party.

Blakeney points out that the TRIPS negotiations were characterised by 'the tension between the desire of the industrialised countries to limit the grounds for compulsory licensing and that of the Group of 77 to facilitate and simplify compulsory licensing'.[120]

In the Brussels text of December 1990, draft Article 34, entitled 'Other Use Without Authorisation of the Right Holder', included a clause on the compulsory licence against non-working, together with the time conditions stipulated in Article 5A(4) of the Paris Convention (chapter 2). This indicated that non-working of foreign patents was still an important concern for developing countries. It proposed in paragraph (n) that:

Authorisation by a PARTY of such use on grounds of failure to work or insufficiency of working of the patented product or process shall not be applied for before the expiration of a period of four years from the date of filing of the patent application or three years from the date of grant of the patent, whichever period expires last. Such

---

[118] Watal (n 62) 320.

[119] According to Gorlin, the word 'predominantly' was inserted (1) to meet the concern of the US Department of Justice which insisted that there are instances in which a compulsory licence could remedy an adjudicated anti-trust violation only if it included permission to supply both foreign and domestic markets, and (2) to avoid market disruption in the markets other than disruptions where unauthorised licence was given. Gorlin (n 49) 36.

[120] JC Ross and JA Wasserman, 'Trade-Related Aspects of Intellectual Property Rights', in TP Stewart (ed), *The GATT Uruguay Round: A Negotiating History (1986–1992)*, Vol II (Kluwer Law and Taxation Publishers, Deventer, Boston, 1993) 2295–6, quoted by M Blakeney, *Trade Related Aspects of Intellectual Property Rights: A Concise Guide to the Trips Agreement* (London, Sweet & Maxwell, 1996) 89.

authorisation shall not be granted [where importation is adequate to supply the local market or] if the right holder can justify failure to work or insufficiency of working by legitimate reasons, including legal, technical or economic reasons.

The Dunkel text of December 1991[121] no longer proposed provisions concerning compulsory licensing against non-working. This was because Article 5A(4) of the Paris Convention was incorporated by virtue of draft Article 2 of the Brussels text.[122] The Dunkel text in draft Article 27 on Patentable Subject Matter referred to the availability of patents and the 'enjoyment of patent rights without discrimination with regard to . . . whether the product is imported or locally produced'. According to Camp and Attaran, the concept of non-discrimination did not emerge from any party's negotiating position but from Dunkel: it was presented to the parties as a 'take-it-or-leave-it' compromise. The concept of non-discrimination was accepted by parties which had been sharply divided on whether importation, and not just manufacture, might be sufficient to meet patentee obligations under the new agreement.[123]

Unable to reach an agreement, negotiators arrived at a compromise that prohibited the issuance of compulsory licensing discriminating between imported and domestically produced goods. Developed countries optimistically thought that no compulsory licensing could be issued because the patented products are merely imported. By using the expression 'whether products are imported or locally produced', developed countries might have been hoping that non-discrimination principles for goods were familiar to the GATT and that this would be acceptable to developing countries.[124]

However, from this wording, the conclusion that working includes importation cannot be drawn. Those countries whose patent law considers only 'manufacturing, selling, using and using the methods' as part of 'working' to the exclusion of importation would not be violating the non-discrimination principles contained in Article 27.1 of the TRIPS Agreement unless they discriminated between domestic and imported products for the acquisition of patents and enjoyment of patent rights.

According to Beier,[125] the institution of compulsory licence against non-working, which was conceived to promote national production, has lost much of its practical significance, at least in industrialised countries. In the era of globalised manufacture and distribution, more efficient means than domestic

[121] Draft Final Act Embodying the Results of the Uruguay Round of Multilateral Trade Negotiations MTN.TNC/W/FA (20 December 1991).(n 60).

[122] UNCTAD-ICTSD, *The Resource Book on TRIPS and Development* (Cambridge University Press, 2005) 467. The *Resource Book* offers commentary on each TRIPS provision, consisting of: 1. terminology, definition, and scope, 2. history of the provision, 3. possible interpretations, 4. WTO jurisprudence, 5. relationship with other international instruments, 6. new developments, and 7. comments, including economic and social implications.

[123] Attaran and Champ (n 114) 378.

[124] S Takakura (n 43) 164.

[125] F-K Beier, 'Exclusive Rights, Statutory Licenses and Compulsory Licenses in Patent and Utility Model Law' (1999) 30, *Int'l Review of Industrial Property and Copyright Law* (IIC) 251–63.

production can be found. Yet, compulsory licensing is still at the centre of the debate as the principal remedy for a complex set of social and economic problems in many developing countries (see chapters 9 and 10).

iii Undisclosed information (Article 39.3 TRIPS)

Protection of pharmaceutical and agricultural chemicals test data submitted to regulatory authorities for marketing approval was another controversial subject in the Uruguay Round negotiations. During the negotiations, the US and the EC requested that this particular type of test data be part of the protection of 'undisclosed information', generally called 'trade secrets' in the US. The EC proposed that the protection of test data is provided within the framework of Article 10bis of the Paris Convention. This meant that this body of information would be treated as private property on the grounds of which protection was claimed to be necessary. India objected to including 'trade secrets' in the mandate of the Negotiating Group, arguing that 'trade secrets' as a category, either undisclosed or unlicensed, do not constitute IPRs.[126]

Concept of Data Exclusivity

At the time of the Uruguay Round negotiations, the US and the EC were particularly concerned about the absence in such developed countries as Canada, Australia and New Zealand of 'data exclusivity' for pharmaceuticals,[127] ie the periods where governments are not allowed to examine the requests for marketing approval of competitor products equivalent to originator products (commonly called 'generics'), based on the clinical data submitted by originator companies. Protection of a fixed term is given to 'data exclusivity' on public policy grounds, evaluating and balancing the cost of clinical data generation including that of failures, and the social benefit of generic entry.

Originator drug companies submit, for marketing approval, the results of physico-chemical, biological or microbiological tests, and pharmacological and toxicological tests obtained through clinical trials that they finance to prove the quality, safety and efficacy of the drug. The drug regulatory authorities then decide on market authorisation. For industries where the R&D process is long, costly and risky, and whose products require the submission, to regulatory

---

[126] 'Trade Secrets cannot be considered to be intellectual property rights. The fundamental basis of an intellectual property right is its disclosure publication and registration, while the fundamental basis of a trade secret is its secrecy and confidentiality. The laws of many developing countries clearly stipulate that the terms "licensor" and "licensee" should not be applied to a transaction involving the supply of confidential know-how, and only expressions such as "supplier" and "recipient" should be used because such know-how cannot be regarded as a licensable right. The observance and enforcement of secrecy and confidentiality should be governed by contractual obligations and the provisions of appropriate Civil Law, and not by intellectual property law.' Communication from India (n 19) para 46.

[127] Gorlin (n 49) 46.

authorities, of data to demonstrate the safety and efficacy of the product, the exclusivity of the data has been recognised for the investment the innovators have to make (in the US, EU and some other developed countries).

Once the period of regulatory protection has expired, competitors can introduce generic medicines, based on an abridged marketing authorisation application. The abridged application procedures differ among countries (chapter 8) but generally do not require the generation of the whole data package based on thorough clinical studies, but only the data necessary to demonstrate that the products are equivalent to the originator products, a much lighter requirement. In developed countries, generally, the regulatory authority may then 'rely' on the originator's data for reference for examining the quality, safety and efficacy of competitor drugs, although the meaning of the term 'rely' has been much debated, even in court.[128] The non-reliance principle means that the regulatory authorities must not rely on the clinical data submitted by the originator when examining the application for approval of competitor products before a certain period of time. This period corresponds to data exclusivity.

Data exclusivity is not always necessary if the drug regulatory approval process is short (such as in the US) leaving a sufficient effective patent length (EPL) after the drug approval.[129] However, for biotech medicines and for drugs for which a long period between patent filing and the start of clinical trials has passed, data exclusivity may be necessary.[130] Furthermore, in countries where judicial systems do not function effectively for enforcing IPR rights, administrative protection is needed. In many technologically advanced developing countries, it often happens that competitor drugs are approved before the originator drugs. There are also countries where the procedures for drug approval itself are unclear, or not established or well-functioning.

Diverging National Laws relating to Marketing Approval

National laws differ radically in relation to the handling of test data submitted to regulatory authorities. The US has its own conception of market exclusivity for newly approved pharmaceutical products which referred to the period of time before a follow-on competitor can enter the market with an abbreviated filing that relies, in whole or in part, on the innovator's data on safety and efficacy.[131] In the US since 1984, regulatory exclusivity for medicines totals five years for new

---

[128] For example, *Bayer Inc v Canada (Attorney General)* [1999] 1 FC 553 (Docket: T-1154-97) http://reports.fja.gc.ca/eng/1998/1999fc23457.html/1999fc23457.html.html.

[129] In the US, the largest increases in competition from generics usually occur 12 to 16 years after a drug is first introduced. FR Lichtenberg and G Duflos, 'The Effect of Patent Expiration on U.S. Drug Prices, Marketing, and Utilization by the Public' Medical Progress Report, No 11 October 2009.

[130] In the US, in March 2010, the House of Representatives passed healthcare reform legislation which included 12 years of data exclusivity for innovator biotech medicines, with allowable six-month extension for conducting pediatric studies specifically requested by the Food and Drug Administration (FDA).

[131] USC 21 § 355(b)(1)(G).

chemical entities (NCEs)[132] and three years for chemical entities which have already been approved for therapeutic use but which require new clinical research.[133] The EU, since the introduction of Directive 65/65, had instituted-partially harmonised conditions of marketing authorisation for pharmaceutical products in which an exclusivity period of six years was provided,[134] although much of the drug regulation was assured under national authorities at the time of the Uruguay Round negotiations.[135] This system was modified by Directive (EC) 2004/27[136] in which new conditions for all-EU market authorisation are delineated.

Each country has its own policy for drug approval, first, to ensure the safety, efficacy and quality of the drugs to be marketed, and, second, to regulate the entry of competitive products, safeguarding at the same time the investment and creativity used in the research of the originator. In certain developing countries, there are arguments that test data protection should be so designed as to reduce the cost of generating data, to facilitate the early marketing of competitive products (see chapter 13).[137]

[132] Food, Drug and Cosmetics Act, s 505 (21 USC § 355(c)(3)(E)(ii)) provides that: 'If an application submitted under subsection (b) for a drug, no active ingredient (including any ester or salt of the active ingredient) of which has been approved in any other application under subsection (b) . . . no application which refers to the drug for which the subsection (b) application was submitted and for which the investigations described in clause (A) of subsection (b)(1) and relied upon by the applicant for approval of the application were not conducted by or for the applicant and for which the applicant has not obtained a right of reference or use from the person by or for whom the investigations were conducted may be submitted under subsection (b) before the expiration of five years from the date of the approval of the application under subsection (b), except that such an application may be submitted under subsection (b) after the expiration of four years from the date of the approval of the subsection (b) application if it contains a certification of patent invalidity or non-infringement described in clause (iv) of subsection (b)(2)(A). Ester or salt are included here because the data package pertaining to them can be protected when drugs which are inactive derivatives, such as ester or salt, are approved as prodrugs'. Prodrugs are medicines which undergo chemical conversion by metabolic processes to become active pharmacological agents in the body. They are useful when the active ingredient may be too toxic to administer, too difficult to be absorbed by the digestive tract, or may destroy the body before it reaches its target. Crystal forms are active and therefore are not mentioned in Section 505 of the above-mentioned US code, but new drugs could be so designed as to include crystal forms.

[133] 21 USC § 355(c)(3)(E)(iii).

[134] Council Directive (EEC) 65/65 of 26 January 1965 on the approximation of provisions laid down by law, regulation or administrative action relating to medicinal products [1965] OJ L22 Art 4(8)(a)(iii). Art 10.1 of this Directive stated that: '. . . applicant shall not be required to provide the results of pre-clinical tests and of clinical trials if he can demonstrate that the medicinal product is a generic of a reference medicinal product which is or has been authorised under Article 6 for not less than eight years in a Member State or in the Community. A generic medicinal product authorised pursuant to this provision shall not be placed on the market until ten years have elapsed from the initial authorisation of the reference product . . .' This exclusivity period of eight years could be extended to 10 years if '. . . one or more new therapeutic indications which, during the scientific evaluation prior to their authorisation, are held to bring a significant clinical benefit in comparison with existing therapies.'

[135] T Cook, *The Protection of Regulatory Data in the Pharmaceutical and Other Sectors* (London, Sweet & Maxwell, 2000).

[136] Directive 2004/27 of 31 March 2004 amending Directive (EC) 2001/83 on the Community code relating to medicinal products for human use,

[137] CM Correa, *Protection of Data Submitted for the Registration of Pharmaceuticals: Implementing the Standards of the TRIPS Agreement* (Geneva, South Center, 2002); R Dinca, 'The "Bermuda Triangle" of Pharmaceutical Law: Is Data Protection a Lost Ship?' (2005) 8(4) *Journal of World Intellectual Property* 517–63.

When examining the New Drug Applications (NDA)[138] under the Federal Food, Drug and Cosmetic Act, the US drug regulator, the Food and Drug and Cosmetic Administration (FDA), examines the existence of patents concerning drugs which are required to be listed in the Approved Drug Products with Therapeutic Equivalence Evaluations (the so-called 'Orange Book').[139] The administrative practice of linking the granting of marketing authorisation for a generic medicinal product to the status of a patent (application) for the originator reference product is often called 'patent linkage'. In Japan, the submission of data concerning patents relevant to new drugs is required and the drug regulatory authority examines the existence of the relevant patents when there are competitor applications. However, the list of patents is not made public. In the EU, by contrast, the drug regulator for marketing approval of generics does not examine the patent information relating to drugs whose authorisation is requested (see chapter 12).

Different Texts during the Uruguay Round Negotiations

At the initial stage of the Uruguary Round negotiations, protection of test data submitted to regulatory authorities was referred to in the Anell text 1A.3, under Article 7: Acts Contrary to Honest Commercial Practices Including Protection of Undisclosed Information. However, the regulatory context in which data is created and submitted was not explicitly mentioned throughout various texts proposed during the Uruguay Round.

The Anell text did not define 'honest commercial practices'. However, Article 1A.1 states that: '. . . PARTIES shall provide in their domestic law the legal means for natural and legal persons to prevent information from being disclosed to, acquired by, or used by others without their consent in a manner contrary to honest commercial practices', if such information is secret (1A.1.1), has the actual [or potential] commercial value (1A.1.2) and has been subject to reasonable steps to keep it secret (1A.1.3),[140] in the course of ensuring effective protection against unfair competition as provided for in Article 10bis of the Paris Convention (1967). However, the broad concept of 'unfair competition' in

---

[138] Under the Federal Food, Drug and Cosmetic Act, the FDA is responsible for approving new drugs before they can be marketed in the US. The FDA is charged with ensuring that the drugs it approves are both safe and effective for its intended uses. 'New drugs' include both 'innovator' and 'generic' drugs. Innovator drugs, or drugs newly discovered, are generally developed under patent by the manufacturer. Generic drugs, or copies of drugs currently on the market, are developed by competitors after a patent has expired or if the innovator patent is not deemed infringed or invalid. Generic drugs must contain the same active ingredients and be manufactured in the same strength and dosage form as the innovator drug.

[139] 21 USC § 355(b)(1), (c)(2). Upon approval of the NDA, the FDA lists and discloses all relevant patents of the approved drug in the so-called Orange Book (Approval Drug Products with Therapeutic Equivalence Evaluation www.accessdata.fda.gov/scripts/cder/ob/default.cfm). Innovator companies are allowed to add to the list all the newly acquired patents relevant to the approved drugs within 30 days.

[140] The Anell text (n 39).

Article 10bis of the Paris Convention[141] had been implemented and interpreted divergently by different members of the Paris Convention. Its meaning remains unclear, particularly in regard to its relation to the antitrust meaning of 'competition' in the relevant product or technology market.

Paragraph 3, entitled 'Government Use', under Section 7 of the Anell text, referred to the protection of test data submitted to regulatory authorities. Article 1.3Aa provided that:

> PARTIES, when requiring the publication or submission of undisclosed information consisting of test [or other] data, the origination of which involves a considerable effort, shall protect such data against unfair exploitation by competitors. The protection shall last for a reasonable time commensurate with the efforts involved in the origination of the data, the nature of the data, and the expenditure involved in their preparation, and shall take account of the availability of other forms of protection.

According to the subsequent subparagraphs, such protection consisted of: (i) a reasonable period of exclusivity of the information for the right holder; and, (ii) an obligation of government not to disclose the data, except to other governmental agencies if necessary to protect human, plant or animal life, health or the environment, with a rule concerning disclosure in the process of obtaining IPR protection and judicial review.[142] Thus, the protection of test data submitted to regulatory authorities for marketing approval from the viewpoint of the safety and efficacy of pharmaceutical chemical products, or the environmental impacts of agricultural chemicals such as pesticides, are placed within the framework of protection of information which is essentially characterised as private trade secrets.

In the Brussels text, protection of test data submitted to regulatory authorities is mentioned in draft Article 4A as follows, under section 7 concerning 'Protection of Undisclosed Information':

> PARTIES, when requiring, as a condition of approving the marketing of *new pharmaceutical products or of a new agricultural chemical product*, the submission of undisclosed

---

[141] Art 10bis concerns 'unfair competition' and provides that:

(1) The countries of the Union are bound to assure to nationals of such countries effective protection against unfair competition. (2) Any act of competition contrary to honest practices in industrial or commercial matters constitutes an act of unfair competition. (3) The following in particular shall be prohibited:

1. all acts of such a nature as to create confusion by any means whatever with the establishment, the goods, or the industrial or commercial activities, of a competitor;
2. false allegations in the course of trade of such a nature as to discredit the establishment, the goods, or the industrial or commercial activities, of a competitor; and,
3. indications or allegations the use of which in the course of trade is liable to mislead the public as to the nature, the manufacturing process, the characteristics, the suitability for their purpose, or the quantity, of the goods.

[142] The Anell text stipulated in 3Ab1 that: 'PARTIES which require that trade secrets be submitted to carry out governmental functions, shall not use the trade secrets for the commercial or competitive benefit of the government or of any person other than the right holder except with the right holder's consent, on payment of the reasonable value of the use, or if a reasonable period of exclusive use is given the right holder . . .'.

test or other data, the origination of which involves a considerable effort, shall [protect such data against unfair commercial use. Unless the person submitting the information agrees, *the data may not be relied upon* for the approval of competing products for a reasonable time, generally *no less than five years*, commensurate with the efforts involved in the origination of the data, their nature, and the expenditure involved in their preparation. In addition, PARTIES shall [protect such data against disclosure, except where necessary to protect the public.][143]

'The new pharmaceutical or agricultural chemical products' in this context normally means new products in the regulatory sense, and not in the meaning of new chemical entities under patent law. This draft stated that, in relation to the term of protection of five years, governments should not rely on the test data to approve competitive products, without the consent of the originator of the data.

However, the terms of protection and the words 'not relied upon' disappeared from the Dunkel text,[144] and the expression 'products which utilise new chemical entities', appeared. Gorlin explains that 'United States negotiators agreed to drop the non-reliance language, because they viewed the phrase as no more than "belts and suspenders", that is, the accepted definition at the time of "protection against unfair commercial use" included non-reliance for a fixed period of time for new chemical entities and the second phrase was, therefore, not needed.'[145] Draft Article 39.3 reads:

> PARTIES, when requiring, as a condition of approving the marketing of pharmaceutical or of agricultural chemical products which utilise new chemical entities, the submission of undisclosed test or other data, the origination of which involves a considerable effort, shall protect such data against unfair commercial use. In addition, PARTIES shall protect such data against disclosure, except where necessary to protect the public, or unless steps are taken to ensure that the data are protected against unfair commercial use.

The meaning of 'new chemical entities' in this text is unclear. Gervais suggests it is practical to consider as 'new', any product which had not previously been submitted for regulatory approval.[146] From a purely textual analysis of this provision, utilising 'new chemical entities' can be interpreted as excluding a new use of a pharmaceutical product, new indications, dosage forms, combinations, new forms of administration, crystalline forms, isomers, etc of existing drugs, unless there is a novel chemical entity involved.[147] However, this does not normally fit the meaning of new medicines under medicinal law.

[143] Emphasis added.
[144] Draft Final Act Embodying the Results of the Uruguay Round of Multilateral Trade Negotiations (n 60).
[145] Gorlin, (n 49) 48.
[146] Gervais explains that 'Although there is little doubt that "products which utilize new chemical entities" need not be new products, it is possible to draw a parallel with the concept of novelty used for patents and industrial designs . . . It would be difficult to conduct a patent-related search of the prior art in each case before deciding on each application', Gervais (n 6) 187.
[147] Correa (n 137) 31.

The Anell text of 23 July 1990 stated that 'PARTIES shall not limit the duration of protection under this section so long as the conditions stipulated at point 1A exist', although the draft of 23 November 1990 contained a bracketed five-year period of non-reliance.[148] However the question of the term of protection of test data submitted to regulatory authorities was left unanswered in the Dunkel text.

The public policy aspects of regulatory data protection therefore are present in national regulatory approval systems, but nowhere in the draft Article 39.3 of the Dunkel text was this explained. The Dunkel text did not provide any clear justification as to why or in what context it was necessary to protect test data, except that the creation of the undisclosed data with commercial value involved considerable effort. This provision has not established either the criteria for judging whether the chemical entities utilised in the submitted drugs are 'new' or whether or not the creation of such data has required 'considerable efforts'.

As it was written in draft Article 39.3, test data protection could be characterised as duplicating patent protection for new drugs. However, in national laws, 'new medicines' to be approved by regulatory authorities are not the same as new molecules in the chemical sense, but based on therapeutic safety and efficacy. According to Taubman, test data protection is conceptually distinct from patent protection, in that the data submitted to regulatory authorities respond more directly to the economics of funding non-inventive but resource-intensive regulatory trials involving public policy issues in terms of economics and equity.[149] Taubman indicates that these two sets of protection have practical linkages: providing efficacy is arguably a subset of the patent law requirement for utility, while safety is arguably cognate with *ordre public* in patent law.[150]

The provision concerning the protection of test data, later adopted as Article 39.3 of the TRIPS Agreement, lacked coherence and clarity. The public policy grounds for protecting data submitted to regulatory authorities for safety and efficacy remained unexplained in the text, leaving the legitimacy of this protection in doubt. Thus, the test data protection in Article 39.3 TRIPS led to arguments that such protection only does harm in developing countries by delaying generic entry, and that clinical test data should be treated as a 'public good'. According to Reichman, for example:

> . . . the drive to protect clinical trial data internationally is but the latest and most far-reaching consequence of the deep structural problems that flow from the failure to treat clinical trials as a national and international public good. So long as this market-distorting anomaly persists, clinical data as a guarantor of public safety will be under-supplied; the scientific benefits of such trials will be impeded; and the drive to keep secret the very data that logically require the highest degree of transparency will

[148] Chairman's Report to the Negotiating Group on TRIPS, including Trade in Counterfeit Goods, Status of Work in the Negotiating GroupMTN.GNG/NG11/W/77 (23 July 1990).

[149] A Taubman, 'Unfair competition and the financing of public-knowledge goods: the problem of test data protection' (2008) 3(9) *Journal of Intellectual Property Law & Practice* 601. Taubman examines public policy aspects of test data protection not only of pharmaceuticals but also of agricultural chemicals.

[150] ibid 598.

produce the rippling legislative distortions and high social costs that now take the form of pseudo-IPRs.[151]

Taking these complex issues into account, the establishment of clear rules of regulatory conditions for marketing approval and good functioning of regulatory authorities would necessarily respond to public needs. Article 39.3 was drafted in such a way that it leaves WTO Members wide flexibility to adopt their own scopes of data protection in the running of regulatory systems for the safety and efficacy of the approved chemical products (see chapter 13).

iv Transitional arrangements (Articles 65–67, 70.8, 79.9 TRIPS)

The Anell text in July 1990 contained section VII relating to transitional arrangements for developing countries to take all necessary steps to ensure the conformity of their laws, regulations and practices with the provisions. However, the period for which non-compliance was allowed (except national treatment and most-favoured nation principles) was not indicated and remained undecided until the Dunkel text. The timeframe for the transitional arrangements was the subject of political, rather than economic discussion.[152] Under section 5 (patents), transitional protection was to be required for the patentable subject matter if a patent had been issued for the product by another party prior to the entry into force of the Agreement, and the product had not been marketed in the territory of the party providing such transitional protection (7A.1(a)–(c)). The right for the patent-owner to submit a copy of the patent to the party providing transitional protection (7A.2 – mailbox application) would also be protected. Developing countries considered this to be compensating, partly, the transitional arrangement for postponing the introduction of product patent protection.

In May 1990, transitional arrangements specifically designed for least-developed country Members (LDCs)[153] were proposed by Argentina, Brazil, Chile, China, Colombia, Cuba, Egypt, India, Nigeria, Peru, Tanzania and Uruguay (mostly non-LDC developing countries) as part of a general counter-proposal to the developed countries' outline of the future IPR Agreement. This proposal submitted to the

---

[151] JH Reichman, 'Undisclosed Clinical Trial Data Under the TRIPS Agreement and Its Progeny: A Broader Perspective', UNCTAD-ICTSD Dialogue on Moving the pro-development IP agenda forward: Preserving Public Goods in health, education and learning, Bellagio, 29 November–3 December 2004, 4.

[152] Watal (n 62) 37. According to Watal, the EC and India made a joint proposal in 1991 under which India agreed to provide for market exclusivity for products before the end of the transition period, and the EC agreed to concede that compulsory licences could be granted for non-working of patents and that a transition period of five years would be given for low-income developing countries as defined by the World Bank; the US objected to this proposal.

[153] The Economic and Social Council of the United Nations, upon proposal by the Committee for Development Policy, regularly establishes the list of LDCs since November 1971. In the 2003 list, the three following criteria are cumulatively applied: a low-income criterion; a human resource weakness criterion; and an economic vulnerability criterion (www.un.org/special-rep/ohrlls/ldc/ldc%20criteria.htm). These criteria are extremely detailed but are somewhat lacking when evaluating human skills or technological and scientific potentials. On LDCs and the WTO, see also ch 5, n 87.

Negotiating Group[154] fully reflected what India and Brazil had advanced earlier. It was composed of two parts: Part I concerning IP and International Trade, and Part II relating to Standards and Principles Concerning the Availability, Scope and Use of IPRs. This proposal emphasised the special needs of the LDCs, as provided in the identical preamble for both Parts I and II as follows:

> Recognizing also the special needs of the least developed countries in respect of maximum flexibility in the application of this Agreement in order to enable them to create a sound and viable technological base.

The Anell text in July 1990 reproduced this preamble *tel quel* as 1B.4 under section IX relating to Trade in Counterfeit and Pirated Goods.[155] The Anell text referred also to LDCs as requiring a longer period of transition. Part III (Standards) and Part IV (Enforcement). Technical advice and cooperation on the part of developed countries was required for all developing countries, but such cooperation concerned only those legislative aspects of implementation of the future agreement in domestic laws and regulations, including the prevention of abuse (2A) as well as training of personnel (2B). Bangladesh, on behalf of LDCs, had proposed that 'Contracting parties shall, if requested, give technical assistance to the LDCs on mutually-agreed terms and conditions to assist in the preparation of domestic regulations relating to this area.'[156] The Bangladesh proposal concerning 'mutually-agreed' technical assistance based on a specific request from LDCs was not incorporated into the TRIPS Agreement. If adopted, the Bangladesh proposal would have made possible technical cooperation adapted to the divergent situations and needs of developing countries.

The 'Commentary' section of the Brussels text further drew attention to the special needs of LDCs, and said: 'A number of developing countries have also stated that the texts should contain greater recognition of the constraints on their administrative capacity and of their development needs, in the light of the provisions in the Declaration of Punta del Este on differential and more favourable treatment of developing countries.' Thus, paragraph 6 of the introduction to the TRIPS part of the Brussels text, as the Preamble of the TRIPS Agreement later adopts, stated:

> Recognising also the special needs of the least developed countries in respect of maximum flexibility in the domestic implementation of laws and regulations in order to enable them to create a sound and viable technological base.

Article 69 of the Brussels text, under section VII, included what was later to be adopted as Article 66 TRIPS. Draft Article 69.1 emphasised the LDCs' special needs and requirements, economic, financial and administrative constraints, and their need for flexibility to create a viable technological base. The draft Article

---

[154] MTN.GNG/NG11/W/71 (n 103).

[155] As well as in Art 1.8 of the Composite Draft Text (Parts I, VI, VII and VIII) 12 June 1990, in Annex of the Anell text.

[156] Proposals on behalf of the Least-Developed Countries–Communication from Bangladesh MTN.GNG/NG11/W/50 (16 November 1989).

provided that the LDCs are not required, insofar as compliance with those provisions requires the amendment of domestic laws, regulations or practices, to apply the provisions of the agreement except Articles 3–5.[157] Draft Article 69.1 also exonerated LDCs from the obligation contained in the draft Article 68.5, ie, for countries benefiting from transitional arrangements to submit, on accession, a schedule setting out its timetable for application of the provisions of the Agreement. The Brussels text did not contain, however, what was later inserted in the Dunkel text, ie, the provisions concerning the extension of the transition arrangements. The Dunkel text provided in Article 66.1 *in fine* that 'the Council shall, upon duly motivated request by a least-developed country PARTY, accord extensions of the transition period'. The period of transition was not yet determined in the Brussels text, but was later agreed to be 10 years, which was included in Article 66.1 of the Dunkel text. The Brussels text included, in its Article 69.2, the duty of developed countries to provide incentives for encouraging transfer of technology as in Article 66.2 TRIPS. Draft Article 69.2 provided that: 'Developed country PARTIES shall provide incentives to enterprises and institutions in their territories for the purpose of promoting and encouraging technology transfer to least-developed country PARTIES in order to enable them to create a sound and viable technological base.'

The purpose of the transitional arrangements for LDCs was somewhat unclear and remained unclarified by Article 66 TRIPS, and later became a source of discussions without sufficient guidance from the text of the Agreement. In 2003, before the Ministerial scheduled in Cancun in September, African States[158] and LDCs[159] submitted proposals concerning transitional arrangements for LDCs. Both proposals suggested that the transition period for LDCs should be automatically postponed, if a viable technological base is not established in the requesting countries. In response to these proposals, developed countries argued that it was difficult to determine whether such a 'viable technological base has been created or not'.[160] In contrast, developing countries advanced that it is easy to determine this, and this disagreement meant that the decision over this subject was not taken. Pires de Carvalho argues that the purpose of the transition period for LDCs is to prepare legal and administrative structures for implementing the TRIPS Agreement, whereas establishing a technological base relates to developed countries' obligations to give incentives for technology transfer.[161]

---

[157] Draft Brussels Art 5 concerned 'Multilateral Agreements on Acquisition or Maintenance of Protection' and stated that: 'The obligations under Articles 3 and 4 above do not apply to procedures provided in multilateral agreements concluded under the auspices of the World Intellectual Property Organization relating to the acquisition or maintenance of intellectual property rights.'

[158] TN/CTD/W/3/Rev.2.

[159] TN/CTD/W/4/Add.1.

[160] Minutes of the TRIPS Council meeting of June 4–5, 2003, IP/C/M/40, 22 August 2003, para 203, fn 2.

[161] Pires de Carvalho, commenting on these proposals, says that the justification or the purpose of the transitional arrangements (Part VI which is the context of Art 66.1) is to 'let countries to dispose of enough time to get acquainted with new legal obligations and to take the legislative, administrative and technical measures necessary for implementing obligations and making them effective'

On the timeframe of the transitional arrangements for developing countries (as opposed to arrangements only for LDCs), the Dunkel text proposed a period of 10 years[162] during which those countries that had not yet made available product patent protection for pharmaceutical and agricultural products, from the date of the entry into force of the TRIPS Agreement, to introduce the so-called 'mailbox' system[163] and grant exclusive marketing rights under certain conditions.[164]

The US pharmaceutical industry criticised the Dunkel draft of 7 January 1992, and expressed its intention to oppose it in Congress unless there were major changes. According to the industry representative, the main point of contention was that the draft gave a transition period of 10 years to countries such as India, Thailand and Brazil, which would, overall, 'undermine US efforts to secure better patent protection through bilateral pressure'.[165]

Later, the Panel in their Report on *India–Patent Protection*, by referring to this negotiating history as a supplementary means of interpretation, confirmed their interpretation of the nature of obligation under Article 70.8(a) to institute a system of mailbox application. Specifically, the Panel interpreted that this provision requires developing countries to establish 'a means' for filing mailbox applications that provide a sound legal basis to preserve both the novelty of the inventions and the priority of the applications in terms of the relevant filing and priority dates. The Panel Reports mentioned that:

> . . . in the negotiation of the TRIPS Agreement the question of patent protection for pharmaceutical and agricultural chemical products was a key issue, which was

and that 'creating a viable technological base is the justification and the purpose of paragraph 2 of Article 66, not of paragraph 1'. N Pires de Carvalho (n 102) 431–3.

[162] Draft Art 65.4 of the Dunkel text proposed that: 'To the extent that a developing country PARTY is obliged by this Agreement to extend product patent protection to areas of technology not protectable in its territory on the general date of application of this Agreement for that PARTY, as defined in paragraph 2 above, it may delay the application of Section 5 of Part II of this Agreement to such areas of technology for an additional period of five years.'

[163] Art 70.8 concerning Protection of Existing Subject Matter, under Part VII relating to Institutional Arrangements – Final Provisions, provided that: 'Where a PARTY does not make available as of the date of entry into force of this Agreement patent protection for pharmaceutical and agricultural chemical products commensurate with its obligations under Article 27, that PARTY shall: (i) provide as from the date of entry into force of the Agreement a means by which applications for patents for such inventions can be filed; (ii) apply to these applications, as of the date of application of this Agreement, the criteria for patentability as laid down in this Agreement as if those criteria were being applied on the date of filing in that PARTY or, where priority is available and claimed, the priority date of the application; and, (iii) provide patent protection in accordance with this Agreement as from the grant of the patent and for the remainder of the patent term, counted from the filing date in accordance with Article 33 of this Agreement, for those of these applications that meet the criteria for protection referred to in sub-paragraph (ii) above.'

[164] Art 70.9 of the Dunkel text proposed that: 'Where a product is the subject of a patent application in a PARTY in accordance with paragraph 8(i) above, exclusive marketing rights shall be granted for a period of five years after obtaining market approval in that PARTY or until a product patent is granted or rejected in that PARTY, whichever period is shorter, provided that, subsequent to the entry into force of this Agreement, a patent application has been filed and a patent granted for that product in another PARTY and marketing approval obtained in such other PARTY.'

[165] H Bale, 'Drug, Textile Makers to Fight Trade Pact', *Journal of Commerce*, 8 January 1992. See also ch 14.

negotiated as part of a complex of related issues concerning the scope of the protection to be accorded to patents and some related rights and the timing of the economic impact of such protection. [166]

v 'Objectives' and 'principles' (Articles 7 and 8 TRIPS)

In the Dunkel text, as in the Brussels text, under Part I: General Provisions and Basic Principles, Article 7 entitled 'Objectives' stated:

> The protection and enforcement of intellectual property rights should contribute to the promotion of technological innovation and to the transfer and dissemination of technology, to the mutual advantage of producers and users of technological knowledge and in a manner conducive to social and economic welfare, and to a balance of rights and obligations.

India argued that Article 7 was a key provision that defines 'the objectives of the Agreement'. Article 8, entitled 'Principles', in the Dunkel text was similar to that in the Brussels text:

> 1. PARTIES may, in formulating or amending their national laws and regulations, adopt measures necessary to protect public health and nutrition, and to promote the public interest in sectors of vital importance to their socio-economic and technological development, provided that such measures are consistent with the provisions of this Agreement.
>
> 2. Appropriate measures, provided that they are consistent with the provisions of this Agreement, may be needed to prevent the abuse of intellectual property rights by right holders or the resort to practices which unreasonably restrain trade or adversely affect the international transfer of technology.

According to Gorlin, as indicated earlier, the negotiators considered these provisions as 'non-operational and hortatory', but during the closing negotiations on the Dunkel text in late 1991, India identified Article 8 as sanctioning exceptions to the TRIPS Agreement.[167] As a result, two parallel attempts were made by developed countries. One attempt sought the insertion of language that would clarify the non-operational character of draft Article 8, ie, 'such measures must be consistent with the provisions of this agreement'. In order for this phrase to be effective for rendering Article 8 non-operational, exceptions permitted under TRIPS must be interpreted narrowly. The other attempt, which failed, was to move Article 8 to the Preamble. It seems that no attempt was made to define such key concepts as 'the protection of public health and nutrition' or the promotion of 'public interest'.

---

[166] *India–Patent Protection for Pharmaceutical and Agricultural Chemical Products–Complaint by the United States (India–Patents (US)*, Panel ReportWT/DS50/R as modified by the Appellate Body Report (adopted 16 January 1998), WT/DS50/AB/R para 7.29 and *India–Patent Protection for Pharmaceutical and Agricultural Chemical Products–Complaint by the European Communitie (India–Patents (EC))s*, Panel Report (adopted 22 September 1998) WT/DS79/R para 7.40.

[167] Gorlin (n 49) 17. On this point, Watal adds that: 'In the preparations to the 1999 Ministerial Conference, India demanded operationalizing these provisions, although it is not entirely clear how this should be done'. Watal (n 62) 293, fn 6.

The *Economic Times New Delhi* in June 1993 interviewed AV Ganesan (then Indian Commerce Secretary), who said:

> ... the crux of the matter is that when the world is moving in one direction, it makes no sense for India to move in the opposite direction. In reality, India has no choice and there is no question of not becoming a party to the Uruguay Round Agreement. At best, India can seek amelioration, which it has done successfully.[168]

Ganesan explained that India's argument was to provide legally binding 'principles and objectives' incorporated in Articles 7 and 8 of IP protection, which would introduce 'flexibilities' to IP agreements. According to Ganesan, this was not necessarily because some countries need a low level of IPR protection, but rather because technology evolves and social contexts change. These factors, he argued, should be taken into consideration in changing IPR protection over time.[169] The definition of 'microorganisms' is an example of such flexibility. He referred to this in 1994:

> Coming now to micro-organisms, the word has not been defined in the TRIPS Agreement. For everything else there are standards, but micro-organisms is not defined and the definition of micro-organism is not there in any international convention either. It is purposely not defined in international conventions also because they do not know where to stop or where to begin with respect to patents of living things.[170]

Soon after the adoption of the Agreement, interpreting TRIPS became a battle over what the TRIPS Agreement posed as specific legal obligations between states, in the light of the diversity of their industrial and technology policies, and national self-interest enhanced through the inevitable process of technological evolution. The EU was also calling for regular reviews of the TRIPS Agreement into the future, as technology advanced.

Two radically opposing positions concerning IPR protection seem to have persisted throughout the Uruguay Round negotiations leading up to the TRIPS Agreement. One position promoted an international instrument specifically for IPR protection. Little discussion, however, seems to have occurred as to how countries without scientific or technological resources would be able to make innovation possible. The other held the view that IPRs are merely private monopoly rights which hinder innovation in developing countries, and that countries therefore should have lenient IP protection for their own 'public policy' purposes, whatever the meaning of 'public'. How the concept of 'public' should be construed was not discussed. Later, the WTO Panel in *Canada–Pharmaceutical Patents*[171]

---

[168] *The Economic Times* (Calcutta, 8 June 1993), cited in H Redwood, *New Horisons in India: the consequences of pharmaceutical patent protection*, (Felixstowe, Oldwicks Press, 1994) 39.

[169] Telephone interview with Ganesan, 7 December 2008.

[170] AV Ganesan's speech at the Workshop on EC–India Perspective on Uruguay Round Agreement, 7 February 1994, Bombay, Council of EEC Chambers of Commerce in India 34–5.

[171] Panel Report, *Canada–Patent Protection of Pharmaceutical Product (Canada–Pharmaceutical Patents (EC))*, WT/DS114/R, adopted 7 April 2000.

and *EC–Geographical Indications*[172] interpreted these notions in discussing the place of Articles 7 ('Objectives') and 8 ('Principles') in the TRIPS Agreement and in relation to IPR protection. Arguably, the burden of proof will be an important issue within the framework of WTO dispute settlement (see chapter 7). The underlying opposing views concerning the role of IPRs in the economic development of developing countries remained a potential source of discord.

Instead of engaging in an interminable debate without facts or evidence, the negotiators in the Uruguay Round appeared to prefer focusing on the benefits offered by the results of negotiations on a wider range of trade issues such as in agriculture and textiles. As a consequence, the so-called 'balance' within the adopted text was political, while the real balance was to be found in wider trade advantages for developing countries in general. On the complex question of public policy and IPRs within the framework of the TRIPS Agreement, Gurry observed in 2003:

> . . . IP and patents were a largely self-contained policy at the international level, responding essentially to the needs and demands of the objectives underlying those policies, which in the case of patents, consisted primarily of the provision of an economic incentive to investment in the creation or commercialisation of new knowledge in the form of invention. More complexity existed at the national level, where the sometimes competitive demands of competition policy, *ordre public* and national security limit or modify the scope and exploitation of patent rights. This unimodular system changed with the conclusion of the TRIPS Agreement. [173]

In the TRIPS Agreement, Gurry explains, the interface between patent policy and other areas of public policy came to be treated primarily from the perspective of the patent system as exemplified by its Article 27 and in the subsequent years, this relationship became increasingly 'complex and interactive.'[174] Great expectations came to be placed on both the TRIPS Agreement and national patent laws that they should respond to complex and difficult public policy issues such as environmental protection or access to medicines. Public policies such as insurance, taxation, encouragement of R&D and subventions to cope with market failure or externalities had been relegated primarily to the domain outside intellectual property law. Today, however, the domain of what should be 'public' has become widely open to discussions in the abstract, to which IP laws are expected to accommodate themselves.

The GATT was, and the WTO continues to be, a forum where governments defend private (mainly export) interests.[175] No matter how important it is to

---

[172] *EC–Protection of Trademarks and Geographical Indications for Agricultural Products and Foodstuffs* Panel Reports (adopted 20 April 2005) WT/DS174/R (complaint by the US) paras 7.209–7.210, WT/DS290/R (complaint by Australia) paras 7.245 – 7.246 ('*EC–Geographical Indications*'). See ch 7 of this book.

[173] F Gurry, 'A Multilateral View of Change in the Patent System', OECD Conference on IPR, Innovation and Economic Performance, Paris (October 2003) ch 22 p 334.

[174] Watal (n 62) 334.

[175] J Pauwelyn, 'WTO dispute settlement: Of sovereign interests, private rights and public goods', in KE Maskus and JH Reichman (eds), *International Public Goods and Transfer of Technology under a Globalized Intellectual Property Regime* (Cambridge, 2005) 817 *et seq*.

formulate public policy under the TRIPS Agreement, the notion of 'public' tends to be an abstract construct which is not dealt with in the Agreement. The focus gradually shifted to the margin of discretion under the TRIPS Agreement, and therefore, to flexibilities.

Industrial situations change, as do social consciences. According to Redwood, pharmaceuticals were not regarded as a key industry in developing countries in the 1980s and early 1990s. Soon after the adoption of the TRIPS Agreement, the issue became more controversial as both the industrial stakes and consciousness about equality of access to medicines as a human right increased (see chapter 8).[176]

---

[176] H Redwood, *Where is the Pharma Industry Going? Insights for the New Millennium* (Felixstowe, Oldwicks Press, 2002) 123.

5

The TRIPS Agreement de Lege Lata: *the Outline*

THE TRIPS AGREEMENT was adopted as part of a single-undertaking. This means that TRIPS applies to all WTO Members, and its provisions are subject to the integrated WTO dispute settlement mechanism which is contained in the Understanding on Rules and Procedures Governing the Settlement of Disputes (DSU).[1] The TRIPS Agreement is composed of a Preamble and the following seven parts:

Part I: General Provisions and Basic Principles
Part II: Standards concerning the Availability, Scope and Use of Intellectual Property Rights
Part III: Enforcement of Intellectual Property Rights
Part IV: Acquisition and Maintenance of Intellectual Property Rights and Related Inter-Partes Procedures
Part V: Dispute Prevention and Settlement
Part VI: Transitional Arrangements
Part VII: Institutional Arrangements; Final Provisions

Part II on standards and Part III on enforcement constitute the core of the TRIPS Agreement. The nature of the different Parts, and their respective importance in interpreting TRIPS provisions, have been discussed extensively in the dispute cases involving the TRIPS Agreement (chapter 7), and in *China–Intellectual Property Rights*,[2] in particular.

PREAMBLE

A preamble generally declares the intention of the parties in entering into the agreement. Without creating binding obligations, preambles of a treaty can provide 'context' for the purpose of treaty interpretation.

The Preamble of the TRIPS Agreement resembles a kaleidoscope of opposing views and perspectives regarding 'trade aspects of IPRs' that were expressed

---

[1] Annex 2 of the Agreement Establishing the WTO.
[2] *China–Measures Affecting the Protection and Enforcement of Intellectual Property Rights (China–Intellectual Property Rights)*, Panel Report (adopted 20 March 2009) WT/DS362/R.

in the 1986 Punta del Este Declaration[3] and the 1988–89 Mid-Term Review by Ministers.[4] These views and perspectives reflect the effort to balance different political considerations.

Recital 1 of the Preamble of the TRIPS Agreement, reflecting both developed and developing countries' perspectives, states that:

> [d]esiring to reduce distortions and impediments to international trade, and taking into account the need to promote effective and adequate protection of intellectual property rights, and to ensure that measures and procedures to enforce intellectual property rights do not themselves become barriers to legitimate trade.

Recitals 2 and 3 further state that the TRIPS Agreement was agreed upon, recognising the need for new rules and disciplines concerning:

(a) the applicability of the basic principles of GATT 1994 and of relevant international intellectual property agreements or conventions;
(b) the provision of adequate standards and principles concerning the availability, scope and use of trade-related intellectual property rights;
(c) the provision of effective and appropriate means for the enforcement of trade-related intellectual property rights, taking into account differences in national legal systems;
(d) the provision of effective and expeditious procedures for the multilateral prevention and settlement of disputes between governments; and
(e) transitional arrangements aiming at the fullest participation in the results of the negotiations (Recital 2);

and the need for a multilateral framework of principles, rules and disciplines dealing with international trade in counterfeit goods (Recital 3).

Recital 4 of the Preamble recognises that IPRs are private rights, and Recital 5 refers to the 'underlying public policy objectives of national systems for the protection of intellectual property, including developmental and technological objectives'. In Recital 6, the Preamble reproduces the statement concerning LDCs proposed by a number of developing countries[5] and recognises 'the special needs of the least-developed country Members in respect of maximum flexibility in the domestic implementation of laws and regulations in order to enable them to create a sound and viable technological base'. Importantly, the Preamble emphasises resolution of IP-related disputes through multilateral procedures (Recital 7). It then calls for a mutually supportive relationship between the WTO and the World Intellectual Property Organization (WIPO – see chapter 2), as well as other relevant international organisations (Recital 8).

Thus, the protection of intellectual property rights (IPRs) became an integral part of the multilateral trading system as embodied in the WTO, and international

---

[3] Ministerial Declaration on the Uruguay Round: Declaration of 20 Sept 1986, GATT, Basic Instruments and Selected Documents (BISD), 33d Supp.19, 25–26 (1987). See ch 4.

[4] MTN.TNC/11 (21 April 1989). See ch 4, n 37.

[5] Communication from Argentina, Brazil, Chile, China, Colombia, Cuba, Egypt, India, Nigeria, Peru, Tanzania and Uruguay, MTN.GNG/NG11/W/71 (14 May 1990) (see ch 4).

cooperation concerning IPRs, which had been confined to a narrow circle of specialists in the previous 100 years, came to be exposed to a larger group of actors dealing with trade rules.

PART I: GENERAL PROVISIONS AND BASIC PRINCIPLES (ARTICLES 1–8)

Nature and Scope of Obligations

The first sentence of Article 1.1 sets out the basic obligation of WTO Members to 'give effect' to the provisions of this Agreement. Members must, therefore, implement, in their domestic law, the protection required by the TRIPS Agreement. The Panel in *China–Intellectual Property Rights* confirmed that Article 1.1 does not offer Members freedom to implement a lower standard, but that Members are free to determine the appropriate method of implementation of TRIPS provisions to which they are required to give effect.[6] The second sentence, 'Members may, but shall not be obliged to, implement in their law more extensive protection than is required by this Agreement, provided that such protection does not contravene the provisions of this Agreement', clarifies that the provisions of the Agreement are minimum standards only, in that they give Members the freedom to implement higher standards, subject to conditions. This sentence makes it clear that the Agreement is not intended to be a harmonisation agreement.[7] The third sentence stipulates that 'Members shall be free to determine the appropriate method of implementing the provisions of this Agreement within their own legal system and practice'. In *Canada–Patent Term*, the Panel noted that the discretion of Members under Article 1.1 to determine the appropriate method of implementing their obligations under the TRIPS Agreement did not extend to choosing which obligation to comply with.[8] Similarly, in *China–Intellectual Property Protection*, the Panel emphasised that the third sentence of Article 1.1 does not permit differences in domestic legal systems and practices to justify any derogation from the basic obligation to give effect to the provisions on enforcement.

Article 1.2 TRIPS provides that: 'For the purposes of this Agreement, the term "intellectual property" refers to all categories of intellectual property that are the subjects of Sections 1 through 7 of Part II.' The Article uses obligations in pre-existing IPR treaties (such as the Paris and Berne Conventions) and supplements them as necessary. These 'categories' include copyrights, patents, trademarks, geographical indications, industrial designs, integrated circuit designs, and undisclosed information. The TRIPS Agreement introduced rules

---

[6] *China–Intellectual Property Rights* (n 2) para 7.513.

[7] A Otten and H Wager, 'Compliance with TRIPS: the Emerging World View', (1996) 29 *Vanderbilt J Trans Law* 391.

[8] *Canada–Term of Patent Protection (Canada–Patent Term)*, Panel Report WT/DS170/R as upheld by the Appellate Body Report (adopted 12 October 2000) WT/DS170/AB/R.

in pioneering fields of technology such as biotechnology, computer programs and semi-conductor integrated circuits, but does not contain rules that are specific to fields such as internet-related copyright protection, software patents, or business models. The inclusion of trade names, not explicitly mentioned in the TRIPS Agreement but included in the Paris Convention, was confirmed by the Appellate Body Report in *US–Section 211 Appropriation Act.*[9]

One of the basic obligations of WTO Members under the TRIPS Agreement is to offer the treatment in regard to the protection of intellectual property (IP) to the persons of other Members, as in the pre-existing IP conventions. Article 1.3 defines who these persons are. The persons are referred to as 'nationals' but include persons, natural or legal, who have a close attachment to other Members without necessarily being nationals.[10] In the case of a separate customs territory Member of the WTO (Hong Kong, China, for example) 'nationals' for the purpose of the TRIPS Agreement means natural and legal persons who are domiciled or who have a real and effective industrial or commercial establishment (footnote 1 to Article 1.3 of the TRIPS Agreement). The criteria for determining who will benefit from the treatment provided for under the Agreement are laid down in the pre-existing IP conventions, ie, the Paris Convention (1967), the Berne Convention (1971), the Rome Convention and the Treaty on Intellectual Property in Respect of Integrated Circuits (although this treaty has not entered into force).[11] Nationals of any country of the Paris Union can enjoy in all the other countries of the Union the advantages that their respective laws grant to nationals (Article 2(1) of the Paris Convention) and no requirement as to domicile or establishment in the country where protection is claimed may be imposed upon nationals of countries of the Union (Article 2(2) of the Paris Convention). Authors' works, whether published or not, are eligible for protection under the Berne Convention (Article 3(1) of the Berne Convention), if the authors are nationals of one of the countries of the Berne Union. Authors who are not nationals of one of the countries of the Union are eligible for protection under the Berne Convention for works first published in one of those countries, or simultaneously in a country outside the Union and in a country of the Union.

---

[9] The Appellate Body found that Members have an obligation to provide protection to trade names in accordance with Art 8 of the Paris Convention, as incorporated by Art 2.1 of the TRIPS Agreement. Art 8 of the Paris Convention stipulates that: 'A trade name shall be protected in all the countries of the Union without the obligation of filing or registration, whether or not it forms part of a trademark.' *US–Section 211 Omnibus Appropriations Act of 1998 (US–Section 211 Appropriations Act)*, Appellate Body Report (adopted 1 February 2002) WT/DS176/AB/R paras 320–54.

[10] Otten and Wager (n 7) 395.

[11] Footnote 2 to Article 1.3 notes that: 'In this Agreement, "Paris Convention" refers to the Paris Convention for the Protection of Industrial Property; "Paris Convention (1967)" refers to the Stockholm Act of this Convention of 14 July 1967. "Berne Convention" refers to the Berne Convention for the Protection of Literary and Artistic Works; "Berne Convention (1971)" refers to the Paris Act of this Convention of 24 July 1971. "Rome Convention" refers to the International Convention for the Protection of Performers, Producers of Phonograms and Broadcasting Organizations, adopted at Rome on 26 October 1961. "Treaty on Intellectual Property in Respect of Integrated Circuits" (IPIC Treaty) refers to the Treaty on Intellectual Property in Respect of Integrated Circuits, adopted at Washington on 26 May 1989. "WTO Agreement" refers to the Agreement Establishing the WTO.'

These provisions are applied to all WTO Members whether or not they are parties to these pre-existing conventions.

Intellectual Property Conventions

Article 2 obliges all WTO Members, even those that are not parties to the Paris Convention, to comply with Articles 1–12 and Article 19 of the Paris Convention (1967) as far as Part II (standards concerning the availability, scope and use of IPRs), Part III (enforcement) and Part IV (acquisition and maintenance of IPRs and related *inter-partes* procedures) are concerned.[12]

National Treatment

Intellectual property rights (IPRs) are held by persons (whether natural or juridical), and, as in the pre-existing IP Conventions, the basic obligation of each Member is to accord the treatment in regard to the protection of intellectual property provided for under the Agreement to the persons of other Members. The national treatment principle prohibits discrimination between a Member's own nationals and the nationals of other Members. In the first sentence of Article 3.1 TRIPS, the principle of national treatment is delineated as follows:

> Each Member shall accord to the nationals[13] of other Members treatment no less favourable than that it accords to its own nationals with regard to the protection of intellectual property, subject to the exceptions already provided in, respectively, the Paris Convention (1967), the Berne Convention (1971), the Rome Convention[14] or the Treaty on Intellectual Property in Respect of Integrated Circuits. . . .

The 'no less favourable' language derives from Article III:4 GATT, about which the Appellate Body in *US–Section 211 Appropriations Act* stated that 'the jurisprudence on Article III:4 of the GATT 1994 may be useful in interpreting the national treatment obligation in the TRIPS Agreement',[15] and referred to the GATT Panel Report in *US–Section 337*.[16] The Appellate Body concluded that

---

[12] See Art 9.1 TRIPS for the Berne Convention, and Art 35 TRIPS for the IPIC Treaty.

[13] A footnote to Art 3 of the Agreement provides that: 'When "nationals" are referred to in this Agreement, they shall be deemed, in the case of a separate customs territory Member of the WTO, to mean persons, natural or legal, who are domiciled or who have a real and effective industrial or commercial establishment in that customs territory.'

[14] The International Convention for the Protection of Performers, Producers of Phonograms and Broadcasting Organisations, known as the Rome Convention, was adopted on 26 October 1961. 91 countries are its contracting parties as of 15 October 2010. In several respects, the Rome Convention is different from TRIPS provisions on the subject.

[15] The Appellate Body report stated that: The Panel was correct in concluding that, as the language of Article 3.1 of the TRIPS Agreement, in particular, is similar to that of Article III:4 of the GATT 1994.' *US–Section 211 Appropriations Act*, Appellate Body Report (n 9) para 242.

[16] *US–Section 337 of the Tariff Act of 1930*, Panel Report (adopted 7 November 1989) BISD 30S/149; see ch 3 p 96.

'even the possibility that non-US successors-in-interest face two hurdles is inherently less favourable than the undisputed fact that US successors-in-interest face only one'.[17] According to the Panel in *EC–Geographical Indications,*

> two elements must be satisfied to establish an inconsistency with this obligation: (1) the measure at issue must apply with regard to the protection of intellectual property; and (2) the nationals of other Members must be accorded 'less favourable' treatment than the Member's own nationals.[18]

The second sentence of Article 3.1 TRIPS stipulates that: 'In respect of performers, producers of phonograms and broadcasting organisations, this obligation only applies in respect of the rights provided under this Agreement.' This clause was inserted so that those WTO Members not parties to the Rome Convention cannot claim that their nationals be accorded the rights that are not guaranteed in their own territory.

Article 3.2 provides for exceptions to national treatment obligation with regard to 'judicial and administrative procedures, including the designation of an address for service or the appointment of an agent within the jurisdiction of a Member'. Article 2(3) of the Paris Convention also exempts from national treatment obligation, 'laws on judicial and administrative procedure'. However, the TRIPS Agreement adds further conditions in which such exceptions are allowed. In language similar to Article XX GATT, Article 3.2 TRIPS requires that the measure in question must be 'necessary' to secure compliance with laws and regulations which are not inconsistent with the provisions of the Agreement and that 'such practices are not applied in a manner which would constitute a disguised restriction on trade'.[19]

Most-Favoured-Nation Treatment

The most-favoured-nation treatment principle forbids discrimination between the nationals of other Members. Article 4, entitled 'Most-Favoured-Nation Treatment', stipulates that: 'With regard to the protection of intellectual property, any advantage, favour, privilege or immunity granted by a Member to the nationals of any other country shall be accorded immediately and unconditionally to the nationals of all other Members.' For the first time, the MFN principle was included in a multilateral IP treaty, although ways in which this could be applied in IP protection were unknown. In most IP cases, those measures not respecting

---

[17] *US–Section 211 Appropriations Act* (n 9) para 265.

[18] *EC–Protection of Trademarks and Geographical Indications for Agricultural Products and Foodstuffs* (*EC–Geographical Indications*), Panel Reports (adopted 20 April 2005) WT/DS174/R (complaint by the US) para 7.175; WT/DS290/R (complaint by Australia) para 7.125.

[19] IP/C/M/12 paras 10–16. The Council for TRIPS referred to the obligations to notify laws and regulations that correspond to the obligations of Arts 3, 4 and 5 of the TRIPS Agreement. It circulated guidelines on 27 February 1997 through a format in IP/C/9 (Analytical Index www.wto.org/english/res_e/booksp_e/analytic_index_e/trips_01_e.htm#fntext25).

the MFN principle could also violate the national treatment principle. The principle's inclusion in the TRIPS Agreement was questioned during the Uruguay Round negotiations.[20] In *US–Section 211 Appropriations Act*, the Appellate Body found that the US measure in question (sections 211(a)(2) and 211(b) of the US Appropriations Act) violated the MFN obligations under the TRIPS Agreement. The apparently nationality-free provisions concerning the 'designated national' could lead to a situation where two 'original owners', one, a Cuban national and another, a non-Cuban foreign national, are discriminated against.[21]

The MFN principle should be helpful for scrutinising certain unilateral or regional arrangements, but certain concepts in Article 4 are not entirely clear. It is difficult to say what constitutes 'advantage, favour, privilege' in IP protection, and which advantages merit being granted to other country nationals based on the MFN principle without the country's consent. For example, a hypothetical requirement that patent filings should be made not only in the language of the country but also in English would offer advantages to English-speaking nationals. However, this measure does not seem to deserve MFN treatment.

The second sentence of Article 4 TRIPS states that the application of the MFN principle is exempted from any advantage, favour, privilege or immunity accorded by a Member:

(a) deriving from international agreements on judicial assistance or law enforcement of a general nature and not particularly confined to the protection of intellectual property;

(b) granted in accordance with the provisions of the Berne Convention (1971) or the Rome Convention authorising that the treatment accorded be a function not of national treatment but of the treatment accorded in another country;

(c) in respect of the rights of performers, producers of phonograms and broadcasting organisations not provided for under the TRIPS Agreement;

(d) deriving from international agreements related to the protection of intellectual property which came to effect prior to the entry into force of the WTO Agreement, provided that such agreements are notified to the Council for TRIPS and do not constitute an arbitrary or unjustifiable discrimination against nationals of other Members. Article (b) and (c) mirror the exceptions to national treatment contained in Article 3. The exception in Article 4 (d) seems to be of limited utility since it only applies to past agreements.

---

[20] A delegate, 'speaking on behalf of a number of developing countries', expressed his scepticism concerning the adoption in the agreement of the MFN principle, as follows: 'The obligation in Article 2 to comply with the major intellectual property conventions was contrary to accepted principles of international law, according to which conventions were binding only upon those countries which had adhered to them. The only exception to this related to conventions codifying general rules of customary international law, which certainly did not apply to the relevant intellectual property conventions. With respect to Article 4, he said that he was still not convinced of the need to include the MFN principle in the text, since it was alien to the intellectual property system, and would in any case be rendered meaningless by the growing list of exceptions written into it.' Note of the Secretariat: Meeting of the Negotiating Group of 1 November 1990 MTN.GNG/NG11/27 (14 November 1990) para 4.

[21] *US–Section 211 Appropriations Act,* Appellate Body Report (n 9) para 319.

Multilateral Agreements on Acquisition or Maintenance of Protection

According to Article 5 of the TRIPS Agreement, national treatment and MFN treatment obligations under Articles 3 and 4 do not apply to 'procedures provided in multilateral agreements concluded under the auspices of WIPO relating to the acquisition or maintenance of intellectual property rights'. This provision excludes the automatic extension to WTO Members of rights under WIPO treaties relating to the acquisition or maintenance of IPRs, such as the Madrid Agreement Concerning the International Registration of Marks and its Protocol, the Hague Agreement Concerning the International Deposit of Industrial Designs, the Patent Cooperation Treaty, the Patent Law Treaty and the Budapest Treaty on the International Recognition of the Deposit of Microorganisms for the Purposes of Patent Procedure (on these agreements, see chapter 2).

Exhaustion

'Exhaustion' refers to the lapse of the exclusive right of distribution of the right holder who loses or 'exhausts' certain rights with regard to one specific product after the first use of the subject matter, once the product has entered the market with the consent of the right holder. For example, the ability of a trademark owner to control further sales of a product bearing its mark is generally considered 'exhausted' after the sale of that product. However, there is no consensus on the question of whether or not and under what conditions the right holder loses or 'exhausts' his rights. Legitimacy of parallel imports depends on the exhaustion regime (eg, national, regional or international) of a country and, therefore, the subject of 'exhaustion' of intellectual property rights has been controversial. The Uruguay Round negotiations did not reach an agreement on any particular exhaustion regime.

Article 6 stipulates that '[f]or the purposes of dispute settlement under this Agreement, subject to the provisions of Articles 3 and 4 nothing in this Agreement shall be used to address the issue of the exhaustion of intellectual property rights.' In other words, this provision excludes the question of the exhaustion of rights from dispute settlement, except provisions of Articles 3 and 4. Therefore, there is some scope for bilateral disputes over the exhaustion of rights.[22] Paragraph 5 d) of the Doha Declaration on the TRIPS Agreement and Public Health[23] states that:

[22] There has been debate on the question of what instruments are relevant in interpreting Art 6. For example, M Bronckers, 'The Exhaustion of Patent Rights under World Trade Organization Law' (1998) 32 *Journal of World Trade Law*; FM Abbott, Second Report to the Committee on International Trade Law of the International Law Association, 'Exhaustion of Intellectual Property Rights and Parallel Importation', July 2000, at the 69th Conference of the International Law Association, rev 1.1.

[23] Declaration on the TRIPS agreement and public health, adopted by Ministerial Conference on 14 November 2001 WT/MIN(01)/DEC/2 (20 November 2001).

The effect of the provisions in the TRIPS Agreement that are relevant to the exhaustion of intellectual property rights is to leave each member free to establish its own regime for such exhaustion without challenge, subject to the MFN and national treatment provisions of Articles 3 and 4.

Possible differences between what this paragraph states and what is provided in Article 6 of the TRIPS Agreement are discussed in chapter 9.

Lawfulness of parallel imports, defined as imports without authorisation from the right holder of patented goods from the third country, depends on the exhaustion regime of a country, ie, whether the country adopts policies of national, regional or international exhaustion. Depending on the policies that a country adopts, right holders may be unable to enforce particular rights in another jurisdiction.

Objectives and Principles

Article 7 is entitled 'Objectives' and provides that: 'The protection and enforcement of intellectual property rights should contribute to the promotion of technological innovation and to the transfer and dissemination of technology, to the mutual advantage of producers and users of technological knowledge and in a manner conducive to social and economic welfare, and to a balance of rights and obligations.' The Article, however, does not define the objectives of the TRIPS Agreement, but states the objectives of the protection and enforcement of IPRs.

Article 8 is entitled 'principles'. According to this provision, Members may, in formulating or amending their laws and regulations, adopt measures *necessary to* protect public health and nutrition, and to promote the public interest in sectors of vital importance to their socio-economic and technological development (Article 8.1). Conditions attached to 'necessary to' in the GATT dispute settlement tradition evolved in the new WTO framework (see chapter 4). Article 8.2 refers to the 'appropriate measures which may be needed to prevent the abuse of IPRs by right holders' that Members may adopt, or the resort to 'practices which unreasonably restrain trade or adversely affect the international transfer of technology'. Articles 8.1 and 8.2 are both accompanied by a clause which states: 'provided that such measures are consistent with the provisions of this Agreement'. This, in turn, depends on how the exceptions to the rights conferred provided under the TRIPS Agreement are interpreted within the fundamental balance between the rights and obligations of the TRIPS Agreement. Articles 7 and 8 and their relation to Article 30 concerning 'exceptions to rights conferred' were discussed in *Canada–Patent Protection of Pharmaceutical Products*.[24] The Panel in *EC–Geographical Indications* noted that 'Article 8 of the TRIPS Agreement sets out the principles of that agreement', and stated that:

[24] *Canada–Patent Protection of Pharmaceutical Products*, (*Canada–Pharmaceutical Patents (EC)*) Complaint by the European Communities and their Member States, Panel Report (adopted 7 April 2000) WT/DS114/R.

These principles reflect the fact that the TRIPS Agreement does not generally provide for the grant of positive rights to exploit or use certain subject matter, but rather provides for the grant of negative rights to prevent certain acts. This fundamental feature of intellectual property protection inherently grants Members freedom to pursue legitimate public policy objectives since many measures to attain those public policy objectives lie outside the scope of intellectual property rights and do not require an exception under the TRIPS Agreement. [25]

PART II: STANDARDS CONCERNING THE AVAILABILITY, SCOPE AND USE OF INTELLECTUAL PROPERTY RIGHTS (ARTICLES 9–40)

In Part II, the TRIPS Agreement sets out the minimum standards of protection to be provided by each Member. The subject matter to be protected, the minimum duration of protection, the rights to be conferred and permissible exceptions to those rights are defined with respect to each of the main areas of intellectual property rights covered by the TRIPS Agreement. During the Uruguay Round negotiations, important provisions contained in pre-existing treaties on IPRs were incorporated and served as a basis for further elaboration in TRIPS. For copyright and 'neighbouring rights', the existing level of protection under the latest Act of the Berne Convention was largely maintained with, however, substantial additions and clarifications. The TRIPS Agreement offers the following clarifications concerning copyright protection given to certain new technologies: computer programs, whether in source or in object code, shall be protected as literary works under the Berne Convention (Article 10.1); and database or other compilation of data or other material shall be protected under copyrights (Article 10.2 TRIPS). Where the level of protection under the previous IPR treaties is higher than the TRIPS Agreement, TRIPS under Parts I to IV do not allow derogations from existing obligations that Members may have to each other under the Paris Convention, the Berne Convention, the Rome Convention and the Treaty on Intellectual Property in Respect of Integrated Circuits (Article 2.2 TRIPS). In the area of patents, the TRIPS Agreement incorporates Articles 1 to 12 and Article 19 of the Paris Convention (1967). It adds substantive rules of protection to set the level of protection considerably higher than the Paris Convention in a number of instances, for example, protection of products.

Copyright and Related Rights (Articles 9–14)

Articles 9–14 concern the substantive standards of copyright protection, including the rights of performers, producers of phonograms and broadcasting organisations, which are called in the TRIPS Agreement 'related rights'. Article 9.1

---

[25] *EC–Geographical Indications*, Panel Reports (n 19) WT/DS174/R (complaint by the US) para 7.210; WT/DS290/R (complaint by Australia) para 7.246. See also ch 7 at p 220.

stipulates that 'Members shall comply with Articles 1 through 21 of the Berne Convention (1971) and the Appendix thereto.' WTO Members are not required to comply with the obligations concerning 'moral rights' provided under Article 6 *bis* of the Berne Convention (Article 9.1, second sentence).[26] Copyright protection, according to Article 9.2, shall extend to 'expressions', but not to 'ideas, procedures, methods of operation or mathematical concepts as such'.

The TRIPS Agreement provides copyright protection to the following works:

- works covered by the Berne Convention, excluding moral rights (Article 9.1);
- computer programs as literary works under the Berne Convention (Article 10.1 TRIPS);
- compilations of data or other material, whether in machine, readable or other form, which by reason of the selection or arrangement of their contents as such that constitutes intellectual creations;[27] however 'the data or material itself' is not protected (Article 10.2 TRIPS);[28]

The TRIPS Agreement recognises rental rights of authors and their successors in title, to authorise or to prohibit the commercial rental to the public of originals or copies of their copyright works, except when rental has not led to widespread copying that impairs the reproduction right[29] (Article 11). It also recognises (as 'related rights') rights of performers, producers of phonograms and broadcasting organisations (Article 14).

In the TRIPS Agreement, internet-related issues such as making available technical protection measures, the liability of internet service providers (ISPs) and others included in the 1996 WIPO Internet Treaties are not covered.

Article 12 of the TRIPS Agreement refers to the minimum term of copyright protection for works of legal persons, such as sound recordings and films under the US law. The term of protection for this category of authors (except for photographic works or works of applied art) is not calculated on the basis of the life of a natural person. Such a term must be 'no less than 50 years from the end of the calendar year of authorised publication, or, failing such authorized publication, within 50 years from the making of the work, 50 years from the end of the calendar year of making.'

---

[26] Art 6 bis of the Berne Convention provides rules for moral rights by which the author has 'the right to claim authorship of the work and to object to any distortion, mutilation or other modification of, or other derogatory action in relation to, the said work, which would be prejudicial to his honor or reputation Independently of the author's economic rights.'

[27] However, Art 10.1 adds that 'such protection, which shall not extend to the data or material itself, shall be without prejudice to any copyright subsisting in the data or material itself.' Protection of computer programs under Arts 10.1 and 10.2 is similar to the law in the US, Europe and Japan.

[28] Without prejudice to any copyright subsisting in the data or material itself.

[29] A phrase, 'A Member shall be excepted from this obligation in respect of cinematographic works unless such rental has led to widespread copying of such works which is materially impairing the exclusive right of reproduction conferred in that Member on authors and their successors in title', was inserted at the insistence of Japan, which could not accept the US proposal for the period of exclusivity of 50 years.

For works of a natural person, the minimum term of protection is the life of the author plus 50 years, as Article 7(1) of the Berne Convention prescribes. This provision of the Berne Convention is incorporated into the TRIPS Agreement through Article 9.1.

Certain limitations or exceptions to the copyrights related to protected work are necessary for the purpose of advancing science and art or other socio-economic and cultural needs, respecting adequately at the same time the rights of the author. Exceptions and limitations could be in the form, for example, of private use, teaching or research. Continental law has provided case-specific limitations or exceptions, whereas the common law tradition has followed the concept of 'fair use' or 'fair dealing'.

Article 13 TRIPS provides that: 'Members shall confine limitations or exceptions to exclusive rights to certain special cases which do not conflict with a normal exploitation of the work and do not unreasonably prejudice the legitimate interests of the right holder.'

Article 9(2) of the Berne Convention concerns 'possible exceptions' to the exclusive right of reproduction conferred to authors of literary and artistic works, and stipulates that: 'It shall be a matter for legislation in the countries of the Union to permit the reproduction of such works in certain special cases, provided that such reproduction does not conflict with a normal exploitation of the work and does not unreasonably prejudice the legitimate interests of the author.'[30] The exceptions in the Berne Convention are incorporated into TRIPS by way of reference under Article 9.1. However, interpretation and application of Article 13 determines the scope of the specific exceptions in domestic law. In *US–Section 110(5) Copyright Act*[31], the relationship of Article 13 TRIPS to Article 9(2) of the Berne Convention (1971) was discussed (chapter 7).

Trademarks (Articles 15–21)

The TRIPS provisions concerning trademarks responded to certain difficulties that companies operating internationally face in both developed and developing countries as a result of local conditions or preferences, whereby trademarks are recognised, registered, maintained or used. The TRIPS Agreement clarifies the criteria of permissibility of these conditions and procedures. The basic rule concerning protectable subject matter is that any sign, or any combination of signs, capable of distinguishing the goods and services of one company from those of

[30] There are other specific exceptions for certain uses of a copyrighted work in the Berne Convention. For example, quotations from works reproduced to the extent justified by the informatory purpose, of addresses, lectures (Art 2 bis(2)) or articles published in newspapers or periodicals on current affairs (Art 10 bis(1)) by the press or broadcasters or lawfully made available to the public (Art 10(1)); or use of literary or Artistic works for teaching, provided that the use is compatible with fair practice (Arts 10(2), 10 bis (2)).

[31] *United States–Section 110(5) of the US Copyright Act (US–Section 110 (5) Copyright Act)*, Panel Report (adopted 27 July 2000) WT/DS160/R.

other companies must be eligible for registration as a trademark, provided that it is visually perceptible.[32]

According to Article 15.1 TRIPS, any 'sign, or any combination of signs', 'capable of distinguishing the goods or services' of one undertaking from those of other undertakings, is protectable, and eligible for registration as a trademark. Alternatively, if signs are not inherently capable of distinguishing the relevant goods or services, Members 'may make registrability depend on distinctiveness acquired through use'.

Article 15.2 states the principle that Members are not prevented from denying registration of a trademark on grounds not indicated in Article 15.1, provided that the conditions do not violate the Paris Convention. In the *US–Section 211 Appropriation Act* case, the Appellate Body recognised a Member's right to impose conditions other than those in Article 15.1. The Appellate Body in this case found that Article 6 *quinquies* of the Paris Convention, obliges Members to accept marks for registration in the same form (ie, 'as is', or '*telle quelle*') as registered in the country of origin.

Article 15.3 TRIPS responded to local requirements which make registrability depend on actual use.[33] Without negating the possibility that Members require actual use of trademarks for registration, Article 15.3 TRIPS stipulates that Members shall not refuse an application for registration 'solely on the ground that intended use has not taken place before the expiry of a period of three years from the date of application.'

In the similar context of responding to local requirements or preferences which hamper international commercial operation beyond the functions of trademarks, Article 20 establishes the principle that 'the use of a trademark in the course of trade shall not be unjustifiably encumbered by special requirements.'[34] The meaning of 'encumbered' and 'requirements' cannot, however, be interpreted broadly. In *Indonesia–Auto*[35], the US took issue with Indonesia's industrial policy programme and invoked Article 20 in conjunction with Article 3 TRIPS (national treatment). According to the US, a foreign right holder's ability to use its pre-existing trademark was 'encumbered' by this programme and by the competitive disadvantage due to the subsidies and tariffs favouring local companies. The Panel did not accept these arguments, firstly because foreign companies entered into arrangements with a local company voluntarily and in the knowledge of consequent implications concerning the use of their trademark, and, secondly, because the US did not sufficiently explain how ineligibility for

---

[32] Otten and Wager (n 7) 399.

[33] The US Lanham Act 15 USC § 1051(b)–(d) was amended during the Uruguay Round negotiations. The US law continues to require actual use as a precondition to completion of registration, but permits an application to be filed prior to such use.

[34] Refers to, for example, use with another trade mark, use in a special form or use in a manner detrimental to its capability to distinguish the goods or services of one undertaking from those of other undertakings.

[35] *Indonesia–Certain Measures Affecting the Automobile Industry (Indonesia–Autos)* Panel Report (adopted 23 July 1998) WT/DS54/R.

benefits accruing under the programme could constitute 'requirements' imposed on foreign trademark holders, in line with Article 20 of the TRIPS Agreement.

Article 16 (exclusive rights), Article 17 (exceptions), Article 18 (term of protection) and Article 21 (licensing and assignment) of the TRIPS Agreement specify a minimum level of protection that Members must guarantee in their domestic legislation. The owner of a registered trademark shall have the exclusive right 'to prevent all third parties without the owner's consent from using identical or similar signs for goods or services which are identical or similar to those in respect of which the trademark is registered, where such use would result in a likelihood of confusion.' The second sentence of Article 16.1 refers to the presumption of the likelihood of confusion when an identical sign for identical goods or services is used. Limited exceptions to the exclusive rights, such as fair use of descriptive terms, are allowed, provided that such exceptions take account of 'the legitimate interests of the owner of the trademark and of third parties'. Members may determine conditions on the licensing and assignment of trademarks, it being understood that the compulsory licensing of trademarks shall not be permitted. The owner of a registered trademark shall have the right to assign the trademark with or without the transfer of the business to which the trademark belongs.

Article 16.2 deals with well-known marks. Although there is no commonly agreed detailed definition of what constitutes a well-known mark,[36] those marks with respect to goods and services which have gained reputation, irrespective of whether they are registered or not, have been protected in the Paris Union countries under Article 6 bis of the Paris Convention (1967). The authorities protect well-known marks whose reproduction, imitation, or translation is liable to create confusion, by refusing or by cancelling the registration, and by prohibiting the use thereof. In many countries, well-known marks are also protected even against use for dissimilar goods and services. In developed countries, courts tend to rely on business realities to determine whether a mark is 'well-known'. Developing countries, by contrast, tend to underplay well-known marks and think that trademark registration is sufficient to prevent free-riding of well-known marks in foreign countries.

Article 16.2 TRIPS introduces three new elements, in comparison to Article 6 bis of the Paris Convention. Firstly, the 'knowledge of the trademark in the relevant sector of the public' shall be taken into account, in determining whether a trademark is well-known. In other words, the mark does not have to be known in the entire Member country (although Article 16.2 does not clarify its geographical scope, ie whether 'the public' is defined as being world-wide or only within the country concerned). Secondly, knowledge in the Member concerned which has been obtained as a result of the promotion of that trademark shall also be

---

[36] The WIPO Joint Recommendation concerning Provisions on the Protection of Well-Known Marks adopted by the Assembly of the Paris Union for the Protection of Industrial Property and the General Assembly of the WIPO at the 34th Series of Meetings of the Assemblies of the Member States of WIPO, September 20 to 29, 1999 www.wipo.int/sme/en/ip_business/marks/well_known_marks.htm.

taken into consideration. Finally, Article 6 *bis* of the Paris Convention (1967) shall apply to services.

Article 17 concerning exceptions, such as Articles 26.2 for design rights and Article 30 for patents, provides that Members may provide 'limited' exceptions to the rights conferred by a trademark, including fair use of descriptive terms, provided that such exceptions 'take account of the legitimate interests' of 'the owner of the trademark and of third parties'. However, Article 21 of the TRIPS Agreement concerning licensing and assignment prohibits compulsory licensing of trademarks. This prohibition is due to the different function that exclusive trademark rights have, in comparison to designs or patents. The purpose of trademarks is to distinguish the goods or services of a particular company from those of others, and, therefore, the use or assignment of the mark by the owner fulfils this purpose.[37]

Geographical Indications (Articles 22–4)

Article 22 of the TRIPS Agreement explains that, for the purpose of the TRIPS Agreement, geographical indications (GIs) are 'indications which identify a good as originating in the territory of a Member, or a region or locality in that territory, where a given quality, reputation or other characteristic of the good is essentially attributable to its geographical origin.' Members have the obligation, first, to refuse or invalidate the registration of a trademark which contains or consists of a GI with respect to goods not originating in the territory indicated, so that it would not 'mislead the public as to the true place'.[38] Secondly, Members must provide legal means for the interested party to prevent acts of misrepresentation as well as unfair competition against the third person using the mark. The above means of protection had already been made available in many countries under Article 10 bis of the Paris Convention.

Article 23 provides for 'additional protection' concerning GIs for wines and spirits. The term 'additional' is used because the protection provided for wines or spirits covers not only the origin but also: (i) the indication in translation, and expressions such as 'kind', 'type', 'style', 'imitation' etc.; (ii) indications which contain or consist of a GI with respect to such wines or spirits not having this origin must be refused or invalidated, *ex officio* if a Member's legislation so permits or at the request of an interested party; and, (iii) the use of GIs for wine and spirits, even when there is no risk of misleading consumers.

Article 24 concerns international bilateral negotiations on this subject and exceptions. Article 24.4 allows 'continued and similar use' by those who have used GIs in a continuous manner with regard to the same or related goods or

---

[37] Beier uses the term 'exploitation right' to characterise the exclusive nature of design or patent rights, whereas 'designation right' refers to trade mark rights. F-K Beier, 'Exclusive Rights, Statutory Licenses and Compulsory Licenses in Patent and Utility Model Law' (1999) 30(3) *IIC* 254.

[38] *Ex officio*, and, if its legislation so permits, at the request of an interested party.

services either: (a) for at least 10 years preceding 15 April 1994; or, (b) in good faith preceding that date. Examples of these are products with foreign GIs which are designated as 'semi-generic' under the US alcohol, tobacco products and firearms (ATF) regulations,[39] such as burgundy, champagne, chablis, chianti and sherry.

Article 24.5 exonerates protection for trademarks which had been applied for or registered in good faith, or where rights to a trademark have been acquired through use in good faith either before the date of application of TRIPS provisions in that Member as defined in Part VI (transitional arrangements), or before the GIs were protected in their countries of origin. Article 24.6 also allows the continued use of GIs of any other Member with respect to goods or services for which the relevant indication is identical with the term customary, in common language, as the common name for such goods or services in the territory of that Member.

Thus, the TRIPS Agreement introduces significant exceptions to GI protection in Article 24. Under its 'built-in agenda' it provides that negotiations shall be undertaken in the Council for TRIPS concerning the establishment of a multilateral system of notification and registration of GIs for wines eligible for protection in those Members participating in the system. (Article 23.4). In addition, Members agree to enter into negotiations aimed at increasing the protection of individual GIs under Article 23 (Article 24.1). It also provides that the Council for Trade-Related Aspects of Intellectual Property Rights (TRIPS Council – see below under Article 68 of the TRIPS Agreement) shall keep under review the application of the provisions under Section III relating to GIs (Article 24.2).

Industrial Designs (Articles 25–6)

According to Article 25, Members must protect industrial designs that are 'independently created' and 'new or original', for at least 10 years. Under the industrial designs protection, the owner has the right to prevent third parties not having the owner's consent from making, selling or importing Articles bearing or embodying a design which is a copy, or substantially a copy, of the protected design, when such acts are undertaken for commercial purposes (Article 26).

Industrial designs may have characteristics such as aesthetic creation that fall under other areas of IP protection, such as copyright, or other industrial property characteristics, such as utility models. The wording 'new' or 'original' indicates that industrial designs could also be protected by copyright. 'Original' is normally an easier condition to fulfil than 'new'. If designs are protected by copyright, the author is not given exclusive rights granted under industrial designs protection, but has a longer term of protection which is recognised without registration procedures. Members may provide such protection, even if designs

---

[39]   27 CFR – Code of Federal Regulations – Title 27.

are not new or original, on the condition that they do not significantly differ from known designs or combinations of known design features. Members may provide that such protection shall not extend to designs dictated essentially by technical or functional considerations (Article 25, second and third sentences).

Special considerations are given to textile designs for Members to ensure that the cost, examination or publication for securing industrial design protection does not unreasonably impair the opportunity to seek and obtain such protection. The wording 'examination' includes the time it takes for examination, and 'publication' implies the period allowed for keeping it secret for a certain period of time (Article 25.2).

Patents (Articles 27–34)

The Paris Convention (1967) contains few substantive provisions concerning patents (see chapter 2). Significantly, the TRIPS Agreement dealt with substantive provisions in relation to patentable subject matter, the scope and effects of patent protection, non-voluntary licensing and government use of patented technologies, and the term of protection.

Availability of patents based on the same patentability criteria for all fields of technology

Article 27 of the TRIPS Agreement establishes patentable subject matter based on the following principles. The first sentence of Article 27.1 provides that patents shall be 'available for any inventions, whether products or processes, in all fields of technology', provided that they are 'new, involve an inventive step and are capable of industrial application'.[40] Members therefore must protect not only processes but also 'products', including pharmaceutical products, and apply the same criteria of patentability for all fields of technology.

Principles of non-discrimination

The second sentence of Article 27.1 provides that patents shall be available and patent rights 'enjoyable' without discrimination as to the place of invention, the field of technology and whether products are imported or locally produced. Under the TRIPS Agreement, therefore, national laws are not allowed to exclude from patentability an entire technological field. Regulations allowing lenient conditions for compulsory licensing in a specific technological field would also be discriminating one field of technology against others, and would not conform to Article 27.1. In making patents available and patent rights enjoyable, it is

---

[40] Footnote 8 to Art 27.1 of the TRIPS Agreement provides that: 'For the purposes of this Article, the terms "inventive step" and "capable of industrial application" may be deemed by a Member to be synonymous with the terms "non-obvious" and "useful" respectively.'

prohibited to discriminate between right holders based on whether their products are imported or locally produced. The formulation 'whether products are imported or locally produced' in Article 27.1 of TRIPS was a compromise, and has different interpretations (see chapters 4 and 7). The US in 2000 took Brazil to WTO dispute settlement procedures on the issue of Article 68 of Brazil's 1996 Industrial Property Law[41] as not conforming to Articles 27.1 (and 28) of the TRIPS Agreement.[42] Article 68 of the Brazilian law stipulates compulsory licensing conditions due to non-exploitation of the object of the patent within the Brazilian territory – for 'failure to manufacture or incomplete manufacture of the product, or also failure to make full use of the patented process' (see chapters 4,7,10,13).[43] As this dispute resulted in a settlement,[44] we have not yet seen detailed analysis by the WTO dispute organs of the meaning of the provision in Article 27.1 which says '. . . patents shall be available and patent rights enjoyable without discrimination as to . . . whether products are imported or locally produced'.

Possible exclusions from patentable subject matter

Article 27.2 provides for possible exclusions from patentability concerning individual cases. Members may exclude from patentability 'inventions, the prevention within their territory of the commercial exploitation of which is necessary to protect *ordre public* or morality, including to protect human, animal or plant life or health or to avoid serious prejudice to the environment, provided that such exclusion is not made merely because the exploitation is prohibited by their law.'

Article 27.3 of the TRIPS Agreement was a result of a complex compromise among different approaches, and over the patentability requirements and exclusions regarding patentable subject matter offered by Article 27.1. Article 27.3(a) concerns permissible exclusions by categories which are 'diagnostic, therapeutic and surgical methods for humans and animals'. Article 27.3(b), often called the 'biotechnology clause', provides that Members may exclude from patentable subject matter 'plants and animals other than microorganisms, and essentially biological processes[45] for the production of plants or animals other than non-biological and microbiological processes'. According to Article 27.3(b), second

---

[41] Law No 9,279 of 14 May 1996; effective May 1997 www.wipo.int/clea/en/text_pdf. jsp?lang=EN&id=515.

[42] On 30 May 2000, the US requested consultations with the Government of Brazil regarding the above measure (WT/DS199/1). The US and Brazil then held consultations on 29 June 2000 and on 1 December 2000, but, at this stage, failed to reach a mutually satisfactory resolution of the dispute and asked for the establishment of a Panel. ibid para 4.

[43] *Brazil–Measures Affecting Patent Protection*, Request for the Establishment of a Panel by the US (9 January 2001) WT/DS199/3.

[44] *Brazil–Measures Affecting Patent Protection*, Notification of Mutually Agreed Solution (19 July 2001) WT/DS199/4, G/L/454, IP/D/23/Add 1.

[45] The European Patent Office (EPO) has used the degree of technical intervention (biotech intervention such as insertion of genes etc) to decide on whether an 'essentially biological process' is patentable (EPO Examination Guidelines, No X-232.2).

sentence, Members must protect plant varieties but have the choice of the form of protection either by patents, an effective *sui generis* system or any combination thereof. The provisions contained in Article 27.3(b) are subject to review (four years after the date of entry into force of the WTO Agreement – on 'built-in agenda', see below p 185).

Exclusive Rights Conferred by a Patent

Article 28 defines the exclusive rights conferred to the patent owner and provides suggestions for what constitutes infringement. Where the patented subject matter is a product, the patent owner has exclusive rights to prevent third parties not having the owner's consent from the acts of 'making, using, offering for sale, selling, or importing' (Article 28.1(a)).[46] 'Importing' is included among the rights conferred, so it is possible for the right holder to stop the import of infringing goods at customs. It is also possible to interpret Article 28 to mean that the right holder can stop patented goods from the third country (parallel trade), if they are imported without his or her consent. However, a footnote to Article 28.1(a) states that '[t]his right, like all other rights conferred under this Agreement in respect of the use, sale, importation or other distribution of goods, is subject to the provisions of Article 6.' Article 6, in turn, provides that, 'For the purposes of dispute settlement under this Agreement, subject to the provisions of Articles 3 and 4 nothing in this Agreement shall be used to address the issue of the exhaustion of intellectual property rights'(see above p 155). The extent to which the right holder can control the import depends thus on the policy of exhaustion of the country in which the patented goods are imported, which will not be a subject of dispute settlement at the WTO.

Where the subject matter is a process, the owner of the process patent has the exclusive right to prevent third parties not having the owner's consent from the act of using the process, and from the acts of using, offering for sale, selling, or importing for these purposes at least the product obtained directly by that process. The expressions 'at least' and the product 'obtained directly' from the processes of genetic engineering or substance, animals, plants may accompany interpretative uncertainties. The effect of process patents depends mainly on whether the derived product can be protected (product-by-process protection) and the rules concerning the burden of proof. In a country where product-by-process protection is assured, the sale of the product using the claimed process infringes the patent.

Article 29 of the TRIPS Agreement concerns disclosure requirements for patent applicants. The first sentence of Article 29.1 obliges WTO Members to require: 1) that applicants describe, in the patent specification (on a 'written description' of the invention, see also chapter 1) 'enablement' conditions in a

---

[46] This right, like all other rights conferred under this agreement in respect of the use, sale, importation or other distribution of goods, is subject to the provisions of Art 6.

manner 'sufficiently clear and complete'; and 2) that the invention be carried out by a person skilled in the art. Most patent laws around the world incorporate the idea that the invention must be described in such a way that a person skilled in the art will be enabled to make and use the invention defined in the claim(s) of the particular application or patent. The purpose of the enablement requirement as codified in 35 USC 112, according to the USPTO, is to ensure that the invention is communicated to the interested public in a meaningful way.[47] The second sentence of Article 29.1 TRIPS states that Members 'may' require the applicant to indicate the 'best mode' for carrying out the invention known to the inventor at the filing date or, where priority is claimed, at the priority date of the application. The best mode is clearly inspired by US law 35 USC 112.[48] Its idea is to prevent inventors from disclosing only what they know to be their second-best embodiment, retaining the best for themselves.[49] The US courts in particular have frequently found broad claims to proteins and DNA sequences to be invalid, for a lack of enablement[50] (see chapter 3). The 'best mode' disclosure sometimes conflicts with the protection of trade secrets. However, the best mode requirement is limited only to what the inventor knows at the time of patent filing (when he may not have completed the work).[51] Article 29.2 of the TRIPS Agreement provides that Members may require an applicant for a patent to provide information concerning the applicant's corresponding foreign applications and grants. This provision seems to aim at facilitating the task of examination, particularly in developing countries.

According to Article 33, 'The term of protection available shall not end before the expiration of a period of 20 years counted from the filing date.' In *Canada–Patent Term*, the Panel and the Appellate Body interpreted the word 'available' in Article 33 to mean 'available, as a matter of right', ie, 'available as a matter of legal right and certainty'.[52]

Article 34 delineates the rules concerning the burden of proof in civil proceedings against infringements of process patents for obtaining a product. Where the alleged infringer's product is structurally identical to the product manufactured by the patented process, the judiciary of Members has the obligation to order the defendant (alleged infringer) to prove that the process to obtain an identical

---

[47] www.uspto.gov/web/offices/pac/mpep/documents/2100_2164.htm.

[48] ibid.

[49] *Re Nelson* 280 F 2d 172, 126 USPQ 242 (CCPA 1960).

[50] PW Grubb, *Patents for Chemicals, Pharmaceuticals and Biotechnology: Fundamentals of Global Law, Practice and Strategy*, 4th edn (Oxford University Press, 2004) 258–61.

[51] 35 USC 112 requires three conditions to be described in the specification: (i) written description; (ii) enablement; and, (iii) best mode. The purpose of the written description requirement is to clearly convey the information that an applicant has invented the subject matter which is claimed (*Re Barker* 559 F 2d 588, 592 n 4, 194 USPQ 470, 473 n 4 (CCPA 1977), or to put the public in possession of what the applicant claims as the invention. See *Regents of the University of California v Eli Lilly* 119 F 3d 1559, 1566, 43 USPQ2d 1398, 1404 (Fed Cir 1997), cert denied, 523 US 1089 (1998). Written descriptions convey more technical knowledge than claims which show the scope of exclusive rights. See for lack of written description, *University of Rochester v GD Searle & Co* 358 F 3d 916, 920–3, 69 USPQ 2d 1886, 1890–93 (Fed Cir 2004) (see ch 3)

[52] *Canada–Patent Term*, Appellate Body Report (n 8) para 91.

product is different from the patented process, if at least either of these following conditions are met: (a) the product obtained by the patented process is new;
or (b) there is a substantial likelihood that the identical product was made by the
process, and the owner of the patent has been unable through reasonable efforts
to determine the process actually used. In the absence of proof to the contrary,
the defendant is presumed to have obtained the product by the patented process.

The above condition (a) had been the rule in most developed countries[53] other
than the US, and (b) is based on Section 104 of the US Patent Law (chapter 4).[54]
This rule concerning burden of proof was introduced due to the fact that it may
be extremely difficult for an owner of a process patent to prove that an identical product was manufactured using his or her patented process. It reverses the
evidential principle that the person asserting a fact must prove it. The terms in
Article 34.1(a) and (b) are based on national law practices and therefore may
not be sufficiently clear. For example, the term 'new' in (a) can be interpreted in
several ways, such as being publicly unknown in a country, or not published in
foreign journals. At what point in time something is to be considered 'new' is
also often unclear. The criteria for determining whether there is 'a substantial
likelihood' or whether 'reasonable efforts' have been made in (b) could be subjective.[55] However, the conditions in (a) and (b) are not cumulative, and therefore, at least possible TRIPS inconsistencies in domestic laws can be avoided.
Thus, Article 34.2 provides that: 'Any Member shall be free to provide that the
burden of proof indicated in paragraph 1 shall be on the alleged infringer only if
the condition referred to in subparagraph (a) is fulfilled or only if the condition
referred to in subparagraph (b) is fulfilled'. Article 34.3 provides that: 'In the
adduction of proof to the contrary, the legitimate interests of defendants in protecting their manufacturing and business secrets shall be taken into account.' If
the product was in fact produced by a different process, the alleged infringer will
have to rebut the presumption, even though he or she may not want to disclose
his or her process to competitors. In these situations, the court must provide the
means by which to protect the defendant's trade secrets. Once evidence is produced by the defendant that eliminates the prima facie presumption, the burden
of proof shifts to the plaintiff.[56]

Article 32 concerns patent revocation and forfeiture and provides that an
opportunity for judicial review of any decision to revoke or forfeit a patent shall
be available. Other rules relating to this subject follow the provisions of the
TRIPS Agreement and the Paris Convention as incorporated in the former.

---

[53] The rule on the reversal of the burden of proof was introduced by the 1891 German Patent Law
(Article 139) and incorporated in the patent laws of Italy, Belgium and Spain.UNCTAD-ICTSD,
Resource Book on TRIPS and Development, (Cambridge University Press, 2005) 497–98,

[54] A Oshima, *Chikujou Kaisetu TRIPS Kyoutei (Detailed Analysis of the TRIPS)* (Tokyo, JMC,
1999) 163–64.

[55] ibid 163–66.

[56] D Gervais, *The TRIPS Agreement: Drafting History and Analysis* (London, Sweet & Maxwell,
1998) 172.

Exceptions to the exclusive rights conferred by a patent

Article 30 provides that exceptions to the exclusive rights conferred by patents may be granted, if these exceptions: (i) are 'limited'; (ii) do not unreasonably conflict with a normal exploitation of the patent; and (iii) do not unreasonably prejudice the legitimate interests of the patent owner, taking account of the legitimate interests of third parties. Article 30 exceptions may involve legislation relating to the general effect on patent owners and authorised parties.

The Panel in *Canada–Pharmaceutical Patents*[57] clarified the meaning of the very abstract provisions in Article 30. The Panel analysed the meaning of the above conditions (i), (ii) and (iii), mostly by analysing their wording, and affirmed that these conditions are basically independent and cumulative (chapter 7).

Limitations on or exceptions to patent rights, such as rights based on prior use,[58] acts done privately and for non-commercial purposes or acts done for certain experimental purposes,[59] exist in most countries' laws or have been recognised by courts. During the Uruguay Round, the negotiators discussed these exceptions and worked towards establishing a list of exemptions to patent rights. However, they found that listing all kinds of nationally divergent exceptions in the TRIPS Agreement would require too many details. Moreover, the scope of these exceptions differed in each country, and court decisions were evolving. Some laws limited the scope of experimental research strictly to scientific and non-commercial research, whereas the US law contained so-called '*Bolar* exemptions' whereby experimental use of patented medicines for submission of clinical data to the Food and Drug Administration (FDA) is exempted from infringement under certain conditions.[60]

As there is no provision concerning exceptions to patent rights in the Paris Convention, Article 9(2) of the Berne Convention served as a model in the drafting of Article 30 of the TRIPS Agreement. As result, the wording of Article 30 TRIPS resembles that of Article 13 TRIPS relating to 'limitations and exceptions'

---

[57] *Canada–Pharmaceutical Patents*, Panel Report (n 28).

[58] Although there are a variety of practices in different countries, the general idea of 'prior use' exception is that the person who had been carrying out or preparing for manufacturing the invention before another person's patent application of the same invention may continue to use it.

[59] *Canada–Pharmaceutical Patents* (n 28) paras 7.20–7.21.

[60] Regulatory exemptions for uses reasonably related to the development and submission of information under a Federal Law which regulates the manufacture, use, or sale of drugs or veterinary biological products). The *Bolar* exemption had been added to the US patent statute 35 USC § 271(e)(1) in 1984, following the ruling of the Court of Appeals for the Federal Circuit (CAFC) in *Roche Prod Inc v Bolar Pharmaceutical Co* 733 F 2d 858 (Fed Cir., cert. denied, 469 US 856 (1984). In this case, a generic manufacturer had used a patented invention to test and apply for marketing authorisation of its version of a patented medicine. The Court decided that this amounted to an infringement of the relevant patents, the common law 'experimental use' defence covering only experimentation for scientific, not commercial, purposes, and the generic manufacturer's activities. This regulatory exemption came to be regulated by the EU in Art 10(6) of Directive 2001/83/EC as amended by Directive 2004/27/EC. In Japan, the Supreme Court in 1999 recognised regulatory exemption in its judgment over the interpretation of Art 69.1 of the Japanese Patent Law (*Otsuka Pharmaceutical Co Ltd v Towa Yakuhin KK*, Case no 1998). On the regulatory exemptions in the Chinese Patent Law, see ch 10.

provided for copyrights and 'related rights'. Article 13 TRIPS, in turn, reproduced the wording of Article 9(2) of the Berne Convention. However, Article 30 is not identical to Article 13. For example, 'taking account of the legitimate interests of third parties' is included in the above condition (iii).

Article 31 is entitled 'Other Use Without the Authorisation of the Right Holder'. Footnote 7 to this provision explains that 'other use' refers to use other than that allowed under Article 30. Article 31(a) TRIPS provides that compulsory licensing shall be considered on 'its individual merits'. No compulsory licensing on bundling of patents or routine issuance would therefore be permitted.

As a result of the negotiation, Article 31 incorporates three very different types of case-by-case use without authorisation of the right holder: government use, authorisation to use the patented technologies by the third party in the market, and state intervention to rectify anti-competitive behaviour, based on national competition laws (chapter 4). Also as a result of the negotiation, Article 31 does not concern grounds for such licensing but regulates, primarily, procedural conditions for the granting of a compulsory licence. Exceptionally, Article 31(c) limits the grounds for compulsory licensing of semi-conductor technology only for public non-commercial use, or to remedy a practice determined by judicial or administrative process to be anti-competitive.

Article 31(b) stipulates a basic procedural rule for such use of patented inventions. The proposed user must, prior to such use, make efforts to obtain authorisation from the right holder on reasonable commercial terms and conditions. Only if such efforts have been unsuccessful within a reasonable period of time, will a compulsory licence be permitted. However, this requirement may be waived in the cases of (i) a national emergency or other circumstances of extreme urgency, or (ii) public non-commercial use. In the case of (i), the right holder shall, nevertheless, be notified as soon as reasonably practicable. In the case of (ii), where the government or contractor knows or has demonstrable grounds to know that a valid patent is or will be used by or for the government, the right holder shall be informed promptly.

Article 31(c)–(j) stipulates additional conditions for compulsory licensing as follows: The scope and duration of such use shall be limited to the purpose for which it was authorized (c); non-exclusive (d), non-assignable, except with that part of the enterprise or goodwill which enjoys such use (e); authorised predominantly for the supply of the domestic market of the Member authorizing such use (f); liable, subject to adequate protection of the legitimate interests of the persons so authorized, to be terminated if and when the circumstances which led to it cease to exist and are unlikely to recur and the competent authority shall have the authority to review, upon motivated request, the continued existence of these circumstances (g); the right holder shall be paid adequate remuneration in the circumstances of each case, taking into account the economic value of the authorisation (h); the legal validity of any decision relating to the authorisation of such use shall be subject to judicial review or other independent review by a distinct higher authority in that Member (i); any decision relating to the remuneration provided in respect of such use shall be subject to judicial review or other independent review by a distinct higher authority in that Member (j).

Article 31(l) provides specific conditions for compulsory licensing on the grounds of a dependent patent, ie where such use is authorised to permit the exploitation of a patent (the second patent), which cannot be done without infringing on another patent (the first patent). According to this provision: (i) the second patent must involve an important technical advance of considerable economic significance in relation to the first patent; (ii) the owner of the first patent shall be entitled to a cross-licence on reasonable terms to use the invention claimed in the second patent; and, (iii) the use authorised must be non-assignable except with the assignment of the second patent.

Article 31(k) provides specific procedural rules for compulsory licensing to remedy a practice determined after judicial or administrative process to be anti-competitive. According to this provision, Members are not obliged to apply the conditions set forth in Article 31(b) and 31(f) above. The need to correct anti-competitive practices may be taken into account in determining the amount of remuneration in such cases. Competent authorities shall have the authority to refuse termination of authorisation if and when the conditions which led to such authorisation are likely to recur.

The amended Article 31 bis of the TRIPS Agreement has not yet entered into force. It is based on the agreement reached at the WTO General Council on 6 December 2005[61] and responds to paragraph 6 of the Doha Declaration on the TRIPS Agreement and Public Health.[62] This amendment transforms into a formal provision the Agreement of the General Council Decision of 30 August 2003[63] concerning the waiver of Article 31(f) for the purposes of production of a pharmaceutical product(s) and its export. For the eligible importing Member, Article 31(h) is also waivered in this Decision (see chapter 9).

Section 6: Layout Designs (Topographies) of Integrated Circuits

The protection of layout designs (arrangements of a two- or three-dimensional layout or topography of an integrated circuit (IC, or 'chip')) is dealt with by the multilateral Treaty on Intellectual Property in respect of Integrated Circuits (Washington Treaty, or IPIC Treaty), signed in Washington on 26 May 1989, but this treaty has not entered in force[64].

[61] General Council Decision of 6 December 2005 (8 December 2005) WT/L/641 ('Amendment of the TRIPS Agreement').

[62] Declaration on the TRIPS agreement and public health, adopted by Ministerial Conference on 14 November 2001 (20 November 2001) WT/MIN(01)/DEC/2.

[63] *Amendment of the TRIPS Agreement–Extension of the Period for the Acceptance by Members of the Protocol Amending the TRIPS Agreement*, General Council Decision of 18 December 2007 (21 December 2007) WT/L/711.

[64] Unacceptable provisions in the IPIC Treaty seem to relate to the term of protection, the treatment of innocent infringers, the applicability of the protection to articles containing infringing integrated circuits, and compulsory licensing. Otten and Wager (n 7) 402.

Articles 2 to 7 (other than paragraph 3 of Article 6), as well as Article 12 and paragraph 3 of Article 16 are incorporated into the TRIPs agreement (Article 35 TRIPS). According to Article 36, importing, selling, or otherwise distributing without authorisation of the owner for commercial purposes an integrated circuit in which a protected layout design is incorporated, or an Article incorporating such an integrated circuit only in so far as it continues to contain an unlawfully reproduced layout design, is unlawful. Finished products, such as personal computers, which include chips which infringe upon IPRs, are themselves also considered to be infringements. However, the rights of the owner do not reach good-faith users, who are nevertheless obliged to pay if they receive a notice of warning. Article 38 provides a minimum term of protection of 10 years (instead of eight years in the IPIC Treaty), counted from the date of filing an application for registration or from the first commercial exploitation wherever in the world it occurs (Article 38.1). If the registration is not required, the minimum term of protection is 10 years from the first commercial exploitation (Article 38.2), although this could be 15 years from its creation. IPIC provisions concerning compulsory licensing were not incorporated in the TRIPS Agreement, and therefore such licensing of layout designs under the TRIPS Agreement relies on its Article 31(a)–(k) (Article 37.2).

Section 7: Protection of Undisclosed Information

Article 39 is the sole Article within Section 7. Paragraph 1 of the Article requires Members to protect effectively 'undisclosed information'referred to in paragraphs 2 and 3, against unfair competition, as provided in Article 10 *bis* of the Paris Convention (1967).

Undisclosed information covers trade secrets and know-how. The concept of trade secrets is often used in the US to designate undisclosed information of commercial or business value, and includes know-how, which refers to technological knowledge for designing or manufacturing the product or information needed for any other technical operations.

Article 10 bis of the Paris Convention requires Contracting Parties to assure effective protection of undisclosed information against 'unfair competition' (which could be 'unfair commercial practice' or 'unfair use'), which is contrary to honest practices in industrial or commercial matters, particularly those: (i) creating confusion with the establishment, the goods, or the industrial or commercial activities, of a competitor; (ii) false allegations in the course of trade of such a nature as to discredit the establishment, the goods, or the industrial or commercial activities, of a competitor; and (iii) indications or allegations the use of which in the course of trade is liable to mislead the public as to the nature, the manufacturing process, the characteristics, the suitability for their purpose, or the quantity, of the goods. The introduction of Article 39 caused undisclosed information to be protected by public international law.

Paragraph 2 refers to unlawful disclosure of information, acquired by, or used by others without the consent of the right holder 'in a manner contrary to honest commercial practices', and paragraph 3 refers to the protection of specific data against 'unfair commercial use.'

The protection of 'undisclosed information' differs significantly between Articles 39.2 and 39.3. According to Article 39.2, which refers broadly to trade secrets,

> natural and legal persons shall have the possibility of preventing information lawfully within their control from being disclosed to, acquired by, or used by others without their consent in a manner contrary to honest commercial practices, if such information satisfies the following conditions:
>
> (a) is secret in the sense that it is not, as a body or in the precise configuration and assembly of its components, generally known among or readily accessible to persons within the circles that normally deal with the kind of information in question;
> (b) has commercial value because it is secret; and
> (c) has been subject to reasonable steps under the circumstances, by the person lawfully in control of the information, to keep it secret.

For the purpose of this provision, a footnote to Article 39.2 of the TRIPS Agreement defines 'a manner contrary to honest commercial practices' to mean 'at least practices such as breach of contract, breach of confidence and inducement to breach, and it includes the acquisition of undisclosed information by third parties who knew, or were grossly negligent in failing to know, that such practices were involved in the acquisition'.

One matter on which TRIPS provisions are implicit or silent is reverse engineering – the process of discovering the technical principle or knowledge behind a product. The purpose of reverse engineering could be either curiosity or commercial – to get a copy product to market more quickly and more cheaply than the original product. In traditional engineering industries (as opposed to newer industries such as the semiconductor chip industry, the computer software industry and the digital content industry), reverse engineering has generally been allowed, mainly because such an approach is generally too costly and time-consuming for the copy product to arrive at the market profitably[65] and the delay normally protects the originator sufficiently to recoup his initial R&D expense. Under patent law, there is no need for reverse engineering, as the patent specification should inform the relevant technical community how to make the invention and the best mode of making it (see chapter 1). Reverse engineering activities normally will not infringe a patent. Under the unfair competition laws of many countries, the owner of trade secrets has no exclusive right to possession or use of the secret information. Protection is available only against 'a wrongful acquisition, use, or disclosure of the trade secret'.[66] Under Article 39.2, this seems to hold also for reverse engineering.

---

[65] For detailed economic and legal analyses of reverse engineering in the industrial sectors, P Samuelson and S Scotchmer, 'The Law and Economics of Reverse Engineering' (2002) 111(7) *The Yale Law Journal* 1575–1663.

[66] American Law Institute, *Restatement of the Law (Third), Unfair Competition* (1995).

Article 39.3 concerns information dealt with in a specific regulatory context for pharmaceutical or agricultural chemical products, ie, clinical or other test data which is submitted to regulatory authorities for marketing approval. It reads:

> [WTO] Members, when requiring, as a condition of approving the marketing of pharmaceutical or of agricultural chemical products which utilize new chemical entities, the submission of undisclosed test or other data, the origination of which involves a considerable effort, shall protect such data against unfair commercial use. In addition, Members shall protect such data against disclosure, except where necessary to protect the public, or unless steps are taken to ensure that the data are protected against unfair commercial use.

According to the wording of Article 39.3, the 'information' referred to is protected because: (i) chemical entities utilised in the submitted drugs are 'new chemical entities'; (ii) the data concerned are 'undisclosed'; and (iii) the origination of the data involved a 'considerable effort'. The reasons for protecting this data therefore seem to be a mixture of the need to protect investment and the need to protect innovative efforts. The scope of the 'products which utilize new chemical entities' in the regulatory process is not necessarily clear. For example, marketing approval of pharmaceutical products is decided from a therapeutic point of view and concerns the safety and efficacy of the drugs to be marketed. Approval also regulates when following copy products should be authorised, safeguarding at the same time the investment and creativity used for the research of the applicant. In such a regulatory process, the therapeutic values of new medicines are not necessarily associated with the chemical forms of the products (see chapter 13).

Two dispute settlement cases under Article 39.3 were resolved by mutually agreed solutions. In the first case, Pakistan and the US agreed[67] that under Articles 70.8 and 70.9 of the TRIPS Agreement, Pakistan was required to establish a system for the filing of patent applications on pharmaceutical and agricultural chemical product inventions by 1 January 1995 and to establish a system to grant exclusive marketing rights to such patent applicants if they meet certain criteria. To fulfil these obligations, Pakistan adopted the necessary measures on 4 February 1997.[68] Consultations under the WTO dispute settlement mechanism were undertaken between the US and Argentina, inter alia, on the protection of test data for pharmaceuticals and agrochemicals. The issues raised seemed to garner a mutually agreed solution of which the Dispute Settlement Body (DSB)[69] was notified (chapters 9 and 12).

---

[67] *Pakistan–Patent Protection for Pharmaceutical and Agricultural Chemical Products* (WT/DS36).

[68] Ordinance No XXVI. The mutually agreed solution was notified on 28 February 1997 (WT/DS36/4)

[69] *Argentina–Patent Protection for Pharmaceuticals and Test Data Protection for Agricultural Chemicals* (WT/DS171); *Argentina–Certain Measures on the Protection of Patents and Test Data* (WT/DS196). Notification of Mutually Agreed Solution WT/DS171/3, WT/DS196/4 (20 June 2002). Concerning the protection of test data, the parties will continue consultations to assess the progress

Section 8: Control of Anti-Competitive Practices in Contractual Licences

Section 8 of the TRIPS Agreement contains only Article 40 and deals with control of anti-competitive practices in contractual licences. Relevant provisions are found in Article 8.2, part of 'the general provisions and basic principles' of Part I of the Agreement, and which provides that there must be '[a]ppropriate measures to prevent the abuse of intellectual property rights by right holders or the resort to practices which unreasonably restrain trade or adversely affect the international transfer of technology.'

Article 40.1 establishes that WTO Members agree that some licensing practices or conditions pertaining to intellectual property rights which restrain competition may have adverse effects on trade and may impede the transfer and dissemination of technology (chapter 4).

Article 40.2 establishes that Members have the right to specify in their legislation appropriate measures to intervene in such practices, 'which may include for example exclusive grantback[70] conditions, conditions preventing challenges to validity and coercive package licensing, in the light of the relevant laws and regulations of that Member.' These measures must be consistent with other provisions of the TRIPS Agreement, and based on case-by-case analysis of anti-competitive effect on competition in the relevant market. Article 40.3 provides for consultation and cooperation among Members, if abuse in the meaning of Article 40 is practiced in the requesting country (chapter 9).

PART III: ENFORCEMENT OF INTELLECTUAL PROPERTY RIGHTS (ARTICLES 41–61)

Part III concerning enforcement is one of the original contributions of the TRIPS Agreement. The pre-existing treaties on IPRs have been silent on the issue of enforcement, whereas the TRIPS Agreement requires Members to provide domestic procedures and remedies so that right holders can effectively enforce their rights. Part III consists of five sections made up of 21 Articles in total: section 1 (Article 41), general obligations relating to all provisions of Part III; section 2 (Articles 42–9), rules on civil and administrative procedures and remedies; section 3 (Article 50), provisional measures; section 4 (Articles 51–60), specific requirements concerning border measures; section 5 (Article 61), criminal procedures. These provisions are sufficiently precise to provide for effective enforcement action, but they recognise differences between national legal systems.

of the legislative process of approval of the related items of the notification, and in the light of this assessment, the United States may decide to continue consultations or request the establishment of a panel related to Art 39.3 of the TRIPS Agreement.

[70] A grantback is 'an arrangement under which a licensee agrees to extend to the licensor of intellectual property the right to use the licensee's improvements of the licensed technology'. H Hovenkamp, MD Janis and MA Lemley, *IP and antitrust: an analysis of antitrust principles applied to intellectual property law* (Aspen Law & Business, 2002) App B-34.

Article 41.1 stipulates that: 'Members shall ensure that enforcement procedures as specified in this Part are *available* under their law so as to permit *effective action* against any act of infringement of intellectual property rights covered by this Agreement, including *expeditious remedies to prevent infringements* and remedies which constitute a *deterrent to* further infringements' (emphasis added). The principle of enforcement in Article 41.1 is not only about 'effectiveness of action'. The sentence that follows, says: 'These procedures shall be applied in such a manner as to avoid the creation of barriers to legitimate trade and to provide for safeguards against their abuse.' Article 41.1 further states that 'These procedures shall be applied in such a manner as to avoid the creation of barriers to legitimate trade and to provide for safeguards against their abuse.'

Procedures for enforcement must be 'fair and equitable' and 'not unnecessarily complicated or costly'(Article 41.2); the decisions should 'preferably' be in writing and reasoned and should be made available at least to the parties to the proceeding without undue delay (Article 41.3). Final administrative decisions are subject to judicial review (Article 41.4).

Significantly, Article 41.5 explicitly states that: 'Members need not set up a special judicial system for the enforcement of IPRs.' This means that it is possible for each country to provide for the enforcement of IPRs in its own laws, including through its civil, criminal, and civil procedure laws. This is in line with the balance struck by Article 1.1 of the TRIPS Agreement concerning the 'nature and scope of obligations', which says that 'Members shall give effect to the provisions of this Agreement . . . Members shall be free to determine the appropriate method of implementing the provisions of this Agreement within their own legal system and practice.' The Panel in *China–Intellectual Property Rights* stated that Article 41.5, which China invoked, is an important provision in the overall balance of rights and obligations relating to the whole enforcement provisions in Part III of the TRIPS Agreement.[71]

Part III contains those provisions which instruct Members to make 'available' certain powers for existing courts and other authorities. The dictionary meaning of 'available' is 'obtainable'. According to the Appellate Body Report in *US–Section 211 Appropriation Act*, 'available' in the context of Article 41 means that 'right holders' are entitled to 'have access to civil judicial procedures that are effective in bringing about the enforcement of their rights covered by the Agreement.' The Panel in *China–Intellectual Property Rights* stated that the obligation to 'have' the authority is not an obligation to 'exercise' authority.' The Panel asserted that the phrase 'shall have the authority' is contrasted with the terminology used in the minimum standards of Part II of the TRIPS Agreement, such as 'Members shall provide.'[72]

---

[71] *China-Intellectual Property Rights* (n 2) para 7.594. See ch 7.

[72] ibid para 7.236. 'Shall have the authority' is used throughout the enforcement obligations in sections 2, 3 and 4 of Part III of the TRIPS Agreement, specifically, in Arts 43.1, 44.1, 45.1, 45.2, 46, 48.1, 50.1, 50.2, 50.3, 50.7, 53.1, 56, 57 and 59.

Section 2 of Part III describes in detail civil and administrative procedures and remedies to be applied by the domestic institutions, according to the principles delineated in Section 1 (Article 41). Article 42 deals with fair and equitable procedures; Article 43, evidence; Article 44, injunctions; Article 45, damages; Article 46, other remedies; Article 47, right of information; Article 48, indemnification of the defendant; Article 49, administrative procedures. Both Sections 1 and 2 of Part III establish 'internationally agreed minimum standards' that Members are bound to implement in their domestic legislation, according to the Appellate Body in *US–Section 211 Appropriation Act*.[73]

Section 3 (Article 50) of the TRIPS Agreement provides that 'the judicial authorities shall have the authority to order prompt and effective provisional measures'. The purpose of these measures is (a) to prevent entry into the channels of commerce in their jurisdiction of imported goods 'immediately' after customs clearance and to preserve relevant evidence in regard to alleged infringement, and (b) to preserve relevant evidence in regard to the alleged infringement. The judicial authorities shall have the authority to adopt these measures even without hearing of parties (*inaudita altera parte*), where appropriate, in particular where any delay is likely to cause irreparable harm to the right holder, or where there is a demonstrable risk of evidence being destroyed (Article 50.2). In these cases, the parties affected shall be given notice, without delay after the execution of the measures at the latest. A review, including a right to be heard, shall take place upon request of the defendant, with a view to deciding, within a reasonable period after the notification of the measures, whether these measures shall be modified, revoked or confirmed (Article 50.4).

Section 4 (Articles 51–60) concerns border measures which are taken primarily at the customs points of the importing country, basically by the initiative of the right holder, to prevent the import of goods suspected of infringing IPRs. Possibilities for establishing rules and procedures concerning border measures had been discussed within the GATT since the Tokyo Round in the 1970s. In the Uruguay Round negotiations, 'establishing a multilateral framework of principles, rules and disciplines dealing with international trade in counterfeit goods' was one of the goals of developed countries.[74] These goals were integrated in the Preamble of the TRIPS Agreement.

The TRIPS Agreement introduces in Article 51 the procedures for the 'suspension of release by customs authorities' concerning the importation of counterfeit trademark or pirated copyright goods. According to the first sentence of Article 51, Members have an obligation to enable a right holder, who has valid grounds for suspecting that the importation of counterfeit trademark or pirated

---

[73] *US–Section 211 Appropriations Act* (n 9) paras 205–7.

[74] The principle of the prohibition of the release for free circulation of counterfeit goods was proposed by the EC in 1987. The text of the Council Reg (EEC) 3842/86 of 1 December 1986, laying down measures to prohibit the release for free circulation of counterfeit goods, was communicated to the Negotiating Group to circulate, for information, in MTN.GNG/NG11/W/3 of 3 April 1987. Reg (EEC) 3842/86 was replaced in 1995 by Reg (EC) 3295/94, and in July 2004, by Reg 1381/2003.

copyright goods may take place, to lodge an application in writing with competent administrative or judicial authorities, for the suspension by the customs authorities of the release into free circulation of such goods. Article 51 adds, in the second sentence, that Members 'may' adopt the same procedures to enable such application for 'other IPRs' such as patents, industrial designs or semiconductor layouts, provided that the requirements of section 4 are met.

Footnote 13 to Article 51 states that 'there shall be no obligation to apply [suspension of release] procedures to imports of goods put on the market in another country by or with the consent of the right holder, or to goods in transit.' The agreement to disagree on the question of parallel trade during the Uruguay Round negotiation is reflected in Article 6. Footnote 13 is the reminder of this disagreement and states that 'Members are not obliged to apply border procedures to imports of goods put on the market in another country by or with the consent of the right holder'. Footnote 13 also says that Members are not required to apply such procedures to goods in transit.[75]

Footnote 14 to Article 51 defines counterfeit and pirated goods for the purposes of the TRIPS Agreement.[76] The definitions of trademark infringement in this footnote can be narrower than trademark or copyright infringements under Article 16 of the Agreement, because the latter includes similar signs for goods or services which are similar to those in respect of which the trademark is registered. Pirated goods, in footnote 14, include only those goods which infringe copyrights or related rights under the law of the country of importation. Such rights may also include the moral rights of authors and performers and the rights of publication.

Article 52 delineates the requirements for the right holder in initiating procedures under Article 51 for the customs authorities to take action. The applicant is required to provide adequate evidence to satisfy the competent authorities that, under the laws of the country of importation, there is prima facie an infringement of the right holder's IPRs. The applicant is also required to supply a sufficiently detailed description of the goods to make them readily recognisable by the customs authorities. As a result of the US proposal to introduce due process when goods are suspended by customs authorities, Article 53 concerning security was introduced.[77] According to Article 53.1, the competent authorities

---

[75] *European Union And A Member State - Seizure of Generic Drugs in Transit* requests for consultations by India (WT/DS408/1,11 May 2010) and by Brazil (WT/DS409/1, 19 May 2010). See ch 14.

[76] '(a) "counterfeit trademark goods" shall mean any goods, including packaging, bearing without authorization a trademark which is identical to the trademark validly registered in respect of such goods, or which cannot be distinguished in its essential aspects from such a trademark, and which thereby infringes the rights of the owner of the trademark in question under the law of the country of importation.

(b) "pirated copyright goods" shall mean any goods which are copies made without the consent of the right holder or person duly authorised by the right holder in the country of production and which are made directly or indirectly from an article where the making of that copy would have constituted an infringement of a copyright or a related right under the law of the country of importation.'

[77] Oshima, (n 54) 233. Art 17A of the Anell Draft proposed that: 'PARTIES shall seek to avoid border enforcement procedures being abused by means of unjustified or frivolous applications. For

shall have the authority to require an applicant to provide a financial security or equivalent assurance, sufficient to protect the defendant. Article 53.2 stipulates that the owner, importer, or consignee of such goods shall be entitled to their release on the posting of a financial security in an amount sufficient to protect the right holder for any infringement.[78]

Other procedural rules concerning border measures include notice of suspension (Article 54), duration of suspension (Article 55), indemnification of the importer and of the owner of the goods (article 56), right of inspection and information (Article 57), *ex officio* action (Article 58), remedies (Article 59) and *de minimis* imports (Article 60). Although Article 58 provides certain rules for official conduct, the TRIPS Agreement imposes no obligation for Members to intervene *ex officio,* as Article 58 states: 'Where Members require competent authorities to act upon their own initiative and to suspend the release of goods . . . .'.

Article 59 requires Members to empower competent authorities to order the destruction or disposal of infringing goods in accordance with the principles of enforcement set out in Article 46. In order to create an effective deterrent to infringement, Article 46 stipulates that the judicial authorities 'shall have the authority to order that goods that they have found to be infringing be, without compensation of any sort, disposed of outside the channels of commerce . . .' and, in regard to counterfeit trademark goods, 'shall not allow the re-exportation of the infringing goods in an unaltered state or subject them to a different customs procedure, other than in exceptional circumstances'.

The Panel in *China–Intellectual Property Rights* found that the interpretation of Article 59 is guided by the common objective set out in Article 46, ie, 'to create an effective deterrent to infringement'[79] and by the principle of proportionality between the remedies specified in the TRIPS provision and any alternative remedies.[80]

Section 5, entitled 'criminal procedures' is made up only of Article 61, which creates an obligation on Members to provide for criminal procedures and penalties 'at least in cases of wilful trademark counterfeiting or copyright piracy on a commercial scale'. Remedies must be 'sufficient to provide a deterrent' to infringement, and the level of penalties applied in these cases must be consistent with that applied for crimes of 'a corresponding gravity'.

---

this purpose, they [may] [shall] require a right holder who has lodged an application according to point 16 to provide a security or equivalent assurance. Such security or equivalent assurance shall not unreasonably deter recourse to these procedures.'

[78] This occurs when the goods have been suspended by customs authorities on the basis of a decision other than by a judicial or other independent authority, and the period provided for in Art 55 has expired without the granting of provisional relief by the duly empowered authority, and provided that all other conditions for importation have been complied with.

[79] *China–Intellectual Property Rights* (n 2) para 7.391. Art 46 explicitly says: 'simple removal of the trademark unlawfully affixed is not sufficient to permit release of counterfeit trademark goods into the channels of commerce other than in exceptional cases'.

[80] *China–Intellectual Property Rights* (n 2) para 7.263.

The meaning of 'commercial scale' is particularly unclear and it is possible to interpret this phrase in several ways. In *China–Intellectual Property Protection* for example, China argued that it should be interpreted to mean 'for profit' or where it has a commercial effect. In the context of a business, however, there are many ways of interpreting profit, including indirect profit. The Panel, in an attempt to clarify the meaning of 'on a commercial scale', set out criteria not only in terms of the nature of activity, but also its relative size in terms of a market benchmark (see chapter 7). [81]

PART IV: ACQUISITION AND MAINTENANCE OF INTELLECTUAL PROPERTY RIGHTS AND RELATED *INTER PARTES* PROCEDURES (ARTICLE 62)

Part IV of the TRIPS Agreement sets out some general rules on the acquisition and maintenance of IPRs, so that unnecessary procedural difficulties in acquiring or maintaining IPRs will not impair the protection required by the Agreement.[82]

Article 62 is the sole Article under Part IV, and establishes the standards concerning the acquisition and maintenance of IPRs under sections 2 to 6 of Part II. This means that these standards do not cover section 1, which concerns copyright and related rights, or section 7 on the protection of undisclosed information. Article 6.1 allows Members to require 'reasonable' procedures and formalities such as examinations and registration for the acquisition or maintenance of these rights, provided that such procedures and formalities are 'consistent with the provisions of this Agreement'. Article 62.2 obliges Members to ensure that granting or registration of the rights are achieved within a reasonable period of time so as to avoid 'unwarranted curtailment of the period of protection'. Article 62.3 extends the application of the right of priority defined in Article 4 of the Paris Convention (1967) to service marks. This provision brings trademark protection to service marks, which had not previously been protected necessarily by trademarks. Article 62.4 sets out that procedures concerning the acquisition or maintenance of intellectual property rights, administrative revocation and *inter partes* procedures such as opposition, revocation and cancellation, are subject to the rules contained in Articles 41.2 and 41.3 of TRIPS. Article 41.2 concerns fair and equitable procedures, and Article 41.3 reasoned decisions. *Inter partes* procedures are initiated by a third party (and not *ex officio* by the administration). Article 62.5 gives Members the obligation to make available a judicial or quasi-judicial authority to review the final administrative decisions in any of the procedures referred to under paragraph 4, such as opposition, revocation and cancellation. If these third party opposition or administrative revocations are unsuccessful, there is no obligation for Members to provide review of such acts, provided that third parties or the administration may challenge invalidation procedures.

---

[81] ibid paras 7.532–7.662.
[82] Otten and Wager (n 7) 403.

PART V: DISPUTE PREVENTION AND SETTLEMENT (ARTICLES 63–4)

Article 63 concerns transparency. Members have the obligation to publish (or, where such publication is not practicable, to make publicly available) laws and regulations, and final judicial decisions and administrative rulings of general application pertaining to the subject matter of the TRIPS Agreement (the availability, scope, acquisition, enforcement and prevention of the abuse of intellectual property rights), in a national language, in such a manner as to enable governments and right holders to become acquainted with them. These obligations are implemented notably through official publications (Article 63.1), notifications to the TRIPS Council (Article 63.2), and bilateral requests for information and access (Article 63.3). Nothing in paragraphs 1, 2 and 3 shall require Members to disclose confidential information which would impede law enforcement or otherwise be contrary to the public interest or would prejudice the legitimate commercial interests of particular enterprises, public or private (Article 63.4).

Article 64 relates to dispute settlement and provides that Articles XXII (consultation) and XXIII (nullification or Impairment) of GATT 1994, as elaborated and applied by the DSU, apply to consultations and the settlement of disputes under the TRIPS Agreement, except as otherwise specifically provided by the TRIPS Agreement itself. Article XXIII.1 of GATT 1994 provides that:

> If any contracting party should consider that any benefit accruing to it directly or indirectly under this Agreement is being nullified or impaired or that the attainment of any objective of the Agreement is being impeded as the result of (a) the failure of another contracting party to carry out its obligations under this Agreement, or (b) the application by another contracting party of any measure, whether or not it conflicts with the provisions of this Agreement, or (c) the existence of any other situation, the contracting party may resort to the dispute procedures, with a view to the satisfactory adjustment of the matter.

However, Article 64.2 TRIPS specifically provides that the above 1(b) and 1(c) of Article XXIII of GATT 1994 (non-violation complaints) shall not apply to the settlement of disputes under the TRIPS Agreement for a period of five years from the date of entry into force of the WTO Agreement. During the period where non-violation complaints are not allowed, the TRIPS Council examines the scope and modalities for these complaints (Article 64.3). Later, paragraph 11.1 of the Decision on Implementation-Related Issues and Concerns, adopted at the Doha Ministerial Conference in 2001 (chapter 9), instructed the TRIPS Council to make a recommendation to the Cancún Ministerial Conference. Until then, Members agreed not to file non-violation complaints under TRIPS. In May 2003, the TRIPS Council chairperson listed four possible recommendations: (1) banning non-violation complaints based on the TRIPS Agreement completely; (2) allowing the complaints to be handled under the WTO's dispute settlement rules as applies to goods and services cases; (3) allowing non-violation complaints, but subject to special 'modalities' (ie ways of dealing with them);

and, (4) extending the moratorium. Based on the General Council decision on 1 August 2004, the moratorium was extended until the Hong Kong Ministerial Conference in 2005, and, there, the moratorium was further extended.[83] The Seventh Ministerial Conference on 2 December 2009 further extended the moratorium until the Ministerial Conference in 2011.

TRIPS dispute procedures are based mostly on DSU provisions as in other WTO disputes and followed by steps, ie, consultation (Article 4 DSU), Panel proceedings (Articles 6–16 DSU) and Appellate Body proceedings (Article 19 DSU). With the adoption by the Dispute Settlement Body (DSB) of a Panel or an Appellate Body report, the implementation phase of the DSB decisions begins. The DSB monitors prompt compliance by the defaulting party with recommendations or rulings of the DSB within a reasonable period of time (Article 21 DSU). A reasonable period of time can be determined through binding arbitration within 90 days after the date of adoption of the recommendations and rulings (Article 21.3(c) DSU). The original panel can also be re-established to assess whether the implementing measures taken by the defendant meet the relevant WTO obligations (Article 21.5 DSU). If the Member concerned fails to bring the measure found to be inconsistent with a covered agreement into compliance therewith, or otherwise to comply with the recommendations and rulings within a reasonable period of time, the parties to the dispute, if so requested, shall enter into negotiations with a view to developing mutually acceptable compensation within 20 days after the date of expiry of the reasonable period of time (Article 22 DSU). If no satisfactory compensation is then agreed within that period, any party having invoked the dispute settlement procedures may request authorisation from the DSB to suspend the application to the Member concerned of concessions or other obligations under the covered agreements (Article 22.2).

The complaining party should first seek to suspend concessions or other obligations with respect to the same sector(s) as that in which the panel or Appellate Body has found a violation (Article 22.3), but if that party considers that it is not practicable or effective to do so, it may seek to suspend concessions or other obligations in other sectors under the same agreement (Article 22.3(b) DSU).[84] This latter is popularly called 'cross-retaliation'. The level of the suspension of concessions authorised by the DSB must be equivalent to that of nullification or impairment (Article 22.4 DSU). The DSB, upon request, must grant authorisation to suspend concessions or other obligations within 30 days of the expiry of the reasonable period of time, unless the DSB decides by consensus to reject the request (Article 22.6 DSU). In a few Article 22.6 arbitration cases, such authorisation has been granted and 'cross-retaliation' in the TRIPS sector considered.[85]

---

[83] Doha Work Program, Ministerial Declaration (22 December 2005) WT/MIN(05)/DEC.

[84] Art 22.3(c) says: 'if that party considers that it is not practicable or effective to suspend concessions or other obligations with respect to other sectors under the same agreement, and that the circumstances are serious enough, it may seek to suspend concessions or other obligations under another covered agreement'.

[85] *EC–Regime for the Importation, Sale and Distribution of Bananas* (Report of the Arbitrator circulated 9 April 1999) WT/DS27/ARB/ECU/Corr.1; *US–Measures Affecting the Cross-Border*

In the EC–*Bananas III* case, Ecuador was authorised to cross-retaliate, considered possible retaliation measures in the TRIPS areas, and found them unrealistic.[86] In the *US–Gambling* case, Antigua and Barbuda was allowed to retaliate in the area of TRIPS Agreement but it is up to this country to establish equivalence between the loss and the amount of retaliation. In the *US–Upland Cotton* case, Brazil was also allowed to retaliate, but the US and Brazil seem to be negotiating for settlement. In cross-retaliation, it is difficult for parties to establish the equivalence between the retaliatory measures and the value of the loss incurred through the original violation of the WTO Agreement. The efficacy and the impacts of cross-retaliatory measures have therefore remained unknown.

PART VI: TRANSITIONAL ARRANGEMENTS (ARTICLES 65–7)

Members are not obliged to apply the provisions of the TRIPS Agreement before the expiry of a general period of one year following the date of entry into force of the WTO Agreement (1 January 1995), except Articles 2, 3 and 4 (Article 65.1). For the application of the provisions of the Agreement except Articles 3, 4 and 5, a transition period of five years from the date of entry into force of the Agreement is given to developing countries (Article 65.2). Article 65.4 allows developing countries a further delay of five years, the application of the provisions concerning product patents protection in Section 5, Part II.

The TRIPS Agreement addresses the situations of developing and least developed countries (LDCs)[87] by providing transitional agreements in Articles 65 and 66 (see chapter 4). Those developing countries (but not LDCs), who do not make available product patent protection to pharmaceutical or agricultural chemical inventions may delay up to ten years the introduction of patent protection to such inventions (Article 65.4). However, during the 10-year transition period, these Members have an obligation to provide as from the date of entry into force of the WTO Agreement, a means by which applications for patents for such inventions can be filed (called 'mailbox application') (Article 70.9).

During the transition period under paragraphs 1, 2, 3 or 4, a 'Member shall ensure that any changes in its laws, regulations and practice made during that

---

Supply of Gambling and Betting Services (Report of the Arbitrator circulated 21 December 2007) WT/DS285/ARB; *US–Subsidies on Upland Cotton* (Report of the Arbitrator circulated 31 August 2009) WT/DS267/ARB.

[86] Ecuador intended to suspend its obligations towards the EC under Art 14 of the TRIPS Agreement and export EU phonograms to third countries without the consent of the EU right holders. However, the Arbitration Panel said all other WTO Members remained bound by their TRIPS obligations towards the EC and therefore would apply Article 51 of the TRIPS Agreement, ie, suspension of the release into free circulation of those phonograms, to the detriment of Ecuador's economic interest.

[87] The WTO recognises as least-developed countries (LDCs) those countries which have been designated by the United Nations as such. As of 1 November 2010, 32 LDCs are members of the WTO. http://www.wto.org/english/thewto_e/whatis_e/tif_e/org7_e.htm There are no WTO definitions of 'developed' or 'developing' countries: they are self-announced. http://www.wto.org/english/tratop_e/devel_e/d1who_e.htm See ch 4 n 153 on LDCs.

period do not result in a lesser degree of consistency with the provisions of the TRIPS Agreement' (Article 65.5). This standstill provision does not seem to prohibit all roll-back measures, but allows the developing country to reduce its level of protection as long as the measure in question is consistent with the Agreement.

Thus, developing country Members were not obliged to introduce patent protection for pharmaceutical and agricultural chemical products until 1 January 2006. However, Article 70.8 requires that, subsequent to the entry into force of the WTO Agreement, developing country members shall grant exclusive marketing rights for a period of five years after obtaining marketing approval in that Member, or until a product patent is granted or rejected in that Member, whichever period is shorter. These provisions hold provided that a patent application has been filed and a patent granted for that product in another Member country and marketing approval obtained in that other Member country.

Table 5.1: Transitional Arrangements

	Principles of national treatment (Art 3) and most-favoured nation treatment (Art 4) and Art 5 (*)	Obligations other than Articles 3, 4 and 5	Obligation to introduce patent protection for agricultural and chemical products
Developed countries	1.1.1996 (Art 65.1 TRIPS)	1.1.1996 (Art 65.1 TRIPS)	1.1. 1996 (Art 65.1 TRIPS)
Developing countries	1.1. 1996 (Art 65.1 TRIPS)	1.1.2000 (Art 65.2 TRIPS)	1.1. 2005 (Art 65.4 TRIPS)
Transition from centralised to market economies	1.1.1996 (Art 65.1 TRIPS)	1.1.2000 (Art 65.3 TRIPS)	1.1.2000 (Art 65.3 TRIPS)
Least developed countries	1.1.1996 (Art 66.1 TRIPS)	1.1.2006 at the adoption of the TRIPS (Art 66.1 TRIPS) and postponed to 1.7.2013 on the bases of the TRIPS Council Decision IP/C/40 of 29.11.2005	1.1.2006 at the adoption of the TRIPS (Art 66.1 TRIPS). The LDC obligations to implement patent and undisclosed data protection for pharmaceuticals were postponed to 1.1.2016 by Decision of the TRIPS Council, IP/C/25 (27. 6.2002) based on para 7 of the Doha Declaration on TRIPS and Public Health (chapter 9)

(*) Article 5: 'The obligations under Articles 3 and 4 do not apply to procedures provided in multilateral agreements concluded under the auspices of WIPO relating to the acquisition or maintenance of IPRs'.

PART VII: INSTITUTIONAL ARRANGEMENTS; FINAL PROVISIONS
(ARTICLES 68–73)

Article 68 concerns the functions of the TRIPS Council. The Council monitors the operation of the TRIPS Agreement and, in particular, Members' compliance with their obligations thereunder, and affords Members the opportunity of consulting on matters relating to the Agreement. Other functions of the TRIPS Council include executing the instructions of Member States (General Council, Ministerial Conference) and pursuing cooperation with the WIPO Cooperation agreement.[88]

Article 71, entitled 'review and amendment', refers also to the function of the TRIPS Council, ie to review the implementation of the Agreement after the expiration of the transitional period (referred to in Article 65.2) two years after that date, and at identical intervals thereafter. The Council may also undertake reviews in the light of any relevant new developments which might warrant modification or amendment of the TRIPS Agreement.

Article 71.2 provides for a special procedure for amending the TRIPS Agreement only when the following conditions are cumulatively met: i) amendments are merely serving the purpose of adjusting to higher levels of IPRs; (ii) which are achieved in other multilateral agreements and in force; (iii) all Members of the WTO are parties to these multilateral agreements; and (iv) may be referred to the Ministerial Conference for action in accordance with paragraph 6 of Article X of the WTO Agreement on the basis of a consensus proposal from the Council for TRIPS. Other amendments must follow the procedures provided in Article X of the WTO Agreement.

Where insufficient agreement was reached during the Uruguay Round negotiations, continued discussions were to be undertaken by the TRIPS Council. These so-called 'built-in agenda' items include the negotiation, review or examination of the provisions concerning: (i) the establishment of a multilateral system of notification and registration of geographical indications for wines eligible for protection in those Members participating in the system (Article 23.4); (ii) the review of the application of the provisions of Section 3 relating to geographical indications (Article 24.2); (iii) the review four years after the date of entry into force of the WTO Agreement of the provisions contained in Article 27.3(b) concerning the protection of plants and animals other than microorganisms; and, (iv) the appropriateness of non-violation complaints of the type provided for under subparagraphs 1(b) and 1(c) of Article XXIII of GATT 1994 (Articles 64.2 and 64.3).

Article 70, entitled 'protection of existing subject matter', sets out specific rules concerning the temporal effects of the application of the TRIPS Agreement on the existing protectable subject matter. Different dates are used for the

---

[88] Concluded with the WIPO in December 2005 and entered into force on 1 January 2006.

Agreement to have effect: the date of its application, the date of its entry into force, the date of the acceptance of the WTO Agreement, and the date when the TRIPS Agreement is known.

According to Article 70.1, the TRIPS Agreement 'does not give rise to obligations in respect of acts which occurred before the date of application of the Agreement for the Member in question'. In *Canada–Patent Term*, Canada argued that the obligations under TRIPS (notably Article 33 on the term of patent protection) did not affect Canada's 'act' of granting a patent prior to the date when TRIPS became applicable. The Panel and the Appellate Body disagreed and found that the term 'acts' denoted the continuing results of acts, ie, those rights that had been created by acts. The date of application refers to the date when the provisions regarding the subject matter became effective for that Member, subject to the transition provisions of the Agreement. According to Article 70.2, Members have an obligation to protect all 'subject matter' existing at the date of application of the TRIPS Agreement for the Member in question (except those which have fallen into the public domain on this date (Article 70.3)). The Appellate Body in the same case referred to Article 27, entitled 'patentable subject matter', which provides that 'patents shall be available for any inventions' and confirms that 'inventions' constitute 'subject matter'.[89] For example, an invention still under patent protection at the time when the TRIPS Agreement is applied in a country whose term of patent protection was 17 years from the date of its grant, benefits from extended protection based on Article 33 TRIPS, whereas an invention whose patent protection has already ended on the date of TRIPS application does not. The Appellate Body upheld the Panel's finding that Article 70.1 does not exclude from the scope of the TRIPS Agreement those patents that existed on the date of application of the TRIPS Agreement for Canada.[90]

The second sentence of Article 70.2 explicitly states that copyright obligations with respect to existing works shall be determined under Article 18 of the Berne Convention (1971) concerning 'works existing on Convention's entry into force' (possibilities of retroactive application). It also states that obligations with respect to the rights of producers of phonograms and performers in existing phonograms shall be determined solely under Article 18 of the Berne Convention (1971) as made applicable under paragraph 6 of Article 14 TRIPS. The dispute brought by the US and the EC against Japan concerned the interpretation of this provision.[91]

---

[89]   *Canada–Patent Term*, Appellate Body Report (n 8) paras 65–6.
[90]   ibid para 60.
[91]   This was the first WTO dispute settlement case involving the TRIPS Agreement, (*Japan–Measures Concerning Sound Recordings*, DS28, the US request for consultations on 9 February 1996), in which the EC joined (DS42, request for consultations on 28 May 1996). The US and the EC claimed that Japan's copyright regime for the protection of intellectual property in sound recordings was inconsistent, inter alia, with Art 14 TRIPS (protection of performers, producers of phonograms and broadcasting organisations). On 7 November 1997, both parties notified a mutually agreed solution.

Article 70.3 provides for a limitation of the remedies available to the right holder as to the continued performance of such prior use, on the date of application of the TRIPS Agreement (for that Member). When a third party has been using the subject matter before the date of acceptance of the WTO Agreement by that Member, the use by that third party becomes an infringement under the legislation in conformity with the TRIPS Agreement. According to this provision, any Member may provide for attenuated remedies, if a significant investment has been made by the third party. However, he or she must provide for the payment of equitable remuneration to the right holder. The India Patents (Amendment) Act 2005, after the transition period of 10 years, introduced product patent protection for pharmaceutical and agricultural chemical products commensurate with the obligations under Article 27 TRIPS. Section 11A(7) of this Act allows those enterprises which were using the inventions to continue manufacturing, if they have made significant investments and produced and marketed the products prior to 1 January 2005, with payment of reasonable royalties

According to Article 70.5 TRIPS, there is no obligation to protect rental rights with respect to computer programs and cinematographic works, against those who purchased the relevant works prior to the date of application of the TRIPS Agreement for that Member.

Article 70.6 states that Members, in applying Article 31, are exonerated from the requirement in Article 27.1 that patent rights shall be enjoyable without discrimination as to the field of technology, if compulsory licensing is issued before the date when the TRIPS Agreement 'became known'.

According to Article 70.7, in the case of IPRs for which protection is conditional upon registration, pending applications for protection at the time of the application of the TRIPS Agreement for that Member are permitted to be amended to claim any enhanced protection provided under TRIPS provisions. However, such amendments shall not include new matter (the second sentence of Article 70.7). In many countries, protection of IPRs such as patents, trademarks, industrial designs, geographical indications, plant varieties and layout-designs of integrated circuits, is conditional on registration.

Article 70.8 refers to the specific obligations for those Members which do not make available patent protection for pharmaceutical and agricultural chemical products, as of the date of entry into force of the WTO Agreement. According to Article 70.8(a), these Members shall provide, notwithstanding the transitional arrangements under Part VI of the TRIPS Agreement, 'a means by which applications for patents for such inventions can be filed as from the date of entry into force of the WTO Agreement'. The Appellate Body in *India–Patents(US)* stated that the 'means' under Article 70.8(a) must allow for 'the entitlement to file mailbox applications and the allocation of filing and priority dates to them'. It endorsed the Panel's finding that provisions under Article 70.8(a) are inseperable from paragraphs (b) and (c) of Article 70.8 and impose an obligation for these Members to provide 'a sound legal basis to preserve novelty and priority as of those dates'.[92] In this case, the Appellate Body corrected the Panel argument that India's approach to providing a legal means for implementing its mailbox obligation did not satisfy the 'legitimate expectations' of the US and private patent owners. According to the Appellate Body, the panel used the concept of 'legitimate expectations', in the sense of a non-violation nullification or impairment cause of action, instead of a violation of India's obligation under the TRIPS Agreement of providing a 'sound legal mechanism'.[93]

Article 70.9 relates to 'exclusive marketing rights' (EMRs) that developing WTO Members which do not provide patent protection for agricultural and pharmaceutical products (transitional period under Article 70.8(a)) must grant. EMRs should be granted by these developing countries in transition (A) when, subsequent to the entry into force of the WTO Agreement, a patent application has been filed in countries (A) and both a patent granted for that product in another Member country (B) and marketing approval is obtained in that other Member country (B). EMRs are valid for a period of five years in countries (A) after marketing approval has been obtained in a Member country (A), or until a product patent is granted or rejected in that Member (A), whichever period is shorter.

EMRs, as provided in Article 70.9, were a result of a compromise between the US demand for a pipeline protection and the opposition, thereto, of developing countries. Pipeline protection generally means administrative protection given in a foreign country between the date of filing and the grant of patents, for those pharmaceutical products which have not yet obtained marketing authorisation in the country where the product was originally developed and patented. EMRs under Article 70.9 are not IPRs in the sense of Article 1.2 TRIPS, because they are not subject to the provisions in sections 1 to 7, Part II of the TRIPS Agreement and, therefore, not subject to the principles that apply to IPRs under the Agreement, such as national treatment, most-favoured nation treatment as well as other provisions pertaining to sections 1 to 7, Part II. In this case, India argued that the expression in Article 70.9 that EMRs 'shall be granted . . .' was different from 'shall be available . . .', in Article 27.[94] Both the Panel and the Appellate Body disagreed with India, for the reason that the term 'right' connotes an entitlement to which a person has a just claim implying general, non-discretionary availability in the case of those eligible to exercise it. They held, therefore, that EMRs could not be 'granted' in a specific case unless there is a mechanism in place that establishes general availability and enables such requests to be made.[95] The Appellate Body considered that India's claim must be examined under Article XVI: 4 of the WTO Agreement which provides that Members shall ensure the conformity of their laws with their WTO obligations.

---

[92] *India–Patent Protection for Pharmaceutical and Agricultural Chemical Products (India–Patents (US))*, Appellate Body Report (adopted 16 January 1998) WT/DS50/AB/R paras 54–7.

[93] ibid para 48.

[94] *India–Patents (US), Appellate Body Report* (n 92) paras 11-4.

[95] ibid para 57.

In this regard, the Appellate Body noted India's acknowledgement that in order to grant EMRs under Article 70.9, the Indian Government would have to enact legislation to that effect. According to the Appellate Body, no such legal basis existed in Indian legislation.[96]

Article 72 stipulates that reservations to the provisions of the TRIPS Agreement are allowed only with the consent of all other Members. Article 73 concerns security exceptions whose intent is to protect Members' rights not to disclose information concerning essential security interests (a), to act to safeguard essential security interest in war, emergency in international relations (b), and to take action in pursuance of its obligations under the United Nations Charter for the maintenance of international peace and security (c).

---

[96] *India–Patents(US)*, Appellate Body Report (n 92) paras 79–80.

6

Various Methods of Interpretation: WTO Agreements and the Vienna Convention on the Law of Treaties

PROBABLY MORE THAN any other international dispute settlement organs, WTO Panels and the Appellate Body have resorted to the rules of interpretation under the Vienna Convention on the Law of Treaties (VCLT)[1] (mainly Articles 31 and 32) as 'customary rules of interpretation of public international law',[2] in examining the cases brought to the WTO dispute settlement procedures. This chapter explores first the VCLT rules of treaty interpretation and then how the WTO Panels and Appellate Body have understood them. The WTO dispute settlement organs have taken a textualist, consensus-forming and formalistic approach to treaty interpretation, probably to a greater degree than Articles 31 and 32 VCLT stipulate. Possible reasons for the particular WTO interpretative discipline are also explored in this chapter.

I WTO AND THE VIENNA CONVENTION ON THE LAW OF TREATIES

A 'Customary rules of interpretation of public international law'

According to Article 64 of the TRIPS Agreement, the WTO rules and procedures for disputes apply to consultations and disputes under the TRIPS Agreement, except when this Agreement itself provides special provisions. The WTO rules

---

[1] The VCLT was adopted in Vienna on 23 May 1969 and entered into force on 27 January 1980 (UN Treaty Series, vol 1155, 331). As of 5 September 2009, 109 countries were parties to the VCLT (Brazil is a signatory but not a party, while France and the US are neither signatories nor parties).

[2] The International Court of Justice (ICJ) has also recognised Art 31 VCLT as reflecting the customary rules of interpretation, in such cases as Guinea-Bissau/Senegal (para 48), El Salvador/Honduras (paras 373, 380), Libyan Arab Jamahiriya/Chad (para 41), Qatar/Bahrain (para 33), and Legality of the Use by a State of Nuclear Weapons (paras 19–22). The ICJ is the principal judicial organ of the United Nations and is established by the UN Charter. Art 38.1 of its Statute stipulates that: '1. The Court, whose function is to decide in accordance with international law such disputes as are submitted to it, shall apply: (a) international conventions, whether general or particular, establishing rules expressly recognized by the contesting states; (b) international custom, as evidence of a general practice accepted as law; (c) the general principles of law recognized by civilized nations; (d) subject to the provisions of Article 59, judicial decisions and the teachings of the most highly qualified publicists of the various nations, as subsidiary means for the determination of rules of law . . .'.

and procedures were established under Articles XXII and XXIII of GATT 1947, and further elaborated and modified in the Understanding on Rules and Procedures Governing the Settlement of Disputes (DSU).

Article 3.7 of the DSU provides that the aim of the dispute settlement mechanism is to secure a positive solution to a dispute, and lists such solutions in order of preference: first, a solution mutually acceptable to the parties to a dispute and consistent with the covered agreements; secondly, withdrawal of the measures concerned, if these are found to be inconsistent with the provisions of any of the covered agreements;[3] thirdly, compensation; and, finally, the suspension of concessions or other obligations under the covered agreements on a discriminatory basis vis-à-vis the other Member, subject to authorisation by the Dispute Settlement Body (DSB)[4] of such measures. According to Article 23 of the DSU, when seeking the redress of a violation of obligations or other nullification or impairment of benefits under the covered agreements, or an impediment to the attainment of any objective of the covered agreements, Members shall abide by the rules and procedures of the DSU and not make a determination to the effect that a violation has occurred.

Article 3.2 of the DSU states that 'the dispute settlement system of the WTO serves to preserve the rights and obligations of Members under the covered agreements . . . [and] to clarify the existing provisions of those agreements . . . in accordance with customary rules of interpretation of public international law'. The reference to customary rules of interpretation was included so that the WTO dispute settlement organs would interpret relevant provisions with a common discipline in public international law.

Unlike GATT panels, which often resorted to negotiating history or preparatory works, the WTO dispute settlement organs are directed by 'customary rules of interpretation of public international law'. Thus the Appellate Body in *US–Gasoline*[5] stated what subsequent Panels repeated: 'the *General Agreement* is not to be read in clinical isolation from public international law'.[6] Article 3.2

---

[3] 'Covered agreements' are those agreements listed in Appendix 1 to the DSU, namely, the Agreement establishing the WTO, the Multilateral Trade Agreements in Annex 1A – Multilateral Agreements on Trade in Goods, Annex 1B – General Agreement on Trade in Services (GATS), and Annex 1C – Agreement on Trade-Related Aspects of intellectual property (TRIPS), as well as other plurilateral trade agreements. The 'Dispute Settlement Body' (DSB) administers the rules and procedures concerning dispute settlements and has the authority to establish panels, adopt panel and Appellate Body reports, maintain surveillance of implementation of rulings and recommendations, and authorise suspension of concessions and other obligations under the covered agreements.

[4] The DSB is established by WTO Members in order to administer the rules and procedures for dispute settlement, establish panels, adopt panel and Appellate Body reports, maintain surveillance of implementation of rulings and recommendations, and authorise suspension of concessions and other obligations under the covered agreements (Art 2 DSU).

[5] *US–Standards for Reformulated and Conventional Gasoline* (*US–Gasoline*), Appellate Body Report (adopted 20 May 1996) WT/DS2/AB/R.

[6] *US–Gasoline* ibid p16. Also *Japan–Taxes on Alcoholic Beverages* (*Japan–Alcoholic Beverages II*), Appellate Body Report (adopted 1 November 1996) WT/DS8/AB/R, WT/DS10/AB/R, WT/DS11/AB/R pp. 10–12; *India–Patent Protection for Pharmaceutical and Agricultural Chemical Products* (*India–Patents (US)*), Appellate Body Report (adopted 16 January 1998) WT/DS50/AB/R para 46.

further binds the WTO dispute settlement organs to the text of the treaty provisions by adding that 'recommendations and rulings of the Dispute Settlement Body (DSB) cannot add to or diminish the rights and obligations provided in the covered agreements.'

Article 31 of the VCLT is entitled 'general rule of interpretation'. According to Article 31.1, 'a treaty shall be interpreted in good faith in accordance with 'the ordinary meaning to be given to the terms of the treaty in their context and in the light of its object and purpose'.[7] Article 31 of the VCLT does not specifically mention well-known axioms of treaty interpretation, such as *ut res magis valeat quam pereat* (the 'effectiveness' principle, which means that treaties must not be interpreted in a way that would reduce any part of a treaty to redundancy or inutility), *exceptio est strictissimae interpretationis* (exceptions should be interpreted narrowly), or *lex specialis derogat legi generali or lex posterior derogat legi priori* provisions (specific subject matter overrides general matters, or later, specific treaty provisions override earlier general ones).[8]

Article 31 of the VCLT provides a method of interpretation, rather than specific principles, which relies mainly on the wording, its context and the object and purpose of the treaty, and makes it possible for the treaty interpreter to resort to these principles, if they are helpful for interpreting the provisions in question and not incompatible with the analysis based on Article 31.[9] The 'effectiveness' principle, for example, has been recognised by many dispute settlement systems today as one of the fundamental principles of treaty interpretation. WTO Panels and the Appellate Body have referred to the effectiveness principle as 'the fundamental tenet of treaty interpretation flowing from the general rule set out in Article 31 of the VCLT'.[10] During the drafting process of the VCLT by the International Law Commission (ILC),[11] the principle of effectiveness was

---

[7]   The ILC considered that the provision on *pacta sunt servanda* explained the meaning of 'good faith'. Art 26 VCLT states: 'Every treaty in force is binding upon the parties to it and must be performed by them in good faith'. MK Yasseen, 'L'interprétation des traités d'après la Convention de Vienne sur le Droit des Traités' (1976) 151 *Recueil des Cours* 20.

[8]   Part of this principle is reflected in Art 30 VCLT. On the question of how the WTO dispute settlement organs have dealt with this principle, see J Pauwelyn, *Conflict of Norms in Public International Law* (Cambridge University Press, 2003).

[9]   RG Wetzel (compilation), D Rauschuning (ed), *Dokumente, The Vienna Convention of the Law of Treaties: travaux préparatoires* (Frankfurt am Main, Alfred Metzner Verlag, 1978).

[10]   *Japan–Alcoholic Beverages II* (n 6) pp12–14. This principle has been important in many later WTO cases. See also, for example, *US–Gasoline* (n 5) paras 25–26; *Argentina–Safeguard Measures on Imports of Footwear*, Appellate Body Report (adopted 12 January 2000) WT/DS121/AB/R para 89; *Canada–Term of Patent Protection'Canada–Patent Term*), Panel Report (adopted 12 October 2000) WT/DS170/R,para 6.50 (as upheld by the Appellate Body Report, WT/DS170/AB/R).

[11]   At its first session, in 1949, the ILC selected the law of treaties as a topic for codification to which it gave priority. The Commission appointed JL Brierly, Sir Hersch Lauterpacht, Sir Gerald Fitzmaurice and Sir Humphrey Waldock as the successive Special Rapporteurs for the topic at its first (1949), fourth (1952), seventh (1955) and thirteenth (1961) sessions. The Commission considered the topic at its second (1950), third (1951), eighth (1956) and eleventh (1959) sessions, and from 1961 to 1966. The ILC had before it the reports of the Special Rapporteurs, information provided by governments as well as documents prepared by the Secretariat: http://untreaty.un.org/ilc/summaries/1_1.htm.

proposed as part of the 'general rule of interpretation'.[12] However, the explicit reference to this principle was removed from the draft because it was considered to make Article 31.1 of the current version of the VCLT redundant.[13]

For treaty interpretation, the WTO dispute settlement organs have emphasised the importance of the wording of treaty provisions in its textual context. The axiom of strict interpretation of exceptions (*exceptio est strictissimae interpretationis*) does not seem to be included in the VCLT rule of interpretation. For the WTO dispute settlement organs, the interpretation of the covered agreements depends primarily on the wording of any provision concerned, including those words phrased as 'exceptions', read in its context and in light of the treaty's 'object and purpose'. This method may not result in a narrow interpretation of exceptions. It could lead to interpretations that strike a balance between two policies, depending on the treaty language. This question will be further examined in the chapter 7, which examines how exceptions in the TRIPS Agreement have been interpreted by the WTO dispute organs.

B The VCLT rule of interpretation

i The role of preparatory work in treaty interpretation

The VCLT rule of interpretation was acceptable to the participating parties in the Vienna Conference probably because this rule allows various principles of treaty interpretation and facilitates broad participation by states. Therefore, many crucial questions for interpretation were left open to the choice of the treaty interpreter. The meaning of the 'object and purpose' of the treaty, and its relation to 'context', is open-ended.

During the elaboration of the draft VCLT at the ILC, the idea of codifying general principles of interpretation itself was met with scepticism.[14] According to Jacobs (1969), various approaches to treaty interpretation regarding the draft

---

[12] Following draft Art 71, entitled 'application of the general rules', draft Art 72, entitled 'effective interpretation of the terms (*ut res magis valeat quam pereat*)', stated that 'in the application of draft Articles 70 and 71, a term of a treaty shall be interpreted as to give it the fullest weight and effect consistent with: (a) its natural and ordinary meaning and that of the other terms of the treaty; and, (b) the objects and purposes of the treaty'. *Yearbook of the International Law Commission* (New York, ILC, 1964) vol II 53.

[13] It was considered that the effective principle was almost synonymous with interpreting the structure of the treaty in good faith, which is stated in Art 31.1 VCLT. Yasseen (n 7) 19.

[14] Sceptical views stated that there could be interpretative 'guidelines', but it would not be appropriate to make the existing principles into a 'rule' or, a fortiori, a rigid rule. *Yearbook of the ILC* (n 12) vol II 53 and 71. The Waldock Report (1964) also pointed out that there were many sceptical opinions over the rules for interpretation, and quoted various authors, including the following: McNair, *Law of Treaties* (1961) 366, C Rousseau, *Principes généraux du droit international public* (1944) 676 et seq, C de Visscher, *Problèmes d'interprétation judiciaire en droit international public* (1963) 50 et seq.

VCLT are broadly classified as follows:[15] (i) a subjective approach (which emphasises the 'intentions' of the parties and tends to refer to the processes of negotiation and drafting leading to the conclusion of the treaty); (ii) a textual approach
(which values the actual wording of the treaty); and (iii) a teleological approach
(which seeks to interpret the treaty through a broad inquiry by the interpreter
into the objects and purposes of the treaty taken as a whole). Controversies over
interpretation have particularly concerned the antithesis between the textualist
and teleological approaches.

Under the textualist approach, which was the predominant position in early
discussions within the ILC, the intentions of the parties are expressed in the
wording of the treaty, which must not be construed in a way that departs from
its ordinary meaning.[16] With the teleological approach, however, a treaty is to
be interpreted by reference to the leading concept of the treaty (for example, the
maintenance of peace, public interest etc), which is not necessarily expressed in
its text, but is nevertheless understood by the interpreter as the general and most
important purpose of the treaty.[17]

A few examples of the teleological approach can also be found in the
arguments by Members in WTO disputes cases. Cuba, as a third party in
Canada–Pharmaceutical Patents,[18] argued that 'the TRIPS Agreement, at all
times, is to be read and interpreted in such a way that the important objectives
and principles it contained were not relegated to the background by the over-
riding application of any of its other provisions.'

At the ILC in the late 1950s, the attempt by Fitzmaurice[19] to establish a single
unified doctrine with the interpretation principles used by the ICJ finally bore
fruit and brought together various principles and methods of interpretation
into what became Article 31 and Article 32 of the current version of the VCLT.
Arriving at a compromise, the textualist and teleological approaches came to

---

[15]   F Jacobs, 'Varieties of Approach to Treaty Interpretation: With Special Reference to the Draft
Convention on the Law of Treaties before the Vienna Diplomatic Conference' (1969) 18(2) *ICLQ*
318–46. On the evolution of different schools of treaty interpretation and their relationship to Arts
31 and 32 VCLT, see also Yasseen (n 7) 3 et seq.

[16]   According to Schwarzenberger, 'Nor is it permissible to read into the text of a treaty anything
which is not to be found there; for the intention of the parties is only relevant to the extent to
which it had found expression in the treaty', G Schwarzenberger, *International Law as Applied by
International Courts and Tribunals* 3rd edn (London, Stevens,1957) 503.

[17]   For example, Judges Alvarez (Chile) and Azevedo (Brazil) of the ICJ used the teleological
approach in their interpretation of treaties. The following dissenting opinion was expressed by Judge
Azevedo concerning the Competence of the General Assembly for the Admission of a State to the
United Nations in the Advisory Opinion of the Court of 3 March 1950: 'Even more than in the
applications of municipal law, the meaning and the scope of international texts must continually be
perfected, even if the terms remain unchanged. This proposition is acceptable to any dogmatic system of law, and even to those who hold that law should be autonomous and free from the interference
of forces, tendencies or influences alien to its proper sphere' (para 4). Judge Alvarez, in his dissenting
opinion in the Reservations to the Genocide Convention case, said these conventions are not established for the benefit of private interest but for that of the general interest (ICJ Reports 1951, 51).

[18]   *Canada–Patent Protection of Pharmaceutical Product (Canada–Pharmaceutical Patents (EC))*,
Panel Report (adopted 7 April 2000) WT/DS114/R para 5.19.

[19]   Member of the ILC (UK) from 1955 to 1960.

occupy a relatively important position, to the detriment of the position valuing the role of preparatory work.

From the textualist perspective, preparatory work should be used only when the application of the general rule of interpretation in Article 31 renders the meaning of a provision in a treaty vague or unclear. Alternatively, from the teleological perspective, it is important for the interpreter to discern the overall purpose of the treaty and give the effect of that purpose.

The role of preparatory work in treaty interpretation, therefore, was marginalised by the fact that both the textualist and the teleological approaches viewed preparatory work only in a secondary sense. At the first session of the Diplomatic Conference which started in Vienna in 1968, the US Delegation led by McDougal[20] argued against a predetermined hierarchy among different elements to be considered for interpretation, and requested that the two Articles, the general rule and the supplementary means of interpretation, be combined into a single Article without establishing a rigid rule.[21] This, however, was not the position adopted at the Diplomatic Conference,[22] and a distinction was made between Article 31 (general rule of interpretation) and Article 32 (supplementary means of interpretation).

According to Article 32 VCLT:

> recourse may be had to supplementary means of interpretation, including the preparatory work of the treaty and the circumstances of its conclusion, in order to confirm the meaning resulting from the application of Article 31, or to determine the meaning when the interpretation according to Article 31: (a) leaves the meaning ambiguous or obscure; or (b) leads to a result which is manifestly absurd or unreasonable.

ii Meaning of the 'object and purpose' of the treaty for interpretative purposes

Draft Article 70, entitled 'general rule of interpretation', did not contain the terms 'object and purpose' until 1966. According to the draft, it was necessary to take into account the 'context of a treaty as a whole' when determining the ordinary meaning of the terms of a treaty. Thus, Article 70.1 of the ILC draft of 1964 read: 'The terms of a treaty shall be interpreted in good faith in accordance with the natural and ordinary meaning to be given to each term: (a) in its context and *in the context of the treaty as a whole*; and (b) in the context of the rules of international law in force at the time of the conclusion of the treaty' (emphasis

---

[20] 'Statement of Professor Myres S McDougal, United States Delegation to Committee of the Whole', (1968) 62 *American Journal of International Law* 1021.

[21] A/CONF.39/C.1/L.156.

[22] The first session of the United Nations Conference on the Law of Treaties was held from 26 March to 24 May 1968 and the second session from 9 April to 22 May 1969. The first session of the Conference was devoted primarily to consideration by a Committee of the Whole and by a Drafting Committee of the set of draft Articles adopted by the International Law Commission. Thirty plenary meetings of the second session considered the Articles adopted by the Committee of the Whole and reviewed by the Drafting Committee.

added).[23] Consideration of 'objects and purposes'[24] of the treaty, by contrast, was proposed as a supplementary means, and not as part of the general rule of interpretation, to be employed in the second step, only 'when the natural or ordinary meaning of the terms of the treaty (i) leaves the meaning ambiguous or obscure or (ii) leads to a result which is manifestly absurd or unreasonable'.[25]

The phrase 'ordinary meaning of the terms' in Article 31.1 VCLT presumes that the intentions of the contracting parties are reflected in the ordinary meaning of the terms of the treaty, and indicates the importance of the wording used in the treaty.[26] However, none of the three elements of interpretation, 'ordinary meaning of the term', 'context', and a treaty's 'object and purpose,' take precedence over any other, and no interpretative principle is established among them. The meaning of 'object and purpose' is particularly unclear and its relationship with 'context' not explained.[27]

As the teleological approach to interpretation gained strength, so the role of the treaty's 'object and purpose' acquired importance. When Article 31 VCLT was finalised at the Diplomatic Conference in Vienna, the 'object and purpose' of the treaty for the purpose of interpreting treaties could still convey at least two different meanings: first, in line with the general structure of the treaty; and, secondly, for the overall purposes of the treaty that the treaty interpreter can philosophically define.

Interestingly, much later, in the WTO *US–Shrimp I*,[28] the WTO Appellate Body Report, quoting the following passage from Sinclair,[29] adhered to the ILC draft version of 1964 which attributes to the 'object and purpose' of the treaty a mere 'supplementary' role for the purpose of interpretation:

> A treaty interpreter must begin with, and focus upon, the text of the particular provision to be interpreted. It is in the language constituting a particular provision, when read in context, that the object and purpose of the states which are parties to the treaty must first be sought. Where the meaning imparted by the text itself is equivocal or inconclusive, or where confirmation of the correctness of the reading of the text itself is desired, it might be useful to refer to the object and purpose of the treaty as a whole for further clarification.[30]

[23]   Third Report on the Law of Treaties, Article 70, Article 72, *Yearbook of the ILC* (n 12) 52–3.

[24]   The 'objects and purposes' of the treaty were expressed in a plural form (Art 31 VCLT uses the terms 'object and purpose').

[25]   As Art 32 VCLT reserves the interpretative role of preparatory work as a supplementary means of interpretation, Art 70(2) of the 1964 draft provided that only the circumstances of: (a) the context and the objects and purposes of the treaty; and (b) the other means of interpretation mentioned in Arts 71 and 72 should be taken into account. *Yearbook of the ILC* (n 12) 52–3.

[26]   Art 31(4) of VCLT adds that '[a] special meaning shall be given to a term if it is established that the parties so intended'. *Yearbook of the ILC* (n 12) vol II 221.

[27]   J Klabbers, 'Some Problems regarding the Object and Purpose of Treaties' (1999) *Finnish Yearbook of International Law*, 138–60; I Buffard and K Zemarek, 'The object and purpose of a Treaty; an Enigma' (1998) 3 *Austrian Review of International and European Law* 311–43,.

[28]   *United States–Import Prohibition of Certain Shrimp and Shrimp Products (Shrimp I)*, Appellate Body Report (adopted 6 November 1998) WT/DS58/AB/R.

[29]   Member of the ILC (UK) from 1982 to 1986.

[30]   *US–Shrimp I* (n 28) para 114. The Appellate Body quotes I Sinclair, *The Vienna Convention on the Law of Treaties*, 2nd edn (Manchester University Press, 1984) 130–1.

C International agreements to be considered for the purpose of interpretation

While the term 'object and purpose' of the treaty in the VCLT was left unde-fined, the VCLT delineated, in detail, those agreements and instruments to be taken into consideration as the 'context' (Article 31.2(a)(b) VCLT) and the sub-sequent agreements, practices and relevant rules of international law to be taken into account, together with the context (Article 31.3(a)(b)(c) VCLT) for the pur-pose of the treaty interpretation. The scope of these elements in Articles 31.2(b) and 31.3(c) was left wide open.

Article 31.2 of the VCLT stipulates that 'the context for the purpose of the interpretation of a treaty' includes not only 'the text, including its preamble and annexes', but also: (a) any agreement relating to the treaty which was made between *all* the parties in connection with the conclusion of the treaty; and, (b) any instrument which was made by one or more parties in connection with the conclusion of the treaty and accepted by the other parties as an instrument related to the treaty (emphasis added).

However, there are no specific provisions in the VCLT which describe whether these agreements or instruments need to have any connection with the treaty in dispute (for example, whether the agreement or instrument, which is referred to in Article 31.2(a) and 31.2(b) of the VCLT, is related to interpretation or is a condition of participation in the treaty to be interpreted).[31]

Article 31.3 of the VCLT adds that, together with the context, the following must be taken into account: (a) any subsequent agreement between the parties regarding the interpretation of the treaty or the application of its provisions; (b) any subsequent practice in the application of the treaty which establishes the agreement of the parties regarding its interpretation; and (c) any relevant rules of international law applicable in the relations between the parties.

Article 31.2(a) of the VCLT stipulates that *all* the parties should participate in an agreement if it is to be considered part of the 'context' for the purpose of interpreting a particular provision in a treaty. However, Article 31.3(b) is silent on the issue of whether 'all the parties' must participate for the subsequent prac-tice to be considered as establishing the agreement of the parties regarding its interpretation. Article 69.3(b) of the 1964 draft of the ILC (Article 31.3(b) of the VCLT) originally referred to, as a factor to be taken into consideration together with the context for the purpose of treaty interpretation, '[a]ny subsequent prac-tice in the application of the treaty which *clearly* establishes the understand-ing of *all* the parties regarding its interpretation'(emphasis added). However,

---

[31] The 1964 draft of the ILC specified the conditions in which certain agreements or instruments could be considered to be the 'context' for determining the meaning of the term of a treaty. The draft Art 70(1)(b) referred to as a context that the treaty interpreter must take into consideration: (a) any agreement arrived at between the parties as a condition of the conclusion of the treaty or as a basis for its interpretation; (b) any instrument or document annexed to the treaty; and (c) any other instru-ment related to, and drawn up in connection with the conclusion of, the treaty.

the terms 'clearly' and 'all' were eventually deleted.[32] This was based on the idea that it is sufficient if 'all parties' at least passively accept the treaty, even if they do not actively apply it. This resulted in a broadening of conditions required to consider subsequent national practices for the establishment of the understanding between the parties for the purpose of interpreting the treaty.[33] The draft required agreements or practices 'among all the parties' for 'subsequent practice' to be considered as establishing an agreement among parties to the treaty.

Article 31.3(c), by contrast, refers to 'the parties', but not to 'all the parties'. Therefore, relevant rules of international law between the disputing parties could be taken into account, together with the context, for interpretative purposes. In other words, when interpreting a provision of a treaty, a treaty interpreter could refer to a very broad range of agreements and instruments together with the context and be selective about which materials to use. The 1964 ILC draft text stated in Article 69.3(c), which later became Article 31.3 (c) VCLT that: 'There shall also be taken into account, together with the context, (a) any agreement between the parties regarding the interpretation of the treaty.[34] The scope of 'relevant rules of international law' in Article 31.3(c) is interpreted to encompass a broad range not only of treaties but also of customary rules and general principles of international law.[35]

D Temporal factors (evolutionary interpretation)

Article 69 of the 1964 ICL draft, which was later adopted as a general rule of interpretation in Article 31 of the VCLT, specified that a treaty shall be interpreted in good faith in accordance with the ordinary meaning to be given to each term: (a) in the context of the treaty and in the light of its objects and purpose; and (b) in the light of the rules of general international law in force at the time of its conclusion.[36] However, in certain disputes over treaty provisions, involving subject matter such as human rights, it may be appropriate to interpret treaty provisions according to the meaning of terms and criteria at the time of

---

[32] Waldock Report, *Yearbook of the ILC* (n 12) vol II 222; MK Yasseen (n 7) 48–9. For the ILC draft Art 27.3(b), Australia proposed the amendment of this sub-paragraph (b) by inserting the word 'common' before the word 'understanding' (A/CONF.39/C.1/L210).

[33] In the drafting history of the VCLT, the possibility to modify multilateral treaties by subsequent practice (1966 Draft Art 38) was incorporated in the provisions of the current Art 41 of the VCLT concerning 'agreements to modify multilateral treaties between certain of the parties only'. Eventually, however, this language was removed. Thus, the possibility to modify treaties under 'subsequent practices related to the treaty interpretation' exists only as customary law and not as part of the law of treaties.

[34] Waldock Report VI, reprinted in RG Wetzel (ed), *The Vienna Convention of the Law of Treaties: Travaux Préparatoires* (Vienna, Alfred Metzner Verlag GmbH, 1978) 239.

[35] Yasseen (n 7) 62–63.

[36] Waldock Report VI (n 34) 105.

interpretation, rather than at the time of the conclusion of the treaty.[37] In some cases concerning environmental protection, science or technology, it may also be appropriate to consider the standards at the time of interpretation.[38]

The question of how to handle changes in international law from the time of the conclusion of the treaty until the time of its interpretation remained unresolved in the 1964 ILC draft,[39] and the phrase, 'at the time of its conclusion', was deleted subsequently. From the reading of Article 31.3(c) VCLT, therefore, it is possible to determine the ordinary meaning of terms using the concepts and criteria at the time of the conclusion of the treaty, or by those which prevail at the time of interpretation of the treaty. The VCLT rule of interpretation, as adopted in 1969, became so flexible that it came to include a broad range of various methods of interpretation.

Later, in 2006, the Study Group of the International Law Commission, in 'Fragmentation of International Law',[40] stated that:

> the appeal of Articles 31 and 32 of the VCLT may be attributable to the fact . . . that they adopt a set of practical considerations . . . general and flexible enough to provide a reasonable response to most interpretative problems. The Articles adopt both an "ordinary meaning" and a "purposive" approach; . . . It is in fact hard to think of any approach to interpretation that would be excluded from Articles 31–32.[41]

According to the Study Group, the textual analysis of Article 31.3(c) reveals a number of aspects of the rules of interpretation. One of these is that the

---

[37] R Higgins suggests: 'There are good reasons for thinking that treaties that guarantee human rights – whether expressly or as an incident of their subject matter – fall into a special category so far as inter-temporal law is concerned' (R Higgins, 'Time and the Law' (1997) 46 *International and Comparative Law Quarterly* 516). On the European Court of Human Rights and 'evolving' interpretation of terms, see JG Merrills, *The Development of International Law by the European Court of Human Rights*, 2nd edn (Manchester University Press, 1995). In the *Tyre v UK* case (25 April 1978, Series A no 26, para 31) the European Court of Human Rights said: '. . . the Convention is a living instrument which . . . must be interpreted in the light of present-day conditions. In the case now before it the Court cannot but be influenced by the developments and commonly accepted standards in general policy of the Member States of the Council of Europe in this field'.

[38] Pauwelyn suggests that WTO Agreements which include regulatory provisions may be adapted to the 'evolutionary' method of interpretation. J Pauwelyn, 'The nature of WTO obligations' (2002) Jean Monnet Working Paper 1/02, New York University School of Law.

[39] Judge Max Huber in *Island of Palmas* (*Arbitration*) (1928) 2 R. Int'l Arb. Awards 831)stated that: 'A judicial fact must be appreciated in the light of the law contemporary with it, and not of the law in force at the time such a dispute in regard to it arises or falls to be settled'(p 845). He distinguished the creation of rights from the existence of rights, and spoke of a principle by which the existence of the right (its continued manifestation) shall follow the conditions required by the evolution of the relevant rules (ibid). The ILC in elaborating the draft text on the law of treaties had determined that the issue of temporal factors was part of the general rules of good faith, and removed the words 'at the time of its conclusion'. There are, however, outstanding concerns over its legal stability, and the general rule of *pacta tertius nec nocent nec procent* was confirmed as a premise. Yasseen (n 7) 64 et seq.

[40] Report of the Study Group of the ILC, finalised by M Koskenniemi, 'Fragmentation of International Law: difficulties arising from the diversification and expansion of international law' A.CN.4/L.702, A/CN.4/L.682, 13 April 2006.

[41] Report of the Study Group of the ILC (n 40) para 427.

sub-paragraph contains no temporal provision.[42] It does not state whether the rules of international law to be taken into account for the purpose of treaty interpretation are to be determined in relation to the date on which the treaty was concluded or alternatively, the date on which the dispute arises. Furthermore, on the question of what scope of 'relevant rules of international law applicable in the relations between the parties' that Article 31.3(c) VCLT requires the interpreter to take into account, together with the context, for establishing what the parties have been understood to have agreed upon, the Report includes:

> the extent to which that other treaty [provided that the parties in dispute are also parties to that other treaty] relied upon can be said to have been 'implicitly' accepted or at least tolerated by the other parties [in dispute] 'in the sense that it can reasonably be considered to express the common intentions or understanding of all members as to the meaning of the . . . term concerned'. [43]

The Report by the Study Group, citing the mode of interpretation by the WTO Appellate Body in the Shrimp I case which remains rather exceptional in the tradition of WTO dispute settlement as we will see below, recommended that this will give effect to 'a good sense of a "common understanding" or a "state of the art" in a particular technical field without necessarily reflecting formal customary law' and help avoid those interpretations that threaten the coherence of the treaty to be interpreted.[44]

II VCLT AND DISPUTE SETTLEMENT AT THE WTO

As the drafting history of the VCLT shows, the original drafts of Articles 31 and 32, which were relatively precise with restrictive conditions concerning the elements to be taken into account for treaty interpretation, came to include various possibilities offering multiple choices to the treaty interpreter, to the extent that even opposing interpretations within the same provision are possible. Although open-ended, flexible rules of treaty interpretation allow diverse parties to participate in multilateral treaties, excessively flexible rules may not be practical in resolving conflicts among opposing interests and legal positions arising between them. Furthermore, overly flexible rules of interpretation may not create the degree of certainty and predictability needed for stable international cooperation.[45] Article

---

[42] Report of the Study Group of the ILC (n 40) para 426(d).

[43] . ibid para 472. The Report of the Study Group quotes in fn 28 the Appellate Body Report in US– Shrimp I, para 130.

[44] ibid. para 472.

[45] The Court of Justice of the European Union, for example, generally relies on the method of interpretation indicated in *Van Gend en Loos* (Case 26/62 [1963] ECR 1) on 5 February 1963, namely, the EC treaty provisions are interpreted in accordance with *'l'esprit, l'économie et le texte'*. Under this rather 'teleological' method, the effectiveness principle has been applied. According to Ehlermann, the difference in style and methodology of interpretation at the WTO dispute settlement 'could hardly be more radical' (C-D Ehlermann, 'Six Years on the Bench of the "World Trade Court" – Some Personal Experiences as member of the Appellate Body of the WTO' (2002) 4 *Journal of*

3.2 of the DSU states that '[t]he dispute settlement system of the WTO is a central element in providing security and predictability to the multilateral trading system.' Article 3.2 DSU affirms that

> [t]he prompt settlement of situations in which a Member considers that any benefits accruing to it directly or indirectly under the covered agreements are being impaired by measures taken by another Member is essential to the effective functioning of the WTO and the maintenance of a proper balance between the rights and obligations of Members.

According to Jackson, 'predictability and security' as well as 'prompt and effective settlement of disputes' are an important part of the underlying fundamental policy objectives of the dispute settlement system, although these goals may conflict with each other somewhat.[46] 'In a broad brush', Jackson interprets the provision in Article 3.2 for the WTO dispute settlement system not to 'add to or diminish rights or obligations' as a 'precautionary admonition against "judicial activism"'.[47] A high degree of pragmatism is necessary to achieve these purposes in a multilateral trading system.

By capitalising on the rule of interpretation based on Articles 31 and 32 of the VCLT, and by adding a systematic discipline to them, the Panels and the Appellate Body gradually formulated an interpretative tradition unique to the WTO.

A Terms of the treaty

The Appellate Body in *Japan–Alcoholic Beverages* clearly adopted a classical, 'textualist' approach characteristic of the 1964 ILC draft rules of treaty interpretation, by quoting scholars of this school. It explained that 'Article 31 of the Vienna Convention provides that the words of the treaty form the foundation for the interpretive process' and quoted ICJ cases where it was stated that 'interpretation must be based above all upon the text of the treaty'.[48] In interpreting the covered agreements, WTO Panels and the Appellate Body focused their attention on the 'ordinary meaning given to the terms', and referred frequently to dictionaries to find those meanings. In *EC–Hormones*, the Appellate

---

World Trade 616). For a 'teleological' method of interpretation to be effective, it would be necessary to have consensus among Member States on the primary purpose of the treaty (such as the creation of a single market) and the fundamental values with respect to the implementation of the treaty, which certainly is not the case with the global participants.

[46] JH Jackson, 'The WTO Dispute Settlement System after Ten Years: The First Decade's Promises and Challenges in The WTO' in Y Taniguchi et al (eds) *The Twenty-First-Century: Dispute Settlement, Negotiations, and Regionalism in Asia* (Cambridge, Cambridge University Press 2007) 32-3.

[47] Jackson, ibid 33.

[48] *Territorial Dispute (Libyan Arab Jamahiriya/Chad)*, Judgment (1994) ICJ Reports 6, 20; *Maritime Delimitation and Territorial Questions between Qatar and Bahrain, Jurisdiction and Admissibility*, Judgment (1995), ICJ Reports 6, 18 are quoted. *Japan–Alcoholic Beverages* (n 6) 12.

Body emphasised that the fundamental rule of treaty interpretation was to read and interpret the words 'actually used', and not words which 'the interpreter may feel should have been used'. The Panel interpreted the word 'risk assessment' in the Sanitary and Phytosanitary (SPS) Agreement to mean 'scientific risk assessment', and not 'risk management which is not scientific but policy exercise involving social value judgments'. Discussions on 'policy exercise involving social value' may be interminable, particularly among parties to a multilateral treaty. According to the Appellate Body, this distinction, which was employed by the Panel to achieve or support what appears to be a restrictive notion of risk assessment, had 'no textual basis'.[49] In other words, for the purpose of interpreting treaties, the emphasis is placed on the parties' original intentions as reflected on the wording, its textual context, but not the general overall purpose of the treaty and inferred philosophically by the treaty interpreter. The Appellate Body explains in footnote 20 in *EC–Hormones* that the treaty's 'object and purpose' is to be referred to in determining the meaning of the 'terms of the treaty' and 'not as an independent basis for interpretation'.[50] Instead, the Appellate Body uses the effectiveness principle to examine the structure of the treaty.

Thus, the Appellate Body has developed a consensual approach to interpretation based on the objective assessment of the wording of treaty provisions. In *EC–Computer Equipment*, the Appellate Body corrected the Panel's view that 'the duty of the interpreter is to examine the words of the treaty to determine the *intentions* of the parties'. According to the Appellate Body, the purpose of treaty interpretation under the general rule of interpretation drawn from the Vienna Convention is to ascertain the 'common intentions' of the parties.[51] Furthermore, these common intentions cannot be ascertained on the basis of the subjective and unilaterally determined 'expectations' of only one of the parties to a treaty.

B 'Object and purpose' of the treaty

The philosophical 'object and purpose' of the treaty as a whole is rarely sought explicitly in WTO dispute settlement. Instead, the effectiveness principle, which explores the meaning of specific terms or provisions in light of the general structure of the treaty, is employed. This interpretative approach which, again, is

---

[49] *EC–Measures Concerning Meat and Meat Products (EC–Hormones)*, Appellate Body Report (adopted 13 February 1998) WT/DS26/AB/R, WT/DS48/AB/R para 181.

[50] The Appellate Body's Report quotes the following authors who rely generally on the textualist approach: Harris, *Cases and Materials on International Law,* 4th edn (1991); Jiménez de Aréchaga, 'International Law in the Past Third of a Century' (1978) I *Recueil des Cours*; Sinclair, *The Vienna Convention and the Law of Treaties,* 2nd edn (1984); Jennings and Watts (eds), *Oppenheims' International Law,* 9th edn (1992) vol I; *Competence of the ILO to Regulate the Personal Work of the Employer* (1926) PCIJ, Series B, No 13: 6, 18; *International Status of South West Africa* (1962) ICJ Reports 128, 336; *Re Competence of Conciliation Commission* (1955) 22 ILR 867, 871.

[51] *EC–Customs Classification of Certain Computer Equipment*, Appellate Body Report (adopted 22 June 1998) WT/DS62 67, 68/AB/R paras 83–4.

found in the earlier ILC draft for the general rule of interpretation, seems to be taken because Members' opinions are potentially divided on how to determine the 'object and purpose' of multilateral agreements. Even at the International Centre for the Settlement of Investment Disputes (ICSID)[52] where the 'object and purpose of the treaty' might appear to be relatively easy to discern, because the preamble states that 'the parties have agreed to the provisions of the treaty for the purpose of creating favourable conditions for the investments of nationals or companies or one of the two states in the territory of the or the state', difficulties nevertheless have arisen in defining the object and purpose of the treaty.[53] For example, in *Palma v Bulgaria*, the Decision on Jurisdiction of 8 February 2005 states that: 'the Tribunal is mindful of Sir Ian Sinclair's warning of the "risk that the placing of undue emphasis on the 'object and purpose' of a treaty will encourage teleological methods of interpretation [which], in some of its more extreme forms, will even deny the relevance of the intentions of the parties"'.[54]

In the dispute settlement cases under the GATT, treaties seem to have been interpreted from an implicitly teleological perspective, in the sense that the aim of maintaining and strengthening the free trade system was assumed important for the Panels.[55] With the establishment of the WTO, however, a wide range of treaties covering areas such as services and IPRs came into play, complicating debates on object and purpose in several ways. First, some of the WTO agreements were conceived not only for the purpose of trade liberalisation but also for necessary regulatory considerations which do not necessarily correspond to trade liberalisation. There could be potential inconsistency and discord in the objects and purposes of different WTO agreements as we have seen in the elaboration of the TRIPS Agreement. Secondly, taking subjective considerations into account by interpreting the object and purpose of a treaty could easily lead to an unstable interpretation. Thirdly, the meaning of Article 31 of the VCLT is unclear. If the language of the treaty in question provides that its purpose is the object and purpose of Article 31 of the VCLT, this interpretation could possibly be not different from a literal interpretation anyway. According to Article 31.1 of the VCLT, the question of which method to use in determining the 'object and purpose' of the treaty is left with the treaty interpreter. If the purpose is

---

[52] ICSID is an autonomous international institution established under the Convention on the Settlement of Investment Disputes between States and Nationals of Other States (ICSID Convention), which sets forth ICSID's mandate, organisation and core functions. The primary purpose of ICSID is to provide facilities for conciliation and arbitration of international investment disputes. As of 26 January 2009, there were 155 signatory States to the ICSID Convention. Of these, 143 had also deposited their instruments of ratification, acceptance or approval of the Convention to become ICSID Contracting States.

[53] *Siemens v Argentina*, ICSID Case No ARB/02/8 (Germany/Argentina BIT). Decision on Jurisdiction, 3 August 2004.

[54] ibid para 193.

[55] See, for example, *US–Restrictions on Imports of Tuna (US–Tuna (Mexico))*, Panel Report DS29/R (unadopted 3 September 1991), BISD 39S/155. Economists tend to assert that the purposes of the GATT and the WTO are not trade liberalisation based on the idea of comparative advantage, but rather trade regulation. See for example, P Krugman, 'What Should Trade Negotiators Negotiate About?' (1997) 35(1) *Journal of Economic Literature* 113–20.

described in the treaty as the 'object and purpose of the treaty', and if the interpreter considers this actually as the treaty's overall 'object and purpose', the interpreter is resorting to the mere 'wording'. Other 'objects and purposes' may be inferred from the structure or the spirit of the treaty in question, or from the political or ideological stance of the interpreter. In any of these cases, opinions will diverge on what the 'object and purpose' of the treaty is. There would be various methods of determining the purpose, the result of the application of which would differ considerably.[56]

C Elements to be taken into consideration for interpretative purposes

WTO Panels and the Appellate Body have tended also to impose strict conditions on the elements to be taken into account, 'together with the context', for the purpose of interpretation, set out in Article 31.3. According to the Appellate Body in *Japan–Alcoholic Beverages*, for recognising as 'subsequent practice' the establishment of the agreement of the parties (Article 31.3(b)), the practice should form a 'concordant, *common* and consistent sequence of acts or pronouncements which is sufficient to establish a discernable pattern implying the agreement of the parties regarding its interpretation.'[57] In other words, an isolated act is too insufficient to be recognised as 'subsequent practice'. The Appellate Body explained in *EC–Chicken Cuts*[58] what Article 31.3 (b) means, and cautions that:

> 'lack of reaction' should not lightly, without further inquiry into attendant circumstances of a case, be read to imply agreement with an interpretation by treaty parties that have not themselves engaged in a particular practice followed by other parties in the application of the treaty. This is all the more so because the interpretation of a treaty provision on the basis of subsequent practice is binding on all parties to the treaty, including those that have not actually engaged in such practice.[59]

---

[56] According to Art 2 of the Treaty establishing the European Community (EC), the 'purpose' of the treaty was the establishment of a common market and an economic and monetary union through policies described in Arts 3 and 4 (repealed by the Treaty on the Functioning of the European Union). Art 3 of the EC treaty covered 21 policy targets, some of which conflicted with each other. For example, the European Court of Justice (ECJ) heard disputes about the discrepancies between Art 3(e), which provided for a policy in the sphere of agriculture and fisheries, and Art 3(g), which provided for competition. The ECJ resolved disagreements on the interpretation of the 'object and purpose of a treaty' by establishing principles of interpretation of the EC Treaty which relied on the analysis of the treaty's structure, spirit, and language.

[57] *Japan–Alcoholic Beverages* (n 6) 13.

[58] *EC–Customs Classification of Frozen Boneless Chicken Cuts*, Appellate Body Report (adopted 12 September 2005) WT/DS269/AB/R, WT/DS286/AB/R 99–110.

[59] ibid para 250. The Appellate Body, quoting the AB report in *Japan–Alcoholic Beverages*, asserted that 'relying on "subsequent practice" for purposes of interpretation must not lead to interference with the "exclusive authority" of the Ministerial Conference and the General Council to adopt interpretations of WTO agreements that are binding on all Members'. In this case, the EC argued that Art IX:2 of the WTO Agreement suggests that any practice relating to the interpretation of the multilateral trade agreements and acceptance thereof must take the form of overt acts that are explicitly submitted for consideration of all WTO Members and adopted by a large majority of the WTO membership.

On the 'relevant rules of international law applicable in the relations between the parties' in the treaty interpretation' in Article 31.3 (c), the position of the WTO dispute organs has not been entirely clear. In *US–Shrimp I*, which dealt with measures presumably intended to promote environmental protection, the Appellate Body considered a wider scope of customary rules in interpreting Article XX (g) of the GATT 1994. In this case, the Appellate Body examined the terms of the Convention on International Trade in Endangered Species of Wild Fauna and Flora (CITES), the Convention on Biological Diversity (CBD)[60] and the Inter-American Convention for the Protection and Conservation of Sea Turtles, to explore the term 'exhaustible natural resources' in Article XX(g) GATT, even though the disputing party was not a party to all the conventions cited. The US, which accepted this approach of the Appellate Body in *US–Shrimp I*, might have resisted it if the WTO-covered agreements had led to an unacceptable interpretation of the treaty terms through rules of international law to which they do not adhere.[61]

This method of interpretation has not been followed subsequently. However, the Panel in *EC–Biotech Products*[62] stated that not the disputing parties alone but all WTO Members must be bound by 'other relevant rules' in order for these rules to be looked at for the purpose of interpreting treaty provisions:

> It may be inferred from these elements that the rules of international law applicable in the relations between "the parties" are the rules of international law applicable in the relations between the States which have consented to be bound by the treaty which is being interpreted, and for which that treaty is in force. This understanding of the term 'the parties' leads logically to the view that the rules of international law to be taken into account in interpreting the WTO agreements at issue in this dispute are those which are applicable in the relations between the WTO Members.[63]

---

[60] The Convention on Biodiversity (CBD) was negotiated under the auspices of the United Nations Environment Programme (UNEP), adopted at the UN Conference on Environment and Development in 1992 (Rio Earth Summit), and came into force on 29 December 1993. A large number of countries – 187 countries and the European Communities as of April 2006; 191 parties in October 2009 – are parties to the Convention, with the notable exception of the United States, which has not ratified it. As stated in Art 1: 'The objectives of this Convention, to be pursued in accordance with its relevant provisions, are the conservation of biological diversity, the sustainable use of its components and the fair and equitable sharing of the benefits arising out of the utilization of genetic resources, including by appropriate access to genetic resources and by appropriate transfer of relevant technologies, taking into account all rights over those resources and to technologies, and by appropriate funding.'

[61] In the interpretation by the Appellate Body in the *US–Shrimp I* case, the important role played by the text of the Preamble of the Agreement establishing the WTO may also be controversial. In interpreting Art XX(g) of the GATT 1994, the Appellate Body noted 'once more that the preamble of the WTO Agreement demonstrates a recognition by WTO negotiators that optimal use of the world's resources should be made in accordance with the objective of sustainable development. As this preamble language reflects the intentions of negotiators of the WTO Agreement, we believe it must add "colour, texture and shading" to our interpretation of the agreements annexed to the WTO Agreement, in this case, the GATT 1994 . . .' (*US–Shrimp I* (n 28) para 153).

[62] *EC–Measures Affecting the Approval and Marketing of Biotech Products* (*EC–Biotech Products*), Panel Report (adopted 21 November 2006)WT/DS291, 292, 293/R.

[63] *EC–Biotech Products* ibid para 7.68. The GATT Panel, which was not bound by customary rules of international law for interpreting the GATT, interpreted Art 31.3(c) of the VCLT strictly by

The Panel in *EC–Biotech Products* referred back to the Appellate Body's analysis in *Shrimp I,* explaining that: 'the Appellate Body drew on other rules of international law because it considered that they were informative and aided it in establishing the meaning and scope of the term "exhaustible natural resources"'. In other words, the mere fact that not all of the disputing parties are parties to a convention does not necessarily mean that the convention cannot shed light on the meaning and scope of a treaty term to be interpreted. The Panel added in footnote 271 to the same paragraph that: 'we note that the Appellate Body did not suggest that it was looking to other rules of international law because it was required to do so pursuant to the provisions of Article 31.3(c) of the Vienna Convention. Indeed, the Appellate Body did not even mention Article 31.3(c).'[64]

D   Temporal factors

At the WTO dispute settlement, the issue of temporality in treaty interpretation had not arisen until the *US–Shrimp I* case. The Appellate Body, in interpreting the term 'exhaustible natural resources' stated that: 'They must be read by a treaty interpreter in the light of contemporary concerns of the community of nations about the protection and conservation of the environment'.[65]

In other words, the Appellate Body in this case took into consideration the situation at the time of interpreting the term of a treaty by the Appellate Body in the *US–Shrimp I* case as follows:

> From the perspective embodied in the preamble of the WTO Agreement, we note that the generic term 'natural resources' in Article XX(g) is not 'static' in its content or reference but is rather 'by definition, evolutionary'. It is, therefore, pertinent to note that modern international conventions and declarations make frequent references to natural resources as embracing both living and non-living resources.[66] According to the Appellate Body, 'from the perspective embodied in the preamble of the WTO Agreement, we note that the generic term 'exhaustible natural resources' in Article XX (g) is not 'static' in its content or reference but is rather 'by definition, evolutionary.[67]

interpreting that it is necessary for the reference materials set out in Art 31.3 to be between 'all' of the parties: *US–Restrictions on Imports of Tuna* (n 55) para 5.19. On this point, see PC Mavroidis and D Palmeter, 'The WTO Legal System: Sources of Law' (1998) 92 *American Journal of International Law* 411–12. The Panel in *EC–Biotech Products* also found that: 'where consideration of all other interpretative elements set out in Article 31 results in more than one permissible interpretation, Article 31.3(c) mandates a treaty interpreter to take into account other rules of international law, for the interpretation in accord with other applicable rules of international law should be settled for'. According to this Panel, it makes sense to interpret Article 31.3(c) as requiring consideration of those rules of international law which are 'applicable in the relations between all parties to the treaty which is being interpreted' (para 7.69).

[64] *EC–Biotech Products* (n 62) para 7.94, fn 271.

[65] Appellate Body Report, *US–Shrimp I* (n 28), paras.154–5.

[66] ibid para 130.

[67] The Appellate Body, in fn 271, mentions that the ICJ adopted this interpretative method in such cases as *Namibia Advisory Opinion* (1971); *Aegean Sea Continental Shelf* (1978); and *Gabcikovo-Nagymaros* (1998). The Appellate Body made a decision which was not followed by subsequent dispute cases.

The 'evolutionary' approach to treaty interpretation was not adopted in subsequent cases, but was more recently confirmed by the Appellate Body in *China–Audiovisual Services*.[68]

The approach to interpretation by the WTO Panels and the Appellate Body has been criticised from several perspectives, for the following reasons, including that (i) there is excessive reliance on dictionaries;[69] (ii) the meaning of the 'context' for interpretative purposes is rigid and confused, in the sense that it sometimes comprises 'factual' (instead of textual) contexts;[70] (iii) there is failure to examine the structure of the treaty as a whole;[71] and (iv) that the object and purpose of the treaty are disregarded.[72] These criticisms questioned the rigid, formal application of Article 31 of the VCLT. However, there were also criticisms from another viewpoint, namely that preparatory work was considered without taking into account the elements set out in the general rule of interpretation (Article 31VCLT).[73]

Despite criticisms and the inevitable evolution towards subtler interpretations adapted to each case and in light of the complexities of facts, however, the positive role played by the cautious, conservative and consensual approach to interpretation described above should also be valorised. This method of interpretation probably allowed the WTO dispute settlement organs to provide

---

[68] The Panel in *China–Measures Affecting Trading Rights and Distribution Services for Certain Publications and Audiovisual Entertainment Products* refers to the interpretation of the term 'exhaustible natural resources' in the above *US–Shrimp I* case in reading GATS Schedules and states that: 'We further note that interpreting the terms of GATS-specific commitments based on the notion that the ordinary meaning to be attributed to those terms can only be the meaning that they had at the time the Schedule was concluded would mean that very similar or identically worded commitments could be given different meanings, content, and coverage depending on the date of their adoption or the date of a Member's accession to the treaty. Such interpretation would undermine the predictability, security, and clarity of GATS specific commitments, which are undertaken through successive rounds of negotiations, and which must be interpreted in accordance with customary rules of interpretation of public international law' (paras 396–7).

[69] H Norn and JHH Weiler, 'EC-Trade Description of Sardines: Textualism and its Discontent' in H Horn and PC Mavroidis (eds), *The WTO Case of 2002* (Cambridge University Press, 2005).

[70] C Valles, 'Challenges in interpreting Schedules of Concessions relying on the rules of treaty interpretation in the Vienna Convention on the Law of Treaties', Sixth Annual WTO Conference, London, 23 May 2006. Valles appreciates that the Appellate Body did not find any error in the Panel's interpretive approach, considering factual contexts in finding the meaning of certain words such as 'flavour, texture, [and] other physical properties' of the products falling under the tariff heading of the Schedules of Concessions. Para 176 of the Appellate Body Report states: 'Interpretation pursuant to the customary rules codified in Article 31 of the Vienna Convention is ultimately a holistic exercise that should not be mechanically subdivided into rigid components. Considering particular surrounding circumstances under the rubric of "ordinary meaning" or "in the light of its context" would not, in our view, change the outcome of treaty interpretation.'. *EC–Chicken Cuts* (n 58).

[71] F Ortino, 'Treaty Interpretation and the WTO Appellate Body Report in US-Gambling: A Critique' (2006) 9(1) *Journal of International Economic Law* 117–48.

[72] D Shanker, 'The Vienna Convention on the Law of Treaties: the dispute settlement system of the WTO and the Doha Declaration on the TRIPS Agreement' (2002) 36(4) *Journal of World Trade* 721–72.

[73] M Matsushita, TJ Schoenbaum and PC Mavroidis. *The World Trade Organization: Law, Practice, and Policy*, 2nd edn (Oxford University Press, 2006) 52.

pragmatic solutions to conflicts, detached from potentially divisive political positions and opposing economic interests of WTO Members. It also allowed the WTO dispute settlement organs to avoid infringing Article 3.2 of the DSU.

7

TRIPS Provisions as Interpreted by the WTO Dispute Settlement Organs

THIS CHAPTER EXAMINES how the WTO dispute settlement organs have interpreted TRIPS provisions. Except for the initial period following the establishment of the WTO, there have been few dispute cases over the TRIPS provisions: only three cases have been appealed. Nonetheless, the reports on these disputes are important guideposts for interpreting TRIPS, especially about the objective and principles of the Agreement, its exceptions and limitations, non-discrimination principles and TRIPS 'flexibility' as understood by the WTO dispute organs. The WTO dispute organs emphasised the importance of the customary rules of international public law in interpreting the TRIPS Agreement, as has been the case for all the WTO-covered agreements, and, in particular, the wording of the treaty provisions to be interpreted. This may be due largely to Article 3.2 of the Understanding on Rules and Procedures Governing the Settlement of Disputes (DSU), which defines the role of the WTO dispute settlement system. According to Article 3.2 of the DSU, this system serves 'to preserve the rights and obligations of Members under the covered agreements, to clarify the existing provisions of those agreements in accordance with customary rules of interpretation of public international law', but cannot add to or diminish the rights and obligations provided in the covered agreements. This disciplined approach to interpreting TRIPS provisions seems to have prevented potential political arguments based on limited market data.

I AN OVERVIEW

From 1 January 1995 to 30 September 2009, there were a total of 399 requests for consultations and 122 Panel and Appellate Body Reports.[1] Of these, only 13 Panel and Appellate Body Reports concerning the TRIPS Agreement were adopted, in a total of eight cases. The findings of Panel Reports are binding only on the parties to the dispute, and although the Appellate Body reports can have a wider impact on legal, systemic questions, there are to date only three Appellate Body reports concerning this Agreement.

---

[1] *Overview of the State of Play of WTO Disputes*, Dispute Settlement Body, Annual Report (5 November 2009) WT/DSB/49/Add.1.

At the initial period after the entry into force of the WTO Agreement, approximately 10 per cent of disputes, a relatively high level, concerned the TRIPS Agreement.[2] Most disputes were over differences between the systems of intellectual property protection in developed countries. For example, the first TRIPS dispute case was brought against Japan by the US, concerning retroactive protection of sound recordings in Japan. This dispute was resolved during the bilateral consultations between the two countries. Several dispute cases were brought to the dipute settlement procedures over the implementation of the TRIPS Agreement in developing countries. Among the total of 29 complaints concerning the TRIPS agreement, 14 cases garnered mutually agreed solutions. Three consultations remain inactive (Table 7.4). In May 2010, two requests for consultations relating to the TRIPS Agreement as well as the GATT 1994 were submitted by developing countries to the Dispute Settlement Body (DSB)[3]. The rate of TRIPS dispute cases dropped sharply after the initial period, as Tables 7.1 – to 7.4 show.

WTO Disputes relating to the TRIPS Agreement

Table 7.1: Disputes where a Panel report (P), or Panel and Appellate Body (AB) Reports are adopted

Disputes		Report (P)(AB) adopted	Complainant	Third parties
India–Patents I (US)	WT/DS50	16 January 1998 (AB)	US	EC
India–Patents II (EC)	WT/DS79	22 September 1998 (P)	EC	US
Indonesia–Autos	WT/D59	23 July 1998 (P)	US	Rep Korea, India
Canada– Pharmaceutical Patent Protection	WT/DS 114	7 April 2000 (P)	EC	Australia, Brazil, Columbia, Cuba, India, Israel, Japan, Poland, Switzerland, Thailand, US
US–Section 110(5) of US Copyright Act	WT/DS 160	27 July 2000 (P)	EC	Brazil, Australia, Canada, Japan, Switzerland

---

[2] The US has initiated many of the approximately 20 major disputes that have been resolved, followed by the EU. The US has taken action against countries including Japan, India, Indonesia, Denmark, Sweden, Greece, Ireland, Canada and Brazil, as well as the EU. The majority of these disputes (10 cases) have been about the protection of patent rights.

[3] *European Union and a Member State–Seizure of Generic Drugs in Transit* (19 May 2010) WT/DS408/1 (India),WT/DS/409/1(Brazil). The dispute between India and the EU in this case, according to press reports, seem resolved in principle, at the 11th EU-India summit on 10 December 2010.

Canada–Patent Term	WT/DS170	12 October 2000 (AB)	US	
Disputes		**Report (P)(AB) adopted**	**Complainant**	**Third parties**
US–Section 211 Appropriation Act	WT/DS176	1 February 2002 (AB)	EC	Nicaragua, Japan
EC–Geographical Indication	WT/DS 174	20 April 2005 (P)	US	Argentina, Australia, Brazil, Canada, China, Chinese Taipei, Colombia, Guatemala, India, Mexico, New Zealand, Turkey
	WT/DS 290	20 April 2005 (P)	Australia	Argentina, Australia, Bulgaria, Cyprus, the Czech Republic, Hungary, India, Malta, Mexico, New Zealand, Romania, the Slovak Republic, Slovenia, Sri Lanka and Turkey
China – Intellectual Property Protection	WT/ DS/362	20 March 2009 (P)	US	Argentina; Australia; Brazil; Canada; EU; India; Japan; Rep Korea; Mexico; Chinese Taipei; Thailand; Turkey

(P) Adopted Panel Reports
(AB) Adopted Appellate Body Reports

Table 7.2 Cases where consultations have been initiated (pending)

Disputes		**Complainant**	**Third parties**
EU–Seizure of Generic Drugs in Tansit(respondents: EU and the Netherlands)	WT/DS408	India	Brazil, Canada, China, Ecuador, Japan, Turkey
	WT/DS409	Brazil	Canada, Ecuador, India, China, Japan Turkey

Table 7.3: Settled disputes

Disputes	Complain-ant	Notification of Mutually Agreed Solution
Portugal–Patent Protection under the Industrial Property Act (WT/DS37)	US	3 October 1996
Japan–Measures Concerning Sound Recordings (WT/DS28, WT/DS42)	US EC	24 January 1997 (US) 7 November 1997 (EC)
Pakistan–Patent Protection for Pharmaceutical and Agricultural Chemical Products (WT/DS36)	US	28 February 1997
Denmark, Sweden–Measures Affecting the Enforcement of Intellectual Property Rights (WT/DS83, WT/DS86)	US	2 December 1998 (S) 7 June 2001 (DK)
Ireland–Measures Affecting the Grant of Copyright and Neighbouring Rights (WT/DS82)	US	6 November 2000
EC–Measures Affecting the Grant of Copyright and Neighbouring Rights (WT/DS115)	US	6 November 2000
EC–Enforcement of Intellectual Property Rights for Motion Pictures and Television Programs (WT/DS124)	US	20 March 2001
Greece–Enforcement of Intellectual Property Rights for Motion Pictures and Television Programs (WT/DS125)	US	20 March 2001
Brazil–Measures Affecting Patent Protection (WT/DSDS199)	US	5 July 2001
Argentina–Patent Protection for Pharmaceuticals and Test Data Protection for Agricultural Chemical Products (WT/DS171)	US	31 May 2002
Argentina–Certain Measures on the Protection of Patents and Test Data (WT/DS196)	US	31 May 2002
China–Measures Affecting Financial Information Services and Foreign Financial Information Suppliers(WT/ DS372)	EC	4 December 2008

Table 7.4: Disputes where consultations continue (inactive)

Disputes	Complainant	Respondent
EC–Patent Protection for Pharmaceutical and Agricultural Chemical Products (WT/DS153)	Canada	EC
US–Section 337 of the Tariff Act of 1930 and Amendments thereto (WT/DS/186)	EC	US
US–US Patents Code (WT/DS/224)	Brazil	US

WTO Panels and the Appellate Body have interpreted the TRIPS Agreement by referring to the customary rules of treaty interpretation, notably the method delineated in Articles 31 and 32 VCLT, in the same cautious and consensual spirit and through the same textualist approach for TRIPS cases as they have for other cases, with, however, certain adaptations to the characteristics of the TRIPS Agreement as a treaty.

TRIPS interpretation has so far relied much on finding the ordinary meaning of the terms in the Agreement, often supported by the effectiveness principle (*ut res magis valeat quam pereat*). Additionally, Panels and the Appellate Body have relied extensively on the provisions in the Paris and Berne Conventions, and their related documents, guidelines and preparatory work, as 'context', 'contextual guidance' or 'extended context' for the purpose of interpreting the TRIPS Agreement. From the previous GATT system, there has been some interpretative guidance for TRIPS dispute cases, but mainly on the issues of national treatment and most-favoured nation principles.

The text of the TRIPS Agreement is brief, and little preparatory work is available. During the Uruguay Round negotiations, the Secretariat Notes and various written proposals from participants were available, but there was no drafting committee to keep track of the processes by which the text of the TRIPS Agreement was adopted. There was no accumulation of experience within the GATT regarding intellectual property rights (IPRs).

When the meaning of a treaty provision is sufficiently clear, no interpretative guidance is sought from the Vienna Convention. In such cases, Panels and the Appellate Body have relied directly on the wording of the Agreement, including its titles and footnotes. In searching for the meaning of 'rights holders' to whom civil judicial procedures should be made available by the WTO Members, the Appellate Body in *US–Section 211 Appropriation Act*[4] simply relied on the footnote to Article 42 TRIPS, which states that: 'For the purpose of this Part [III], the term "right holder" includes federations and associations having legal standing to assert such rights'.[5] Under the TRIPS Agreement, therefore, procedures should be available not only to those who obtain IPRs, but also to any party which has legal standing to assert such rights. Footnotes were also examined to determine the meaning of 'nationals' of the customs territory (footnote 1 to Article 1.3 TRIPS – see chapter 5),[6] and whether principles of national treatment apply to the use of IPRs generally, or if they only apply to 'those matters affecting the use of IPRs specifically addressed in the TRIPS' (footnote to Article 3.1).[7] The

---

[4] *United States–Section 211 Omnibus Appropriations Act of 1998 (US–Section 211 Appropriation Act)*, Appellate Body Report (adopted 1 February 2002) WT/DS176/AB/R.

[5] ibid para 8.99.

[6] *EC–Protection of Trademarks and Geographical Indications for Agricultural Products and Foodstuffs (EC–Geographical Indications)*, Panel Reports (adopted 20 April 2005) WT/DS174/R (complaint by the US) para 7.165, WT/DS290/R (complaint by Australia) para 7.215.

[7] *Indonesia–Certain Measures Affecting the Automobile Industry* Panel Report (adopted 23 July 1998) WT/DS54/R, WT/DS55/R, WT/DS59/R, WT/DS64/R and Corr 1,2,3,4 para 11.29 (*Indonesia– Autos*).

Panel and the Appellate Body, in dealing with TRIPS cases, have referred also to GATT Panel Reports and the 1994 GATT.[8] In *EC–Geographical Indications*,[9] the Panel referred to the GATT report on *US–Section 337*,[10] as well as the Panel and Appellate Body reports in *US–Section 211 Appropriation Act*, and stated that national treatment relates to 'effective equality of opportunities' of the nationals of Members with regard to the protection of IPRs, to the nationals of the Member concerned.[11]

When the examination of 'preparatory work' for the elaboration of the TRIPS Agreement was needed, the text, guidelines and model laws relating to the relevant provisions of the Paris or Berne Conventions were often referred to as 'contextual guidance' or 'contextual support'. In examining the historical context of TRIPS provisions in terms of previous IP treaties, the Appellate Body in *US–Section 211 Appropriation Act* stated that Article 6 *quinquies* of the Paris Convention offered 'contextual support'.[12] These concepts relating to 'context' in interpreting TRIPS do not necessarily derive from Article 31 VCLT.

II TRIPS INTERPRETED BY WTO DISPUTE ORGANS

A 'Context' for the purpose of Interpreting TRIPS

Article 2 TRIPS concerning 'intellectual property conventions' stipulates in para 1 that '[i]n respect of Parts II, III and IV of this Agreement, Members shall comply with Articles 1 through 12, and Article 19 of the Paris Convention (1967)', while Article 9 concerning 'Relation to the Berne Convention' provides that 'Members shall comply with Articles 1 through 21 of the Berne Convention (1971) and the Appendix thereto'.[13]

---

[8] The Panel in *EC–Geographical Indications* defined the relationship between the GATT 1994 and the TRIPS Agreement as follows: 'The Panel notes that there is no hierarchy between the TRIPS Agreement and GATT 1994, which appear in separate annexes to the WTO Agreement. The ordinary meaning of the texts of the TRIPS Agreement and GATT 1994, as well as Article II:2 of the WTO Agreement, taken together, indicates that obligations under the TRIPS Agreement and GATT 1994 can co-exist and that one does not override the other.' *EC–Geographical Indications* (n 6) (US) para 7.208, (Australia) para 7.258.

[9] *EC–Geographical Indications* (n 6).

[10] *US–Section 337 of the Tariff Act of 1930*, Panel Report (adopted 7 November 1989) BISD 36S/345 (see chs 3 and 4).

[11] *EC–Geographical Indications*, (n 6), (US) paras 7.126–37, (Australia) paras 7.176–87.

[12] According to the Appellate Body in *US–Section 211 Appropriations Act* (n 4) para 139, 'To resolve this question, we look to the context of Article 6 *quinquies* A(1). We find that there is considerable contextual support for the view that the requirement to register a trademark "as is" under Article 6 *quinquies* A (1) does not encompass all the features and aspects of that trademark . . .'. In this case, the EC referred to Article 6 *quinquies* as 'contextual guidance' (para 18) and 'contextual support' (para 143).

[13] Art 2.1 stipulates *in fine* that: '. . . Members shall not have rights or obligations under this Agreement in respect of the rights conferred under Article 6 *bis* of [the Berne] Convention or of the rights derived therefrom'. Part II, Part III and Part IV concern standards concerning the availability, scope and use of intellectual property rights, enforcement of intellectual property rights, and acquisition and maintenance of intellectual property rights and related *inter partes* procedures, respectively.

The Panel in *US–Section 211 Appropriation Act* interpreted the words 'in respect of' in Article 2.1 as limiting the incorporation of the provisions of the Paris and Berne Conventions to mean 'in respect of what is covered by those parts of the TRIPS Agreement identified therein'.[14] The Panel also held that the phrase 'intellectual property' in Article 1.2 designated all categories of IP that are 'the subject of Sections 1 through 7 of Part II'. For the question of whether trade names are included as the subject of protection under the TRIPS Agreement, the Panel did not find among the titles the word 'trade name' and excluded from the categories of intellectual property included under the TRIPS. The negotiating history of Articles 1.2 and 2.1 of the TRIPS Agreement was not conclusive. The Appellate Body examined the wording of Article 1.2 TRIPS and held that Article 1.2, which refers to 'the subject of Sections 1 through 7 of Part II', deals not only with the categories of intellectual property indicated in each section *title*, but with other *subjects* as well, as with the protection of *sui generis* rights, which is not found as a title but which is included under Article 27(3)(b) TRIPS[15]. The Appellate Body examined also Article 8 of the Paris Convention which covers only the protection of trade names, and reached the following conclusion: if the intention of the negotiators had been to exclude trade names from protection, there would have been no purpose in including Article 8 in the list of Paris Convention (1967) provisions incorporated into the *TRIPS Agreement*. The Appellate Body emphasised the need to give meaning and effect to all terms of a treaty.[16] Thus, the Appellate Body relied on the effectiveness principle rather than on the 'preparatory work', and quoted *US–Gasoline*[17] and *Japan–Alcoholic Beverages II*[18] in this regard.[19]

The Panel in *US–Section 110(5) Copyright Act*[20] analysed also the extent to which the minor exceptions doctrine forms part of the Berne Convention *acquis* and whether this principle has been incorporated into the TRIPS Agreement, by virtue of Article 9.1 TRIPS, together with Articles 1–21 of the Berne Convention (1971). For determining whether this doctrine, which primarily concerns *de minimis* use for the Panel, is part of the Berne Convention and the TRIPS Agreement, or forms a 'context' within the meaning of Article 31 VCLT, the Panel explored the intention of the parties[21] as reflected in the wording of relevant documents. The

---

[14] *US–Section 211 Appropriation Act,* Panel Report WT/DS176/R para 8.30.

[15] *US–Section 211 Appropriation Act,* Appellate Body Report (n 4) para 335.

[16] ibid para 338.

[17] *United States–Standards for Reformulated and Conventional Gasoline,* Appellate Body Report (adopted 20 May 1996) WT/DS2/AB/R 106.

[18] *Japan–Taxes on Alcoholic Beverages,* Appellate Body Report (adopted 1 November 1996) WT/DS8/AB/R, WT/DS10/AB/R, WT/DS11/AB/R.

[19] Ibid para. 338.

[20] *US–Section 110(5) of US Copyright Act,* Panel Report (adopted 27 July 2000) WT/DS160/R para 6.66. The EC argued that Art 10(2) WCT which incorporated the three-step test constituted the 'subsequent practice' following Art 13 TRIPS.

[21] The Panel quotes Sinclair (*The Vienna Convention on the Law of Treaties,* 2nd edn (Manchester University Press, 1984) 129) and the ILC documents (*Yearbook of the International Law Commission* (New York, ILC, 1966) vol II 221.

Panel found that the minor exceptions doctrine forms part of the 'context' within the meaning of Article 31.2(a) of the Vienna Convention, of at least Articles 11 and 11 *bis* of the Berne Convention (1971).[22] The Panel then looked into the preparatory work, notably in the documents of the TRIPS Negotiating Group, which confirmed that the information concerning this doctrine was provided by the International Bureau of WIPO,[23] and that no record exists of any party challenging the idea that the minor exceptions doctrine is part of the Berne *acquis* on which the TRIPS Agreement was to be built. From this, the Panel concluded that, in the absence of any express exclusion in Article 9.1 of the TRIPS Agreement, the incorporation of Articles 11 and 11 *bis* of the Berne Convention (1971) into the Agreement included the entire *acquis* of these provisions, including the possibility of providing minor exceptions to respective exclusive rights.[24] Although it is not exactly reflected in the language of Article 9.1 TRIPS, the Panel concluded that 'if that incorporation should have covered only the text of Articles 1–21 of the Berne Convention (1971), but not the entire Berne *acquis* relating to these Articles, Article 9.1 of the TRIPS Agreement would have explicitly so provided.'[25]

The Panel relied not only on various kinds of 'context' for treaty interpretation, but on a 'general principle of interpretation' to establish the legal status of the minor exceptions doctrine. According to the Panel, in the area of copyright, the Berne Convention and the TRIPS Agreement form 'the overall framework for multilateral protection'. Furthermore, most WTO Members are also parties to the Berne Convention. For the Panel, adopting a meaning that would reconcile the texts of different treaties and avoid conflict between them, is a general principle of interpretation, based on public international law's presumption against conflicts.[26] The Panel did not recognise either Article 10(2) of the 1996 WIPO Copyright Treaty (WCT – see chapter 2), as a subsequent treaty on the same subject matter within the meaning of Article 30 VCLT[27], or subsequent agreements

[22] *US–Section 110(5) Copyright* Act, Panel Report (n 20) para 6.62.

[23] GATT document MTN.GNG/NG11/6, paragraphs 39 and 40 and Annex. *US–Section 110(5) Copyright Act,* Panel Rerport (n 20) para 6.64).

[24] *US–Section 110(5) Copyright Act,* Panel Report (n 20) para 6.63.

[25] ibid para 6.62. Normally, however, in relation to the *acquis* of the preceding treaty, only those which are included would be explicitly referred to, as in the accession treaties to the European Union.

[26] *US–Section 110(5) Copyright Act,* Panel Report (n 20) para 6.66. The Panel referred to the previous Appellate Body Reports, for example, in *Canada–Certain Measures Concerning Periodicals* (adopted 30 July 1997) WT/DS31/AB/R p.19, *EC–Regime for the Importation, Sale and Distribution of Bananas* (adopted 25 September 1997) WT/DS27/AB/R paras 219–22 and *Guatemala– Antidumping Investigation Regarding Portland Cement from Mexico* (adopted 25 November 1998) WT/DS60/AB/R para 65.

[27] Arguing that Art 13 of the TRIPS Agreement clarifies and articulates the scope of the minor exceptions doctrine, which is applicable under the TRIPS Agreement, also relied on Art 30 VCLT concerning 'successive treaties relating to the same subject-matter' and referred to Art 10(2) of the WIPO 1996 Copyright Treaty (WCT) which specifically refers to the three-step principle. The US also argued that that the signatories of the WCT, which include the EC (and its Member States) and the US, commonly recognised the minor exceptions doctrine in Article 10 of the WCT. The Panel however, did not consider the WCT as 'successive treaties relating to the same subject-matter' in respect of Art 13 TRIPS, or as 'subsequent practice in the application of the treaty which establishes the agreement of the parties regarding its interpretation' as defined in Art 31.3(b) of the VCLT.

on the interpretation of a treaty within the meaning of Article 31.2(b) VCLT, or subsequent practice within the meaning of Article 31.3 VCLT. However, as all 127 signatories to the TRIPS Agreement in the WTO took part in all of the WCT meetings, the Panel held that it is also relevant to seek 'contextual guidance' in the WCT when developing interpretations that avoid conflicts within the over-all framework of multilateral copyright protection, except where these treaties explicitly contain different obligations.[28] The Panel concluded, therefore, that the TRIPS Agreement and the WCT should be interpreted consistently with each other.[29]

In an attempt to identify the scope and the level of protection provided by TRIPS provisions incorporating previous IPR treaties, the WTO Panels and the Appellate Body have resorted thus to different kinds of treaty 'context', which are not necessarily within the meaning of Article 31 VCLT. In *Canada–Pharmaceutical Patents*,[30] the Panel considered that Article 9(2)[31] of the Berne Convention for the Protection of Literary and Artistic Works (1971) is a 'rule of international law which the interpreter must consider, together with the context' which falls under Article 31.3(c) of the VCLT, and referred to it as 'an important contextual element for the interpretation of Article 30 of the TRIPS Agreement', calling this provision 'extended context'.[32]

The analysis of the 'context' for the purpose of interpretation based on the VCLT rule, determines important questions such as whether the scope of excep-tions and the level of protection differs between the Berne Convention and the TRIPS Agreement based on Article 13.

The main difference between Article 9(2) of the Berne Convention (1971) and Article 13 of the TRIPS Agreement is that the former applies only to the repro-duction right, whereas Article 13 does not contain an express limitation in terms of the categories of rights under copyright to which it may apply.[33]

The EC (today the European Union) argued that the provisions of Article 13 of the TRIPS Agreement and those of Article 11(1)(ii) and Article 11 *bis* of the Berne Convention provided different standards. The EC contended that parties to the Berne Convention could not agree that another treaty (ie the TRIPS Agreement) reduces the Berne Convention's level of protection. From

---

[28] *US–Section 110(5) Copyright Act*, Panel Report (n 20) para 6.70.

[29] ibid paras 6.66–6.70. *Indonesia–Certain Measures Affecting the Automobile Industry,* Panel Report (n 7) para 14.28. The meaning of 'the conflict among the WTO agreements' is an event when compliance with one provision of a WTO agreement leads to the violation of another provision of a WTO agreement (*Guatemala–Anti-Dumping Investigation Regarding Portland Cement from Mexico*, Panel Report (adopted 25 November 1998) WT/DS60/AB/R para 65).

[30] *Canada–Patent Protection of Pharmaceutical Products (Canada–Pharmaceutical Patents)*, Panel Report (adopted 7 April 2000) WT/DS114/R.

[31] Art 9(2) of the Berne Convention stipulates: 'It shall be a matter for legislation in the countries of the Union to permit the reproduction of such works in certain special cases, provided that such reproduction does not conflict with a normal exploitation of the work and does not unreasonably prejudice the legitimate interests of the author'.

[32] *Canada–Pharmaceutical Patents*, Panel Report (n 30) para 7.15.

[33] *US–Section 110(5) Copyright Act,* Panel Report (n 20) para 6.74.

the wording or the context of Article 13 of the TRIPS Agreement, according to the EC, the Berne *acquis* could not be considered to be incorporated in the TRIPS Agreement. The EC contended therefore that Article 13 applied only to the rights newly adopted under the TRIPS Agreement.[34] The US argued that the TRIPS Agreement incorporates the substantive provisions of the Berne Convention (1971), and that Article 13 TRIPS provides the standard by which to judge the appropriateness of limitations or exceptions, with which s 110(5) is compliant. According to the Panel, Article 11 *bis*(2)[35] of the Berne Convention (1971) and Article 13 TRIPS cover different situations.[36]

Reports of successive revision conferences of the Berne Convention refer to 'implied exceptions' allowing Member countries to provide limitations and exceptions to certain rights. The so-called 'minor exceptions' doctrine concerns those minor exceptions to the right of public performance, a concept which is close to the notion of 'fair use'.[37] The doctrine is not explicitly described in terms of exceptions in the Berne Convention, which refers to the conditions allowing national laws to provide for exceptions, using a three-step test, with respect to Articles 11 and 11 *bis*, and other exclusive rights (such as the right of translation) of the Berne Convention. The three-step test is a standard by which limitations on exclusive copyrights are confined to 'certain special cases' which do not conflict with 'normal exploitation of the work', do not 'unreasonably prejudice the legitimate interests of the author', and are applied to the right of reproduction.[38]

Article 13 of the TRIPS Agreement imposes three conditions to be met for testing permissibility of exceptions or limitations to the exclusive rights. These conditions represent situations that are 'certain special cases', '[do] not conflict with a normal exploitation of the work' and '[do] not unreasonably prejudice the legitimate interests of the right holder'. If these three conditions are met, a government may choose between different options for limiting the right in question, including use free of charge and without an authorisation by the right

---

[34] ibid para 6.78.

[35] *US–Section 110(5) Copyright Act,* Panel Report (n 20) para 6.87. Art 11 *bis*(2) authorises Members to determine conditions under which lectures, addresses and other works of the same nature which are delivered in public may be reproduced by the press, broadcast, communicated to the public by wire and made the subject of public communication as envisaged in Art 11 *bis*(1) of this Convention, when such use is justified by the informatory purpose.

[36] According to the Panel Report para 6.87, 'Article 11bis(2) authorizes Members to determine conditions under which the rights conferred by Article 11bis(1)(i–iii) may be exercised. The imposition of such conditions may completely replace the free exercise of the exclusive right of authorizing the use of the rights embodied in subparagraphs (i–iii) provided that equitable remuneration and the author's moral rights are not prejudiced. However, unlike Article 13 of the TRIPS Agreement, Article 11bis(2) of the Berne Convention (1971) would not in any case justify use free of charge.'

[37] The minor exceptions doctrine was proposed in the General Report of the WIPO Secretariat, presented at the Brussels Diplomatic Conference (1967) and considered in the Stockholm Treaty amending the Berne Convention (1971). This amendment was agreed upon at the Stockholm Diplomatic Conference. *US–Section 110(5) Copyright Act,* Panel Report (n 20) para 6.64.

[38] Art 9(2) of the 1971 Berne Convention provides that: 'It shall be a matter for legislation in the countries of the Union to permit the reproduction of such works in certain special cases, provided that such reproduction does not conflict with a normal exploitation of the work and does not unreasonably prejudice the legitimate interests of the author.'

holder. The Panel, in interpreting these three conditions in *US–Section 110(5) Copyright Act*, applied the effectiveness principle, which requires the treaty interpreter to give a distinct meaning to each of the three conditions and to avoid a reading that could reduce any of the conditions to 'redundancy or inutility'.[39]

B 'Object and Purpose' of the TRIPS Agreement

At the close of the Uruguay Round negotiations, developed countries considered Articles 7 and 8 only 'hortatory', whereas developing countries regarded them as describing the objectives and principles of the TRIPS Agreement affecting rights and obligations of the Members under the Agreement (see chapter 4). The question of what the 'object and purpose' of the TRIPS Agreement are has increasingly become contentious, as access to medicines and transfer of technology, as well as other possible public policy issues in IPR protection come to be debated. In these discussions outside the disputes settlement procedures, the legal statuses and the interpretative roles of Articles 7 and 8 TRIPS became divisive issues.

Only in a few dispute cases, have Panels and the Appellate Body dealing with TRIPS provisions been faced with the question of what the overall object and purpose of the Agreement is. In one of the earlier TRIPS dispute cases, *India–Patents (US)*,[40] the Appellate Body for the purpose of interpreting Article 70.8(a), referred to the Preamble, and said that: 'The Panel's interpretation here is consistent with the object and purpose of the TRIPS Agreement.' According to the Appellate Body, the object and purpose of the Agreement is, inter alia, 'the need to promote effective and adequate protection of intellectual property rights'.[41]

The identification of the 'object and purpose of the treaty' for interpreting TRIPS provisions, for the WTO dispute settlement organs, has been based mostly on textual analyses, with some exceptional cases where the Panel did not exclude considerations of facts and policies. In *Canada–Patent Term*,[42] the Appellate Body stated that their task was to give meaning to the phrase, 'acts which occurred before the date of application', and to interpret Article 70.1[43] in a way that is in accord with the rest of the provisions of Article 70.1 and their context, having particular regard to the object and purpose of the treaty.[44] In this case, however, the Appellate Body added that: 'we note that our findings in this appeal do not in any way prejudice the applicability of Article 7 or Article 8 of the TRIPS Agreement

---

[39] *US–Section 110(5) Copyright Act*, Panel Report (n 20) para 6.97.
[40] *India–Patent Protection for Pharmaceutical and Agricultural Chemical Products*, complaint by the US (*India–Patents (US)*), Panel Report WT/DS50/R as modified by Appellate Body Report (adopted 16 January 1998) WT/DS50/AB/R.
[41] *India–Patents (US), Appellate Body Report*, WT/DS50/AB/R (n 40) para 57.
[42] *Canada–Term of Patent Protection (Canada–Patent Term)*, Appellate Body Report (adopted 12 October 2000) WT/DS170/AB/R.
[43] Art 70 concerns 'Protection of Existing Subject Matter', and provides in para 1 that: 'This Agreement does not give rise to obligations in respect of acts which occurred before the date of application of the Agreement for the Member in question . . .'
[44] *Canada–Patent Term* Appellate Body Report (n 42) para 54.

in possible future cases with respect to measures to promote the policy objectives of the WTO Members that are set out in those Articles. Those Articles still await appropriate interpretation.'[45]

Two years later, the Panel Report in *Canada–Pharmaceutical Patents* dealt with the question of the 'object and purpose' of the TRIPS Agreement and,[46] following the general rule of interpretation in accordance with Article 31 of the VCLT, identified what follows. Article 7 of TRIPS is not the only purpose of the TRIPS Agreement. Article 7 mentions that the purpose of the IPR system is the premise of the Agreement, and so the object and purpose of the treaty will also depend on other provisions. Even if the exceptions in Article 30 of the TRIPS Agreement allow certain limitations of the exclusive rights as provided in Article 28, they must not change the fundamental balance between the rights and obligations of the TRIPS Agreement. Thus, for the Panel in *Canada–Pharmaceutical Patents*, the 'object and purpose' of the TRIPS Agreement in the meaning of Article 31.1 VCLT is inferred from the general structure of the agreement in which the balance of rights and obligations is struck.

The Panel in *EC–Geographical Indications* explicitly stated that many measures to achieve public policy objectives are different from intellectual property protection itself, and therefore outside the scope of the TRIPS Agreement. The Panel explained that the nature of intellectual property rights provides for the grant of negative rights to prevent certain acts. This fact leaves Members free to pursue legitimate public policy objectives which normally lie outside the scope of intellectual property rights without resorting to exceptions under the Agreement. The Panel Report thus delineated the principles in Article 8.1 (see chapter 5, p 157).[47]

C Determining the Scope of Exceptions

i Are exceptions interpreted narrowly? From GATT to WTO

As stated earlier, the VCLT rule of interpretation does not include the axiom that 'exceptions should be interpreted narrowly'. GATT Panels adopted this approach more often than the WTO dispute settlement organs, particularly concerning Article XX (see chapter 4). The most apparent difference between the GATT Panels and the WTO in dealing with 'exceptions', concerns the interpretation of Article XX GATT. In *US–Gasoline*, the Appellate Body stated:

[45] ibid para 101.

[46] Canada argued that each element of Art 30 of the TRIPS Agreement should be analysed on the basis of its particular language, and in the specific context in which it appeared. That was what the Appellate Body had done in the *Shrimps* case (*United States–Import Prohibition of Certain Shrimp and Shrimp Products (US-Shrimp I)*, Appellate Body Report (adopted 6 November 1998) WT/DS58/AB/R paras 129–31) and – contrary to the EC's theory – it had taken the objective of the WTO Agreement, as stated in its preamble, into account in establishing the 'ordinary meaning' of Art XX. *Canada–Pharmaceutical Patents* (n 30) para 4.41.

[47] *EC–Geographical Indications* (n 6) (US) paras 7.209–7. 210, (Australia) paras 7.245–7.246.

The relationship between the affirmative commitments set out in, e.g., Articles I, III and XI, and the policies and interests embodied in the "General Exceptions" listed in Article XX, can be given meaning within the framework of the General Agreement and its object and purpose by a treaty interpreter only on a case-to-case basis, by careful scrutiny of the factual and legal context in a given dispute, without disregarding the words actually used by the WTO Members themselves to express their intent and purpose.[48]

The Appellate Body compared its approach with that under the GATT, and found a similar approach taken also by the GATT Panel, in the 1987 Herring and Salmon Report. The Appellate Body in *US–Gasoline* noted that:

> . . . as the preamble of Article XX indicates, the purpose of including Article XX(g) in the General Agreement was not to widen the scope for measures serving trade policy purposes but merely to ensure that the commitments under the General Agreement do not hinder the pursuit of policies aimed at the conservation of exhaustible natural resources.[49]

The Panel in *EC–Geographical Indications* considered that most public policies are formulated outside IPR protection, without regard to the issue of IPR protection.[50] However, there may be arguments that good public policies can be realised through the use of exceptions to IPRs, such as 'fair use' of copyrighted works or regulatory exceptions to patent rights. For example, the interpretation of Article 17 which refers to 'fair use' of descriptive terms could refer to some public policies.[51] There may therefore be arguments that TRIPS exceptions must be interpreted widely to allow certain public policy objectives, such as public health or fair use.

Fundamentally for the WTO dispute organs, it is the VCLT rule, ie, the analysis of 'the terms of the treaty in their context and in the light of its object and purpose', that determines the perspective taken by the treaty interpreter. In what follows, the Appellate Body explains that the word 'exception' alone cannot determine how this provision should be interpreted:

> The general rule in a dispute settlement proceeding requiring a complaining party to establish a *prima facie* case of inconsistency with a provision of the *SPS Agreement* before the burden of showing consistency with that provision is taken on by the defending party, is *not* avoided by simply describing that same provision as an "exception". In much the same way, merely characterising a treaty provision as an "exception" does not by itself justify a "stricter" or "narrower" interpretation of that provision than would be warranted by examination of the ordinary meaning of the actual treaty words, viewed in context and in the light of the treaty's object and purpose, or, in other words, by applying the normal rules of treaty interpretation.[52]

[48] *US–Gasoline*, Appellate Body Report (n 17) 17–18.
[49] ibid 17.
[50] See above p 219 and ch 5.
[51] Art 17 provides that: 'Members may provide limited exceptions to the rights conferred by a trademark, such as fair use of descriptive terms, provided that such exceptions take account of the legitimate interests of the owner of the trademark and of third parties'.
[52] *EC Measures Concerning Meat and Meat Products (EC–Hormones)*, Appellate Body Report (adopted 13 February 1998) WT/DS26/AB/R, WT/DS48/AB/R para 104.

The WTO method of interpreting exceptions is based thoroughly on the VCLT rule and, apparently, differs from interpreting exceptions narrowly, as shown, for example, in the following judgment at the European Court of Human Rights:

> [the Court is] faced not with a choice between two conflicting principles [human rights of the individual and the restrictions necessary for democratic society] but with a principle of freedom of expression that is subject to a number of exceptions which must be narrowly interpreted.[53]

Many dispute settlement organs, including the European Court of Human Rights (ECHR), relied to some extent on the effectiveness principles[54] but have developed their own policies of treaty interpretation without specifically referring to or turning away from the VCLT rule of interpretation. The Court referred to the VCLT rule of interpretation in early cases such as *Golder v UK*[55] in 1975, before the entry into force of the VCLT.[56] However, the ECHR developed its own interpretative principles, among which is the principle that exceptions should be interpreted restrictively when they concern self-standing rights/principles which cannot be easily balanced against other policy considerations, such as the right to freedom of expression provided in Article 10 of the European Convention on Human Rights and Fundamental Freedoms. Ultimately, however, the ECHR also engages in a balancing exercise between different policies. For the WTO-covered agreements which are of a commercial nature, there seems to be no norm with authority that is automatically accepted and that stands out from others. The above difference in the interpretative methods relating to exceptions therefore concerns this kind of balancing. Significantly for the WTO Agreements, the question of burden of proof is important in arguing for exceptions.

ii VCLT and Exceptions and Limitations to the Rights Conferred under the TRIPS Agreement

The scope of exceptions or limitations to the rights conferred under the TRIPS Agreement may require special consideration. There are pre-existing IP conventions with provisions concerning exceptions to the rights conferred and specific

---

[53] *Sunday Times v UK* (1978) Series A no 30 para 65. Art 10(2) of the European Convention on Human Rights and Fundamental Freedoms provides that: 'The exercise of these freedoms, since it carries with it duties and responsibilities, may be subject to such formalities, conditions, restrictions or penalties as are prescribed by law and are necessary in a democratic society, in the interests of national security, territorial integrity or public safety, for the prevention of disorder or crime, for the protection of health or morals, for the protection of the reputation or rights of others, for preventing the disclosure of information received in confidence, or for maintaining the authority and impartiality of the judiciary.'

[54] JG Merrills, *The Development of International Law by the European Court of Human Rights*, 2nd edn (Manchester University Press, 1995) 98 et seq.

[55] *Golder v UK* (1975) Series A no 18; see also *Kamasinski v Austria* (1989) Series A no 168.

[56] It stated that Arts 31–33 of the VCLT constituted generally accepted principles of international law (para 29) and that: 'As stated in Article 31 para. 2 of the Vienna Convention, the preamble to a treaty forms an integral part of the context. Furthermore, the preamble is generally useful for determining the "object" and "purpose" of the instrument to be construed' (para 34).

provisions, relating to exceptions in the TRIPS Agreement, for separate categories of IPR. How provisions in the TRIPS Agreement concerning exceptions are interpreted, therefore, depends in part on how the treaty interpreter views the relationship between the relevant TRIPS exceptions provisions and provisions in the IP Conventions which are incorporated in the TRIPS Agreement.

According to the Panel in *EC–Geographical Indications*, the scope of the exceptions in the TRIPS Agreement must be interpreted based on the terms of the provision in their context, in light of the 'object and purpose' of the Agreement as follows:

> The ordinary meaning of the terms in their context must also be interpreted in light of the object and purpose of the agreement. The object and purpose of the TRIPS Agreement, as indicated by Articles 9 through 62 and 70 and reflected in the preamble, includes the provision of adequate standards and principles concerning the availability, scope, use and enforcement of trade-related intellectual property rights. This confirms that a limitation on the standards for trademark or GI protection should not be implied unless it is supported by the text.[57]

The Panel responds to an argument made by Australia that there was an 'implied limitation' on the rights in Article 16 – implied from the relationship between Article 16 (which is in Part II – Standards concerning the Availability, Scope and Use of Intellectual Property Rights) and Articles 3 and 4 in Part I (General Provisions and Basic Principles) of the TRIPS Agreement. The Panel responded that such a limitation had to be supported by the text, and found that it was not so supported.[58]

iii Exceptions and public policy considerations

The Panels in *US–Section 110(5) Copyright Act* and in *Canada–Pharmaceutical Patents* examined extensively the scope of exceptions in Article 13 (entitled 'Limitations and Exceptions') and Article 30 (entitled 'Exceptions to Rights Conferred') of the TRIPS Agreement. Both Panels followed an interpretative method based on the customary rules of interpretation as understood and developed by the WTO dispute settlement organs in non-TRIPS cases, examined the extent to which pre-existing intellectual property treaty provisions were incorporated and looked into the negotiating history of the TRIPS Agreement. Although the Panel in *US–Section 110(5) Copyright Act* was innovative in its use of economic data, both Panels emphasized the wording of the relevant provisions which they analysed in detail. The Panel in *Canada–Pharmaceutical Patents* recognized public policy implications of Article 30 without, however, expounding on substantive issues.

---

[57] *EC–Geographical Indications*, Panel Reports (n 6) (US) para 7.584, (Australia) para 7.620.
[58] ibid (US) para 7.584, (Australia) para 7.620.

a Article 13 TRIPS (Limitations and Exceptions)

The Panel relied basically on the VCLT method of interpretation to find the criteria for judging the scope of the exceptions and limitation under Article 13 TRIPS which provides that:

> Members shall confine limitations or exceptions to exclusive rights to certain special cases which do not conflict with a normal exploitation of the work and do not unreasonably prejudice the legitimate interests of the right holder.

In this case, the European Communities and their Member States alleged that the exemptions provided in subparagraphs (A) and (B) of Section 110(5) of the US Copyright Act were in violation of the US's obligations under Article 9.1 of the TRIPS Agreement, together with Articles 11(1)(ii)[59] and 11 *bis*(1)(iii)[60] of the Berne Convention (1971). Section 110(5) of the US Copyright Act provides for limitations on exclusive rights granted to copyright holders for their copyrighted work, in the form of exemptions for broadcast by non-right holders of certain performances and displays, namely, (A)'home style exemption' (for 'dramatic' musical works) and (B)'business exemption' (works other than 'dramatic' musical works, eg the playing of radio and television music in public places such as bars, shops, restaurants, etc). For the EC, the above exemptions under the US law could not be justified under any express or implied exception or limitation permissible under the Berne Convention (1971) or the TRIPS Agreement.[61]

Article 9.1 TRIPS stipulates that 'Members shall comply with Articles 1 through 21 of the Berne Convention (1971) and the Appendix thereto . . .'. Article 13 of the TRIPS Agreement, in Section 1 concerning copyright and related rights, provides three conditions in which limitations and exceptions to exclusive rights are allowed. According to Article 13, 'Members shall confine limitations or exceptions to exclusive rights to certain (i) special cases; (ii) which do not conflict with a normal exploitation of the work; and, (iii) do not unreasonably prejudice the legitimate interests of the right holder.

The Panel and the parties agreed that these conditions are cumulative because the principle of effective treaty interpretation requires that the Panel avoids any reading that could reduce any of the conditions to redundancy or inutility.[62]

The Panel found that the language of Article 13 TRIPS is similar to that in Article 9(2) of the Berne Convention, except that Article 9(2) applies only to the right of reproduction, whereas Article 13 has no such limitation. The Panel also noted at the outset that: 'Article 13 cannot have more than a narrow or limited operation. Its tenor, consistent as it is with the provisions of Article 9(2) of the

---

[59] Refers to any communication to the public about the performance of dramatic and musical works.

[60] Refers to public communication by loudspeaker or any analogous instrument transmitting, by signs, sounds or images, the broadcast of the work pertaining to broadcasting and related rights.

[61] Whether or not the scope of exceptions to copyright differs between the Berne Convention and the TRIPS Agreement (ie, the applicability of Art 13 TRIPS to Arts 11 *bis*(1) and 11(1) of the Berne Convention (1971) as incorporated into the TRIPS Agreement) was discussed in this context.

[62] *US–Section 110(5) Copyright Act* (n 20) para 6.97.

Berne Convention (1971), discloses that it was not intended to provide for exceptions or limitations except for those of a limited nature.'[63] Having considered the examples of the minor exceptions in the context of the Berne Convention as well as national laws, the Panel concluded that Article 13 is a narrow exception which is allowed only if its scope is *de minimis*.[64] This analysis was based on the wording of the provision in its context and facts from national laws, not because of the general principle that exceptions must be interpreted narrowly. In the light of the minor exceptions doctrine which was recognised as being incorporated into Article 13 of the TRIPS Agreement, the Panel analysed each term,[65] first of all textually,[66] but also through economic data which represented the actual and potential effects of the exemptions.[67]

The EC argued that the exceptions should be related to a legitimate policy purpose. In examining the scope and meaning of 'certain special cases', the Panel rejected equating the term 'certain special cases' with 'special purpose'. The Panel explained that: 'It is difficult to reconcile the wording of Article 13 with the proposition that an exception or limitation must be justified in terms of a legitimate public policy purpose'.[68] According to the Panel, 'special cases' in Article 13 require that a limitation or exception in national legislation should not only be clearly defined, but also 'narrow in its scope and reach'.[69] Interestingly,

---

[63] ibid para 6.97.

[64] *US–Section 110(5) Copyright Act* (n 20) para 6.93.

[65] In considering each of the three conditions, the Panel used the following methodology: 'We will look at the defined and limited scope of the exemptions at issue under the first condition, and focus on the degree of conflict with normal exploitation of works under the second condition. In relation to the third condition, we will examine the extent of prejudice caused to the legitimate interests of the right holder in the light of the information submitted by the parties.' *US–Section 110(5) Copyright Act*, Panel Report (n 20) para 6.99.

[66] For example, the Panel held that there were two connotations to the term 'normal': one of an empirical nature, ie what is regular, usual, typical or ordinary, and another somewhat more normative, if not dynamic, approach, ie conforming to a type or standard. According to the Panel, Art 31 VCLT suggests a harmonious interpretation which gives meaning and effect to both connotations of 'normal'. If 'normal' exploitation was equated with full use of all exclusive rights conferred by copyright, the exception clause to Art 13 would be devoid of meaning. Therefore, 'normal' exploitation clearly means something less than full use of an exclusive right. *US–Section 110(5) Copyright Act*, Panel Report (n 20) paras 6.166–6.167.

[67] The Panel explored among GATT/WTO dispute cases in which actual and potential effects were taken into account when assessing the consistency of exemptions. The Panel found that actual trade effects have not been considered as indispensable for finding inconsistency with the national treatment principle in Art III.4 GATT. This was because there was potential for adverse effects on competitive opportunities and equal competitive conditions for foreign products (in comparison to like domestic products), *US–Section 110(5) Copyright Act, Panel Report* (n 20) para 6.185. The Panel was cautious in interpreting provisions of the TRIPS Agreement in the light of concepts that have been developed in GATT but, 'given that the agreements covered by the WTO form a single, integrated legal system', found it appropriate to develop interpretations of the legal protection conferred on intellectual property right holders under the TRIPS Agreement which are not incompatible with the treatment conferred to products under the GATT, or in respect of services and service suppliers under the GATS, as the Appellate Body in EC- Bananas III (European Communities – Regime for the Importation, Sale and Distribution of Bananas, Appellate Body Report WT/DS27/AB/R (adopted 11 December 2008 (Ecuador) 22 December 2008 (US)) case has shown.

[68] *US–Section 110(5) Copyright Act*, Panel Report (n 20) paras 6.105 and 6.111–6.112.

[69] ibid para 6.112.

the EC contended in this case that the US exemption is not based upon a 'valid' public policy or other exceptional circumstance that makes it inappropriate or impossible to enforce the exclusive rights conferred.[70] The Panel did not interpret Article 13 of the TRIPS Agreement from an a priori conception of public policy, with the intention of achieving appropriate balance based on such conceptions.[71] Interestingly, the Panel rejected the idea that the first condition of Article 13 requires 'a value judgment on the legitimacy of an exception or limitation'.[72]

The Panel added, however, that 'public policy purposes could be of subsidiary relevance for drawing inferences about the scope of an exemption and the clarity of its definition'. It then reiterated that what is important for the interpretation of Article 13 is that the statements from the legislative history indicate an intention of establishing an exception with a narrow scope, and that the intention of Article 13, which incorporates the context of Arts 11 and 11 *bis* of the Berne Convention (1971), is to allow exceptions as long as they are *de minimis* in scope.[73]

Concerning the second condition that exceptions must 'not conflict with a normal exploitation of the work', the Panel, after examining the ordinary meaning of the words, held that 'normal exploitation' means something less than the full use of an exclusive right[74] and that work includes 'all' of the relevant exclusive rights attached to the work.

The US argued that whether or not the exception conflicts with normal exploitation should be judged by economic analysis of the degree of 'market displacement', ie, the forgone collection of remuneration by right holders. The Panel supported the EC argument that proof of actual trade effects has not been considered an indispensable prerequisite for a finding of inconsistency with the national treatment clause of Article III of GATT and it is rather 'a potentiality of adverse effects on competitive opportunities and equal competitive conditions for foreign products, in comparison to like domestic products'.[75] In applying this GATT model of analysis to a TRIPS case, the Panel explained that:

> We wish to express our caution in interpreting provisions of the TRIPS Agreement in the light of concepts that have been developed in GATT dispute settlement practice. . . . Given that the agreements covered by the WTO form a single, integrated legal system, we deem it appropriate to develop interpretations of the legal protection conferred on intellectual property right holders under the TRIPS Agreement which are not incompatible with the treatment conferred to products under the GATT, or in respect of services and service suppliers under the GATS, in the light of pertinent dispute settlement practice.[76]

---

[70] *US–Section 110(5) Copyright Act,* Panel Report (n 20) para 6.154.
[71] ibid paras 6.11–6.12.
[72] *US–Section 110(5) Copyright Act,* Panel Report (n 20) para 6.157.
[73] ibid para 6.158.
[74] *US–Section 110(5) Copyright Act,* Panel Report (n 20) para 6.166–6.167.
[75] ibid para 6.185.
[76] *US–Section 110(5) Copyright Act,* Panel Report (n 20) para 6.185.

The Panel analysed the preparatory work for the Berne Convention's 1967 Revision Conference and arrived at the following criteria for judging whether the second condition was met: an exception or limitation to an exclusive right in domestic legislation rises to conflict with a normal exploitation of the work, if uses that are covered by that right but exempted under the exception or limitation, enter into economic competition with the ways that right holders normally extract economic value from that right to the work, depriving them of significant or tangible commercial gains.[77] The Panel rejected the US approach after the 1976 law amendment following the *Aiken* judgment[78] which equates 'normal exploitation' with 'normal remuneration' in a given market, at a particular point in time. The Panel further recalled that the US law exempts communication to the public of radio and television broadcasts, while the playing of musical works from CDs and tapes (or live music) is not exempted.[79]

On the third condition of Article 13, ie, 'not unreasonably prejudic[ing] the legitimate interests of the right holder', the US argued that the focus should be placed on whether the right holder is 'harmed by the effects of the exception' and whether that prejudice is 'unreasonable'. The Panel observed that this third condition implies a three-step test, ie, the determination of the terms 'legitimate interests' at stake and the extent of 'prejudice' to judge what amount of prejudice reaches the level of what is considered to be 'unreasonable'.[80] The Panel stressed the need to take into account potential revenue loss and the need for right holders to own their rights such that they can engage in agreements like collective management organisations in the first place. Based on the economic impact of the provisions in US law for 'normal use' and 'legitimate interest of the right holder' incurred by the exemptions,[81] the Panel concluded that the US, which had the burden of proof in invoking the exception of Article 13, failed to demonstrate that the business exemption did not unreasonably prejudice the legitimate interests of the right holder.[82]

---

[77] ibid para 6.183.

[78] In the *Aiken* case (*Twentieth Century Music Corp v Aiken* 422 US 151 (1975)), prior to the passage of the 1976 Copyright Act, the US Supreme Court held that an owner of a small restaurant was not liable for playing music for his customers by means of an ordinary FM radio with outlets to four speakers in the ceiling because the size of the shop was very small (1,055 square feet, of which 620 square feet were open to the public) and the receiver size was 'commonly found in private homes'. This decision was considered as representing the 'outer limit of the exemption' (HR Rep No 94-1476, 94th Cong.).

[79] *US–Section 110(5) Copyright Act*, Panel Report (n 20) paras 6.206–6.207.

[80] ibid para 6.222.

[81] The use of copyrighted works under the exemption provision and the potential effects of using the exemptions were evaluated, based on the commercial or technical conditions of the US market. 'Normal use' in the US was determined by analysing the royalties one ought to have received if there had been no exemption rule. 'Legitimate interests of the right holder' were assessed, based on a quantitative analysis of the extent of economic value the right holder should have gained (including potential profits) under the commercial and technological conditions in the market at that time, and in the near future, that would be lost due to the exemption to exclusive rights.

[82] *US–Section 110(5) Copyright Act*, Panel Report (n 20) paras 6.248–6.250.

The Panel's method of interpretation of the scope of exception and limitations in Article 13 of TRIPS shows that the burden of proof concerning the consequences of an exception is more crucial than its justification in words, ie, a public policy, self-standing right or principle. Based on the analyses of data brought by the parties based on this methodology, the Panel concluded that the business exemption did not meet the requirements of TRIPS Agreement Article 13 and was inconsistent with Berne Convention Articles 11 *bis*(1)(iii) and 11(1) (ii) as incorporated into the TRIPS Agreement by TRIPS Agreement Article 9.1.[83]

In *US–Section 101 (5) Copyright Act*, there was no debate on the dimension of public policy largely because of the wording of Article 13 of the TRIPS Agreement. According to the Panel, the phrase 'certain special cases' in Article 13 of the TRIPS Agreement is not the equivalent of 'for a special purpose' and does not refer to justifiable in the sense of normative policy (such as public policy or special circumstances). However, 'for a special purpose' is also included in 'certain special cases', so it is possible to interpret that Article 13 also has a public policy dimension. It would be possible under the TRIPS Agreement to consider public policy considerations for copyright protection to the extent that the scope of 'minor exception' allows.

b Articles 30 TRIPS (Exceptions to Rights Conferred)

The Panel in *Canada–Pharmaceutical Patents*[84] adopted a method of interpretation even more textualist than that in *US–Section 101 (5) Copyright Act* in that it did not resort to economic data in judging whether the 'regulatory exception' (popularly called the '*Bolar* exemption'[85]) for drug marketing authorisation and the 'stock-piling' exception provided by the Canadian Patent Act[86] could be considered to fall within the scope of exceptions provided by Article 30 of the TRIPS Agreement. Article 30 TRIPS provides that:

> Members may provide limited exceptions to the exclusive rights conferred by a patent, provided that such exceptions do not unreasonably conflict with a normal exploitation of the patent and do not unreasonably prejudice the legitimate interests of the patent owner, taking account of the legitimate interests of third parties.

Canada, in interpreting the conditions of exceptions stipulated in Article 30 TRIPS to the exclusive rights conferred on the patent-owner under Article 28

---

[83] ibid para 7.1(b).

[84] *Canada–Pharmaceutical Patents*, Panel Report (n 30).

[85] 35 USC § 271(e)(1). See ch 5, n 60.

[86] s 55.2(1) of the Canadian Patent Act provided that 'It is not an infringement of a patent for any person to make, construct, use or sell the patented invention solely for uses reasonably related to the development and submission of information required under any law of Canada, a province or a country other than Canada that regulates the manufacture, construction, use or sale of any product' (regulatory exemption). S 55.2(2) stipulated that 'It is not an infringement of a patent for any person who makes, constructs, uses or sells a patented invention in accordance with subsection (1) to make, construct or use the invention, during the applicable period provided for by the regulations, for the manufacture and storage of Articles intended for sale after the date on which the term of the patent expires' (stock-piling exemption).

TRIPS, called attention to Articles 7 and 8.1 TRIPS, as relevant to the object and purpose of Article 30.[87] According to Canada, Article 7 declares that one of the key goals of the TRIPS Agreement was a balance between the IPRs created by the Agreement and other important socio-economic policies of WTO Member governments. For Canada, Article 8 elaborates upon the socio-economic policies in question, with particular attention to health and nutritional policies.[88] With respect to patent rights, Canada argued that: 'these purposes call for a liberal interpretation of the three conditions stated in Article 30 of the Agreement, so that governments would have the necessary flexibility to adjust patent rights to maintain the desired balance with other important national policies'.

The EC, on the other hand, argued that Articles 7 and 8 describe a balancing that had already taken place during the TRIPS Agreement negotiations and that the negotiations were not intended to allow a Member to 'renegotiate' the overall balance. The EC pointed to the last phrase of Article 8.1, which requires that socio-economic policies that Canada refers to must be consistent with the obligations of the TRIPS Agreement.[89] For the EC, the first paragraph of the Preamble and Article 1.1 demonstrated that the basic purpose of the TRIPS Agreement was 'to lay down minimum requirements for the protection and enforcement of intellectual property rights'.[90]

The Panel stated the view that 'Article 30's very existence amounts to a recognition that the definition of exclusive rights contained in Article 28 would need certain adjustments', but that 'the three limiting conditions attached to Article 30 testify strongly that the negotiators of the Agreement did not intend Article 30 to bring about what would be equivalent to a renegotiation of the basic balance of the Agreement'.[91] The Panel considered that the exact scope of Article 30's authority will depend on the specific meaning given to its limiting conditions. For the Panel, therefore, the scope of exceptions to the patent rights conferred must be determined by analysing the wording of Article 30 in the context of relevant TRIPS provisions, including Articles 7 and 8.1.

Article 30 of the TRIPS Agreement stipulates three conditions which the Panel considered to be cumulative.[92] The exception must (1) be 'limited'; (2) not 'unreasonably conflict with normal exploitation of the patent'; and (3) not 'unreasonably prejudice the legitimate interests of the patent owner, taking account of the legitimate interests of third parties'. The language of Article 30 resembles that of Article 13 TRIPS, since the drafters drew the same inspiration from Article 9(2) of the Berne Convention as they did for Article 13 TRIPS. However, in condition (3) of Article 30, in contrast to Article 13, the phrase, 'taking account of the legitimate interests of third parties' is added which, according to the Panel in this case, leaves room for public policy consideration.

---

[87] *Canada–Pharmaceutical Patents,* Panel Report (n 30) para 7.23.
[88] *ibid* para 7.24.
[89] *Canada–Pharmaceutical Patents,* Panel Report (n 30) para 7.25.
[90] *ibid* para 7.25.
[91] *Canada–Pharmaceutical Patents*, Panel Report (n 30) para 7.26.
[92] ibid para 7.20.

The Panel interpreted the first condition, 'limited exception', to connote a 'narrow exception – one which makes only a small diminution of the rights in question'.[93] For the Panel, this concerned *legal rights* which must be 'measured by the extent to which the exclusive rights of the patent owner have been curtailed', rather than by the size or extent of the economic impact. Canada argued that whether or not an exception to exclusive rights is 'limited' depends on whether the right holder has lost an exclusive right to sell, which is one of the five exclusive rights set out in Article 28 of the TRIPS Agreement, ie, making, using, offering for sale, selling or importing.[94] However, the Panel argued that if the right to sell was the only important right, there would be no point in setting out five rights in Article 28 of the TRIPS Agreement.[95] The Panel disagreed also with the EC on the methodology of 'counting' the number of legal rights impaired, and instead articulated a standard under which 'the extent to which the patent owner's rights have been curtailed must be measured'.[96] For the Panel, the stockpiling provision violates the criteria of 'limited exception' as there are no limitations on the quantity of production for stockpiling.

Concerning the second condition, that exceptions must not 'unreasonably conflict with a normal exploitation of the patent', the parties differed on the meaning of 'normal'. According to the Panel, the term 'normal' has a combined meaning of two possible dictionary meanings, ie, 'what is common within a relevant community', and 'a normative standard of entitlement'.[97] No economic criteria for judging whether the effects of the Canadian law 'unreasonably conflict with a normal exploitation of the patent' were developed or applied in this case. The Panel held therefore that a right to extended term of protection due to regulatory delays falls *outside* the bounds of 'normal'[98] as the patent term erosion of this kind is an unintended consequence of the conjunction of the patent laws with product regulatory laws, which is not applicable to the vast majority

---

[93]   *Canada–Pharmaceutical Patents*, Panel Report (n 30) para 7.30.

[94]   This right, like all other rights conferred under this Agreement in respect of the use, sale, importation or other distribution of goods, is subject to the provisions of Art 6.

[95]   However, the Panel disagreed with the EC on the methodology of 'counting' the number of legal rights impaired, and instead articulated a standard under which 'the extent to which the patent owner's rights have been curtailed must be measured'. The Panel pointed out that a very small act could potentially violate all five rights conferred under Art 28.1, but for all practical purposes leave the owner's rights intact (*Canada–Pharmaceutical Patents*, Panel Report (n 30) para 7.32).

[96]   *Canada–Pharmaceutical Patents*, Panel Report (n 30) para 7.34.

[97]   ibid para 7.54.

[98]   The parties essentially agreed that 'exploitation' involves 'the extraction of commercial value from the patent by "working" the patent,' either by selling the product or licensing others (para 7.51). However, Canada argued that market exclusivity occurring after the 20-year patent term expires should not be regarded as 'normal'. The Panel was unable to accept this as a categorical proposition (para 7.56) but disagreed also with the EC's assertion that the mere existence of the patent owner's rights to exclude was a sufficient reason, by itself, for treating all gains derived from such rights as flowing from 'normal exploitation'. In the Panel's view, the EC's argument contained no evidence or analysis addressing to the various meanings of 'normal' – neither a demonstration that most patent owners extract the value of their patents in the manner barred by s 55.2(1), nor an argument that the prohibited manner of exploitation was 'normal' in the sense of being essential to the achievement of the goals of patent policy.

of patented products.[99] For these reasons, the Panel concluded that Canada's regulatory review provision does not conflict with a normal exploitation of patents under TRIPS Agreement Article 30.[100]

As for the meaning of condition (3) of Article 30, ie, that the exception must not 'unreasonably prejudice the legitimate interests of the patent owner, taking into account the legitimate interests of third parties', the Panel relied on the dictionary definition. It interpreted the word 'legitimate' as a normative claim calling for protection of interests that are 'justifiable' in the sense that they are 'supported by relevant public policies or other social norms', and then looked into the preparatory work of Article 9(2) of the Berne Convention. The Panel concluded that the concept of 'legitimate interests' in Article 30 are construed as a broader concept than legal interests.[101] The EC invoked the time lost to the effective patent protection due to regulatory delays in obtaining marketing approval, but the Panel rejected the EC claim that this situation creates a 'legitimate interest' for the patent holder. The Panel asserted that this interest was 'neither so compelling nor so widely recognized' to constitute a 'policy norm' that would fall within TRIPS Agreement. According to the Panel, the concept of 'legitimate interests' should not be used to decide, through adjudication, a normative policy issue that was still obviously a matter of unresolved political debate.[102] From this, the Panel concluded that Canada had demonstrated that the regulatory review provision did not prejudice 'legitimate interests' of affected patent owners within the meaning of Article 30.[103]

Thus, in evaluating the scope of exceptions allowed under Article 30, the Panel took a thoroughly 'textualist' approach. Intense discussions followed as to the extent to which this formalism is suited to intellectual property protection. The Panel's extreme caution in confining itself to a textual approach for interpreting TRIPS provisions may partly be explained by the existence of potential political and industrial conflicts which could involve polarising debate. The formal, textual approach in *Canada–Pharmaceutical Patents* seems to have preempted endless political arguments, although the fact that no economic or social realities behind abstract concepts have been taken into consideration has left many other questions open to future debates.

The Panel in *Canada–Pharmaceutical Patents* stated that the non-discrimination rule delineated in Article 27.1 applied also to exceptions. This gave rise to various criticisms, including those relating to research tool patents in biotechnology, as we will see below.

---

[99] *Canada–Pharmaceutical Patents*, Panel Report (n 30) paras 7.54–7.58.

[100] ibid para 7.59.

[101] *Canada–Pharmaceutical Patents*, Panel Report (n 30) para 7.69.

[102] ibid para 7.82.

[103] *Canada–Pharmaceutical Patents*, Panel Report (n 30) para 7.83.

D Non-Discrimination Principles in the TRIPS Agreement

i National Treatment Principle and IP protection

National treatment and most favoured nation principles, commonly called 'non-discriminatory principles', have been pivotal in trade liberalisation in goods throughout the GATT and the WTO history, and central to trade disputes and their settlement within these institutions. These principles are also enshrined in Part I of the TRIPS Agreement as basic principles, in Articles 3 and 4, respectively, but they had to be adapted to be applied to intellectual property owned by persons.

In the TRIPS context, these GATT principles apply specifically to the ways in which IPR 'protection' is accorded to nationals and non-nationals, which include, according to footnote 3 to Article 3, 'matters affecting the availability, acquisition, scope, maintenance and enforcement of intellectual property rights as well as those matters affecting the use of intellectual property rights specifically addressed in this Agreement.' In *Indonesia–Autos*,[104] therefore, the US argued, as an ancillary complaint, that the Indonesian law and practices at issue, as far as they concerned the use of trademarks, were inconsistent with Article 3 TRIPS, national treatment and Article 20 of the TRIPS Agreement.[105]

The Appellate Body in *US–Section 211 Appropriation Act* considered that Article III:4 GATT, which concerns equality of competitive opportunities for domestic and imported products, could serve as a 'useful context', even to this TRIPS dispute.[106] The relevant standard for its examination of Article 3.1 TRIPS concerning national treatment was 'whether the measure provides effective equality of opportunities as between these two groups in respect of protection of intellectual property rights'.[107] The Panel in *EC–Geographical Indications*, admitted further that the language of Article 3.1 is similar to the language of GATT Article III:4,[108] but that the latter requires that 'no less favourable treatment must be given to like products'. The Panel suggested that this combination of elements, the basic principles of GATT 1994 and of relevant international intellectual property agreements or conventions, characterises new TRIPS rules and disciplines as expressed in the preamble to the TRIPS Agreement.[109]

The Panel in *EC–Geographical Indications* examined whether the difference in treatment affected the 'effective equality of opportunities' for nationals of the defendant Member's country with regard to the 'protection' of IPR, to the

---

[104] *Indonesia–Autos* (n 7).

[105] Art 20 of the TRIPS Agreement stipulates that the use of a trade mark in the course of trade shall not unjustifiably be encumbered by special requirements, in a manner detrimental to its capability to distinguish the goods or services of one undertaking from those of other undertakings.

[106] *US–Section 211 Appropriation Act* (n 4) para 242.

[107] *EC–Geographical Indications*, Panel Report (n 6) (US) paras 8.129–8.131, (Australia) paras 8.179–8.181.

[108] ibid (US) para 7.127, (Australia) para 7.163.

[109] *EC–Geographical Indications*, Panel Report (n 6) paras 7.184–7.187.

detriment of nationals of other Members.[110] In this regard, the Panel quoted the Appellate Body in *Korea–Various Measures on Beef*, in a dispute concerning formally different treatment, and drew the conclusion that '[a] formal difference in treatment between imported and like domestic products is thus neither necessary, nor sufficient, to show a violation of Article III:4'.[111] The Panel in *EC–Geographical Indications* viewed that even if the provisions of the Regulation in question were formally identical in the treatment that they accorded to nationals of other Member countries, the standard from which to assess whether the measure violates Article 3.1 must be the 'effective equality of opportunities' with regard to the protection of IPRs. On this basis, the Panel concluded, with respect to the EC objection procedures, that there was 'less favourable treatment to the nationals of other Members', inconsistent with Article 3.1 of the TRIPS Agreement.[112]

ii Non-discrimination Principles in Article 27.1 TRIPS

a Discrimination as to whether products are imported or locally produced

The second sentence of Article 27.1 of the TRIPS Agreement includes a set of non-discrimination principles specific to the Agreement, and stipulates that 'patents shall be *available* and patent rights *enjoyable* without discrimination as to the place of invention, the field of technology and whether products are imported or locally produced'(emphasis added).

The US, in *Brazil–Measures Affecting Patent Protection*,[113]took the issue of discrimination as to 'whether products are imported or locally produced' in Article 27.1 TRIPS. In January 2001, the US requested the establishment of a Panel over the conformity of Article 68 of Brazil's 1996 Industrial Property Law[114] with regard to Articles 27.1 and 28 of the TRIPS Agreement.[115] Article 68(1)I of Brazil's Industrial Property Law provides that 'the following [also] occasion a compulsory license: [I] non-exploitation of the object of the patent within the Brazilian territory for failure to manufacture or incomplete manufacture of the

---

[110] The Panel noted that the objection procedures in the disputed EC Regulation do not concern the location of the geographical area to which the GI referred, but the place where the objector resided or was established. The Panel therefore recognised the close link between nationality, on the one hand, and residence and establishment, on the other.

[111] *Korea–Measures Affecting Imports of Fresh, Chilled and Frozen Beef*, Appellate Report (adopted 10 January 2001) WT/DS161/AB/R, WT/DS169/AB/R para 7.208.

[112] *EC–Geographical Indications* (n 6) (US) para 7.345, (Australia) para 7.395.

[113] Request for the Establishment of a Panel by the US (9 January 2001) WT/DS199/3.

[114] Law No 9,279 of 14 May 1996; effective May 1997. www.wipo.int/clea/en/text_pdf.jsp?lang=EN&id=515.

[115] On 30 May 2000, the US requested consultations with the Government of Brazil pursuant to Art 4 of the Understanding on Rules and Procedures Governing the Settlement of Disputes (DSU) and Art 64 of the TRIPS Agreement (to the extent that it incorporates by reference Art XXII of the General Agreement on Tariffs and Trade 1994) regarding the above measure (WT/DS199/1). The US and Brazil then held consultations on 29 June 2000 and on 1 December 2000, but failed to reach a mutually satisfactory resolution of the dispute. ibid para 4.

product, or also failure to make full use of the patented process, except cases where this is not economically feasible, when importation shall be permitted; . . .'. Article 68(1)II provides that 'commercialization that does not satisfy the needs of the market' would also be a reason for such licensing. Furthermore, Article 68(4) allows parallel trade of products manufactured according to a process or product patent. Article 68(5) adds that 'The compulsory license can be requested when three years have elapsed since the patent was granted.'

According to the US, Article 68 of Brazil's industrial property law 'discriminates against US owners of Brazilian patents whose products are imported into, but not locally produced in Brazil. Article 68 also curtails the exclusive rights conferred on these owners by their patents. As such, Brazil's local working requirement appears inconsistent with its obligations under Article 27.1 and Article 28 of the TRIPS Agreement.'[116]

Under the Paris Convention, whether or not importation is considered as 'working' of the patented inventions is left to the discretion of its Members (chapter 2).[117] During the Uruguay Round negotiations, the US and some developed countries attempted to make this view prevail,[118] but developing countries opposed it and attempted to make it obligatory for protection of foreign patents that products be manufactured locally.[119] The resulting compromise was the prohibition in Article 27.1 TRIPS of discrimination as to 'whether products are imported or locally produced' (chapter 4).

Article 27.1 of the TRIPS Agreement does not deal with the meaning of 'working' a patent. Under Article 27.1, therefore, unless imported products are discriminated against in favour of locally produced ones 'in the acquisition and enjoyment of patent rights', considering only local production as 'working' of the patented inventions per se would not violate the TRIPS Agreement.

It is apparent from the wording of Article 68 of Brazil's Industrial Property Law that 'exploitation' means local manufacturing, and the lack, or incomplete manufacture, or failure to make full use of the patented process thereof on the territory of Brazil 'may' result in compulsory licensing. However, importation can be allowed to substitute for local working in the event that local manufacturing is not 'economically viable', and if such authorisation is given. The provi-

---

[116] Article 42 of the Brazilian Industrial Property Law provides that: 'A patent confers on its title-holder the right to prevent a third party from, without his consent, producing, using, offering for sale, selling or importing for these purposes.'

[117] Art 5A(4) of the Paris Convention reads: 'A compulsory license may not be applied for on the ground of failure to work or insufficient working before the expiration of a period of four years from the date of filing of the patent application or three years from the date of the grant of the patent, whichever period expires last.'

[118] According to Gorlin, 'the importation/locally produced non-discrimination has implications that go beyond compulsory licensing. For example, Spanish patent law formerly required that the patentee produce the product locally in order to be entitled to a preliminary injunction in a patent infringement action'. JJ Gorlin, *An Analysis of the Pharmaceutical-related Provisions of the WTO TRIPS (IP) Agreement* (IP Institute, 1999) 23.

[119] A Attaran and P Champ, 'Patent Rights and Local Working Under the WTO TRIPS Agreement: An Analysis of the U.S.-Brazil Patent Dispute' (2002) 27 *Yale Journal of International Law* 365–80.

sion therefore is not mandatory and, depending on the economic circumstances, importation is allowed. For example, imported medicines might achieve a lower price than if they were domestically produced. The provision still imposes conditions on imported products which locally manufactured products escape.

Brazil, in turn, requested consultations with the US concerning the consistency, with regard to Articles 27 and 28, of allegedly discriminatory measures under Chapter 18 of the US Patent Act (inventions made possible by US federal funding) as discriminating against non-US nationals (DS244).[120] After several consultations, the issues raised in the US case against Brazil garnered a mutually agreed solution, of which the DSB was notified on 19 July 2001.[121] The parties agreed to settle by mutual consultation if a party decides to issue a compulsory licence. Incidentally, the US, by raising these disputes, provoked moral indignation and world-wide media mobilisation against US obstruction of Brazil's AIDS programme.[122]

The case was settled, and therefore we have missed the opportunity for a clarification by a WTO Panel as to the exact nature and extent of the prohibition of discrimination in Article 27.1 in relation to compulsory licensing on the grounds of non-working of patents. The meaning of 'working' of patents remains unclear, after a hundred-year history of controversies since the beginning of the Paris Convention (chapter 2). In fact, the patent laws of many countries contain similar provisions to Brazil's, concerning compulsory licensing based on non-exploitation or insufficient exploitation. Section 83 of India's Patents Act and the Patent Law of China are examples that we will examine in chapters 9 and 10.

b The meaning of discrimination under Article 27.1

The second sentence of Article 27.1 TRIPS provides that '. . . patents shall be available and patent rights enjoyable without discrimination as to the place of invention, the field of technology and whether products are imported or locally produced.' In comparison to the principles of national treatment and most favoured nation treatment that do not use the word 'discrimination' but are defined in precise terms, non-discrimination principles in Article 27.1, according to the Panel in *Canada–Pharmaceutical Patents,* are one of the variously defined forms of discrimination among WTO provisions. Non-discrimination provisions in Article 27.1 therefore involve issues specific to the TRIPS Agreement.

The Panel in this case emphasised that those TRIPS provisions that deal with so-called non-discriminatory principles, such as the national treatment and most

---

[120] *United States–US Patents Code,* Request for Consultations by Brazil (7 February 2001) WT/DS224/1.

[121] (19 July 2001) WT/DS199/4, G/L/454, IP/D/23/Add.1. The Parties agreed, if it should be deemed necessary for Brazil to apply Art 68 to grant compulsory licences on patents held by US companies, to hold prior talks on the matter, and that Brazil would not proceed with further dispute settlement action regarding ss 204 and 209 of US patent law.

[122] C Passarelli and T Veriano Jr, 'Good Medicine: Brazil's Multifront War on AIDS' (2001) 35(5) *NACLA Report on the Americas* 35–52.

favoured nation provisions of Articles 3 and 4, do not use the term 'discrimination'.[123] Furthermore, *Canada–Pharmaceutical Patents* concerned minimum standards of protection in Part II, and not the basic principles in Part I.[124]

According to the Panel, the ordinary meaning of the word 'discriminate' is potentially broader than these more specific types of discrimination, such as the national treatment and most-favoured-nation provisions of Articles 3 and 4.[125] The Panel stated that 'discrimination' is a term to be avoided whenever more precise standards are available, and it is impossible to treat the concept of discrimination in Article 27 TRIPS as applications of a general concept of discrimination derived from the rulings under the GATT or WTO, each being based on the precise legal text at issue.[126] The Panel further stated that:

> [the word 'discrimination'] certainly extends beyond the concept of differential treatment. It is a normative term, pejorative in connotation, referring to results of the unjustified imposition of differentially disadvantageous treatment.[127]

The Panel considered that claims against both formal (de jure) and practical (de facto) discrimination are possible under the TRIPS Agreement. According to the Panel, discrimination may arise from explicitly different treatment, sometimes called 'de jure discrimination', but may also arise from ostensibly identical treatment which, due to differences in circumstances, produces differentially advantageous effects, sometimes called 'de facto discrimination'.[128]

The US argued in *Canada–Pharmaceutical Patents* that 'discrimination' inconsistent with Article 27.1 should be distinguished from mere differentiation[129] by assessing 'whether the measure in question applied differentially to pharmaceuticals effectively and consistently accorded less favourable treatment in the enjoyment of rights to pharmaceutical inventions, as compared to inventions in other fields of technology'.[130]

Significantly, the Panel Report in *Canada–Pharmaceutical Patents*[131] stated that the non-discrimination rule delineated in Article 27.1 is applicable to both Articles 30 and 31.[132] According to the Panel, this is because Article 30 refers explicitly to 'exceptions to the exclusive rights conferred by a patent', and not to 'exceptions to non-discriminatory rules.' On this question, the Panel concluded that:

---

[123] *Canada–Pharmaceutical Patents*, Panel Report (n 30) para 7.94.
[124] ibid paras 7.209–7.210.
[125] *Canada–Pharmaceutical Patents*, Panel Report (n 30) para 7.94.
[126] ibid para 7.98.
[127] *Canada–Pharmaceutical Patents,* Panel Report (n 30) para 7.94.
[128] ibid para 7.94.
[129] The US referred to *US–Section 337 of the Tariff Act of 1930,* BISD 36S/386 para 5.11, according to which 'the mere fact that imported products are subject to legal provisions that are different from those applying to products of national origin is in itself not conclusive in establishing inconsistency with Article III:4 of the GATT, in the sense that it has to be assessed whether or not such differences in the legal provisions applicable do or do not accord to imported products less favourable treatment.'
[130] *Canada–Pharmaceutical Patents,* Panel Report (n 30) para 5.36(b)(3)(ii).
[131] ibid para 7.93.
[132] *Canada–Pharmaceutical Patents,* Panel Report (n 30) para 7.91.

Nor was the Panel able to agree with the policy arguments in support of Canada's interpretation of Article 27. To begin with, it is not true that being able to discriminate against particular patents will make it possible to meet Article 30's requirement that the exception be 'limited'. Article 30 exception cannot be made 'limited' by limiting it to one field of technology, because the effects of each exception must be found to be "limited" when measured against each affected patent.[133]

The Panel added a reason that the anti-discrimination rule of Article 27.1 applies to exceptions of the kind authorised by Article 30:

> It is quite plausible, as the EC argued, that the TRIPS Agreement would want to require governments to apply exceptions in a non-discriminatory manner, in order to ensure that governments do not succumb to domestic pressures to limit exceptions to areas where right holders tend to be foreign producers.[134]

The Panel's interpretation that the principle of non-discrimination also applied to exceptions was criticised by scholars as mere textual analysis (although the above reason seems rather non-textualist).[135] Canada argued that the scope of Article 30 would be reduced to insignificance if governments were required to treat all fields of technology in the same way. It may be far more difficult to meet the requirement that Article 30 exceptions be 'limited', if all exceptions must apply to every product. Canada's view was taken from the perspective that it is more appropriate for exceptions to be formulated in a way that can limit them to certain technical fields (such as biotechnology), because the range of exceptions could thus be limited.

c 'Discrimination' and 'differentiation'

Would legal provisions which specifically concern certain technological fields violate the non-discrimination principle set forth in Article 27.1 of the TRIPS Agreement? The Panel in *Canada–Pharmaceutical Patents* stated that Article 27 does not require all exceptions in Article 30 to apply to all products. According to the Panel, this provision 'does not prohibit *bona fide* exceptions to deal with problems that may exist only in certain product areas'.[136] Moreover, to the extent that the prohibition of discrimination does limit the ability to target certain products in dealing with certain national policies referred to in Articles 7 and 8.1, 'that fact may well constitute a deliberate limitation rather than a frustration of purpose'.[137]

The Panel thus introduced the concept of *bona fide* differential measures to which the non-discrimination principle in Article 27.1 of the TRIPS Agreement may not be applied. The Panel does not define this concept or delineate its scope,

[133] *Canada–Pharmaceutical Patentss,* Panel Report (n 30) para 7.92.

[134] ibid para 7.92

[135] For example, see GB Dinwoodie and R Cooper Dreyfuss, 'International Intellectual Property Law and the Public Domain of Science' (2004) 7 *Journal of International Economic Law* 431–48.

[136] *Canada–Pharmaceutical Patents,* Panel Report (n 30) para 7.92.

[137] ibid para 7.92.

except for giving some indicia as to what 'discrimination' is, compared to bona fide differentiating treatment. By default, *bona fide* measures are normative, not pejorative, without a discriminatory purpose, intent or effect; they do not constitute a means of protecting domestic industry.

Abbott stretches the scope of this statement by the Panel and draws the following conclusion from the Panel Report on *Canada–Pharmaceutical Patents*:

> Pharmaceutical producers have argued that Article 27:1 prohibits WTO Members from adopting compulsory licensing legislation that is specifically directed at the pharmaceutical sectors. The panel report in the *Canada–Generic Pharmaceuticals* case rejected this line of analysis. While Article 27:1 of the TRIPS Agreement may preclude some forms of differentiation among fields of patented inventions, it certainly does not preclude all differentiation. It prohibits only differentiation that is "discriminatory".[138]

According to Abbott, 'the term "discrimination" in TRIPS 27:1 should be read flexibly':

> The panel states that governments are permitted to adopt different rules for particular product areas, provided that the differences are adopted for bona fide purposes. The Panel did not attempt to provide a general rules regarding what differences will be considered *bona fide*. . . . It should be obvious that the factors that will support the grant of compulsory licenses in the field of pharmaceuticals will not be the same as the factors that support the grant of compulsory licenses in, for example, the field of machine tools or internet auctions . . . logically there will be internal regulatory *differences* in the way in which requests for compulsory licenses are treated; and that these differences may not be *discriminatory*. [139]

From this, Abbott interprets that 'the constraint imposed by Article 27.1 on compulsory licensing to address public health emergencies is that 'differential regulations be adopted for a *bona fide* purpose – that they be adopted in good faith', which may amount to a revision of Article 27.1.[140]

If special procedures for compulsory licensing specifically for pharmaceuticals are justifiable under Article 27.1, which provides that patent rights must be

---

[138] F Abbott 'The TRIPS-legality of measures taken to address public health crises: Responding to USTR-State-industry positions that undermine the WTO' in RE Hudec, JD Southwick and DLM Kennedy (eds) *The Political Economy of International Trade Law: Essays in Honour of Robert E Hudec* (Cambridge University Press, 2002) 326.

[139] ibid 326–7.

[140] The open-ended issues of 'bona fide differentiation' in *Canada–Pharmaceutical Patents* seems to have become a policy reference. A paper prepared by Keith Maskus in November 2009, as a contribution to the OECD project on Environmental Policy and Technological Change, states that:'an early WTO dispute settlement panel ruled that this provision only bars unjustified distinctions in patent law among technological areas and does not bar differences in legislation and processes based on legitimate policy preferences.' K Maskus, 'Differentiated Intellectual Property Regimes for Environmental and Climate Technologies' (2009) OECD Working Party on National Environmental Policies ENV/EPOC/WPNEP6 para 49, 15–16. The paper concludes that: 'Economists and legal scholars have long argued that IPRs should be differentiated by field to reflect varying industry innovation characteristics and the relative power of IPRs to influence activity in different sectors. As Abbott (2009) notes, there are many examples of fundamental variations in legislation among the United States, EU, Japan, India and other countries. Thus, policy actions can be taken at the national and regional levels within the flexible bounds set out by TRIPS.'

enjoyable without discrimination regarding the field of technology, all kinds of measures taken for social and political purposes in a specific field of technology may then be justified. Each industry will then lobby for legislation in its own interest. Moreover, what is presented as *bona fide* by one Member could well be considered by others as constituting an industrial interest or a policy protecting domestic industry against foreign technologies. The Panel insisted on avoiding this situation, which was probably the intention of the agreement reached during the Uruguay Round (see chapter 4).[141]

For the Panel in *Canada–Pharmaceutical Patents*, the non-discriminatory principles in Article 27.1 covers exceptions, so that the measure in question would not leave the door open to various industrial or social policies to be accepted as escaping from the principle. After considering various meanings of 'discrimination', the Panel avoided defining a general concept of discrimination but referred to the limited scope of the non-discrimination principles in Article 27.1 which prohibits discrimination only in relation to the place of invention, the field of technology, and whether products are imported or produced locally.

Given the very broad range of issues that might be involved in defining the word 'discrimination' in Article 27.1 of the TRIPS Agreement, the Panel decided that it would be better to defer attempting to define that term at the outset, but instead to determine which issues were raised by the record before the Panel, and to define the concept of discrimination to the extent necessary to resolve those issues.[142] In any case, according to the Panel, '[r]ecommendations and rulings of the DSB cannot add to or diminish the rights and obligations provided'[143] and, therefore, the statement about bona fide differentiation in the Panel Report in *Canada–Pharmaceutical Patents* could not be extrapolated to mean something more than the text of Article 27.1 provides.

d Differential treatment to ensure equal treatment across technologies?

In fact, the scope of application for the non-discrimination principle involves many substantive technological and legal issues that cannot be resolved through textual analysis of the provisions of the TRIPS Agreement alone, as Dinwoodie and Dreyfuss argue.[144]

There have been adjustments in patent laws responding to regulatory requirements specific to technological fields. For example, the US Patent Act provides for restoration of patent terms for human drugs, food additives and medical devices whose commercialisation has been delayed by lengthy regulatory procedures by the Food and Drug Administration.[145] Such delays shorten the effective

---

[141] *Canada–Pharmaceutical Patents*, Panel Report (n 30) para 7.92
[142] ibid para 7.98
[143] Art 3.2 of the Understanding on Rules and Procedures Governing the Settlement of Disputes (DSU).
[144] Dinwoodie and Dreyfuss (n 135) 434–6.
[145] 35 USC § 157.

length of patent protection (EPL – see chapter 13) from 20 years to only 8–12 years on average. Article 67.2 of the Japanese Patent Act does not specify a technical field, but the relevant legislative decree specifies that the extension of the term of patent protection is allowed only for medicines, agricultural chemicals and veterinary medicines. Other countries, such as Switzerland, Australia, Israel and the EU have adopted similar systems of patent term extension for the same reason.[146]

The EU grants patent term extension only to medicinal and agricultural chemical products. In *Canada–Pharmaceutical Patents*, the Panel took up the issue of 'regulatory review exception' when discussing the concept of 'legitimate interest' in Article 30 TRIPS[147] On 2 December 1998, Canada requested consultations with the European Communities on the patent term extension of medicinal and pharmaceutical products but this case remains inactive.[148] According to Canada, Council Regulation (EEC) 1768/92 and European Parliament and Council Regulation (EC) 1610/96 of 23 July 1996 concerning the creation of a supplementary protection certificate for plant protection products (SPC)[149] are inconsistent with the EU's obligations not to discriminate on the basis of field of technology, as provided by Article 27.1 of the TRIPS Agreement, because these Regulations only apply to pharmaceutical and agricultural products. However, these measures are instituted with a view to assuring non-discriminatory treatment of inventions across different technological fields, because special circumstances of particular sectors disadvantage the inventions in these sectors. Patent Examination Guidelines, for example, are also elaborated often to respond to specific characteristics of different technological fields, such as pharmaceutical, biotechnology, and software fields. To ensure equally effective protection for all technical fields, different treatment of different technologies may be necessary. The Panel in *Canada–Pharmaceutical Patents* did not take up these debates, but it did not entirely close the possibility of considering these questions.

---

[146] *Canada–Pharmaceutical Patents,* Panel Report (n 30) para 7.78.

[147] The Panel stated that: 'It is an unintended consequence of the conjunction of the patent laws with product regulatory laws, where the combination of patent rights with the time demands of the regulatory process gives a greater than normal period of market exclusivity to the enforcement of certain patent rights. It is likewise a form of exploitation that most patent owners do not in fact employ. For the vast majority of patented products, there is no marketing regulation of the kind covered by Section 55.2(1), and thus there is no possibility to extend patent exclusivity by delaying the marketing approval process for competitors' (*Canada–Pharmaceutical Patents,* Panel Report (n 30) para 7.57), and concluded that: 'Notwithstanding the number of governments that had responded positively to that claimed interest by granting compensatory patent term extensions, the issue itself was of relatively recent standing, and the community of governments was obviously still divided over the merits of such claims' (para. 7.8).

[148] *EC–Patent Protection for Pharmaceutical and Agricultural Chemical Products,* Request for consultations WT/DS153/1 (7 December 1998). The request states: 'In Canada's view, Council Regulation (EEC) No. 1768/92 and European Parliament and Council Regulation (EC) No. 1610/96 are incompatible with the obligation of the European Communities and their Member States not to discriminate on the basis of field of technology (as found in Article 27.1 of the TRIPS Agreement), since they only apply to pharmaceutical and agricultural chemical products.'

[149] [1996] OJ L198/30.

e Differential patentability and enforcement mechanisms for innovation?

Among the questions raised by third parties in the proceedings in *Canada–Pharmaceutical Patents,* the Panelconsidered whether measures that are limited to a particular area of technology – de jure or de facto – are necessarily 'discriminatory' by virtue of that fact alone. Whether under certain circumstances they may be justified as special measures needed to restore equality of treatment to the area of technology in question was a related issue that the Panel did not touch upon.[150]

Indeed, to encourage innovation, affirmative action has been taken, and this may be necessary in different fields.[151] Due to the differing natures of technical fields and the ways in which innovations occur, there may be differing treatment, depending on these technological characteristics and measures to equalise conditions for availability and enjoyment of patents in all fields. Differentiation in different fields of technology may be necessary to ensure non-discriminatory treatment among technologies.

In US academic circles, Barton, for example, asserted that in order to foster innovation in the field of biotechnology, patents should not be granted for tests and research tools, such as coordinate data in the three-dimensional structure of a protein.[152] According to Burk and Lemley, on the other hand, the criteria for judging non-obviousness (which depends on the common technical knowledge of a 'person having ordinary skill in the art' (an average expert)) vary significantly with regard to different fields of technology. To foster innovation in biotechnology, they argue, it is desirable to allow right holders to encompass a wide scope of claims, to raise requirements for non-obviousness and to lower enablement requirements in this particular field.[153]

There have been discussions over the criteria for determining whether the patent claims satisfy the patentability requirement of 'inventive step' (non-obviousness) in such new fields as gene patents (chapter 3). Patenting a structure of DNA sequences with potential functions which have not yet been disclosed, it was argued, would deter subsequent innovation and fail to accord equitable remuneration for contributions made to the state of the art. Certain industries, academia and other critics of the patent system also maintained that the prevalence of biotechnology research tool patents negatively influence scientific research. In the US, adjustments relating to patentability to different technological fields are achieved through court decisions, and the law remains general and abstract, covering all technological fields.

---

[150] *Canada–Pharmaceutical Patents* (n 30) para 7.105 fn 439.
[151] DL Burk and MA Lemley, 'Is Patent Law Technology-Specific?' (2002) 17 *Berkeley Tech. Law Journal.*
[152] JH Barton, 'United States Law of Genomic and Post-Genomic Patents' (2002) 33 *International Review of Industrial Property and Copyright Law.*
[153] Burk and Lemley (n 151).

f European legislation and non-discrimination in Article 27.1

In Europe, legislative measures to limit the scope of DNA-related patent protection in biotechnology to those functions disclosed in the patent have been introduced. These laws have been formulated with the intention of responding to broad allegations that strong patent rights could create barriers to follow-up research, and thus hinder technological advance (chapter 3).[154] It was feared that, if all these potential functions and uses are claimed in the basic patent, subsequent researchers may have difficulty innovating and collecting economic rewards, which would reduce the incentive to invest in scientific and technological R&D to discover new functions.[155]

As these legislations specify or imply the field of technology concerned (DNA-related inventions), and as these limitations on patentability do not exist for other chemical substances, they could be characterised as discriminatory in the sense of Article 27.1. Product patent protection normally includes possible uses of the DNA in the future, as well as the processes to produce that patented DNA. DNA sequences may have various functions such as coding for a multiplicity of proteins (which may function as medicines, antibodies, receptors for specific viruses, nucleic acid probes to locate particular parts of DNA sequences, etc) and can be used for different purposes, such as diagnosis and drug targeting.

In Switzerland, Article 40b of the amended Swiss Federal Law on Patents for Inventions contains a special provision relating to research tools which provides that: 'Whoever intends to use a patented biotechnological invention as an instrument or means in research, is entitled to a non-exclusive licence.' The Swiss Patent Act affords the same scope of patent protection to biotechnological inventions, regardless of whether or not the patented subject matter can be used as a research tool. However, when a third party wishes to use a patented invention as a research tool, this party may ask for a non-exclusive licence of this patented technology from the courts. According to the Swiss Institute of Intellectual Property, compulsory licensing is possible for the purpose of preventing research tool patents from unreasonably restraining research, mainly in the field of health care. Because licences are given on individual merits, the Institute argues, this provision is consistent with TRIPS, in particular with Article 31(1)(a). According to the same Institute, the TRIPS Agreement allows differentiated treatments of inventions, most radically in Article 27.3(b) which allows Members to exclude plants and animals from patentability. Based on the principle that *major continet in se minus,* the Swiss Institute affirms that differential treatment of research tool inventions in Article 40b therefore should be allowed.[156] However, it seems accepted that once protection is given, gene patents

---

[154] eg, French Patent Law L.613-2-1 (2004) and Art 1(a)(3) of the German Patent Law, modified by law L.611-18 (2004) See ch 3.

[155] See eg *University of Rochester v G D Searle & Co Inc, Monsanto Company, Pharmacia Corporation, and Pfizer Inc* 375 F 3d 1303, CAFC, 2 July 2004 (ch 3, n 112).

[156] 'The greater contains the lesser'. Interviews at the Swiss Institute of Intellectual Property, 20 April 2009.

must fulfil the requirements of non-discriminatory 'enjoyment' of patent rights under Article 27.1 and not Article 27.3(b) of the TRIPS Agreement.

Pyrmont explores the question of conformity of these European laws vis-à-vis Article 27.1 of the TRIPS Agreement and in the light of (i) various arguments about the characteristics of DNA sequences, including those denying that these are products,[157] (ii) possible justifications of differential treatment that are provided in other TRIPS provisions (Articles 7, 8 and 27.2), using the criteria of 'discrimination' developed in the Panel Report provided in *Canada–Pharmaceutical Patents*. After examining the types of arguments that support or reject the conformity of these measures to Article 27.1 TRIPS, Pyrmont concludes that restricting the scope of gene patents to the disclosed purpose while maintaining the principle of absolute product protection for all other technical fields violates the non-discrimination requirement of Article 27.1 TRIPS,[158] and that product patent protection of DNA sequences so far has had only an insignificant negative impact, particularly on genetic testing.[159]

On the other hand, the 'purpose-bound' approach to DNA sequences may be justified by the different ways in which claims are interpreted in different fields of technology, to give, overall, a fair treatment to inventions in these fields. Claims relating to a chemical compound cover potential uses which are not claimed in the patent specification. However, they do not cover other chemical compounds which comprise the first compound as a part of their structure. The claims interpretation is limited because the doctrine of equivalents is rarely applied to these claims. In the field of machinery, by contrast, patent rights cover the machine and its uses and functions, but even if the entire machine (a motor vehicle, a crane, etc) is not claimed, the patentee's right over the part which is claimed can be asserted against another machine. The doctrine of equivalents is often applied when these claims are interpreted.

There is no logical reason to equate claims over DNA sequences to those over machines, and there is considerable area for doubt in deciding how much scope should be given to DNA claims. The legislatures of certain European countries seem to have decided that DNA sequences are like machines, and that a very limited scope should be given to their claims. This has not yet been proven to be the best method. The US decides these questions judicially, an approach that seems better adapted to changing frontiers of technology.[160] An approach in which patentability is micromanaged, and different rules for the scope of claims

---

[157] Pyrmont cites SCHRELL, 2001 GRUR 782,785 et seq. WPW Pyrmont, 'Special Legislation for Genetic Inventions–A Violation of Article 27(1) TRIPS?', in WPW Pyrmont et al (eds), *Patents and Technological Progress in a Globalized World: Liber Amicorum Joseph Straus* (MPI Studies on Intellectual Property, Competition and Tax Law, Berlin and Heidelberg, Springer, 2007) 209.

[158] idid 304. The author states also that 'the Belgian provision appears to violate Article 28 as the exemption for the use of inventions for research purposes constitutes a significant incursion on the rights of research tool patent owners that could hardly be qualified as a limited exception permissible under Article 30'.

[159] Pyrmont cites the BRCA 1 and BRCA 2 patents drawing the attention however that these controversies relate to the function disclosed in the patents. Pyrmont (n 159) 301.

[160] See *University of Rochester v Searle et al* (n 155).

for each field of technology are legislated does not seem appropriate, as this could be ill-fitting with the progress of technology.[161] Rather than enacting a technology-specific patent law, elaborating clear guidelines and educating the judiciary in new technologies would be a better response.

g Patent rights 'enjoyable' without discrimination

Article 27.1 establishes a non-discriminatory principle regarding not only the 'availability' of patents but also the enjoyment of patent rights. The Dutch Court in *Monsanto v Cefetra*[162] (chapter 3), asked a fourth question for a preliminary judgment: 'Is it possible, in answering the previous questions, to take into consideration the TRIPS Agreement, in particular Articles 27 and 30 thereof?' The Court of Justice of the European Union (Court of Justice) answered the question succinctly, as follows:

> . . . the above interpretation of Article 9 of the Directive "does not appear to conflict unreasonably with a normal exploitation of the patent" and does not "unreasonably prejudice the legitimate interests of the patent owner, taking account of the legitimate interests of third parties", within the meaning of Article 30 of the TRIPS Agreement.[163]

The fact that Monsanto did not claim the soy meal in the patent specification seems to be the cause of the failure of its infringement case. However, the Court of Justice might have handled the fourth question too quickly. For example, the Advocate General stated that:

> Specifically, Article 27 of the TRIPS Agreement is concerned exclusively with patentability. In the present case, no problem of patentability arises, since it is not disputed that Monsanto has the right – which it has actually exercised – to patent the DNA sequence which makes soya resistant to Glyphosate. The point of contention between the parties is merely the extent of the protection which must be recognised as accruing to the invention.[164]

The stipulation in Article 27 of the TRIPS Agreement that 'patents shall be available and patent rights enjoyable without discrimination as to the place of invention, the field of technology and whether products are imported or locally produced' refers also to enforcement'. As for Article 30, the Advocate General affirms, using the general term of 'purpose-bound' protection and without detailed examination, that:

> Above all, in fact, to recognise purpose-bound protection does not mean providing for *exceptions* from the scope of protection of a patent: what is defined in narrow terms rather, is the *extent* of the right itself, which is not recognised in respect of uses other than those described in the patent application. There is no obligation under the TRIPS Agreement to recognise that the protection accruing to DNA sequences is "absolute"

---

[161] Pyrmont (n 159) 304.
[162] *Monsanto v Cefetra*, Case C-428/08 6 July 2010.
[163] ibid para 76.
[164] *Monsanto v Cefetra* (n 162) para 75.

– that is to say, protection in respect of all possible uses, including even unforeseen and future uses.[165]

Exceptions and limitations to the rights conferred are not necessarily termed 'exceptions', as the WTO dispute settlement organs have shown, and their scope is interpreted in accordance with the VCLT rule, taking into account not only laws but also the facts of the case. The Court of Justice may not have paid adequate attention to these issues.

On the complex question of the scope of claims and innovation in biotechnology, realities of R&D and empirical evidence will guide the future discussions which may lead to a proper balance. At any rate, there seem to be fewer controversies[166] over gene patent infringement cases.[167] Today, attention seems to be focused on the diagnostic use of genes (chapter 3).

E TRIPS Flexibilities

i What are 'TRIPS flexibilities'?

In the TRIPS Agreement, the explicit reference to 'flexibility' is made only in the context of the transition period[168] allowed for the Least Developed Countries (LDCs – see chapter 4 n 153, chapter 5 n 87) Members. Article 66.1 exonerates LDCs of the TRIPS implementation obligations, other than Articles 3, 4 and 5, during the transition period, stipulating the following:

> In view of the special needs and requirements of LDC Members, their economic, financial and administrative constraints, and their need for flexibility to create a viable technological base, such Members shall not be required to apply the provisions of this Agreement, other than Articles 3, 4 and 5, for a period of 10 years from the date of application as defined under paragraph 1 of Article 65.

The sixth Recital in the Preamble recognises the needs of LDCs for 'maximum flexibility' in the domestic implementation of laws and regulations with a view to creating a sound and viable technological base. Flexibility in this context is de jure exoneration of obligations except those contained in Articles 3, 4 and 5.

---

[165] ibid para 76.

[166] See for example, ch 3, n 115.

[167] In *Monsanto v Cefetra* (n 162), on the question of whether Articles 27 and 30 of the TRIPS Agreement affect the interpretation given of Article 9 of the Biotech Directive 98/44/EC, the Court of Justice of the European Union simply stated that: '. . . it should be pointed out that an interpretation of Article 9 of the Directive limiting the protection it confers to situations in which the patented product performs its function does not appear to conflict unreasonably with a normal exploitation of the patent and does not "unreasonably prejudice the legitimate interests of the patent owner, taking account of the legitimate interests of third parties", within the meaning of Article 30 of the TRIPS Agreement' (para 76). On the Advocate General's Opinion, see M Kock, 'Purpose-bound protection for DNA sequences: in through the back door?' (2010) 5(7) *Journal of Intellectual Property Law & Practice* 495–513.

[168] Initially for 10 years from the date of application as defined under para 1 of Art 65 and later extended until 1 July 2014. See ch 5.

There are substantive provisions in the TRIPS Agreement which leave open the possibility for a wide range of interpretations due to the fact that they are not written clearly, or are written without sufficient detail.[169] There are also those, such as Article 27.3(b), which offer options to Members concerning the patentability of biotechnology inventions that have not been objects of the WTO dispute settlement procedures. Some other provisions of the Agreement allow, by their wording, a certain margin of discretion to Members (for example, where it says 'Members may', 'shall not be obliged to', 'shall be free to determine') and may be characterised as 'flexible'. In any case, any international treaties including the TRIPS Agreement leave a certain margin of discretion to participating parties in interpreting its provisions, subject to appropriate norms of interpretation and rules for dispute settlements.

Furthermore, Article 1.1 of the TRIPS Agreement, entitled 'Nature and Scope of Obligations', contains such wording in the second and third sentences. Article 1.1 provides that:

> Members shall give effect to the provisions of this Agreement. Members may, but shall not be obliged to, implement in their law more extensive protection than is required by this Agreement, provided that such protection does not contravene the provisions of this Agreement. Members shall be free to determine the appropriate method of implementing the provisions of this Agreement within their own legal system and practice.

The second sentence of Article 1.1 indicates that the provisions of the Agreement are not only the minimum standards but offer 'flexibility' to Members for instituting a higher level of protection to intellectual property rights covered by the TRIPS Agreement, subject to certain conditions.

Since the adoption of the Doha Declaration on the TRIPS Agreement and Public Health, adopted at the WTO Doha Ministerial Conference in November 2001,[170] specific notions, such as compulsory licences, exceptions to the rights conferred and the freedom of Members to establish its own regime for such exhaustion,[171] have been thought of as TRIPS 'flexibilities.' Furthermore, the

---

[169] Flexibility, according to the Oxford English Dictionary, 2nd edn (Oxford, Clarendon Press; New York, Oxford University Press, 1989), 1049–50), is: '1. capability of being bent, pliancy, the quality of yielding to pressure, 2. susceptibility of modification or alteration, capacity for ready adaptation to various purposes or conditions, freedom from stiffness or rigidity'. Apparently, flexibilities are not just ambiguities (which means: 'capability of being understood in two or more ways; double or dubious signification, ambiguousness', according to the Oxford English Dictionary at 386).

[170] The Doha Declaration on the TRIPS Agreement and Public Health (Doha Declaration on Public Health) was adopted at the Doha WTO Ministerial on 14 November 2001 (WT/MIN(01)/DEC/2, 20 November 2001) and was later confirmed by a Decision of the TRIPS Council of 27 June 2002 (WT/MIN(01)/DEC/2.1 July 2002).

[171] Paragraph 5d) of the Doha Declaration on Public Health states that: 'The effect of the provisions in the TRIPS Agreement that are relevant to the exhaustion of intellectual property rights is to leave each member free to establish its own regime for such exhaustion without challenge, subject to the MFN and national treatment provisions of Articles 3 and 4.' Article 6 of the TRIPS Agreement does not contain the identical provision. Article 6 TRIPS provides that: 'For the purposes of dispute settlement under this Agreement, subject to the provisions of Articles 3 and 4 nothing in this Agreement shall be used to address the issue of the exhaustion of intellectual property rights.'

concept of 'flexibilities' has often been interpreted as a method of TRIPS interpretation allowing the reduction of the level, the scope or the effects of IPR protection.

Recently, the WIPO Committee on Development and Intellectual Property (CDIP) proposed defining 'flexibilities' as 'legal tools that countries can use as they see fit in their national developmental plans and within the framework of the mandatory standards of international obligations'.[172] This concept is based on the understanding of the TRIPS Agreement, that:

> A different approach is taken in the TRIPS Agreement [compared to the Paris Convention on the Protection of Industrial Property], which lays down the minimum substantive standards of protection that must be provided by WTO Members. There is a common understanding among experts that those standards were set broadly at the current level of developed countries at the time of the negotiations of the Uruguay Round; therefore a reduction of *the room for manoeuvre* was the consequence of the inclusion of new minimum substantive standards.[173]

Based on this understanding of the TRIPS Agreement, the paper explains that:

> The term 'flexibilities' means that there are different options through which TRIPS obligations can be transposed into national law so that national interests are accommodated and yet TRIPS provisions and principles are complied with.[174]

The paper then classifies these 'flexibilities' into two major categories: those regarding transition periods, and 'substantive' flexibilities in the TRIPS Agreement. The paper takes into account the process of acquisition of the right, the scope of the patent right and to the use and enforcement of patent right in delineating 'flexibilities' in the TRIPS provisions relating to patents and deals additionally with 'five specific flexibilities', which are: compulsory licenses and government use, exhaustion of rights, research exemption, regulatory review exception, and utility models. The paper purports to explain the options that these flexibilities contain so that developing countries might use them in the implementation of the TRIPS Agreement according to their national policy choices.[175]

For the five 'specific' cases of flexibilities such as compulsory licensing or research exemptions, the WIPO flexibility paper defines 'the basic notion and then mention[s] some of the elements that allow different implementation approaches'[176] by reference to certain types of exceptions to and limitations on the rights conferred on patent owners, for example.

---

[172] WIPO Committee on Development and Intellectual Property (CDIP), Fifth Session, 'Patent Related Flexibilities in the Multilateral Legal Framework and their Legislative Implementation at the National and Regional Levels' (Geneva, WIPO Secretariat 26–30 April 2010) (WIPO flexibility paper) para 9.

[173] ibid para 20.

[174] WIPO flexibility paper (n 172) para 34.

[175] ibid para 21 fn 187.

[176] WIPO flexibility paper (n 172) para 45 fn 187.

Thus, much has been said and written about TRIPS flexibilities. In past WTO dispute cases, different Parties to disputes relating to the TRIPS Agreement invoked various concepts of 'flexibilities' to defend a wide margin of national discretion. More recently, in *China–Intellectual Property Rights*,[177] the Panel used the notion of flexibility to clarify the limit of national dicretion left by a succinct provision contained in Article 61 of the TRIPS Agreement, through the application of customary rules of public international law. The Panel understood the scope of 'flexibility' to be based on the ordinary meaning of the term and used the method of treaty interpretation developed by the WTO dispute settlement organs to interpret provisions of WTO agreements.

This approach may differ from those that have generally been adopted in political discussions. The meaning of flexibilities, therefore, varies significantly among those who use the word. We examine the understanding of the concept of flexibility through two examples: the ways in which certain WTO Members invoked flexibility in specific disputes and the understanding by the Panel of this concept in interpreting Article 61 of the TRIPS Agreement in *China–Intellectual Property Rights*. The Panel interpretation in this case was significant in that it shed light on certain provisions in Part III (enforcement of intellectual property rights, Articles 41–61) of the TRIPS Agreement which set out procedures for domestic enforcement both internally and at the border. Article 61 TRIPS is a single article in the fifth Section in Part III and deals with criminal procedures. According to Article 61, Members must 'make available' (see chapter 5) the domestic procedures and penalties to be applied, at least in cases of wilful trademark counterfeiting and copyright piracy on a commercial scale; sufficient sanctions to provide a deterrent, consistent with the level of penalties applied for crimes of corresponding gravity; criminal measures in appropriate cases for the seizure, forfeiture and destruction of the infringing goods and of materials and instruments used to produce them.

The clarification of the concept of 'flexibilities' that the Panel made in *China–Intellectual Property Rights* is important not only for interpreting the enforcement chapter of the TRIPS Agreement, but also for other TRIPS provisions.

ii 'Flexibilities' invoked by parties to WTO disputes

WTO Member countries, including the US, have resorted to the concept of flexibility to justify the disputed national measures on the grounds of national discretion given by the TRIPS Agreement, thus easing the tension in interpreting TRIPS. India, which has been one of the promoters of 'TRIPS flexibilities', did not seem to have relied specifically on this term in the WTO disputes, either in *India–Patents (US)*[178] or *Canada–Pharmaceutical Patents* (as a third party) when the extent to which Article 1.1 authorises national discretion was discussed.

---

[177] *China–Measures Affecting the Protection and Enforcement of Intellectual Property Rights*, Panel Report (adopted 20 March 2009) WT/DS362/R.

[178] *India–Patents (US)*, Appellate Body Report (n 40).

The US, by contrast, was one of the first users of the concept of 'flexibility' in its arguments in WTO disputes. It submitted in *US–Section 110(5) Copyright Act* that Article 1.1, second sentence, offers 'flexibility' to Members to determine for themselves whether a particular case represents an appropriate basis for an exception stipulated in Article 13 TRIPS.[179]

Parties to the disputes (including third party participants) also invoked Article 1.1, Article 7 (entitled 'objectives') which explains the objectives of the protection and enforcement of IPR, and Article 8.1 (entitled 'principles') which refers to measures 'necessary to protect public health and nutrition' also as providing flexibilities, particularly in *Canada–Pharmaceutical Patents*. Canada's argument was examined earlier when the scope of exceptions in Article 30 TRIPS was analysed.

In *China–Intellectual Property Rights*, China argued that Articles 59 and 61, read in conjunction with Article 1.1 were also characterised as being 'flexible'. In this case, particularly, China, as well as third parties such as Cuba, Argentina, Brazil and Thailand, invoked 'flexibility' which Members should enjoy in the enforcement of IPRs covered by the TRIPS Agreement. In this WTO dispute settlement case, the US claims included that: (i) China's measures for disposing of confiscated goods that infringe intellectual property rights are inconsistent with Article 59[180] of the TRIPS Agreement; and, (ii) China's criminal procedures and penalties to be applied in cases of wilful trademark counterfeiting, or copyright piracy on a commercial scale, fail to meet its obligations under Article 61, in the first two sentences, as well as in Article 41.1 of the TRIPS Agreement.[181] In the discussions concerning claim (i) above, the US claimed that the measures of destruction or disposition to be ordered against infringing goods establish a mandatory sequence of steps on the basis of Article 59. The US questioned what decisions China Customs is permitted by law to take in particular circumstances, and took issue with the customs measures permitting destruction only in 'highly limited circumstances'.[182]

---

[179] The US submitted that: 'the TRIPS Agreement does not elaborate on the criteria for a case to be considered "special" and WTO Members have flexibility to determine for themselves whether a particular case represents an appropriate basis for an exception to exclusive rights' (para 22). The US Submission in the same case further asserted that the 'interpretation of the TRIPS Article 13 criteria' requires 'a fact-intensive analysis by the Panel that takes into account all the circumstances of an individual case. Article 13 is intended to be a flexible mechanism to evaluate numerous different exceptions in many different contexts and legal systems. It does not impose any "per-se" rules with respect to any of the criteria in the Article. Rather, the permissibility of exceptions under TRIPS Article 13 must necessarily be determined on a case-by-case basis' (para 27). Attachment 2.1 to the Panel Report, First Written Submission of the US (26 October 1999). *US–Section 110(5) Copyright Act*, Panel Report (n 20).

[180] Art 59 is under section 4 (special requirements related to border measures), Part III (enforcement of IPRs) and stipulates that: 'Without prejudice to other rights of action open to the right holder and subject to the right of the defendant to seek review by a judicial authority, competent authorities shall have the authority to order the destruction or disposal of infringing goods in accordance with the principles set out in Article 46. In regard to counterfeit trademark goods, the authorities shall not allow the re-exportation of the infringing goods in an unaltered state or subject them to a different customs procedure, other than in exceptional circumstances.'

[181] ibid para 3.1.

[182] *China–Intellectual Property Rights*, Panel Report (n 177) para 7.250.

China argued that Article 59 must be read in conjunction with Article 1.1 of the TRIPS Agreement (chapter 5) and, therefore, that the obligation in Article 59 to grant 'authority' to order destruction does not mean that 'Members must make a grant of unfettered and unguided discretion and that domestic agencies must have the absolute power to order destruction of infringing goods in any circumstance whatsoever.'[183]

Cuba, as a third party participant in this case, advanced a similar argument that, in as much as Part II (Standards Concerning the Availability, Scope and Use of Intellectual Property Rights) of the TRIPS Agreement, and in particular Section 5 (Patents) were subject to the regulations of Part I (General Provisions and Basic Principles), the provisions of Article 7 (Objectives) and Article 8 (Principles) were particularly relevant for these purposes, together with the last sentence of Article 1.1 (Nature and Scope of Obligations). Cuba said this was because they allowed WTO Members some flexibility in complying with the obligations stemming from the TRIPS Agreement.[184]

The US counter-argument was that Article 1.1 of the TRIPS Agreement only offers flexibility in 'how a Member implements TRIPS obligations and does not exempt a Member from full compliance with TRIPS obligations'.[185] The US argued that Chinese Customs measures at issue provided for three disposal options besides destruction, but none of these disposal options was in accordance with the principles set out in Article 46, and that all preclude authority to order destruction.[186]

Article 61 is the sole Article under Section 5, entitled 'Criminal Procedures', and stipulates that:

> Members shall provide for criminal procedures and penalties to be applied at least in cases of wilful trademark counterfeiting or copyright piracy on a commercial scale. Remedies available shall include imprisonment and/or monetary fines sufficient to provide a deterrent, consistently with the level of penalties applied for crimes of a corresponding gravity. . . .

With regard to the issues relating to the examination of the second claim above regarding Article 61, China argued that the US bears a significantly higher burden of proof than normal, because their claim concerns criminal law matters. According to China, the Panel should 'treat sovereign jurisdiction over police powers as a powerful default norm, departure from which can be authorised only in light of explicit and unequivocal consent of State parties', based on the 'interpre-

---

[183]   ibid para 7.198. China said that 'Chinese law sets forth criteria that reflect an official preference for the use of disposition methods besides destruction but Customs has the discretion to determine whether the criteria are met and therefore which disposition method is appropriate', and argued that 'donation to social welfare bodies and sale to the right holder constitute disposal outside the channels of commerce in such a way as to avoid harm to the right holder'.

[184]   *China–Intellectual Property Rights*, Panel Report (n 177) para 518.

[185]   ibid para 7.199.

[186]   *China–Intellectual Property Rights*, Panel Report (n 177) para 7.254. Where any of these three options are available, the authorities are not authorised to order destruction of the infringing goods.

tative canon' of *in dubio mitius*[187] which, it submits, has a particular justification in the realm of criminal law.[188] The doctrine of *in dubio mitius* advocates that the disputed measures should be deemed not inconsistent with the agreement in question, if there are any ambiguities in the disputed provision. The US, quoting the Appellate Body Report on the *EC-Hormones*[189] case, responded that the principle of *in dubio mitius* is valid only when there is doubt in interpreting the application of Article 31 VCLT, whereas there is no doubt in this case.[190]

On the substantial issue of thresholds, the US asserted that China's criminal sanctions were insufficient, resulting in a haven for certain counterfeit and pirated goods.[191] According to the US, although China has additional administrative enforcement, only criminal procedures and penalties can fulfil the obligations in Article 61 of the TRIPS Agreement.[192]

China responded with the following arguments: none of the enforcement provisions contained in Article 41.5 TRIPS can be read to require Members to set out low-scale, high-resource thresholds for criminalisation; China's criminal enforcement is based on its legal structure and other laws relating to commercial crimes, and their thresholds of prosecution reflect the significance of various illegal acts for China's public and economic order; its system of administrative enforcement of intellectual property infringement operates separately from its criminal enforcement system;[193] the criminal thresholds for counterfeiting and piracy are, therefore, reasonable and appropriate.

---

[187] The Appellate Body in *EC-Hormones* (n 52) para 165 fn 154, recognised the principle as 'supplementary means of interpretation', and quoted R Jennings and A Watts (eds), *Oppenheim's International Law*, 9th edn (Oxford University Press, 1992) vol. 1 1278 which says: 'The principle of *in dubio mitius* applies in interpreting treaties, in deference to the sovereignty of states, is widely recognized in international law as a "supplementary means of interpretation", and has been expressed in the following terms; "If the meaning of a term is ambiguous, that meaning is to be preferred which is less onerous to the party assuming an obligation, or which interferes less with the territorial and personal supremacy of a party, or involves less general restrictions upon the parties".'

[188] *China–Intellectual Property Rights,* Panel Report, (n 177) para 7.497.

[189] *EC–Hormones,* Appellate Body Report (n 52).

[190] *China–Intellectual Property Rights,* Panel Report (n 177) para 7.498.

[191] The fixed term of imprisonment under Art 213 of Chinese Criminal Law for non-authorised use of a registered trade mark, if the circumstances are serious, is set at not more than three years or criminal detention; the crime shall also, or shall only, be fined; if the circumstances are egregious, the offender shall be sentenced to fixed-term imprisonment of not less than three years but not more than seven years and shall also be fined. Art 1 of China's Judicial Interpretation No 19 says: '. . . shall also, or shall only, be fined . . . and . . . shall be considered as there are other serious circumstances under Article 217 of the Criminal Law . . .'.

[192] On the characteristics of the Chinese penalties relating to criminal measures against illegal business operation, the Panel observes that, in accordance with the definition of 'illegal business operation volume' in Art 12(1) of Judicial Interpretation No 19 [2004] 447, these thresholds are calculated in terms of the price of goods. Naturally, the volume of goods required to meet the threshold is inversely proportional to the value of those goods. Therefore, the threshold is flexible enough to capture a small number of high-value goods or a large number of low-value goods. However, where the number of goods multiplied by the value of the goods is less than the threshold and is not captured by any alternative applicable threshold, no criminal procedures and penalties will apply (para 7.470).

[193] The thresholds are calculated over a prolonged period of time and flexible enough and appropriate to capture a small number of high-value goods or a large number of low-value goods. Public security authorities tend to focus more on infringement above the criminal thresholds.

As a third party participant to this case, Argentina argued that China's measures did not appear to be inconsistent with Article 61 of the TRIPS Agreement, as Article 1.1 provided China with the flexibility to implement enforcement provisions in a way compatible with its existing constitutional and regulatory framework.[194] Concerning the claim under Article 41.1 of the TRIPS Agreement, Argentina submitted that China's measures do not appear to be inconsistent with the Agreement. Article 41.1 should be viewed in light of the following: Article 1.1, which provides flexibility in implementation; Article 41.2 which requires Members to ensure that enforcement procedures are fair and equitable; and Article 41.5 which renders the obligation in Article 41.1 relative, not absolute.[195] Thailand argued that the absence of a definition of 'commercial scale' in the TRIPS Agreement was a built-in flexibility recognising the different legal systems of Members, and, that every Member could adopt the interpretation it deemed appropriate.[196]

China referred to the second sentence of Article 61 on remedies and noted that it contains an element of flexibility in its reference to 'the level of penalties applied for crimes of a corresponding gravity'.[197] It argues that if Members were not required to impose meaningful punishment for low-level crimes, they should not be required to enforce low-level intellectual property crimes either.

iii Panel's analysis of 'flexibilities'

The Panel in US – Section 110(5) Copyright Act disagreed with the US argument concerning its interpretation of the scope of flexibility of Article 1.1, saying that the US itself acknowledged that 'the essence of the first condition is that the exceptions be well-defined and of limited application and that they cannot cause unreasonable prejudice to the legitimate interests of the right holder'.[198] In other words, the wording, context, object and purpose of Article 13 TRIPS attaches specific limiting conditions to such an exception. It is therefore the TRIPS Agreement which regulates exceptions, and not the discretion of Members.

In *Canada–Patent Term*,[199] the Panel noted that the discretion of Members under Article 1.1 to determine the appropriate method of implementing their obligations under the TRIPS Agreement did not extend to choosing which obligation to comply with. Similarly in *China–Intellectual Property Rights,* the Panel emphasised that the third sentence of Article 1.1 does not permit differ-

---

[194] *China–Intellectual Property Rights,* Panel Report (n 177) para 7.484.

[195] ibid para 7.678.

[196] *China–Intellectual Property Rights,* Panel Report (n 177) para 7.493.

[197] ibid para 7.597. Based on the analysis of the Chinese measures in question, the Panel observed that, in accordance with the definition of 'illegal business operation volume' in Art 12(1) of Judicial Interpretation No 19 where the number of goods multiplied by the value of the goods is less than the threshold and is not captured by any alternative applicable threshold, no criminal procedures or penalties will apply. Ibid para 7.470.

[198] *US–Section 110(5) Copyright Act,* Panel Report (n 20) para 6.103.

[199] *Canada–Patent Term,* Panel Report (adopted 12 October 2000) WT/DS170/R, as upheld by the Appellate Body Report, WT/DS170/AB/R para 6.94.

ences in domestic legal systems and practices to justify any derogation from the basic obligation to give effect to the provisions on enforcement.[200]

For the Panel, the exact scope of flexibilities depends on the specific meaning given to its limiting conditions in relevant provisions (see above p 222 on the delimitation of the exceptions provided for the rights conferred)[201] and, therefore, the words of those conditions must be examined with particular care. Both the goals and the limitations stated in Articles 7 and 8.1 must obviously be considered, as well as those of other provisions of the TRIPS Agreement which indicate its object and purposes. In other words, in as much as conditions of exceptions are TRIPS-regulated, Members cannot decide their scope at its discretion.

The Panel, in *China–Intellectual Property Rights,* examining the nature of the obligation in the first sentence of Article 59 which says: 'competent authorities "shall have the authority" to order certain types of remedies with respect to infringing goods . . .'.[202] The Panel analysed not only the text, context, object and purpose of the provision, but looked also into the circumstances of conclusion as well as the records of the negotiation of the TRIPS Agreement when justified by the VCLT.[203] Following these analyses, it asserted that the phrase 'shall have the authority'[204] can be contrasted with terminology used in the minimum standards of protection in Part II of the TRIPS Agreement.[205] The obligation in

---

[200] *China–Intellectual Property Rights*, Panel Report (n 177) para 7.513.

[201] *Canada–Pharmaceutical Patents,* Panel Report (n 30) para 7.26.

[202] The Panel stated: 'the fact that Article 59 [TRIPS] addresses the authority to order remedies implies that the obligations continue until the time that a remedy has been ordered. The text of the Article does not indicate any other limitation on the temporal scope of the obligations. Therefore, the obligation that competent authorities "shall have the authority" to make certain orders applies from the time that competent authorities find that goods subject to suspension at the border are infringing, right up until the time that a remedy is ordered.'(*China–Intellectual Property Rights*, Panel Report (n 177) para 7.234.)

[203] The Panel explained in paras 7.238 and 7.241 that: 'given the potential importance of this interpretation to the operation of Part III of the TRIPS Agreement, the Panel notes that it is confirmed by the circumstances of conclusion of the Agreement'. For example, Composite Draft Text of 12 July 1990, MTN.GNG/NG11/W/76, quoting the Appellate Body in its report on *EC–Computer Equipment* (para 86) and *EC–Customs Classification of Frozen Boneless Chicken Cuts* (adopted 12 September 2005) WT/DS269/AB/R, WT/DS286/AB/R para 284. The latter report quotes I Sinclair, *The Vienna Convention on the Law of Treaties*, 2nd edn (Manchester University Press, 1984) 141, who says that recourse to the circumstances of conclusion of a treaty 'permits, in appropriate cases, the examination of the historical background against which the treaty was negotiated'. In para 7.260, the Panel had recourse to the records of the negotiation of the TRIPS Agreement to resolve the ambiguity of the third sentence of Art 46 (for example, Part IV of document MTN.GNG/NG11/W/76, Chairman's revised draft text of 13 November 1990, and document no 2814, MTN.TNC/W/35/Rev.1 dated 3 December 1990 entitled 'Draft Final Act Embodying the Results of the Uruguay Round of Multilateral Trade Negotiations – Revision' in fnn 202–5). This provision refers to 'such requests', although the previous sentences do not refer expressly to any requests. According to the Panel, the content of the third sentence clearly relates to materials and implements as addressed in the second sentence, but could equally relate to infringing goods as addressed in the first sentence.

[204] 'Shall have the authority' is used throughout the enforcement obligations in ss 2, 3 and 4 of Part III of the TRIPS Agreement, specifically, in Arts 43.1, 44.1, 45.1, 45.2, 46, 48.1, 50.1, 50.2, 50.3, 50.7, 53.1, 56 and 57.

[205] Such as 'Members shall provide' protection, or that certain material 'shall be' protected.

Article 46[206] that certain authorities 'shall have the authority' to make certain orders reflects inter alia that orders with respect to specific infringements are left to enforcement authorities' discretion, and obliges Members to ensure that enforcement procedures as specified in Part III are 'available' under their law, so as to 'permit' effective action against infringement, which addresses the potential for action.[207] According to the Panel, the existence of a disposition method *not* required by Article 59 does not, in itself, lead to WTO inconsistent action, to the extent that such authority mandates a disposition method in any given circumstance it may preclude authority that *is* required by Article 59.[208]

This said, the Panel finds the fourth principle in Article 46 (the action with respect to orders for the destruction or disposal of infringing goods) pertinent to Article 59.[209] This principle, according to the Panel, is guided by the common objective set out in Article 46, ie 'to create an effective deterrent to infringement'[210] and by the principle of proportionality. The Panel emphasises that the phrase 'other than in exceptional cases' must be interpreted in light of the object of that Article, namely, 'to create an effective deterrent to infringement'[211] and narrowly circumscribed, in order to satisfy the description of 'exceptional'. According to the Panel,[212] a low rate of cases involving a simple removal of the trademark does not fulfil the condition that these should be 'exceptional cases' within the meaning of the fourth sentence of Article 46: first, because 'exceptional cases' as incorporated in Article 59 should be assessed in terms of a proportion of all cases of infringing goods seized at the border; and secondly, such an approach to goods that have already been found to be counterfeit trademark goods would amount to a margin of tolerance of further infringement (ie, not creating an effective deterrent).[213] For these reasons, the Panel concluded that China's Customs measures are inconsistent with Article 59 of the TRIPS Agreement, as it incorporates the principle set out in the fourth sentence of Article 46.[214] A certain level of national discretion in the enforcement action in Part III is thus recognised, but the principle of enforcement is TRIPS-regulated and depends on the wording, context and the objective of the relevant TRIPS provisions.

---

[206]   TRIPS Art 46 states: 'In order to create an effective deterrent to infringement, the judicial authorities shall have the authority to order that goods that they have found to be infringing be, without compensation of any sort, disposed of outside the channels of commerce in such a manner as to avoid any harm caused to the right holder, or, unless this would be contrary to existing constitutional requirements, destroyed . . .'.

[207]   *China–Intellectual Property Rights,* Panel Report (n 177) para 7.348. According to the Panel, the protection granted in Part III is generally the responsibility of private rights-holders and therefore the fact that there appear to be circumstances in which Customs departs from the terms of the measures indicates that the measures are not as mandatory as they appear on their face.

[208]   ibid para 7.252.

[209]   *China–Intellectual Property Rights,* Panel Report (n 177) para 7.269.

[210]   Art 46 explicitly says 'simple removal of the trademark unlawfully affixed is not sufficient to permit release of counterfeit trademark goods into the channels of commerce other than in exceptional cases' (*China–Intellectual Property Rights* (n 180) para 7.283).

[211]   *China–Intellectual Property Rights,* Panel Report (n 177) para 7.391.

[212]   ibid para 7.392.

[213]   *China–Intellectual Property Rights,* Panel Report (n 177) para 7.393.

[214]   ibid.para 7.394.

On the application of Articles 31 and 32 of the VCLT to the threshold penalty question, the Panel made a general statement as follows:

'The Panel acknowledges the sensitive nature of criminal matters and attendant concerns regarding sovereignty. These concerns may be expected to find reflection in the text and scope of treaty obligations regarding such matters as negotiated by States and other Members. Section 5 of Part III of the TRIPS Agreement [consisting only of art 61], dedicated to criminal procedures and remedies, is considerably briefer and less detailed than the other Sections on enforcement in Part III.'

Thus the Panel said with regard to Article 61 that: 'brief as it is, the text of Section 5 also contains significant limitations and flexibilities'.[215] According to the Panel, however, 'the customary rules of treaty interpretation oblige the treaty interpreter to take these limitations and flexibilities into account in interpreting the relevant provision'.[216] The Panel judged that the VCLT rule of interpretation applies to Article 61.[217] It emphasised, in particular, that it should be analysed within the context of Article 41.1,[218] for which Article 41.5 plays an important role, in order to find TRIPS-regulated principles and specific obligations of Members.

In applying the customary rule of treaty interpretation, it interpreted Article 61 as containing legal obligation for the following reasons: it uses the word 'shall', indicating that it is mandatory.[219] This interpretation is confirmed by Article 41, the first provision of Part III of the TRIPS Agreement and forms part of the context of Article 61.[220] Against China's argument that Article 61 defers to national discretion to define the rights being infringed upon, the Panel asserted that the Agreement contains substantive obligations in Part II and Part III. It also drew attention to Article XVI:4 of the WTO Agreement,[221] where the first sentence of Article 1.1 sets out the basic obligation that Members 'shall give effect' to TRIPS provisions.[222] This suggests that, in some cases, the scope of

---

[215] *China–Intellectual Property Rights*, Panel Report (n 177) para 7.501.

[216] ibid para 7.501.

[217] *China–Intellectual Property Rights*, Panel Report (n 177) para 7.501.

[218] Art 41.1 requires that the enforcement procedures under TRIPS permit effective action but prohibit that to be trade barriers to legitimate trade. Art 41.5 states: 'It is understood that this Part does not create any obligation to put in place a judicial system for the enforcement of intellectual property rights distinct from that for the enforcement of law in general, nor does it affect the capacity of Members to enforce their law in general. Nothing in this Part creates any obligation with respect to the distribution of resources as between enforcement of intellectual property rights and the enforcement of law in general.'

[219] *China–Intellectual Property Rights*, Panel Report (n 177) para 7.503.

[220] TRIPS Art 41.1: 'Members shall ensure that enforcement procedures as specified in this Part are available under their law so as to permit effective action against any act of infringement of intellectual property rights covered by this Agreement, including expeditious remedies to prevent infringements and remedies which constitute a deterrent to further infringements. These procedures shall be applied in such a manner as to avoid the creation of barriers to legitimate trade and to provide for safeguards against their abuse'.

[221] Art XVI: 4 of the WTO Agreement: 'Each Member shall ensure the conformity of its laws, regulations and administrative procedures with its obligations as provided in the annexed Agreements'.

[222] *China–Intellectual Property Rights*, Panel Report (n 177) para 7.513.

TRIPS-regulated obligations on Members may be wider than it appears. Some uses of the term 'flexibilities' may be interpreting the scope of discretion that TRIPS provisions grant to states more broadly than they actually permit. In these cases, 'flexibilities' may not be considered TRIPS-compliant at WTO dispute settlements.

The Panel interpreted the words 'commercial scale' in accordance with the VCLT rules, taking into account the benchmarks in the marketplace relevant to the provisions concerned. When the term of the treaty is unclear, as in the case of the words 'commercial scale', the Panel, applying the VCLT rule, said that the ordinary meaning of a treaty term must be ascertained according to the particular circumstances of each case, unless any party thinks a 'special' meaning should be given to it.[223] Quoting *EC–Chicken Cuts*,[224] the Panel explains how the analysis of 'ordinary meaning' should take into account the 'flexibilities' of the term and says that, 'importantly, the ordinary meaning of a treaty term must be seen in the light of the intention of the parties as expressed in the words used by them against the light of the surrounding circumstances'.[225] The Panel observes that what is typical or usual in commerce is a flexible concept. None of the terms, 'deterrent', 'corresponding gravity' and 'commercial scale', are precise, but all depend on circumstances, which vary according to the differing forms of commerce and of counterfeiting and piracy to which these obligations apply.[226]

The Panel then examined whether any state practice following the adoption of Article 61 might have helped establish what the agreement among the parties was in adopting the provision. However, it found that the practice examined did not correspond to 'subsequent practice' in the meaning of Article 31.3(b) of the VCLT according to the WTO criteria, ie, a common, consistent, discernible pattern of acts or pronouncements.[227] It then looked into preparatory work during the Uruguay Round negotiations,[228] notably the Model Provisions prepared by the WIPO Committee of Experts on Measures Against Counterfeiting and Piracy. However, it only led to the conclusion that the records of the TRIPS negotiations do not disclose any discussion of the meaning of the phrase 'on a commercial scale'.[229]

---

[223]   ibid para 7.558.
[224]   *EC –Chicken Cuts* (n 203) para 175.
[225]   *China–Intellectual Property Rights,* Panel Report (n 177) para 7.537.
[226]   Ibid para 7.578. The Panel explored the dictionary definition of 'scale' and 'commercial', the patent laws of countries when the WIPO commentary on 'commercial scale' was elaborated on (this referred to the working of inventions, or failure to work inventions 'on a commercial scale'), to find that there is insufficient indication that the meaning ascribed to the term 'on a commercial scale' in such legislation and that this was not what was intended by the negotiators of the TRIPS Agreement when they used the term in the first and fourth sentences of Art 61.
[227]   *China–Intellectual Property Rights,* Panel Report (n 177) para 7.581.
[228]   ibid paras 7.567–7.588.
[229]   *China–Intellectual Property Rights,* Panel Report (n 177) para 7.589.

In examining whether or not China's thresholds capture all cases on a 'commercial scale', the Panel took into account physical evidence and the impact that piracy or counterfeiting has on the commercial marketplace.[230]

The Panel emphasises that the terms used in the first sentence of Article 61, in particular 'commercial', are technology-neutral and considered that a 'commercial scale' can apply to various forms of commerce depending on the evolution and competition in the market place at the time the provision is interpreted, and took the following approach:

> The Panel sees no reason why those forms of commerce should be limited to the forms of commerce that existed at the time of negotiation of the TRIPS Agreement. Accordingly, the application of the term 'commercial scale' can adjust to different situations, and refer to a different relative magnitude or extent, degree or proportion, depending on the facts. However, subsequent technological developments do not alter the considerations relevant to the interpretation of the terms used in Article 61.[231]

Following analysis of the meaning of 'commercial scale', the Panel decided that solely on face value, it could not distinguish between acts that, in China's marketplace, are on a commercial scale, and those that are not.[232] According to the Panel, the US did not provide data regarding products and markets or other factors that would demonstrate what constituted 'a commercial scale' in the specific case of China's marketplace. The Panel insisted on the need for substantive evidence to prove the US argument, which the US did not provide. The Panel did not, therefore, accept that Members have discretion in determining what 'commercial scale' means through simple analysis of the wording. The Panel instead limited such discretion (ie, flexibility) in emphasising that this concept depends on the characteristics of the market. The Panel also avoided Members' eventual defence of national measures by arguing that Article 61 considerations are out-of-date because they were negotiated in the last century.

During the Uruguay Round negotiations, a call for constructive ambiguities allowed diplomatic compromises and gave leeway for leaving out what could not be agreed upon (chapter 4). These constructive ambiguities in more than a few of the TRIPS provisions – as in many other multilateral treaties – leave a margin of discretion to WTO Member States, as exemplified by their arguments in the above cases.

The WTO dispute organs have applied the VCLT rule of interpretation to analyse the TRIPS provisions that contain flexibilities and have indicated where the limits lie in the national discretion given by the treaty. Subsequent chapters of this book will examine in depth how the concept of flexibilities evolved with the Doha Declaration, and how they come to be applied in the national implementation of the TRIPS Agreement.

---

[230] ibid para 7.496. The US alleged that China's thresholds are tied only to finished goods and therefore ignore other indicia of commercial scale operations, such as the impact that the piracy or counterfeiting has on the commercial marketplace and by extension, right holders (para 7.653).

[231] *China–Intellectual Property Rights,* Panel Report (n 177) para 7.657.

[232] ibid para 7.661.

Part III

Access to Medicines

8

The AIDS Epidemic and TRIPS

P RIOR TO THE adoption and entry into force of the TRIPS Agreement, a
tragic epidemic was emerging in the early 1980s. HIV/AIDS became a global
disease, severely affecting many developing countries. This chapter retraces how
AIDS medicines were made available but not accessible for low-income people in
these countries. Both developed and developing country governments were slow
to realise the severity of the situation in developing countries and the need to act
accordingly. Research-based pharmaceutical companies acted in their 'business
as usual' way. International solidarity among non-governmental organisations
(NGOs) and Indian generic drugs companies was formed around the issue of
access to inexpensive medicines. In this process, patents and the behaviour of
research-based multinational drug companies came to be viewed as the cause
of the denial of access to medicines. Policies to produce medicines locally were
also revived.

I AVAILABILITY OF AIDS DRUGS

A Scientific Discovery of Human Immunodeficiency Virus (HIV)

Acquired immunodeficiency syndrome (AIDS)[1] is caused by an RNA[2] retrovirus (a virus that carries its genetic material in RNA rather than DNA).[3] This
retrovirus destroys organs of the human immune system such as CD4+ T cells[4]
and macrophages. HIV is an RNA virus and has an affinity for the CD4 molecule, which is on the surface of certain lymphocytes called CD4+ T cells.
Macrophages also have CD4 molecules on their cell surfaces. HIV invades and

---

[1] AIDS leads to a series of opportunistic infections resulting from the damage to the human
immune system caused by the human immunodeficiency virus (HIV).

[2] Ribonucleic acid; see ch 3 n 5.

[3] A virus is a particle too small to be seen with a light microscope and is capable of independent
metabolism and reproduction within a living host cell. It consists of a core of nucleic acid (DNA
or RNA), surrounded by a protein coat. Within a host cell, the virus initiates the synthesisation of
viral proteins and undergoes replication. Mature viruses are released while the host cell is damaged.
Viruses consist of either DNA or RNA, but like hepatitis B, there are exceptional cases where viruses
consist of both. Viruses are categorised according to various factors such as genome, structure,
infected host (such as human or other animal), pathogenicity, or whether the virus has a membrane.

[4] A type of lymphocyte, vital organs for the immune system.

fuses with CD4+ T cells and, using reverse transcriptase enzyme, transcribes its RNA into DNA. The viral DNA is then integrated into the genetic make-up of the host DNA and becomes a provirus. Via transcription, the provirus then forms a core of HIV RNA and other composite elements such as gag proteins, reverse transcriptase, integrase, protease, and other viral proteins. These are assembled into retroviral cores beneath the cell plasma membrane before they bud through the host CD4+ T cells. When they are released from CD4+ T cells, some of the core viral proteins are not mature and need to be cleaved by viral protease in order for a mature HIV particle to be formed and begin to infect another CD4+ T cell.

The discovery of the virus causing AIDS was achieved through scientific competition among groups of researchers at the National Cancer Institute (NCI, part of the National Institute of Health (NIH)) group led by RC Gallo, Harvard University, and the Pasteur Institute (France) group led by Luc Montagnier. In May 1983, these researchers published their respective articles, relating to the relationship between AIDS symptoms and the virus that they had isolated, in *Science*.[5] According to Gallo, HTLV-III (human T-lymphotrophic virus Type III) was the pathogen of AIDS.[6] For Montagnier, an isolated LAV (lymphade-nopathy-associated virus) in a patient with generalised lymphadenopathy, was the AIDS pathogen.[7] Following their publications, opinion was divided in the US and France as to whether these two retroviruses were the same.

An inquiry by the US Congress brought the argument to an end, and in May 1986 the virus was given the single name of HIV by an international nomenclature committee. Having experienced several disputes over scientific information such as this, the Pasteur Institute, which had been relatively unconcerned with intellectual property rights, also became sensitive to obtaining certain rights over its scientific discoveries. Since these could now be used in the diagnostics, prevention of infection and treatment of diseases or in further research on pharmacological agents, they began patenting their research results, as was the usual practice in the United States. The licence revenue of the Pasteur Institute allowed it to invest in further research. In 2004, roughly 40 per cent[8] of basic research investment in the Institute's biotechnology department came from licence fees from technologies that its researchers had developed.[9] Virological research on HIV/AIDS has led the

[5] The Gallo research group published that HTLV-1 was the pathogen of ATL (RC Gallo et al, 'Isolation of human T-cell leukaemia virus in acquired immunodeficiency syndrome (AIDS)' (1983) 220 *Science* 865–7), while Montagnier et al of the Pasteur Institute, published that HTLV, which is a type-C RNA tumour virus, was the pathogen of AIDS (L Montagnier et al, 'Isolation of a T-lymphotropic retrovirus from a patient at risk for acquired immunodeficiency syndrome (AIDS)' (1983) 220 *Science* 868–71).

[6] RC Gallo et al, 'Frequent detection and isolation of cytopathic retroviruses (HTLV-III) from patients with AIDS and at risk for AIDS' (1984) 224 *Science* 500–3.

[7] L Montagnier et al, 'T-lymphocyte T4 molecule behaves as the receptor for human retrovirus LAV' (1984) 312 *Nature* 67–768; F Clavel, 'Deficient LAV1 Neutralising Capacity of Sera from Patients with AIDS or Related Syndromes' (1985) 325 *The Lancet* 879–80.

[8] Of which approximately 30% comes from government subvention.

[9] Interview with Danielle Berneman, Director of the Licensing Division, Pasteur Institute, 5 October 2005.

Pasteur Institute, the New York Blood Center, and the American Biotechnology Laboratory to obtain basic patents for HIV/AIDS diagnostics (eg equipment), not only in the US, Europe and Japan, but also in South Africa.

B Development of Antiretroviral Drugs

Discovering HIV to be the cause of AIDS and ascertaining the HIV life cycle were key to developing AIDS drugs. Following the isolation of HIV and the identification of its life cycle, the development of AIDS drugs was relatively smooth. Antiretroviral (ARV) drugs provide a mechanism for blocking one stage or another in the life cycle of HIV. ARVs help maintain the patient's immune status by preventing reproduction and replication of HIV.

AZT (abbreviated from its chemical name, azidothymidine – generic name, zidovudine),[10] the first ARV, was developed by Burroughs Wellcome, the US subsidiary of the Wellcome Foundation (UK). In the emergency phase of the AIDS epidemic in the early 1980s,[11] the Clinical Data Examination Committee of the US Food and Drug Administration (FDA) suspended the placebo test, and granted authorisation to market AZT, based only on the test data of several hundred patients.[12] One stage in the life cycle of HIV is the synthesis of DNA from viral RNA by reverse transcriptase. AZT inhibits the action of reverse transcriptase by supplying a base analogue (of nitrogen-infused thymidine), mimicking a DNA base, which stops elongation of the HIV DNA chain.

The AZT compound had been known for 20 years before AZT was marketed as an AIDS drug. In 1964, researchers at the Detroit Cancer Institute had synthesised the compound as an anti-cancer drug but without any preclinical data or statement relating to its therapeutic use.[13] In 1980, an article by E de Clercq and others of the University of Leuven referred to AZT's first medical indication as antiviral, antimetabolic and antineoplastic against normal viruses (ie not

---

[10] A drug has the following kinds of names, according to http://www.fda.gov/fdac/features/2005/405_confusion.html: (1) a chemical drug name is given by International Nonproprietary Name (INN) Programme Quality Assurance and Safety: Medicines World Health Organization, based on the chemical structure; (2) an INN (International Non-proprietary Name) generic name (non-proprietary) for pharmaceutical substances, based on its structure. For a combination product, each of the related mono-products are viewed as separate INNs; and, (3) a commercial name (brand name) given by the company which developed or sells the drug.

[11] AIDS was first reported in the United States in 1981. In Europe, symptoms, which were regarded as African regional diseases, began to be reported in the 1950s among sailors, and studies have been recorded in France since the 1970s. B Seytre, *L'Histoire de la recherche sur le SIDA* (*Que sais-je?* no 3024) (Paris, Presses Universitaires de France, 1995).

[12] A placebo in the clinical study context is to give physiologically inert treatment to the patient either for the improvement of the patient's condition, or to compare the patient's condition with placebo with that of similar patients who receive no treatment at all. It is morally impossible to continue placebo treatment, if the patient's life is at stake. In this case, the clinical study (Phase III, in particular) is suspended.

[13] JP Horowitz et al, 'Nucleosides. V. The Monomesylates of 1-(2-Deoxy-O-D-lyxofuranosyl) thymine' (1964) 29 *The Journal of Organic Chemistry* 2076–78.

retroviruses), such as herpes simplex virus and vaccinia virus.[14] In 1985, the *in vitro* activity of this compound against the HIV virus was reported by Mitsuya and other researchers at the National Cancer Institute (NCI including RC Gallo), Duke University and Burroughs Wellcome.[15]

Following AZT, several less toxic, more easily tolerated ARVs using 'nucleoside reverse transcriptase inhibitors' (NRTIs) were developed. Stavudine (2', 3'-Didehydro-3'-deoxythymidine, or d4T) belongs to the same therapeutic class in terms of chemical structure and blocking mechanisms. It was developed by the Yale research team and licensed to Bristol Myers Squibb (BMS) which, after nearly 10 years of clinical studies, obtained US FDA marketing authorisation in 1994. This NRTI antiretroviral was sold as Zerit.

Both AZT and d4T lack -OH at a saccharide 3'-hydroxyl group, and these artificial nucleic acid bases compete with deoxythymidine (which is a natural nucleic acid base) in order to be incorporated into growing viral DNA chains. Hence, if AZT or d4T is incorporated into a DNA chain instead of deoxythymidine, the growth of that 'chain' through a 3'-hydroxyl group is halted and further elongation of viral DNA is inhibited.

Stavudine (d4T) improved the existing ARVs because it has a lower short-term toxicity than AZT. The discovery of AZT was a breakthrough, while d4T is considered a typical incremental improvement over AZT, seven years after AZT's marketing in March 1987. Names and years of FDA approvals of the other NRTIs are as follow:[16] didanosine (brand name Videx, approved in 1991), zalcitabine (brand name Hivid, approved in 1992 but currently discontinued by the manufacturer), lamivudine (brand name Epivir, approved in 1995), abacavir (brand name Ziagen, approved in 1998), emtricitabine (brand name Emtriva, approved in 2003), and nucleotide reverse transcriptase inhibitor (NtRTI) tenofovir (brand name Viread, approved in 2001).

Another type of ARV, referred to as a 'non-nucleoside reverse transcriptase inhibitor' (NNRTI) was also developed following NRTIs. The NNRTI type of ARV binds directly to reverse transcriptase and blocks its functioning by changing its structure. These include nevirapine (brand name Viramune), delavirdine (brand name Rescriptor) and efavirenz (brand name Sustiva or Stocrin).

Since 1995, other kinds of ARVs called 'protease inhibitors' (PIs) have been marketed. PIs prevent long precursor proteins from being cleaved by viral pro-

---

[14] E de Clercq et al, 'Antiviral, antimetabolic and antineoplastic activities of 2- or 3-amino or -azido-substituted deoxyribonucleosides' (1980) 29 *Biochemical Pharmacology* 1849–51.

[15] H Mitsuya et al, '3-azido-3-deoxythymidine (BW A509U): An Antiviral Agent that Inhibits the Infectivity and Cytopathic Effect of Human T-Lymphotropic Virus Type III/Lymphadenopathy-Associated Virus in vitro' (1985) 82 *Proceedings of National Academy of Sciences* 7096–100.

[16] The US FDA list of originator drugs used in the treatment of HIV infection is found at www.fda.gov/ForConsumers/byAudience/ForPatientAdvocates/HIVandAIDSActivities/ucm118915.htm; for approved generic formulations of antiretroviral drugs used in the treatment of HIV infection, see www.fda.gov/ForConsumers/ByAudience/ForPatientAdvocates/HIVandAIDSActivities/ucm118944.htm; for FDA approved and tentatively approved Antiretrovirals in association with the US President's Emergency Plan Expedited Review Process, see www.fda.gov/InternationalPrograms/FDABeyondOurBordersForeignOffices/AsiaandAfrica/ucm119231.htm.

tease to produce the mature virus, the final stage of the HIV life cycle. Thus, these inhibitors lead to an increase in the ratio of immature viruses which are not infectious. The cell population infected by HIV and the amount of HIV in the body declines, so that the number of CD4+T cells increases and there is a gradual recovery of immune function. In the US, currently nine PIs are available. A newer NNRTI ARV, etravirine (brand name Intelence) was approved for marketing by the US FDA on 18 January 2008. Approval by regulators in other developed countries followed. Etravirine is considered to be appropriate only for treatment-experienced adults who have evidence of viral replication and HIV strains resistant to other ARVs.

Other new classes of ARVs include entry inhibitors such as enfuvirtide (brand name Fuzeon) and maraviroc (brand name Selzentry) and integrase inhibitors such as raltegravir (brand name Isentress).

C 'Use' Patents

Burroughs Wellcome applied for a patent for a new use for the AZT compound, based on the compound's activity against HIV retroviruses, in March 1985,[17] before the publication of the last article, and in September 1985.[18]This was because the AZT compound had already been known as having activity against 'normal' DNA viruses, and been developed as a cancer drug.

The US Patent and Trademark Office (USPTO) granted the first AZT patent on 9 February 1988.[19] Its claim 1 is: 'A method of treating a human having acquired immunodeficiency syndrome comprising the oral administration of an effective acquired immunodeficiency syndrome treatment amount of 3-azido-3-deoxythymidine to said human.' According to section 101 of the US Patent Act, whoever invents or discovers any new and useful (a) process, (b) machine, (c) manufacture, or (d) composition of matter, or (e) any new and useful improvement thereof, may obtain a patent therefore.[20] In other words, a new use of a known compound is patentable. A claim type, 'a method of preventing or treating disease X by administering compound S to a human in need thereof in an amount effective for preventing or treating the disease X' is therefore possible in the US.

Specific features of a substance or new uses for a substance can be inventive and considered inventions (whether the invention is a product or process). This can take any descriptive form, including a specific use, formulation, or method of use. In the US, therapeutic methods used to be regarded as patentable without restriction. In 1996, the US Congress added restrictions on remedial

[17] EP17, 325, ZA8, 305, 031, JP61, 071, 360, USP1984-646, 658, AU8, 546, 668, for example.
[18] EP136, 798, AU8, 432, 276, ZA8, 406, 354, DK840, 450, JP60, 100, 523, CA1, 245, 982, USP1983-526, 573, for example.
[19] USP 4,724, 232.
[20] 35 USC § 101. Sildenafil citrate, which was not effective against 'unstable angina, hypertension, congestive heart failure, atherosclerosis', etc, was marketed later as Viagra, and is another example of a patent grant for new use.

action against infringements by medical practitioners' 'performance of a medical or surgical procedure on a body'.[21] In the US today, therefore, medical or surgical, therapeutic and diagnostic methods performed on a human body can be patented, even though asking for injunctions or claiming damages against such acts is not possible.

Under the European Patent Convention (EPC), by contrast, claiming a method of treatment on a human or animal body is not allowed (see chapter 3), and this exclusion from patentability is permitted under Article 27.3(a) of the TRIPS Agreement, which states that: 'Members may also exclude from patentability: (a) diagnostic, therapeutic and surgical methods for the treatment of humans or animals'.

Article 52(4) EPC 1973 stated that:

> European patents shall not be granted in respect of "methods for treatment of the human or animal body by surgery or therapy and diagnostic methods practised on the human or animal body". Methods for treatment of the human or animal body by surgery or therapy and diagnostic methods practised on the human or animal body shall not be regarded as inventions which are susceptible of industrial application within the meaning of paragraph 1. This provision shall not apply to products, in particular substances or compositions, for use in any of these methods.

It therefore became possible to claim 'a (known) substance S for use as a medicament', if the claim is written, 'a pharmaceutical composition comprising compound S and pharmaceutically acceptable carrier'. In other words, a European patent may not be granted for the use of a substance or composition for the treatment of the human or animal body by therapy, but may be granted when directed to the use of a substance or composition for the manufacture of a medicament for a specified new and inventive therapeutic application. According to the Decision of the Enlarged Board of Appeal G5/83 in 1984, a first medical indication could obtain purpose-limited protection for a known substance.[22] Pursuant to the EPC amendments which entered into force on 29 November 2000, Article 52(4) EPC 1973 was deleted but the same provision was placed under Article 53(c).[23] In the amended text of Article 54(5) EPC 2000, it was made clear that claiming diagnostic or therapeutic use of products is allowable under the EPC.[24]

---

[21] 35 USC § 287(c)(1):'With respect to a medical practitioner's performance of a medical activity that constitutes an infringement under s 271(a) or (b) of this title, the provisions of ss 281, 283, 284 and 285 of this title shall not apply against the medical practitioner or against a related health care entity with respect to such medical activity.

'Medical activities' are defined in 35 USC § 287(c)(2)(A) as: 'the performance of a medical or surgical procedure on a body, but shall not include (i) the use of a patented machine, manufacture, or composition of matter in violation of such patent, (ii) the practice of a patented use of a composition of matter in violation of such patent, or (iii) the practice of a process in violation of a biotechnology patent'.

[22] *Eisai*, Decision of 5 December 1984, [1985] OJ EPO 64.

[23] The EPC was adopted on 5 October 1973, revised by the Act revising Art 63 EPC of 17 December 1991 and the Act revising the EPC of 29 November 2000.

[24] Art 54 EPC concerns 'novelty' and was amended as follows: '(1) An invention shall be considered to be new if it does not form part of the state of the art;' and, '(5) Paragraphs 2 and 3 shall

For second pharmaceutical use claims, the so-called 'Swiss type', ie 'the use of compound S in the manufacture of a medicament for the treatment or prophylaxis of disease X', can also be accepted. However, the mere use, ie the German '*Verwendung*' type of 'the use of compound S for treating the disease X' is not allowable because it violates Article 52(4), EPC 1973, (G5/83). The 'Swiss-type' claims are acceptable only in the case of new uses of a medicament. They have not been allowed for other types of medical treatment, such as a new use of a known laser surgery system.[25] Furthermore, a real pathological condition must be defined in the second medical use (T241/95[26]). In T1020/03,[27] however, the decision of the Technical Board of Appeal of 29 October 2004, changed the previous decisions of the European Patent Office (EPO), in expanding the allowable type of the claims directed to the new dosage, or route, or interval of administration for the same active ingredient and for the same medical indication, while complying with the above provisions.

Thus, for AZT, for example, the European Patent (EP) 196,185, Claim 1 is formulated as follows: 'A pharmaceutical formulation comprising as active ingredient, 3'-azido-3'-deoxythimidine and at least one pharmaceutically acceptable carrier therefor'. In patent EP 291,633, a separate application for EP 196,185, but claiming the same Convention priority, claim 12 is formulated as the 'use of 3'-azido-3'-deoxythimidine in the manufacture of a medicament for the treatment or prophylaxis of a human retrovirus infection'.

In Japan, 'use' as a therapeutic method is not patentable because it is not considered as meeting the 'industrial applicability' requirement. However, 'a pharmaceutical composition comprising compound A for treating the disease X' is patentable and so the 'second medical use' is substantially patentable.[28] Thus, the formula, 'a pharmaceutical agent for preventing and/or treating disease X

also not exclude the patentability of any substance or composition referred to in paragraph 4 for any specific use in a method referred to in Article 53(c), provided that such use is not comprised in the state of the art.'

[25] The Board stated in T 227/91 *Codman* [1994] OJ EPO 491 that 'a surgical use of an instrument is not analogous to a therapeutic use . . ., since the instrument is not consumed in the application and could be repeatedly used for the same or even for other purposes as well . . . Medicaments, on the other hand, are expended in the process of use and have only a once for all utility'.

[26] The Board in T 241/95 [2001] OJ EPO 103 concerning the Swiss-type second medical use claim of a substance X in a 'condition which is capable of being improved or prevented by selective occupation of the serotonin receptor', held that this functional definition was unclear because no test was disclosed and it was therefore impossible to determine whether the therapeutic effects were a result of the newly discovered property of X of occupying the serotonin receptor or any other known or unknown property of that substance.

[27] 'IGF-1/Genentech' – 3.3.04 29.10.04 ([2007] OJ 4, 204).

[28] Art 29(1) of the Japanese Patent Law states that industrial application is a requirement for obtaining a patent but does not explicitly exclude from patentability diagnostic, therapeutic or surgical methods on the human body. The Examination Guidelines have treated diagnostic, therapeutic or surgical methods as not susceptible to industrial use. However, if the invention is a product, even if it is used for treatment, the actual production of this product is considered an industrial application, and therefore it is patentable. Recently, arguments supporting the patentability of diagnostic and therapeutic methods have increased as rapid developments in fields such as regenerative medicine and gene therapy have taken place.

comprising compound A (of which a first indication is already known) as the active ingredient' is allowable. The Japanese patent 1,721,193, for AZT, Claim 1 is formulated as 'a pharmaceutical composition for treating or preventing the human retrovirus infections comprising 3'-azido-3'-deoxythimidine as the active ingredient and a pharmaceutically acceptable carrier'.

D Administration of AIDS Drugs

At present, no single antiretroviral (ARV) is sufficient to treat HIV infection and therefore a combination of ARVs is necessary. The appropriate combination is to be determined by specialist doctors based on the various factors of the diagnoses, such as CD4 counts, HIV viral load, side-effects, the state of opportunistic infections and drug resistance.[29] In 1996, successful viral suppression with a combination of triple ARVs including a protease inhibitor (PI) was described by David Ho *et al* at the International AIDS Conference in Vancouver and the concept of highly active antiretroviral therapy (HAART) was introduced. This allowed for combining suitable ARVs, in order to suppress the viral load and avoid development of a resistant virus. Although the original HAART clinical trial was done using a combination of two nucleoside reverse transcriptase inhibitors (NRTIs) and one PI, a combination of ARVs such as two NRTIs or two NRTIs plus one PI, for example, became standard treatment.[30] After numerous clinical trials, in general, currently HAART is comprised of combinations of two NRTIs plus one ritonavir-boosted PI (as described below; some are non-boosted) or two NRTIs plus one non-nucleoside reverse transcriptase inhibitor (NNRTI). The most recent guidelines of the Department of Health and Human Services (DHHS) also include two NRTIs plus an integrase inhibitor. Different sets of multiple ARVs came to be called the 'AIDS cocktail'. Several years later, it became the standard of care to combine ARVs according to resistance of the particular virus.[31]

Formulations began to be manufactured which combined two or three ARVs, simplifying patient intake. For example, GlaxoSmithKline (GSK) marketed Combivir, which is a combination of lamivudine (3TC, brand name Epivir) and zidovudine (AZT, brand name Retrovir), as well as Trizivir, a combination of AZT, 3TC and abacavir (brand name Ziagen). Abbott sells its combination of two PIs (lopinavir and ritonavir), under the brand name Kaletra. Ritonavir (brand name Norvir) is hard to tolerate because of its side-effects when used in doses high enough to work as a single PI. Ritonavir serves better as a booster for

---

[29] When drugs for neutralising the pathogen are insufficiently effective, for various reasons (dosage failure, for example), an organism becomes resistant to the drug.

[30] For certain types of HIV infection, such as mother-to-child infection, a single ARV was used. This is no longer the case in developed countries. A mother needs to be treated in the same way as non-pregnant women with a combination regimen.

[31] Department of Health and Human Services (DHHS) http://aidsinfo.nih.gov/contentfiles/AdultandAdolescentGL.pdf.

other PIs, making them increase their concentrations and last longer in the blood because it inhibits an enzyme in the liver that metabolises other PIs.[32]

Kaletra was initially used as a second-line ARV in patients with treatment failure. In 2005, a tablet formulation was marketed which does not require refrigeration, an improvement over the capsule. In 2006, Gilead received authorisation from the US FDA to manufacture and sell Truvada, which is a combination of tenofovir (brand name Viread) and emtricitabine (brand name Emtriva). In July 2007, the US FDA and in December the European Medicinal Agency (EMEA) authorised the selling of Atripla, a once-daily pill consisting of tenofovir, emtricitabine and efavirenz (brand name Sustiva or Stocrin). It was developed as a result of cooperation between Gilead and Bristol Myers Squibb (BMS) and offered another option in initial regimens which are relatively easy to administer. In the US, six combination formulas of ARVs are available. Those formulas were developed to significantly decrease pill burden and to increase patients' adherence to HAART regimens. In current pharmaceutical developments, there are several possibilities for HAART regimens. These are as follows: (1) treatments that combines two NRTIs and one NNRTI to avoid PI side-effects, such as abnormal fat distribution and metabolic abnormalities; (2) the use of PIs such as ritonavir-boosted PIs or nevirapine manufactured by Boehringer Ingelheim (brand name Viramune) to avoid side- effects on the central nervous system caused by efavirenz; or, (3) the use of NRTI-sparing regimens to avoid long-term side-effects due to NRTIs.

E New Modes of Blocking HIV

HIV mutates frequently and its RNA is integrated into host white blood cells, called T-cells, and some T-cells infected with HIV become latent. For this reason, a permanent cure is difficult to achieve and constant research to develop new drugs with new modes of blocking HIV is necessary.

New AIDS drugs are developed with the aim of blocking the process of fusion to or entry into the cell. One entry inhibitor, manufactured by Roche, is enfuvirtide (brand name Fuzeon), an injectable fusion inhibitor, which binds the subunit of viral glycoprotein (gp) 41 and prevents the virus attaching to the cell.

Chemokine receptor type 5 (CCR5), a protein on the surface of immune cells like T cells and macrophages, acts as a chemokine attractant to guide the migration of cells.[33] Around the year 2000, US researchers discovered that CCR5s functions

---

[32] *Gary Schor v Abbott Laboratories* (US Court of Appeals for the 7th Circuit, 26 July 2006).

[33] Chemokines belong to a family of small cytokines which are proteins, peptides or glycoproteins secreted by cells. Cytokines include a diverse family of polypeptide regulators that are produced widely throughout the body by cells of different embryological origin. They function as signalling molecules and are used extensively in cellular communication like hormones and neurotransmitters. Chemokine is a general term for cytokine, which functions to control migration and activation of specific white blood cells from blood vessels to into inflamed tissues. Cytokines control the replication of neighbouring cells by using the proteins secreted by cells. Cytokines that control lymphocytes are called

as a viral co-receptor, guiding HIV to its target cells.[34] A compound that blocks the functioning of CCR5, therefore, could be an effective ARV drug. It would prevent the virus from entering uninfected cells by blocking the predominant route of entry, instead of fighting HIV inside white blood cells. There were several competing entry inhibitors that block the interaction between CCR5 and HIV in clinical trials, including PRO140 (Progenics), vicriviroc (Schering Plough), aplaviroc (GW-873140) (GSK) and maraviroc (Pfizer). Some were terminated, however, due to safety concerns over liver toxicity and increased risk of cancers. Another difficulty was that HIV could use another co-receptor CXCR4 to enter the cells. On 6 August 2007, seven years after the identification of CCR5's function as a major HIV co-receptor, the US FDA granted accelerated approval to maraviroc (brand name Selzentry), making it the first approved agent in this drug class. Earlier, on 1 July 2003, US patent 6,586,430 was granted for the invention of new chemical compounds with particular use as CCR5 modulators, preferably antagonistic, of the activities of chemokine CCR5 receptors.

AIDS drugs which act on viral integrase (integrase inhibitors or strand transfer inhibitors) are also being developed. Integrase inhibitors block the process of DNA strand transfer from the viral genome to the host genome. Raltegravir, manufactured by Merck (brand name Isentress) which was approved by the US FDA on 12 October 2007, is one such medicine.

F Further Challenges

As ARV therapies advanced between 1995 and 1998, AIDS-related mortality decreased dramatically and conditions improved for HIV patients in developed countries.[35] However, it is very easy for HIV to mutate, so strains of the virus that are resistant to therapeutic agents can easily emerge. In 1996, it was estimated that HIV replicates approximately 10 billion virions (viral particles) per day. HIV reverse transcriptase is not perfect and may, on average, make one spontaneous error (mutation) each time a viral genome is replicated. HIV does not have a mutation repair capability during replication, so many HIV mutations (heterogeneous or variant strains) coexist. If a patient continues to have a high level of HIV, mutant viruses accumulate within the body, and if treatment is given after mutant viruses emerge, drug resistant strains constitute a majority of the HIV viral population.

lymphokines and cytokines that control actions between white blood cells are called interleukins. Since the migration and activation of white blood cells serves a critical function in the protective response of the body's immune system, it is anticipated that chemokines will help treat problems such as allergies and autoimmune inflammations. To date, more than 50 chemokines have been identified.

[34] When HIV infects vital cells in the human immune system such as helper T cells, macrophages, and dendritic cells, the HIV gp120 glycoprotein binds with CD4 on the surface of those cells. It also binds with CCR5, which is a complementary receptor, and through the activity of gp41, the membrane of the virus fuses with the cell membrane and 'infection' occurs. It has been verified that when CCR5 is absent, cells show a strong resistance to HIV infection.

[35] In the US, the AIDS-related mortality rate dropped by one-third, from 17 to 5 out of every 100,000 people.

Drug-resistance refers to a condition in which a normally effective dose of a drug no longer inhibits the growth of a virus or bacterium. When a virus becomes resistant to drugs, the effective level of drugs necessary to inhibit growth changes, and drug-resistant strains emerge. If the amount of ARV drugs in the blood is insufficient, resistant viruses (viruses against which the medication is ineffective) emerge and replicate to a greater degree than susceptible viruses (viruses against which medications are effective).[36] One of the most significant difficulties faced in using antiretroviral treatment (ART) to treat HIV is the ease with which drug-resistant strains of HIV can emerge.[37] Thus, for AIDS treatments, it is necessary that: (1) the treatment continues with the correct dosage and through the correct method; (2) at least two of the combined drugs are effective and the virus does not become resistant to them; and, (3) the combination of ARVs maintains the HIV viral load at a level below the limit of detection. As the toxicity and side-effects of AIDS drugs are significant and the rate of mutation of the virus is high, no definitive link has been established between the quality of specific ARVs and drug resistance.[38] Drug resistance cannot be taken lightly, as drug-resistant strains of HIV are transmitted globally. Thus, the difficulties in producing second-line ARVs to ameliorate treatment failure with the initial regimens, lead to global consequences, including economic ones. Clinical studies are always in progress and the International AIDS Society–USA (IAS–USA) Drug Resistance Mutations Group regularly reviews new data on HIV drug resistance and updates and publishes a list of mutations associated with antiretroviral drug resistance.[39] A recent study undertaken by Hirsch et al includes drug resistance examinations of those new drugs using a new mechanism, such as maraviroc. The results of this study are included in the 2008 Recommendations of an International AIDS Society–USA Panel.[40]

---

[36] MS Hirsch et al, 'Antiretroviral Drug resistance testing in Adults with HIV Infection: Implications for Clinical Management' (1998) 279(24) *Journal of the American Medical Association (JAMA)*, 41. The 2008 version is in Hirsh et al, 'Antiretroviral Drug Resistance Testing in Adult HIV-1 Infection: 2008 Recommendations of an International AIDS Society–USA Panel', www.jk-aids-stiftung.de/news/pdf/Hirsch-CID.pdf. Also in SM Hammer et al, 'Antiretroviral Treatment of Adult HIV Infection. 2008 Recommendations of the International AIDS Society–USA Panel' (2008) 300(5) *JAMA* 555–70. Also see the Department of Health and Human Services (DHHS) guidelines at http://aidsinfo.nih.gov/contentfiles/AdultandAdolescentGL.pdf.

[37] RC Gallo and L Montagnier, 'Un vaccin préventif efficace demandera encore bien des années de recherches: Nos propositions pour le sida' *Le Figaro*, 2 June 2003, 14 ; 'Drug-resistant AIDS: the next tsunami' *Turkish Daily News*, April 2006; R Sutthenta et al, 'HIV-1 drug resistance in Thailand: Before and after National Access to Antiretroviral Program' (2005) 34 *Journal of Clinical Virology* 272–6; S Sungkanuparph et al, 'Options for a Second-Line Antiretroviral Regimen for HIV Type 1 Infected Patients Whose Initial Regimen of a Fixed-Dose Combination of Stavudine, Lamivudine, and Nevirapine Fails' (2007) 44 *Clinical Infectious Diseases* 447–52; S Sirivichayakul et al, 'HIV drug resistance transmission threshold survey in Bangkok' (2008) 2 *Antiviral Therapy* 109–13.

[38] R McEnery, 'If effective, pre-exposure prophylaxis for HIV will offer many opportunities, but also numerous challenges' (2008) 12(6) *IAVI Report*, www.iavireport.org/archives/2008/Pages/IAVIReport12(6)PrEP-Work.aspx.

[39] VA Johnson et al, 'Update of the Drug Resistance Mutations in HIV-1' (2008) 138 *International AIDS Society–USA Topics in HIV Medicine*, www.iasusa.org/pub/topics/2008/issue5/138.pdf.

[40] Hammer et al, 'Antiretroviral Treatment of Adult HIV Infection' (n 37) 276, Table 2.

Currently, in the US, there are 23 ARVs available (seven NRTIs, four NNRTIs, nine PIs, two entry inhibitors, and one integrase inhibitor). Of these, two new PIs, tipranavir, manufacture by Boehringer Ingelheim (brand name Aptivas) and darunavir, manufactured by Tibotec (brand name Prezista), were developed to treat viruses resistant to available PIs and one NNRTI, etravirine manufactured by Tibotec (brand name Intelence), was developed for viruses resistant to available NNRTIs. As mentioned previously, raltegravir, enfuvirtide and maraviroc were developed to work during various steps of the viral life cycle so that they could still be effective if the previous treatment failed. For example, as long as the virus uses the CCR5 receptor alone, maraviroc can be administered. Recently, darunavir and raltegravir have been approved even for treatment-naïve patients by the FDA. Maraviroc was also supported as an initial treatment ARV, given accelerated approval, and subsequently approved on 20 November 2009. These new ARVs could be very difficult to obtain in resource-limited countries.

The 2010 revised WHO Guidelines[41] address primarily the problems of developing (ie, resource-limited) countries. They recommend that national programmes should develop policies for third-line therapy that take into account the conditions for funding, sustainability and the provision of equitable access to HAART (conditional recommendation, low quality of evidence)[42]. The WHO Guidelines differ from the Guidelines of the Department of Health and Human Services (DHHS)[43] and of the International AIDS Society-USA (IAS-USA) in several respects. One of these differences is that the WHO Guidelines recommend darunavir as a third-line HAART medicine when first- or second-line ARV treatment has failed. The WHO Guidelines include raltegravir (integrase inhibitor) and etravirine (a new type of NNRTI)[44] among a third-line therapy. The DHHS Guidelines consider darunavir and raltegravir as first-line therapy ARVs (see chapter 11).

Recently, there seems to have been a general decrease in the marketing rate of new AIDS drugs, which has prompted institutions such as the National Institutes of Health (NIH), the largest funder of HIV/AIDS drug development in the world, to adopt incentive policies. In 1997, there were 125 AIDS drugs at a developmental stage, but by 2001–02 this number was said to have dropped to approximately 80. GSK, Roche and others did not enter the new AIDS drug market, and many biotech companies licensed out their inventions. For example, GSK halted clinical trials of its CCR5 anti-HIV drugs because of issues such as side-effects on the liver and increased risk of malignancies. New players, like Panacos, Schering Plough and Pfizer have entered the field.[45]

[41] WHO, Antiretroviral therapy for HIV infection in adults and adolescents: Recommendations for a public health approach 2010 revision (Geneva, 2010).

[42] ibid 58.

[43] Guidelines for the Use of Antiretroviral Agents in HIV-1-Infected Adults and Adolescents (Developed by the DHHS Panel on Antiretroviral Guidelines for Adults and Adolescents – A Working Group of the Office of AIDS Research Advisory Council (Washington, DC, December 2009) www.aidsinfo.nih.gov/contentfiles/AdultandAdolescentGL.pdf.

[44] 2010 WHO Guidelines 58–59.

[45] http://napwa.org.au/pl/2008/09/aids-2008-is-the-hiv-drug-pipeline-drying-up.

There have been no new Big Pharma entrants. This could lead to clinical trials problems if and when a third generation of HIV/AIDS drugs is needed. The burden of future uncertainties seems to have prevented a significant increase in efforts against HIV/AIDS, compared with other illnesses such as diabetes and cardiovascular diseases.[46]

However, the portfolio of available AIDS drugs is not so unhealthy as that of drugs in development. Table 8.1 shows a comparison of HIV/AIDS drugs in the pipeline in 2009 with drugs for other diseases.

Table 8.1: Drugs in development, HIV/AIDS compared with other diseases

Disease	Drugs in Development*
Cancer	750
HIV/AIDS	109 (of which approximately 20 are vaccines)
Heart Disease/Stroke	277
Infectious Diseases	338
Mental Illness	197
Neurological Disorders	547

*Either in clinical trials or under FDA review.
Some medicines are listed in more than one category.

Source: 'Drugs in Development' (www.phrma.org/read_reports)/PhRMA, Chain Drug Review, Dec 17, 2008 (http://findarticles.com/p/articles/mi_hb3007/is_21_29/ai_n29398196/).

II AFFORDABILITY OF MEDICINES: CONTINUOUS CHALLENGE

A Access to ARVs in Developing Countries

Thus, various ARVs have been marketed since 1987 offering different ways to administration, depending on patients' infection situations. At the inception of ARV marketing, approximate market sizes were known only for the US and Europe. The price for ARVs in the US is extremely high, currently $10,000 to $15,000 per patient per year. This is because these ARVs are new and still patent protected; their market volume is relatively small; and some patients have relatively high incomes and insurance.

Around 1990, the overall pharmaceutical market in developing countries comprised less than 13 per cent of the world market.[47] Of the total, Africa's

---

[46] http://www.cid.harvard.edu/cidinthenews/articles/ap_042001.html.
[47] The market share of emerging economies has started to grow. In 2006, the share was approximately 19%. It rose to 23% in 2007.

share was 1.1 per cent, and South Africa's was approximately 1 per cent.[48] Since that time, the emerging pharmaceutical markets such as China, Russia, Brazil, Turkey, the Republic of Korea, Mexico and India have expanded considerably and will continue to do so in the future.[49] Today, the overall drug market of developing countries is estimated to be approximately 19 per cent of the world market. However, the overall South African pharmaceutical market has shrunk, and currently makes up only 0.35 per cent of the world market.

Although South Africa is a developing country, it has a high income class, a clinical trial system and a drug manufacturing infrastructure. When the wealthy class in a poor country forms the 'market' for a drug, it is difficult for a company to determine what its patent and drug pricing strategy should be in that country. Research-based pharmaceutical companies at this time are pursuing a traditional pricing policy often called 'cherry picking', targeting the wealthy class exclusively, by setting drug prices at the same levels as in developed countries.

The problem of purchasing power gaps in a country is usually resolved through policies taken by the government of that country, or international procurement systems through international and national organisations, but drug companies could also practise what is usually called differential pricing[50] which could be efficient for the companies themselves. However, concerning the initial pricing of AIDS drugs, the originator companies apparently followed traditional 'global' pricing policies for ARVs and paid little attention to patient access and affordability problems.

Higher than competitive prices (on the concept of 'competitive price' see Chapter 1) for patented drugs are often justified by the patent-holders' need to recover the cost of R&D, including clinical studies to ensure the safety and efficacy of the medicines, which is said generally to be two-thirds of the entire cost of the drug R&D, starting from basic science (see chapters 3 and 12). Innovative medicines could also lead to savings in healthcare costs, making new treatments possible and probably providing alternatives to non-drug inputs such as invasive operations,[51] or reducing the necessary recovery time. However, the strategy of tailoring patents and prices to the upper class has had a disastrous consequence in the AIDS pandemic situation. The fact that ARV drug prices were affordable only for sufficiently insured patients in developed countries and the wealthy

---

[48]   Interview, Pharmaceutical Manufacturers' Association of South Africa (PMA), 13 May 2005.

[49]   The Brazilian pharmaceutical market expanded by nearly 30% from 2006 to 2009. Over the same period, the size of the Indian pharmaceutical market increased by 15% and is expected to continue to increase by 10% annually in the future. Similarly, the Chinese market increased by 22% in the same period. The seven emerging pharmaceutical markets (Brazil, China, India, Mexico, Russia, the Republic of Korea and Turkey) altogether are predicted to expand by 13–16% in 2010 and 13–16% in the next five years. The Chinese pharmaceutical market has grown annually by 20% in the same period and, by 2013, will constitute 20% of world pharmaceutical market growth. www.ims-japan.co.jp/japanese/pr_20091008.php.

[50]   Differential pricing includes issues such as discriminatory pricing and rebates that are used to meet the drug pricing policies of various countries. However, in this case, this should probably be referred to as preferential pricing. PM Danzon 'At what price?' (2007) 449 *Nature* 176–9.

[51]   SO Schweitzer, *Pharmaceutical Economics and Policy*, 2nd edn (Oxford University Press, 2007).

classes in developing countries was bound to open political discussions among those who cared, ie, patients and civil society groups. Markets where there were no patents on ARVs soon began to get supplies from less expensive Indian producers.

High prices, together with the underdeveloped state of health care systems in many developing countries and general lack of financial resources have made it difficult for most patients to get access even to old, unpatented drugs. Annual per capita public expenditures for pharmaceuticals are low in most developing countries, and the high potential in this vast public sector market is yet to be realised. According to a 1986 World Bank report,[52] annual per-person outlays for pharmaceuticals were of the order of US$0.56 in low-income economies, US$1.40 in lower middle-income economies and US$5.60 in upper middle income economies. For nine countries for which data was readily available, the Bank found that the private sector's share in national pharmaceuticals expenditures was at least one half (in Zimbabwe for examples), more commonly two-thirds, and in select countries more than 90 per cent (Pakistan and Thailand).[53] More recent figures from the WHO suggest similarly that out-of-pocket payments for pharmaceuticals in developing countries are extremely high.[54] The average percentage of expenditure on drugs, as a percentage of total health expenditure, is relatively low and stable in developed countries (7–20 per cent in 2006).[55] In developing countries, however, it is 24–66 per cent on average.[56] It remains unclear whether this is due to inadequate healthcare services and infrastructure, or whether the services in these countries are inexpensive.

B Compulsory Licences and Local Production

i International Solidarity for Affordability of AIDS Drugs

Among the civil society groups which organised campaigns for access to medication, there are organisations such as Médicins sans Fronti res (MSF) that are devoted to extending medical and nursing care to developing countries in a state

---

[52] HK Lashman, 'Pharmaceuticals in the Third World: An Overview', PHN Technical Note 86-31, Population, Health and Nutrition Department, World Bank, November 1986 (1986 World Bank Report).

[53] ibid at 11–12.

[54] The following numbers are from 2002 and for selected countries, percentages of GDP paid out of pocket (includes out-of-pocket payments for people covered by both public and private insurance): Bangladesh 64, Cameroon 69, Côte d'Ivoire 73, Cyprus 57, Democratic Republic of Congo 70, Ecuador 57, Egypt 58, Georgia 80, Ghana 59, Guinea 84, India 78, Indonesia 48, Kenya 45, Malaysia 50, Nigeria 67, Pakistan 65, Philippines 47, Sri Lanka 49, United Republic of Tanzania 38, Venezuela 46, Vietnam 62. WHO, *Make Every Mother and Child Count* (Geneva, WHO Press, 2005).

[55] OECD, Health Data 2008. www.oecd.org/document/27/0,3343,en_2649_34631_40902299_1_1_1_1,00.html.

[56] For Eastern Europe/CIS, this rate is 15–30%, WHO *Make Every Mother and Child Count* (n 54).

of emergency.[57] There are also organisations working towards development and social justice, such as Oxfam, Consumer International and Third World Network. In the US, CPTech (today named Knowledge Ecology International), part of a consumer organisation founded by Ralph Nader, began a critical information campaign on intellectual property issues. CPTech cooperated closely with WF Haddad[58] who is known in particular for his international efforts to promote generic drugs. Together with the Indian National Working Group on Patents, which was made up of members of the Indian government and civil society groups, CPTech also led an international movement questioning the public health role of the TRIPS Agreement in favouring US multinationals. MSF and Health Action International (HAI) later joined this movement and together they developed the 'Access to Medicines Campaign.' This international movement received wide public support, including that of the WHO and other UN organisations such as the United Nations Development Programme (UNDP) and the World Bank.

The following constitutional challenge in South Africa by 39 research-based pharmaceutical companies was a trigger. It led to the subsequent movement in various parts of the world, ultimately leading the way to the Doha Declaration on Public Health and the TRIPS Agreement.[59]

In February 1998, 39 Members of the Pharmaceutical Manufacturers' Association of South Africa (PMA) filed a lawsuit arguing that the amendment in December 1997 made to the Medicines and Related Substances Control Amendment Act 101 of 1965 (Medicines Act)[60] infringed the Constitution of South Africa.[61] By the amendment, section 15C entitled 'measures to ensure supply of more affordable medicines in certain circumstances so as to protect the health of the public' was inserted in the Medicines Act.[62] The main argu-

---

[57]   MSF is a humanitarian, non-governmental organisation providing medical care and services to people in situations of natural calamities, armed conflict, refugee camps, particularly in developing countries facing endemic disease (http://www.msf.org/msfinternational/aboutmsf/). It was established in 1971, by French doctors responding to the experience of the Biafra situation. MSF received the Nobel Peace Prize in 1999.

[58]   A generic drugs manufacturer (Schein Pharmaceutical etc), founder of the generic trade association, the Peace Corps and the poverty program, initiated and negotiated the 1984 Drug Price Competition and Patent Restoration Act (Hatch-Waxman) www.cptech.org/events/wb06022003/bh-bio.html.

[59]   WT/MIN(01)/DEC/2 adopted on 14 November 2001 para 3: 'We also recognize the concerns about its effects on prices.'

[60]   No 18505 Government Gazette, 12 December 1997.

[61]   *PMA v President of the Republic of South Africa*, Case No. 4183/98 sworn 18 February 1998, High Court of South Africa (Transvaal Provincial Division).

[62]   Act No 57 of 1978. S 15C gives the Minister of Health the power to authorise parallel trade or compulsory licensing, even in contradiction to South Africa's Patent Law and prescribes in particular: '(a) notwithstanding anything to the contrary contained in the Patents Act 1978 determine that the rights with regard to any medicine under a patent granted in the Republic shall not extend to acts in respect of such medicine which has been put onto the market by the owner of the medicine or with his or her consent; (b) prescribe the conditions on which any medicine which is identical in composition, meets the same quality standard and is intended to have the same proprietary name as that of another medicine already registered in the Republic but which is imported by a person other than the person who is the holder of the registration certificate of the medicine already registered and which originates from any site of manufacture of the original manufacturer as approved by the

ment by PMA companies was that section 15C was unconstitutional because it gave broad discretionary power to the Minister of Health without specifying under what conditions (for what diseases, for example) this power could be exercised, and without giving right holders the opportunity of prior consultation (as Article 31(b) of the TRIPS Agreement provides).[63]

That these pharmaceutical companies responded with a lawsuit on such a grave issue without even proposing alternative solutions to the urgent public epidemic problem shocked the conscience of the international community.[64] Thousands of protestors marched on the Pretoria High Court in support for the South African Government. MSF alone obtained 250,000 signatures from all over the world. Civil society groups, not only from South Africa, such as Treatment Action Campaign, but from the entire world protested against the PMA companies. In their campaigns, they quoted President Nelson Mandela, who said that: 'the pharmaceuticals are exploiting the situation that exists in countries like South Africa – in the developing world – because they charge exorbitant prices which are beyond the capacity of the ordinary HIV/AIDS person. That is completely wrong and must be condemned'.[65]

Paralleling this lawsuit, in 1996, the United States Trade Representative (USTR) placed South Africa on its 'watch list' of countries, and initiated negotiations to bring it into line with Article 31 of the TRIPS Agreement. During the Uruguay Round, the US insisted that disputes relating to the TRIPS Agreement be resolved through the WTO dispute settlement procedures. The case of the South African Medicines Act, for them, was a test case on how TRIPS could be used. This approach also was criticised heavily by civil society groups. Following the meeting between the next South African President Mbeki and US Vice-President Gore in September 1999, South Africa was removed from this list. In May 2001, President Clinton recommended that the USTR take tolerant measures towards the statutory amendments made by the South African government.

The first ARVs were major innovations (new use of a known compound originally for therapeutic use for cancer) and priced accordingly for rich, industrialised markets. But even in the US in the 1980s, their prices were too high for a large number of uninsured and under-insured patients. In the series of international events that followed in South Africa and Thailand that attracted world attention, the original concern was not so much the practice of patent protection but the affordability of AIDS drugs and the allegation of a decisive link between IPR and denial of access.

council in the prescribed manner, may be imported; (c) prescribe the registration procedure for as well as the use of the medicine referred to in paragraph (b).'

[63] Meeting with the PMA at the WHO's Commission on Intellectual Property, Innovation and Public Health (CIPIH) consultation meeting in June 2005.

[64] At around the same time, there were demonstrations against GSK Mumbai, based on the sheer rumour that this company was filing a lawsuit in Ghana against the import in Ghana of Duovir (a combination drug of AZT-3TC), produced by Cipla, that infringed on GSK'S patents (*Express India*, 22 February 2001).

[65] O Quist-Arcton, 'South Africa: Battle Against Pharmaceutical Giants Continues' 17 April 2001, http://allafrica.com/stories/200104170346.html.

As we will see below, for the vast majority of medicines recognised as essential medicines by the WHO, patent problems were not relevant, since very few such medicines remain under patent. The chronic problem in developing countries has been that medicines needed are not available for various reasons (such as the mismatch between prescription and available medicines).[66] The fact that even generics are unaffordable in many of the least developed countries where there is no product patent protection indicates that problems of access extend well beyond the issue of patent protection.

It is not in the least developed countries but rather in those developing countries with wealthy classes that research-based pharmaceutical companies tend to file for patents, and it is in these countries with their technical capacity for copying and their ability to undertake R&D, that conflicts over IPRs occur. It is also in the emerging economies that there is continuing extreme poverty in large segments of their populations, together with wealthy classes. In these developing countries with relatively developed technological skills, the idea of domestic production is often supported for the moral and political reason of assuring self-reliance. It is also widely believed in these countries that domestic production would reduce drug prices. Since the 1970s, many countries with certain technological skills have attempted to nurture their own domestic pharmaceutical industries (see chapter 9). Intellectual property rights in this situation can be seen as the sole obstacle to the local production of medicines. Regulations concerning scientific and clinical research (biological and genetic resources), as well as requirements concerning safety, efficacy and quality of medicines, are often unclear in these countries, and also become sources of political conflict. As the discussions on the affordability of medicines in these countries have intensified, the idea of dynamic welfare through innovation has received less attention than arguments that patents only hinder access to medicines.

C Important Roles Played by Indian Generic Producers

The originator companies in the early 1990s, by ignoring patient access and affordability problems, opened the political field to civil society groups and Indian generic producers, who soon found commercial markets in non-patented countries.

The chairman and managing director of the Indian generic company Cipla, YK Hamied, took the lead in providing inexpensive drugs to African countries[67] and helped establish the credibility of the civil society movements and solidarity between the civil society groups and Indian producers. At that time, there was no protection for product patents in India, so Cipla was able to begin producing ARVs which had been patented in the US, Europe, and South Africa. He exported combination ARVs, attracting world-wide attention, including

---

[66]   1986 World Bank Report (n 52).

[67]   Cipla promised to sell AIDS drugs to MSF for $350 a year (one dollar a day) per patient and began exporting these medicines.

media news reports on the BBC and in the *New York Times*.[68] Cipla and MSF claimed that patents were preventing AIDS drugs from being sold at affordable prices to those who needed them, and therefore requested that the South African Government issue compulsory licences for all patents on AIDS drugs. Cipla increased its production capacity by exporting ARVs to Africa and subsequently established its reputation by passing quality tests conducted by the US FDA and international organisations such as the WHO.

On 10 March 2001, the *New York Times* published an article about the remarkable changes that had taken place for AIDS patients in Africa.[69] According to this article, these occurred because Cipla had asked the South African Government for permission to sell inexpensive knock-off versions of eight of the 15 ARVs that, in varying combinations, are used in the AIDS cocktails for $600 per year per patient – a small fraction of the $10,000 to $15,000 that Americans pay. The pharmaceutical giant Merck offered the ARV sales at cost ($600 per patient per year for the protease inhibitor Crixivan, and $500 per patient per year for another antiretroviral, Sustiva, marketed overseas as Stocrin).

In this humanitarian campaign, a confluence of views emerged among civil society groups, the Indian generics community and academics in the US who criticised the Bayh-Dole Act (chapter 3 p 97) and patenting or licence policies of the NIH. Discussions in the US on the 'public' nature of medicinal patents were adapted to conditions in developing countries and came to contain powerful arguments against multinational companies' pharmaceutical patents and the TRIPS Agreement in these countries.

Chairman Hamied of Cipla argued that 'large pharmaceutical companies' did not really own the patents.[70] He gave the example of Brystol Myers Squibb (BMS), which manufactures stavudine. Hamied said:

> the original inventor is Yale University, and the patent is held by the US government. BMS pays the US government for Yale University royalties. AZT is not a Glaxo product, but was developed by the National Institute of Health. I am simply asking these companies to give me a licence, in the same way they have one from the US government.

Health policy-oriented civil society groups protested against the patent and licence policies of the NIH and from 2000 to 2001 demonstrated against the high price of BMS's stavudine (d4T). These groups also demanded intervention by the Federal Trade Commission (FTC), alleging patent abuse by drug companies. MSF, HAI and CPTech Health Gap complained that the high price of paclitaxel (Taxol)[71] and fluconazole (Diflucan)[72] violated section 5 of the FTC Act.

[68] SK Sell and A Prakash, 'Using Ideas Strategically: The Contest Between Business and NGO Networks' (2004) 8(1) *Intellectual Property Rights, International Studies Quarterly* 143–75.

[69] 'Africa's AIDS War', *New York Times* (10 March 2001).

[70] KS Jayaraman, 'Taste of their own medicines', *New Scientist* (31 March 2001).

[71] Taxol is used to treat breast cancer, lung cancer, and ovarian cancer. It is also used to treat AIDS-related Kaposi's sarcoma. The high price of Taxol is often attributed to the scarcity of the yu tree, which provides a key ingredient.

[72] An antifungal medicine for opportunistic diseases following HIV infection, www.fda.gov/downloads/Drugs/GuidanceComplianceRegulatoryInformation/Guidances/ucm086187.pdf.

Later, in 2006, CPTech complained that Gilead (a US bioventure company) licensed tenofovir and emtrisitavine patents in India, despite the fact that there were no patents established in India. CPTech complained to the FTC that Gilead was partitioning world markets through their global patent strategy.[73] Gilead licenses several Indian manufacturers to produce and sell tenofovir.[74]

D International Organisations

Not only research-based pharmaceutical companies, but international organisations and governments of developed countries as well were slow to respond to the urgent pharmaceutical needs arising from the HIV/AIDS pandemic.

The WHO is one of the specialised agencies of the UN and was established on 7 April 1948. The WHO was originally created to respond to problems relating to epidemic outbreaks in different regions, but its expectations are high, as the Preamble of the WHO Constitution states, inter alia, that 'health is a state of complete physical, mental and social well-being, and not merely the absence of disease of infirmity'. Its objective as stated in Article 1 is: 'the attainment by all peoples of the highest possible level of health'. Article 2 of the Constitution delineates the WHO's broad range of activities, such as: '(a) to act as the directing and co-ordinating authority on international health work; . . . and (u) to develop, establish and promote international standards with respect to food, biological, pharmaceutical and similar products'. Therefore, the task of the WHO is not only to combat diseases, especially key infectious diseases, but also to promote the health of people in a broad sense.

In 1977, the WHO Health Assembly adopted Resolution WHA 28.66 which laid the foundation for the WHO Essential Medicines policy. Since then the WHO has been investigating social and economic requirements for treatments[75] and has developed a list of approximately 300 essential drugs, known as the List of Essential Medicines, which is revised roughly once every two to three years. Each WHO member country can adopt its own list, modelled on the WHO's list.

In combating the AIDS epidemic, however, the UN itself, rather than the WHO, took the initiative[76] and in 1996 established the Joint United Nations

---

[73] KEI request for investigation into anticompetitive aspects of Gilead Voluntary Licenses for patents on Tenofovir and Emtricitabine (12 February 2007). www.keionline.org/misc-docs/ftcgile-ad12feb07.pdf.

[74] Gilead licenses tenofovir to Indian generic manufacturers (10 October 2006). www.i-base.info/htb/v7/htb7-10/Gilead.html.

[75] In the past, affordability was one of the factors considered for establishing the list of essential medicines. Interview with HV Hogerzeil, Director, Department of Essential Medicines and Pharmaceutical Policies, WHO, Geneva, 2 June 2005.

[76] According to several staff members of the WHO Department of HIV/AIDS (interviews in May 2005), successive WHO directors general in the 1990s have concentrated more on other health issues than HIV/AIDS, such as the conclusion of the WHO Framework Convention on Tobacco Control, for example. Civil society groups and WHO staff members took the lead on HIV/AIDS issues, particularly concerning medicines.

Programme on HIV/AIDS (UNAIDS) with a view to mobilising financial, human and technical resources to support an effective response. Co-sponsors include UNHCR, UNICEF, WFP, UNDP, UNFPA, UNODC, ILO, UNESCO, WHO and the World Bank.[77]

As part of the UN's coordinated efforts to cope with the AIDS epidemic, the WHO HIV/AIDS Programme came to provide technical support to WHO Member States to help them scale up HIV treatment, and increase access to drugs and diagnostics.[78] Although WHO policy orientations changed over time,[79] AIDS medicines and diagnostics service (AMDS) within the WHO HIV/AIDS Department came to play an important role in the implementation of the HIV/AIDS Programme. AMDS organises a network for supply management of HIV commodities and brokers cooperation between technical partners, funding agencies, manufacturing companies and other organisations. The WHO and NGOs came together to combat AIDS and adopted various strategies to facilitate the supply of ARVs to generic drug manufacturers in developing countries, whom they believed should play an important role in providing solutions. In this context, IPR protection and research-based pharmaceutical companies together came to be the target of criticism.

E WHO promotion of quality generics

The public health situation in developing countries could greatly improve if effective preventive measures for disease were taken, affordable originator or generic drugs with guaranteed safety, efficacy and quality entered the market, medical care were provided through insurance and a medical system were put into place. Attempts to realise these goals often face difficulties when governments lack the political will to implement viable public health policies or provide human and financial resources for sustainable healthcare systems. Often, medicines do not reach patients as a result of the diversion of medicines in the distribution process or when specialised channels for medical treatment are lacking. There are often situations where there are only expensive, new drugs that only the wealthy can purchase, or available copy drugs are without quality guarantees.

The WHO Prequalification Project was established in 2001 for HIV/AIDS, malaria and tuberculosis medicines. Under this Project, manufacturers (both for brand name products and generics) can submit data about the quality, safety and efficacy of their products to the WHO assessment teams. These data include details of the purity of all ingredients used in manufacture, finished products,

---

[77] www.unaids.org/en/AboutUNAIDS/Secretariat/default.asp. UNAIDS has five focus areas for a more effective global response to AIDS: mobilising leadership and advocacy for effective action on the epidemic providing strategic information and policies to guide efforts in the AIDS response worldwide, tracking, monitoring and evaluation of the epidemic – the world's leading resource for AIDS-related epidemiological data and analysis, engaging civil society and developing partnerships.

[78] www.who.int/hiv/en/.

[79] The first director was Dr Texeira, the head of Brazil's AIDS Programme. Directors of this Department have changed more than 10 times since the inception of WHO's HIV/AIDS Programme.

including the stability and the rate of dissolution, and the results of *in vivo* bioequivalence tests. Their standards of evaluating the quality specifications of medicines and the manufacturing sites are based on the principles and practices agreed to by the world's leading regulatory agencies and adopted by the WHO Expert Committee on Specification for Pharmaceutical Preparations.[80] The names of drugs that are approved for quality are published, while the names of those which are not approved are not.[81] By encouraging the candidate companies to improve their production standards, this project promotes high-quality generics production by developing countries.[82]

The WHO prequalification approval process became an important measure of the safety, efficacy and quality of the medicines for HIV/AIDS, malaria and tuberculosis including those procured by international funds such as UNICEF, the Global Fund and US President's Emergency Plan for AIDS Relief, PEPFAR. For example, on 30 April 2005 the Global Fund introduced the rule that grant funds may only be used to procure pharmaceutical products that meet the requirements of being either prequalified by the WHO or approved by a stringent regulatory authority[83] such as the US FDA. Some developing countries persist in protesting against this rule as it could disadvantage their domestic companies.

III THE ROAD TO THE DOHA DECLARATION ON PUBLIC HEALTH

When the world became aware of the seriousness of the AIDS pandemic and its social and economic consequences, particularly in developing countries, there was controversy over the causal relationship between patents and the lack of access to medicines. In these discussions, information on basic facts about patents, markets, pricing and national regulations in developing countries and their health policies were lacking, and this remains so even today.

A Patents and Access to Medicines

In the late 1990s, fierce disputes arose among multinational pharmaceutical companies, academics and civil society groups regarding whether and how patent protection of ARVs influenced access to medicines in developing countries.

[80] www.who.int/mediacentre/factsheets/fs278/en/index.html.

[81] As of 20 November 2009, 42 brand name medicines and 65 generic medicines were found to meet the WHO prequalification standards. These included 62 antiretrovirals and 33 medicines for HIV/AIDS-related diseases; two antimalarials and six drugs for the treatment of tuberculosis: 'New edition of WHO prequalification list to include four new anti-AIDS medicines', www.who.int/mediacentre/news/releases/2004/pr49/en/.

[82] www.who.int/mediacentre/factsheets/fs278/en/. Interview with L Rago, Coordinator, Quality Assurance and Safety of Medicines, 30 September 2009. Also see R Laing et al, '25 Years of the WHO Essential Medicines Lists: Progress and Challenges' (2003) 361 *The Lancet* 1723–29.

[83] Stringent regulatory authority means (a) a member of the Pharmaceutical Inspection Convention or an entity participating in the Pharmaceutical Inspection Cooperation Scheme; or (b) a member of the International Conference on Harmonisation of Technical Requirements for the Registration of Pharmaceuticals for Human Use.

In 2001, Attaran and Gillespie-White published their survey results on the existence of patents on ARVs in African countries.[84] According to the study, 15 out of 16 ARVs were protected by patent in South Africa, but on average, only three ARVs are protected in an African country. According to the study, an important reason for the high prices was the lack of any effective public market. To begin with, the purchasing power of patients would be insufficient in any country in the absence of medical insurance. Very few governments were providing ARVs during the initial period in the 1990s and therefore the medicines were available only through the private sector that targeted the elite classes. These high private sector prices were used for price comparisons at the time. Once a public market is created, preferential prices become possible in response to increased demand on the part of supplying firms. In his paper, Attaran argued that the causes of the lack of access to medicines lie far more in the failings of systems and poor purchasing power than in patents. The cost of medicines is determined by the structure of demand, such as government regulation and patient numbers, the size of the wealthy class, and the medical infrastructure. It proposes that the problem should therefore be solved through international aid.

Civil society groups criticised the above view and CPTech, in particular, calling the simple counting of patents in the above studies meaningless, arguing that the competitive market entry of important AIDS drugs is impossible for the following reasons:[85]

1. Patients' choice of appropriate treatment cocktails is restricted by patents.[86] Not noted is the fact that, while ritonavir is not patented anywhere in Africa, Kaletra (comprised of 80 per cent lopinavir and 20 per cent ritonavir) is patented in South Africa.[87]

2. Both Attaran and PhRMA surveys omit Trizivir (a combination of AZT+3TC+abacavir taken twice a day, a product sold by GSK), and the Attaran paper only briefly notes improvements (in dosage form) made to existing drugs.

3. Entry into the South African market (where the income level is relatively high and there are a large number of patients) is important for generic suppliers

---

[84] A Attaran and L Gillespie-White, 'Do Patents for Antiretroviral Drugs Constrain Access to AIDS Treatment in Africa?' (2001) 286 *JAMA*.

[85] www.cptech.org/ip/health/africa/dopatentsmatterinafrica.html.

[86] CPTech shows various mechanisms by which the selection is restricted. A three-drug HAART regimen consists usually of two NRTI products and abacavir, NNRTI or a PI. In developed countries, a three-NRTI combination such as AZT+3TC+abacavir is no longer recommended. The best choices, considering both toxicity and efficacy, for the two-NRTI drugs are d4T, 3TC, AZT or ddI; however, d4T and AZT cannot be taken together. The least expensive generic three-drug regime is d4T/3TC/nevirapine, but at least one of them is patented.

[87] While competitive analyses of AIDS cocktails may be relevant, each case requires a specific analysis. See for example *Schor v Abbott Labs* (Case No 05-3344, 7th Cir 26 June 2006), antitrust civil case in the US involving Kaletra. The district court dismissed the complaint, saying that 'monopoly leveraging' does not violate the antitrust laws unless it takes a particular form, such as a tie-in sale, predatory pricing or refusal to deal. In any case, an analysis of each market situation will be needed.

in order to achieve economies of scale, but entry is hindered by patents, particularly of Kaletra and abacavir.

4. The surveys do not mention patents on generic three-drugs-in-one-pill versions of d4T+3TC+nevirapine or AZT+3TC+nevirapine, which combine products sold by different US or European companies, and which are now only available from Indian generic suppliers.

First of all, patent searches are always limited by the choice of database and methodologies and, from patent data, speculation on their social implications is risky.

Table 8.2 shows countries in which some of the basic AIDS medicines-related patent applications had been filed (searched in August 2005) This table is based on information provided by the International Patent Documentation Center (INPADOC), a data collection maintained by the European Patent Office (EPO). While it is possible to rely on INPADOC as a source of public information on patents, it only covers information on 73 countries and regions, and excludes information from countries such as Thailand and Malaysia. INPADOC covers information on five broad regional patent systems: the African Regional Industrial Property Organisation (ARIPO) for anglophone Africa;[88] the African Intellectual Property Organisation (OAPI) for francophone Africa;[89] the Eurasian Patent Office (EAPO);[90] the EPO; and WIPO international application based on the Patent Cooperation Treaty (PCT). However, it is still difficult to get information on whether a patent in fact exists or, a fortiori, whether or not it is valid in a specific country. According to the WIPO report of 2000 on Patent Protection and Access to HIV/AIDS Pharmaceuticals in Sub-Saharan Africa,[91] although patent holders knew of the existence of patents, they were reluctant to cooperate with surveys.[92] For many governments of developing countries, having a 'patent system' is a negotiating tool that can be used to bargain with developed countries.[93]

---

[88] The members of ARIPO are Botswana, Gambia, Ghana, Kenya, Lesotho, Malawi, Mozambique, Namibia, Sierra Leone, Sudan, Swaziland, Tanzania, Uganda, Zambia, and Zimbabwe. www.aripo. org/.

[89] The members of OAPI are Benin, Burkina Faso, Cameroon, Central African Republic, Chad, Congo, Equatorial Guinea, Gabon, Guinea, Guinea Bissau, Ivory Coast, Mali, Mauritania, Niger, Senegal, and Togo.

[90] The Eurasian Patent Convention, effective in August 1995, establishes an interstate system for the protection of inventions on the basis of a single patent valid for Turkmenistan, Belarus, Tajikistan, Russia, Azerbaijan, Kazakhstan, Kyrgyzstan, Armenia and Moldova; www.eapo.org/index_eng.html.

[91] WIPO, *Patent Protection and Access to HIV/AIDS Pharmaceuticals in Sub-Saharan Africa* (International Intellectual Property Institute, 2000) www.wipo.int/about-ip/en/studies/pdf/iipi_hiv. pdf. There was a response rate of approximately 50% to questionnaires used for this report.

[92] In the case of this Report, 50% answered the questionnaire.

[93] Interview with WIPO staff, June 2006.

Table 8.2 AIDS Medicines-related patent applications by countries

	medicines	Applicant(s)	patent no.	filing date	Regional/National Patent Offices					total
					North & Central America	South America	Asia and Oceania	Europe	Africa	
1	zidovudine	GlaxoSmithKline plc	EP0196185	1986	CA, US (2)	-	AU, HK, IL, JP, KR, NZ, PH, SG (8)	EP, AT, CS, CY, DD, DE, DK, ES, FI, GB, HU, IE, LV, MC, PL, PT (16)	AP, ZA (2)	28
2	abacavir sulfate	GlaxoSmithKline	EP0317128	1988	CA, MX, US (3)	-	AU, JP (2)	EP, AT, DE, DK, ES, FI, GB, GR, HU, PT (10)	ZA (1)	16
3	sanilvudine	Bristol-Myers Squibb	EP0398230	1990	CA, US (2)	-	AU, CN, JP, KR, NZ (5)	EP, AT, GB, CZ, DD, DE, DK, ES, FI GR, HU, IE, NO, PL, PT, RU, SK (17)	EG, ZA (2)	26
4	nevirapine	Boehringer Ingelheim	EP0393529	1990	CA, US (2)	-	AU, HK, IL, JP, KR, NZ, SG (7)	EP, AT, DD, DE, DK, ES, FI, GR, HU, IE, LU, NL, NO, PT, RU (15)	AP, OA, ZA (3)	27
5	saquinavir mesylate	Roche	EP0432695	1990	CA, MX, US (3)	BR (1)	AU, CN, HK, ID, IL, IN, JP, KR, SG (9)	EP, AT, BG, CZ, DE, DK, ES, FI, GB, GR, HR, HU, IE, LT, LU, LV, MC, MT, NL, NO, PL, PT, RO, RU, SI, SK (26)	OA, EG, MA, MW, ZA, ZW (6)	45
6	lamivudine	IAF BIOCHEM INT	WO9117159	1991	CA, US (2)	-	AU, CN, HK, IL, JP, KR, NZ, SG, TW (9)	EP, BA, BG, CS, FI, GB, HR, HU, IE, MD, NO, PL, PT, RO, RU, SI, SK (17)	AP, EG, MA, OA, ZA (5)	33

Table 8.2 (*cont.*)

	medicines	Applicant(s)	patent no.	filing date	Regional/National Patent Offices					total
					North & Central America	South America	Asia and Oceania	Europe	Africa	
7	ritonavir	Abbott Laboratories	WO9217176	1992	CA, MX, US (3)	BR (1)	AU, HK, IL, JP, KR, NZ (6)	EP, AT, CH, DE, DK, ES, GR, HU, IE, IT, NL, PT (12)	ZA (1)	23
8	indinavir sulfate ethanolate	Merck	WO9309096	1992	CA, MX, US (3)	BR (1)	AU, CN, HK, IL, JP, KR, NZ, SG (8)	EP, AT, GB, CY, CZ, DE, DK, ES, FI, GB, GR, HR, HU, LV, NO, PL, PT, RO, RU, SI, SK (21)	ZA (1)	34
9	efavirenz	Merck	WO9403440	1993	CA, MX, US (3)	-	AU, CN, HK, IL, JP, KR, NZ, SG, TW (9)	EP, AT, GB, CZ, DE, ES, FI, GR, HR, HU, LU, LV, NL, NO, PL, PT, RO, RU, SI, SK (20)	ZA (1)	33
10	lopinavir	Abbott Laboratories	WO9721685	1996	CA, US (2)	BR (1)	AU, CN, HK, IL, JP, NZ, TW (7)	EP, AT, CZ, DE, DK, ES, HU, PT (8)	ZA (1)	19
11	atazanavir sulfate	Bristol-Myers Squibb	WO9936404	1998	US (1)	BR (1)	AU, CN, HK, IL, JP, NZ, TR, TW (8)	EP, AT, BG, CZ, DE, DK, EE, ES, HU, LT, LV, NO, PL, PT, RO, RU, SK (17)	ZA (1)	28

EP, AP, OA are counted as one country. On the country code see Annex, section 1, List of States, Other Entities and Intergovernmental Organizations, Handbook on Industrial Property Information and Documentation http://www.wipo.int/export/sites/www/standards/en/pdf/03-01.pdf

There are many other difficulties in acquiring accurate information on the existence of patents. To start with, it is not easy to establish the relationship between the product on the market, and the patent. Even if a search is limited to product patents only, this might include selection patents and derivative products such as isomers and polymorphs. Furthermore, the specifications of the patent do not always clearly describe the pharmacological effects or therapeutic use of the drug (see chapter 12). When filing for a patent, the applicant takes into account not only existing patents, but also possible subsequent patents which he or she might file in the future. If the claims of drug efficacy are broad, this will prevent other companies from applying for similar patents. However, it might also make it impossible to acquire subsequent patents for the applicant company itself, if the efficacy is meticulously described. In the case of new breakthrough drugs, it is even more difficult to decide the extent to which the pharmacological effects and drug efficacy should be described, because there could be other concurrent applications, as well as competing literature published by universities.

One of the reasons why there is a considerable number of patent applications, even in the least developed countries, seems to be the existence of the two regional patent cooperation areas in Africa. In the 1990s, regional cooperation for patent applications was promoted in view of factors such as cost. Fifteen countries which were former French colonies joined the OAPI while 15 nations which were former British colonies formed the ARIPO (AP), and in adopting product patents, neither has made medicines unpatentable. The OAPI (OA) does not have an examination system, so applicants are automatically granted patents simply by filing an application. In the early 1990s, originator pharmaceutical companies also seemed to have taken it for granted that patent applications should be made to exclude generic drugs in potentially important markets. More recently, since there has been growing criticism of these companies, there have been fewer patent applications in developing countries. A few major pharmaceutical companies have declared that they do not apply for patents on ARVs in Africa, except in South Africa, or enforce their rights.

Combination drugs, which have been most important in Africa, seem to be patented extensively in the region. Not only originators, but also generic companies are filing for patents, particularly in African countries. For example, GSK's Combivir (lamivudine+zidovudine, EP513, 917, US5627, 186 etc) is patented extensively in Africa (South Africa, ARIPO, etc). Cipla's joint venture, CIPLA-Medpro (Pty) Ltd, filed for a formulation patent of Triomune, a combination drug of lamivudine, stavudine, nevirapine (3TC+d4T+NVP) in South Africa and on the basis of this priority right, at ARIPO, with the designation of Ghana, Gambia, Kenya, Lesotho, Malawi, Mozambique, Sierra Leone, Sudan, Swaziland, Tansania, Uganda, Zambia and Zimbabwe. The patent was granted in South Africa in 2002 (ZA2001-10499) but the patent status in other African countries is not known from the data base.

In 2005, the US patent on AZT expired and, in October 2005, Roxane Laboratories (Columbus, Ohio, US), Ranbaxy (Graogon, India), and Aurobindo

(Hyderabad, India) received approval from the US FDA for their applications for generic drugs. As a result, AZT can now be purchased in the US for around $7 per 300 mg. Ranbaxy applied for WHO prequalification in addition to US FDA approval and expanded its export market. After Ranbaxy received approval, Hetero also received approval from the US FDA for nevirapine and in August 2007 Cipla received US FDA approval for a paediatric formulation distributed by PEPFAR, which is a combination of 3TC, d4T, and nevirapine.

For new types of HIV/AIDS, patent search could help identify possible causes of the lack of supply. Combinations and other various formulations of ARVs could be held by both originator and generic companies (chapter 11). It is, however, too limited an approach to concentrate on the patent factor in addressing the access to medicines issues. Most essential medicines are rarely under patent protection that would effectively prevent generic entry (p 292).

B United Nations and the TRIPS

i First UN Conference on HIV/AIDS and Developing Countries

Civil society groups have been the major organisations committed to providing medical treatment in poor countries and were instrumental in bringing the AIDS problems of developing countries to the fore of international discussions. At the Press Conference of the First Special Session of the UN General Assembly on HIV/AIDS, from 25 to 27 June 2001, Kofi Annan stated that the Session was historic for two reasons. First, because 'the world is at long last waking up to the gravity of the HIV/AIDS crisis', and secondly because of the strong role played by non-governmental activists in 'setting the pace in care and prevention, and in advocating greater action at national and international levels'. For Annan, the proactive role of NGOs came despite the fact that '. . . I am sorry to say, the response in other quarters has often been painfully slow'.[94]

Brazil argued that it was through 'local production' of pharmaceuticals, in particular, that developing countries could cope with the epidemic. Brazil had been implementing an effective AIDS programme since 1996, earlier than other developing countries. It provided a model of how to cope with the epidemic, the importance of which the Brazilian Minister of Health emphasised at the same session:

> The reason for the affordability of our policy is the local production of drugs. Brazil produces 8 generic versions of non-patented antiretroviral drugs at low costs. Most of the medicines provided by Brazilian laboratories are much cheaper than those imported. Last year, only 2 imported drugs amounted to as much as 36% of the whole purchase costs of antiretroviral medicines. Nevertheless, effective or potential competition from the local companies is inducing foreign industries to bring their costs down on average by 70%.[95]

---

[94] www.un.org/News/dh/latest/sg_20010627.htm.
[95] Statement by Senator José Serra, Minister of Health of Brazil.

The Brazilian Minister went on to discuss the relationship between 'local production' and the TRIPS Agreement as follows:

> The TRIPS Agreement itself, for all its provisions on scientific knowledge protection, contains measures allowing for the promotion of public health. We are pleased that this Special Session has acknowledged the efforts of countries to develop domestic industries in order to increase access to medicines and protect the health of their populations. It has also recognized that affordability of drugs is a significant factor in the fight against the epidemic.

Certain developing countries such as Brazil and India had started import substitution policies in pharmaceuticals in the 1970s. 'Local production' was an attractive concept as this meant, for developing countries, replacing high-priced multinational products with locally produced ones which were considered to be cheaper.[96] This was achieved in India, but not in all developing countries (chapters 10 and 11).

More than 20 years ago, in 1986, a World Bank Report[97] offered some insights into what was required in sustaining viable 'local production' of pharmaceuticals in developing countries. It pointed out that the industrial policy objective of a country (commercial profit of local companies) often conflicted with the pursuit of health policy (the optimum pharmaceuticals product mix). Therefore, care should be taken in determining policy, institutional and investment priorities in the sector.

The Report estimated that developing countries produced 11 per cent of the total volume of pharmaceutical production in the world. It noted, however, that definitions of pharmaceutical products were not standardised across the world (for example, whether veterinary medicines were included or not). The breadth of this involvement was heavily concentrated in just a few key countries, namely Argentina, Brazil, Egypt, India, and Mexico, as well as in the latter phases of production, ie, formulation of finished products, packaging, promotion and marketing and distribution. Among these activities, a significant portion, ranging from 18 to 100 per cent, with a median value of 70 per cent, was held by transnational corporations (at that time, the countries where the market share of transnational corporations was below 50 per cent were limited to Egypt and Korea).[98]

The Report warned that local production tended to be costly,[99] due mainly to the difficulties of attaining economies of scale, which in turn were caused

---

[96] G Velasquez, *l'Industrie du medicament et le tiers monde* (Paris, Edition l'Harmattan, 1983) 93–94.

[97] 1986 World Bank Report (n 52).

[98] ibid 35–36.

[99] The 1986 World Bank Report (n 53) 2–3 stated that: 'In depth Bank analysis of the salient techno-economic characteristics of the world pharmaceuticals industry underscores, however, that the vast majority of developing countries cannot, and in the medium term, will not be able to make pharmaceuticals locally more cheaply than they can buy them from existing products. Their strong comparative disadvantage in local pharmaceuticals production vis-à-vis existing international manufacturers is due to numerous factors, among the most important of which are: (1) the lack of strong domestic research capacity, given the rapid pace of innovation in both products and process technology in this industry; (2) the significant economies of scale of R&D, production, and marketing,

by insufficient R&D activities, technical skills and infrastructure, including formulation technologies, as well as inefficient distribution.[100] The Report also indicated that state-owned production and/or distribution companies, set up in the belief that their non-profit orientation would not necessarily permit the manufacture and distribution of pharmaceuticals more cheaply than the private sector, proved to be economically unsuccessful (except in Hungary). According to this Report, state-owned companies lacked the flexibility and creativity required in the highly competitive international pharmaceuticals market.[101]

Over 20 years have passed since this analysis in the 1986 World Bank Report was published. Today, this Report is criticised as being too negative about the efficiency of 'local production' of medicines in developing countries.[102] There have indeed been considerable changes in the pharmaceutical industrial sector globally, some of which were not foreseen by this Report. The most notable is that major companies from India have become globally competitive in the intervening period. India is now a leading player in the production of generic medicines and has increased its competitiveness in this field. China is increasing its domestic production and market and increasing its export of pharmaceutical ingredients. The current situation is evolving into one that was not entirely envisioned in the 1986 World Bank Report. At the same time, there are still some state-run enterprises in developing countriesthat have been unable to attain economies of scale for the reasons that the 1986 World Bank Report advanced (ie, a reduction in average costs[103] as production volumes increase, for R&D, production and marketing).

---

as contrasted to the small average developing country domestic market size and export potential; (3) the foreign exchange intensity of pharmaceuticals operations, reflecting the importance of imports for acquisition of the key production inputs from technology and equipment, to raw materials and/or intermediates – the major category of manufacturing costs; and (4) the undeveloped state of distribution and marketing networks of reaching potential markets. The significant economies of scale underlie the high degree of specialization, the resultant interdependence among countries to meet their total supply needs, and the consequently highly competitive, yet oligopolistic market structure of the industry.' The Report suggested that: 'Overall, the joint pursuit of health and industrial objectives and pharmaceuticals in the developing countries often raises serious conflicts in determining policy, institutional and investment priorities in each sector, and commonly leads to substantial inefficiency in the use of scarce resources.' Ibid 3.

[100] The retail price of non-prescription drugs is relatively lower than prescription drugs, so it is necessary to keep costs low during their formulation process. This requires low-cost formulation technology that can be used for commercial production.

[101] 1986 World Bank Report (n 52) 36–37.

[102] For example, see N Homedes et al, 'The World Bank, Pharmaceutical Policies, and Health Reforms in Latin America' (2005) 35(4) *International Journal of Health Services* 691–717.

[103] Average costs refer to the total cost per unit of output, where marginal costs are the additional costs resulting from the company producing an extra unit of output. Average costs are high if fixed costs, such as capital investments, are high and production output is low. Sunk costs are fixed costs that cannot be recovered by, for example, transferring such costs to an alternative use. Investments in R&D are typically considered fixed costs, but are also often sunk costs (this is also true of advertising costs). There are also 'economies of scope', which are related to economies of scale. An economy of scope exists when costs are lowered through centralising production, rather than producing several different products at separate companies.

There have also been changes in the conditions in which medicines are developed, produced and distributed, particularly with the development of new drug technology driven by biotechnology. Drug discovery and development have become increasingly dependent on science, and the role of universities and biotech ventures has become more important. Research institutions and venture businesses contribute increasingly to the discovery of potential medicinal compounds, and relatively small-scale bio-ventures have become indispensable in developing innovative compounds into products.

There are today opposing arguments about the optimum size of companies and the success of drug development.[104] Significantly, the size of the pharmaceutical markets, particularly those for generic products, in emerging economies is increasing rapidly and there is a general trend for large research-based pharmaceutical companies to acquire or form strategic alliances with emerging-country generic companies for the purpose of expanding their operations in and from these rapidly growing markets. Multinational companies started to distribute world-wide those generic drugs produced in emerging economies (see Chapters 10 and 11). Increased globalisation of R&D, production and distribution of pharmaceuticals has made the 'local production' issue much more complex than it was in 1980s. Achieving the economies of scale needed for domestic industry has remained an unresolved issue.

ii Access to Medicines as a Human Right

Another significant change that has occurred since the 1986 World Bank Report is that access to new, patented medicines is beginning to be thought of as a human right and, in the context of the AIDS pandemic, has gained global support. In 1998, the UN Sub-Commission on the Promotion and Protection of Human Rights[105] adopted a series of resolutions entitled 'Intellectual Property Rights and Human Rights'. These resolutions pinpointed places where international human rights norms might be in conflict with the TRIPS Agreement, although it was unclear whether these were questions of law or fact, and if these concerned ongoing problems or anticipated future problems. Access to medicines, IPRs and other issues which were vaguely related, or even unrelated, were put into various resolutions. For example:

---

[104] P Cuatrecasas, 'Drug discovery in jeopardy' (2006) 116(11) *Journal of Clinical Investigation* 2837–42.

[105] The Sub-Commission is the main subsidiary body of the Commission on Human Rights and was established by the Commission in 1947 as the UN Sub-Commission on Prevention of Discrimination and Protection of Minorities, until its title was changed in 1999 to the Promotion and Protection of Human Rights. Its main functions are: (a) to undertake studies concerning the prevention of discrimination of any kind relating to human rights and fundamental freedoms and the protection of racial, national, religious and linguistic minorities; (b) to perform any other functions which may be entrusted to it by the Economic and Social Council or the Commission. www.unhchr.ch/html/menu2/2/sc.htm.

- Resolution 1998/8 of 20 August 1998 reminded all governments of the primacy of human rights obligations over economic policies and agreements (para 3); requested the Special Rapporteur on globalisation and its impact on the full enjoyment of human rights to include consideration of the human rights impact of the implementation of the TRIPS Agreement in their next report (para 8).
- Resolution 2000/7 of 9 November 1998 declared that since the implementation of the TRIPS Agreement did not adequately reflect the fundamental nature and indivisibility of all human rights, including the right of everyone to enjoy the benefits of scientific progress and its applications, the right to health, the right to food and the right to self-determination, there were apparent conflicts between the intellectual property rights regime embodied in the TRIPS Agreement, on the one hand, and international human rights law, on the other (para 2).
- Resolution 2001/21 again urged governments to fully take into account existing state obligations under international human rights instruments in the formulation of proposals for the ongoing review of the TRIPS Agreement, in particular in the context of the Ministerial Conference of the World Trade Organization to be held in Doha in November 2001 (para 6).[106]

iii Patents, Essential Medicines and the TRIPS Agreement

In 1998, the Health Minister of Zimbabwe encouraged the participation of civil society groups when the WHO List of Essential Medicines was revised. These citizens groups alerted the governments of developing countries to the fact that AIDS drugs under patent protection were also included in the WHO's List of Essential Medicines. In the 1992 list of some 300 medicines, about 10 were still under effective patent protection in developed countries.[107] Incidentally, on the list adopted in March 2005, 16 out of 311 drugs listed as essential, including 13 ARVs and Coartem (artemisinin-based malaria drug), were probably under patent protection in developed countries. Of these, six (the antibiotic azithromycin (Zithromax), Coartem and ARVs (AZT (off-patent today), abacavir, lamivudine, nelfinavir and nevirapine) were patented in many developing countries, but nine others were patented in only a few developing countries. The Essential List dated March 2007 included 10 ARVs and their combinations which are still

---

[106] Decision of the Commission on Human Rights in its Resolution 2001/30 of 20 April 2001 to encourage the High Commissioner for Human Rights to strengthen the research and analytical capacities of her Office in the field of economic, social and cultural rights and to share her expertise states that: 'Reiterating that actual or potential conflict exists between the implementation of the TRIPS Agreement and the realization of economic, social and cultural rights, in particular the rights to self-determination, food, housing, work, health and education, and in relation to transfers of technology to developing countries.'

[107] 1. albendazole, 2. cytarabine, 3. ivermectin, 4. ketoconazole, 5. iperacillin, 6. captopril, 7. ciprofloxacin, 8. mefloquine, 9. eflornithine, 10. vecuronium bromide. Of these, 9. and 10. are for emergency purposes, 6., 7. and 8. are designated as essential but only when 1.–5. cannot be obtained. http://mednet3.who.int/EMLib/DiseaseTreatments/Medicines.aspx

under patent protection in developed countries.[108] However, the large majority of the WHO essential medicines are off-patent.

The main underlying assumption seems to be that most medicines are under patent protection, and that the existence of patents inevitably leads to higher prices of medicines, as expressed in the Doha Declaration on the TRIPS Agreement and Public Health.[109]

As a result of the cooperation between civil society groups and developing country governments over essential medicines, the WHO Secretariat drafted a Revised Drug Strategy which expanded the scope of exceptions in Article 30 of the TRIPS Agreement concerning 'exceptions to rights conferred' to medicines, and promoted the active use of compulsory licenses (Article 31 of the TRIPS Agreement).[110] For civil society groups actively engaged in the access to medicines campaign, patents are preventing access to medicines and, therefore, the rules in the TRIPS Agreement concerning patent protection should be re-examined.

In 1999, the WHO Health Assembly adopted a resolution called the 'WHO Medicines Strategy' (WHA54.11) in which compulsory licensing was determined to be the most important means by which to ensure health policies in developing countries. When this resolution was adopted, CPTech identified US compulsory licensing cases (many of which are premerger examination cases of the Federal Trade Commission (FTC)) and emphasised the contradictory position of the US in trying to prevent other countries from doing the same as it does. Health Groups referred to this WHO assembly as the 'referendum to support compulsory licenses'.[111]

Later, in a series of discussions on access to medicines at the TRIPS Council of the WTO, many developing countries drew WTO Members' attention to the aforementioned resolution on the WHO Medicines Strategy.[112] These countries suggested that 'the impact of international trade agreements [notably the TRIPS Agreement] on access to, or local manufacturing of, essential drugs and on the development of new drugs needs to be further evaluated'. In addition, they advocated that the WTO should be 'part of various UN agencies' cooperation in strengthening pharmaceutical policies and practices, including those applicable

[108] The following ARVs are still under patent protection in major developed countries: abacavir, didanosine (generic in the US), emtricitabine, lamivudine, stavudine (generic in the US), tenofovir disoproxil fumarate, zidovudine (generic in the US), efavirenz, nevirapine, indinavir, lopinavir + ritonavir, nelfinavir, ritonavir, saquinavir, efavirenz + emtricitabine + tenofovir, emtricitabine* + tenofovir, stavudine + lamivudine + nevirapine (not manufactured in the US), zidovudine + lamivudine, zidovudine + lamivudine + nevirapine (not manufactured in the US).

[109] Doha Declaration on the TRIPS Agreement and Public Health para 3: 'We also recognise the concerns about its effects on prices.' See ch 9.

[110] Revised Drug Strategy WHA52. 19 (24 May 1999). www.who.int/gb/EB_WHA/PDF/WHA52/e19.pdf.

[111] SK Sell, *Private Power, Public Law: The Globalization of Intellectual Property Rights* (Cambridge Studies in International Relations, 2003) 149.

[112] Notably African Group, Barbados, Bolivia, Brazil, Cuba, Dominican Republic, Ecuador, Honduras, India, Indonesia, Jamaica, Pakistan, Paraguay, Philippines, Peru, Sri Lanka, Thailand, Venezuela. See submission by these countries (29 June 2001) IP/C/W/296 paras 10–11.

to generic drugs and intellectual property regimes in order further to promote innovation and the development of domestic industries'.[113] There is a persistent criticism in developing countries that originator pharmaceutical companies' huge and increasing R&D expenditures are leading to higher prices for medicines. Concerns about possible future increase in prices were discussed generally as though the impact of patents on prices was immediate and direct. Patents, by definition, allow the right holder or his/her licensee to raise prices. However, the question of whether or when this occurs, to which product, and to what extent, depends on other factors in a specific market situation. Actual generic prices are difficult to ascertain in any country, because published prices ignore discounts negotiated between suppliers and purchasers.

Nor have the social, political or administrative factors causing the lack of access to medicines been analysed. As a consequence, few data are available on the conditions of access in these markets. Often, there are few medicines, whether brand names or generics, or doctors in developing country markets – this is often the fundamental problem. In the years leading up to the WTO Ministerial Conference in Doha, the view that the TRIPS Agreement was preventing access to medicines in developing countries rapidly prevailed.

iv   Access to Medicines: Proposals at the WTO

With these objectives in view, amendments to TRIPS provisions, mostly relating to the scope of patentable inventions (Article 27.3(b)) or general exceptions (Article 30), were proposed by certain developing countries and discussed at the TRIPS Council. In 1999, for example, in a paper prepared for the WTO Ministerial Conference planned in Seattle, Venezuela proposed that a clause should be added to Article 27.3(b) that 'essential medicines' should not be patentable.[114] A similar proposal concerning Article 27.3(b) was made by Cuba, Dominican Republic, Egypt, El Salvador, Honduras, India, Indonesia, Malaysia, Nigeria, Pakistan, Sri Lanka and Uganda to exclude from patentability the list of essential drugs of the WHO.[115]

In early 2001, Zimbabwe's ambassador to the WTO proposed that a special TRIPS Council meeting be held to discuss the TRIPS Agreement and access to medicines. This was held in June 2001 where, in preparation for the WTO Ministerial Conference in Doha in November 2001, African Group, Cuba, India and some Latin American countries proposed[116] the ideas that are later delineated in the Doha Declaration on the TRIPS Agreement and Public Health

---

[113]   ibid para 11.

[114]   Preparations for the 1999 Ministerial Conference (Seatle), Proposals Regarding the TRIPS Agreement (para 9(a)(ii) of the Geneva Ministerial Declaration), Communication from Venezuela (6 August 1999) WT/GC/W/282 para II-3.

[115]   'Implementation Issues to be Addressed Before/At Seattle', Communication from Cuba, Dominican Republic, Egypt, El Salvador, Honduras, India, Indonesia, Malaysia, Nigeria, Pakistan, Sri Lanka and UgandaWT/GC/W/354 (11 October 1999) para 27.

[116]   Submission Ip/C/W/296 (n 112).

(chapter 9). This paper affirmed that the TRIPS Agreement does not undermine the legitimate right of WTO Members to formulate and implement measures to protect public health, and made the following recommendations:

- TRIPS provisions should be interpreted in light of the objectives and principles set forth in Articles 7 and 8;
- compulsory licences and parallel imports are essential tools for governments to carry out public health policies;[117]
- the argument advanced by research-based pharmaceutical companies that parallel trade would destroy the means to implement 'differential pricing' should be refuted.[118]

Cuba submitted a paper[119] emphasising that compulsory licensing should be used not only in emergency situations, but also to ensure that countries are not dependent solely on imports of medicines[120] and that 'Ongoing research into new medicines for both longstanding and new diseases must not be the cause of, or effectively result in, the sidelining of the most sacred of all human rights, the right to life, because the considerable expense involved, constantly mentioned but never proven, has to produce returns.'[121]

In August and September 2001,[122] the TRIPS Council held additional sessions for discussions on access to medicines. On 19 September 2001, a draft Declaration was presented for the circulation in the General Council by Zimbabwe on behalf of a group of developing countries. In addition to the ideas delineated in the previous paper submitted in June 2001 from a group of developing countries, this draft included the proposal that 'Under Article 30 of the TRIPS Agreement, Members may, among others, authorize the production and export of medicines by persons other than holders of patents on those medicines to address public health needs in importing Members.'[123] A group of developed countries proposed their preambular text, entitled 'Access to medicines for hiv/aids and other pandemics', which emphasised the importance of public drug procurement, distribution, education

---

[117] The paper cited in fn 1 of para 29 that: 'In the United States under anti-trust laws, from August 1941 to January 1959 there were 107 judgments (13 in litigated cases and 94 by consent) in which patent rights were restricted. The use of compulsory licences continued after that date: "literally tens of thousands of patents have been compulsorily licensed in the United States (Scherer, 1998, p.106), in more than a hundred cases. In one single case (*US Manufacturers Aircraft Associations Inc.*), about 1,500 patents were compulsorily licensed (Finnegan 1997, p. 139; Goldestein, 1977, p. 123)" – in *Intellectual Property Rights and the Use of Compulsory Licenses: Options for Developing Countries*, by Carlos Correa (Geneva: South Center, October 1999).'

[118] Submission IP/C/W/296 (n 112) para 37.

[119] Communication from Cuba (5 July 2001) IP/C/W/299.

[120] ibid. para 5.

[121] Communication from Cuba (n 119) para 13.

[122] www.wto.org/english/news_e/news01_e/trips_drugs_010919_e.htm.

[123] Draft Ministerial Declaration, Proposal by the African Group, Bangladesh, Barbados, Bolivia, Brazil, Cuba, Dominican Republic, Ecuador, Haiti, Honduras, India, Indonesia, Jamaica, Pakistan, Paraguay, Philippines, Peru, Sri Lanka, Thailand and Venezuela (4 October 2001) IP/C/W/312,WT/GC/W/450.

and technical assistance.[124] Hong Kong China also circulated an informal draft on 21 September dealing with compulsory licensing of foreign production, to overcome the problem of countries without domestic capacity.[125]

The WTO Members understood the seriousness of the failures of the Ministerial Conference in Seattle and widely incorporated the proposals of the developing countries. This contributed to the successful opening of a new round of trade negotiations, which began at the Ministerial Conference in Doha in November 2001.

Celso Amorim, Brazil's Minister of External Relations, who was one of the leaders promoting the adoption of the Doha Declaration, later affirmed that:

> Our intention in adopting the Doha Declaration was to open up a space where patients of developing countries can breathe under the cluster of patent protection from which they suffer. Such a space was realised by TRIPS flexibilities, on the basis of which the rights conferred to the right-holders can be restricted notably by interpreting Articles 7 and 8 as the objective of the TRIPS Agreement.[126]

The adoption of the Doha Declaration on the TRIPS Agreement and Public Health was indeed a significant turn in the ways in which the public viewed the balance of interests within the TRIPS Agreement.

v International Aid Efforts, Finally

Developed country governments and multinational pharmaceutical companies were slow to understand the situations of HIV/AIDS in developing countries, as we have seen above. Concrete international measures to remedy the financial difficulties in developing countries in improving access to AIDS medicines were finally taking shape when the arguments of developing countries had already been formed around patents and the TRIPS Agreement.

While concerns were expressed by various international organisations, the idea of establishing an international fund to fight AIDS was initially developed by G8 leaders at their 2000 meeting in Okinawa, then at the African Summit on HIV/AIDS, Tuberculosis and other related infectious diseases (Abuja, Nigeria, 26 – 27 April), and at the UN General Assembly Special Session on AIDS in June 2001, where a commitment to create such a fund was made. In 2001 the Global Fund to Fight AIDS, Tuberculosis and Malaria was established. The Global Fund Secretariat is based in Geneva and manages the grant portfolio by screening submitted proposals, disbursing money to grant recipients and implementing grant funding.[127] For each country, the Country Coordinating Mechanism (CCM) is set up by key stakeholders and submits proposals to the Global Fund.

---

[124] 'Preambular language for ministerial declaration' IP/C/W/313. (4 October 2001) Contribution from Australia, Canada, Japan, Switzerland and the United States.
[125] www.wto.org/english/news_e/news01_e/trips_drugs_010919e.htm.
[126] Interview, WHO/CIPIH Meeting in Brasilia, 1 February 2005.
[127] www.theglobalfund.org/en/structures/?lang=en.

The Global Fund Board is composed of representatives from donor and recipient governments, civil society, the private sector, private foundations, and communities living with and affected by the diseases. The Board's main task is to establish strategies and policies, make funding decisions and set budgets.[128]

The US has played a prominent role in bilateral aid on HIV/AIDS issues. The US Congress together with USAID, the Centres for Disease Control and Prevention (CDC) and the US National Institutes of Health (NIH) approved a PEPFAR commitment, announced in January 2003, of US$15 billion.[129] The Clinton Foundation also joined in working towards obtaining generic drugs to be used against AIDS, tuberculosis, and malaria.[130]

There could be various other factors besides patents, such as transfer prices, taxes, middlemen's exploitation and high distribution costs that play a role in determining the price of drugs and that contribute to the high prices of new drugs. The degree of influence of these factors depends on the market situation and the particular regulations in a given country. For example, distribution costs and consumption taxes within developing countries tend to be high, while tariffs on pharmaceutical products in many African countries are around 20 per cent and sometimes even reach 30 per cent. Multinational companies' pricing policy is another decisive factor, and could also assist in the access to medicines.

In May 2001, before Indian generic drugs entered the market, six major producers of AIDS drugs dramatically lowered the prices of AIDS treatments sold in Africa to levels of around one-fifth of the retail price in the US and Europe (Accelerating Access Initiative, AAI).[131] In around 2000, ACT-UP, an AIDS patients' group, demanded that the price of AIDS medicines be lowered in the US as well. The current prices of generic AIDS drugs are occasionally higher than those of name brands, particularly in low-income countries in Africa.

IV INTRICATE RELATIONS BETWEEN DRUG REGULATIONS
AND IPR LAWS

A. Definitions of 'Generic' Drugs

A note of caution is necessary concerning the definition of 'generic' medicines. Whether a medicine is generic or not depends on both IPR protection and national regulatory rules for marketing approval. However, national laws do not necessarily use the term 'generic' (see Chapters 4, 5, 10, 11 and 13). Generic drugs are typically approved by regulatory authorities, if the therapeutic equivalence to the original

---

[128] Requests related to AIDS drugs comprise over 65% of all applications for the Global Fund funding.

[129] www.pepfar.gov/about/index.htm.

[130] www.clintonfoundation.org/what-we-do/clinton-hiv-aids-initiative/.

[131] The Accelerating Access Initiative is supported by UNAIDS, the WHO, UNICEF, the UN Population Fund (UNFPA), and the World Bank. By September 2006, 738,000 AIDS patients were receiving triple-drug therapy through this programme.

product is proven and the safety and quality of the generic drug have been verified through the abbreviated procedure. This compares to a lengthy and onerous approval procedure for new drugs.

Generic medicines, as approved for marketing by national pharmaceutical regulatory authorities, are considered to meet the national standards for safety, efficacy and quality. However, these standards and their implementation vary across countries.

Among the countries whose regulatory standards conform to internationally-agreed industry standards such as the ICH standards,[132] drug quality standards are more or less harmonised. For the approval of generic medicines among ICH countries, therapeutic equivalence is verified through clinical trials conducted on a small number (10 to 20) of healthy adult volunteers, testing whether the absorption and metabolism levels (in vivo bioavailability BA) are equivalent to those found in the original products. If the absorption and metabolism pattern of the active ingredient in the blood that is tested is proven to be equivalent to the original product, this verifies the equivalence of the drug's potency (bioequivalence BE).[133] In many other countries only the proof of BA and BE (often substituted by simple dissolution data) is required, and for some countries, BE is not necessary. In certain Latin American countries, pharmaceutical products whose biological equivalence is not tested are called similares (similar drugs)[134] and are differentiated from generics, but are allowed under pharmaceutical laws. There are also countries with no clear rules for generic approval.[135] Some countries rely on the marketing approval of foreign countries. Recently, the WHO has been using the expression 'multisource drugs' to denote various kinds of 'generic' medicines from the regulatory perspective. Therefore, generics for one country may not be generics for another country, depending on the IPR protection and pharmaceutical regulatory standards.

National legislation differs as to whether and how drug regulatory authorities take into account the situation of IPR protection (ie clinical test data protection and patents) when they examine the request for drug marketing approval. In the US and Canada, all the patents relating to the originator products are registered

---

[132] Members of the International Conference on Harmonisation of Technical Requirements for Registration of Pharmaceuticals for Human Use (ICH) are six parties that represent the regulatory bodies and research-based industry associations in the European Union, Japan and the USA. Additional ICH members include observers such as the WHO and Canada, and other non-voting members.

[133] For example, USC 21 § 320.1 defines bioequivalence as 'the absence of a significant difference in the rate and extent to which the active ingredient or active moiety in pharmaceutical equivalents or pharmaceutical alternatives becomes available at the site of drug action when administered at the same molar dose under similar conditions in an appropriately designed study'. On bioavailability and bioequivalence, see, for example, the US Food and Drug Administration (FDA) Guidance for Industry (US Department of Health and Human Services, Food and Drug Administration, Center for Drug Evaluation and Research (CDER), March 2003) www.fda.gov/downloads/Drugs/GuidanceComplianceRegulatoryInformation/Guidances/ucm070124.pdf

[134] N Homedes1 and A Ugalde, 'Multisource drug policies in Latin America: survey of 10 countries' (2005) 83 (1) Bulletin of the World Health Organization 64-71.

[135] PAHO-BE Workgroup on Bioequivalence, Mexico City, 4–5 August 2003. http://new.paho.org/hq/index2.php?option=com_docman&task=doc_view&gid=312&Itemid=646.

and made public. Regulators take into account the patent status of the product when approving marketing of generics. The EU medicinal authorities do not look into the patent status of the drug for marketing approval. In Japan and China, regulators take into account the patent status for generic approval (see chapters 11, 12 and 13).

The WHO's work on medicinal standards is based on its resolutions, adopted in 1971 (EB47.R29) and in 1984 (WHA37.23) referring to the organisation's role in the establishment of internationally acceptable basic requirements for drug registration. A collection of materials relating to national drug regulations, product assessment and registration, called *Marketing Authorization of Pharmaceutical Products with Special Reference to Multisource (Generic) Products*, was compiled and published in 1999 and has since been renewed.[136] The *Manual for a Drug Regulatory Authority* contains general provisions and prerequisites for regulatory control and operating activities, guiding principles for small drug regulatory authorities and principles of review of applications for marketing authorisation of generic medicines, including guidelines for stability testing and establishing interchangeability (bioequivalence guidelines).

The esoteric and technical worlds of IPR and regulatory sciences are rarely considered by the public or by each other, but they rapidly became subjects of public debate in the discussions over access to medicines.

B. International Organisations and Definition of Generics

The WTO explains the term 'generic' based solely on trademarks and patents, without referring to pharmaceutical regulatory aspects.[137] According to the WTO website explanation: 'dictionaries tend to define a "generic" as a product – particularly a drug – that does not have a trademark'; generics are 'copies of patent drugs' which are made by other manufactures, 'either sold under the name of the chemical ingredient (making them clearly generic), or under another brand name (which means they are still generics from the point of view of patents)'. In April 2001, the WTO website added the following passage to specify that those products manufactured in a country without pharmaceutical patent protection or under compulsory licence or in parallel trade are also 'generics':

> the product could be generic because the patent has expired, or there never was a patent. Or it could be because the drug is being copied outside patent protection, for example in a country that still does not provide patent protection for pharmaceuticals . . . if a pharmaceutical is patented in a country and is illegally copied (infringing patent protection) in that country, it is not 'generic', particularly if it is also illegally

---

[136] WHO/DMP/RGS/98.5, WHO, 1999. *Quality Assurance of Pharmaceuticals*, Volume 1, 1977, included the *International Pharmacopoeia* and related activities, international trade in pharmaceuticals and their distribution, quality control laboratories, counterfeit products, and basic tests for pharmaceutical products.

[137] www.wto.org/English/tratop_e/trips_e/factsheet_pharm03_e.htm.

marketed under a registered trademark. Similarly, 'parallel imports' . . . are also not generics.

This explanatory wording was revised again in 2006 to distinguish generics from 'illegal' drugs from the point of view of IPRs:

> Whether a drug is generic is one question. Whether it infringes intellectual property rights and is pirated or counterfeit is a separate question. Generic copies are legal from the patent point of view when they are made after the patent has expired or under voluntary or compulsory licence – but pirated and counterfeit products are by definition illegal.[138]

The WHO website defines a generic drug as 'a pharmaceutical product usually intended to be interchangeable with an innovator product – that is, manufactured without a licence from the innovator company and marketed after the expiration date of the patent or other exclusive rights'. This website explains generics particularly from a pricing point of view and concludes that:

> generic drugs are frequently as effective as, but much cheaper than, brand-name drugs. . . . Because of their low price, generic drugs are often the only medicines that the poorest can access. The TRIPS Agreement does not prevent governments from requiring accurate labelling or allowing generic substitution. Indeed, it is argued that competition between drug companies and generic producers has been more effective than negotiations with drug companies in reducing the cost of drugs, in particular those used to treat HIV/AIDS.[139]

On the question of patents and pricing in developing countries, little data has been available for a long time and this remains the position today. However, a few studies have been undertaken on ARV pricing for international procurement using the Price Reporting Mechanism (PRM) database of the Global Fund Price Reporting Mechanism,[140] which highlighted a subtle gap between commonly held opinions and facts.

Kubo and Yamane used different methods of regression analysis on the Global Fund transaction prices of ARVs in 2007 and 2009.[141] The main findings of the 2007 study were the following.

---

[138] This book takes a similar approach to the WTO's and calls all copy drugs 'generic', regardless of the characteristics from the regulatory perspective, ie, bioequivalent or not, or GMP status, for example.

[139] www.who.int/trade/glossary/story034/en/index.html.

[140] Chien, Colleen. 2007. "HIV/AIDS Drugs for Sub-Saharan Africa: How do brand and generic supply compare?" PLoS ONE, issue 3, e278.

[141] K Kubo and H Yamane, 'Determinants of antiretroviral drug prices: An analysis of Global Price Reporting Mechanism (GPRM) data', Institute of Development Studies, www.ide.go.jp/English/Publish/Download/Jrp/pdf/jrp_142_05.pdf; http://web.theglobalfund.org/prm/. A total of 4,053 transactions that took place between June 2003 and December 2006, of which 2,638 were ARVs with complete information on Incoterms, were analysed. This represents approximately 40% of the developing country ARV market. Patent information on each drug analysed was found in Médecins Sans Frontières, *Drug patents under the spotlight: Sharing practical knowledge about pharmaceutical patents* (2003).

1. Branded drugs supplied by originator pharmaceutical firms tend to be priced higher than their generic counterparts in middle-income countries, but this premium disappears in the lowest-income countries. This, however, does not necessarily mean that patents are the cause of lower prices. It is possible that these prices are due to endogenous factors, such as policy or political elements, and not to patents.
2. Originator firms tend to offer lower prices in developing countries with a high prevalence of HIV infection.
3. Meeting quality standards does not cause the increase of prices; in fact the price of ARV drugs that have been pre-qualified by the WHO is lower.[142]
4. Firms tend to charge higher prices when supplying their home country market. It is possible that local firms may be awarded contracts even if they are not the most competitive bidder. In those countries where state-run monopoly companies exist, prices also tend to be higher.

Improving on this regression analysis, the same authors compared pricing behaviours of generic and research-based pharmaceutical companies. The 2009 analysis[143] confirmed earlier findings and added new ones. For example, the winning bidder is more likely to be an originator firm in countries with higher per capita GDP and a larger patient population, because they are selective about which tenders to enter (ie, there is a tendency to refrain from entering certain low-income countries having local pharmaceutical manufacturing capabilities); there is a tendency for originator companies to offer lower prices in countries with low per capita GDP, but such behaviour is not found among generic firms.

The findings of these two studies may suggest, first of all, that governments of low-income developing countries have much to gain by negotiating directly with originator companies to obtain acceptable prices. Secondly, local production (particularly by state monopoly companies) may not always be the most efficient means of ensuring access to these medicines, in terms either of price or quality. Finally, donor countries are advised to increase the size of recipient groups in such a way that a large number of patients can be covered by one procurement programme. For instance, grouping together several recipient countries may make it easier to obtain quantity discounts from manufacturers.

Later, in July 2010, at the WHO-WIPO-WTO Joint Technical Symposium on Access to Medicines: Pricing and Procurement Practices, a presentation

---

[142] Before April 2005, the Global Fund rules did not require the approval of the WHO prequalification or regulatory authorities requiring more stringent drug standards of such bodies as the US FDA and, therefore, ARVs procured by the Fund before this date included some that did not meet the WHO prequalification standards.

[143] 'Determinants of HIV/AIDS Drug Prices for Developing Countries: Analysis of Global Fund Procurement Data' in H Uchimura (ed) *Making Health Services More Accessible in Developing Countries: Finance and Health Resources for Functioning Health Systems* (Basingstoke, Palgrave Macmillan 2009) 137–72.

was made by Laing showing that some findings refute conventional wisdom on generic and brand ARV prices.[144]

With regard to other medicines, there is little empirically tested data on the existence of IPR, pricing and general accessibility conditions.

C. Confusion about Generics and Sub-Standard Medicines

When access problems are discussed only as an IPR issue, drug safety, efficacy and quality issues tend to be overlooked, whereas in reality, they constitute an important part of healthcare and economic considerations. Drawing attention to the public health and economic problems of spurious drugs, the Report of the WHO Commission on Intellectual Property, Innovation and Public Health (CIPIH) noted in 2006 that:

> Quality of medicines is a source of great concern worldwide, particularly in many developing countries. Recent reports indicate that the availability of substandard and counterfeit drugs has reached a disturbing proportion in developing countries. Use of poor-quality drugs has serious health consequences and wastes scarce resources. Other human costs of poor-quality medicines include loss of work and income resulting from death, disability, or extended duration of disease.[145]

According to this Report, 25 per cent of the medicines consumed in poor countries are 'counterfeit' or 'substandard'.[146] A WHO survey of counterfeit medicines, completed in 20 countries between January 1999 and October 2000, found that 60 per cent of spurious medicine cases occurred in poor countries. This means that one quarter of the expenditure on drugs in poor countries is being wasted, a fact which should be taken into account.

The use of the term 'counterfeit' medicines became controversial in recent years, however, when the International Medical Products Anti-Counterfeiting Taskforce (IMPACT) discussed a definition of counterfeit medicines. Created in February 2006 by the WHO,[147] IMPACT is a global coalition of all stakeholders, including NGOs, enforcement agencies, pharmaceutical manufacturers associations and drug and regulatory authorities. It suggested in May 2008 that a medical product is counterfeit when there is 'a false representation in relation to its identity, history or source, its container, packaging or other labelling information'.[148]

India and the Indian Pharmaceutical Alliance (IPA) argue that the reference to 'history' in this definition suggests patent infringement and that this might

---

[144] R Laing, 'Procurement, selection, prequalification, pricing and monitoring of medicines' 16. http://www.wto.org/english/tratop_e/trips_e/techsymp_july10_e/laing_e.pdf.

[145] CIPIH Report, 2006, www.who.int/intellectualproperty/documents/thereport/ENPublicHealth Report.pdf, 105–6.

[146] ibid, 124.

[147] www.who.int/impact/en/index.html.

[148] 'Counterfeit definition worrys Pharmas', *Business Standard* (New Delhi, 21 May 2008).

affect Indian exports because it wrongly leads the public to believe that generics are counterfeits.[149] Therefore, they call for maintaining the original WHO definition of counterfeit medicines[150], ie, those that are 'deliberately and fraudulently mislabelled with respect to identity and/or source' and separating the issue from 'spurious drugs'[151] with wrong ingredients, without active ingredients, or with insufficient ingredients or with fake packaging.

The above precision is important, because the meaning of the word 'counterfeit' differs in the two separate worlds of IPR and regulatory sciences. In the IPR world, the TRIPS Agreement refers only to 'counterfeit trademark goods' and footnote 14 of article 51 states that:

> for the purposes of this Agreement: (a) 'counterfeit trademark goods' shall mean any goods, including packaging, bearing without authorization a trademark which is identical to the trademark validly registered in respect of such goods, or which cannot be distinguished in its essential aspects from such a trademark, and which thereby infringes the rights of the owner of the trademark in question under the law of the country of importation; . . .

This definition of 'counterfeit' is not irrelevant to 'counterfeit medicines' because fake or substandard medicines are 'deliberately and fraudulently mislabelled' (WHO definition). However, fake or substandard medicines should be dealt with from a larger, public health regulatory perspective with various administrative or criminal measures. Effective adherence to good manufacturing practices and supply chain management is an essential starting point for addressing this problem, but measures based on IP rights, and trademark rights, in particular, are also helpful. Medical accidents often result from the similarity of product names even when the distribution network is secure.

---

[149] 'New counterfeit definition a threat to generics, says India', *SCRIP World Pharmaceutical News* (30 May 2008).

[150] According to the WHO definition, counterfeit drugs are 'deliberately and fraudulently mislabelled with respect to identity and/or source. Counterfeiting can apply to both branded and generic products and counterfeit products may include products with the correct ingredients or with the wrong ingredients, without active ingredients, with insufficient active ingredient or with fake packaging'. www.who.int/trade/glossary/story034/en/index.html.

[151] According to ch IV, s 17B of India's Drugs and Cosmetics Act, 1940, the following is a 'spurious drug': (a) if it is manufactured under a name which belongs to another drug; or (b) if it is an intimation of, or is a substitute for, another drug or resembles another drug in a manner likely to deceive or bear upon it or upon its label or container the name of another drug unless it is plainly and conspicuously marked so as to reveal its true character and its lack of identity with such other drug ; or (c) if the label or container bears the name of an individual or company purporting to be the manufacturer of the drug, which individual or company is fictitious or does not exist; or (d) if it has been substituted wholly or in part by another drug or substance; or (e) if it purports to be the product of a manufacturer of whom it is not truly a product.

9

Doha Declaration and Beyond

THE DECLARATION ON the TRIPS Agreement and Public Health,[1] adopted at the WTO Doha Ministerial Conference in 2001, responded to growing concerns about the implications of the TRIPS Agreement for access to medicines. It declares that the TRIPS Agreement does not and should not prevent members from taking measures to protect public health. The Declaration refers to 'flexibilities' that this Agreement provides and ensures that WTO Members may resort to such flexibilities, including compulsory licensing, to cope with public health problems.

This chapter describes the content of the Declaration and different views about the nature and scope of the flexibilities that the Declaration refers to. The relationship between the TRIPS Agreement and the Doha Declaration is also explored. Albeit with extremely limited data, this chapter looks into the circumstances in which certain compulsory licences were issued during the ten years after the adoption of the Declaration. The chapter examines administrative and court IP policies on compulsory licensing in some of the rapidly industrialising, middle-income developing countries, with a view to exploring how public interest could be intermingled with industrial policy considerations.

I THE ADOPTION OF THE DOHA DECLARATION

A Doha Development Agenda (DDA)

At the Fourth Ministerial Conference which took place from 9 to 11 November 2001 in Doha, Qatar, WTO Members agreed to launch the ninth multilateral negotiations to be carried out since 1948, defining its work programme in the Ministerial declaration of 14 November 2001. The main areas of negotiations were agriculture, market access for industrial goods, services, trade facilitation, WTO rules (ie, trade remedies, fish subsidies, and regional trade agreements) and development.[2] The Conference also adopted the Decision on Implementation-Related Issues and Concerns,[3] which identifies ways to resolve the difficulties

---

[1] The Doha Declaration on the TRIPS Agreement and Public Health WT/MIN(01)/DEC/2(20 November 2001).

[2] Ministerial Declaration adopted on 14 November 2001, WT/MIN(01)/DEC/1(20 November 2001).

[3] Ministerial Decision adopted on 14 November 2001, WT/MIN(01)/17(20 November 2001).

and resource constraints faced by developing countries in implementing the current WTO Agreements. Those implementation issues on which no clarification was made were not included in this Decision, but were included among the items to be negotiated,[4] and the approximately 20 remaining issues were to be addressed as a matter of priority by the relevant WTO bodies, to report to the Trade Negotiations Committee (TNC) for discussion on possible inclusion as issues to be negotiated.[5] Those issues which the TNC decided to give a negotiating mandate would become part of the work programme. This entire package was called the Doha Development Agenda (DDA).

Concerning the TRIPS Agreement, the following declarations were made in the Ministerial Declaration:

1. the importance of implementing and interpreting the TRIPS Agreement in a manner supportive of public health, by promoting both access to existing medicines and research and development into new medicines;[6]
2. the establishment of a multilateral system of notification and registration of geographical indications for wines and spirits;[7]
3. the examination as implementation issues of the built-in agenda, ie, the review of Article 27.3(b), the relationship between the TRIPS Agreement and the Convention on Biological Diversity (CBD),[8] the protection of traditional knowledge and folklore, and other relevant new developments raised by Members pursuant to Article 71.1.

In undertaking 3 above, the Decision notes that, 'the TRIPS Council shall be guided by the objectives and principles set out in Articles 7 and 8 of the TRIPS Agreement and shall take fully into account the development dimension'.

B The Doha Declaration: What It Says

The Doha Declaration on the TRIPS Agreement and Public Health (Doha Declaration) was adopted at the WTO Ministerial Conference on 14 November 2001, outside of the Work Programme. The Ministers recognised 'the gravity of the public health problems afflicting many developing and least-developed countries, especially those resulting from HIV/AIDS, tuberculosis, malaria and other epidemics' (paragraph 1) and stressed 'the need for the WTO TRIPS Agreement

---

[4] Ministerial Declaration (n 2) para 12(a).

[5] ibid para 12(b).

[6] Ministerial Declaration (n 2) para 17.

[7] ibid para 18. Issues related to the extension of the protection of geographical indications provided for in Art 23 to products other than wines and spirits were to be addressed as an implementation issue in the sense of para 12 of the Ministerial Declaration. While geographical indications (GI) under Art 22 are protected to avoid the use in a manner which 'misleads the public as to the geographical origin of the goods', protection of GI on wine and spirits is given without this condition under Art 23. The latter therefore is called additional protection.

[8] See chs 6 n 60 and 10.

to be part of the wider national and international action to address these problems' (paragraph 2). It expressed the concern that patents have an impact on prices, while recognising that IP protection is important for the development of new medicines (paragraph 3).

The main message of the Doha Declaration is in the first sentence of paragraph 4. The Ministers agree that 'the TRIPS Agreement does not and should not prevent Members from taking measures to protect public health'. At the same time, the Ministers, 'reiterating [their] commitment to the TRIPS Agreement, affirm that the Agreement can and should be interpreted and implemented in a manner supportive of WTO Members' right to protect public health and, in particular, to promote access to medicines for all' (second sentence of paragraph 4).

The third sentence of paragraph 4 states: 'In this connection, we reaffirm the right of WTO Members to use, to the full, the provisions in the TRIPS Agreement, which provide flexibility for this purpose.' Paragraph 5 reiterates the phrase 'while maintaining our commitments in the TRIPS Agreement', and recognises that the above flexibilities include:

a) in applying the customary rules of interpretation of public international law, each provision of the TRIPS Agreement shall be read in the light of the object and purpose of the Agreement as expressed, in particular, in its objectives and principles;

b) each Member has the right to grant compulsory licences and the freedom to determine the grounds upon which such licences are granted;

c) each Member has the right to determine what constitutes a national emergency or other circumstances of extreme urgency, it being understood that public health crises, including those relating to HIV/AIDS, tuberculosis, malaria and other epidemics, can represent a national emergency or other circumstances of extreme urgency; and,

d) the provisions in the TRIPS Agreement that are relevant to the exhaustion of intellectual property rights leave each Member free to establish its own regime for such exhaustion without challenge, subject to the most-favoured nation and national treatment provisions of Articles 3 and 4.

Paragraph 6 refers to the difficulties that WTO Members may face, even if a compulsory licence is issued, if they have insufficient or no manufacturing capacity in the pharmaceutical sector. The Ministers instructed 'the Council for TRIPS to find an expeditious solution to this problem and to report to the General Council before the end of 2002.'

Paragraph 7 reaffirms the provision concerning the transfer of technology to LDCs under Article 66.2 of the TRIPS Agreement and extends the transition periods for LDCs regarding pharmaceutical products in implementing and applying Sections 5 (patents) and 7 (undisclosed data) of Part II of the TRIPS Agreement until 1 January 2016, renewable upon requests in accordance with Article 66.1.

C Legal Status of the Declaration

All commentators agree that the following decisions taken by the TRIPS Council in pursuance of the Doha Declaration on Public Health are legally binding. The TRIPS Council, by Decision IP/C/25 of 27 June 2002[9], decided that least-developed country Members will not be obliged, with respect to pharmaceutical products, to implement or apply Sections 5 (patents) and 7 of Part II (undisclosed data) of the TRIPS Agreement or to enforce rights provided for under these Sections until 1 January 2016. This decision was taken following the 'instructions' of the Ministerial Conference to the Council for TRIPS contained in paragraph 7 of the Doha Declaration on Public Health which the Council considered as constituting a duly motivated request by the least-developed country Members for an extension of the period under Article 66.1 of the TRIPS Agreement. The TRIPS Council Decision L/540, adopted on 30 August 2003 pursuant to paragraph 6[10] of the Declaration, establishes the mechanisms for compulsory export licensing for countries with insufficient or no capacity to manufacture medicines (on paragraph 6 system, see below p 314).[11]

All commentators consider the Declaration to be an important political and moral declaration with practical implications. Many commentators hold that the Declaration does not change Members' rights and obligations under the TRIPS Agreement, although it has become politically more difficult to exercise these rights.[12] Correa, on the other hand, asserts that the Declaration is a 'Ministerial decision with legal effects on the Members and on the WTO bodies, particularly the Dispute Settlement Body and the Council for TRIPS.' According to Correa, the Declaration implies that 'public health-related patents may be treated differently from other patents'.[13]

The Declaration does not indicate that it is an 'authoritative interpretation', as defined in Article IX.2[14] of the Agreement Establishing the WTO, and its

[9] TRIPS Council Decision IP/C/25 (1 July 2002). A more general extension of transition periods was granted to LDCs by the decision of the TRIPS Council on 29 November 2005 regarding the general implementation of TRIPS obligations (except for Articles 3 and 4 of the Agreement) until 1 July 2013. IP/C/40 (30 November 2005). See chp 5, Table 5.1, for transition periods for LDCs.

[10] 'We instruct the Council for TRIPS to find an expeditious solution to this problem and to report to the General Council before the end of 2002.'

[11] Implementation of para 6 of the Doha Declaration on the TRIPS Agreement and public health WT/L/540 and Corr 1. (1 September 2003).

[12] See for example, J Schott, 'Comment on the Doha Ministerial' (2002) 5(1) *Journal of International Economic Law (JIEL)* 195.

[13] C Correa, 'Implications of the Doha Declaration on the TRIPS Agreement and Public Health', June 2002 http://www.who.int/medicines/areas/policy/WHO_EDM_PAR_2002.3.pdf viii. Abbott treats this Declaration as a decision of Ministers that would 'prove significant in supporting interpretations that promote the protection of public health'. FM Abbott, 'The Doha Declaration on the TRIPS Agreement and Public Health: Lighting a Dark Corner at the WTO' (2002) 5(2) *JIEL* 470.

[14] Art IX of the Agreement Establishing the WTO (WTO Agreement) provides for decision making rules at the WTO. Its para 2 provides that: 'the Ministerial Conference and the General Council shall have the exclusive authority to adopt interpretations of the WTO Agreement and of the Multilateral Trade Agreements.' In the case of an interpretation of a Multilateral Trade Agreement in Annex 1, they shall exercise their authority on the basis of a recommendation by the Council

adoption did not follow the procedures foreseen in the above Article. Its draft was negotiated in the TRIPS Council and was sent to the General Council.[15] Jackson observes that the Doha Declaration gives the impression that it was adopted only by those Ministers who participated in the meeting concerned, and not by the Ministerial Conference.[16] The Declaration was adopted at the Doha Ministerial Conference but the Ministerial Conference did not take the three-quarters majority decision required to adopt an 'authoritative interpretation'. If the Declaration is not an 'authoritative interpretation' that requires a procedure less onerous than those for treaty amendments delineated in Article X of the WTO Agreement, it is, a fortiori, not an amendment of the TRIPS Agreement.

Correa considers this Declaration to have the same effects as an authoritative interpretation, in particular, 'in providing an agreed understanding on certain aspects of the TRIPS Agreement in paragraph 5' and in creating a 'binding precedent for future panels and Appellate Body reports'.[17]

However, even if we consider the Doha Declaration as equivalent to a non-binding authoritative interpretation, the legal effects of authoritative interpretation do not amount to 'subsequent agreements' or 'subsequent practice' within the meaning of Articles 31.3(a) and (b) of the VCLT, according to Ehlermann and Ehring. These authors state that:

> From a formal point of view, it is questionable whether a panel and the Appellate Body could rely on a non-binding authoritative interpretation for more than a mere reference or confirmation of legal findings the Panels have developed independently of such authoritative interpretation.[18]

D Confirmation of TRIPS or New Rules for Interpreting TRIPS?

According to Correa,[19] 'spelling out some of the available flexibility [of the TRIPS Agreement] was the main objective of the Declaration on the TRIPS

overseeing the functioning of that Agreement (the TRIPS Council for the TRIPS Agreement). According to Art IX.2, the decision to adopt an interpretation shall be taken by a three-quarters majority of the Members. Only the Ministerial Conference and the General Council, on the recommendation of the TRIPS Council, can take a decision to adopt an interpretation by a three-quarters majority of the Members. According to Ehlermann and L Ehring, the authoritative interpretation is 'an invention of the Uruguay Round', but 'in the early days of the GATT, the Chairman of the Contracting Parties, often resolved questions of interpretation through rulings that were tacitly or expressly accepted or put to a roll-call vote'. D Ehlermann and L Ehring, 'The Authoritative Interpretation Under Article IX:2 of the Agreement Establishing the World Trade Organization: Current Law, Practice and Possible Improvements' (2005) 8(4) *JIEL* 805.

[15] There seem to have been only minor changes in the text of the draft Declaration. Its title was changed from 'the TRIPS Agreement and Access to Medicines' to 'the TRIPS Agreement and Public Health', and the words 'shall not' in Art 4 were changed to 'does not and should not'.

[16] J Jackson, '*Doha Kakuryou Kaigi no Insho* (Impressions from the 4th WTO Ministerial Conference)' (2002) 35(2) *Keizai Sangyo Janal* (*Journal of Economy and Industry*) (in Japanese) 12.

[17] Correa (n 13) 44.

[18] Ehlermann and Ehring, 'The Authoritative Interpretation Under Article IX:2 of the Agreement Establishing the World Trade Organization' (n 17) 807–08.

[19] Correa (n 13) 13.

Agreement and Public Health'. However, there is no definition of TRIPS flexibility and there seem to have been widely diverging understandings of this concept when the Doha Declaration was adopted as it is today. Among the proposals submitted to the TRIPS Council prior to the adoption of the Doha Declaration, the EU, for the special discussion on IP and access to medicines before the Doha Ministerial, referred to flexibility as follows:

> The EC and their Member States consider that procedural safeguards are important to guarantee legal security. Article 31 nevertheless leaves some flexibility in cases of national emergency and other circumstances of extreme urgency, or when the subject matter of the patent is required for public non-commercial use. Although Article 31 does not itself contain tailor-made solutions to any specific problem raised in the debate on access to health, it does leave WTO Members the freedom to determine the grounds for granting compulsory licences, provided the terms of the Article, and of other provisions of the Agreement, are met, and it allows for swift action in case of emergency or extreme urgency.[20]

The paper submitted on 29 June 2001 by the African Group, Barbados, Bolivia, Brazil, Dominican Republic, Ecuador, Honduras, India, Indonesia, Jamaica, Pakistan, Paraguay, Philippines, Peru, Sri Lanka, Thailand and Venezuela[21] argued that the TRIPS Agreement offers flexibilities first, by its interpretation in light of the objectives and principles set forth in Articles 7 and 8, secondly, by not limiting the grounds for governments to issue compulsory licences, and thirdly, by legitimising parallel imports. The paper also indicated that such remedies for access to medicines as differential pricing should not limit the flexibility of the TRIPS Agreement in any of its provisions such as parallel trade and compulsory licensing.[22]

The developing country paper for Doha emphasised that Article 7 is 'a key provision that defines the objectives of the TRIPS Agreement'[23] and elaborated particularly on the notion of Article 8 as expressing the principles of the TRIPS Agreement:

> In Article 8, the TRIPS Agreement affirms that Members may adopt measures to protect public health, among other overarching public policy objectives, such as nutrition and socio-economic and technological development. Any interpretation of the provisions of the Agreement should take into account the principles set forth in Article 8. The reading of such provision should confirm that nothing in the TRIPS Agreement

---

[20] Communication from the European Communities and their Member states to the TRIPS Council, for the special discussion on intellectual property and access to medicines, June 20, 2001 IP/C/W/280 (12 June 2001).

[21] IP/C/W/296 (20 June 2001) ('developing country paper for Doha'),

[22] ibid para 37. The paper also says that differential pricing (or tiered pricing), not being an IP issue, should not be covered by the TRIPS Agreement but in other international fora, such as the World Health Organization (WHO) (para 35).

[23] Developing country paper for Doha (n 21) para 18. The summary of this paper states that 'Each provision of the TRIPS Agreement should be read in light of the objectives and principles set forth in Articles 7 and 8.'

will prevent Members from adopting measures to protect public health, as well as from pursuing the overarching policies defined in Article 8.[24]

Significantly, the paper ignored the phrase *in fine* of Article 8.1,[25] which says 'provided that such measures are consistent with the provisions of this Agreement' (see chapters 4 and 5).

In elaborating on paragraph 5a) of the Doha Declaration, the EU seems to have mitigated this interpretation which limits the 'object and purpose' of the TRIPS Agreement solely to Articles 7 and 8. Thus the phrase 'in applying the customary rules of interpretation of public international law' was inserted, and the specific reference to Articles 7 and 8 was deleted from the final version of the Declaration, to be replaced by 'its objectives and principles', which are not limited to Articles 7 and 8.[26] Paragraph 5a), therefore, does not seem to propose anything radically different from the method of interpretation based on the customary rules of interpretation taken by the Panel in *Canada–Pharmaceutical Patents*[27]. This Panel interpreted the objectives and principles of the TRIPS Agreement from various relevant TRIPS provisions, such as Articles 1, 27 and 28, together with the Preamble, as offering a context for interpretative purposes, rather than only Articles 7 and 8. From a legal point of view, therefore, paragraph 5a) does not seem to provide a special interpretative rule for pharmaceutical products[28] within the TRIPS Agreement.

Does the Doha Declaration create a special regime for pharmaceutical products, relating to compulsory licensing?[29] Paragraph 5b) says that 'each Member has . . . the freedom to determine the grounds upon which such licences are granted'. In any case, Article 31 does not take the 'grounds' approach, but a 'conditions' approach (see chapter 4) and, therefore, the TRIPS Agreement allows Members to determine the grounds for compulsory licensing. Such grounds may be limited by the conditions delineated in Article 31 and other provisions of the TRIPS Agreement.

Members may differ in their understanding of what constitutes 'grounds' and what are 'conditions'. The EC, in one of its Trade Barriers Regulation (TBR)

---

[24]   ibid para 22.

[25]   Art 8.1 of the TRIPS Agreement reads: 'Members may, in formulating or amending their laws and regulations, adopt measures necessary to protect public health and nutrition, and to promote the public interest in sectors of vital importance to their socio-economic and technological development, provided that such measures are consistent with the provisions of this Agreement.'

[26]   Interviews with JC van Eeckhaute, European Commission, DG Trade, 20 June 2002 and 7 September 2003. Also by the same author, 'The debate on the TRIPS Agreement and access to medicines in the WTO: Doha and beyond' (2002) 5 *Pharmaceuticals Policy and Law* 11–24.

[27]   *Canada–Patent Protection of Pharmaceutical Products (Canada–Pharmaceutical Patents)*, Panel Report (adopted 7 April 2000) WT/DS114/R (see ch 7).

[28]   The scope of the Doha Declaration seems to be 'Sections 5 and 7 of Part II of the TRIPS Agreement with regard to pharmaceutical products', as indicated by para 7 of the Declaration, although this leaves room for interpretation.

[29]   The word 'compulsory licence' is used in the Doha Declaration, whereas the title of Art 31 is 'other use without authorisation of the right holder'.

Reports in 2008[30] asserted that the stipulation of 'reasonable commercial terms' in Article 76 of the Taiwan Patent Act[31] is no more than a procedural requirement, and treating it as a substantive ground for issuing compulsory licences (ie, on the grounds of 'high prices') runs counter to Article 31, read in conjunction with Article 28. Likewise, a mere 'refusal to deal' cannot be a sufficiently substantive basis for the grant of a compulsory licence, if there are no associated competition law violations. According to the EC, if a mere refusal to deal without anti-competitive behaviour, could be grounds for compulsory licensing, the exclusive rights granted to right holders pursuant to Article 28 of TRIPS would be voided of a large part of their substantive value, since their exclusive nature could be brought to an end simply by a failure to deal, thus rendering Article 31(k) redundant. Furthermore, national competition law jurisprudence shows that the 'refusal to deal' of a patent owner is a permissible activity that might only be considered illegal when the patent owner is in a position of market power and the refusal is linked to abuse of that market power.[32]

Whatever the EC interpretations concerning specific provisions of Articles 31 and 28, the Doha Declaration 'reiterates' the commitment of WTO Members under the TRIPS Agreement (paragraph 4, Doha Declaration). The text of the TRIPS Agreement is not changed by the Doha Declaration (except for the above-mentioned decisions adopted by the TRIPS Council) but there are radically divergent opinions as to whether the Declaration has changed the rules of TRIPS interpretation, as we have observed. Reading and interpreting the Doha Declaration independently of TRIPS provisions or without applying the international customary rules of treaty interpretation would amount to adding a layer of 'super-flexibility' to the flexibilities already included in the TRIPS provisions.

Treaty provisions granting a margin of discretion to the parties may be characterised as having 'flexibilities'. Undefined concepts of 'flexibilities' without any rules for interpreting their scope could offer an additional margin of discretion by showing that the TRIPS Agreement can legitimately be interpreted and implemented by national laws to alleviate TRIPS obligations without violating the Agreement. This is supported by the commonly held notion that this would *ipso facto* solve socio-economic problems allegedly created by IPRs.

On the question of compulsory licensing, the Doha Declaration, examined in conjunction with TRIPS Agreement provisions, does not seem to go beyond the textual flexibilities provided in the TRIPS Agreement, ie, a certain scope of national discretion; rather, it supports those provisions. Under the TRIPS Agreement, Members are free to choose the grounds on which to issue

---

[30] Chinese Taipei TBR Investigation Report, *Compulsory licensing of CD-R patents* (January 30, 2008) (hereafter 'China Taipei TBR Report'), http://trade.ec.europa.eu/doclib/docs/2008/january/tradoc_137633.pdf.

[31] Art 76 of the Taiwan Patent Act stipulates that: 'in the case of an applicant's failure to reach a licensing agreement with the patentee concerned under reasonable commercial terms and conditions within a considerable period of time, the Patent Authority may, upon an application, grant a right of compulsory licensing to the applicant to put the patented invention into practice'.

[32] China Taipei TBR Report (n 30) 37. On 'market power', see ch 1.

compulsory licences, provided that they followed the procedural requirements (chapters 4 and 5). The Declaration supported the legitimacy of compulsory licensing, provided that the provisions of the TRIPS Agreement are respected. The radical effects of the Declaration seem to be mainly political and moral. Developing country Members had been uncertain about the reactions of others to compulsory licences. Today, it would be more constraining for Members to bring dispute cases to the WTO regarding the ways these licences are issued relating to pharmaceuticals in light of the relevant TRIPS provisions.

On the other hand, the wording of the Doha Declaration concerning exhaustion differs slightly from the TRIPS provision on the same subject. Paragraph 5 d) of the Declaration states that:

> The effect of the provisions in the TRIPS Agreement that are relevant to the exhaustion of intellectual property rights is to leave each member free to establish its own regime for such exhaustion without challenge, subject to the MFN and national treatment provisions of Articles 3 and 4.

Article 6 of the TRIPS Agreement, by contrast, provides that:

> For the purposes of dispute settlement under this Agreement, subject to the provisions of Articles 3 and 4 nothing in this Agreement shall be used to address the issue of the exhaustion of intellectual property rights.

According to the latter provision, a Member is not 'free to establish its own regime for such exhaustion without challenge' and the exhaustion policy of a Member could be inconsistent with Article 28 TRIPS. Although this could not be dealt with by the WTO dispute settlement procedures, questions concerning the exhaustion policy could be brought to bilateral dispute procedures.

So, how would the WTO Panel interpret the Doha Declaration when dealing with TRIPS pharmaceutical cases?

Footnote 1 of Article IX of the Agreement Establishing the WTO states that 'The body concerned shall be deemed to have decided by consensus on a matter submitted for its consideration, if no Member, present at the meeting when the decision is taken, formally objects to the proposed decision.' The Doha Declaration could therefore be considered to have been adopted at the Ministerial Conference by consensus. The dispute organs, in practice, would have to take this into account one way or another, if the parties to a dispute invoke the Declaration. Parties that do not recognise the relevance of the Declaration to the case in dispute would have difficulties in the Declaration not being interpreted by the Panel, although the disputing party could refute the public health nature of the case, in order to place the case outside the scope of the Declaration.

The Declaration would guide the dispute settlement organs' interpretation of relevant TRIPS provisions, and the socio-economic context of the case in question may also be looked into. This will probably occur after an analysis of relevant TRIPS provisions in accordance with the rules of customary law. The Panels and Appellate Body have interpreted flexibilities in the text of the TRIPS provisions which prima facie would permit a scope of national discretion, which may not coincide with the readings of the TRIPS provisions based on the VCLT rules of treaty interpretation.

The above exploration leads us to the following conclusion. Rather than determining its formalistic status and insisting on its effects on the TRIPS Agreement with a view to establishing a doctrine or a theory of reduced TRIPS obligations (or increased national discretion), simply accepting the moral appeal of the Doha Declaration may offer more possibilities for realistic cooperation to promote access to medicines. As we will see below, public health policies involve all kinds of private interests and industrial policies. It is therefore better to consider this Declaration not as a legally prescriptive requirement but as a moral standard and a political commitment, so access to medicines can be achieved widely and effectively in different situations.

E Implementing Paragraph 6 of the Doha Declaration

i Rising expectations

After the adoption of the Doha Declaration, training seminars and consultations on its implementation followed. Non-governmental organisations (NGOs) and some developing country diplomats discussed how to implement the Declaration and how to practice compulsory licensing. For example, in 2002, at an NGO Conference on the implementation of the Doha Declaration, B Pécoul, Director of the MSF Access to Essential Medicines Campaign at that time, stated that:

> compulsory licensing has undergone a dramatic transformation: no longer a pariah, compulsory licensing is now considered an important policy tool in top-level policy circles. No developing country has actually yet issued a compulsory license on a pharmaceutical, but the way is open for compulsory licensing to become the rule rather than the exception.[33]

In the years prior to and after the adoption of the Doha Declaration, the WHO organised training seminars on TRIPS flexibilities that provided information on national legislation or on ARV prices. In these seminars on compulsory licensing, Article 31(f) of the TRIPS Agreement was increasingly viewed as an obstacle specifically impeding 'developing countries that have domestic drug production capacity (e.g. India) from exporting medicines to those that do not (e.g. Togo)'.[34] Article 31(f) says that compulsory licences are 'authorized predominantly for the supply of the domestic market of the Member authorizing such use'. If Article 31(f) were to prevent the export of medicines to countries without manufacturing capacity, it was argued that 'compulsory licensing [would be] a meaningless measure for many LDCs'.[35]

[33] Conference Report, 'Implementation of the Doha Declaration on the TRIPS Agreement and Public Health: Technical Assistance – How to Get It Right' (28 March 2002) 5, www.haiweb.org/campaign/access/ReportPostDoha.pdf.
[34] ibid 4.
[35] Conference Report (n 33) 4.

The disadvantages of compulsory licensing in a small market situation were also pointed out. The example of the Republic of Korea was provided, where a patient group was 'trying to get a compulsory license for Gleevec'.[36] It was argued that in such a country, 'the relatively small patient population makes it economically impractical to build a factory to produce the drug'. In April 2002, groups of citizens and patients petitioned the Korea Patent Office to issue a compulsory licence for Gleevec.[37] Another prediction from these seminars was that the import of the raw material from India or China under compulsory licensing would bring about 'economies of scale and comparative advantage'.[38]

ii   30 August solution to paragraph 6 question

If patents in a country prohibit third party production, then compulsory licensing would, theoretically, allow either local producers to manufacture copies, or the country issuing such licences to import the medicines in question. As mentioned above, Article 31(f) of the TRIPS Agreement has been criticised for preventing a small country without production capacity from obtaining cheap medicines from abroad under a compulsory licence. Paragraph 6 of the Doha Declaration instructed the TRIPS Council to find an expeditious solution by December 2002 to the problem faced by WTO Member countries without pharmaceutical manufacturing capacity where compulsory licensing would not be effective.

Diverse proposals were made regarding a solution to this problem. Several developing countries (Bolivia, Brazil, Cuba, China, Dominican Republic, Ecuador, India, Indonesia, Pakistan, Peru, Sri Lanka, Thailand and Venezuela) proposed that the TRIPS Council should recommend that an authoritative interpretation of Article 30 (limited exceptions to the rights conferred) of the TRIPS Agreement be adopted by the General Council, so as to recognise the right of WTO Members to 'authorise local producers to make, sell and export patented public health-related products, without the consent of the patent holder, to address public health needs in another country'.[39] Because the act of 'exporting' is not enumerated among the

---

[36] Gleevec (imatinib mesylate) is a medicine to treat chronic myeloid leukemia (see ch 10).

[37] Submitted by HeeSeob Nam and SungHo Park in 2002 on behalf of People's Health Coalition for Equitable Society, Association of Physicians for Humanism, and Korean Pharmacists for Democratic Society. The text of the petition can be found at http://glivec.jinbo.net/Request_for_CL_Final_version.htm. On 5 March 2003 the Korean Patent Office (KPO) turned down the request for licensing submitted in 2002, for the following reasons: 'By importing the drug in question, the economic burden of patients will be lighter. However, in a situation where economic and social crisis is not acute, issuing compulsory licences of the drug patent because its prices are high, the purpose of patent protection, which is to provide incentives to the public at large for technological innovation and industrial development by granting time-bound exclusivity to the inventor will be damaged. In deciding on whether to issue a compulsory licence, these opposing interests should be weighted with care.' Japanese Patent Office report on Outlines of the institution of compulsory licensing in Korea, www.jpo.go.jp/shiryou/toushin/shingikai/pdf/strategy_wg09/file4_3.pdf.

[38] Conference Report (n 33) 5.

[39] IP/C/W/355 (24 June 2002) para 8. This paper emphasises local manufacturing and TRIPS 'flexibilities' explained in paper IP/C/W/296 (developing country paper for Doha, n 23), and asserts the importance of technology transfer as the objective of the TRIPS Agreement.

exclusive rights conferred by the patent in Article 28 of the TRIPS Agreement, the paper explained, this solution does not 'unreasonably prejudice the legitimate interests of the patent owner', which is a requirement of Article 30. For these exporting countries, this solution had 'the advantage of avoiding burdensome procedures relating to the grant of compulsory licences'.[40]

The March 2002 TRIPS Council allowed Members to present their preliminary views on the possible solution to the problem identified under paragraph 6 of the Declaration on the TRIPS Agreement and Public Health. At this meeting, four basic options were put on the table: an authoritative interpretation based on Article 30; an amendment to Article 31 in order to overcome the restriction, under Article 31(f), to the possibility to export products manufactured and/or sold under a compulsory licence; a dispute settlement moratorium with regard to the non-respect of the restriction under Article 31(f); or a waiver with regard to Article 31(f).

The EC speculated on the solutions based on Article 30 and Article 31,[41] but later, in June 2002, proposed a solution based on the amendment of Article 31(f) of the TRIPS Agreement.[42] The US proposed a moratorium or waiver to be approved in advance, 'which would provide the manufacturing country with certainty that its production and export of the product under the waiver will not be subject to challenge.'[43] Both the EU and the US specified that the product scope should be based on the Doha Declaration, which covers 'the grave public health problems afflicting Africa and other developing and least developed countries, especially those resulting from HIV/AIDS, malaria, tuberculosis, and other epidemics.' The US insisted on limiting the scope of the products to include medicines to treat 'epidemics', as expressed in the Doha Declaration.[44] Since 2002, Members have been unable to agree on the scope of diseases to be covered by the mechanism to be adopted in response to the paragraph 6 question. Several developing countries insisted that 'diseases' should include chronic diseases such as asthma, obesity and diabetes, which they considered to be diseases that affect public health in developing countries. In the meantime, on 27 December 2002, the US, Switzerland and Canada decided not to resort to the WTO dispute settlement procedures, if Article 31(f) were waived by a Member.

---

[40] ibid para 10.

[41] The EC considered two possible solutions, amending Article 31(f) or interpreting Article 30 in a way which would allow production for export, to certain countries and under certain conditions, of products needed to combat serious public health problems. Concept Paper relating to Paragraph 6 of the Doha Declaration on the TRIPS Agreement and Public Health, Communication from the European Communities and their Member StatesIP/C/W/339 (4 March 2002) para 7.

[42] Paragraph 6 of the Doha Declaration of the TRIPS Agreement and Public Health, Communication from the European Communities and their Member States IP/C/W352 (20 June 2002).

[43] Second Communication from the United States IP/C/W/358 (9 July 2002).

[44] The EU specified the scope of beneficiary countries as follows: 'Members that would qualify for importing these products would be developing country members, focussing especially on least developed country members and low income members, with no or insufficient domestic manufacturing capacity, or, in case that product is patented in that member, no or insufficient manufacturing capacity other than that of the patent holder of the product in that member.' IP/C/W352 (n 42) para 12.

The solution to the paragraph 6 question, namely, the situation of countries without the capacity to manufacture the medicines they require, was agreed upon on 30 August 2003 when the General Council adopted Decision L/540.[45] By this decision, the obligations of an exporting Member under Article 31(f) of the TRIPS Agreement are waived when a Member manufactures and exports a pharmaceutical product to eligible importing Members. For the purpose of this decision, 'pharmaceutical product' means any patented product, or product manufactured through a patented process, of the pharmaceutical sector needed to address the public health problems as recognised in paragraph 1 of the Declaration. Active ingredients necessary for its manufacture and diagnostic kits needed for its use are included (para 1(a)).

Eligible Members are either LDCs or Members that have established insufficient or no manufacturing capacities in the pharmaceutical sector for the product in question in one of the ways set out in the Annex to Decision L/540. The products exported under the paragraph 6 system must fulfil several conditions. They are to be: (i) only the amount notified to the Council for TRIPS as necessary to meet the needs of the eligible importing Member(s); (ii) identified through specific labelling or marking and packaging and/or special colouring/ shaping; (iii) provided in the quantities and with the characteristics posted by the licensee on a website (paragraph 2). For the exporting Member, adequate remuneration is to be paid to the right holder, taking into account the economic value of the authorisation for the importing Member in accordance with Article 31(h), but for the importing Member, this obligation is waived. The scope of the diseases to be covered by the paragraph 6 system was much discussed during the negotiations but ultimately remained unspecified (paragraph 3).

The importing Members must take reasonable measures within their means against the risk of trade diversion, to prevent re-exportation of the products imported into their territories under the system, with technical or financial assistance from developed country Members if the importing Member is a developing or LDC country (paragraph 4). Members must ensure the availability of effective legal means to prevent the diversion of the products produced under the paragraph 6 system (paragraph 5). 'With a view to harnessing economies of scale for the purposes of enhancing purchasing power for, and facilitating the local production of, pharmaceutical products', the regional trade agreement (RTA) falls under the paragraph 6 system if at least half of the RTA Members are LDCs and the Members concerned share the health problem in question. In this case, the obligation under Article 31(f) of a Member of the RTA is waived (paragraph 6(i)). This will not prejudice the territorial nature of the patent rights in question, but regional patents to be applicable in the above Members should be promoted, and developed countries should provide technical cooperation to this end (paragraph 6(ii)). Members recognise the desirability of promoting the transfer of technology in order to overcome the problem identified in paragraph 6 of the Declaration

---

[45] WT/L/540 (and Corr.1) (n 11), www.wto.org/english/tratop_e/trips_e/implem_para6_e.htm.

(paragraph 7). The Council for TRIPS shall review annually the functioning of the system (paragraph 8). This Decision is without prejudice to the rights, obligations and flexibilities that Members have under the provisions of the TRIPS Agreement other than paragraphs (f) and (h) of Article 31 and also to the extent to which pharmaceutical products produced under a compulsory licence can be exported under the present provisions of Article 31(f) of the TRIPS Agreement (paragraph 9). Non-violation complaints are not applied concerning measures taken in conformity with the waivers contained in this Decision (paragraph 10). Decision L/540 terminates for each Member on the date on which an amendment to the TRIPS Agreement replacing its provisions takes effect for that Member (paragraph 11; see below).

When Decision L/540 was adopted on 30 August 2003, the Chairperson stated that: 'before adopting this decision, I would like to place on the record this Statement which represents several key shared understandings of Members regarding the decision to be taken and the way in which it will be interpreted and implemented.'[46] His first point was that the system to be established based on paragraph 6 of the Doha Declaration should be used in good faith to protect public health and 'not be an instrument to pursue industrial or commercial policy objectives.' His second point was that anti-diversion measures (special colouring or shaping) should be applied 'not only to formulated pharmaceuticals produced and supplied under the system but also to active ingredients produced and supplied under the system and to finished products produced using such active ingredients'. His third point was that 'any issues arising from the use and implementation of the Decision must be resolved expeditiously and amicably'.

F The First Amendment to the TRIPS Agreement

Paragraph 11 of Decision L/540 instructed[47] the TRIPS Council to initiate, by the end of 2003, work on the preparation of an amendment to the TRIPS Agreement with a view to its adoption within six months.[48]

On 6 December 2005, after a lengthy debate on which method to use to transform the 30 August 2003 waiver into a formal amendment, the General Council[49] adopted Decision L/641 amending Article 31 of the TRIPS Agreement.[50] Decision L/641 adopts a Protocol of Amendment which, upon the entry into force of the Protocol pursuant to Article X of the WTO Agreement, should be amended as

---

[46] General Council 'Chairperson's statement' at the General Council meeting on 30 August 2003. www.wto.org/english/tratop_e/trips_e/gc_stat_30aug03_e.htm.

[47] 'The amendment will be based, where appropriate, on this Decision and on the further understanding that it will not be part of the negotiations referred to in paragraph 45 of the Doha Ministerial Declaration.' para 11 of the Decision WT/L/540 (n 11).

[48] The waivers granted in Decision L/540 terminate for each Member on the date on which an amendment to the TRIPS Agreement replacing its provisions takes effect for that Member.

[49] General Council Decision of 6 December 2005, WT/L/641.

[50] www.wto.org/english/news_e/pres05_e/pr426_e.htm.

set out in the Annex to this Protocol, 'by inserting Article 31 *bis* after Article 31 and by inserting the Annex to the TRIPS Agreement after Article 73'. The new Article 31 *bis* and Annex of the TRIPS Agreement are attached to the Protocol of Amendment, which, in turn, is attached to Decision L/641[51]. Article 31 *bis* allows pharmaceutical products manufactured under compulsory licences to be exported to countries lacking production capacity. An annex to the TRIPS Agreement sets out definitions and notification procedures for avoiding the diversion of pharmaceuticals to other markets, developing regional systems to allow economies of scale, and annual reviews in the TRIPS Council. An 'appendix' to the annex (originally an annex to the 2003 decision) deals with assessing lack of manufacturing capability in the importing country.

One of the reasons why it took more than two years to adopt the text for the amendment was uncertainty over whether the Chairperson's statement of 30 August 2003 would be part of the amendment, notably the statement that the system drawn up relating to the problem posed by paragraph 6 of the Doha Declaration 'would not be used as an instrument to pursue industrial or commercial policy objectives'. The announcement of the 11 Members that they would only use the system as importers in situations of national emergency or other circumstances of extreme urgency was included in the Chairperson's statement, but not in Decision L/540. The US, Canada, Japan and the Republic of Korea considered the Chairperson's statement to fall under Article 31.2(a) VCLT and constitute an 'agreement relating to the treaty which was made between all the parties in connection with the conclusion of the treaty'. However, there was no evidence that all parties to the TRIPS Agreement had agreed to the statement. The US government insisted that the Chairperson's statement, together with Decision L/540, form part of the August 30 agreement and that this statement be included as a footnote to the amended Article 31(f). It was decided that Decision L/540 would be reproduced in the amendment and that the Chairperson's statement would be read when the amendment to Article 31 was adopted.

The entry into force of this amendment requires the ratification by two-thirds of the WTO Members. Upon ratification, the amendment becomes immediately effective in the countries that ratify it. The deadline was originally set for 1 December 2007 but the General Council extended it to 31 December 2009[52] and then to 31 December 2011.[53] For each of the remaining Members, the waiver will continue to apply until they accept the amendment and it takes effect.

[51] www.wto.org/english/tratop_e/trips_e/wtl641_e.htm.
[52] General Council Decision of 18 December 2007, WT/L/711.
[53] General Council Decision of 11 November 2009, WT/L/785.

II TEN YEARS AFTER THE DOHA DECLARATION

A Compulsory Licences in Developing Countries

For a few years after the adoption in August 2003 by the TRIPS Council of Decision L/540 concerning the paragraph 6 system, certain developing countries, international organisations such as the WHO and civil society groups may have continued to expect that compulsory licensing would effectively and invariably solve the access to medicines problems. Manuals were prepared in cooperation with the World Bank.[54]

Compulsory licensing could have contributed to solving urgent problems when surrounding circumstances have supported it, but this required much more time than expected. Few data are available about what happened after the compulsory licences were issued. As in the case of Brazil, compulsory licensing may have primarily been a negotiating instrument for reducing the price of HIV/AIDS antiretrovirals (ARVs) in many countries.

CPTech (see chapter 8) provides web information on 'Examples of Health-Related Compulsory Licenses'. These examples include, in particular, compulsory licences that were issued in Africa, Asia and Latin America after the Doha Declaration, mostly for ARVs or Tamiflu (oseltamivir).[55]

Several African countries have issued compulsory licences for ARVs since 2002, notably for standard combination drugs (3TC-d4T-NVP). In Zimbabwe, in May 2002, the Minister of Justice Affairs declared an emergency and granted a licence to Varichem Pharmaceuticals to make, use or import generic HIV/AIDS medicines for government use, for a period of six months, which was later extended.[56] Mozambique,[57] on 5 April 2004, and Zambia, on 21 September 2004, granted the local subsidiaries of Pharco (Egypt) licences to produce a fixed-dose combination (3TC-d4T-NVP) at royalties to the originator not exceeding 2 per cent and maximum 2.5 per cent of sales, respectively.[58]

The Zambian order of licence explains that the three originators had refused a licence for the combination drug to be marketed in Zambia.[59] The situation surrounding the issuance of a compulsory licence is unclear, and the country appears to rely on the importation of Indian generics. CPTech provides information on compulsory licences for similar purposes in Cameroon in January

---

[54] See for example FM Abbott and RV van Puymbroeck, 'Compulsory Licensing for Public Health: A Guide and Model Documents for Implementation of the Doha Declaration Paragraph 6 Decision' (August 2005) World Bank Working Paper No 61.

[55] www.cptech.org/ip/health/cl/recent-examples.html.

[56] Notice based on Section 35 Patents Act (Zimbabwe) www.cptech.org/ip/health/c/zimbabwe/zim05242002.html.

[57] www.cptech.org/ip/health/c/mozambique/5apr04-moz-cl.pdf.

[58] http://lists.essential.org/pipermail/ip-health/2004-September/006959.html.

[59] www.cptech.org/ip/health/c/zambia/zcl.html at http://lists.essential.org/pipermail/ip-health/2004-September/006959.html.

2005,[60] Ghana in October 2005 and Eritrea in June 2005,[61] but no further information is available on what happened afterwards.

On 29 September 2004, the Minister of Trade and Consumer Affairs in Malaysia ordered a licence to import didanosine (ddI), zidovudine (AZT) and lamivudine+zidovidine (Combivir) from India (Cipla) as supplies for public hospitals for two years. However, an agreement was then reached between the Government and the originator.[62] The royalty rate to the originator is 0.5 per cent of the net selling value.[63]

On 25 November 2005, Taiwan granted compulsory licensing for Tamiflu (oseltamivir) antiviral for the treatment of avian flu,[64] with a view to developing a stockpile for the national inventory through 31 December 2007. Actual manufacturing by Taiwanese companies did not seem to occur and cooperation was re-established with the right holder.

On 29 November 2006, the Thai Government announced a compulsory licence to import (from India) and locally produce efavirenz for government use until 31 December 2011, and that a royalty fee of 0.5 per cent of the Government Pharmaceutical Organization (GPO) total sale value of the imported or locally produced efavirenz would be paid to the right holder.[65] The GPO announced that they would start producing locally in June 2007 at a price of less than half the originator price.[66] This, however, has not yet been achieved. According to the GPO, domestic production of efavirenz will start in 2011.[67] On 25 January 2007, the Government announced two additional compulsory licences for government use of antiretroviral Kaletra (LPV+RTV) and the heart disease drug Plavix (clopidogrel bisulphate).[68] The royalties to the originator were fixed at the same rate as efavirenz.

---

[60] www.essentialinventions.org/docs/cameroon/.

[61] www.cptech.org/ip/health/cl/Eritrea.png.

[62] www.cptech.org/ip/health/cl/recent-examples.html#Malaysia. Later, on 5 October 2004, compulsory licences for lamivudine (3TC) and nevirapine (NVP) products, and in March 2007 for Stocrin (efavirenz) at 0.5 per cent royalties were said to have been issued but no further information is available. On 5 October 2004 Indonesia issued compulsory licences to manufacture for government use 3TC and NVP, until the end of the patent term in 2011 and 2012, respectively.

[63] CP Tech, http://lists.essential.org/pipermail/ip-health/2004-December/007233.html.

[64] ICTSD 'Taiwan Issues Compulsory License for Tamiflu', http://ictsd.org/i/ip/39838/.

[65] www.cptech.org/ip/health/cl/thailand/.

[66] www.cptech.org/ip/health/cl/recent-examples.html.

[67] Interview on 30 May 2010.

[68] www.cptech.org/ip/health/c/thailand/thai-cl-clopidogrel_en.pdf. Plavix (clopidogrel) is a medicine for inhibiting blood clots in coronary arterial disease, peripheral vascular disease, and cerebrovascular disease, adapted to those patients for whom substitute drugs, such as aspirin, could have adverse effects. Its number needed to treat (NTT) (patients needed to be treated to prevent one additional bad outcome) is relatively high. Centre for Evidence Based Medicine, www.cebm.net/index.aspx?o=1044. In Japan, clopidogrel was approved in January 2007.

There are ways to evaluate to what extent a medicine is substitutable. For example, aspirin can be substituted with clopidogrel, another thrombus-formation inhibitor that has antiplatelet activity. A small amount of aspirin is sufficient for thrombus-formation inhibition and its side-effects (except for ulcer patients) can be negligible. However, even a small amount of aspirin sometimes causes side-effects in the stomach or intestines. The use of suppositories or enteric-coated tablets can reduce these side-effects. As an antiplatelet medicine, ticlopidine hydrochloride could be a substitute for

On 11 March 2008, in Thailand, further compulsory licences were issued for four cancer drugs: Taxotere (docetaxel), Femara (letrozole), Tarceva (erlotinib) and Gleevec (imatinib masylate). In April 2008, the new Thai Government announced that it would continue the previous policy of issuing compulsory licences to lower prices if originator prices are more than 5 per cent higher than the lowest generic prices, at a royalty rate of 0.5 per cent of the sales prices when they are high and at 2 per cent when they are low.[69] In August 2008, efavirenz was imported from India (Emcure Pharmaceuticals)[70] and, today, two other medicines are also imported from India (Kaletra by Matrix Laboratory and Plavix, Cadila Healthcare).[71] Concerning Gleevec, the originator company continued to distribute it free of charge at public hospitals and therefore it did not become the subject of compulsory licensing. For the three cancer drugs Taxotere, Femara and Tarceva, compulsory licences were confirmed and the import from India planned. However, Thai oncologists were sceptical about whether effective treatment could be provided using the imported products unknown to medical doctors in Thailand, and refused to issue prescriptions.[72] Today, these two cancer drugs do not seem to be in wide use in Thailand.[73]

On 4 May 2007, the Brazilian Government issued a decree allowing for the production or importation of efavirenz without the consent of the right holder for use in the national HIV/AIDS programme at a royalty rate of 1.5 per cent.[74] The decree followed negotiations to obtain a 40 per cent price reduction, which seems not to have been achieved. In Brazil, compulsory licensing has primarily been a negotiating tool for price agreements. The prices of ARVs in Brazil are generally lower than in some small and poor countries where the prices of patented drugs are extremely high. The following data by UNITAID[75] shows that

aspirin. For the treatment of angina, a broader category of thrombus disease, there are Ca blockers (15), $\alpha\beta$ (alpha beta receptor) blockers (4), β (beta receptor) blockers (23), coronary vasodilators (6) and anticoagulants (2), etc. The number in brackets indicates a rough estimation of the number of substitutable medicines. Source: Japan Pharmaceutical Information Centre (JAPIC), Medicine Collection 2010 and others.

[69] 'Facts and Evidence on the 10 Burning Issues Related to the Government Use of Patents on Three Patented Essential Drugs in Thailand, Document to Support Strengthening of Social Wisdom on the Issue of Drug Patent', The Ministry of Public Health, and The National Health Security Office, Thailand, February 2007, 11.

[70] 'Aids drugs now available', *The Bangkok Post* (5 August 2008).

[71] Information provided by the Thai Ministry of Public Health on 11 March 2008.

[72] ibid.

[73] Confirmed by a GPO personnel, 30 May 2010.

[74] http://portal.saude.gov.br/portal/aplicacoes/noticias/noticias_detalhe.cfm?co_seq_noticia= 29719.

[75] UNITAID, a new type of international organisation launched on 19 September 2006 on the initiative of Brazil and France, takes advantage of a better organisation of recipient markets combined with innovative financing, and facilitates access to treatment for HIV/AIDS, malaria and tuberculosis for developing countries. UNITAID's Membership grew from five countries (Brazil, Chile, France, Norway and the UK) in 2006 to 29 countries and one foundation (Bill & Melinda Gates Foundation) in 2008. The majority of UNITAID's Member countries are African. UNITAID's financing comes mainly from a solidarity levy on airline tickets, but Norway provides finances from its CO2 emission taxes and the UK from its ODA budget. UNITAID has committed to provide funds of up to US$4 million in 2010, out of which at least 85% must be distributed to low-income countries. www.unitaid.eu/fr.

the price of Kaletra in Brazil is even lower than that procured by the Global Fund (see chapter 8).

Prices of Kaletra: differences by country (2005)

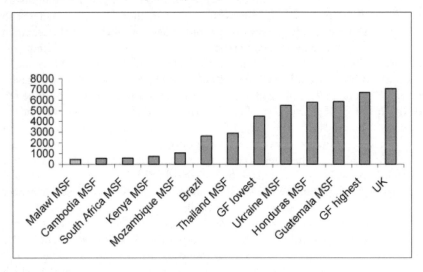

'Intellectual Property Rights and Medicines Procurement Patent Pools', Note by Médecins Sans Frontières (MSF) for consideration by the Ministry of Foreign Affairs (France) and UNITAID, 1 June 2006.

GF=Global Fund

On 14 April 2010, Ecuador granted a compulsory licence for ritonavir, an antiretroviral drug, to Eskegroup SA, the local distributor for Cipla.[76] According to *IP Watch*, the method of calculating royalties that was adopted was the 'tiered royalty method' (TRM), recommended in the UNDP/WHO document, 'Remuneration guidelines for non-voluntary use of a patent on medical technologies'.[77] The TRM takes as a base royalty 4 per cent of the high-income country price, adjusted to relative income per capita, and for countries facing a particularly high burden of disease, relative income per person with the disease. According to this document, the TRM 'provides a more rational framework for sharing the costs of research and independent of manufacturing costs, and vary directly with proxies for therapeutic value (the high income price) and capacity to pay.[78]

---

[76] 'Ecuador Grants First Compulsory Licence, For HIV/AIDS Drug', *IP Watch* (22 April 2010).
[77] J Love, CP Tech, 'Remuneration guidelines for non-voluntary use of a patent on medical technologies', WHO, Health Economics and Drugs TCM series No 18, www.who.int/medicines/areas/technical_cooperation/WHOTCM2005.1_OMS.pdf.
[78] ibid 64.

B Under WTO's Export Licensing System

i Options under the paragraph 6 system

All WTO Member countries are eligible to use the paragraph 6 system adopted on 30 August 2003. When Decision L/540 was made by the WTO General Council, 23 developed countries[79] announced that they would not import medicines under this system. Since then, the EU has been enlarged to include an additional 12 countries.[80] Eleven other WTO Members[81] announced that they would only use the system as importers in situations of national emergency or other circumstances of extreme urgency, although this was not included in Decision L/540 but only in the General Council Chairperson's statement.

As of 15 October 2010, thirty-one WTO Members ratified the TRIPS amendment of 2005.[82] While waiting for the amendment to become effective, the WTO General Council Decision of 30 August 2003 (the paragraph 6 system) was implemented in different ways in national laws, of which the Canadian CMAR is one example.

ii Canada and the paragraph 6 system

The WTO General Council Decision of 30 August 2003 was implemented in Canada by the Act to amend the Patent Act and the Food and Drugs Act of 2004, which came into force on 14 May 2005.[83] Canada's Access to Medicines Regime (CAMR)[84] was established based on this legislation. It amended the Patent Law, the Food and Drugs Law and associated regulations to address public health problems of developing and least-developed countries, especially those resulting from HIV/AIDS, tuberculosis, malaria and other epidemics. (Schedule 1 is a list of drugs and medical devices for export under the CAMR). Eligible countries (schedules 2–4), which include non-WTO Members, must make arrangements with pharmaceutical companies based in Canada[85] and royalties paid to the right holder vary according to the importing country's position on the UN Human Development Index. The authorised export agreement is valid for two years, renewable once.

---

[79] Australia, Austria, Belgium, Canada, Denmark, Finland, France, Germany, Greece, Iceland, Ireland, Italy, Japan, Luxembourg, Netherlands, New Zealand, Norway, Portugal, Spain, Sweden, Switzerland, the United Kingdom and the US.

[80] Czech Republic, Cyprus, Estonia, Hungary, Latvia, Lithuania, Malta, Poland, Slovak Republic, Slovenia, Romania and Bulgaria.

[81] Hong Kong China, Israel, Korea, Kuwait, Macao China, Mexico, Qatar, Singapore, Chinese Taipei, Turkey and the United Arab Emirates.

[82] www.wto.org/english/tratop_e/trips_e/amendment_e.htm.

[83] http://laws.justice.gc.ca/en/showdoc/cs/P-4/bo-ga:s_21_01//en#anchorbo-ga:s_21_01.

[84] www.camr-rcam.gc.ca/index_e.html.

[85] Non-governmental organisations can assist countries to obtain and distribute drugs and medical devices through the CAMR and can also obtain and distribute generic drugs on their own. Eligible countries may be able to obtain funding to support their purchase of medicines, although not directly through CAMR.

The CAMR reflects the WTO Chairperson's statement on 30 August 2003 that the paragraph 6 system was not to be 'an instrument to pursue industrial or commercial policy objectives'. To ensure that the regime is used in good faith, right holders may challenge a compulsory licence in court.[86] If the average price of the product to be manufactured is equal to or greater than 25 per cent of the average price in Canada of the equivalent product sold by or with the consent of the patentee, the transaction is considered 'commercial in nature' (Patent Law 21.17(1)). In this case, the patentee may, on notice given by the patentee to the person to whom an authorisation was granted, apply to the Federal Court for an order under 21.17(3) and the Federal Court will make a determination based on '(*a*) the reasonable return sufficient to sustain a continued participation in humanitarian initiatives; (*b*) the ordinary levels of profitability in Canada; and (*c*) the international trends in prices as reported by the UN for the supply of such products for humanitarian purposes.' If the Federal Court determines that the agreement is commercial in nature, it may 'make an order, on any terms that it considers appropriate, (a) terminating the authorization; or (b) requiring the holder to pay, in addition to the royalty otherwise required to be paid, an amount that the Federal Court considers adequate to compensate the patentee for the commercial use of the patent' (21.17(3)).[87]

The amending legislation creating the CAMR included a clause calling upon the Minister of Industry to review the relevant provisions of the Patent Act (sections 21.01 to 21.19) within two years of its coming into force. There was much debate before and after the enactment of this legislation which continues, along with the changing world opinion on the issue of TRIPS and access to medicines. Amidst conflicting opinions about how burdensome it is under the CAMR to export medicines, and the doubts about the competitiveness of Canada's high generic prices,[88] Bill S-393 was presented in 2009 by a Senator, with a view to simplifying it to establish a system of one licence to allow shipments of the same medication to multiple countries without needing new approvals for each shipment.[89]

Under the WTO's paragraph 6 system, one example of export to Rwanda was achieved under compulsory licence in Canada for a fixed-dose combination (FDC) of AZT +3TC+NVP (TriAvir) manufactured in Canada by Apotex. On 17 July 2007, Rwanda's Government Centre for Treatment & Research on AIDS

---

[86]   www.camr-rcam.gc.ca/intro/regime_e.html.

[87]   The Canadian Patent Law 21.17(4) provides that: '. . . if the Federal Court makes an order terminating the authorization, (a) requiring the holder to deliver to the patentee any of the product to which the authorization relates remaining in the holder's possession as though the holder had been determined to have been infringing a patent; or (b) with the consent of the patentee, requiring the holder to export any of the product to which the authorization relates remaining in the holder's possession to the country or WTO Member named in the authorization.'

[88]   Attaran pointed out that Canada's pricing of generic medicines is not competitive, as shown, for example, by Apotex's price which is three times higher than the same FDC already being sold by Ranbaxy in Rwanda. A Attaran, 'AIDS drugs fiasco a tale of red tape', 9 August 2009, www.business-humanrights.org/Categories/Individualcompanies/A/Apotex.

[89]   http://www.hemophilia.ca/files/Petition%20House%20of%20Commons%20-%20C-393.pdf.

(TRAC) notified the TRIPS Council that it would import 260,000 packs of the FDC for two years.[90] The Canadian Government, for its part, notified the TRIPS Council on 5 October 2007 that it had authorised Apotex to export TriAvir to Rwanda.[91] Glaxo Smith Kline (GSK), Shire and Boehringer Ingelheim, the three right holders, gave their consent to Apotex to manufacture FDC and, in 2009, to continue the operation.[92]

iii Attempts in India

India, for its part, added a new sub-section 92A when its Patents Act 1970 was amended in 2005, in light of the paragraph 6 system. In the Indian Patents (Amendment) Act, 2005, compulsory licences are provided in sections 82 to 94 of Chapter 16 and government use, section 47[93] of Chapter 8 and sections 99–103 of Chapter 16. The basic procedure is based on section 84, which provides that any person interested may make an application to the Controller for grant of compulsory licence on a patent at any time after the expiration of three years from the date of the grant of the patent if the patent is not worked in India or is inadequately supplying Indian markets (see below p 340). Under the section 84 procedure, the Indian patent law has, since 1970, provided that insufficient supplies in India's export market could be grounds for issuing compulsory licences in India (section 84(7)(a)(iii)). The second type of compulsory licensing is provided in section 92, according to which the Indian Government can, at any time after the sealing thereof, make available compulsory licences to work the invention in particular circumstances of national emergency or extreme urgency or in cases where public non-commercial use is required, 'including public health crises, related to HIV/AIDS, malaria or other epidemics'. Section 92 is similar to the previous system, which 'endorsed' every patent granted in the sectors of foods, medicines or other chemical processes with the words 'licence of right' so that any person could work the patent without the authorisation of the rights-holder (see chapter 2).

Section 92A, added in the 2005 amendment, provides another compulsory licensing procedure for 'export of patented pharmaceutical products in certain exceptional circumstances', reflecting the WTO August 30 Decision. According to this provision, compulsory licensing shall be available for the manufacture and

---

[90] Notification under para 2(A) of the Decision of 30 August 2003 on the Implementation of Paragraph 6 of the Doha Declaration on the TRIPS Agreement and Public Health, Rwanda IP/N/9/RWA/1(19 July 2007) http://portal.saude.gov.br/portal/aplicacoes/noticias/noticias_detalhe.cfm?co_seq_noticia=2971.

[91] Notification under para 2(C) of the Decision of 30 August 2003 on the Implementation of Paragraph 6 of the Doha Declaration on the TRIPS Agreement and Public Health: Canada IP/N/10/CAN/1(8 October 2007) to which the authorisation by the Commissioner of Patents for compulsory licence is attached.

[92] www.apotex.com/global/about/press/20070920.asp, www.news-medical.net/news/20091020/GlaxoSmithKline-to-allow-Apotex-continue-manufacturing-their-drug-in-Rwanda.aspx.

[93] For recent case law relating to government use, see *Chemtra Corp v Union of India and Others* (CS(OS) No 930 of 2009, Delhi High Court, 3 August 2009).

export of patented pharmaceutical products to any country having insufficient or no manufacturing capacity in the pharmaceutical sector to address public health problems. A compulsory licence must be granted in the importing country to allow importation of the patented pharmaceutical products from India, if there are relevant patents.

In September 2007, an Indian generic company, Natco (Hyderabad), requested compulsory licensing under section 92A from the Indian Patent Office (IPO) to export 3000 tablets (150 mg) of Erlonat, its version of Tarceva (erlotinib hydrochloride). Tarceva is designed to block tumour cell growth by targeting the protein called the Human Epidermal Growth Factor Receptor 1 (HER1/EGFR) and is prescribed for patients with advanced-stage non-small cell lung cancer (NSCLC) who have received at least one prior chemotherapy regimen (see chapter 12). It was approved in the US by the FDA on 18 November 2004.[94] Natco is offering Erlonat (a branded generic version of erlotinib) for sale over the Internet and via Indian wholesalers.[95]

The Indian patent for Tarceva was granted to Pfizer and OSI Pharmaceuticals in July 2007.[96] OSI entered into a marketing agreement with Hoffman-La Roche for distribution of erlotinib outside the US. There was no patent in Nepal, but the Nepalese authorities had given authorisation for the import of Erlonat and, in the state of Andhra Pradesh, export authorisation was granted for 9000 tablets (150 mg). According to Decision L/540, the importing country must notify the Council for TRIPS of its intention to use the system as an importer (paragraph 1(b)), and the exporter country must make a determination based on the importer country's notification concerning (i) the names and expected quantities of the product needed and (ii) confirmation that it has insufficient or no manufacturing capacities in the pharmaceutical sector for the product(s) in question and (iii) that the pharmaceutical product is patented in its territory.

Natco also requested a compulsory licence to export to Nepal Suninat, its version of Sutent (sunitinib malate).[97] Sutent is a new targeted anti-cancer treatment for patients with gastrointestinal stromal tumors (GIST), a rare stomach cancer, and advanced kidney cancer, and was approved on 30 January 2006 by the FDA. This medicine is administered to treat patients with advanced GIST or who are unable to tolerate treatment with Gleevec (imatinib mesylate),[98] which was approved in the US in May 2001 by the FDA, also to treat a rare refractory cancer called chronic myeloid leukemia (CML). The Indian Sutent patent[99] was

[94] www.accessdata.fda.gov/scripts/cder/drugsatfda/index.cfm?fuseaction=Search.DrugDetails.

[95] http://www.natcopharma.co.in/solid_tumors.html; http://www.ec21.com/ks-erlotinib-natco/; http://www.star-line.co.jp/a2/chemist/tarceva_erlotinib.html

[96] The compound was developed by Genentech, patented by Pfizer/OSI Pharmaceuticals in developed countries, but marketed in India by Roche. Tarceva was approved by the US FDA on 19 November 2004.

[97] www.accessdata.fda.gov/scripts/cder/drugsatfda/index.cfm?fuseaction=Search.Overview&DrugName=SUTENT.

[98] 10 May 2001 www.accessdata.fda.gov/scripts/cder/drugsatfda/index.cfm?fuseaction=Search.Overview&DrugName=GLEEVEC.

[99] Patent No 209251 (pyrrole substituted 2-indolinone protein kinase inhibitors), date of publication of granted patent, 10 May 2007.

granted in 2007 to Sugen and Pharmacia & UpJohn and licensed to the Indian subsidiary of Pfizer.

Responding to the request for a compulsory licence for Tarceva, in March 2008 the IPO organised a hearing with the interested parties[100] on the basis of the assistant controller's decision and explanation that Pfizer had a right to be heard.[101] While Pfizer/Roche contended that the absence of a hearing would have seriously prejudiced the rights of Pfizer/Roche, and due process in determining the patentee's rights including 'adequate remuneration' for the compulsory licence, Natco argued that compulsory licence under section 92 is mandatory and does not permit a hearing, and that such a licence must be granted promptly, with the royalty rates determined by the patent office. Citing the Doha Declaration, which refers to the 'gravity of public health problems that developing countries were facing, and sought to "balance the needs" of both patent holders and countries facing an urgent need to provide affordable medicines to its people', Natco argued that the common law doctrine of natural justice recognised that the right to be heard could be dispensed with 'in situations that required prompt action in the public interest'. Natco referred to the WHO/UNDP 'Remuneration Guidelines for Non-Voluntary Use of a Patent Medical Technologies'[102] to determine 'adequate remuneration in such circumstances without the involvement of the patentees'. The IPO organised the hearing probably in the absence of accurate data on the circumstances in Nepal and for the necessity to establish how this corresponded to the public health situation.[103] Natco subsequently withdrew the requests to the IPO.[104]

Following these discussions, Pfizer established a programme to deliver free patient assistance to two leading cancer hospitals in Nepal.[105]

The adoption of the paragraph 6 system in 2003 was an important action by the WTO so that patent rules would not stand in the way of exports for humanitarian purposes of more affordable medicines to countries that do not have manufacturing capacity. Today, there are many international mechanisms to facilitate access to medicines including international procurement, partnerships and technical assistance offering greater choice to countries to obtain medicines, of which the paragraph 6 system is an integral part.

---

[100] For the record of this hearing, see Lawyers Collective, 'Natco's application for CL for Export – Hearing in the Delhi Patent Office' (20 March 2008). http://commonslaw.freeflux.net/blog/archive/2008/03/20/commons-law-natco-s-application-for-cl-for-export-hearing-in-the-delhi-patent-office.html.See also '*Natco vs Roche/Pfizer*: Hearing on the Right to Hearing', *Spicy IP* (21 March 2008). See ch 12.

[101] *Spicy IP*, 'Natco's Doha CL Application: Patent Office Rules in Favour of Pfizer'(5 July 2008).

[102] Lawyers Collective (n 100). For 'Remuneration guidelines', see n 87.

[103] 'Natco's Doha CL Application: Patent Office Rules in Favour of Pfizer', Spicy IP, 5 July 2008.

[104] 'Breaking News – Gilead files tenofovir appeal at IPAB', Spicy IP (7 December 2009)

[105] 'Pfizer to launch free Sutent access programme in Nepal', *Livemint* (3 November 2010)

C Compulsory licences through competition law application

i Competition Law and Refusal to License

Article 40.2 of the TRIPS Agreement allows Members to adopt appropriate measures to prevent or control 'licensing practices or conditions that may in particular cases constitute an abuse of intellectual property rights having an adverse effect on competition in the relevant market'. Members do not have unlimited discretion in legislating such national measures, because anti-competitive effects in the relevant market must be evaluated on a case-by-case basis (on 'relevant markets' see chapter 1, footnote 69). Article 40.2 stipulates also that these measures must be adopted 'consistently with the other provisions of this Agreement' such as national treatment obligations (Article 3) and transparency (Article 63).

In the mutually agreed solution in the WTO dispute cases, *Argentina–Patent Protection for Pharmaceuticals and Test Data Protection for Agricultural Chemicals* and *Argentina–Certain Measures on the Protection of Patents and Test Data*,[106] Argentina confirmed that if any of the situations defining 'anti-competitive' practices in Article 44 of its Law on Patents and Utility Models were found to exist, such a finding would not in and of itself warrant an automatic determination that a patent owner is engaging in an 'anti-competitive' practice. Argentina and the US agreed that, to justify the granting of a compulsory license by the Argentine Patent Office (INPI), a prior decision must have been handed down by Argentina's Competition Commission establishing the existence of an 'abuse of a dominant position' for the practice in question.

Article 40 of the TRIPS Agreement refers to the application of national competition laws, among which there is no substantive harmonisation. For example, in the US, IP licensing could come under scrutiny under section 1 or section 2 of the Sherman Act (as well as section 5 of the Federal Trade Commission (FTC) Act). [107] For section 2 of the Sherman Act which prohibits monopolisation, the proof of acquisition or maintenance of monopoly power has been much debated.[108] For example, whether or not it is necessary to show specific intent[109] and how to distinguish exclusionary conduct from competitive behaviour have raised complex questions.[110] In the US, under the Patent Law, defendants in an infringement action or a contract action can claim that the patentee has 'misused' his patent and therefore is not entitled to the requested relief. Examples of patent misuse are tying (which, it was believed, extended the legal monopoly to tied product market),[111] refusal to license, resale price maintenance, price discrimination, non contest covenant, mandatory package licensing, etc.

---

[106] Notification of Mutually Agreed Solution WT/DS171/3, WT/DS196/4 (20 June 2002).

[107] s 1 of the Sherman Act (US Code Title 15-1) prohibits 'contract, combination in the form of trust or otherwise, or conspiracy, in restraint of trade or commerce among States, or with foreign nations'. On s 2 of the Sherman Act, see ch 4 n 58.

[108] United States v Grinnell Corporation (384 U. S. 563, 570–571 (1966)).

[109] Spectrum Sports Inc. v McQuillan (506 US 447, 459 (1993)).

[110] United States v Microsoft Corporation, D C Cir. 2001.

[111] Motion Picture Patents v Universal Film Manufacturing (243 U. S. 502 (1917)).

Article 102 of the of the Treaty on the Functioning of the European Union TFEU (formerly Article 82 EC[112])prohibits abuse of a dominant position but the proof of 'abuse of dominant position' gave rise to debate over the treatment of the refusal to license. In most countries, unilateral refusal to deal (license) generally does not raise competition problems, but each country has different criteria for recognising when the refusal becomes a competition problem. For example, a dominant firm's refusal to license is not itself illegal under EU competition law,[113] but, under certain special circumstances, can be analysed as contrary to Article 102 of the TFEU. In a few very recent cases, licensing was ordered by the European Commission.[114] The Court of Justice of the European Union (Court of Justice) has developed parameters for analysing these circumstances.[115] No US

[112] The Treaty Establishing the European Community.

[113] A dominant firm's refusal to license is not 'in itself' an abuse, unless it is coupled with other conduct, for example, refusal to supply spare parts (*Volvo v Veng* Case C-238/87, [1988] ECR 6211).

[114] *Magill* (Commission Decision 89/205/EEC of 21 December 1988 relating to a proceeding under Article 86 of the EEC Treaty (IV/31.851 Magill TV Guide/ITP, BBC and RTE) (OJ 1989 L 78, p. 43)) and *Microsoft* (Commission Decision 2007/53/EC of 24 March 2004 relating to a proceeding pursuant to Article 82 [EC] and Article 54 of the EEA Agreement against Microsoft Corp (Case COMP/C-3/37.792 – Microsoft) (OJ 2007 L 32, p. 23)). In the latter case, in addition to the parameters of 'exceptional circumstances', circumstances particular to the case, such as the network effects, the company's exceptional market share and duration of dominance, the non-existence of the risks that ordering interoperability could lead to mere copying of the whole product and the lock-in effects of users, seem to have contributed to the analysis.

[115] The Court of Justice held that refusal to deal generally is not illegal under EU competition law but in 'exceptional' circumstances where the following conditions are met, it could be considered to be abuse of a dominant position. Whether or not these conditions are open-ended, case-specific ones is not entirely clear. In the *Magill case*, these 'exceptional circumstances' were identified as the following: the refusal to license prevents the introduction of a new product; the refusal to license is not objectively justified; the refusal to license excludes a rival from a 'secondary market' (Joined Cases C-241/91P, C-242/91 P *RTE and ITP v Commission* [1995] ECR I-743). In this case, the refusal to provide basic information by relying on national copyright provisions was considered to be preventing the appearance of a new product, a comprehensive weekly guide to television programmes, for which there was a potential consumer demand and constituted a breach of Art 102(b) TFEU. In *Tiercé Ladbroke v Commission* (Case T-504/93[1997] ECR 927), the Court of Justice rejected an attempt by Ladbroke to invoke Magill because (inter alia) the refusal to supply the applicant could not fall within the prohibition laid down by Article 102 TFEU, unless it concerned 'a product or service which was either essential for the exercise of the activity in question, in that there was no real or potential substitute, or was a new product whose introduction might be prevented, despite specific, constant and regular potential demand on the part of consumers'(The Commission had rejected a complaint by Ladbroke, a company operating betting shops in Belgium, which sought to force operators of French horse races to provide a license transmission of sound and pictures of the races in the betting shops in Belgium). Under *Magill*, the essential for the activity in question requirement was an alternative to, and not cumulative with, the 'new product' requirement. (Further, in a case not involving IPRs but a distribution network, the Court of Justice in Oscar Bronner (Case C-7/97 Oscar Bronner GMbH & Co KG v Mediaprint [1998] ECR I-7791) delineated that denial of access is abusive if: it is likely to eliminate all competition on the neighboring market; there is no objective justification and; the access or service is indispensable to operate on the neighboring market "inasmuch as there is no actual or potential substitute" for it.) In *IMS Health* (Case C-418/01 [2004] ECR I-5039), the Court held the exceptional circumstances to be when: it is likely to eliminate all competition in the neighbouring market; there is no objective justification; and the access or service is indispensable for operating in the neighbouring market in as much as there is no actual or potential substitute for it. In the IMS Health case, the concept of 'duplication' as opposed to 'new product' became the centre of discussion and the Court of Justice appears to have eliminated *Magill*'s secondary market requirement. In *Microsoft* (Case T-201/04 [2007] ECR II-1491), the General Court (formerly Court

court has imposed antitrust liability for a unilateral refusal to license intellectual property unless there was additional illegal conduct.[116]

ii Competition Law Application and Licensing of ARV patents in South Africa

Towards the end of 2002, 12 civil society groups and individuals from South Africa complained to the Competition Commission of South Africa that the high price of ARVs (such as AZT, 3TC, avacabir, amprenavir, Combivir, Trizivir) of GlaxoSmithKline South Africa (Pty) Ltd (GSK) and nevirapine of Boehringer Ingelheim (BI) amounted to abuse of a dominant position under South African competition law.[117] The complainants argued that these medicines were not substitutable considering their respective side-effects and the difficulties of applying them in combination treatment. For example, CPTech's argument was based

of First Instance, CFI) held that, in order for the refusal by an undertaking that owns a copyright to give access to a product or service that is indispensable for carrying on a particular business to be treated as abusive, it was sufficient that three cumulative conditions be satisfied, namely, that: refusal prevents the emergence of a new product for which there is a potential consumer demand; it is unjustified; and it is such as to exclude any competition on a secondary market (Microsoft, para 330).

[116] See for example *Image Technical Services v Kodak*, 125 F 3d 1195. In certain cases involving refusal to deal where no intellectual property is involved, US courts took, for example, the following positions. In *Aspen Skiing Co v Aspen Highlands Skiing Corp* 472 US 585 (1985), the US Supreme Court ruled that the petitioner's abrupt refusal to provide access, which resulted in a sudden loss in the respondent's share of the market, constituted exclusionary conduct. In determining whether the petitioner's conduct might properly be characterised as exclusionary, the Court considered (1) the impact on consumers, (2) the impact on competitors, and (3) 'valid business reasons'. The Court confirmed that there was an 'obligation to continue' to provide access which had been granted up to that point, but that the actual act of refusing to cooperate with a competitor did not constitute a violation of law. According to the Court, however, even a firm with monopoly power has no general duty to engage in a joint marketing programme with a competitor; the absence of an unqualified duty to cooperate does not mean that every time a firm declines to participate in a particular cooperative venture, that decision may not have evidentiary significance, or that it may not give rise to liability in certain circumstances. In the *Trinko* case (*Verizon Communications Inc v Law Offices of Curtis V Trinko, LLP* 540 US 398 (2004)) the US Supreme Court held that the complaint alleging breach of Verizon's Telecommunication Act duties to share its network with competitors did not state a claim under the Sherman Act. The Department of Justice (DOJ) and the Federal Trade Commission (FTC) submitted a brief as amici curiae, stating that placing a burden on competitors to have to help rivals to an 'unreasonable' extent is justifiable only when the relevant conduct by that company is exclusionary or predatory.

[117] The content of the Competition Act of South Africa (1998) is similar to the EU competition law but differs from it in that the South African law explicitly refers to 'excessive pricing as a form of abuse of dominant position' (Article 8(a)) and essential facilities (Article 8(b)). If a dominant company in the relevant market controls production facilities, transport services, power transmission facilities or distribution networks, etc, and refuses its competitors access to these facilities without any justifiable reason so that business activities cannot be carried out (or if it is economically and technically impossible to duplicate these facilities), these facilities (or information) may be called 'essential facilities' and the dominant firm's behaviour might constitute abuse, depending on the context of a particular case. Competition authorities in Europe, the US and Japan have not used the concept of 'essential facilities' to determine illegality from the competition law point of view, but there has been debate on what facilities could be considered 'essential', what is included under the term 'facilities', and on what conditions competition law can intervene.

on the theory of 'essential facilities' and others on 'excessive pricing'.[118] While competition authorities are normally reluctant to evaluate whether or not prices are high, because they are not price regulators, the South African Competition Commission started investigating the case. It then found that GSK and BI abused their dominant positions by denying a competitor access to an essential facility, by excessive pricing and by engaging in an exclusionary act in their respective anti-retroviral (ARV) markets,[119] and by doing so contravened the Competition Act of 1998. On 16 October 2003, the Competition Commission notified the two companies of its intention to bring the case to the Competition Tribunal.[120] According to one Commissioner, these companies' excessive pricing (section 8(a)), refusing access to essential facilities (section 8(b)) and exclusionary acts had 'an anticompetitive effect that outweighed technological, efficiency or other pro-competitive gains (section 8(c))' and that 'it was plausible that each of the firms refused to license their patents to generic manufacturers in return for a reasonable royalty'.[121] The Commission's market analyses were not made public.

On 16 December 2003,[122] the complainants and the aforementioned pharmaceutical companies concluded a settlement agreement, under which the parties agreed to undertake the following:

- to extend to the private sector, the voluntary licence which had already been granted to Aspen Pharmacare (Aspen) in October 2001 in respect of the public sector;
- to grant up to three more voluntary licences on terms no less favourable than those granted to Aspen (maximum royalty rate of 5 per cent);
- to permit the licensees to export relevant ARVs to sub-Saharan Africa; and,
- where the licensee does not have manufacturing capability in South Africa, GSK will permit the importation of the drugs for distribution in South Africa.[123]

[118] Hazel Tau explained that the prices of these products were excessively high in comparison to generic drugs which have passed the WHO's prequalification and are sold internationally at the lowest price. The calculation of high prices in this complaint is explained in Hazel Tau et al, 'Statement of complaint in terms of section 49B(2)(b) of the Competition Act of 1998', www.tac.org.za/Documents/DrugCompaniesCC/HazelTauAndOthersVGlaxoSmithKlineAndOthersStatementOfComplaint.doc; www.tac.org.za/Documents/DrugCompaniesCC/HazelTauAndOthersVGlaxoSmithKlineAndOthersStatementOfComplaint.doc; T Avafia et al, 'The ability of select sub-Saharan African countries to utilise TRIPs Flexibilities and Competition Law to ensure a sustainable supply of essential medicines: A study of producing and importing countries' ICTSD, UNCTAD and Tralac, 2006, www.iprsonline.org/unctadictsd/docs/Trade%20and%20Competition%2030%203%2006%20final%20Edit1%20_2_%20_2_.pdf.

[119] 'Competition Commission finds pharmaceutical firms in contravention of the Competition Act', Competition Commission Media Release No 29 (16 October 2003).

[120] Competition Commission Press Releases, No 29 (16 October 2003) and No 32 (7 December 2003).

[121] Competition Commission Media Release No 29 ibid.

[122] Settlement Agreement entered into between 12 complainants and GSK South Africa, Glaxo Group Ltd and the Wellcome Foundation. On 10 December 2003, the parties reached an agreement. One NGO which had filed a complaint and failed to reach a settlement in this dispute contested GSK in an antitrust court. The NGO won on 6 December 2006 and GSK's appeal of this decision was rejected.

[123] Settlement Agreement ibid.

Because the South African Competition Commission did not publish its analyses or findings on market definition/dominance and the parties' conduct, it is difficult to evaluate the soundness of this competition analysis. However, the result was positive in the sense that these licences granted and implemented on the basis of sound business principles and in appropriate conditions facilitated patient access to ARVs in sub-Saharan Africa. There was no longer a need to pass the requirements of paragraph 6 of the 30 August 2003 WTO Agreement under Chapter 6 of the Doha Declaration. These licences contributed also to local generic companies' business expansion.

Technology licence transfers to generic drug companies were already undertaken prior to the South African Competition Commission's intervention. Aspen had received licences from GSK and Shire to manufacture and sell their ARVs for free, as long as the medicines were used for WHO or the South African Government programme for AIDS treatment. Thirty per cent of profits from the sale of these drugs are given either to NGOs or the Government's AIDS education programmes. The ARVs produced under this agreement are supplied to government medical institutions at one-third of the market price, and they now account for 20 to 25 per cent of the drugs used in the government medical programmes.[124]

In 2002, Aspen also received licences from Boehringer which strengthened Aspen's competitiveness vis-à-vis other generics in the ARV market.[125] Through joint ventures with Matrix (India), Aspen produces active pharmaceutical ingredients for Nigeria, Tanzania, Zimbabwe, Kenya, Ethiopia and Mozambique; markets which represent approximately 43 per cent of all Africans needing HAART. In January 2005, Aspen won fast-track approval (tentative) from the FDA for developing country markets of the generic 3TC+ AZT combination and nevirapine as part of the Presidential Emergency Plan for AIDS Relief (PEPFAR)[126] and the Clinton Foundation. The 2003 settlement promoted further technology transfer and exports to sub-Saharan countries other than South Africa.

The South African drug market was valued at US$150 million in 2002, which amounts to US$35 per person. Public health programmes face financial difficulties and private health insurance only covers 18 per cent of the population. In South Africa, there are competitive generic companies such as Aspen Pharmacare,[127] Adkock/Ingram and other joint ventures with Indian companies such as Timbalami and Cipla/Medpro which seem devoted to business under licence. The impact of

---

[124] Interview with Jon Pender, Vice President, Government Affairs at GSK on 3 August 2007.

[125] Generics (UK) and Merck Generics (RSA).

[126] See ch 7 and URL below: www.fda.gov/InternationalPrograms/FDABeyondOurBordersForeign Offices/AsiaandAfrica/ucm119231.htm. As of 6 October 2009, 'more than 100 products have been assessed by the FDA and either fully or tentatively approved in association with the PEPFAR program. Of these, 29 have been new products and 71 have been generic copies of previously authorized antiretroviral products in the United States. Twenty-two of these new products are new combinations or regimens that have not previously been authorized in the United States. In addition, there are seven new pediatric products considered innovative for patients in developing economies.' www. fda.gov/NewsEvents/Newsroom/PressAnnouncements/ucm185416.htm.

[127] Aspen Pharmacare is Africa's largest generic company, with capital of approximately US$50 million. For seven successive years, Aspen's business grew by 40%. *Financial Times*, 1 April 2006.

Indian companies has been considerable in this region and, with respect to AIDS drugs, 85 per cent of the ARVs supplied by the Global Fund are provided by exports from Indian companies.[128] Today, Aspen has grown into a global generic company through its ARV transactions and is contributing to the South African regional supply of ARVs. In 2009, GSK bought a 16 per cent stake in Aspen Pharmacare.

D   National Courts and the Doha Declaration

The Doha Declaration has been quoted by domestic courts in many countries, including Thailand and India. Among the first examples was the Thai Central Intellectual Property and International Trade Court (CIPITC).[129] This was the only case in the world where an AIDS drug patent was enforced in a developing country.[130] No other ARV patent rights were enforced in developing countries.

In Thailand, on 9 May 2001, an AIDS patients' organisation, AIDS Access Foundation (AAF), together with the Ministry of Health, brought a lawsuit for the cancellation of Bristol-Myers Squibb's (BMS) ARV patent[131] to the CIPITC. This lawsuit was brought forward in the context of the Thai Government Pharmaceutical Organisation's (GPO) attempt to produce this medicine in spite of BMS' patents on this medicine.

The application for a patent for Vidax (didanosine, ddI), was filed on 7 July 1992 by BMS at the Thai Department of Intellectual Property Rights (DIP).[132] Subsequently, on 13 May 1997, BMS submitted another application to amend the claim by deleting, from claims 1 and 2, the phrase 'from about 5 to 100 mg per dose'.[133] BMS was said to have expanded its rights in this way, because the GPO had started producing generic ddI tablets at a dosage of 150 mg, which was not covered by the BMS patent claim.[134] In 1999, the GPO requested that DIP grant a compulsory license for the BMS patent on ddI. However, this was unsuccessful due to the reluctance of other government agencies.[135]

In the initial judgment, the CIPITC, in judging the plaintiffs' standing, quoted the WTO 2001 Doha Declaration on Public Health and the TRIPS Agreement to

---

[128] CV Chien, 'HIV/AIDS Drugs for Sub-Saharan Africa: How Do Brand and Generic Supply Compare?' (2007) 2(3) Santa Clara University School of Law Legal Studies Research Paper No 07-41, *PLoS ONE*.

[129] The CIPITC was established on 1 December 1997 to deal with intellectual property rights issues such as counterfeit goods exported from Thailand.

[130] Telephone interview with Pascale Boulet, Médecins sans Frontières, Geneva, 7 July 2006.

[131] Based on s 53 of the Thai Patent Act. *Aids Access Foundation, Mrs Wanida Chaichana and Mr Hurn Ruangsuksud v Bristol-Myers Squibb Company and the Department of Intellectual Property*, Judgment, 1 October 2002 (34/2544, 93/2545).

[132] 'A combination formula offering better oral use of dideoxy purine nucleosides which provides positive effects for the treatment of AIDS'. Medicines and their active pharmaceutical ingredients were not patentable under the 1979 Thai Patent Act 9(2), but the 1992 Patent Act, which entered into effect on 1 August 1992, included them as subjects of patent protection.

[133] This phrase, incidentally, is found in the Australian and Japanese patents.

[134] It is estimated that in Thailand more than 600,000 people are infected with AIDS.

[135] MSF – Belgium, 'Civil Society Movement: To Revoke the Thai Patent on ddI' (Bangkok, 2004) 3–6.

say that 'the treatment of life and health of the human is more important than any other property and this is recognized internationally . . .'.[136] Despite the Thai courts' usually dualist approach to treaties and domestic law, the judges in this case seemed to take into account the situation of the country by referring to the international Declaration. This is, however, an obiter dictum and the Court actually recognised the locus standi of the plaintiffs on the basis of s 54(2), which refers to 'any interested person'.[137]

The plaintiffs appealed to the Court, arguing that the ddI tablet dosage patent did not satisfy the novelty requirement, and that it was invalid.[138] According to the Court, the Doha Declaration insists that TRIPS be interpreted and implemented in order to promote the rights of the Members to protect the public health of countries, and therefore, those in need of the medicine are also interested parties to the grant of the patent.[139]

On 1 October 2002, the CIPITC upheld the plaintiffs' request that the phrase 'from about 5 to 100 mg per dose' be inserted into the defendant's patent. BMS and the co-defendant appealed to the upper court and the AAF filed a new lawsuit with the Upper Court, claiming that the tablet patent lacked novelty and therefore the patent itself was invalid. In 2004, a settlement, whose content remains confidential, was reached.[140] On 17 January 2004, BMS declared, in court, their intention to terminate their ddI patent in Thailand and withdrew their court appeal.[141]

Several years later, TRIPS flexibilities and the Doha Declaration came to be quoted in various national courts, some examples of which will be referred to in chapters 11 and 13.

---

[136]   CIPITC judgment (n 138) 6.

[137]   Section 54 of the Thai Patent Act stipulates that: 'Any patent granted not in compliance with the provisions of Section 5, 9, 10, 11 or Section 14 shall be invalid. The invalidity of a patent may be challenged by any person. A petition to cancel an invalid patent may be submitted to the Court by any interested person or the public prosecutor.'

[138]   Subsequently, DIP granted a patent to BMS but without the phrase 'from about 5 to 100 mg per dose'. The plaintiffs argued that the deletion of this phrase was in breach of s 20 of the Patent Act concerning the modification of the material part of the invention. The plaintiffs further argued that the GPO attempted to manufacture ddI tablets of more than 100 mg per dose to sell at a price of about Baht 20 each. According to the plaintiffs, this would not have been possible if the scope of the patent claim of the defendant was so wide and, therefore, prejudiced the human rights of the patients to access proper medical treatment. CIPITC judgment (n 131) 4.

[139]   The CIPITC judgment states that 'The Court views that the Defendant as the holder of the Patent has an absolute power to prevent the others to seek any benefit from the invention of DDI, whether to manufacture for use, for sale, or to import such medicine in the [Thai] Kingdom, without the consent from the Defendant. Since the medicine is one of the fundamental factors necessary for human being, as distinct from other products or other invention that the consumers may or may not choose for consumption. . . . It was insisted that the TPIPS be interpreted and implemented so as to promote the rights of the Members to protect the countries' public health, especially, the promotion and support of the access to medicine of the people as a whole. Therefore, the injured parties from the grant of Patent are not limited to the manufacturers or the sellers of medicine protected by the Patent. The patients or those in need of the medicine are also interested parties to the grant of the Patent'. CIPITC judgment (n 131) 7.

[140]   CIPITC judgment (n 131) 63–66.

[141]   MSF-Belgium (n 135)/19.

III COMPULSORY LICENSING AND INDUSTRIAL POLICY

A The Nature of the Doha Declaration

In the discussions leading to the Doha Declaration, many arguments were made on the assumption that, but for patents, local production of medicines would provide a cheaper stream of safe generics. The Doha Declaration, in paragraph 5, refers to compulsory licensing and parallel trade as examples of TRIPS flexibilities, but does not say these are the best methods of ensuring access to medicines. Parallel trade, the international trade of patented products that occurs mainly to take advantage of exchange rates, rarely occurs in medicines, except in the EU, where it is politically encouraged for market integration. If it did occur globally, prices in developing countries would rise while those in developed countries would fall in the long run, so policies of international exhaustion may not necessarily provide a long-term solution to access problems. Parallel import of relatively low-priced patented medicines from neighbouring countries is feasible, but this seems to be a localised and limited solution. Alternatively, 'parallel import' of patented medicines may refer to products coming from a country without patent protection over the product, or circulating under compulsory licences. If the right holder has not recouped remuneration from the first sale of these products, he or she may retain the right to stop such imports, given that the theory of exhaustion is usually based on the prohibition of double remuneration.[142]

Compulsory licences had been a central issue in the access to medicines debate. However, as Reichman et al point out, 'What seems clear is that compulsory licenses may be used more effectively in some circumstances than in others, and broad general statements obscure these factual nuances.'[143] Compulsory licensing presupposes that the local manufacturing or import sources of products are quality-assured and that the cooperation of the patent-holder is not needed to provide the necessary know-how for designing, manufacturing and administering the product. Pharmaceutical production requires relatively less know-how than other technological fields (see chapter 1), but such production must be economically efficient for the country and must not cause it to forgo better choices, including humanitarian cooperation, in either the short or long term. Compulsory licensing is seen by many as a guarantee of better priced products or technologies but it may not necessarily be cost-effective if, for example, the cost of manufacturing for a small market and the cost of assuring quality are taken into account.

---

[142] See, for example, on the question of injunction on the import of a patented product from a country without patent protection, *Merck v Stephar*, Case 187/80 [1981] ECR 2063, and for a product under compulsory licence, *Merck v Primecrown*, Case C-267, 268/95 [1996] ECR; *Pharmon BV v Hoechst*, Case 19/84[1985] ECR 2281.

[143] J Reichman et al, 'Non-voluntary Licensing of Patented Inventions: Historical Perspective, Legal Framework under TRIPS, and an Overview of the Practice in Canada and the United States of America', UNCTAD/ICTSD Issue Paper No 5, September 2002, 24.

The patenting and pricing behaviour of multinational pharmaceutical firms attracted the attention of the international community, particularly because brand name firms set a high price for AIDS medicines in the first years of marketing. But for patents, it was argued, generic manufacturers could offer lower prices than their originator counterparts and introduce a certain degree of competitive pressure. However, most essential medicines indicated by the WHO, which guides the national selection (antibiotics, analgesics, anti-allergics, anti-tuberculosis, etc) are off-patent, and patented essential medicines are mostly AIDS medicines (see chapter 8).

There is a wide range of medicine access problems and causes that the Declaration does not cover. One of the most difficult obstacles to the access to medicines would be the lack of adequately trained medical personnel to prescribe and administer appropriate medicines, as well as the lack of health insurance in developing countries. Even when medicines are patented, many factors other than IP protection could cause high prices, such as small market size, distribution costs, abusive behaviours of specific companies, etc, which are not inherent in IPRs.

In discussions leading up to the Declaration, the idea that affordability is possible only by limiting intellectual property rights was accepted as given, while other options were not discussed. At the WTO, discussions on such options as differential pricing,[144] the establishment of public procurement schemes or effective forms of international cooperation were excluded as being 'outside the purview of the TRIPS Agreement':

> Differential pricing should in no way be used to limit the flexibility of the TRIPS Agreement in any of its provisions. Given that the issue is not within the sphere of discussions on intellectual property rights, it should not be covered by the TRIPS Council, but rather by other intergovernmental international organizations, such as the World Health Organization.[145]

As a result, the focus in the access to medicines debate has been on IPRs only. Each specialist advocates a solution specific to the problem that he or she has singled out from the complex reality; for example, for J Sacks, the widespread use of mosquito nets and fertilizer is the solution to malaria and poverty in Africa.[146] This mindset could yield one valid solution to a specific problem, but such a solution would be difficult to apply generally to other problems or use to solve complex problems. The obstacles to access to medicines differ from one country to another and, in most cases, IPRs are probably not the main obstacle. Considering IP protection as the only factor preventing access to medicines may,

---

[144] Differential pricing by originator pharmaceutical firms is a pricing policy whereby prices are set higher in high-income countries and lower in low-income countries (this does not include policies of rebates, etc). This could contribute to the expanded use of new pharmaceuticals in developing countries, while preserving the returns to R&D in the most lucrative markets.

[145] Developing country paper for Doha IP/C/W/296 (n 22) summary and para 35. .

[146] JD Sachs and JJ Myers, 'The End of Poverty: Economic Possibilities for Our Time', 30 March 2005, www.cceia.org/resources/transcripts/5132.html#1.

in certain situations, divert governments' focus from establishing a viable public health policy with a more equitable and coordinated management of financial and human resources.

C 'Public Interest' in Complex Realities

Compulsory licensing could be an effective solution in certain situations, but, in the complex reality, could be a tool of politics, or an inefficient industrial policy. In the aforementioned China-Taipei TBR Report, the European Commission raised the issue that Chinese Taipei 'interferes gravely with the free operation of the market', using compulsory licensing 'as an industrial policy instrument, and not as a limited exception to the use of patent rights'.[147] Compulsory licensing requires public intervention based on well-founded, clearly explained public goals. Article 8.1 of the TRIPS Agreement refers to measures 'necessary to' protect public health and nutrition, implying that a mere designation of 'public health' is insufficient for compulsory licensing to be in conformity with the Agreement.

Compulsory licensing could also be part of lucrative political operations. On 2 August 2002, two months after Pfizer's entry into the local market to sell Viagra,[148] the Egyptian Ministry of Health announced it would authorise 12 local companies to produce a generic version of the drug, to sell at one-twentieth of Pfizer's market price of about $5.20 for each 50-milligram pill.[149] According to the *New York Times*, the President of the department within Egypt's Ministry of Health that administers pharmaceuticals said: 'We have to think of the interests of the poor people.' Article 23(2) of the Egyptian Intellectual Property Law[150] allows the Minister of Health to grant compulsory licensing when 'the quantity of medicines available fails to meet national needs due to the poor quality or a prohibitive price or in public health emergencies, without prior negotiations with the right holder'.[151]

---

[147]   Chinese Taipei TBR Report (n 34) 89–90.

[148]   RA Castellano, 'Note, Patent Law for New Medical Uses of Known Compounds and Pfizer's Viagra Patent' (2006) 46 *IDEA* 283, 284; I Shirasu, 'Defense of the Chinese Pharmaceutical Market: the Annulment of the PRB Decision on the Viagra Patent' (in Japanese) (2006) 4(48) *IP Prism* 289–290; RC Bird and DR Cahoy, 'The Impact of Compulsory Licensing on Foreign Direct Investment: A Collective Bargaining Approach' (2008) 45(2) *American Business Law Journal* 24.

[149]   'We will definitely grant market authorization for all Egyptian companies that applied to produce Viagra': A Allam, 'Investment, Egypt Tries Patent Laws', *New York Times* (4 October 2002), http://www.nytimes.com/2002/10/04/business/worldbusiness/04EGYP.html.

[150]   As cited in Castellano, 'Note' (n 148) 289, www.nytimes.com/2002/10/04/business/worldbusiness/04EGYP.html.

[151]   *Intellectual Property Law*, www.egypo.gov.eg/inner/english/PDFs/law2002e.pdf. Upon the request of the Minister of Health, when the quantity of patented medicines made available fails to adequately meet the national needs, due to their poor quality or if they are offered at a prohibitive price, or if the patent is related to medicines addressing critical cases, incurable or endemic diseases or products used in the prevention of these diseases, or where the invention is related to the medicines, their manufacturing process, the raw materials necessary for their preparation or the process of manufacturing of those materials. According to the *New York Times*, the drug was covered by the data protection provisions in a 2000 ministerial decree as well as by the patent provisions in the new

Concerning compulsory licences, except when courts issues decisions, accurate data and explanations are often lacking on the processes and reasons leading to such licensing. According to the *New York Times*, prior to Pfizer's market entry into Egypt, Viagra from Syria and India had been widely available in Egypt for years, for as much as $40 a pill; it dropped to $1 after Pfizer's drug became available. It seems that local pharmaceutical companies raised a 'storm after the exclusive rights were issued to Pfizer in June, accusing the Ministry of Health of helping multinational drug companies to exploit Egypt's poor.'

In Argentina, also, local companies requested marketing authorisation for similarly structured compounds for Viagra which were ready for production, after Pfizer obtained marketing approval.[152] Subsequently, the protection of test data for pharmaceuticals and agrochemicals became one of the subjects of the WTO dispute settlement between the US and Argentina, which led to the above-mentioned settlement agreement.[153]

In the these cases, the US initiated consultations in 1999 with Argentina on the conformity of a series of provisions in the Argentine patent and pharmaceutical regulatory law with regard to the TRIPS Agreement. Switzerland joined the dispute as a third party. Under Argentina's pharmaceutical law, in which data protection as provided in Article 39.3 of the TRIPS Agreement is stipulated, generic versions of new drugs such as Viagra received marketing authorisation. In other cases, compulsory licensing under the patent law and competition law had been issued. Medicines under compulsory licence were priced regularly at somewhat lower prices (shadow pricing). Nine consultations were held between June 1999 and April 2002 over these questions, leading to a settlement agreement between the US and Argentina.

D Different IPR Court Policies and Local Industries

The Viagra patent represents new use of a known compound[154] and can be non-patentable or contestable in certain jurisdictions. If its patent is successfully invalidated, Viagra can be a lucrative source of profits for competitor companies. In

---

law. In all these cases, the decision of granting a non-voluntary licence shall be notified promptly to the owner of the patent. Allam, 'Investment, Egypt Tries Patent Laws' (n 149).

[152] Art 5 of Argentine Law No 24.766. Castellano (n 148); Bird and Cahoy, 'The Impact of Compulsory Licensing on Foreign Direct Investment' (n 148); M Edelman, 'The Argentine Trade Tango: Out of Step on Intellectual Property Protection' (1999) 172 *AdTI Issue Brief* 1–7, hwww.adti.net/new_zuberi_uploaded/IP/Argentine_Trade_Tango.html.

[153] *Argentina–Patent Protection for Pharmaceuticals and Test Data Protection for Agricultural Chemicals* (WT/DS171); *Argentina–Certain Measures on the Protection of Patents and Test Data* (WT/DS196) (n 106). Concerning the protection of test data, the parties will continue consultations to assess the progress of the legislative process of approval of the related items of the notification, and in the light of this assessment, the US may decide to continue consultations or request the establishment of a panel related to Art 39.3 of the TRIPS Agreement.

[154] The invention relating to the use of sildenafil citrate for the treatment of erectile dysfunction (EDF).

China, relatively sophisticated administrative and judicial institutions dealt with the pressures from domestic industry. The Viagra patent application was filed by Pfizer under the Patent Cooperation Treaty (PCT – see chapter 2). On 19 September 2001, the Chinese patent, with one single claim,[155] was granted by the Chinese State Intellectual Property Office (SIPO). Immediately, 13 complaints from one individual and 12 Chinese drug-makers were filed with the Patent Re-examination Board (PRB), challenging the validity of the patent. These companies argued that a person skilled in the art would not understand whether the compound in the single claim was the preferred compound used in the clinical test, demonstrating its therapeutic function. The PRB declared the patent invalid in July 2004 on the grounds that the description of the invention in the patent specification was inadequate and did not fulfil the enablement requirements provided by Article 26 of the Chinese Patent Law.[156] The PRB followed the jurisprudential lead of the US in using a tight application of the written description doctrine on a second use patent.[157]

In October 2004, Pfizer filed an appeal against the ruling with the Beijing First Intermediate People's Court. On 2 June 2006, this Court revoked the invalidation decision of the PRB. On 7 September 2007, the Beijing People's High Court upheld the Viagra patent until 2014. According to the High Court, the compounds for selectively inhibiting the cyclic guanosine monophosphate phosphodiesterse (cGMP139-PDE)[158] were explained by five classes in a certain order[159] as the fifth class constituted by nine compounds (sildenafil is included) selected from the fourth class; the compound in the single claim among the nine preferred compounds is thus described in the specification.

The High Court's view was that, for medical inventions, test data, rather than a single technical solution based on a technical idea, was necessary to prove patentability, and the technical effects should be shown by the test data of the preferred embodiments. As to the second medical use of inventions, test data are required for a person skilled in the art to be persuaded that the claimed use will achieve the stated technical objective of carrying out the claimed invention. It was estimated that in 2005, the legitimate and underground markets combined for ED drugs in China was CNY 20 billion (US$3.0 billion).[160] It was a battle for an attractive market. Many countries denied patentability or exclusivity to Viagra, and their reasons vary.[161] Many commentators praised local companies

---

[155] The single claim of the Viagra patent is related to the second medical use of sildenafil.

[156] Art 26 of the Chinese Patent Law states that 'the description shall set forth the invention or utility model in a manner sufficiently clear and complete so as to enable a person skied in the relevant field of technology to carry it out . . .'.

[157] Castellano (n 155) 284: Shirasu (n 148) 22–27.

[158] A nucleotide derived from guanosine triphosphate (GTP). cGMP acts as a second messenger activating intracellular protein kinases in response to the binding of membrane-impermeable peptide hormones to the external cell surface which widens blood vessels resulting from relaxation of smooth muscle cells.

[159] Shirasu (n 148) 24.

[160] ibid 28.

[161] Castellano (n 148) 288.

for resorting to legal means instead of marketing their copies anyway,[162] and some regretted that these companies did not invest in research in developing from the eight other compounds a better drug[163]. In August 2004, at around the same time as Pfizer appealed to the court, GlaxoSmithKline decided to abandon its patent in China for rosiglitazone – a major ingredient of its popular diabetes drug Avandia – which, as in Pfizer's Viagra case, was challenged by local pharmaceutical manufacturers. As local industries grow, patent challenges by local companies will increase substantially.

E Public Interest and Industrial Policies

Patent laws (and other special laws or competition law) of most WTO Members allow government agencies to issue compulsory licences. Many of these laws refer to 'public interest', and/or issues that could be interpreted as forming part of the public interest, such as public health and the environment. Among various countries, however, the 'public' or 'public interest' is defined in widely different terms. Some are more national security-oriented and others include market considerations, including prices and the interest of domestic industry. In China, official Patent Law commentary, such as *New Patent Law Commentary* and *People's Republic of China Commentary of the Patent Law*, provides the following examples of 'state emergency' within the Patent Law: invasion by enemies, uprisings and danger to the security of the state. According to the same source, 'emergency' means natural hazards, epidemics or situations where the security of the state, people or property are affected.[164] Some other countries provide economic grounds for issuing compulsory licenses, such as non-affordable prices, supply shortages not only in the domestic market but also in export markets (India), or conditions that adversely affect the transfer of technology (India, Egypt).

According to section 84(1)(a) of India's the Patents (Amendment) Act, 2005, any interested person may make an application to the Controller for grant of a compulsory licence at any time after the expiration of three years from the date of the grant of a patent when, on any of the following grounds if: the reasonable requirements of the public with respect to the patented invention have not been satisfied, and section 84(7)(a) further provides that:

> For the purposes of this Chapter, the reasonable requirements of the public shall be deemed not to have been satisfied if, by reason of the refusal of the patentee to grant a licence or licences on reasonable terms, (i) an existing trade or industry or the development thereof or the establishment of any new trade or industry in India or the trade or industry of any person or class of persons trading or manufacturing in India is prejudiced; or (ii) an existing trade or industry or the development thereof or the establish-

---

[162] P Yu, 'Viagra's Upside' (2004) Oct. *IP Law & Business US* 49; Shirasu (n 148) 28.

[163] Shirasu (n 148) 28.

[164] S Nakajima, *Commentary on the Chinese Patent Law and Regulations Article by Article* (in Japanese, Keizai Sangyou Chousakai, 2006) 588.

ment of any new trade or industry in India or the trade or industry of any person or class of persons trading or manufacturing in India is prejudiced; or(iii) a market for export of the patented article manufactured in India is not being supplied or developed; or(iv) the establishment or development of commercial activities in India is prejudiced; . . .

The history of patent laws shows that 'public interest' covers a wide range of national interests and social welfare. The institutions of compulsory licensing have developed under the influence of various ideas, one of which is that governments should intervene in certain market situations for the sake of public interest, which often includes domestic industrial policy considerations (see chapter 10).

To safeguard public interest, which is a mission of all governments, it seems important that governments ensure the public nature and, as much as possible, economic viability of the objectives for compulsory licensing.

Table 9.1 compares compulsory licensing provisions in the legislation of selected WTO Members, including emerging economies.

Table 9.1: Compulsory licensing provisions

	State of extreme emergency	Non-working or insufficient working	High price or market demand	Para 6 mechanism (export licensing)	Dependency	Public interest	Remedies to anti-competitive behaviour	Government use
China	○	○(1)		○	○	○	○	
Thailand	○	○(2)	○(3)		○	○	○	○(4)
India	○	○(2) (5)	○(2) (6)	○	○	○	○	○
Taiwan	○	○			○	○	○	○
Brazil	○	○(2)		○	○	○	○	
Egypt	○	○(1)	○(7)		○	○(8), (9)	○	
Rep. of Korea	○	○(2)	○	○	○	○	○	○

Key

(1) At any time after the expiration of three years from the grant of a patent or four years from the date of application, whichever is later.

(2) When three years have elapsed since the patent was granted.

(3) Thailand Patent Act 1999 Article 46(2): 'no product produced under the patent is sold in any domestic market, or that such a product is sold but at unreasonably high prices or does not meet the public demand, without any legitimate reason.'

(4) Thailand Patent Act 1999 Article 51: 'In order to carry out any service for public consumption or which is of vital importance to the defence of the country or for the preservation or realization of natural resources or the environment or to prevent or relieve a severe shortage of food, drugs or other consumption items or for any other public service.'

(5) Revocation of patents after the expiration of two years from the date of the order granting the first compulsory licence.

(6) See section 84(7)(a).

(7) Article 23(2) of Egypt's Law on the Protection of Intellectual Property Rights: 'Upon the request of the Minister of Health, when the quantity of patented medicines made available fail to adequately meet the national needs, due to their poor quality or if they are offered at a prohibitive price, or if the patent is related to medicines address-ing critical cases, incurable or endemic diseases or products used in the prevention of these diseases, or where the invention is related to the medicines, their manufacturing process, the raw materials necessary for their preparation or the process of manufac-turing of those materials.'

(8) Article 23(1)(a) of Egypt's Law on the Protection of Intellectual Property Rights: 'Public non-commercial interest. This includes the preservation of national security, health, environment and food safety.'

(9) Article 23(1)(c) of Egypt's Law on the Protection of Intellectual Property Rights: 'Support of national efforts in vital sectors for economic, social and technological development, without unreasonable prejudice to the rights of the patent owner and taking into consideration the legitimate interests of third parties.'

Part IV

IP and Industrial Policies

10

Emerging Economies' IP and Industrial Policies

THIS CHAPTER RETRACES the past and present intellectual property policies relating to pharmaceutical industrial development of middle income developing countries, many of which are often referred to today as emerging economies. Although the original spirit of IP protection in encouraging creativity may not be as narrow as this, IP policies could be tools of industrial development if they are combined with coordinated efforts to promote scientific and technical skill and knowledge as well, to encourage innovative business management and market growth.

The development of the Japanese Patent Law and its role in increasing the competitiveness of R&D and their results in the pharmaceutical sector may offer a comparative example, as Japan's economy, during several decades in the second half of the twentieth century, could be characterised as an emerging economy at that time.

I INTELLECTUAL PROPERTY PROTECTION AS INDUSTRIAL POLICY TOOLS

A Patent Protection of chemicals, pharmaceuticals and foods

The chemical industry grew during a period of fierce competition in the first three decades of the twentieth century. Until World War I, Germany's chemical industry, which had grown fast since the turn of the century,[1] was generally reckoned to be far ahead of all other countries and was regarded as 'the Pharmacy of the World'. At that time, the US chemical industry was mainly of pharmaceutical origin.[2] Chemical development in the US came later, with American

---

[1] JP Murmann, 'Chemical Industries after 1850', *Oxford Encyclopedia of Economic History* (Oxford University Press, 2002); LF Haber, *The Chemical Industry 1900–1930: international growth and technological change* (Oxford, Clarendon Press, 1971).

[2] There were pharmaceutical companies which grew out of pharmacies (compounding and dealing mainly with medicines of botanical and mineral origin) and those that ventured into pharmaceuticals via synthetic chemicals and dyestuffs. Companies that grew mainly or totally out of pharmacies include Merck (German and American), Schering, GSK, Abbott, Eli Lilly, Wyeth and others; those that started out from synthetic chemicals include Hoechst and Rhone-Poulenc (now part of Sanofi-Aventis) and ICI (now part of AstraZeneca). Today, these differences are blurred as a

leadership during and after World War II. In the UK, the British Key Industry Protection policy for the chemical industry in the years after 1917 is said to have helped the UK catch up with US and German chemical industries.

Some companies moved from the chemical industry to pharmaceuticals, which came to be organised as an industry in the 1930s.[3] UK and Swiss companies attempted to catch up with the most advanced German and US pharmaceutical technologies by licensing or by inventing around internationally available new technologies, aided by relatively weak domestic patent protection regimes. By the 1940s, latecomers such as Italy, Japan and India had also acquired varying degrees of technical skills in organic chemistry. These countries watched closely the evolution of technologies of more advanced countries in this field and studied the patent laws of these countries, with a view to adjusting their own. Patent laws in technological latecomer countries with relatively high skill levels incorporated industrial policy dimensions in a mirror-image response to patent protection in more advanced countries. Some categories of inventions were excluded from patentability, particularly where, as today, such exceptions were easily justifiable and accepted due to the popular belief that patents always raise prices and prevent a general and sustained supply of goods.

Since the enactment of its Patent Act in 1790, the US has not restricted patentability to particular fields of technology, including chemical substances, medicines or foods and beverages. The UK had granted patent protection for chemical substances inventions, but from 1919 stopped doing so until 1949, when product patent protection was restored. Medicines and foods were patentable throughout, but there were special rules based on public interest in the Patents Act of 1949 until the enactment of the 1977 Patents Act (see chapter 2). Subsequently, the UK Patent Act was amended in 1999 in conformity with the TRIPS Agreement and EC case law.[4]

In France, the first Patent Law was adopted in 1791 and amended in 1844. This law recognised the patentability of chemical and food inventions, but not medicines. In 1941, the system of visa by the Ministry of Health granted a period of exclusivity of six years to medicines and, in 1959, patent protection of medicines was established also by a special law. In 1968, the latter was integrated in the Patent Law and the visa system came to control only safety and efficacy of medicines. In Germany, chemical, drug and food substances were not protected by patent until 1967. It was only in 1978 that Switzerland and Italy introduced product patent protection, and in Spain, Portugal and Norway, as late as 1992.

---

result of mergers and more recent developments in biotechnology. For an historical account of the origins of the industry in pharmacy, synthetic chemistry and microbiology, see H Redwood, *The Pharmaceutical Industry: trends, problems and achievements* (Felixstowe, Oldwicks Press, 1988) 6–35.

[3] The discovery of the first effective synthetic product for an infectious disease, Salvarsan, was in 1905, but the pharmaceutical industry actually developed with the commercialisation of the sulphonamides between 1935 and 1940. For an historical account of the origins of the industry in pharmacy, synthetic chemistry and microbiology, ibid 6–35.

[4] *Commission v UK*, Case C30/90, [1992] ECR I-829.

Japan's first patent protection regulation in 1871[5] but the country had no special rule regarding product patents until 1889, when the patent law made food and medicine inventions unpatentable, presumably for social and moral reasons. Japan became a party to the Paris Convention in 1899. In 1919, chemical substances became unpatentable.

It was explained that the inadequate wartime supply of chemical products from Germany led to this decision, encouraging domestic production. It was also held widely in Japan, as in India later, that in France and Germany, product patent protection prevented research in the field.[6] The reintroduction in Japan of product patents for chemicals, pharmaceuticals and foods was discussed from the 1950s, but the actual introduction of such protection was retarded, due to public and industrial opinion that argued in favour of 'public interest'.

In 1958, at the fifth revision Conference of the Paris Convention in Lisbon, the BIRPI[7] tabled a draft proposing that each Member recognise the patentability of chemical substances under certain conditions encouraging the working of these patents through licensing.[8] At that time, there were 25 Members with laws that protected chemical substances, but Members such as France, Italy, Austria, Hungary and Czechoslovakia objected.[9] The Paris Convention was therefore not amended on this point, and the draft resolution proposed by Germany was adopted instead. The resolution urged that the Paris Union study the possibility of providing patent protection for new chemical products in national legislation, given that inventions must be protected to promote technological progress.[10] Product patents are necessary to protect pharmaceutical inventions, because most process patents can be circumvented by those with technological skills in chemistry (and, later, in biotechnology).

In Japan, the appropriateness of introducing product patent protection was considered since the 1950s,[11] in the light of the proposals made at the Lisbon Conference and in consideration of Japan's domestic technological level, until product patent protection was finally introduced in 1976. In Japan, adopting the standards of the most developed countries was regarded as desirable, and pat-

---

[5] The Japanese Patent Regulation was first enacted in 1871, only for Japanese nationals. However, this soon became obsolete, due to its failure in encouraging domestic creativity in an open, global context. A new Patent Law was adopted in 1899 when Japan became a Member of the Paris Convention based on the principle, inter alia, of national treatment. The current law was promulgated in 1995 and has since been through numerous revisions. www.wipo.int/clea/en/text_pdf.jsp?lang=EN&id=2678.

[6] H Iwata et al, *Busshitsu no Chishiki (Knowledge about Product Patents, in Japanese)* (Tokyo, Tusho-Sangyo Chosakai, 1975) 3–7.

[7] Bureaux Internationaux Réunis pour la Protection de la Propriété Intellectuelle (the predecessor to the World Intellectual Property Organization (WIPO)), ch 2.

[8] Iwata et al (n 6) 11.

[9] Conférence de Lisbonne: Documents préliminaire (6–31 October 1958) http://ftp.wipo.int/pub/library/ebooks/Internationalconferences-recordsproceedings/LisbonneConference1958/.

[10] This resolution obtained 27 supporting votes, no objections and 12 abstentions. Iwata et al (n 6) 12.

[11] The Sub-Committee of the Industrial Property Rights Committee in 1957 considered this a matter that needed to be addressed in the near future. I Neary, 'Patent legislation and the Japanese pharmaceutical industry' (1990) 2(2) *Japan Forum* 208.

ent protection was seen as beneficial for technological creativity. Most chemical industry representatives supported the introduction of product patent protection. They felt that too much R&D effort was spent on exploring different processes of producing chemical products patented abroad and on litigation, and that product patents would make R&D more effective. However, it took two decades for Japan's pharmaceutical industry to gain confidence in its ability to compete with foreign companies.[12]

The Japanese Patent Law[13] still retains some of the expressions of earlier days, when encouraging local invention was seen as a means of technological and industrial development and the industry looked to foreign examples for the optimum methods and levels of protection. The Japanese Patent Law is one of the few patent laws in the world to have explicitly defined invention; most patent laws have simply defined criteria by which to recognise inventions.[14] Article 2, paragraph 1, of the Japanese Patent Law defines invention as 'the highly advanced creation of technical ideas by which a law of nature is utilised'.

This definition was introduced in 1959 and was influenced by German academic writings of the nineteenth century, when the laws of nature were important for machines and heavy industry at that time.[15] Based on this definition, certain types of ideas, such as in relation to methods of solving mathematical formulas, unfinished inventions and certain types of business models, have not been accepted as inventions, either because they were not considered to be technical ideas, or did not utilise a law of nature (chapter 12). This rigid statutory definition of invention has not prevented the advancement of biotechnology, but it may become obsolete in the future with further advancement of science and technology.

Another expression which is also a remnant of the past is Article 1 of the Japanese Patent Act, which states its objective to encourage inventions by promoting their protection and utilisation so as 'to contribute to the development of industry'. Article 29(1) of the Japanese Patent Law stipulates that 'any person who has made an invention which is industrially applicable may obtain a patent therefor', excluding those inventions which were publicly known, worked or described,[16] but leaves the explanation of 'inventive step' until Article 29(2). This

---

[12] Iwata et al (n 6) 208.

[13] Patent Law No 121 of 13 April 1959, as last amended by Act No 109 of 2006.

[14] Mexico's Industrial Property Law is another example of a patent law that contains an explicit definition of invention: 'any human creation that allows matter or energy existing in nature to be transformed for utilisation by man for the satisfaction of his specific needs shall be considered an invention' (Art 15). Based on this concept, the Mexican law stipulates that any invention that is new and that is the result of an inventive step and is susceptible to industrial application within the meaning of this Law is patentable, with the exception of: (a) processes that are essentially biological processes for obtaining, reproducing and propagating plants and animals; (b) biological and generic material as found in nature; (c) animal breeds; (d) the human body and the living matter constituting it; and (e) plant varieties (Art 16). Industrial Property Law of 25 June 1991, last amended by the Decree of 26 December 1997.

[15] German jurist Josef Kohler's definition of invention was adopted.

[16] 'In a distributed publication or made available to the public through electric telecommunication lines prior to the patent application' is added *in fine*.

is probably because the requirement of inventive step is inherent in the concept of invention. The reason why the patentability criterion of 'industrial application' is emphasised may be related to the stated objective of the law. Based on Article 1, inventions which can be used in pure science have not been patentable, because it is thought that the legal monopoly over such inventions could hinder industrial development. By the same token, therapeutic methods directly dealing with the human body for health reasons have not been considered as 'industry', and so not patentable, although the latter thinking is increasingly contested due to new biotechnology therapies working directly on human genes for treatment purposes. Diagnostic methods using extracted parts of the body, such as blood or urine, have already been patentable, because they are not considered as part of the human body. However, the fear that hospitals may become profit-maximising 'companies' animates still today the resistance of the Japanese medical profession to making therapeutic methods patentable. Article 32 of the Japanese Act is entitled 'unpatentable inventions' and stipulates that inventions liable to contravene public order, morality or public health shall not be patented, notwithstanding section 29. This provision, however, has never been used as a reason for the final rejection of a patent. Significantly, the Japanese Patent Law[17] has maintained provisions relating to the conditions for compulsory licensing in three situations: on the grounds of non-working after four years have lapsed since the filing date of the application (Article 83), when a patented invention would utilise another person's patented invention, registered utility model or registered design (Article 92), and when the working of a patented invention is particularly necessary for the public interest (Article 93). The Guidelines on Compulsory Licences, amended in 1997, provide that compulsory licences be issued in conformity with the TRIPS Agreement.[18] In fact, these provisions have not been used either.

B Indian Patents Act 1970

In India, under British colonial rule, the first Act relating to patent rights was passed in 1856; it was replaced by the Indian Patents & Designs Act in 1911. After gaining independence in 1947, India's government appointed B Tek Chand to lead the Patents Enquiry Committee (1948–50),[19] and, subsequently, Justice Ayyangar to advise the government with a view to amending the Patents Act. The 400-page Ayyangar Report[20] meticulously compared the patent systems of the

[17] Conditions for compulsory licensing are stipulated in Arts 72, 79–83 and 92–97 of the Japanese Patent Law.

[18] Amended on 24 April 1997.

[19] The Tek Chand Committee Report led to the adoption of the Indian Patents and Designs (Amendment) Bill 1950, but lapsed. P Narayanan, *Patent Law,* 2nd edn (Calcutta, Eastern Law House, 1985) 5–7.

[20] R Ayyangar, *Report on the Revision of the Patent Law* (New Delhi, 1959) (Ayyangar Report), see also ch 2.

world, their historical development and functioning in industrial development, particularly in the US, the UK, Germany and other European countries, Canada, the Soviet Union and East European countries. He studied the provisions of the Paris Convention and the Lisbon revisions discussions in particular. The Report also examined the recommendations of the Patents Enquiry Committee that led to the 1953 Indian Patents Act Bill, and criticised many of its recommendations.

The Ayyangar Report asserted that 'patents are taken [by foreign companies in developing countries] not in the interests of the economy of the country granting the patent or with a view to manufacture there but with the main object of protecting an export market from competition from rival manufacturers particularly those in other parts of the world.'[21] The Report argued that: 'the conservation of foreign exchange is a matter of prime importance [for India] . . . that any increase in the price of the patented products imported into the country must to that extent be a disadvantage to the nation's economy'.[22] According to the Report, if the right holder was the monopoly supplier of a product whose patent was not worked in India, it would be possible that India would be deprived of alternative supplies of that product at cheaper prices.[23]

Justice Ayyangar argued that the patent system had been universally accepted for well over a century and would encourage Indian inventors in the future, although they took only a small share in the benefits of that system at that time.[24] For this to happen, he argued, certain conditions must be fulfilled: (i) technical education and scientific diffusion and the number of persons reaching high proficiency by such education and science; (ii) massive production of industrial production which could absorb the products of the education and develop the instinct for research and direct it to useful and productive channels; (iii) patent procedures in India to assure working of foreign patents in India, opposition procedures, compulsory licensing, and government use of inventions including use by corporations owned and controlled by government; and (iv) special provisions for food and medicines.[25]

According to Justice Ayyangar, therefore, the scope of patentable inventions in India must be determined in light of India's economic position and the degree of scientific and technological progress of the country. Interestingly, he distinguished two categories of non-patentable inventions: those inventions which were universally not patentable, and those inventions for which patents were not at that moment permitted under Indian law due to the state of its economy.[26] The Ayyangar Report criticised the Patents Enquiry Commission's recommendation that the term 'invention' should be given a wider meaning than in the past, asserting that having a wide scope of patentable inventions would be disadvantageous to India. According to Justice Ayyangar:

[21] ibid 11.
[22] Ayyangar Report (n 20) 17.
[23] ibid 15–17.
[24] Ayyangar Report (n 20) 19.
[25] ibid 9–125.
[26] Ayyangar Report (n 20) 20–21.

It does not need much argument to establish that, if the scope of patentable inventions were widened, the persons to benefit would be mostly inventors in the highly advanced industrial countries and for the use of these inventions which are not subject to patents in any country of the world other than in the United Kingdom, the industries in India would have to pay a tax in the shape of royalty.[27]

For the same reason, the Ayyangar Report also opposed the Tek Chand Committee recommendation that India should adhere to the Paris Convention for India's economic interest (see chapter 2). This was in view particularly of developed countries' tendencies to propose strengthening patent protection substantially; for example, the product patent protection of chemical inventions and the restriction on the use of compulsory licensing, as shown at the Lisbon revision conference.[28]

The Ayyangar Report opposed product patent protection,[29] but urged that processes should be patentable for the following industrial reasons:

To render even the process unpatentable is I consider not in [the] public interest as the grant of exclusive rights to the process which an inventor has devised would accelerated [*sic*] research in developing other processes by offering an economic inducement to the discovery of alternative processes leading again to a larger volume of manufacture at competitive prices.[30]

The Indian Patents Act 1970, was inspired by the views and analyses of Judge Ayyangar, although the general framework of the UK Patents Act 1949 was largely retained.[31] The Act reflects the thinking that the country's patent law should be micromanaged to fit the strengths and weaknesses of its industry, and so the international norms should be flexible to allow such national interest. Underlying this Report was the message that the narrower the scope of patent protection, the fewer patents would be held by foreigners, and the opportunity for the development of Indian industry would increase. The Report also encouraged the thinking that India's patent law should make it difficult to patent the types of technologies for which multinationals tend to apply for protection in India.

The Patents Act 1970, entered into force on 20 April 1972. It defined inventions, non-inventions and those inventions that are not patentable.

An 'invention' was defined in section 2(1)(j) of the Act as:
any new and useful:

(i)   art, process, method or manner of manufacture;
(ii) machine, apparatus and other Article;
(iii) substance produced by manufacture, and any new and useful improvement of any of them.[32]

---

[27] ibid 22.

[28] Ayyangar Report (n 20) 117–19.

[29] ibid 'Restrictions on the Patentability of Inventions' 20–40.

[30] Ayyangar Report (n 20) 42.

[31] Narayanan, *Patent Law* (n 19) v, and AK Bagchi, 'India Patents Act and Its Relation to Technological Development in India: a Preliminary Investigation' (1984) Feb. *Economic and Political Weekly* 291–93.

[32] http://ipindia.nic.in/ipr/patent/patents.htm.

The meaning of 'manufacture' and the 'substance produced by manufacture' in the definition of 'invention' (section 2(1)(j)) was interpreted narrowly by the Indian Patent Office, until the Kolkata High Court held in the *Dimminaco* case in 2000 that the term 'manufacture' does not exclude from patentability the process of preparing a product that contains a living substance.[33] Basheer argues that the Indian Patent Office has conserved 'policy-style reasoning' that can be traced back to the Ayyangar Report which formed the 'very basis for the current Indian patent regime'.[34]

The Indian Patent Act 1970 enumerates the following list of 'what are not inventions' within the meaning of this Act in section 3, under Chapter II, entitled 'Inventions not Patentable':[35]

(a) invention which is frivolous or which claims anything obvious contrary to well established natural laws; (b) an invention the primary or intended use of which would be contrary to law or morality or injurious to public health; (c) the mere discovery of a scientific principle or the formulation of an abstract theory; (d) the mere discovery of any new property of new use for a known substance or of the mere use of a known process, machine or apparatus unless such known process results in a new product or employs at least one new reactant; (e) a substance obtained by a mere admixture resulting only in the aggregation of the properties of the components thereof or a process for producing such substance; (f) the mere arrangement or re-arrangement or duplication of known devices each functioning independently of one another in a known way; (g) a method or process for testing applicable during the process of manufacture for rendering the machine, apparatus or other equipment more efficient or for the improvement or restoration of the existing machine, apparatus or other equipment or for the improvement or control of manufacture; (h) a method of agriculture or horticulture; (i) any process for the medicinal, surgical, curative, prophylactic or other treatment of human beings or any process for a similar treatment of animals or plants to render them free of disease or to increase their economic value or that of their products.

Some of the items designated in paragraphs (a), (b), (c) and (f), such as mathematical formulae, would be universally non-patentable. Part of the above list, (i) for example, is shared by other jurisdictions such as Japan and, later, the European Patent Convention (EPC). Others, by contrast, are not common in other patent laws. Some of these provisions seem original to India and may describe 'inventions not patentable' in India due to the development stage of India's economy, as suggested by Justice Ayyangar. The list of those non-inventions and inven-

---

[33] *Dimminaco AG v Controller of Patents Designs & Others* (2002) IPLR July 255, Kolkata High Court. In 1998, the Patent Office rejected the patent application by Dimminaco, a Swiss biotech company which was a subsidiary of American Home Products, for a preparation process for infectious bursitis vaccine for poultry. The Controller of Patents interpreted the meaning of 'living thing' broadly and rejected the patentability of live vaccine on several grounds, one of which was that the term 'manufacture' did not include a process resulting in a living substance.

[34] S Basheer, '"Policy Style" Reasoning at the Indian Patent Office' (2005) *Intellectual Property Quarterly* 313.

[35] Chapter I of the Patents Act is entitled 'Inventions not Patentable' and, under this chapter, s 3 provides for 'what are not inventions'.

tions that are not patentable by the criteria specific to India became longer and more complex as the Act went through amendments in 2002 and 2005.

However, trying to outline the comprehensiveness of what is not an invention in brief, abstract sentences is difficult to begin with. Furthermore, the word 'mere', which appears frequently in section 3, creates a vast field of negation and blurs the scope of what is not negated. There is no country that recognises as an invention a mere principle or abstract theory, or that recognises as novel the mere discovery of a new property or a mere admixture of a known substance. In practice, much would depend on the practices of the IPO, clear examination guidelines and court decisions.

On the other hand, the non-patentability of medicines, foods or substances produced by chemical processes was very clear. Section 5 of the Indian Patents Act 1970, entitled 'Inventions where only methods or processes of manufacture Patentable', excluded from patentability inventions (a) claiming substances intended for use, or capable of being used, as food or medicines; or (b) relating to substances prepared or produced by chemical processes including alloys, optical glass, semi-conductors and inter-metallic compounds; only patent protection on methods or manufacturing processes was provided to inventions (section 5(1)). As Justice Ayyangar had recommended, only process patent protection was provided for food and medicines, for five years from the date of sealing of the patent, or seven years from the date of the patent, whichever period should be shorter (section 53(1)(a)), in comparison to the patent term of 14 years from the date of the patent (section 53(1)(b)) granted to other inventions.

Furthermore, there was a system of 'licences of right' (see chapter 2) under which the Controller of Patents automatically 'endorsed' medicines, foods and chemical processes from the commencement of the Patents Act 1970, or from the expiration of three years from the date of sealing of the patent under the Indian Patents and Designs Act 1911, whichever is later,[36] so that any person could work the patent without the authorisation of the patent owner. Finally, the compulsory licensing provisions of the Act are broadly worded (see chapter 9) to make such

---

[36] ss 86 to 88 of the Indian Patents Act 1970 stipulated the objects and procedures for licences of rights. S 86(1) provided that: 'At any time after the expiration of three years from the date of the sealing of a patent, the Central Government may make an application to the Controller for an order that the patent may be endorsed with the words "Licences of right" on the ground that the reasonable requirements of the public with respect to the patented invention have not been satisfied or that the patented invention is not available to the public at a reasonable price.' S 87 provided that inventions relating to: (i) substances used or capable of being used as food or as medicine or drug; (ii) the methods or processes for the manufacture or production of any such substance as is referred to in sub-clause (i); or (iii) the methods or processes for the manufacture or production of chemical substances (including alloys, optical glass, semi-conductors and inter-metallic compounds), were endorsed with the words 'Licences of right'.

s 88(1) provided another type of 'licences of right', ie, 'any person who is interested in working the patented invention in India may require the patentee to grant him a licence for the purpose on such terms as may be mutually agreed upon . . . and that: (2) 'if the parties are unable to agree on the terms of the licence, either of them may apply in the prescribed manner to the Controller to settle the terms thereof.'

licensing readily available for a wide range of grounds, including non-working of the patent in India, as well as other grounds such as public interest, unreasonable prices or insufficient supplies in both domestic and export markets.[37]

According to Ganesan (see chapter 4):

> The cumulative effect of all these provisions is that the Indian Patents Act, 1970 virtu-ally provides no patent protection in food, pharmaceutical and chemical sectors. It must be remembered that it takes anywhere between seven to ten years for a drug to be brought into the commercial market from the date of the patent application, whereas the term of the patent-and that too a process patent-is only seven years under the Indian law. No company is, therefore, interested in taking out a patent in India. The 'licence of right' and 'compulsory licensing' provisions of the Indian law are indeed and 'over kill'of the subject matter; there has been no need to use them since the com-ing into force of the Patents Act in April, 1972. [38]

In fact, the Controller of Patents issued compulsory licences on only four occa-sions following the enactment of the Patents Act in 1970.[39]

Following the entry into force of the Patents Act 1970, the policy was success-ful in reducing foreign patents to insignificant numbers, as Table 10.1 shows.[40]

Table 10.1: Applications for patents, Indian and foreign, before and after the Patents Act 1970

	Applications for patents		Patents sealed		Patents in force	
	Indian	Foreign	Indian	Foreign	Indian	Foreign
1968	1,110	4,248	426	3,704	3,547	37,816
1979–80	1,055	1,925	516	1,657	2,786	14,476

The legitimacy of patent protection was difficult for different segments of the Indian society to agree upon, because it depended, among other things, on how multinational companies behaved.[41] Furthermore, the acceptability of patent pro-tection seems to have depended on the prices of goods, as well as on the oppor-tunities that it offered to domestic industry, as the Ayyangar Report predicted. How could these concerns be reconciled with the limited goal of patent protec-tion, which is to encourage long-term scientific and technological endeavours not

[37] s 83(1) stipulates the grounds for seeking compulsory licences and stipulates that: 'At any time after the expiration of three years from the date of the sealing of a patent, any person interested may make an application to the Controller alleging that the reasonable requirements of the public with respect to the patented invention have not been satisfied or that the patented invention is not available to the public at a reasonable price and praying for the grant of a compulsory licence to work the patented invention.'

[38] AV Ganesan, 'The GATT Uruguay Round Agreement: Opportunities and Challenges' (1994) Rajiv Gandhi Institute for Contemporary Studies Paper No 8, 8.

[39] Confirmed in an interview with TC James, former Director, Intellectual Property Division, Department of Industrial Policy and Promotion, Ministry of Commerce and Industry, New Delhi, 28 November 2008.

[40] Bagchi, 'India Patents Act and Its Relation to Technological Development in India' (n 31) 293.

[41] Ayyangar Report (n 20) 'Is the Patent System Necessary in India?' 18.

guaranteed to bear fruit? If the perspective is thus set, the weight of public interest is much greater than that of investing in and promoting scientific and technological endeavours to make IP protection meaningful. It seems that the initial policy choice and way of looking at things influenced the future course of events.

In late-comer countries with relatively high levels of technology, patent laws incorporate industrial policy elements and may allow more room for state intervention to encourage domestic industry to invest in research or to compete with more competitive foreign companies. Retrospectively, the situation in Japan differed from that in India. The main difference was that in Japan there was a simple optimism about patent protection and the legitimacy of the system, even though, for a long time, the Japanese domestic pharmaceutical industry lacked confidence in competing with foreign companies. In Japan, the patent protection system was a highly specialised institution for encouraging companies to invest in R&D; there were no political discussions on its social implications. Medicine prices, for example, were taken care of by price regulation and the insurance system. The industrial and social policy considerations underlying the Indian Patents Act seem to be much more complex.

II PRE-TRIPS IMPORT SUBSTITUTION POLICIES FOR PHARMACEUTICALS

A India's Success in Building a Pharmaceutical Industry

According to Redwood, 'the Patents Act, 1970, was the instrument that made it possible for the Indian-owned industry to expand rapidly, because the Act legalised "copying" of drugs that are patentable as products throughout the industrialised world but unprotectable in India.'[42] Later in 2009, a commentary was made in the context of the EU India FTA negotiations that the absence of IP protection was what had promoted the Indian pharmaceutical industry:

> the strengthening of IPR protection sought by the EU may contribute to limit rather than to foster Indian industrial and technological development which – like developed countries earlier – substantially relies on a flexible IPRs regime. A good illustration is the strong development before the introduction of pharmaceutical product patents in 2005 of the Indian pharmaceutical industry, which has become a major world supplier of pharmaceutical active ingredients and medicines.[43]

However, a weak IP protection policy alone could not have led to India's successful development of a domestic pharmaceutical industry. There seem to have been multiple factors that made it possible for India to achieve the economies of scale; skills in organic chemistry and the ability to cheaply manufacture expensive

---

[42] H Redwood, *New Horizons in India: Consequences of Pharmaceutical Patient Protection* (Felixstowe, Oldwicks Press, 1994) 1.

[43] C Correa, 'Negotiation of A Free Trade Agreement European Union-India: Will India Accept Trips-Plus Protection?' June 2009, http://www.oxfam.de/download/correa_eu_india_fta.pdf 5.

products patented in the US and Europe, which gave price advantages to India's products, were key. This was made possible particularly by a well-coordinated national scientific leadership in disseminating technologies to private companies, creating an educational infrastructure that enabled in-house know-how to flourish.[44]

According to Chaudhuri, national chemical or pharmaceutical laboratories such as the National Chemical Laboratory (NCL), Central Drug Research Institute (CDRI) and Indian Institute of Chemical Technology (IICT) conducted research on manufacturing technologies under the leadership of the Council of Scientific and Industrial Research (CSIR). Many Indian companies, such as Cipla, Ranbaxy, Lupin, Nicholas Piramal and Wockhardt, benefited from the activities of these laboratories.[45] Cipla (see chapter 9), for example, collaborated with NCL and IICT in particular and successfully launched products like vinblastine sulphate and vincristine sulphate (anti-cancer drugs), salbutamol (anti-asthma drug), zidovudine (AZT, see chapter 8). The process for manufacturing zidovudine was developed by IICT after the organisation was approached by the Indian Council of Medical Research.

During the last 30 years, the CSIR has filed 25 per cent of all the process patent applications in India. Funding for the CSIR's research came primarily from government funds, but there was also considerable investment by industry. As a technical expert and businessman, Chairman Hamied of Cipla also played an important role in the development of India's pharmaceutical industry. The policy of linking knowledge and family capital abroad to Indian educational institutions and then to actual manufacturing allowed the creation of in-house know-how in the 1980s.[46] This factor, as well as India's export markets in the then Soviet Union[47] and Central and Eastern Europe allowed some economies of scale, although the significant increase in Indian export of pharmaceuticals only started in the late 1990s. Another factor in India's success was the collaboration between business and the national laboratory started by a group of business-minded scientists, government officials and industrialists.[48]

Other policy instruments included foreign exchange and business regulations, restrictions on the import of finished formulations, high tariffs, local content requirements and ownership control by company law. In the pharmaceutical field specifically, they have allowed 13 multinationals to produce only certain active pharmaceutical ingredients that have high technological standards and formulation processes.[49]

[44] S Chaudhuri, *The WTO and India's Pharmaceuticals Industry: Patent Protection, TRIPS, and Developing Countries* (New Delhi and New York, Oxford University Press, 2005) 34–36.

[45] Chaudhuri, ibid 34–36.

[46] Chaudhuri, *The WTO and India's Pharmaceuticals Industry* (n 44) 15–59.

[47] S Matsui accounts for the barter trade in Indian pharmaceuticals with the Soviet Union at this period. 'Patent Protection for New Drug Creation and Criticisms by Developing Country' (in Japanese) 2006 (10) *AIPPI Journal* 2-11.

[48] Chaudhuri, *The WTO and India's Pharmaceuticals Industry* (n 44) 36.

[49] ibid 133–38.

More than 10,000 domestic companies began producing low-cost pharmaceuticals between 1970 and 1995. India also succeeded in ending its dependence on imports and instead began to rely on domestic production, including active pharmaceutical ingredients. This led to approximately 30 major companies growing into a globally competitive generic drug industry which now exports 40 per cent of its production. Export products were often based on reverse engineering and copying. Reverse engineering is the practice of analysing the components of another company's products and, by deconstructing the production process, grasping the product's system and production method to develop one's own products. Reverse engineering is generally legal under patent law (the TRIPS Agreement leaves it to Members). According to Redwood, 'the only flaw in the policy was the expectation that the abolition of patents would encourage original pharmaceutical research and development in India: it did not.'[50]

When the 1970 Patent Act was introduced, Indian companies held a total market share of around 32 per cent in India, but by 1998, this figure increased to 68 per cent.[51] The entry barrier to the Indian pharmaceutical market is not high and the market is competitive. Wockhardt is an example of a small-scale company that grew to be one of India's top companies.

Table 10.2: Market Shares of Foreign Companies and
Indian Companies in India's Pharmaceutical Industry (%)

Year	Foreign Companies	Indian Companies
1952	38	62
1970	68	32
1978	60	40
1980	50	50
1991	40	60
1998	32	68
2004	23	77

Source: S Chaudhuri, *The WTO and India's Pharmaceuticals Industry*, (Oxford University Press, 2005) 18.

---

[50] H Redwood, *Brazil: The Future Impact of Pharmaceutical Patents* (Felixstowe, Oldwicks Press, 1995) 3.
[51] ibid 3.

B Brazil's Import Substitution Policies

Import substitution policies associated with lax IP protection of the 1970s led to varying economic results in different countries, especially developing countries such as India, Thailand, Bangladesh and countries in Latin America. In Latin America, governments promoted import substitution industrialisation (ISI) policies in technology-intensive industries, particularly for pharmaceuticals, through the restriction of IPRs and state-owned and managed economic enterprises in the post-World War II era. In these countries, patent protection of chemical substances and, in Brazil, even process patents for manufacturing pharmaceuticals, were abolished.[52]

Brazil was one of the 11 original Paris Convention Members (1884) and had a long tradition[53] of offering patent protection. However, in 1945, the country's legislation was modified to exclude from patentability inventions relating to foodstuffs, medicines, materials and substances obtained by chemical means or processes. In 1969, process patent protection for pharmaceuticals was also eliminated entirely from the Brazilian Industrial Property Code, with a view to domestically producing active pharmaceutical ingredients (APIs) and intermediary products.

To encourage national production, the Brazilian government implemented a policy of centralised purchasing to promote local production of medicines. Import taxes on medicines were levied at prohibitive levels whilst at the same time the intermediary inputs for local production were taxed mildly and local production was subsidised.[54] To develop the skills necessary for domestic production, Companhia de Desenvolvimento Tecnologico was established to coordinate R&D, and state-run companies such as Nordeste Quimica SA and Norquisa became active in production.

The abolition of pharmaceutical patent protection was intended to protect domestic companies from powerful multinational corporations, with the expectation that the former would invest in local manufacturing of the most promising active chemical substances. However, in 1980 and 1994, domestic companies held 28 per cent and 30 per cent, respectively, of the market share in Brazil and multinationals 70 per cent and 72 per cent. The share of domestic companies increased by only 2 per cent.[55]

---

[52] B Salama and D Benoliel, 'Pharmaceutical Patent Bargains: The Brazilian Experience' (February 2009) http://ssrn.com/abstract=1340349, 5–8.

[53] JAZ Bermudez and MA Oliveira, *Intellectual Property in the Context of the WTO TRIPS Agreement: challenges for public health* (Rio de Janeiro, Oswaldo Cruz Foundation, 2004) 153–54.

[54] ibid 129–30; Salama and Benoliel, 'Pharmaceutical Patent Bargains: The Brazilian Experience' (n 52) 5.

[55] Redwood, *Brazil: The Future Impact of Pharmaceutical Patents* (n 51) 3.

Table 10.3: Brazil's Trade in Medicinal and Pharmaceutical Products, in 100 million US$

	1988	1989	1990	1991	1992
Exports (1)	69.7	70.4	78.0	99.7	111.1
Imports (2)	180.6	258.7	367.0	425.8	372.9
(2)–(1)	110.9	188.3	289.0	326.1	261.8

Source: *United Nations Trade Statistics Yearbook 1992*, as cited in Redwood, Brazil: *The Future Impact of Pharmaceutical Patents* (n 50) 5.

The elimination of patent protection did not cause domestic industry to flourish, due partly to fierce competition in the world market of APIs and intermediaries (Table 10.3). Teaching focused on theory was successful at Brazilian universities, but the skills and know-how necessary in chemical synthesis for producing ingredients and intermediaries with sufficient purity were not accumulated. Government subsidies dissipated and, by 1990, 1,700 chemical pharmaceutical factories had shut down.[56] Today, Brazil imports most of its active pharmaceutical ingredients from India and China.

Brazil's economy has depended heavily on its exports to the US; a situation which US multinationals generally used as leverage for negotiations. The United States Trade Representative (USTR) pressured such countries as Argentina, Brazil, India, Singapore, Turkey and Mexico under section 301 of the US Trade Act (see chapter 3) from the end of the 1980s. In 1993, Brazil was placed on the priority watch list (but in 1995, demoted to the watch list).

C China's IP Policy before WTO Accession

China's policy contrasts with the policies of countries that weakened patent protection for the development of their domestic pharmaceutical industries. In China, the initial stages of intellectual property protection began during the 1980s along with the introduction of a policy of opening the country to foreign business. In this decade, the Trademark Law (1982),[57] the Patent Law (1984)[58]

---

[56] F Orsi et al, 'Intellectual Property Rights, Anti-AIDS Policy and Generic Drugs: Lessons from the Brazilian Public Health Program,' in J-P Moatti et al (eds), *Economics of AIDS and Access to HIV/AIDS Care in Developing Countries, Issues and Challenges* (Paris, Agence Nationale de Recherches sur le Sida, 2003).

[57] In China, the Trademark Office is part of the State Administration Industry and Commerce, whereas the Patent Office is under the State Intellectual Property Office (SIPO).

[58] Patent Law (Adopted at the Fourth Meeting of the Standing Committee of the Sixth National People's Congress on 12 March 1984; amended in accordance with the Decision of the Standing Committee of the Seventh National People's Congress on Amending the Patent Law of the People's Republic of China at its 27th Meeting on 4 September 1992; amended again in accordance with the Decision of the Standing Committee of the Ninth National People's Congress on Amending the Patent Law of the People's Republic of China adopted at its 17th Meeting on 25 August 2000). The text of the Patent Law 2000 is found at www.wipo.int/clea/en/text_pdf.jsp?lang=EN&id=860, that of the Patent Law 2009 at www.csptal.com/en/en_z.asp?id=120.

and the Copyright Law (1990) were all enacted. Subsequently, relevant laws and regulations were revised in the 1990s, in preparation for prospective membership of the WTO. By the First Patent Amendment Act, which entered into force in January 1993, product patents, as well as use and formulation patents, were introduced. China became a WTO member on 11 December 2001.

According to Ganea and Haijun, China's IP laws resulted from 'commitments made in order to become an accepted member of the world trade community rather than from recognition that IP laws would foster innovation and economic development in the domestic context'.[59] China realised that, without IP protection, desired technology-intensive and IP sensitive investment would stay away. It was probably for these reasons that China agreed to grant administrative protection of a maximum of seven and a half years for pharmaceutical inventions patented in the US, European Community Member countries and Japan.

Whatever Chinese companies or researchers think about IPR protection, however, the Chinese Government seems to consider that becoming a 'leader in technology' cannot be achieved without respecting intellectual property rights. Confidence in patent protection is popularly justified by the oft-quoted story of the four ancient great inventions of China[60] which are the compass, gunpowder, papermaking and printing which, it is humourously maintained, could have yielded great income to China had they been patented.

The Chinese Patent Law was adopted on 12 March 1984 and was revised three times: on 4 September 1992, 25 August 2000 and 29 December 2008. China introduced product patent protection in the second amendment, in Article 11.

China's overall policy of encouraging foreign direct investment (FDI) as part of its efforts to raise the technological levels of domestic companies avoided direct confrontation of domestic and foreign companies over IPRs, as reflected in some of its court cases (see chapter 9 and below p 385). The Chinese Government has used various means, including subsidising filing fees, to encourage domestic companies to file patents. The result has been a rapid increase in the number of domestic filings by Chinese residents. Foreign patenting by Chinese entities initially lagged far behind domestic ones, probably for technological reasons, but, in absolute number, increased rapidly. Another possible reason for the relatively low level of Chinese patenting abroad was the obligation introduced by the second amendment of the Patent Law in 1992 for Chinese applicants to file first in China. This system was modified by the third amendment of the Patent Law, as shown later in this chapter. China became the fifth largest PCT user in 2009, with a strong growth rate of 29.7 per cent, representing some 7,946 international applications.[61]

---

[59] P Goldstein and J Straus, *Intellectual Property in Asia: Law, Economics History and Politics* (Heidelberg, Springer, 2009) 38.

[60] http://en.wikipedia.org/wiki/Four_Great_Inventions_of_ancient_China#Origins.

[61] IP Watch, 'International Patent Filings Dip in 2009 amid Global Economic Downturn', 8 February 2010.

III TRIPS AGREEMENT AND EMERGING ECONOMIES

The TRIPS Agreement took a radical step in comparison to the Paris Convention, in making it obligatory to protect not only processes, but also 'products', with the provisions of transition periods of 10 years for developing countries and until 2010 for LDCs (extended until 31 December 2015 – see chapters 5 and 9).

It is generally in the emerging economies that patents tend to become controversial. First of all, foreign direct investment increases where the market size is important. These markets are generally those countries with a large population with a rising income, albeit of limited classes, and with the capacity to imitate and technological skills to produce, creating conflicts over intellectual property. Secondly, there are rising expectations for better healthcare in these countries not only among high income classes but particularly among a large segment of poor people.

A India's TRIPS Implementation

i TRIPS Challenge

Certain technological sectors of India will want reasonable protection for IPR (to build their own inventive industries) and may also be willing to make concessions in that direction in order to gain other major trade advantages with developed country markets, generally. India accepted the TRIPS Agreement in a single undertaking in 1994 based mainly on a desire to preserve within the framework of the WTO the principle of most-favoured nation treatment and access to other world markets.

In 1994, Ganesan explained the implications of the TRIPS Agreement for India. He asserted that India's copyright law was ahead of the provisions of the TRIPS agreement[62] in the matters of software and protection against piracy of cinematographic works; he said that protection of trademarks, trade secrets and industrial designs were on a par with generally accepted international standards.[63]

In the area of patents, however, he warned that:

> there is no meeting ground between the provisions of the Indian Patents Act, 1970 and the norms and standards for protection incorporated in the TRIPS agreement ... the TRIPS agreement requires product patents to be given in all fields of technology without exception; the duration of the patent to be at least 20 years uniformly; compulsory licence to be given on the individual merits of a case but only after approaching the patent owner for obtaining a licence on reasonable commercial terms and conditions; the burden of proof in the case of process patents (that lead directly to new products) to be placed on the

[62] Computer software had been protected as a literary work since 1983, and, in 1994, a bill was pending before the Parliament for amending the Copyright Act, inter alia, for the protection of performers, sound recordings and broadcasting organisations.

[63] Ganesan, 'The GATT Uruguay Round Agreement: Opportunities and Challenges' (n 38) 8.

defendant in the circumstances prescribed; patent rights being available equally regardless of whether the products are locally produced or imported; and so on.[64]

Ganesan then turned to the major concern at the time: that the implementation of the TRIPS Agreement might result in soaring medicine prices. He pointed out that it would be important to distinguish the price of drugs that were patented from those that were not, and suggested that:

> it is unlikely that drugs covered by patents will exceed 10 to 15% by value of the total drug market in our country at any time in the foreseeable future. There is no reason why the prices of drugs not covered by patents should rise so steeply because of the patent system.[65]

India, as a developing country Member of the WTO, was under an obligation to bring its laws and regulations into line with the TRIPS Agreement by 1 January 2000 (Article 65.2), institute the mailbox application system (Article 70.8) and grant exclusive marketing rights as from the entry into force of the WTO Agreement, if it does not introduce patent protection of agricultural and chemical products (Article 70.9). It was further required to introduce product patent protection (Article 65.4) by 1 January 2005 (see chapter 5).

Subsequent to the adoption of the TRIPS Agreement, the Indian Patents Act 1970 was amended in 1999, 2002 and 2005. The mailbox application mechanism and the mechanism for granting exclusive marketing rights (EMRs) were introduced by the Patents (Amendment) Act 1999, after a WTO dispute on this question, *India–Patents*[66]. Then, by the Patents (Amendment) Act 2002, which

---

[64] ibid.

[65] Ganesan, 'The GATT Uruguay Round Agreement: Opportunities and Challenges' (n 38) 10. Later, in a brochure published in 1999, Ganesan analysed the new drugs patented abroad that were introduced in the Indian market in the five calendar years 1994–98: AV Ganesan, *The Implications of the Patents (Amendment) Ordinance, 1999,* (New Delhi, Indian Council for Research on International Economic Relations, 1999) Annex I 36–37.

[66] *India–Patent Protection for Pharmaceutical and Agricultural Chemical Products*, Complaint by US (DS50) (adopted 16 January 1998) WT/DS50/AB/R. The Ordinance that would have introduced the mechanism for mailbox applications and the EMR was not adopted, due to the dissolution of Parliament on 10 May 1996. India's Government notified the TRIPS Council that the 'administrative instructions' issued in April 1995 effectively continued the mailbox system that would have been established by the Ordinance. The Appellate Body held that the system put in place by the Presidential decree did not provide the 'means' by which mailbox applications for patents for pharmaceutical and agricultural chemical products could be securely filed in the meaning of Art 70.8(a) of the TRIPS Agreement, because applications filed under the administrative instructions could be rejected by the court under the contradictory mandatory provisions of the existing Indian Patents Act of 1970. S 5(a) of the Act provides that substances '. . . intended for use, or capable of being used, as food or as medicine or drug' are not patentable. According to the Appellate Body and the Panel, the following provisions are mandatory: s 12(1) of the Indian Patents Act 1970 requires the Controller to refer that application and that specification to an examiner, and s 15(2) states that the Controller 'shall refuse' an application in respect of a substance that is not patentable. The Appellate Body maintained that it is unclear whether India's 'administrative instructions' would prevail over the contradictory mandatory provisions of India's Patents Act, providing a 'sound legal basis to preserve novelty of inventions and priority of applications as of the relevant filing and priority dates'. The Appellate Body, emphasising the importance of the legal stability and predictability of the implementing measures, maintained that India's 'administrative instructions' for receiving mailbox applications are inconsistent with Art 70.8(a) of the TRIPS Agreement.

came into effect on 20 May 2003, the 20-year patent term, reversal of the burden of proof for process patent infringements, and changes in the conditions for compulsory licensing were introduced. Last, the Patents (Amendment) Act 2005, adopted on 5 April 2005, put agricultural-chemical and pharmaceutical product patent protection into full effect retroactively as of 1 January 2005, after the full use of the 10-year transition period provided for by Article 65.4 of the TRIPS Agreement (see chapter 5).

The amendments in 2002 included provisions concerning the term of patent protection to conform to Article 33 of the TRIPS Agreement, and Section 53 provided a term of 20 years after the date of filing of the application for the patent.[67] India acceded to the Paris Convention for the Protection of Industrial Property (Paris Convention) and the Patent Cooperation Treaty (PCT) which entered into force for India in December 1998. The amendments of 2002 also reflected these changes. Provisions concerning compulsory licensing were also modified.

The amendment in 2002 of India's Patents Act 1970 left to a later day the implementation of the product patent protection, which developing countries including India were required to introduce by 1 January 2005.

Concerns were expressed that India's generic industry would lose its competitiveness, if product patent protection were introduced. Scherer warned that India, like Italy in the past, was in danger of losing its first-mover advantage of supplying medicine at 50–65 per cent of the original price before the entry of generic companies in developed countries, who normally wait for the patent expiry of the medicines they manufacture. India, without product patent protection, had the advantage of freely copying those new medicines patented abroad. The timing of their market entry gave them advantages over other generic companies, because they were able to put their medicines on the market before the price went down due to the entry of many generic companies.[68] Indian companies also had the marketing skills and knowledge to export products that were patented abroad and expensive in large markets to markets where there were no patent restrictions. India's generic manufacturers were becoming increasingly competitive and global. The patents for the top 10 pharmaceuticals (such as Lipitor (atorvastatin, a cholesterol-lowering medication), Zyprexa (olanzapin, for schizophrenia treatment), and Neutrogin (lenograstim, for treatment of anemia) were expiring around 2010. According to Scherer, the Patents (Amendment) Act 2005, therefore, should introduce quid pro quo provisions necessary to counter the negative effects of the TRIPS Agreement on domestic industries.[69]

Concerns had been expressed also over the possible social consequences of India's reintroduction of product patents. Civil society groups such as Médecins

---

[67] S 53(1) was substituted in 2002. S 27 was deleted in 2005.

[68] FM Scherer, 'Losing the first mover advantage: India should focus on new drug development to offset the harm, if any' Times (India) (7 April 2005).

[69] Indian companies were able to manufacture products in India patented in other countries because there was no patent protection of substances in India. This gave India an advantage over generic drug industries in developed countries, which had to wait for patents to expire before producing and selling generics.

Sans Frontières, considering India as 'the number one source of affordable medicines',[70] warned against India introducing product patent protection:[71]

> Sick people in India and around the world depend on the willingness of Indian produc-
> ers to carry out the research to develop and manufacture affordable generic versions of
> second-line AIDS drugs and other new medicines. India has a long history of fighting
> for protection of public health over intellectual property: it led developing countries'
> resistance to the TRIPS Agreement during the Uruguay Round of WTO negotiations,
> and also played a key role during the 2001 WTO ministerial conference in Doha, which
> resulted in the adoption of the Doha Declaration on TRIPS and Public Health. Unlike
> other developing countries, it has also waited as long as was permitted by TRIPS before
> introducing patents on pharmaceutical products. In the new post-2005 TRIPS context,
> it is crucial that India continue to develop policies that promote access to medicines,
> not just out of responsibility to its own people, but as a lifeline to patients in other
> developing countries.[72]

However, in the specific historical context of that time, there was high hope in India that the country was becoming an innovative developing country. In December 2004, when the Ordinance[73] amending the Indian Patents Act 1970 was adopted by the Indian Parliament, K Nath, Minister of Commerce & Industry, assured the public, stating that India's larger pharmaceutical industry was becoming more innovative than in the past, spending much more on R&D than in the past and, therefore, the concerns and fears expressed by various sections were wholly misplaced.[74]

Amidst considerable political opposition, Indian biotechnology companies joined forces with the CSIR[75] which started calling for the introduction of product patents as part of a strategy to make India an 'innovative' developing country. In 2004, the sales volume of India's biotechnology companies was up 36.5 per cent from the previous year, to a total of US$1.07 billion.[76] Biogeneric medicines such as human insulin and interferon α were being produced at a relatively

---

[70] Procurement & Supply Management (PSM) Workshop, Nairobi, Kenya (2–9 December 2004), Third-World Network, Asian Regional Workshop on the WTO/TRIPS Agreement and Access to Medicines, Kuala Lumpur, Malaysia (28–30 November 2004).

[71] 'Will the lifeline of affordable medicines for poor countries be cut? Consequences of medi-cines patenting in India' (2005) Briefing document, Médecins Sans Frontièreshttp://www.who.int/hiv/amds/MSFopinion.pdf, 2.

[72] FM Scherer and J Watal, 'Post-TRIPS Options for Access to Patented Medicines in Developing Countries' (2001) Commission on Macroeconomics and Health, Working Paper Series, Paper No WG 4:1, 15–16.

[73] The third amendment to the Patents Act 1970, was introduced through the Patents (Amendment) Ordinance 2004 (effective 1 January 2005). This Ordinance was later replaced by the Patents (Amendment) Act 2005 (Act No 15 of 2005) on 4 April 2005 with retroactive effect from 1 January 2005. http://ipindia.nic.in/ipr/patent/patents.htm.

[74] According to Nath, the larger Indian companies are spending in the region of 6 to 8 % of their turnover on R&D, whereas the norm for major MNCs is 12%.K Nath's Statement on the Ordinance relating to Patents (Third) Amendment, 27 December 2004. http://commerce.nic.in/pressrelease/pressrelease_detail.asp?id=1309.

[75] 'Transforming India into a Knowledge Power', Report of the Pharmaceutical Research and Development Committee, November, 1999.

[76] *BioSpectrum*, Annual Report 2005, Bangalore.

reduced cost,[77] and company-induced incremental innovations such as oral insulin by Biocon were also emerging. At that time, outsourcing to Indian companies of clinical studies by multinationals was expanding rapidly – this also required strengthened patent protection.[78]

ii Patent Law Controversies

Patentable subject matter

The Indian Patents Act, like most other patent laws of the world, generally precludes discoveries from patentability. However, the difficult question is how to draw a clear line between where discovery ends and invention begins, and what the criteria are between 'living' and 'non-living' things occurring in nature (see chapter 3).[79] This is a question whose answer may change with technological changes and has not yet been entirely settled in developed countries. In the meantime, continuous investment has been made through patent protection of biotech inventions (chapter 3).

In the 2002 amendment, the phrase 'or discovery of any living thing or non-living substance occurring in nature' was added to the previous provision under section 3(c),[80] to exclude them from patentability. Why the Indian Parliament decided, at this juncture in history, to exclude from patentability the 'discovery

[77] SE Fren et al, 'India's health biotech sector at a crossroad' (2007) 25 *Nature Biotechnology*.

[78] According to GV Prasad (Dr Reddy's), 75% of the world's top 50 pharmaceutical companies conduct their clinical trials in India (Economist Conference, March 2007), and outsourcing to India of R&D was expected to reach US$2 billion by 2010 (PharmaTimes.com *Clinical News*, 14 March 2007). About 280 companies are operating for the production of bio-generics, of which approximately 20 are engaged in export. The Hepatitis B vaccine manufactured by Shanta Biologics (60% of the stocks are owned by l'Institut Mérieux) occupies 40% of UNICEF's procurement. The Serum Institute of India is the world leader in terms of sales in the production of measles vaccines, and Biocon has world-wide sales of insulin and Panacea Biotech polio vaccines.

[79] The 2008 Draft Patent Manual of Patent Practice and Procedure (Patent Office, India) www.patentoffice.nic.in/ipr/patent/DraftPatent_Manual_2008.pdf distinguishes discovery from invention by stating that 'a discovery adds to the amount of human knowledge by disclosing something already in existence, which has not been seen before, whereas an invention adds to the human knowledge by creating a new product or process involving a technical advance as compared to the existing knowledge'. Draft Manual (2008) 4.4.4, referring to s 3 (c) of the Patent Act, cites *Kirin-Amgen v Hoechst Marion Roussel* [2005] RPC 9 but without explaining how this case is relevant. 4.4.1. From the 2010 Draft Manual this reference disappeared while the short explanation above remained. No further clarification seems to have been added to the 2010 Draft.

[80] Other amendments to s 3 included the following. In cl (i), after the words 'prophylactic,' 'diagnostic, therapeutic' were inserted, and 'or plants' were omitted. Cl (g) of s 3 was omitted. The following clauses were added to s 3 as non-patentable inventions: (j) plants and animals in whole or any part thereof other than micro-organisms but including seeds, varieties and species and essentially biological processes for production or propagation of plants and animals; (k) a mathematical or business method or a computer programme per se or algorithms; (l) a literary, dramatic, musical or artistic work or any other aesthetic creation whatsoever including cinematographic works and television productions; (m) a mere scheme or rule or method of performing mental act or method of playing game; (n) a presentation of information; (topography of integrated circuits; (p) an invention which, in effect, is traditional knowledge or which is an aggregation or duplication of known properties of traditional known component or components.

of living thing[s] or non-living substance[s] occurring in nature', is not clear. It is often said that this amendment resulted from the commonly held concern that foreign companies may patent India's traditional knowledge if living things were patentable. India had been active in discussing the implementation issues of the Convention on Biological Diversity (CBD),[81] which deals with genetic and biological materials. The Indian Patent Office (IPO) emphasises that section 3(c) only excludes from patentability 'the mere' discovery of living things, and that it allows the scope of patentability similar to the European Patent Convention and the Chakrabarty criteria in the US (see chapter 3).[82] Section 10(4)(d)(ii), most of which was inserted by the 2002 amendments, provides the conditions for patent specifications when they mention a biological material. The conditions are based both on the Budapest Treaty (see chapters 2 and 3) and the CBD.[83]

Significantly, most people in India ignore the words 'the discovery of' in section 3(c), and seem to believe that India excludes 'living things' from patentability. They seem to believe that anything related to plants, animals and genes is unpatentable in India.[84] Historically, for the development of the biotech industry, patent protection of inventions relating to microbiological, biological or genetic technologies has been useful. This was probably why the Report of the Technical Expert Group on Patent Law Issues (Mashelkar Committee – chapter 12), established later by the Indian Government in April 2005, included as part of its mandate to provide its views on the meaning of microorganisms.[85]

The Amendment in 2002 also added section 3(j), which reads: 'plants and animals in whole or any part thereof other than microorganisms but including seeds, varieties and species and essentially biological processes for production or propagation of plants and animals [are not patentable]'. The IPO explains that

---

[81] For the CBD see ch 6, n 60. *The Relationship between the TRIPs Agreement and the Convention on Biological Diversity and the Protection of Traditional Knowledge*, Submission by Bolivia, Brazil, Cuba, Dominican Republic, Ecuador, India, Peru, Thailand, Venezuela IP/C/W/403 (24 June 2003).

[82] Interview at the Indian Patent Office (Kolkata) on 22 December 2009.

[83] s 10(4)(d)(ii) of the Indian Patents Act, amended in 2005 provides that: 'if the applicant mentions a biological material in the specification which may not be described in such a way as to satisfy clauses (a) and (b), and if such material is not available to the public, the application shall be completed by depositing [the material to an international depository authority under the Budapest Treaty] and by fulfilling the following conditions, namely: – (A) the deposit of the material shall be made not later than the date of filing the patent application in India and a reference thereof shall be made in the specification within the prescribed period; (B) all the available characteristics of the material required for it to be correctly identified or indicated are included in the specification including the name, address of the depository institution and the date and number of the deposit of the material at the institution;(C) access to the material is available in the depository institution only after the date of the application for patent in India or if a priority is claimed after the date of the priority;(D) disclose the source and geographical origin of the biological material in the specification, when used in an invention.'

[84] Interview with CM Gulhati, Editor, *Monthly Index of Medical Specialities (MIMS India)*, New Delhi, 25 November 2009.

[85] The Technical Expert Group on Patent Law Issues was set up by the Government of India, Ministry of Commerce & Industry, Department of Industrial Policy & Promotion on 5 April 2005, mainly to examine the conformity of the amended s 3(d) of the Patents (Amendments) Act, 2005. The report was submitted in December 2006 and revised in March 2009.

this standard is equivalent to that of the European Patent Convention (EPC).[86] However, according to the latter, animals and plants and any part thereof are patentable unless these technologies do not specify animal or plant varieties.

From the text, 'microorganisms' are patentable in India, but they are difficult to define,[87] as the discussions at the WTO below show. India had a relatively narrow definition of microorganisms. There is no internationally agreed-upon scientific basis for the distinction between plants, animals and microorganisms nor is there agreement on what criteria should be applied to determine which living things are microorganisms. The *Concise Oxford Dictionary* defines a microorganism as 'an organism not visible to the naked eye, *e.g.*, bacterium or virus'.[88] However, microorganisms are capable of reproducing themselves, whereas viruses require host cells to do so. Some argue that viruses are not microorganisms for this reason. The criteria for defining microorganisms could depend also on the level of biotechnology and related observatory, isolation or conservation technologies.

Within the TRIPS Council discussions on Article 27.3(b), which is part of the built-in agenda (see chapter 5), divergent views have been expressed with regard to microorganisms. The African group generally held that there is no scientific or other rationale for distinguishing between plants and animals on the one hand, and microorganisms on the other, and that these should not be patentable, since they are living things which can only be discovered, not invented.[89] Some countries argued that microorganisms, like other biological and living organisms, should be excluded altogether from patentability.[90] However, human intervention is required to isolate a particular microorganism, as a microorganism exists in nature together with varieties of other microorganisms.

At the WTO TRIPS Council, the view has also been expressed that there is no consensus on the meaning of the term 'microorganism' in the scientific community,[91] and that the scientific definition of microorganisms only comprises bacteria, fungi, algae, protozoa and viruses.[92] India and Pakistan questioned whether biological material such as cell lines, enzymes, plasmids, cosmids and

---

[86] Interview at the Indian Patent Office, Kolkata, 22 December 2009.

[87] Communication from the European Communities and their Member States to the Council for TRIPS of 17 October 2002, IP/C/W/383, 1.

[88] This was part of the US argument (IP/C/W/209). Review of the Provisions of Article 27.3(b): Summary of Issues Raised and Points Made, Note by the Secretariat (Revision) (9 March 2006) IP/C/W/369/Rev.1 para 23.

[89] Kenya on behalf of the African Group, IP/C/W/163(8 November 1999).

[90] Kenya, IP/C/M/28 para 152; Bangladesh, IP/C/M/42 para 103. Bangladesh argued that in the event that living organisms remain patentable, a provision should be incorporated into the TRIPS Agreement to the effect that patents must not be granted without the prior consent of the country of origin in order to affirm its compatibility with the CBD and the International Treaty on Plant Genetic Resources for Food and Agriculture (ITPGRFA).

[91] Brazil, IP/C/M/29 para 146; Japan, IP/C/W/236; Switzerland, IP/C/W/284; Venezuela, IP/C/M/29 para 199.

[92] Zimbabwe, IP/C/M/39 para 111.

genes should qualify as microorganisms.[93]These materials are extremely important as research tools in biotechnology (see chapter 3) and, where they fulfil the requirements for patentability, have been patented in developed countries. For example, a genetically modified plasmid (Cohen-Boyer's invention) is a simple strand of DNA and therefore is not necessarily a 'living thing'; however, it has been an important research tool for genetic engineering (see chapter 3). India and Brazil also argued that: 'the term [microorganism] is obviously intended to have a special meaning in the context of patentability and the dictionary explanation and example of a bacterium or virus do not necessarily concern 'patentable microorganisms'.[94]

At the WTO TRIPS Council, the Republic of Korea suggested a pragmatic approach[95] that individual Members should determine and apply the term in their national jurisdictions in accordance with Article 1 of the Budapest Treaty (chapters 2 and 12),[96] and not seek to define the term. According to Korea, patent experts have a fairly clear idea of the term, but the issue is complex and therefore it is better left to each Member's patent offices and experts to determine. In Japan, for example, a formal definition of the term 'microorganisms' is not given due to the fact that such a definition would not be responsive enough to accommodate the emergence of new inventions in the rapidly evolving microbiology.[97] Therefore, Japan provides a non-exhaustive list of microorganisms instead of a formal definition, within the framework of the inexhaustible list in the JPO implementing guidelines for biological inventions.[98] This list includes yeast, moulds, mushrooms, bacteria, actinomyces, unicellular algae, viruses, protozoa, etc (some of which are clearly not microorganisms), and further includes undifferentiated animal or plant cells as well as animal or plant tissue cultures that are not necessarily 'microorganisms' (while the Budapest Treaty only concerns the deposit of 'microorganisms'). When the national deposit organisations are unable to conserve the biological material for technical or safety reasons,

---

[93] India, IP/C/M/25 para 70; Pakistan, IP/C/M/26 para 65. India proposed in IP/C/W/161 (3 November 1999, para 7) that (a) patents on all life-forms be excluded from patentability or, it this is not possible, (b) patents based on traditional/indigenous knowledge and essentially derived products and processes from such knowledge be excluded; or at least: (c) disclosure of the country of origin of the biological resource and associated knowledge.

[94] Brazil, IP/C/M/29 para 146; India, IP/C/M/30 para 168.

[95] Korea, IP/C/M/35 para 225.

[96] If an invention is related to a microorganism not easily accessible by a skilled person, the patent applicant must deposit the microorganism with International Depository Authorities under the Budapest Treaty or other appropriate depository authorities, and must submit to the relevant patent office the certificate issued by the relevant depository authority. This is a measure to ensure that a skilled person can 'carry out' the invention based on the description of the application together with the actual microorganism that is deposited with and available from the Authority. Art 1 of the Budapest Treaty provides that: 'The States party to this Treaty constitute a Union for the international recognition of the deposit of micro-organisms for the purposes of patent procedure.'

[97] *Review of the Provisions of Article 27.3(b)*, Japan's View IP/C/W/236 (11 December 2000) 3.

[98] Japanese Patent Office (JPO), February 1997.

a home deposit system is introduced to promote research and development activities. Thus, the underlying purpose is to promote biotech R&D and inventions by offering patent protection to the widest possible range of materials.

During the consultations in the WTO dispute cases, *Argentina – Patent Protection for Pharmaceuticals and Test Data Protection for Agricultural Chemicals* and *Argentina – Certain Measures on the Protection of Patents and Test Data*, Argentina and the US analysed the legislation and practice of Argentina in the light of Article 27.3(b) of the TRIPS Agreement and discussed a series of questions concerning patentability of microorganisms and other subject matter such as a variety of chemical compounds. These discussions included the patentability of: microorganisms, per se (eg, yeasts, bacteria, unicellular organisms); a composition that includes as one element a microorganism (eg, a culture containing a yeast, bacterium, etc); a chemical compound having a structure identical to a chemical compound isolated from a plant, animal, microorganism or other naturally occurring source; a purified composition containing a chemical compound having a structure identical to a chemical compound isolated from a plant, animal, microorganism or other naturally occurring source, such that the composition is not identical to a composition containing the chemical compound as it would be found in its natural state.[99] Pursuant to this analysis, the Government of Argentina elaborated and published guidelines about its practices relating to patentability of microorganisms in INPI Resolution 633/2001.[100]

In India, under what conditions would natural products synthesised in the laboratory be patentable? Would a virus; isolated genes with functions; a medicinal compound identical to a natural product but metabolised for better efficacy and safety; or antibiotics extracted, purified and produced from nature, be eligible? The text of the Indian Patents Act, alone, is too brief to indicate the scope of patentability and therefore, further clarification and predictability would depend on the IPO guidelines and court decisions. The IPO explains that the Indian standard is equivalent to that of the European Patent Convention (EPC).[101]

Some other countries today exclude certain 'living things' or 'organisms' (whose scope is not always clear) from patentability even when they are isolated from nature (see chapter 3 for new developments in the US). Chapter II of the Brazilian Industrial Property Law of 1996 deals with patentability and its section I defines patentable inventions and utility models.[102] Article 10 under this section enumerates what are not considered to be inventions or utility models. Among them, Article 10 (IX) provides that 'all, or part of natural living beings and biological materials found in nature, even if isolated therefrom, including the

---

[99] Notification of mutually agreed solution WT/DS171/3, WT/DS196/4(20 June 2002) para 7.
[100] Official Gazette, 22 October 2001.
[101] Interview at the IPO (Kolkata) on 22 December 2009.
[102] 14 May 1996, No 9.279. Amendments No 10.19614 February 2001, www.wipo.int/clea/en/details.jsp?id=547&tab=2.

genome or germoplasm[103]of any natural living being, and the natural biological processes'[104] are not inventions.

Compulsory licensing and local working requirements

Another challenge from the TRIPS Agreement concerned compulsory licensing, particularly with regard to local working requirements. Relevant provisions in the TRIPS Agreement (Articles 27.1, 28 and 31) are ambiguous on this question. From the wording of TRIPS Article 27.1, interpreting 'working of the patented invention' as excluding importation is not inconsistent with TRIPS unless this results in discrimination between imported goods and those manufactured locally.[105]

Article 83 of India's Patents Act 1970 provided that:

(a) patents are granted to encourage inventions and to secure that the inventions are worked in India on a commercial scale and to the fullest extent that is reasonably practicable without undue delay; and (b) they are not granted merely to enable patentees to enjoy a monopoly for the importation of the patented Article.

The amendment of 2002 added Articles 83(c)–(g) to include a long list of considerations, starting from transfer and dissemination of technology; social and economic welfare; not impeding protection of public health and nutrition; promoting public interest, especially in sectors of vital importance for the socio-economic and technological development of India; preventing abuses; not unreasonably restraining trade or adversely affecting the international transfer of technology; and ending with the availability of inventions at reasonably affordable prices to the public.

The conditions attached to the procedures and the grounds for compulsory licensing in the Indian Patents Act have been modified to conform with the Paris Convention and the TRIPS Agreement, but controversies remain today, as we will examine below.

---

[103] A collection of genetic resources for an organism.

[104] Other items which are not considered inventions are: I. discoveries, scientific theories, and mathematical methods; II. purely abstract conceptions; III. commercial, accounting, financial, educational, advertising, raffling, and inspection schemes, plans, principles or methods; IV. literary, architectural, artistic and scientific works, or any aesthetic creation; V. computer programs per se; VI. presentation of information; VII. rules of games; VIII. surgical techniques and methods, as well as therapeutic or diagnostic methods, for application to human or animal body.

[105] According to DG Shah, Secretary General of the Indian Pharmaceutical Alliance of Indian drug makers, 'working the patent in the local market could only mean local manufacture. Import can be considered as working of the intellectual property right in smaller markets, as it will be unviable'. And according to S Basheer, 'India could argue its regime is geared towards creating employment and facilitating technology transfer. By importing drugs, drug makers are denying this to the country'. 'Foreign drug companies may lose exclusivity for some drugs in India', *Pharma China* (New Delhi, 5 February 2010).

iii India's Patents (Amendment) Act 2005

In March 2005, the Indian Parliament introduced groundbreaking revisions to its Patents Act with the aim of achieving compliance with the TRIPS Agreement. These revisions took effect retroactively from 1 January 2005. The amendment reflected the discussions which had taken place between 1995 and 2005 on the possible implications of amendments, relevant case law in different countries and a diversity of opinions from industry, civil societies and professional groups.

Safeguards against possible social impacts

A series of important compromise solutions were provided as possible safeguards against the possible socio-economic impacts of introducing the India Patents (Amendments) Act 2005. First, section 11A(7) allows those enterprises which have made significant investments and producing and marketing products prior to 1 January 2005 to continue production of those products. The patentowner is entitled only to receive reasonable royalties[106] from the continued manufacturing of the product. The right holder can file an action in court over whether royalties are 'reasonable', but not institute infringement proceedings against such producers.

The second major compromise related to the opposition systems: the provision concerning pre-grant opposition in section 25(1) of the Patent Act 1970 was maintained; the post-grant opposition system was introduced in section 25(2);[107] and revocation procedures were reinstated in section 64(1)(f) of the Amendment Act 2005. Opposition or revocation proceedings are brought to the Controller of the Patent Office. Pre-Grant opposition can be instituted by 'any person', in writing, against the granting of a patent after it has been published in the Patent Office Journal.[108]

---

[106] See Art 70.4 TRIPS (ch 5). According to S Julaniya, former Director, Dep't of Industrial Policy Promotion, Indian Ministry of Commerce, 3% is considered to be 'reasonable' in general (Interview on 22 August 2006).

[107] Post-grant opposition can be filed only by any 'interested person' within 12 months of the publication date of the patent grant, at the appropriate office. For both pre-grant and post-grant opposition, the main grounds include: wrongful attainment; obviousness or lack of inventive step; non-patentable subject matter; and anticipation by the traditional knowledge in India or elsewhere. The Controller makes the decision after hearing the parties concerned, and after taking into consideration the recommendation of the Opposition Board. The Controller's decision may be appealed to at the Intellectual Property Appellate Board (IPAB) which is an intermediate quasi-judicial body established on 1 January 2007. Decisions of the IPAB can be appealed to India's High Court. There are differences in the grounds for opposition in s 25 and those for revocation in s 64(1). The most notable difference is that ss 25 (1)(e) and (2)(e) lay the condition for opposition that the claimed invention is obvious and 'clearly' does not involve any inventive step; whereas s 64(1)(f) does not require that the invention 'clearly' does not involve inventive steps, for patents to be revoked. In cases where an element of doubt exists, the Controller may allow the issue to be decided by the High Court.

[108] The notice of opposition is given in the prescribed form at the appropriate office along with a written statement setting out the nature of the opponent's interest; the facts upon which the opponent bases his or her case; the relief which the opponent seeks; and the evidence. A copy of the statement and evidence is to be provided to the patentee. On 15 July 2010, the High Court of Delhi,

In India, pre-grant opposition proceedings have been filed by patient groups or competitors and involved, inter alia, Combivir, Viread(tenofovir), Gleevec and Tamiful.[109] The first biotech product patent[110] granted to Pegasys (interferon alpha-2a) survived a post-grant opposition.[111] Later, in 2010, Valcyte (valgancyclovir hydrochloride)[112] faced post-grant oppositions from domestic drug makers and patients groups.[113] On 30 April 2010, the assistant controller ordered to amend this patent to process claims restricted to single process.[114] Novartis' patent no 202350, for 'a medicament containing formoterot and mometasone furoate' faced post-grant oppositions and was revoked on 4 August 2010 on the grounds of lacking inventive-step.

There were, however, in total only 395 pre-grant oppositions in India between 1 January 2005 and 30 November 2009,[115] which seems to be a small number. In Japan, there was also a pre-grant opposition procedure until 1996 and a vast number of such oppositions from competitors are recorded: 6620 cases in 1993, 7419 cases in 1994 and 8549 cases in 1995.[116] However, there was no opposition from patient groups in Japan, probably because health insurance coverage is wide and patients do not have to pay a high price for medicines. Therefore, consumers do not associate patents with the question of access to medicines.

in *Snehalatha v UOI and others*, clarified that the actual date of grant of a patent is the day on which the Controller makes a decision to grant a patent, and not the date of grant of the patent certificate. http://lobis.nic.in/dhc/SMD/judgement/15-07-2010/SMD15072010CW35162007.pdf.

[109] On 23 March 2009, the IPO rejected Gilead's patent application covering Oseltamavir (and certain other) compositions (Gilead had licensed its patent to Roche for production). According to Spicy IP, the decision stated that the application: (i) lacked inventive step, (ii) failed to comply with s 3(d), and (iii) failed to sufficiently disclose the invention claimed and that the key reason for rejection was that no evidence was submitted to demonstrate increased efficacy – apart from increased solubility and unsubstantiated statements. 'The Swine Flu Outbreak: Cipla on a Patent Roll', Spicy IP, 29 April 2009. On the IPO decisions on *Gleevec*, see ch 12 of this book.

[110] Patent IN198952 was granted to Hoffmann-la-Roche and published on 19 May 2006. Post-grant opposition was filed under s 25(2) by Wockhardt and the Sankalp Rehabilitation Trust.

[111] Pegasys patent claims covers physiologically active branched PEG-IFN alpha conjugate and a method for producing it with increased anti-proliferative activity and decreased antiviral activity. The opposition argued that the advantages of PEG interferon (better physical and thermal stability, protection against susceptibility to enzymatic degradation) are naturally generated processes and, therefore, there was no inventive step. Roche pleaded that the anti-proliferative activity of the PEG interferon is much higher than that of interferon or other PEG interferon conjugates. Roche insisted also that the conjugate of this invention is non-immunogenic and, therefore, elicits virtually no antibody formation. The Controller considered that none of the documents cited by the opponents, neither in isolation nor in combination, explained how the antiviral activity was decreased and how the anti-proliferative Interferon activity increased while being used as a PEG conjugate with high molecular weight and decided that the invention was novel and had an inventive step.

[112] In January 2009, the Assistant Patent Controller rejected the pre-grant opposition and granted a patent IN 207232. The opponents argued that this invention lacked novelty.

[113] Cipla, Ranbaxy and Matrix Laboratories, Network for People Living with HIV-AIDS and Tamil Nadu Networking People with HIV-AIDS.

[114] Cipla's product was launched in spite of Roche's patent. Roche filed cases against Cipla in the Bombay High Court for patent and trademark infringements. The High Court asked Cipla to change its brand name in the trade mark case; the patent litigation is still pending.

[115] Interview with KS Kardam, Deputy Controller of Patents & Designs, Patent Office, Government of India, Ministry of Commerce and Industry on 19 December 2009.

[116] JPO database.

Patentable subject matter and patentability criteria

The India Patents (Amendment) Act 2005 omitted section 5 of the Patents Act of 1970 (see above p 353) and thus inventions claiming substances intended for use, or capable of being used, as food or medicines again became patentable. At the same time, in order to adjust to the disadvantages that patent protection may incur industrially and socially, India adopted a series of measures in the 2005 amendments, notably by limiting conditions to patentability, in addition to those introduced in 2002.

The definition of an 'invention' in section 2(1)(j) had been substituted by the amendment in 2002 to read: 'invention" means a new product or process involving an inventive step and [which is] capable of industrial application'. At the same time, section 2(1)(ja) was added to explain that '"an inventive step" is a feature that makes the invention not obvious to a person skilled in the art.' Section 2(1)(ja) was substituted further by the amendment in 2005 to read: '"inventive step" means a feature of an invention that involves technical advance as compared to the existing knowledge or having economic significance or both and that makes the invention not obvious to a person skilled in the art.'[117]

The list in section 3 of what are not considered as inventions became longer and increasingly complex, when it was amended in 2002 and 2005. Section 3(b), according to which in the previous text: 'an invention the primary or intended use of which would be contrary to law or morality or injurious to public health [is not patentable]', was amended in 2002 to read: 'an invention the primary or intended use of which or commercial exploitation would be contrary to public order or morality or which causes serious prejudice to human animal or plant life or health or to the environment [is not patentable].' The language is similar to that of Article 27.2 of the TRIPS Agreement, but this TRIPS provision concerns possible exclusions from patentability concerning individual cases, on the condition that they are 'necessary to' protect '*ordre public* or morality, including to protect human, animal or plant life or health or to avoid serious prejudice to the environment, provided that such exclusion is not made merely because the exploitation is prohibited by their law' (see chapters 4 and 5).

Section 3(d) of the Indian Patents Act 1970, stipulated against the patentability of 'the mere discovery of any new property or new use for a known substance or of the mere use of a known process, machine or apparatus unless such known process results in a new product or employs at least one new reactant'. Therefore, a 'new use of a known substance or process' continued was unpatentable. In the 2004 Order, however, the phrase 'a mere new use' was adopted and therefore a new use could be patentable. This was then reversed in the text of section 3(d) in the 2005 Amendment by the deletion of the word 'mere' from 'a mere new use' to leave simply 'a new use'. As a result, any new use of a known substance

---

[117] According to s 2.1(ta), 'pharmaceutical substance' means any new entity involving one or more inventive steps. In the legislative process, there was a proposition that only a 'new chemical entity' could be considered a drug, to the exclusion of combination drugs or methods of administration.

again became unpatentable. Section 3(d) of India's Patents (Amendment) Act 2005 reads as follows:

> the mere discovery of a new form of a known substance which does not result in the enhancement of the known efficacy of that substance or the mere discovery of any new property or new use for a known substance or of the mere use of a known process, machine or apparatus unless such known process results in a new product or employs at least one new reactant.

> Explanation: For the purposes of this clause, salts, esters, ethers, polymorphs, metabolites, pure form, particle size, isomers, mixtures of isomers, complexes, combinations and other derivatives of known substance shall be considered to be the same substance, unless they differ significantly in properties with regard to efficacy.

Section 3(d) also denies patentability of the derivatives or combinations of known-substances, unless 'they differ significantly in properties with regard to efficacy'. Notably, the derivatives described in the Explanation closely resemble those enumerated in the EC Regulation laying down Community procedures for the authorisation and supervision of medicinal products[118] as substances eligible for consideration as 'generic medicinal product'.[119] This provision is therefore a mirror image of pharmaceutical intellectual property protection abroad, well adapted to India's important export market for generic medicines, as well as India's large domestic market for generics. DG Shah of the Indian Pharmaceutical Association (IPA) explains that, in fact, the export of Indian generics will increase much more than the domestic market, and therefore, this Explanation in section 3(d) makes sense.[120] These restrictions on what is patentable clarified what is copiable in pharmaceuticals and were designed to cushion the shock of new composition-of-matter protection under the 2005 Act, amended in compliance with TRIPS, as new molecules will no longer be copiable until the relevant Indian patents have expired.

Thus, India dealt with the difficult situation for its domestic industry by raising the standards of patentability. Incidentally, the Japanese patent system at the time of the introduction of product patent protection in 1976 did the opposite. It opted for narrow patents to encourage local innovation to be patented. This

---

[118] Regulation (EC) 726/2004 of the European Parliament and of the Council of 31 March 2004 laying down Community procedures for the authorisation and supervision of medicinal products for human and veterinary use and establishing a European Medicines Agency introduced 10-year data protection of pharmaceutical products in Article 10.1. http://ec.europa.eu/enterprise/pharmaceuticals/eudralex/vol-1/consol_2004/human_code.pdf.

[119] Art 10.2(b) of the above Regulation defines, for the purposes of this Regulation: 'generic medicinal product' shall mean a medicinal product which has the same qualitative and quantitative composition in active substances and the same pharmaceutical form as the reference medicinal product, and whose bioequivalence with the reference medicinal product has been demonstrated by appropriate bioavailability studies. The different salts, esters, ethers, isomers, mixtures of isomers, complexes or derivatives of an active substance shall be considered to be the same active substance, unless they differ significantly in properties with regard to safety and/or efficacy. In such cases, additional information providing proof of the safety and/or efficacy of the various salts, esters, or derivatives of an authorised active substance must be supplied by the applicant.'

[120] Interview with DG Shah, Secretary General of the IPA in Osaka, 13 April 2010.

encouraged competition between relatively small-scale domestic companies and highly competitive multinationals. First, examiners at the Japan Patent Office (JPO) were encouraged to interpret patent claims literally, ie only those claims supported by examples were permissible.[121] Japan had a patentability requirement similar to other developed countries, but patent scope was narrow, which made it easier for Japanese firms with fewer R&D resources to enter the market thanks to their own invention, rather than wait until important patents expire. This practice persisted until 1995, when patent examination guidelines were revised to widen the interpretation of claims. Secondly, the Japanese practice, until 1988, of allowing only one claim per patent created 'holes' in the technology space which could be exploited by Japanese firms.[122] This contrast with the Indian approach may be explained by the fact that in Japan there was no competitive generic industry and efforts were concentrated on encouraging local inventions. Abusive or exploitative behaviours of multinational companies may have been much more marked in the past in developing countries.

The balance of considerations underlying certain patent laws of developing countries seems, therefore, to be more complex than in developed countries. UNCTAD discussions in the 1970s (chapter 2) showed that these developing countries considered it necessary to use the 'flexibility'[123] of the Paris Convention, which hardly regulated substantive rules of patent protection, and to maintain the possibility of state intervention over the working of patented foreign inventions and licensing terms. The less the patent protection, it was thought, the better for all developing countries, as this would control import and allow local production. Much attention was paid to the issues of employment and local manufacturing in evaluating the functioning of patent laws, and relatively less effort was made to encourage local invention. Relatively less interest was taken in turning traditional knowledge into significant technological inventions to make local businesses, or attracting investment to create local R&D infrastructure, for example.

Compulsory licensing

Subtle adjustments were made also to conditions and procedures relating to compulsory licensing in response to the TRIPS Agreement. The provisions relating to 'licences of rights' in sections 86–88 were withdrawn in 2002. However, Mueller finds that the framework for granting compulsory licences under section 92 is reminiscent of India's former 'license of right' procedure.[124] The section 92 procedure, unlike those under section 84, empowers the Central Government to

---

[121] T Saiki, 'On the Relationship between the Pharmaceutical Industry Development and Patent Protection' (in Japanese) (2003) 13 *Chizai Prism*.

[122] M Sakakibara and L Branstetter 'Evidence from the 1998 Japanese Patent Law Reforms' (2001) 32(1) *Rand Journal of Economics* 77–100.

[123] UNCTAD, TD/B/AC.11/19, 95.

[124] J Mueller, 'The Tiger Awakens: The Tumultuous Transformation of India's Patent System and the Rise of Indian Pharmaceutical Innovation' (2007) 68(3) *University of Pittsburgh Law Review* 599–600.

declare that compulsory licences should be granted in circumstances of national emergency, in circumstances of extreme urgency or in other cases requiring public non-commercial use at any time after the sealing of the patent.

In the Indian Patents Act of 2005, the amendment added an explanation to section 84(6) to clarify that the 'reasonable period' for licensing negotiations with the right holder before the application for compulsory licence is construed as a period not ordinarily exceeding six months.

Another subtle revision in 2005 was that section 90(1)(vii) was substituted to read: 'the [compulsory] licence is granted with a predominant purpose of supply in the Indian market and that the licensee may also export if the need be, in accordance with Section 84(7)(a)(iii)'.[125] This latter provision stipulates that the reasonable requirements of the public shall be deemed not to have been satisfied if, by reason of the refusal of the patentee to grant a licence or licences on reasonable terms, 'a market for export of the patented Article manufactured in India is not being supplied or developed'. Independently of this provision, a new section 92A on compulsory licence for export of patented pharmaceutical products for any country having insufficient or no manufacturing capacity in the pharmaceutical sector for the concerned product to address public health problems, if compulsory licence is granted by such country (s 92A(1)).

As for the meaning of 'working of patented inventions' in the Indian Patents Act, the Indian Patents (Amendment) Act 2005 seems to preserve the thinking that the working of patents for the Indian domestic market and industry are necessary in exchange for the protection given to the patent. The 'working of the patented invention' in the Indian Patents Act is likely to be interpreted as requiring manufacture of the invention in India rather than any other form of 'working' the invention, including importation. This is assumed from the wording, for example, of section 83(b), which states that patents are not granted 'merely to enable patentees to enjoy a monopoly for the importation of the patented Article', or section 84(7)(e), which applies 'If the working of the patented invention in the territory of India on a commercial scale is being prevented or hindered by the importation from abroad of the patented Article, . . .'

A complex set of justifications and philosophical considerations for granting, protecting and enforcing a patent is provided in Article 83[126] This Article enumerates general considerations to be taken into account in issuing compulsory licensing. The meaning of 'working' the patented invention in the Indian Patents Act (1970, 2002, 2005) is not entirely clear, but Article 84(c) allows application, three years after the grant of the patent, for compulsory licensing on the grounds

---

[125] Before the amendment in 2005, s 90(1) (vii) read: 'the [compulsory] licence is granted with a predominant purpose of supply in the Indian market and in the case of semi-conductor technology, the licence granted is to work the invention for public non-commercial use and in the case, the licence granted to remedy a practice determined after judicial or administrative process to be anti-competitive, licensee shall be permitted to export the patented product.'

[126] Art 83 stipulates that: 'Without prejudice to the other provisions contained in this Act, in exercising the powers conferred by this Chapter, regard shall be had to the following general considerations, namely: . . .'.

of non-working or inadequate working, and for the revocation of patents two years after the issuance of such licence. Under section 146(2) and Rule 131(2), every patentee or licensee is obligated to furnish the details to the Controller of the extent to which the patented invention has been worked on a commercial scale in India within three months of the end of each year and within two months whenever required by the Controller. Refusal or failure to supply information is punishable with a fine (of up to Rs10 lakh) and a person who furnishes information or a statement which is false and which he either knows or has reason to believe to be false or does not believe to be true shall be punishable with a fine or with imprisonment, which may extend to six months, or both.[127]

The 2008 Draft Manual of Patent Practice and Procedure (note 79) states that 'patents are granted for the purpose of encouraging inventions that will enhance industrial development and, therefore, should be worked in its fullest extent within the territory of India.'[128] The Draft Manual draws attention, however, to the provisions that 'failure to work the patented invention within the territory of India will be considered with respect to the facility available in India for the working of the invention . . . provision of importation of patented article is allowed, but the mere importation of patented articles when there is a possibility of manufacturing within India will be a factor that will receive consideration.'

B Brazil's Implementation of the TRIPS Agreement

In 1996, Brazil amended its Industrial Property Law,[129] as required by the TRIPS Agreement, one year after its entry into force. Brazil did not avail itself of the five-year transition period, or of the 10-year transition period for introducing product patent protection, both of which were allowed to developing countries under the TRIPS Agreement. In Articles 230–31 of the Law, Brazil even introduced pipeline product protection, which is not required under the Agreement (see chapter 4). Subsequently, foreign direct investment and the share of imports to Brazil increased, but the strength of multinational corporations within the country seems to have been reinforced.[130]

Brazil's approach to patent law is straightforward and provides safeguards that had already been accepted in the general history of patent law and notably in the tradition of the Paris Convention. Article 68 of Brazil's Industrial Property Law of 1996 concerning compulsory licensing for non-working conditions in the tradition of the Paris Convention was questioned by the US under Articles

---

[127] s 122 on sanctions on refusal or failure to furnish required information.

[128] para 18.1.1 of c 18.1 'Working of Patented Invention'.

[129] The Industrial Property Act was amended by Law 9279/96 on 14 May 1996 which entered into force on 17 May 1997.

[130] Salama and Benoliel, (n 52) 6.

27, 28 or 31 of the TRIPS Agreement, but the case led to a settlement agreement (chapter 7).[131]

In 2001, Article 229-C was added to the Brazilian Industrial Property Law. This provision gives the National Health Surveillance Agency (ANVISA)[132] the authority to review patent applications claiming pharmaceutical products or processes. The question of granting patents for pharmaceutical products or processes depends on prior approval of ANVISA. It has been discussed whether this measure conforms to Article 27.1 of the TRIPS Agreement.[133] However, Article 27.1 does not specify that the examination of novelty, inventive-step and industrial applicability must be made by one agency.

The Brazilian Industrial Property Law reflects the discussion on the transfer of technology that animated the UNCTAD before the adoption of the TRIPS Agreement. Title VI of the Law is 'Transfer of Technology and Franchising'. It stipulates in Article 211 that 'the INPI shall register the contracts involving transfer of technology, franchising and similar contracts in order that they may become effective with regard to third parties'. Thus, the registration of technology transfer agreements is obligatory in Brazil.

Brazil has been one of the leaders and pioneers in the world-wide discussions on IPR and access to medicines (chapter 9) and constantly showed diplomatic skills in the multilateral negotiations that led to the adoption of the Doha Declaration and the paragraph 6 system for developing countries without pharmaceutical manufacturing capacity.

Bill 22/2003, which proposed to exclude pharmaceutical products and processes for the treatment or prevention of HIV/AIDS from patentable subject matter, was approved by the Brazilian House of Representatives in June 2005 without, however, resulting in final adoption. The House in 2006 also proposed a draft resolution to invalidate all pharmaceutical patents under pipeline product protection. Brazil's patients' group, Network for People Integration, expressed its opposition to Brazil's Industrial Property Office (INPI), claiming that the tenofovir patent lacked novelty and inventive step. It also challenged the validity of Kaletra's patent on the basis that the drug was under pipeline protection and lacked novelty.[134] These movements gradually focused on the concept of 'the right to choose the quality of patents' to ensure public health. In 2007, at the Intergovernmental Conference at the Pan American Ministerial Conference of Health Ministers (PAHO) in Washington DC, this concept was proposed by the Brazilian Government, without, however, being adopted.

---

[131] *Brazil–Measures Affecting Patent Protection,* Request for the Establishment of a Panel by the US WT/DS199/3 (9 January 2001)and the settlement agreement WT/DS199/4, G/L/454, IP/D/23/ Add.1 (19 July 2001).

[132] www.anvisa.gov.br/eng/index.htm.

[133] AIPPI seminar on the 'Brazilian Industrial Property Code, Trademarks and Licensing' (Tokyo, 14 October 2008) by Veirano Advogados.

[134] www.abiaids.org.br.

C China's Integration in the Global IP System

Today, the Chinese opinion on patent protection has been diversified to include critical views, but the Chinese Government seems to maintain its thinking generally that becoming a 'leader in technology' cannot be achieved without respecting intellectual property rights. The discussions on the third amendment of the Chinese Patent Law, initiated on 25 August 2000, were carried out particularly from the point of view of strengthening the technological capabilities of domestic companies.

i. Third amendment of the Patent Law

On 27 December, 2008, amid intensified domestic discussions, the Sixth Session of the Standing Committee of the 11th Chinese People's Congress approved the third amendment to the Chinese Patent Law, to be effective from 1 October 2009. China's Patent Office which is under the State Intellectual Property Office of the Peoples' Republic of China (SIPO), subsequently adopted the Implementing Regulation for the new Patent Law on 9 January 2010, which came into effect on 1 February 2010. In the amended Chinese Patent Law, the following new provisions seem to indicate China's renewed interest in technology transfer as well as in encouraging Chinese companies to strengthen their patent portfolio to win 'the global patent war'.[135]

Towards internationalisation

The new law encourages Chinese citizens (companies and individuals)[136] to obtain international patents[137] by abolishing the obligation on the Chinese to file first in China. The previous law enacted in 2000 (Chinese Patent Law 2000) specified in Article 20 that those Chinese citizens who intend to file an application in a foreign country for a patent for inventions made in China must ask for the service of a patent agent designated by SIPO and comply with the provisions contained in Article 4 of this law. Article 4 of the Chinese Patent Law (1984, 1992, 2000 and 2008) stipulates that, if an invention for which an application has

---

[135] P Ganea, 'The Amended Chinese Patent Law: Implications for Foreign Rights Holders' (in Japanese) (2010) 80 *Institute of Intellectual Property*, Tokyo 17.

[136] The 'Chinese entity' includes three types of companies that foreigners could be authorised to establish in China on the basis of Chinese law (ie, Chinese-foreign equity joint ventures, China-foreign contractual joint ventures, and wholly foreign-owned enterprises) but did not include foreign companies.

[137] Art 20.1 of the Patent Law 2000 required a Chinese company applying for patents for inventions completed in China to file a patent application in China first, before any foreign filing. However, the previous law did not say what a foreign applicant was required to do in the same situation. Foreign-owned companies could assign patent applications for inventions completed in China to one of their foreign entities to be filed outside of China first, in the name of that foreign entity. In the third amendment revision process, it was proposed that foreign companies also follow the previous procedure for domestic companies of filing first in China before acquiring foreign patents. In the third amendment, this proposal was rejected.

been filed touches upon national security or other vital interests of the State and is required to be kept secret,[138] it is handled by relevant state regulations.[139] This system of authorisation had been criticised on the grounds that it would delay the filing of Chinese citizens' patent applications in other countries.

However, under the Patent Law 2008, SIPO is required: (1) to inform the applicant within four months upon the filing of the request if it believes that a national security review is necessary; and (2) to decide within four months whether the invention relates to national security such that it shall be kept confidential. If within the six-month statutory period SIPO has not responded, a favourable decision is assumed, and the applicant is free to file a patent application in a foreign country first. For applicants whose inventions are considered related to national security,[140] it is possible to make PCT filings applications in China only after a security check by the State Council. Delays in application may disadvantage the applicants, who may therefore opt to file in China first anyway.

Another aspect of the third amendment indicating China's willingness to be part of the global system of patent protection is that the new law has adopted an absolute novelty standard such that any prior public disclosure anywhere in the world, including public use, can be cited as a prior art, destroying the novelty of the proposed inventions and utility models (Article 22).[141] The new law has also raised the novelty requirement for designs by requiring that the design be substantially different from existing designs and from the combinations of existing design characteristics (Article 23). The new novelty standard will have a significant impact on the way in which patent validity is challenged in China. For example, under the previous law, public use outside China does not destroy novelty and is irrelevant in invalidation proceedings.

Promoting domestic inventions

For multinational companies conducting research in collaboration with Chinese universities or companies,[142] the most significant new provision in the third

---

[138] Violation of the national security review requirement will result in the loss of patent rights in China.

[139] Accordingly, if a Chinese person or a Chinese company intended to submit an application for a patent to a foreign country in connection with an invention made by a Chinese person in China, the first application should be made to the Chinese Patent Office, after which an application could be made to another country through an agency in China designated by SIPO.

[140] eg, certain Chinese herbal medicines are included among technologies that are regarded as state secrets in China whose export is prohibited.

[141] Previously, China had a mixed novelty standard. This was because qualifying prior art consisted of publication in China and abroad, but only inventions practised or publicly made known in China, but not abroad.

[142] Art 15 provides that: 'If the co-owners of a patent application right or patent right have an agreement on the exercise of those rights, the agreement shall apply. If there is no such agreement, any co-owner may independently exploit or license others to exploit the patent through ordinary licences; any royalties obtained through licensing others to exploit the patent shall be distributed amongst all the co-owners. Except for the situation provided in the above paragraph, the exercise of a jointly-owned patent application right or patent right shall be consented to by all co-owners.'

amendment concerns co-ownership of patent rights. It was enacted probably to accelerate transfer of technology. New Article 15 of the Chinese Patent Law allows unilateral exploitation of patent rights by the co-owner without the consent of joint owners, unless otherwise agreed upon. According to the new provision, the joint co-owner 'may independently exploit or license others to exploit the patent through ordinary licences' but must share the royalties obtained thereof with other joint owners. The Amendment does not stipulate how the royalties are to be distributed. Consent by all joint owners is required if the invention is to be exploited in other ways.

Clarifying pharmaceutical regulatory exemptions

At the same time, the third amendment adopted a provision similar to the *Bolar* exemption available in the US[143] and other developed countries, to allow production, use and importation of patented pharmaceutical products or medical equipment for the purpose of obtaining regulatory approval for pharmaceutical products and medical equipment (new Article 69.5). In the Chinese Patent Law 2000, Article 63.4 provided that 'where any person uses the patent concerned solely for the purposes of scientific research and experimentation [shall be deemed an infringement of the patent right]'. Due to wording limiting the scope of exception only to 'scientific research and experimentation', no Chinese courts interpreted this to refer to the regulatory experimental *(Bolar)* exemption (chapter 5, n 60).

Before the 2008 amendment, a Chinese court, on 20 December 2006, implicitly recognised the *Bolar* exemption in *Sankyo v Wangsheng Drug Industry Co Ltd*, but this was not based on Article 63.4.[144] The court in this case held that the defendant used the same compounds and manufacturing method as patented by Sankyo. The court also held that Wangsheng used the Sankyo technology not for immediate, commercial purposes or direct sales, but for the purpose of clinical trials, with a view to applying for regulatory approval of the production. The court resorted to Article 11, which prohibits acts that infringe the rights of the patent holder,[145] to affirm that the limited production of the patented compounds to establish the safety and efficacy of the drug for eventual application for marketing

---

[143] See ch 5 n 53.

[144] *Sankyo v Wangsheng Drug Industry Co Ltd,* Second Beijing Intermediate People's Court, Civil Judgment No 04134/2006. On 24 September 2003, the Sankyo Corporation had obtained Chinese patent ZL 97126347.7, for the methods for manufacturing pharmaceutical compositions of a series of compounds 'for olmesartan medoxomil'. These compounds are antagonists of angiotension II used in the treatment and prophylaxis of hypertension, including diseases of the heart and circulatory system. Upon knowledge of the production by Wangsheng Drug Industry Co of the same product, Sankyo and its licensee, Shanghai Sankyo Corporation, sued Wangsheng for infringing the above patent at the Second Beijing Intermediate People's Court.

[145] Art 11 provides that unless 'otherwise provided for in this Law, no entity or individual may, without the authorization of the patentee, exploit the patent, that is, make, use, offer to sell, sell or import the patented product, or use the patented process, or use, offer to sell, sell or import the product directly obtained by the patented process, for production or business purposes.'

approval to the PRC's State Food and Drug Administration (SFDA) was not violating Article 11. In the absence of an explicit provision corresponding to regulatory experimental exemption, or of experimental exemptions which could be interpreted flexibly, the court had only Article 11 as the legal basis for its judgment. In this case, the Court added that the marketing of the generic products should wait for SFDA approval and subsequently seems to have deterred the marketing of the generic version of olmesartan medoxomil.

Two years later, the third amendment introduced Article 69 (formerly Article 63), which enumerates those acts not considered to be infringements and explicitly mentions experimental exceptions in its paragraph 5, which reads:

> For the purpose of providing the information needed for the administrative approval, manufacture, use, import of a drug or a medical apparatus, and exclusively for such manufacture any import of a patented drug or a patented medical apparatus.

The new provision in Article 69.5 is a clear message encouraging Chinese generic manufacturers.

International exhaustion of patent rights

The third amendment introduced also the principle of patent exhaustion in which importing, using, selling, or offering to sell patented products or products produced directly by a patented process does not constitute infringement in China where such products were first sold by the patentee or its licensee. Thus, the new patent law recognises parallel trade.

Disclosure of origins for genetic resources

The third amendment explicitly prohibits the granting of a patent for any invention and creation for which genetic resources were acquired or used in violation of Chinese laws or regulations (Article 5(2)). For such inventions, the amendment requires that the applicant shall explain in the filing document attached to the patent specification, both the direct and original sources of the genetic resources (Article 26(5)). If the original source cannot be identified, the applicant must explain why. The Implementing Regulation requires the applicant to submit a certificate that demonstrates that access to such a genetic resource was lawfully obtained. Failure to disclose the source of genetic resources could result in the refusal of a Chinese patent (Article 44.1(1), 44.2 of the Implementing Regulation). If, on the other hand, the examiner considers the lack of disclosure of the origin of the genetic resources used in the invention as insufficient disclosure of the invention in the specification (Article 26.3 of the Patent Law), this could be a ground for invalidity of the patent (Article 65.2 of the Implementing Regulation). The Chinese Patent Law does not provide a definition of genetic resources, nor does it limit genetic resources to those in China. However, Article 26 of the Implementing Regulation defines genetic resources as 'entities having human, plant and animal genetic functions with actual or potential values' and includes human genetic resources. The insertion of the word 'potential' widens the scope of disclosure obligation. It appears also that genetic resources for which the Chinese Patent Law requires disclosure include those obtained outside of China, because the form to fill in for such disclosure, prepared by the Patent Administration Division of the State Council, requires the name of the country where the resource is obtained.

The Convention on Biological Diversity (CBD)[146] has not been explicitly cited as the basis for introducing this requirement, either in the amended Patent Law or in the new Implementing Regulation. In their commentaries, SIPO Legal Affairs' Division refers to the CBD as the origin of the new Article 5(2) and 26(5) of China's Patent Law relating to the disclosure of origin of genetic resources.

The CBD provides a framework of goals, policies and obligations, and leaves the contracting parties to determine the specific measures to be applied within their borders. At the international level, the CBD allows the Conference of the Parties (COP), which consists of all governments and regional organisations that have ratified the treaty, to adopt those approaches, as appropriate and as far as possible, in the vast fields of relevance covered by the CBD. Among the topics addressed by the COP are access to genetic resources, prior informed consent as a condition for access (PIC), and benefit sharing in the case of genetic resources (ABS). The Bonn Guidelines[147] concerning ABS were adopted at COP 6 in 2002, and in 2006, at COP 8, a 2010 target to negotiate an international regime was set. However, many provisions in the CBD vaguely define scopes. For example, Article 2 of the CBD stipulates that 'biological resources' include genetic resources, organisms or parts thereof, populations, or any other biotic component of ecosystems with actual or potential use or value for humanity, although a COP 2 Decision as well as the Bonn Guidelines made it clear that human genetic resources are not included in its scope.[148] On 30 October 2010, the COP 10 of the CBD held in Nagoya adopted the Protocol on Access to Genetic Resources and the Fair and Equitable sharing of Benefits (ABS Protocol). This Protocol clearly includes within its scope of application traditional knowledge associated with genetic resources, but did not bring further precision as to the scope of genetic resources for which the ABS rules are applicable. Article 3.1 of the ABS Protocol refers to the benefits arising from the 'utilization' of genetic resources.

---

[146] See ch 6 n 62.

[147] The Bonn Guidelines on Access to Genetic Resources and Fair and Equitable Sharing of The Benefits Arising out of their Utilization (UN Doc UNED/CBD/COP/6/2C (27 May 2002))

[148] COP 2 Decision II/11 (6–17 November 1995), para 2. The Bonn Guidelines state that: 'All genetic resources and associated traditional knowledge, innovations and practices covered by the Convention on Biological Diversity and benefits arising from the commercial and other utilization of such resources should be covered by the guidelines, with the exclusion of human genetic resources.'(I.A.C9).

Compulsory licensing

Since its first adoption in 1984, Chapter VI of the Chinese Patent Law has contained provisions concerning compulsory licensing, and the third amendment clarified the procedures and introduced several new provisions. The third amendment inserts the Paris Convention condition that a compulsory licence cannot be issued unless the patentee has not exploited or has not sufficiently exploited the patent rights without any reasonable grounds within three years since the date that the patent rights were granted and four years since the date of filing (Article 48(1)). New Article 48(2) refers to remedies to monopolistic behaviour.[149] Article 54 contains a new provision concerning compulsory licensing under Article 48 and requires proof that requests for licensing have been made for authorisation from the right holder to exploit the patent on reasonable terms and conditions but that such efforts have not been successful within a reasonable period of time. It also adds provisions concerning semiconductors (new Article 52) limiting the compulsory licence to use for the purpose of public interest.[150] New Article 53 introduces the terms of Article 31(f) of the TRIPS Agreement that compulsory licensing is predominantly for the supply of the domestic market. China implemented the WTO General Council's Decision WT/L540 of 30 August 2003 concerning paragraph 6 of the Doha Declaration (see chapter 9) through SIPO's Measures for the Compulsory Licensing of Patents Relating to Public Health Issues. The amendment incorporates these measures and contains new rules that restrict the general scope of compulsory licensing while making it more feasible and likely for compulsory licences to be granted in the area of pharmaceuticals (new Article 50). In the past, no compulsory licensing was granted by SIPO.

Restoration of the term of patent protection not adopted

The proposed restoration of the term of patent protection, due to regulatory delays, was not adopted. This is due to the fact that China is exploring ways to supply affordable generic drugs and putting as much effort as possible into stabilising its finances and avoiding social instability against the possibilities of high drug prices. As of 2008, of approximately 1300 ingredients used in synthetic drugs produced in China, 97 per cent were generic; of the 62 per cent of these generic drugs available on the market, 14 per cent were brand-generic drugs; and

---

[149] 'Where it has been legally determined that the enforcement of the patent right by the patentee is an act of monopoly, to avoid or to eliminate the adverse effects caused to competition'. Art 55 of China's Anti-Monopoly Law provides that: 'This Law is not applicable to conduct by business operators to exercise their legitimate intellectual property rights in accordance with intellectual property laws and relevant administrative regulations; however, this Law is applicable to the conduct of business operators to eliminate or restrict market competition by abusing intellectual property rights.'

[150] Concerning compulsory licensing, the previous provisions remain when a national emergency or any extraordinary state of affairs occurs, or where the public interest so requires (Art 49), as well as when the exploitation of the later invention depends on the exploitation of the earlier invention and involves important technical advance of considerable economic significance (Art 50).

9 per cent were drugs which were protected by patent rights.[151] Chinese generic companies are far less internationalised than their counterparts in comparable developing countries such as India, as evidenced by the appearance of Indian generic companies operating in China. For example, Matrix, an Indian company, in joint venture with the Chinese Mchem group,[152] exports active pharmaceutical ingredients and intermediaries.[153]

ii The Judiciary and intellectual property rights

In many infringement or validity cases in China, courts seem to be attempting to respond favourably both to domestic and foreign industries using various patent law theories, including the doctrine of equivalents (chapter 3), the *Bolar* exemption and enablement. This sometimes (as in the *Pfizer* (Viagra) and *Sankyo* cases above) resulted in these attitudes appearing contradictory, ie, the courts appeared to be siding with domestic companies, even though the foreign companies won the case, or vice versa. This is shown, for example, through judgments in certain important patent-infringement suits against Chinese companies where foreign companies prevailed. For example, in *Astellas Pharma Inc v Shenzhen Tsinghua Yuanxing Pharmaceutical Co Ltd (TY)*, a doctrine of equivalents was adopted by courts, without which the results might have been different. In this case, an infringement lawsuit was instituted against TY by Astellas concerning its patent ZL90100544.4, entitled 'the method of preparation of tetrahydrobenzimidazole derivatives'.[154] Astellas complained that TY employed one of the three methods it had claimed. The Second Intermediary People's Court of Beijing compared the plaintiff's patent method and the defendant's method, and found that the two methods had the same second reactant and the same product. According to the court, they differed in that the defendant's method substituted boc (tert-butoxycarbonyl) for H in the first reactant. However, according to the evidence available, it could have been concluded that boc was easily subjected to acidolysis and easily removed, and was a conventional protective group. Therefore, the first reactants with the boc group and the H group had 'the same main structure and achieve the same function and effect by the same means', and therefore, TY's method fell within the scope of Astellas' patent and constituted an infringement upon its patent right.[155] According to the court, those skilled in the art can think of the feature

[151] Japan Pharmaceutical Manufacturers' Association (JPMA), *Kenkyushiryo no 404* (in Japaese, June 2010) 82–83.

[152] Mchem group manufactures pharmaceutical products ranging from basic chemicals, intermediates, active pharmaceutical ingredients to finished dosage forms with a group turnover of about $35 million. 'Matrix takes control of Chinese firm Mchem' *Business Standards* (Hyderabad, 27 September 2005).

[153] www.mchem.net/. The Indian company, Matrix, is acquiring companies in Europe in order to operate globally.

[154] Astellas had filed an application for this patent on 2 February 1990, before China introduced product patent protection in 1992, and this patent was granted by SIPO on 15 November 1995. TY was producing ramosetron hydrochloride injections, and argued that its method of production differed from the one claimed in the Astellas patent.

[155] *Er-Zhong-Min-Chu-Zi* No 11763.

of boc without making inventive efforts. In opposition to the Beijing Court judgment of 22 September 2006, TY appealed to the Higher People's Court of Beijing, which upheld the original judgment on 2 July 2007.[156]

The attitudes of the judiciary seem to be evolving with the overall Chinese policy of promoting industrial competitiveness by technological improvement, to achieve a socialist state (see chapter 11). This will mean the state ultimately assuming the management of IPR rights, balancing various interests under the abstract concept of 'public interest'. A recent case outside the pharmaceutical field, but in an equally sensitive area of energy/environmental protection, serves as an example. The High Court of Fujian, in a patent infringement case involving an invention relating to an exhaust gas purification system comprising a NOx conversion catalyst device in sewage treatment plant designs and technologies, refused to order an injunction, despite the fact that the infringement was recognised by the court.[157] On 12 May 2008, the court decision referred to the importance of 'balancing the need for patent protection and the need to protect public interest properly'. Typically, the court cited the US Supreme Court judgment in *eBay v MercExchange*,[158] which said that a permanent injunction should not automatically be issued based on a finding of patent infringement. According to the US Supreme Court, courts should apply and weigh the traditional four-factor test to determine by equitable discretion if an injunction should be ordered, which requires a plaintiff to demonstrate that: (1) it has suffered an irreparable injury; (2) remedies available at law are inadequate to compensate for that injury; (3) considering the balance of hardships between the plaintiff and defendant, a remedy in equity is warranted; and (4) the public interest would not be disserved by a permanent injunction. On 21 December 2009, China's Supreme Court supported the decision by the Fujian High Court and stated that 'when social or public interest is damaged, this Court does not suspend the act of infringement'.[159]

Parallel to this court case, on 5 June 2008, the State Council of the People's Republic of China adopted a National Intellectual Property Strategy. Among the specific tasks for which advanced development plans should be elaborated and strategic patents be obtained, it enumerated the following sectors as the key industry sectors: biology, medicine, information, new materials, advanced manufacturing, new energy, oceanography, resources, environmental protection, modern agriculture, modern transportation, aeronautics and astronautics.[160] As part of the Guiding Principles of China's IP strategy, it states in paragraph 20:

> Balance the need for patent protection and the need to protect public interest properly. While strengthening patent right protection in accordance with law, we need to

---

[156] *Gao-Min-Zhong-Zi* No 38.
[157] Fujian High Court, *Min-Zhi-Chu-Zi* No. 4.
[158] *eBay v MercExchange* 547 US 338 (2006).
[159] Supreme Court, *Min-San-Zhong-Zi* No. 8.
[160] D Friedmann, 'China´s National IP Strategy 2008: Feasible Commitments Or Road To Nowhere Paved With Good Intentions?' 15 September 2008, www.mondaq.com/article.asp?articleid=66196.

improve the compulsory licensing system and make good use of exception provisions. We need to work out relevant policies that are rational to ensure that the public is able to obtain necessary products and services in a timely and sufficient manner whenever a public crisis happens.[161]

[161] Strategy para 20, as translated in Friedmann, 'China's National IP Strategy 2008' (n 163).

11

Pharmaceutical Industries, R&D and Public Health in Emerging Economies

E MERGING COUNTRIES HAVE been extremely successful in expanding their trade and growth, but they have little in common with each other in terms of their IP policies, the state of research and development (R&D) or public health. IP policies are far from being a sufficient framework both for R&D and public health policies, which require their own framework and political will. On the other hand, there seems to be insufficient coordination between IP policies and R&D efforts in some of these countries. In the sense that IP protection purports to encourage long-term R&D efforts and accumulation of R&D infrastructure, there seems to be room for more thought and discussion on how to integrate these two policies. Although available data are not sufficient for describing and analysing the complete situation of R&D and its results in emerging economies, different R&D policies and patenting behaviour of companies in these countries are compared, with a view to understanding the patterns in which patent protection is used.

I GLOBAL PATENT FILINGS BY EMERGING COUNTRIES' ENTERPRISES

A International and Domestic Patent Filing Patterns

Global patenting makes possible the commercialisation of a wide range of technologies and, today, developing country enterprises are participating in larger technology markets and increasing global competition. In 2004 Morel et al showed the number of patent filings in the US in all fields of technology based on per capita GDP, which demonstrated how important it is for universities, research institutions and companies in developing countries to obtain patents in the US, with its exceptionally large market.[1] In 2009, amidst the general decline in international patent filing due to the economic downturn, China became the fifth largest PCT user (chapter 10).[2] The differences in the ways companies and

---

[1] C Morel et al, 'Health Innovation in Developing Countries to Address Diseases of the Poor', Bellagio Conference on Diseases of Poverty: The Role of Public-Private Partnerships in Developing Countries, 10–13 May 2004. www.sciencemag.org/cgi/reprint/309/5733/401.pdf, 6.

[2] 'First-Ever Drop In Filings Under Patent Cooperation Treaty Seen In 2009', *IP Watch* (8 February 2010). International patent filings under the Patent Cooperation Treaty (PCT) fell by 4.5% in 2009.

institutions in developing countries apply for patents at home and in foreign countries reflect not only their technological competitiveness, but also national industrial policies in the context of a global economy and institutions. Over time patent filing patterns in specific fields of technology can also show trends in the scientific and technological policies of different countries. Patenting patterns of companies from different emerging economies reflect the different industrial and R&D policies of each country.

The following Section explores the global strategies of developing country patent applicants in the fields of pharmaceuticals and biotech medicines. The International Patent Classification (IPC)[3] classifications A61K and C12N are used as proxies for counting the number of medicinal inventions and the number of biotechnological medicines or therapies, respectively, in the following codes for countries and regions: AR (Argentina); ARIPO (African Regional Intellectual Property Organisation, an intellectual property organisation consisting of 15 English-speaking countries in Africa); BR (Brazil); CN (China); CU (Cuba); IN (India); MX (Mexico); OAPI (African Intellectual Property Organisation);[4] ZA (Republic of South Africa); US (United States); EPO (European Patent Office); WO (World Intellectual Property Organisation); PCT (Patent Cooperation Treaty); and JP (Japan). The 'nationality' of the applicant can pose problems. There is no international rule concerning the nationality of patent applicants and their applications may provide information based on different notions of nationality. For example, the word 'Brazilian' referred to in the patent application could refer to a local Brazilian company or a Brazilian subsidiary of a multinational corporation. In many patent databases, the nationality of the applicant is not shown. In WO PCT publications, for example, Japanese nationality is attributed to Pfizer Japan Inc (Pfizer's Japanese subsidiary) even though the nationality of Pfizer Japan is perceived by many to be American. In Japan, the patent office does not attribute any nationality to companies.

Originally, a survey on A61K pharmaceutical patent filings at different patent offices was carried out by Momsen, Leonardos and Cia in Brazil in 2003.[5] Their data on nationality were based on the names of applicants and listed only the companies in the relevant developing countries to the exclusion of multinational corporations. In the following study, by contrast, a proxy of nationality is used. The number of applications under A61K and C12N, for which the applicant claimed the right of priority for country X, was considered to be the number of applications from country X. To identify published patent applications[6] submitted by

---

[3] The IPC is a hierarchical system of language-independent symbols for the classification of patents and utility models, according to the different areas of technology to which they pertain. It was established by the Strasbourg Agreement in 1971. www.wipo.int/classifications/ipc/en/.

[4] The OAPI consists of 15 francophone countries in Africa, where since applications are in principle not examined, filing of an application means that a patent is automatically granted (see ch 8).

[5] Momsen, Leonardos and Cia, Rio de Janiero. The author is grateful for their information discussed on 25 April 2006 at the 50th Anniversary of the AIPPI Japanese Group, Tokyo (on file with author).

[6] The patent filings in Table 11.3 are based on the publication year and, therefore, are later than the dates of actual filing.

enterprises operating in developing country X in their home country and in foreign patent offices, such as the US Patent and Trademark Office (USPTO), the European Patent Office (EPO), the Japan Patent Office (JPO) and the WO, the advanced search function of the EPO database (esp@cenet)[7] is used. For most countries, at least until 1998 (the year India joined the Paris Convention and the PCT), there was very little difference between these two methods of identifying the nationality of the applicants.

Another methodological problem is that there are increasing differences in the number of applications published recently by developing countries with figures appearing in different databases. Among different data bases, a large numerical gap is evident especially, since 1998, in the case of India. The number of applications filed by Indian nationals in India since 2000 (through PCT or the Paris route) is far greater in the case of the Dialog DWPI database than on Espacenet. This would suggest that a considerable number of Indian patent applications abroad were not based on priority application in India, and probably not in the US, either. The data, based on priority country, therefore, seem to be imperfect for India. However, they do reflect the overall tendency of Indian companies to rapidly increase their patenting activities abroad. For applicants from other countries, this problem does not occur and there is little discrepancy in the application numbers obtained through different data bases.

B Diversity of Filing Patterns among Companies in Developing Countries

Brazil's A61K patent filings in Brazil increased in the late 1990s, but decreased subsequently. There has been no significant increase in PCT applications. It seems that Brazilian applicants have little interest in markets outside Brazil.

Table 11.3: Brazil's Pharmaceutical (A61K) Patent Filing Publications

	1995	1996	1997	1998	1999	2000	2001	2002	2003	2004	2005	2006	2007	2008
BR	38	17	54	60	87	359	180	142	155	229	242	230	185	236
CN	1	0	1	1	2	2	2	3	4	4	2	5	8	6
MX	0	0	0	1	0	0	0	0	3	11	12	4	4	1
OAPI	0	0	1	0	0	0	0	1	0	1	0	1	0	0
ZA	2	2	0	1	1	1	0	0	1	0	0	0	1	1
US	1	1	1	4	5	3	7	13	20	20	18	16	17	31
EP	3	0	4	4	8	7	5	11	15	12	19	17	25	22
JP	4	0	3	3	4	3	7	4	7	6	6	8	8	11
WO	4	5	1	11	10	3	17	22	16	26	27	31	36	43

---

[7] http://ep.espacenet.com/advancedSearch?locale=en_EP.

In Brazil, it has been possible to acquire product patents since 1996. Research and development is taking place in fields such as vaccines and other biotech medicines at state-run laboratories and other scientific institutions – some results of which must be the subject of patent applications filed principally in Brazil – but this is not strongly reflected in the number of applications.

Table 11.4: Brazilian Companies' Biotechnology (C12N) Patent Filing Publications

	1995	1996	1997	1998	1999	2000	2001	2002	2003	2004	2005	2006	2007	2008
BR	10	1	9	15	13	65	27	37	21	23	37	36	27	40
CN	0	0	0	0	1	0	1	1	0	2	2	0	2	0
MX	0	0	0	0	0	0	0	0	1	0	0	0	0	0
OAPI	0	0	0	0	0	0	0	1	0	1	0	2	0	0
ZA	1	0	0	0	1	0	0	0	2	0	1	0	0	0
US	0	0	0	1	0	0	3	4	7	5	3	2	2	3
EP	2	0	1	1	5	1	0	2	3	3	5	2	0	5
JP	1	1	0	1	0	0	1	0	1	1	3	2	1	4
WO	3	0	0	5	1	0	3	9	3	7	4	1	8	7

There has been an increase in the number of A61K applications filed in the US by Indian companies since 1998. The rapid increase also in the number of WO applications is due to the fact that India took part in PCT that year. Since then, according to the Dialog DWPI database, there have been more applications made by companies with Indian nationality than are shown in the tables below. Patents filed by Indian companies in foreign countries were for inventions concerning the processes for manufacturing admixtures (formulations, combinations) or derivatives forms (eg polymorphs, isomers thereof) of medicines.

Table 11.5: Indian Companies' Pharmaceutical (A61K) Patent Filing Publications

	1995	1996	1997	1998	1999	2000	2001	2002	2003	2004	2005	2006	2007	2008
ARIPO	0	0	0	0	0	0	0	0	0	0	1	2	1	1
BR	0	0	0	0	0	5	8	14	19	30	39	21	18	21
CN	0	1	0	0	3	4	9	8	16	25	47	48	36	51
IN	56	61	148	78	144	149	127	132	239	121	0	0	0	0
MX	0	0	0	0	0	0	0	4	13	35	30	14	28	17
ZA	1	2	3	0	4	2	3	8	17	30	18	26	21	25
US	0	0	4	10	17	24	44	62	68	104	101	129	181	171
EP	1	1	2	0	3	11	13	33	44	49	89	93	99	165
JP	0	1	2	8	8	1	1	16	16	35	37	35	25	62
WO	0	0	0	1	6	32	43	68	112	180	198	254	297	290

Indian patent filings for biotechnology inventions are steadily increasing, although the absolute number is not high. In comparison to the recent past when plant-based research was predominant, there seems to be more research on relatively advanced biotechnology, such as methods of preparation of human embryonic stem cells or the use thereof, for example. However, for these inventions, the priority right is not claimed in India but in the US or WO. Increased vaccine research is also reflected in these data.

The State Intellectual Property Office of the People's Republic of China (SIPO) granted many patents to domestic applicants. The number of pharmaceutically related patent filings, particularly of patent classification A61K[8] which includes pharmaceutical ingredients, is voluminous, of which 30 per cent are traditional Chinese medicines (TCM).[9] Ninety per cent of patent filings for TCM are made by domestic companies and, between 1985 and 2000, these amounted to approximately 20,000 filings. Most of them are combinations and not really backed by scientific research. Approximately 50 per cent of Western medicine filings are made by foreign companies.

Table 11.6: Domestic and Foreign Applications for A61K Patents

	Total Filings	Domestic	Foreign
2002	4987	3480	1507
2003	5681	4237	1444
2004	6816	5061	1755

Source: SIPO. In 2002, of 4987 filings, 1520 applications were related to traditional medicines, 1447 to organic chemical and medicinal preparations, new usages of medicines and cosmetics, 606 to biological preparations and 1414 in other sub-classes under A61K.[10] The SIPO statistics use A61K based on the International Patent Classification (IPC),[11] although national classifications can differ slightly from each other.

[8] A61K relates to formulations intended for medicine, dentistry and cosmetics, pharmaceutical preparations including organic active ingredients, as well as carbohydrates and their derivatives. Normally, if the invention is to some extent connected with pharmaceuticals, the A61K classification is granted as the main or secondary classification. Applications for new compounds that function as pharmaceutical products receive an A61K sub-class. A61K38 is a medicinal preparation with undetermined constitution from algae, etc. and is most likely a traditional medicine.

[9] In China, there are approximately 4000 non-Chinese medicines manufacturers, and 1000 TCM manufacturers, employing 400,000 TCM specialists and 500,000 workers. The central state regulation of TCM started in 1985. The Traditional Chinese Medicine Varieties Protection Ordinance (No 106) entered into force on 1 January 1993. For this, the purpose and content of TCM protection (as opposed to patent protection of TCMs) were more or less clarified. Protection is provided for substances extracted from natural products, formulations and artificially created products whose patent protection expired or that have not been suited for patent protection, lacking novelty and inventive step.

[10] Normally, if the invention is to some extent connected with pharmaceuticals, the A61K classification is granted as the main or secondary classification. Applications for new compounds that function as pharmaceutical products receive an A61K sub-class (such as A61K38, which is a medicinal preparation with undetermined constitution, from algae, etc, ie traditional medicines), and the chemical structure of the compound is used for the main classification. A61K subclasses such as A61K48/00 and A61P35/00 include biotech medicines, inventions or gene therapy.

[11] The IPC is an international patent classification scheme that indicates the technical details of an invention. The IPC is a hierarchical system of language-independent symbols for the classification of patents and utility models, according to the different areas of technology to which they pertain. It was established by the Strasbourg Agreement in 1971, www.wipo.int/classifications/ipc/en/. Each country has a slightly different scope for A61K, and thus the SIPO classification is used here.

The Chinese government is focusing increasingly on the scientific potential in China through life science education and research activities. Centralised, long-term projects have been re-instituted to make biotechnology China's strongest technology in the twenty-first century[12]. Thus, the Chinese C12N filings in the US have increased considerably, as Table 11.7 shows. The outstanding numbers, however, could be caused by a few individuals, and may not indicate a long-term trend.

Table 11.7:   Chinese Companies' Biotech (C12N) Patent Application Filing Publications

	1995	1996	1997	1998	1999	2000	2001	2002	2003	2004	2005	2006	2007	2008
ARIPO	0	0	0	0	0	0	0	0	0	0	0	0	0	0
BR	1	0	1	0	4	0	1	1	0	6	1	1	1	3
CN	111	123	177	236	239	436	2010	2845	1135	1207	1778	1960	2242	2,825
MX	0	0	0	1	0	0	0	1	0	3	1	0	1	2
OAPI	0	0	0	0	0	0	0	0	0	1	0	0	0	0
ZA	3	0	0	0	0	0	0	0	0	2	0	0	0	1
US	3	2	3	6	3	3	6	16	25	50	27	36	18	31
EP	8	2	2	11	5	2	9	9	16	24	16	15	15	24
JP	5	5	2	3	2	2	1	14	8	20	15	15	16	17
WO	4	6	9	3	7	18	899	268	34	65	48	48	48	64

Although Cuba is not an 'emerging' or market economy, the country's biotech medicines development policy and its use of the global patent systems for technology trade (licensing) may be of interest to other developing countries.

Cuban companies are filing applications in advanced industrialised and developing countries for patents for bio-pharmaceutical substances. On the espace@net data base, as of 20 June 2010, there are in Cuba 115 publications of patents filings which refer to C12N and 294 to A61K from residents of different countries. The number of applications in the US from Cuban residents is increasing (43 for C12N and 115 for A61K).[13] As Table 11.8 shows, Cuban residents rarely file patents in Cuba (in total, 122 A61K and 82 C12N filing publications on the espace@net data base), but use patent protection systems overseas. Few foreign companies file for patents in Cuba, although there are filings of more than three US-based entities (universities/companies) according to the Espace@net database.

---

[12]   Y Li, *Imitation to Innovation in China: The Role of Patents in Biotechnology and Pharmaceutical Industries* (Cheltenham, Edward Elgar, 2010) 30-42.
[13]   The *Centro de Immunologia Molecular* in Cuba has filed 'recombinant antibodies and fragments recognizing ganglioside N-clycolyl-GM3 and use thereof in the diagnosis and treatment of tumours' for patents not only at the EPO and in Japan, but also in developing countries such as Botswana, Belize, Ghana and Gambia.

Table 11.8: Cuban Companies' Biotech (C12N) Patent Application Filing Publications

	1995	1996	1997	1998	1999	2000	2001	2002	2003	2004	2005	2006	2007	2008
BR	2	0	2	1	2	5	2	1	1	7	5	1	3	4
CN	1	3	1	3	2	3	2	1	0	5	6	4	4	1
MX	0	0	1	3	0	0	0	2	1	3	6	2	2	0
ZA	0	1	0	1	1	0	0	0	2	4	5	3	3	2
US	0	0	2	3	1	1	1	5	3	5	4	7	6	2
EP	5	2	1	4	2	4	2	1	4	3	7	5	4	2
JP	1	4	0	1	3	1	5	2	1	5	1	12	1	4
WO	1	0	3	5	3	0	1	5	4	7	3	3	2	0
CU	26	8	0	0	0	0	0	0	0	0	2	1	13	5

It was Cuba's determination and quest for self-sufficiency in food and medicinal supplies in the US embargo situation that led to a policy of selectively promoting biological scientists and engineers.[14] Medicuba, an organisation that handles pharmaceutical production, as well as imports and exports of medical equipment and products, was established in 1972 and began the production of bio-similar products approved elsewhere.[15] After local outbreaks of meningitis, dengue fever and conjunctivitis in the 1980s, the Cuban Government set up various scientific institutes specialised in biotechnology.[16] The CIGB was established in 1986[17] and, by 1991, 53 such scientific, manufacturing and commercial entities were organised under the Health and Agriculture Ministries. Heber Biotec SA is one of the 'spin-off' commercial arms, and owns the exclusive rights for commercialisation of the technologies developed by the CIGB and seven other biotech institutions.[18] Biomedical research, clinical studies, drug production and commercialisation abroad were integrated into a 'closed cycle' strategy.[19]

Since the launch of recombinant streptokinase in 1993, the focus was placed on the production of innovative biogenerics. In 1993, Cuba produced 1150 vaccines and medicines (vaccines against meningitis B, etc), diagnostic test drugs and 132 generic medicines, and they exported products amounting to US$1 billion.[20] Currently, 40 per cent of Cuba's active pharmaceutical ingredients are imported from China, and the ratio of domestic production is also relatively high.

Most patented products developed in Cuba are biosimilars with some incremental innovation: haemophilus influenza type B synthetic vaccine, recombinant

[14] R de Silva Rodriguez, *Biotechnology in Cuba* (Tokyo, Centre for Genetic Engineering and Biotechnology (Centro de Ingeniería Genética y Biotecnología, CIGB), 2009) (see ch 3).

[15] In 1987 Cuba began to export US$70 million worth of pharmaceuticals. RS Tancer, 'The Pharmaceutical Industry in Cuba' (1995) 17(4) *Clinical Therapeutics* 1–8.

[16] E Lopez et al. 'Taking stock of Cuban biotech' (2007) 25(11) *Nature Biotechnology* 1215.

[17] ibid.

[18] EL Mola et al, 'Biotechnology in Cuba: 20 years of scientific, social and economic progress' (2006) 13(1) *Journal of Commercial Biotechnology*.

[19] De Silva Rodriguez, *Biotechnology in Cuba* (n 13) 20.

[20] N Homedes et al, 'The World Bank's role in shaping pharmaceutical policies in Latin America', presented at the Fifth World Congress: 'Investing in Health', International Health Economics Association, Barcelona (10–13 July 2005); P Grogg, 'Health – Cuba: Nearly 80 Percent of Medicines Produced Locally', Inter Press Service (19 March 2001).

vaccine for hepatitis-B, thrombolytic recombinant streptokinase, granulocyte, colony-stimulating factor and alpha and gamma interferons, all came to be patented and licensed internationally.[21]

In 2004, three cancer vaccines developed by the Cuban Centre of Molecular Immunology (CMI) were licensed through a Canadian company to a US bioventure company, CancerVax. Indian biotech companies have been swift in associating with these projects. For example, Panacea created a joint venture in 2002 with Heber Biotec to develop a vaccine for hepatitis-B and Biocon conducted phase II trials of a monoclonal antibody cancer drug developed by CIMAB, one of Cuba's cancer drug research institutes, marketing the product (BIOMab-EGFR (rhMAb)) in 2008 under a licensing agreement.

Most of these products may not be brand new molecular entities (NME), first in class, or innovator drugs, but considerable technological improvements seem to be added. For example, IFN-gamma enveloped in plasmids (IL-2) seems to have relatively high scientific and technological quality. The patent for the invention entitled 'method for enhancing healing of diabetic foot ulcers by injecting epidermal growth factor[22]'was registered in the US on 16 December 2008 (US 7465,704 also WO 03/053458, etc). It is certainly a limited, new use invention of a known substance, but the idea of directly injecting EGF for the treatment of diabetic foot ulcers seems to have been evaluated highly by the USPTO and other developed country patent offices. An oncology company in Canada, YM BioSciences Inc, commercialises nimotuzumab, a humanised monoclonal antibody that targets the EGFR with an improved side-effect profile compared to other marketed EGFR-targeting products.

Cuban biotechnology research seems to be directed towards developing medicines for treatment of diseases with a high death rate, both in Cuba and elsewhere in developed countries: heart disease, malignant neoplasm, vascular disease, pneumonia and influenza.[23] The country has adopted the International Conference on Harmonisation of Technical Requirements for Registration of Pharmaceuticals for Human Use (ICH)[24] standards. This allows Cuban medicinal products to be used directly for the application for market authorisation in developed countries.

Heber Biotec SA and Cuban research and manufacturing institutions carry out extensive commercial operations in the world. For example, the applicant of

---

[21] eg, a recombinant chimeric protein, Interferon Chimeric Antagonist (ANTHI), was created comprising a fragment of 60 amino acids from the N-terminal region of the human interleukin 2 (IL-2) and fused to the N-terminal of the extracellular region of the alpha chain of the receptor for IFN gamma. WO 2003/95488, EP 1550672, US 2007-160575, JP 2006-506958, CN 1662555, CA 2485439, BR 304827, RU 2322455.

[22] Epidermal growth factor (EGF) is a small mitogenic protein involved in mechanisms such as normal cell growth, oncogenesis, and wound healing.

[23] De Silva Rodriguez, *Biotechnology in Cuba* (n 14).

[24] The ICH gathers together the regulatory authorities and industry experts of Europe, Japan and the US to discuss scientific and technical aspects of product registration. The main objective of the ICH is to make recommendations on ways to achieve greater harmonisation in the interpretation and application of technical guidelines and requirements for product registration, to avoid duplicating the testing carried out during the research and development of new medicines. www.ich.org/cache/compo/276-254-1.html. See ch 8 n 132.

the patent WO 2004.094477, 'recombinant antibodies and fragments recognising ganglioside N-clycolyl-GM3 and use thereof in the diagnosis and treatment of tumours', is the *Centro de Immunologia Molecular* (CIM).[25] This application was made through the PCT not only for the US, Europe and Japan, but also for such countries as Botswana, Belize, Ghana and Gambia. The export markets for Cuban products include developed countries and Latin American countries such as Argentina, Brazil, Colombia and Mexico.[26]

II PHARMACEUTICAL INDUSTRY AND R&D POLICIES

These global patterns of patenting by companies of emerging economies reflect their countries' policies, industrial structure and realities relating to R&D. Efforts for long-term pharmaceutical and biotechnology R&D have begun in some of the rapidly growing countries. The scale of investment and policies for encouraging innovation differ considerably across these countries.

A India's Industrial and Commercial Success

The major Indian pharmaceutical companies have been highly successful in venturing into developed country markets since the late 1990s. This contrasted with the past, when they exported and distributed their products mostly in the Soviet Union, Eastern Europe and developing countries.[27] Around 2001, Indian generic companies applied to have approval for 40 medicines (mostly formulation drugs) through the US FDA Abbreviated New Drug Application (ANDA)[28]

[25] The specification refers to 'se purificaron los productos de la digestion y se ligaron con el ADN del vector fagomindo pHG-1m (Heber Biotec SA Cuba)'.

[26] Cuban companies have registered more than 1800 international patent applications across most regions of the world. De Silva Rodriguez, *Biotechnology in Cuba* (n 14).

[27] S Chaudhuri, 'Ranbaxy Sell-out: Reversal of Fortunes', *Economic & Political Weekly* (19 July 2008) 12.

[28] The Drug Price Competition and Patent Restoration Act of 1984 (Hatch-Waxman Act, Pub L No 98-417) allowed manufacturers to submit an Abbreviated New Drug Application (ANDA), rather than a New Drug Application (NDA), to obtain marketing approval, if the generic contains the same active ingredients previously demonstrated safe and effective to the FDA by the innovator. For this purpose, generic applicants must demonstrate that: (1) the generic drug contains the same active ingredients; (2) the generic drug is identical in strength, dosage, and route of administration; and (3) the generic drug is bioequivalent to the innovator product (21 U 355G)(2)(A). Once an application is submitted, the FDA has 180 days to review the application and send the applicant a letter which says either 'approved', 'approvable' or 'not approvable'. Abbreviated new Drug Applications (ANDA) with Paragraph IV certifications can be submitted to the FDA under sections 21 and 35 USC. Applicants seeking approval certify: (I) that patent information concerning the drug for which investigations described in para (1)(A) were conducted has not been filed with the FDA; or(II) that such patent has expired; or (III) of the date on which such patent will expire; or (IV) that such patent is invalid or will not be infringed by the manufacture, use, or sale of the new drug for which the application is submitted (21 USC §355(j)(2)(A)(vii)). If the applicant made a certification as described in subcl (IV) of para (2)(A)(vii), the approval shall be made effective immediately unless an action is brought for infringement of a patent which is the subject of the certification before the

procedures under the Drug Price Competition and Patent Term Restoration Act (Hatch-Waxman Act 1984). In 2007, companies from India received 132 ANDA approvals, while US companies received 169.[29] The number of Drug Master Files (DMF – information related to drug production) submitted in advance by Indian companies to the FDA with respect to active pharmaceutical ingredients (APIs) also increased. According to Chaudhuri, these companies with DMFs and/or ANDAs in the USA exported drugs worth Rs 206,552.3 million, which constituted about 70 per cent of India's total drugs exports in 2007–08. India is the largest filer of DMFs, with 274 compared to only 90 from China.[30]

By 2007, India ranked third in terms of volume (8 per cent)[31] and 14th in value in the global pharmaceutical market.[32] Recent export growth has reached nearly 30 per cent per year, and exports have become the major source of income for the three major Indian generic companies: Ranbaxy, Cipla, and Dr Reddy's.[33] The main export markets for finished pharmaceutical products from India are Russia, South-East Asia, Africa, Latin America, China and Hong Kong. However, bulk exports of active pharmaceutical ingredients from India, which account for more than 50 per cent of the international trade in bulk drugs, are sent all over the world, including to Europe and the US.[34] Indian drugs cost about one-tenth of the international price, their production costs are one-fifth, and R&D costs are one-eighth of those in developed countries.[35] The Report of the Task Force,

expiration of 45 days after the date on which the notice described in para (2)(B) is received (21 USC § 355(j)(5)(B)(iii)). If such an action is brought, the FDA does not approve the drug application for 30 months, unless the court decides the patent in question to be invalid or not infringed. The first generic company to file an ANDA containing a Paragraph IV certification is granted 180 days of marketing exclusivity against competing generics (21 USC 355(j)(5)(B)(iv)(I) and (II)) from the first date of manufacture or the date of the appeals court judgment on invalidity or non-infringement, whichever is earlier. It is during the 180-day exclusivity period that the first applicant under Paragrph IV makes important opportunistic profits, after which the entry of many generics reduces the prices considerably. The Federal Trade Commission (FTC) recommended in its 2002 study on 'Generic Drug Entry Prior to Patent Expiration' (www.ftc.gov/os/2002/07/genericdrugstudy.pdf) that only one automatic 30-month stay per drug product per ANDA to resolve infringement disputes over patents listed in the Orange Book (see ch 4) prior to the filing date of the generic applicant's ANDA. The amendment was introduced in December 2003 and entered into force on 7 January 2004 (21 USC § 355(j)(5)(F)). According to these provisions, generic applicants lose the 180-day exclusivity if the product is not marketed within 75 days from the date of the ANDA approval; generic companies can ask the court to modify or delete from the Orange Book patents deemed inappropriate.

[29] S Chaudhuri, 'Indian Pharmaceutical Industry after TRIPS', Paper presented at the technical consultation held on 11 December 2009 in New Delhi, as part of the United Nations Development Programme (UNDP) project on '5 years into Product Patent Regime: India's response', to be published by the UNDP, 19.

[30] ibid 19.

[31] Brazil ranked ninth.

[32] Ministry of Finance, India, 2008.

[33] In addition to these three companies, Wockhardt, Sun Pharmaceuticals and Lupin also export significant volumes. Nearly 30% of India's domestic market is occupied by the top 10 companies. Sanofi-Aventis, a foreign company, is managing to break into the top 10 companies in India.

[34] Interview with P Johri, Deputy Secretary, Department of Chemicals and Petrochemicals, Ministry of Chemicals and Fertilisers, 16 August 2005.

[35] India has been able to achieve such low prices because of (i) low production equipment costs, (ii) low wages, and (iii) low pharmaceutical ingredient (bulk) production costs. In 2009, there were 119 Indian company factories approved by the US FDA. D Panda, Joint Secretary, Ministry of Health

Ministry of Commerce & Industry of India, in 2008, summarised India's global trade role as follows and promoted measures to further its export:

India with its significant advantage of low cost of innovation, low capital requirements and lower costs in running facilities, well established manufacturing processes, R&D infrastructure, is strategically well positioned to emerge as "Health Keeper" of the world.[36]

Table 11.1 shows the dramatic increase of Indian products in the US market. This may be explained by the rapid increase of active pharmaceutical ingredients and the most profitable exports of generics, where generic exporters success-fully challenged US patents, obtaining six-month exclusivity granted to the first generic to enter the market under the ANDA Paragraph IV system. The relative decline from 2007 to 2008 of Indian exports to the US may have been a reflection of the relative decline of the success rate of Indian companies in Paragraph IV litigations there. Notably, the value share of Indian pharmaceutical exports in the world total was only 1.5 per cent in 2000, 2.0 per cent in 2007 and 2.2 per cent in 2008.[37] The relatively low value-added transactions show that exporting innovative drugs with new technological components would have brought much more revenue to Indian companies. This, however, does not seem to be among the current policy objective of the Indian government.

Table 11.1: India's Exports and Imports of Pharmaceutical Products (HS-30),38 2000–08

		2000	2007	2008
Exports in million US$		883	3864	5111
	US	5.2%	22.4%	18.7%
	Africa	22.4%	21.7%	23.9%
	EU27	15.4%	15.5%	19.2%
	Latin America	7.4%	7.4%	8.0%
	Middle East	6.9%	4.6%	4.1%
	ASEAN+6	14.0%	8.2%	7.3%
Import total in million US$		145	696	925
Export & Import Total in million US$		739	3,167	4,185

Source: K Shiino, 'Basic Knowledge of India's Economy' (2009) JETRO 99.

& Family Welfare Government of India Drug Regulatory Framework & New Initiatives in India (July 2009).

[36]   Ministry of Commerce & Industry, 'Strategy for Increasing Exports of Pharmaceutical Products' (2008) 9.

[37]   K Shiino,'Basic Knowledge of India's Economy' (in Japanese) (JETRO, 2009) 99.

[38]   HS stands for the Harmonized Commodity Description and Coding System of tariff nomen-clature, based on the classification by the World Customs Organization (WCO). HS-30 includes pharmaceutical products and human or animal substances prepared for therapeutic purposes.

In parallel with the 30 major, export-oriented generic companies, and other 220 medium-size companies, there are more than 6000 registered, small-scale drugs businesses in India. Their productivity has not been high due to protection given by lax standards,[39] but recently, they have been under severe competitive pressure due to improved quality standards.[40] In India, Good Manufacturing Practice (GMP) standards were introduced in 1986[41] and upgraded to the WHO-GMP level in 2001.[42] In 2003, responding to wide-ranging national concerns about spurious/counterfeit/sub-standard drugs, an Indian Government report recommended measures to tighten regulatory control.[43]

B Emerging Economies' R&D Infrastruture

In the late 1990s, several of the major Indian pharmaceutical companies considerably increased their investments in R&D. Member companies of the Indian Pharmaceutical Alliance (IPA) [44]increased by 15 times their R&D expenditure between 1995 and 2006.[45] Moreover, through alliances with multinationals, and by acquiring European and US companies, these Indian companies appeared to be attempting to partially transform themselves into R&D companies. The top 10 companies hold a 30 per cent share of the Indian market and among these, companies such as Dr Reddy's, Ranbaxy, and Piramal began by investing as much as 8 per cent of their sales into R&D.[46] To ensure that R&D does not put stress on

[39] A Fujimori, A Kamiike and T Sato, 'Empirical Analysis of the Productivity of Small-scale Indian Pharmaceutical Companies' March 2009. Research Paper on 'Factors of Sustainable Economic Development' (In Japanese).

[40] 'Lack of clarity in Drugs Act may hit generic companies', The Economic Times (India) (Mumbai, 31 August 2009).

[41] sch M of the Drug, Cosmetics Act 1945.

[42] Since 11 December 2001, those companies which do not fulfil the GMP standards have been unable to obtain licences for import, manufacturing, storage, sales and distribution of medicines, or approval from the State Drug Control Administration.

[43] The amendment that came into force on 10 August 2009 provides for stricter punishment for companies charged with manufacturing 'adulterated' or 'spurious' drugs. Under the new law, evidence of both adulteration and manufacture of spurious drugs needs to be established for a person to be convicted, but the punishment is increased from five to 10 years' imprisonment, and could extend to life. The monetary fine has also been increased to Rs 100,000 from Rs 10,000. Ministry of Health and Family Welfare, Report of the Expert Committee on a Comprehensive Examination of Drug Regulatory Issues, including the Problem of Spurious Drugs, 2003. According to this Report, the extent of sub-standard drugs varied from 8.19 to 10.64%, and of spurious drugs from 0.24 % to 0.47% (p 76).

[44] The IPA was formed in November 1999 with leading generic companies that collectively account for about 30% of the domestic pharmaceutical market and contribute one-third of the total pharmaceutical exports from the country. www.medisourceasia.com/weblinks/indian_asso.htm#IPA.

[45] Interview with DG Shah, Secretary-General of the IPA, 13 April 2010, on file with author.

[46] Ranbaxy's R&D costs in this period were 9.5% of its sales and it had 300 researchers involved in the development of treatments for infectious diseases and urinary system diseases. Dr Reddy's R&D costs were 12.3% of its sales and it had 310 researchers working on developments in fields such as anticancer drugs, cardiovascular drugs, and antibacterial agents. Wockhardt's R&D costs were 8% of its sales and it had 400 researchers working on the development of treatments related to infectious diseases. Torrent's R&D costs were 9% of its sales and it had 525 researchers working on diabetes drugs, anti-obesity drugs, and cardiovascular drugs. Besides these companies, Lupin's R&D costs were 1% of its sales, with 170 researchers, and Piramal's R&D costs 3.7% of its sales, with 400

their generic drug divisions, these companies were taking measures such as establishing finance companies. The development of India's biotechnology companies through venture capital and alliances with multinationals was also prominent.[47]

Apparently, the company size, in terms of either capital or personnel numbers, is not yet sufficient to make independent R&D sustainable, even though the costs required to develop pharmaceuticals in India are extremely low in comparison with Europe and the US. Some major Indian companies are also orienting themselves towards the development of global drugs through mergers, although it will be difficult for them to conduct clinical trials with Indian capital alone. On the domestic market, on the other hand, the lack of pharmaco-vigilance may be caused by insufficient staffing and experience at the state level.[48]

Industrial R&D expenditure generally has increased in India over the 10 years between 1995 and 2006. The R&D expenditure of leading industry groups is the highest in the pharmaceutical sector. During 2002–03, the industrial sector R&D spending was the highest in drugs & pharmaceuticals, accounting for 28.7 per cent, followed by transportation and chemicals (other than fertilisers) at 21.3 per cent and 7.6 per cent respectively. [49] In India, public expenditure on industrial R&D is spent mostly in the defence sector (41.9 per cent), followed by fuels (22.1 per cent) and electronics equipment and electricals (14.2 per cent).[50] This shows that the public industrial sector investment in new frontiers of technology such as biotechnology has not yet been significant. Moreover, during 2000–02, India's public and private spending on R&D per capita was US$3.53, much less than that in China ($12.15), Brazil ($22.55) and far less than that in the US (US$962.15), Japan ($976.58) and Sweden ($1104.20). These statistics are not really comparable unless they are adjusted by purchasing power parity (PPP). However, these figures give a rough idea about the priority given to public R&D policy by each government. The developing countries whose per capita GDP was between US$1000 and US$10,000 spent more than US$20 per capita R&D, with the exception of Argentina ($11.03), Egypt ($2.20), Thailand ($5.01) and Venezuela ($14.48). Public R&D spending in Pakistan was $1.13 and that of Sri Lanka, $1.46. Although emerging economies with large populations may face difficulties in increasing public R&D expenditure, it is striking that the per capita public industrial R&D expenditure of some

researchers. These companies were also strengthening their license-in and license-out agreements with developed countries, developing Drug Delivery Systems (DDS), and attempting to strengthen joint research activities. S Miyazawa, 'Asia-Pacific Committee Report' (JPMA, November 2006) 3.

[47] BioSpectrum India (Bangalore), *BioSpectrum Survey 2006*, http://biospectrumindia.ciol.com/; S Mani, 'A Review of Issues with Respect to India's National System of Innovation' (2006) http://globelics.org/index.php?module=htmlpages&func=display&pid=12.

[48] WHO official, 'Indian rate of reporting in pharmacovigilance reporting alarming', Pharmabiz.com (Bangalore, 17 April 2007). This article says that Sweden, which has a population of 9 million, has between 250 and 300 drug regulatory officials overseeing operations, while the absolute number of controllers is one tenth of that of Sweden in India.

[49] Government of India, Research and Development Statistics 2004–05, www.nstmis-dst.org/ContentsPage.htm, 29–30. The original data come from the UNESCO Institute for Statistics (UIS), *UNESCO, World Development Indicators 2004/2005* (World Bank, 2005).

[50] ibid.

middle-income countries was close to that of LDCs (Nepal $1.50) and that there was a huge gap of R&D expenditure between developed countries and middle-income developing countries.[51] This is significant because middle-income developing countries, with their relatively high technological capacities, could have contributed more to global innovative efforts.

During 2002–03, there were 115,936 researchers in India, whereas the figure for China was 805,171 (other figures were 1,239,910 for the US and 645,795 for Japan).[52] The number of researchers per 1 million habitants in India was 110, whereas this figure was 7431 for Finland, 5171 for Sweden and 5085 for Japan.[53]

The scale of R&D in emerging economies was generally increasing. The percentage share of developing countries in the total R&D expenditure showed an increasing upward trend during 2000–02. Among the developing countries, Brazil and China spent 1.04 per cent and 1.23 per cent of GDP on their R&D, respectively, while India spent 0.80 per cent of its GDP on R&D. India's R&D share of its GDP has remained stable at the rate of 0.7–0.9 per cent since the early 1990s. For developed countries, on average, the figure is 2.3 per cent (Japan 3.11 per cent, US 2.67 per cent).[54]

The above statistics suggest that national (public) infrastructure and long-term perspectives for innovative R&D in frontier technologies may be slower to develop in India than in China, for example, where the national educational infrastructure is solidly expanding. General statistics also suggest that pharmaceuticals and biotechnology in India could at best follow its most successful pioneer field, which is information technology (IT). India is the largest exporter of computer information services in the world (22.5 per cent),[55] but its overall IT industrial competitiveness has been reported as not being as proportionately high. For example, the Economist Intelligence Unit has undertaken studies based on their benchmarks, detailing the conditions of: (1) the overall business environment, (2) infrastructure, (3) human capital, (4) the legal environment, (5) the R&D environment, and (6) support for industry development.[56] According to these reports, India ranked 48th in the world in 2008 and 44th in 2009, whereas China moved from 50th to 39th. India is strong in improving the cost of applied manufacturing programmes, notably customised software. However, the basic inventions tend to move from the US to India.

In the years around 2000, there was a high expectation both in India and around the world that Indian pharmaceutical companies would rapidly turn into research-based enterpreises (see chapter 10 p 364). By 2001, Dr Reddy's had

---

[51] Government of India, Research and Development Statistics 2004–05 (n49) 49–50. 49–52.

[52] Government of India, Research and Development Statistics 2004–05 (n49) 49–50. The original data come from the UNESCO Institute for Statistics (UIS), *UNESCO, World Development Indicators 2004/2005* (World Bank, 2005) 49–52.

[53] Government of India, Research and Development Statistics 2004–05 (n 49) 52.

[54] ibid 50–51.

[55] Shiino (n 37) 79.

[56] Resilience amid turmoil: Benchmarking IT industry competitiveness 2009', http://global.bsa.org/2009eiu/study/2009_eiu_global.pdf.

nine molecules in the pipeline, one of which was licensed out to Novo Nordisk. Ranbaxy had eight, one of which was licensed to Schwarz Pharma (Germany). There was a considerable number of molecules at the preclinical stage, and all of them concerned 'incremental innovation', notably new modes of administration, new uses of known compounds or derivatives thereof.[57] Some 30 molecules were clinically promising and many of them were licensed to Western multinationals. However, R&D situations in 2004 looked less brilliant. Few drug candidates were at clinical trials. The Novo Nordisk and Schwarz licences failed in clinical trials. Torrent had licensed one molecule to Novartis but the contract was terminated in 2005.[58] It is reported that Piramal Healthcare has four (two anti-cancer and two diabetes), Cadila Healthcare, five, and Lupin, four (two anti-psoriasis, one TB, one migraine). Dr Reddy's has two (one diabetes and one anti-cancer) and is working on a host of programmes. Glenmark has five molecules (diabetes, osteoarthritis, asthma, neuropathic pain, rhueumatoid arthritis).[59] One of these molecules, oglemilast, for asthma, which was licensed to Forest Labs (US) at Phase II (asthma), failed in clinical trials in 2010.[60]

In January 2010, *Businessworld* published a table entitled 'Where Have the Molecules Gone?'[61] As reasons for their disappearance, the magazine cites lack of focus and strategy in research; lack of talent (few scientists have experience in new drug development); and the fact that US drug regulator FDA is clearing fewer drugs than before. According to this magazine, 'not all of those in the running to discover a new drug have lost hope yet. But the wild optimism has died out.'[62]

DG Shah asserts that 'India needs more time for creating medicines of Indian origin'.[63] Certainly; it took 20 years for Japanese companies to become research-based. The total number of molecules in the pipeline in India seems to be less than that of a single R&D-based company in developed countries, and there are no miracles in the scientific world. Chaudhuri explains the main type of research that is being undertaken in India today:

> Even at the pre-clinical stage, Indian companies are not engaged with all the R&D involved. Indian companies are not involved in basic research of target identification for new drugs. They rely on the basic research of others and adopt an approach called

[57] Interview with DG Shah (n 45).

[58] According to Chaudhuri, 'Torrent, for example entered into an agreement with Novartis in 2002 for the development of AGE breaker compound for the treatment of heart disease and diabetes. In 2004 the compound was out-licensed to Novartis. The agreement was terminated in 2005 when Novartis decided not to proceed further with the compound. Torrent is now trying to develop it on its own and explore other options. Torrent received only $0.5 million initially and then $3 million from Novartis. This was too small an amount for a large MNC such as Novartis to have any stake in the project. Dr Reddys has suffered several similar setbacks'. S Chaudhuri, 'Indian Pharmaceutical Industry after TRIPS' (n 29) 32.

[59] Research undertaken by S Chaudhrui, on file with author.

[60] 'Glenmark stops oglemilast (GRC3886) development programme for COPD & asthma with Forest', 20 May 2010. www.dancewithshadows.com/pillscribe/glenmark-stops-oglemilast-grc3886-development-programme-for-copd-asthma-with-forest/.

[61] 'Death of a Dream' (30 January 2010) *Businessworld*.

[62] ibid.

[63] Interview with DG Shah (n 45).

'analogue research'. This entails working on certain pre-identified targets for specific diseases to develop molecules that alter the target's mechanism in the diseased person.[64]

An explanation given by many former Indian officials and pharmaceutical industry people, is that India is committed to innovation that is 'genuine',[65] not 'incremental', which is the purpose of instituting section 3(d) of the Indian Patents (Amendment) Act 2005. In order to support drug R&D, the Department of Pharmaceuticals in the Ministry of Chemicals and Petrochemicals is planning to set up a fund of US$430.5 million to help R&D, 'with the vision to make India one of the top five global pharmaceutical innovation hubs by 2020'.[66]

The Indian pharmaceutical industry business model may be returning to efficient manufacturing of known products, both small molecules, biogenerics, and contract clinical trials and manufacturing. Chaudhuri therefore considers India's mission as being a highly competitive, cost-efficient generics provider for the world and particularly for developing countries.[67] Chaudhuri has advocated that India re-negotiate at the WTO the obligation to protect products:

> [B]ut the pull factor of immense export opportunities was systematically highlighted particularly by those who wanted to show that TRIPS was not bad for India. . . . Thus, events in India since TRIPS confirm the old fears that until late in the development phase, product patent protection may not be good for a country. Developing countries are unlikely to derive much economic benefit from TRIPS. The TRIPS agreement should be renegotiated. In the shorter run, the flexibilities available under TRIPS should be taken full advantage of.[68]

Others, like McKinsey, predict great success for India, provided that it improves IPR protection and fills the gaps that exist in healthcare spending and infrastructure facilities, low insurance penetration and lack of certain specialised disciplines and capabilities.[69] The major Indian generic industry has been economically and politically successful, both domestically and internationally. The outsourcing sectors such as contract manufacturing and large-scale contract research organisations (CRO) for clinical studies are also achieving marked success.[70] However, for their R&D efforts to be more successful, more contribution

[64] Chaudhuri, 'Indian Pharmaceutical Industry after TRIPS' (n 29) 30.

[65] 'India wants genuine inventions and genuine R&D', according to NN Prasad, former Joint Secretary at the DIPP (Department of Industrial Policy and Promotion, Indian Ministry of Commerce), then Chef de Cabinet to the Director General of WIPO. 'Innovation Policy Needs National Focus, Use of TRIPS Obligations, Panellists Say', *IP Watch* (20 July 2009); TC James, *Patent Protection and Innovation: Section 3(d) of the Patents Act and Indian Pharmaceutical Industry* (Mumbai, Indian Pharmaceutical Alliance, c/o Vision Consulting Group, 2009) ('TC James Report') 28 (see also ch 12).

[66] IBEF, Pharmaceuticals, April 2010.

[67] Chaudhuri, 'Ranbaxy Sell-out: Reversal of Fortunes' (n 27) 13.

[68] ibid 13.

[69] 'Indian pharmaceuticals market will grow 10–14%; to touch $40 billion by 2015: McKinsey' 30 November 2009. See also 'China and India tell a tale of two CMO markets', SCRIP (30 April 2010).

[70] According to the SCRIP article 'China and India tell a tale of two CMO markets' 'IP still remains one of the key inhibitors for these two countries in achieving their full contract manufacturing potential', *SCRIP* (30 April 2010) 27.

from a wider spectrum of researchers, scientists and ventures will be needed. Encouraging domestic inventions requires a coherent, long-term policy to create a self-sustaining R&D infrastrucuture. As Penrose once remarked:

> one of the effects of patents is supposed to be to assist the small man with few resources to protect his position against the large well-financed firm . . . and one can argue that a domestic patent system may protect a local inventor from having his ideas taken over without his permission and without adequate compensation by multinational enterprises operating in the country; it may also make possible foreign licensing by the occasional domestic inventor, for as countries develop, their own inventors may after all be expected to become increasingly important.[71]

Smoothly functioning market incentive systems and regulatory institutions would boost domestic inventors' research efforts, all the more necessary for original research to be undertaken and its results to be tested, evaluated and commercialised. For this purpose, practices that give legitimacy to public institutions such as IPR protection, clinical studies and regulatory approval systems will be helpful.

C China's Pharma/Biotech Industries and R&D

i State policy to boost biotechnology

In China, the Government seems to have been increasingly committed to plans for national technological advance, although the results of drug discovery and development research are not yet clearly identifiable. R&D of biotech medicines has been encouraged by successive National Development Plans and is emphasised in the country's 11th five-year plan. The number of registrations of what are called 'biology medicines' (medicines using biological materials) now exceeds 3000. This extraordinary number seems to be due partly to terminological and taxonomic reasons: the Chinese concept of biology medicines includes not only vaccines and recombinant substances, but also a wide range of medicines based on biological materials. Medicines using recombinant technologies registered in China include Actylyse (made by Boeringer Ingelheim), recombinant tissue plasminogen activator Gendicine (Shenzhen SiBionoGeneTech), recombinant Human Ad-p53 Injection Erythropoietin (Kirin/Kyowa Hakko), and Recombinant Human Erythropoietin Injection, which are grouped together with numerous other pharmaceutical substances using biological materials. Some 2684 patent applications corresponding to the patent classification C12Q1/68 (see above p 389) were filed from 1985 to 2008.[72]

---

[71] E Penrose, 'International Patenting and the Less-Developed Countries' (1973) 83 *The Economic Journal* 770. See ch 2.

[72] In one year, there were numerous biotech medicine patents but this seems to have been due to the fact that one applicant applied for international patents simply to obtain government subsidies or tax reductions.

The aspiration of the Chinese Government to create a high-technology based country with their concomitantly positive attitude towards IP is reinforced in the 11th Five-Year Plan of National Economy and Social Development (2006–10). This plan emphasises the importance of national interest, protection of domestic industry and resources and R&D investment by domestic industry. The plan re-centralised the projects which had once been decentralised and allocated resources for long-term purposes, as the earlier methods tended to result in short-termism. The main focus of the government is biotechnology, for which the 11th Five-Year Plan (2011–15) is specifically established.

SIPO, China's State Intellectual Property Office, promotes patenting activities of Chinese citizens:

> One of the principal targets in the 11th Five-Year Plan is to see the emergence of a group of enterprises with their own IP, brands and international competence advantages . . . IPR protection is of great significance in encouraging independent innovation and optimizing a favourable environment for innovation and invention, and is also beneficial to reducing international IP conflicts.[73]

Chinese domestic companies' patent filings were further accelerated by the 10th Five-Year Plan for National Patent Work, of 2006–11, which emphasises the policy of reinforcing Chinese industrial competitiveness by technological improvement.[74] In December 2009, the total number of patent filings in China was the highest in the world.

Today in China, there are several pharmaceutical companies which have commenced R&D of pharmaceutical products. On average, they invest about 2 per cent of their sales revenue in R&D.[75] The Government has been encouraging biotechnology and generic biomedicine, and between 1996 and 2000 it provided US$205 million to support these fields, and $731 million between 2000 and 2005.[76] It has continued to strengthen its assistance policies since then. In Shanghai, research activities of public institutions such as Materia Medica[77] and the Chinese Academy of Science are increasingly supported by multinational companies such as GSK, Novartis and Bayer. Other multinationals such as Novo Nordisk, Astrazeneca and Eli Lilly also invest in R&D activities in China.

China is becoming competitive in the field of chemistry, particularly for chemical materials or bulk medicines such as antibiotics, vitamins, and sulphanilamide.[78] Although as of 2005 no Chinese company had filed an ANDA (see footnote 28) with the US FDA, there were 55 factories in China which had

---

[73] www.china.org.cn/english/China/208356.htm.

[74] www.sipo.gov.cn/sipo_English/laws/developing/200904/t20090414_450778.html.

[75] C Grace, *The Effect of Changing Intellectual Property on Pharmaceutical Industry Prospects in India and China: Considerations for Access to Medicines* (DFID Health Systems Resource Centre, 2004) 44.

[76] ibid. Other figures are indicated by Y Li (n 12) 49.

[77] www.simm.ac.cn/English/English.htm; www.simm.ac.cn/index.html.

[78] Grace, *The Effect of Changing Intellectual Property on Pharmaceutical Industry Prospects in India and China* (n 75) 13.

been approved by the FDA to produce active pharmaceutical ingredients and there were dozens of factories which were filing DMF applications.[79] Domestic pharmaceutical companies are mainly government-owned, and they suffer from chronic overproduction and losses.[80] These companies are currently focused on supplying the China's domestic market and now occupy approximately 70 per cent of it at present.

Many of the Chinese companies manufacturing biological/biotech medicines started as contract research organisations (CROs). Some, such as Wuxi Pharma Tech, China's biggest CRO, also make ingredients for drugs used in clinical trials.[81]

ii Regulatory institutions

The State Food and Drug Administration of the People's Republic of China (SFDA) examines the safety and quality of drugs, and grants marketing authorisation. In 1984, around the same time as the enactment of the Patent Law, the Drug Registration Regulation (DRR)[82] was adopted. Under this Regulation, there are six registration categories of medicines, under which several subcategories are listed:

1. New chemical entities never marketed in any country ('new drugs').
2. Drug preparations with different methods of administration and not marketed in any country.
3. Drugs marketed outside China.
4. Drug substances and their preparations with changed acid or alkaline radicals (or metallic elements), but without any pharmacological changes (and with the original drug entity already approved in China).
5. Drug preparations with changed dosage forms, but no change of administration route, and the original preparation already approved in China.
6. Drug substances or preparations following national standards (products may be authorised under a generic-type application that allows the company to avoid submitting clinical trial information).

---

[79] Grace, *The Effect of Changing Intellectual Property on Pharmaceutical Industry Prospects in India and China* (n 75) 50.

[80] www.buyusa.gov/china/en/pharmaceuticals.html.

[81] It started trading on the New York Stock Exchange. In fact, Wuxi acquired a US bioventure, AppTec Laboratory Services, for US$151 million, in order to complement Wuxi's chemical activities with AppTec's biologics testing, R&D and manufacturing. Wuxi assumed US$11.7 million of AppTec's debt. Then, in May 2010, Charles River Laboratories International Inc. agreed to buy Wuxi to expand in China, where revenue from drug-testing services is growing by as much as 30% a year. 'FTC approves Chinese pharma takeover', 25 January 2008'; 'Charles River to Buy WuXi PharmaTech for $1.6 Billion (Update4)', Bloomberg, 26 April 2010.

[82] The first revision of the DRR was issued in 2005 and the latest revision was adopted in May 2007 and entered into effect on 1 October 2007.

A safety surveillance system was instituted for the first five of the six registration categories (Article 66 of the Regulation).[83] New drugs are under 'surveillance' based on the Drug Registration Regulation.[84] During this surveillance period, the SFDA does not accept registration applications for identical product types by other applicants.[85] When the surveillance period for a new medicine is finished, the third party applicant can ask for marketing authorisation of the medicine as a copy medicine under registration category 6. This functions like the post-marketing surveillance period in Japan under the Pharmaceutical Law, which de facto protects market exclusivity of the new drug. The administrative protection of pharmaceuticals and protection of 'new medicines' is under the jurisdiction of the SFDA.

On 15 September 2002, the Implementing Order (no 360) of the Drug Registration Regulation (DRR) entered into force. Article 35 of the DRR delineates the principle of protection of clinical data submitted to pharmaceutical regulatory authorities for marketing approval for new chemical ingredients.[86] Based on Article 35 of the Drug Registration Regulation, Article 20 of the Implementing Order introduced provisions based on China's understanding of Article 39.3 of the TRIPS Agreement relating to the protection of data submitted to regulatory authorities for marketing authorisation. According to Article 20 of the Implementing Order, China protects self-generated and undisclosed test and other clinical data submitted for the approval of medicines containing new chemical entities and does not approve the use of such data for drug registration by other applicants for six years, unless the originator so agrees.[87]

---

[83] Art 66 of the DRR is related to the surveillance period of new drugs and states that 'the SFDA, as required for the protection of public health, shall establish a surveillance term for new drugs having received production approval. The surveillance term shall be calculated from the date approval was received for production of the relevant new drug and will last for a maximum of five years. The SFDA shall not approve changes to the production or formulation and importation of the drug by another company during the surveillance term of such new drug.'

[84] Last amended on 10 July 2007 by the SFDA Ordinance No 28 and entered into force on 1 October 2007.

[85] The regulation provides that registration applications which have already been received for identical products types by other applicants which have not yet been approved for clinical testing will also be rejected.

[86] Art 35 of the DRR stipulates that: 'The government shall protect against unfair commercial use by any other person the undisclosed clinical data and other data that are generated as well as submitted by a manufacturer or a marketer in obtaining new chemical ingredients. Within 6 years from the date of obtaining the approval of manufacturing or marketing a drug containing new chemical ingredients, any other application for manufacturing or marketing a drug containing new chemical ingredients by using the above mentioned data without the express consent of the original applicant shall not be approved by the drug administration authorities, unless "the submitted data were generated by the subsequent applicant himself". The drug administration authorities shall not disclose the data mentioned above, except the following situations: (1) the need of public interest; and (2) measures have been taken to ensure such data is protected against unfair commercial use.'

[87] Art 20 stipulates *in fine*, however, it states that the medicine can be approved if the applicant asserts that he/she himself/herself generated the data. Applications should be submitted by different administrative routes, depending on the categories of medicines, after which the SFDA can decide what types of data (complete versus summary/published data, scientific literature, etc) are necessary. Documentation on the development of new drugs and on GMP certification of the production site is now required for marketing approval.

Therefore, China protects new medicines (although the scope of protection differs) through two sets of laws: one is the DRR, which provides drug 'surveillance' for five years; and, the other is Article 20 of the Implementing Order which provides six-year data protection to new chemical entities.

The Regulation which is currently in force since 1 October 2007 narrowed the scope of new medicines which can be approved. Prior to the revision, 'new medicines' included drugs which had been partially modified, including new formulations of ones which had been approved. Under the current law, however, drugs which are already approved for production and which have had their formulation or administration route changed, or a new indication, are no longer considered new drugs.

Articles 11 and 12 of the DRR establish the conditions for patent linkage. 'Patent linkage' is a practice of linking regulatory approval for a generic medicine to the patent status of the originator product.[88] According to this Regulation, an applicant for market authorisation must submit a statement declaring that a patent has not been infringed and the SFDA is paid to publicise the applicant's statement and explanation.

D Brazil's Pharmaceutical Industry and R&D

The fact that, in Brazil, biotechnological research is livelier than research in the small-molecule pharmaceuticals manufacturing industry[89] may be attributed to the interest taken by Brazilian scientific research institutes, as well as the comparatively low R&D costs of biotech. It has been pointed out, however, that the results of university research may not have been sufficiently commercialised.[90] More recently, it has been argued that the quality of state intervention for industrial innovation is compromised by political factors and does not necessarily lead to concerted efforts by private and public actors.[91] In addition, state regulations concerning 'natural products' and 'living things' seem to be highly complex. Article 10(IX) of the current Industrial Property Law, for example, specifies that 'natural living beings, in whole or in part, and biological material, including the genome or germ plasm of any natural living being, when found in nature or isolated therefrom, and natural biological processes', are not patentable, on the

---

[88] See also ch 12.

[89] In 1995, Redwood stated: 'There is a widely held view is that "it is now too late for Brazil"to build up competitive expertise in research involving chemical synthesis of novel pharmaceutical compounds. That may or may not be true: generally speaking, it is never too late to conduct research if it is sufficiently original and creative. In any event, it is certainly not too late to concentrate on chemical process development if the right climate of encouragement can be promoted.' H Redwood, *Brazil: The future impact of pharmaceutical patents* (Felixstowe, Oldwicks Press, 1995) 55.

[90] H Thorsteinsdóttir *et al*, 'Different Rhythms of Health Biotechnology Development in Brazil and Cuba' (2005) 2(3) *Journal of Business Chemistry* www.businesschemistry.org at 104; Redwood, *Brazil: The future impact of pharmaceutical patents* (n 89) 51–57.

[91] B Salama et al, 'Pharmaceutical Patent Bargains: the Brazilian Experience', http://works. bepress.com/bruno_meyerhof_salama/45/ 23–32.

grounds that these cannot be considered to be inventions. This may cause difficulties in licensing the results of biotechnological research.

Brazil, having again attempted domestic production of APIs in the late 1990s, seems to have reoriented its policy to focus now on the generic formulation industry. ANVISA, a regulatory agency for quality, marketing authorisation of medicines and drug prices was established in 1999.[92] In the same year, regulation of marketing authorisation for generics was introduced and approximately 80 generics whose bioequivalences were established were marketed for the first time in 2000. Since then, generics approved by ANVISA have rapidly increased and in 2007, the total number of 3074 is 344 times greater than it was in 2002[93]. The Government has encouraged the production and sale of generic drugs and created 15 state-run generic drug companies, although drug prices have decreased little.[94] However, the nascent generics industry 'helped the government in revamping its network of public laboratories, which produce medicines and vaccines for the public health system', which produces today approximately 3 per cent of the national production in monetary value and 10 per cent in unit numbers.[95]

In Brazil, the market share of generic drugs in 2003 was 5.5 per cent in value terms, but this had increased to 11.6 per cent by 2007. Sales of generics during the first half of 2007 came to US$329 million. With some estimating that Brazil's generic market will grow to 22.8 per cent of its total pharmaceutical market by 2011,[96] the Brazilian Government is calling for the creation of an environment which will develop Brazil's global generic drug industry.[97] In addition to new medicines and generics, there is another category of medicines which is prevalent in Latin America called *similares* (chapter 8), which are authorised without bioequivalence. Brazil introduced requirements for the bioequivalence of these in December 2005.[98]

Historically, according to Salama and Benoliel, developing countries have used patent law instrumentally to foster local industries, but there is a trade-off between innovation and dissemination. However, this has become increasingly difficult to balance, due to the absence of success in creating new drugs of Brazilian origin, the subsidies that are not used as effectively as needed, and the difficulties in creating a competitive local generic industry.[99]

---

[92] Law 9.782 of 26 January 1999.

[93] Espicom Business Intelligence, *The World Generic Market Report 2003* (Chichester, Espicom Business Intelligence, 2002) 20–23.

[94] ibid 20–23.

[95] Salama et al, 'Pharmaceutical Patent Bargains: the Brazilian Experience' (n 91) 6. According to its fn 30, 'This network of 18 laboratories is spread in various public administration entities such as the Ministry of Health, the Armed Forces, state governments and universities. Existing production capacity is estimated at 11 billion pharmaceutical units per year.'

[96] SCRIP World Pharmaceutical News, 4 July 2007.

[97] 'Generic Drugs Market in Brazil Report 2007: 2011 Examines the Chief Reasons Why All Major Generic Players Are Heading to Brazil to Manufacture and Sell Their Drugs', *Business Wire* (Dublin/Brazil, 9 December 2007).

[98] ibid.

[99] Salama and Benoliel, 'Pharmaceutical Patent Bargains: The Brazilian Experience' (n 91) 17–31.

II HEALTHCARE AND ACCESS TO MEDICINES IN THE MEDIUM INCOME DEVELOPING COUNTRIES

Thus, medium-income developing countries with little or no patent protection over medicines during the 1970s adopted greatly differing IPR policies in aligning themselves with the TRIPS Agreement. Their public health policies differ even more considerably.

While pharmaceuticals represent only one among many health inputs, new drugs may provide an alternative to non-drug inputs such as invasive operations.[100] Expenditure on pharmaceuticals takes up a substantial percentage of total health spending. In 2000, this ratio was 19.2 per cent in low income countries as a group. This is higher than the corresponding figure for high income countries, 13.8 per cent.[101] However, in the same year, actual per capita expenditure on pharmaceuticals was estimated to be only $4.40 per year in low income countries, while it was $396 per year in high income countries.[102] Thus, there appears to be a considerable disparity between the role of pharmaceuticals in rich countries and in poor countries. While there are many factors involved in determining the level of pharmaceutical expenditure and various interpretations thereof, the low level of drug expenditure in developing countries may be reflecting a more severe lack of access than that in higher income countries. Table 11.2 shows WHO's estimates of pharmaceutical expenditure across different income level countries in 2000.

Table 11.2: Measured world pharmaceutical expenditure, by per income clusters, 1990–2000

Income cluster	Measured expenditure level US$ million at exchange		Share of world total %		Share of expenditure on health %	
	1990	2000	1990	2000	1990	2000
WHO Member States	245,000	440,300	100	100	14.2	15.2
High-income	196,019	345,758	80.2	78.7	13.0	13.8
Middle-income	41,916	82,740	17.1	18.8	22.5	24.8
Low-income	6,568	10,675	2.7	2.4	20.8	19.2

Source: WHO, *The World Medicines Situation* (Geneva, WHO, 2004) 42.

[100] SO Schweitzer, *Pharmaceutical Economics and Policy*, 2nd edn (New York, Oxford University Press, 2007) 3–17, 141–54.
[101] WHO, *The World Medicines Situation* (Geneva, WHO, 2004).
[102] ibid 45.

The majority of essential medicines as defined by the WHO are not affected by patents because many such medicines are off-patent or under ineffective protection (chapter 8). However, some diseases require the use of newer, patented drugs for basic treatment. For example, darunavir and raltegravir, which are considered third-line HIV/AIDS treatment medicines in developing countries (chapter 8) may be difficult to access for many reasons including patents, even though they are not patented in poor countries.[103] The actual situation of each medicine differs from pre-conceived notions, and, therefore requires verification for objective evaluation[104]. High-priced patented drugs are universally accessible for patients only when they are covered by health insurance. Otherwise, they remain luxury goods for the wealthy, even in developed countries.

Lack of access to essential drugs has been particularly severe for AIDS patients infected by HIV. As recently as 2003, only 7 per cent of the people needing treatment for AIDS in low- and middle-income countries were actually receiving treatment.[105]

In 2007, the Chinese Government promised to extend health insurance to all Chinese citizens by 2020[106] and finalised a healthcare reform programme in 2009. The first phase of the reform will seek to expand basic medical insurance cover to 90 per cent of the population by 2011. A lot depends on how local governments interpret and fund the central policy.[107]

In the past, the Chinese Government rarely expressed its opinion overtly and directly concerning intellectual property protection and access to medicines, although it often shared the views of developing countries.[108] Recently, the Chinese Government has become more active in expressing its views on the subject of access to medicines, as it becomes more conscious of domestic

---

[103] It has been argued that the existence of patents in India would prevent access to related medicines in poor countries. For the so-called second- and third-line treatment ARVs, the patent situation in India is as follows. Etravirine product patent 204,028 exists. There is no application for product patent for raltegravir. Applications for inventions relating to atazanavir, darunavi and etravirine have been filed but no patents have been granted. As darunavir and ritonavir inventions date before 1995, there is no product patent application (there is a ritonavir-related patent 209,151). There are more than 100 ritonavir-related patents held by Indian generic companies and a few by originators.

[104] See for example, WHO-WIPO-WTO Joint Technical Symposium, Access to medicines: pricing and procurement practices(Geneva, 16 July 2010) http://www.wto.org/english/tratop_e/trips_e/techsymp_july10_e/techsymp_july10_e.htm

[105] WHO, *Progress on Global Access to HIV Antiretroviral Therapy: A Report on "3 by 5" and Beyond* (Geneva, WHO, 2006) 19.

[106] 'China Puts Healthcare at the Top of the Agenda' *Medical News Today* (1 November 2007).

[107] NHK special TV programme, 'Healthcare for 1.3 billion people' (in Japanese), 3 November 2008.

[108] In the process leading to the adoption at the WTO of the para 6 system, for example, China was among the developing countries that recommended an authoritative interpretation of Art 30 of the TRIPS Agreement (see ch 8). Para 6 of the Ministerial Declaration on the TRIPS Agreement and Public Health, communication from Bolivia, Brazil, Cuba, China, Dominican Republic, Ecuador, India, Indonesia, Pakistan, Peru, Sri Lanka, Thailand and Venezuela (24 June 2002) IP/C/W/355.

healthcare challenges. HIV/AIDS alone[109] will increasingly be a challenge and could absorb a significant proportion of its health expenditure[110]

In India, per capita expenditure on health in 2002 was US$30.[111] In 2005, 15.5 per cent of medical services were funded publicly, and across the country there were one million doctors (the number of doctors per patient is much lower than in Brazil), 350,000 technical support staff, 865,000 nurses, and 16,000 hospitals. Between 25 per cent and 30 per cent of the income of the medical system comes from the wealthier class. Health insurance is nearly non-existent with private health insurance covering only 0.4 per cent of the population and government health insurance covering 3.4 per cent of the population. Patients pay for medicines in both government hospitals and private hospitals.[112] The development of an efficient generic drug industry does not seem to have resulted in the expected level of improved access to pharmaceuticals in India.[113]

Public spending on general healthcare in India seems to have fallen significantly below the level necessary for a nation-wide impact.[114] India's lagging domestic health insurance and medical services market seems to push the good quality generic drugs to be produced for the export market. According to the Organisation of Pharmaceutical Producers of India (OPPI),[115] only 35 per cent of Indian people had access to modern medicines, against 85 per cent in China and 43 per cent in Africa. More recently, the Department of Industrial Policy and Promotion (DIPP), Government of India, published a Discussion Paper on Compulsory Licensing which indicates that most of the 2 to 2.5 million cancer patients are 'unable to afford the cost of expensive anti-cancer medicines' and

[109] The estimated cumulative number of HIV positive people in China reported at the end of October 2007 was 223,501,State Council AIDS Working Committee Office, UN Theme Group on AIDS, *UNGASS country progress report–PR China* (2008) ii.

[110] The Chinese Government initially regarded HIV/AIDS as a 'foreign disease', to be kept out of China, although it gradually developed a national plan for the prevention of HIV/AIDS starting in 1987. By the early 2000s, there were approximately 130 overlapping regulations in the provinces and, where the infection rate is particularly high, there is hardly any viable structure for treatment. J Balzano and J Ping, 'Coming out of Denial: An Analysis of Aids Law and Policy in China (1987–2006)' (2006) 3(2) *Loyola International Law Review* 188–90. In Yunnan where there was not a single regulation until March 2004.ibid. 207.

[111] Source: WHO, www.who.int/hiv/HIVCP_IND.pdf.

[112] T Kuroki, 'Medical Supplies Systems in India' (in Japanese) (7 August 2007). www.yakuji.co.jp/entry3281.html.

[113] 50% to 80% of the Indian population are not able to access all the medicines they need and 649 million people (the largest such sector in the world, according to the WHO World Medicines Report in 2004) are without access to essential medicines. Society for Economic and Social Studies New Delhi and Centre for Trade and Development, New Delhi, in collaboration with WHO Country Office for India, 'Economic Constraints to Access to Essential Medicines in India' www.healthpolicy.cn/rdfx/jbywzd/gjjy2/yd/yjwx/201002/P020100227571385215688.pdf.

[114] General government expenditure on health as a percentage of total government expenditure in India was 3.3% in 2000 and 3.4% in 2006, one of the lowest in the world: WHO, 'Health Workforce, Infrastructure, Essential Medicines', *World Health Statistics* (Geneva, WHO, 2009).

[115] 'Foreign drug companies may lose exclusivity for some drugs in India', *Pharma China* (New Delhi, 5 February 2010).

only 300,000 out of 2.5 million HIV/AIDS patients have access to medicines.[116] The paper explains that: 'The big gap indicates the near non-accessibility of the medicines to a vast majority of the affected population mainly because of the high cost of these medicines.'[117] As the price of drugs is not the only obstacle to access to medicine, more comprehensive, community healthcare programmes with sustainable finance may be helpful.

The Brazilian Government has been a pioneer and active in dispensing AIDS treatments and preventing new HIV infections. The AIDS programme started in 1996[118] and has provided free access to ARVs, dispensed by specialised physicians and through local communities and with civil society groups, to approximately 150,000 patients.[119] The integrated community healthcare programme has achieved excellent results in preventing the endurance of the epidemic and serves as a model for developing countries. The Brazilian AIDS programme is relatively self-reliant and does not resort to funding from international programmes such as the Global Fund for the procurement of ARVs.[120] The Government negotiates prices with multinational drug companies, relying on the cost of local production as a benchmark.

The Brazilian Government undertook to manufacture, under the leadership of the Oswald Cruz Foundation (FIOCRUZ)[121] National Institute for Health, Farmanguinhos, seven kinds of AIDS drugs which had been patented abroad before Brazil introduced product patent protection in 1996. Initially, Brazil's response to the AIDS epidemic was to promote domestic production of active pharmaceutical ingredients, something that Brazil had long been hoping to achieve. To produce domestically active pharmaceutical ingredients and intermediary products and export ARVs through industrial development, the ANVISA designated and encouraged 19 state enterprises, with uneven performance.[122]

Far-Manguinhos is said to supply roughly 40 per cent of the AIDS drugs used in the Brazilian Government's AIDS programme, although the percentage of active pharmaceutical ingredients from India, China, and South Korea totalled 74 per

---

[116] Department of Industrial Policy and Promotion (DIPP), Discussion Paper on Compulsory Licensing, August 2010. http://dipp.nic.in/CL-DraftDiscussion.doc. On access to medicines for HIV/AIDS patients, see also S Guennif, 'AIDS in India, public health related aspects of industrial policy and intellectual property rights in a developing country' (2004) CSH Occasional Paper, No 8, Delhi, French Research Institutes in India.

[117] DIPP, Discussion Paper on Compulsory Licensing (n 91) para 16.

[118] Based on Federal Law 9313 of 13 November 1996.

[119] In 2007, 730,000 people were estimated to be living with HIV in Brazil.

[120] In 2005, Brazil took a strong position against the US administration's attempt to link US$40 million in HIV/AIDS grants to an anti-prostitution pledge based on two 2003 US laws. 'Brazil refuses U.S. AIDS funds, rejects conditions', *Wall Street Journal* (2 May 2005) www.walnet.org/csis/news/world_2005/wallstreet-050502.html.

[121] The Oswaldo Cruz Foundation (FIOCRUZ) is part of the National Health Ministry and a research institute performing basic and applied research on tropical diseases. 'The Brazilian government has announced plans for the local production of a generic version of Merck & Co's HIV treatment Stocrin', *Pharma Times* (UK, 23 September 2008).

[122] JS Mendonca et al, 'High quality production of generic in Brazil – Far-Manguinhos experience'. International Conference on AIDS, 7–12 July 2002; 14: abstract no E11510.

cent in 2002 and reached 94 per cent in 2003.[123] Brazilian companies are involved only in the formulation process, and 75 per cent of production costs are from the costs of the active pharmaceutical ingredients. In 1999, price regulations were revised and tariffs on AIDS drugs and cancer drugs were lowered from 20 per cent to 3 per cent. Between the 1980s and 2004, the Brazilian drug market relied on imports and its export markets were limited to neighbouring counties and other countries where Portuguese is spoken. There has been no aggressive effort to globally commercialise Brazilian products, for example, by printing medication instructions in English. The cost of AIDS treatment in the Government's programme has risen since 2003, due not only to the increase of patients needing second-line ARVs, but also to the cost of domestic production.[124]

Brazil's 1971 Constitution[125] provides for the right to life (Article 5), the right to health (Article 6), the protection of the federal and local governments (Article 23), and universal health insurance (Article 194). In many legal disputes, lower courts have stated that access to medicine is secured by the Constitution, and have ordered the government to take emergency measures (within 48 hours). This interpretation of the Constitution has also been supported by the Supreme Federal Court, which may burden medical financing.

Healthcare is one of the priority issues for the Brazilian government, and UNICEF statistics, for example, show a general improvement in child mortality, which is one indicator of health policy achievement.[126] Its policy facilitating access for medicines for chronic diseases also seems to have achieved positive results, although opinions differ on this issue. The Brazilian Government has made various promises regarding healthcare to its citizens every year which have contributed to budget deficits.

In 2007 a survey of six low- and middle-income countries was presented on the availability and affordability of medicines to treat chronic diseases (cardiovascular disease, diabetes, chronic respiratory disease and glaucoma) and to provide palliative cancer care.[127] Brazil had relatively high availability of both originator and generic medicines in the public and private sectors, and generic drugs are provided generally free of charge in the public sector. The availability of insulin preparations to treat diabetes was poor in all six countries surveyed except Brazil. However, the price level in Brazil varied considerably: for example, aspirin costs 30 times, hydrochlorothiazide 25 times and propranolol eight times their international reference prices. The survey's authors, Mendis et al, recommended from the overall survey results that improvements in availability

---

[123] C Grace, *The Effect of Changing Intellectual Property on Pharmaceutical Industry Prospects in India and China* (London, DFID, 2004) 14. Brazil's exports of pharmaceuticals totalled US$314 million. Brazilian Federation of Pharmaceutical Industry (FEBRAFARMA), February 2005.

[124] AS Nunn et al, 'Evolution of Antiretroviral Drug Costs in Brazil in the Context of Free and Universal Access to AIDS Treatment' (2007) www.hsph.harvard.edu/pihhr/files/NunnPlos.pdf, 7.

[125] www.v-brazil.com/government/laws/constitution.html.

[126] www.unicef.org/infobycountry/brazil_statistics.html.

[127] S Mendis et al, 'The availability and affordability of selected essential medicines for chronic diseases in six low- and middle-income countries' (2007) 85(4) *Bulletin of the World Health Organization*.

and affordability require a mix of policies that specifically address a country's circumstances, particularly policies related to governance and management efficiency, as well as a realistic assessment of local supply options. Strategies to lower prices would include adequate and sustainable financing through national and international sources, pooling procurement and other arrangements to improve purchasing efficiency, eliminating taxes and tariffs, regulating mark-up charges. These recommendations seem to apply across the countries examined in this chapter.

Part V

TRIPS Flexibilities and National Implementation

12

TRIPS Flexibilities and National Implementation

(1) Patentable Subject Matter and Patentability Requirements

THE WTO PANEL explained in China – Intellectual Property Rights[1] that the nature of obligation and the scope of national discretion which is allowed differ between Part II and Part III of the TRIPS Agreement.[2] Part II introduces TRIPS-regulated substantive minimum standards concerning the availability and scope of, and exceptions to IPR, whereas Part III relates to enforcement of IPRs and allows considerable discretion to enforcement authorities as to the means to attain the goals delineated by the TRIPS Agreement. There are, however, provisions also in Part II which leave significant policy options to Members. Notable examples include Article 27 concerning patentable subject matter, and Article 39.3 relating to test data submitted to regulatory authorities for marketing approval. This chapter explores how certain TRIPS 'flexibilities' have been interpreted and recommended as being beneficial to developing countries. India is examined here because of the country's leading role in these discussions. This chapter also addresses the question of 'evergreening', which section 3(d) of the Indian Patents (Amendment) Act 2005 purports to prevent for public health reasons.

I TRIPS FLEXIBILITIES RELATING TO PATENTABLE SUBJECT MATTER

A Suggestions made by International Bodies on the Patentability Criteria for Developing Countries

Article 27 under section 5 (patents) of Part II of the TRIPS Agreement, entitled 'Patentable Subject Matter', provides flexibilities in relation to patentable subject matter and patentability requirements, as well as for the possible exclusions from

---

[1] *China–Measures Affecting the Protection and Enforcement of Intellectual Property Rights(China –Intellectual Property)*, Panel Report (adopted 20 March 2009) WT/DS362/R. See ch 7.
[2] The Panel notably compared the language utilised in Part II and Part III (see chapters 5 and 7).

patentable subject matter. Article 27.1, first sentence, stipulates that 'patents shall be available for any inventions, whether products or processes, in all fields of technology, provided that they are new, involve an inventive step and are capable of industrial application.' It thus makes it obligatory that Members grant patents irrespective of whether the invention is a product or a process, and irrespective of the field of technology. Members cannot exclude from patent protection whole classes of inventions in fields of technology. Article 27.1 further provides that 'patents shall be available and patent rights enjoyable without discrimination as to the place of invention, the field of technology and whether products are imported or locally produced.' Thus, Members are not allowed to impose conditions of grant and enjoyment of patent rights which amount to discriminating one field of technology against others.

Article 27.2 regulates the conditions of exclusion concerning individual cases and provides that Members may exclude from patentability 'inventions, the prevention within their territory of the commercial exploitation of which is necessary to protect *ordre public* or morality', and Article 27.3 allows exclusion from patentability of certain categories of inventions (see chapters 4 and 5).

Many commentators and international organisations have made policy recommendations on the flexibilities that Article 27 of the TRIPS Agreement offers. For example, the UNCTAD-ICTSD *Resource Book on TRIPS and Development* (*The Resource Book*)[3] explains in detail where flexibilities lie in the TRIPS Agreement. An explanatory note to the book states that its purpose is to provide a 'sound understanding of WTO Members' rights and obligations', with a view to clarifying 'the implications of the Agreement, especially highlighting the areas in which the treaty leaves leeway to Members for the pursuit of their own policy objectives, according to their respective levels of development.'[4]

The Resource Book cites Article 27 as one part of the Agreement that contains a variety of flexibilities, including the fact that it does not define what an 'invention' is and provides suggestions that Members may consider,[5] such as:

- limiting 'invention' only to 'technology' (to the exclusion of business method or software),[6] given the wording 'in all fields of technology' in Article 27.1 of the TRIPS Agreement and the example of the EPO Patent Examination Guidelines;
- opting for a narrow scope of patentability relating to plants and animals, confining it to microorganisms that have been genetically modified;[7]
- excluding cells, genes, and other sub-cellular components from patentability because they are not visible but are not 'microorganisms' and therefore are not subject to the obligation under Article 27.3(b).[8]

---

[3] UNCTAD-ICTSD, *The Resource Book on TRIPS and Development* (Cambridge University Press, 2005 – hereafter Resource Book). See ch 4 n 122.

[4] *The Resource Book* (n 3) xi.

[5] ibid (n 3) 393.

[6] *The Resource Book* (n 3) 358–66.

[7] ibid (n 3) 393.

[8] *The Resource Book* (n 3) 392–93.

The Resource Book further asserts that with patentability requirements, ie, novelty, inventive step and industrial applicability, not being harmonised, they may be implemented 'according to what is most appropriate for their specific level of development'. As a criterion of 'industrial applicability', for example, it states that Members may require that the invention result in a 'true' industrial product.[9] The book stresses that 'in some countries, including in the United States, the low standard of inventiveness applied has led to the grant of a large number of patents on minor or trivial developments, often aggressively used to artificially extend the duration of protection and to block legitimate competition.'[10] It suggests therefore that 'given the market disruption and costs that patents granted on low or non-inventive developments may cause', developing countries may set high criteria for defining an inventive step.[11] The underlying assumption, as explained above, is that the high standards of inventiveness reduce the number of patents on minor or trivial inventions and create a more competitive environment which lowers prices. *The Resource Book* cites *Global Economic Prospects and the Developing Countries,* published by the World Bank (2001), as saying that developing countries 'could set high standards for the inventive step, thereby preventing routine discoveries from being patented.'

In a similar vein, *The Resource Book* raises an interpretative question, *inter alia*, as to whether Article 27.1 obliges Members to protect 'uses' as such, for instance, new uses of known products, in addition to products and processes.[12] *The Resource Book* points out that because the TRIPS Agreement only obliges them to grant patents for products and processes (Article 27.1), it is left unclear whether the protection for processes covers uses or methods of use. WTO Members are therefore free to decide whether to allow the patentability of the uses of known products, including for therapeutic use, and are certainly free to adopt the Swiss formula approach.[13]

---

[9] ibid (n 3) 358–59.

[10] The Resource Book cites J Barton, 'Reforming the patent system', 287 (2000) *Science* 1933–1934.

[11] *The Resource Book* (n 3) 360.

[12] In the US, patents on uses are confined to a particular 'method-of-use,' which does not encompass protection of the product as such. Under the European Patent Convention (EPC – see chapters 2 and 3), the patentability of a known product for a new specific purpose is allowed. Thus, the identification of the first medical indication of a known product may permit patenting of the product. In cases where an application refers to the second medical indication of a known pharmaceutical product, however, an obstacle to patentability arises. Patent applications over the therapeutic use of a known product essentially are instructions to the physician about how to use a certain substance to treat a particular disease. Such a new use, hence, is equivalent to a method of therapeutic treatment, which is not patentable.

[13] Art 53(c) EPC 2000 (Art 52(4) EPC 1973) excludes from patentability 'methods for treatment of the human or animal body by surgery or therapy and diagnostic methods practiced on the human or animal body' but adds *in fine* that 'this provision shall not apply to products, in particular substances or compositions, for use in any of these methods' providing exception for 'substances or compositions'. Thus, claiming diagnostic or therapeutic use of products is allowable under Art 53(c). According to the Decision of the Enlarged Board of Appeal G5/83 in 1984, a first medical indication could obtain purpose-limited protection for a known substance. It therefore became possible to claim 'a (known) substance S for use as a medicament', if the claim is written, 'a pharmaceutical composition comprising compound S and pharmaceutically acceptable carrier' (Swiss formula). In

The preface to the WHO-UNCTAD-ICTSD 2007 Working Paper entitled 'Guidelines for the Examination of Pharmaceutical Patents: Developing a public health perspective' by Correa (WHO-UNCTAD-ICTSD Pharmaceutical Guidelines) states that:

> the [2001 Doha] Declaration enshrines the principles that agencies such as WHO have publicly advocated and advanced, namely, the reaffirmation of the right of WTO Members to make full use of the flexibilities of the TRIPS Agreement in order to protect public health and promote access to medicines. An important flexibility in this respect is the right of WTO Members to define the patentability criteria as referred to under the TRIPS Agreement in accordance with their particular national priorities. This may be an important tool for the promotion of genuinely new and inventive pharmaceutical products. [14]

According to the WHO-UNCTAD-ICTSD Pharmaceutical Guidelines, the TRIPS Agreement does not define the criteria of 'novelty, inventive step and industrial applicability' and therefore, each WTO Member has discretion to determine the criteria and recommends, notably, that:

- combinations of known active ingredients should be deemed non-inventive as the synergy between the components are obvious to a person skilled in the art. However, if a new and non-obvious synergistic effect is properly demonstrated by biological tests and appropriately disclosed in the patent specifications, this could be considered as a basis for patentability;[15]
- new formulations, compositions and processes for their preparation should generally be deemed obvious, but could exceptionally be patentable, if a truly unexpected or surprising effect is obtained;
- new doses of known products for the same or a different indication do not constitute inventions;
- new salts, ethers, esters and other forms of existing pharmaceutical products can generally be obtained with ordinary skills and are not inventive, but, exceptionally, if appropriately conducted clinical tests data, described in the specifications, demonstrate unexpected advantages in properties as compared to what was in the prior art, are patentable;
- processes to obtain polymorphs may be patentable in some cases if they are novel and meet the inventive step standard;

---

other words, a European patent may not be granted for the use of a substance or composition for the treatment of the human or animal body by therapy, but may be granted when directed to the use of a substance or composition for the manufacture of a medicament for a specified new and inventive therapeutic application. In the text of Art 54(5) EPC 2000, this is stated clearly. See also chs 3 and 8.

[14] C Correa,'Guidelines for the Examination of Pharmaceutical Patents: Developing a public health perspective' 2007. http://ictsd.net/downloads/2008/06/correa_patentability20guidelines.pdf, vii–viii. The idea that stopping minor innovation will encourage 'genuine' innovation seems to be well-received in India. See, eg, 'Don't destabilise or create uncertainty on the IPR regime', *The Hindu* (3 August 2007); 'Innovation Policy Needs National Focus, Use of TRIPS Obligations, Panelists Say', *IP Watch* (20 July 2009).

[15] ibid 8.

- claims relating to the use, including the second indication, of a known pharmaceutical product can be refused, inter alia, on grounds of lack of novelty and industrial applicability;
- polymorphism is an intrinsic property of matter in its solid state. Polymorphs are not created, but found. Patent offices should be aware of the possible unjustified extension of the term of protection arising from the successive patenting of the active ingredient and its polymorphs, including hydrates/solvates. Processes to obtain polymorphs may be patentable in some cases if they are novel and meet the inventive step standard;
- single enantiomers (optical isomers) should generally not be deemed patentable when the racemic mixture was known but processes for the obtention of enantiomers, if novel and inventive, may be patentable;
- claims relating to the use, including the second indication, of a known pharmaceutical product can be refused, inter alia, on grounds of lack of novelty and industrial applicability.

The US, Europe and Japan have considerably different constructions and legal formulations in delineating the scope of patentable inventions (see chapter 3; see also footnotes 11 and 12 of this chapter). In the European countries, certain kinds of inventions were excluded by statutes, whereas in the US, patentability questions have been decided judicially. While statutory determination may lead to certain predictability, judicial determination could be adaptable to the nature of inventions that evolve with science, technology and market conditions, depending, however, on how objectively and competently the standards are actually applied. The Expert Group on Biotechnological Inventions for the European Commission emphasises that fundamental concepts in patent law, such as discovery, invention or technical character, are 'subject to evolution'.[16]

Additionally, the timing of examination among different jurisdictions tends to create differences in the evaluation of prior art and, therefore, of 'inventive step'. According to a 2007 report of the Japanese Patent Office (JPO),[17] the most common reason for rejecting patent applications is lack of inventive step. This happens slightly more often in Japan than in the US or in Europe. This is mainly because the relevant prior art in the form of scientific and technological literature consulted by the JPO is later in time than the US or the EPO, due to the system in Japan of not examining the application unless such a request is made formally. In most countries, however, the lack of 'inventive step' can be dealt with effectively by applicants and amended by subsequent action improving the specifications, in contrast to rejection on the grounds of lack of novelty. Importantly, the perspective from which patent offices or courts examine patents

---

[16] S J R Bostyn, 'Patenting DNA sequences (polynucleotides) and scope of protection in the European Union: an evaluation' (2004) (European Commission; Directorate-General for Research Food Quality and Safety, 2004) 12.

[17] According to the Report (2007) by the Opposition Division of the Japanese Patent Office, 90% of the first letter of rejection cases lacked inventive steps.

is that properly administered patent protection ultimately and generally contributes to innovation and encourages R&D.

The Resource Book seems to be proposing that it is in the interest of developing countries if TRIPS provisions are interpreted to allow a narrow scope of IPR protection and to create high hurdles for granting patents. It explains that:

> . . . at least from the medium- and long-term perspective, the economic effects of the patent provisions depend largely on the levels of development of countries and sectors concerned, the speed, nature and cost of innovation, as well as on the measures developing countries may take in adopting the new framework. The introduction of patents will entail sacrifices in static efficiency while benefits for most developing countries in terms of dynamic efficiency are uncertain . . . particularly to the extent that research and development of drugs for diseases prevalent in developing countries (such as malaria) continues to be neglected.[18]

Broadly speaking, the content and the level of patent examination may depend on the scientific and technological capabilities of a given society. However, between the actual patent law provisions on patentability and its economic effects on matters such as prices, there seem to be many intervening market and institutional factors such as the size of the market, entry and investment conditions, price regulations, etc. There may not be many patent applications anyway in less developed countries. How the patentability criteria should be determined in relation to 'the levels of development of countries' remains unclear.

The Resource Book, on the question of patent protection of biotechnologies relating to animals and plants, for example, cites the recommendations adopted by the UK Commission on Intellectual Property Rights (CIPR):[19] 'Those developing countries with limited technological capacity should restrict the application of patenting in agricultural biotechnology consistent with TRIPS, and they should adopt a restrictive definition of the term "microorganism".'[20]

Would a reduced scope of patentable subject matter and higher patentability standards, particularly of inventive-step, lead necessarily to a lesser number of patents, a reduction of product prices, and otherwise always be helpful for developing countries? In what ways would restrictions on the patentability of certain chemical forms help public health? And would the choice of policy on patentability depend always on the stage of development, as the CIPR suggests?

---

[18] *The Resource Book* (n 3) 358.

[19] Commission on Intellectual Property Rights, *Integrating Intellectual Property Rights and Development Policy* (London, CIPR, 2002). www.iprcommission.org/papers/pdfs/final_report/CIPRfullfinal.pdf

[20] *The Resource Book* (n 3) 411.

B R&D on Natural Products

Natural product (NP)-based pharmaceutical R&D[21] has been almost totally abandoned by large pharmaceutical companies[22] for technological[23] and other reasons.[24] However, natural products or NP-derived product research could still be attractive sources of research, technology and know-how transfer for R&D.[25] It could create both local business and opportunities for scientific and technological learning. For example, inventions relating to biochemistry (micro-organisms or enzymes and peptides) contain on average many more scientific citations, in comparison to inventions in other technological fields.[26] One of the reasons is that in biochemistry fields, researchers undertaking basic research and applied research tend to overlap.[27]

[21] Natural products (NP) includes: terrestrial microorganisms, terrestrial plants, terrestrial verte-brates, and marine organisms used as templates for synthetic modification.

[22] Among 15 NP or NP-derived drugs in Phase III clinical trials or registration in December 2003, there were 10 total syntheses, four semisyntheses (showing importance of lead optimisation for anti-cancer drugs) and one NP rammoplanin (antibacterial) (MS Butler, 'The role of natural product chemistry in drug discovery' (2004) 67 *Journal of Natural Product (J Nat Prod)* 2148.

[23] Between 1981 and 2002, NP drugs occupied 28% of all NCEs launched onto the market, and NP-derived drugs, 24% (DJ Newman et al, 'Natural Products as Sources of New Drugs over the Period 1981–2002' (2003) 66 *J Nat Prod* 1022) contributing as lead compounds for further modifica-tion during drug development for anti-cancer or anti-hypertensive areas. NP-based drug develop-ment was not amenable to high throughput biological assays, which came to be used predominantly after 2000 for anti-cancer, anti-infective functions exploration. Historically, complex antibiotics are all semi-synthetic products of clinical, pharmacological and chemical studies since the 1940s. Since the 1970s, mechanism-based screening was used for anti-lipidemic drugs (statins), and since the 1980s, high throughput screening (HTS) was used for automatic testing of large collections of compounds for activity as inhibitors or activators of a specific biological target (receptors, enzymes etc). Today, a few Big Pharma companies (including Novartis, part of Wythe and Merck) undertake NP-based R&D. Relatively large numbers of Japanese companies engage in this type of R&D in such fields as food, additives, pharmaceuticals and cosmetics.

[24] The disadvantages of NP-based or NP-derived R&D are: rare success rate (only 200,000 NP drugs, out of 22 million chemical entities) (DJ Newman et al (n 23)); high probability of arriving at a known chemical entity after a long period of R&D; competition from HTS; competition further from other drug discovery processes; uncertain or complex national rules for the supply.

[25] Of the 520 new medicines approved between 1983 and 1994, 39% were derived from natural products, the proportion of antibacterials and anti-cancer agents of which was over 60%; between 1990 and 2000, a total of 41 drugs derived from natural products were launched on the market by major pharmaceutical companies. Reasons for the abundance of 'bioactive' substances may be the defence against mammals, insects, fungi, bacteria and viruses. DJ Abraham (ed), *Burger's Medicinal Chemistry and Drug Discovery*, 6th edn (New York, John Wiley, 2003) vol 1 (Drug Discovery) 848.

[26] J Michel and B Bettels, 'Patent citation analysis' (2001) 51(1) *Scientometrics* 185–201; Tamada et al, 'Science Linkages in Technologies Patented in Japan' (2004) RIETI Discussion Paper Series 04-E-034 (1993–Oct 2001 data over 650,000 patents). Both studies indicated that scientific citations were most frequent in the following subfields of biochemistry: microorganisms or enzymes (C12N – 60.1%; Organic chemistry – peptides (C07K) – 58.6%) whereas the average of all EP applications was 11.95%. Michel and Bettels, 'Patent citation analysis' Table 4, 197 (1999 data).

[27] In 1993, Jaffe et al examined the relationship between citations and spillovers, and tested the extent of spillover localisation for all technological fields. Their findings are that corporate patents are more often self-cited, and self-cites are more often localised, but localisation is more likely to fade for the university patents (40% of knowledge spillovers do not come from the same primary patent class). AB Jaffe et al, 'Geographic localization of knowledge spillovers as evidenced by patent citations' (1993) 108 *Quarterly Journal of Economics* 577–98.

Scientific and technological undertakings in biochemistry could also be adapted to the scale of neglected-disease medicines research. The discussions on the Convention on Biological Diversity (CBD)[28] and its relation to IPR protection have led developing countries to focus mainly on how to prevent biopiracy; they probably are not sufficiently considering the possibilities of direct investment, their own biological and biotechnological R&D, or licensing the results of their R&D.

It certainly is necessary to prevent the plundering of biological resources and of ideas couched in traditional knowledge[29] from developing countries without appropriate reward. Patents are related to traditional knowledge in as much as they are granted by virtue of novelty, inventive step and industrial applicability. If biological resources and/or related traditional knowledge constitute prior art for the invention for which the patent is sought, examiners should take this into account to avoid granting erroneous patents.[30] It is also a common understanding and practice in all countries that a mere 'discovery' of something already existing in nature is not patentable (see chapter 3). Ways to commercialise innovative products using biological resources vary in different fields such as seeds, food, cosmetics or medicines, depending, for example, on the number of players in the market and the ways in which biological resources contribute to innovation.[31] Developing

---

[28] Art 1 of the CBD refers to 'the conservation of biological diversity, the sustainable use of its components and the fair and equitable sharing of the benefits arising out of the utilization of genetic resources'. The CBD delineates other principles, such as protection of the traditional knowledge of indigenous and local communities (Art 8(j)) and 'sovereign rights of Contracting Parties over their genetic resources' (Art 15(1)). Art 16 of the CBD is entitled 'Access to and Transfer of Technology. In this context, Art 16(5) CBD refers to intellectual property rights and stipulates the obligation for Contracting Parties to cooperate, so that 'such rights are supportive of and do not run counter to its objectives'.

Various international organisations have developed projects which cover issues related to the CBD. For example, the Food and Agricultural Organization (FAO) called for the revision and expansion of the 1983 International Undertaking on Plant Genetic Resources (adopted by the FAO Conference in 1983 and deals with access to plant genetic resources for food and agriculture) to be in harmony with the CBD; to deal also with access on mutually agreed terms for plant genetic resources. For these purposes, the International Treaty on Plant Genetic Resources for Food and Agriculture (ITPGRFA) was adopted by the FAO Conference on 3 November 2001 and went into effect in June 2004 (as of 15 October 2010, 27 countries are contracting parties). The ITPGRFA addressed the ex situ collections and farmers' rights issues that are not addressed in the CBD. Similarly, the World Intellectual Property Organization (WIPO) created the 'Intergovernmental Committee on Intellectual Property and Genetic Resources, Traditional Knowledge and Folklore' in 2000 to discuss possible ways to protect traditional knowledge and folklore.

[29] The CBD refers to intellectual property rights in Art 16(5), which stipulates the obligation for Contracting Parties to cooperate, so that 'such rights are supportive of and do not run counter to its objectives'. The Bonn Guidelines adopted by the Conference of the Parties (COP) suggest that countries with users of genetic resources could consider 'measures to encourage the disclosure of the country of origin of the genetic resources and of the origin of traditional knowledge, innovations, and practices of indigenous and local communities in applications for intellectual property rights'.

[30] To prevent foreign and domestic patent offices from overlooking traditional knowledge that constitutes prior Art, documenting traditional knowledge is helpful.

[31] See ch 1 n 24. One of the factors to be taken into consideration in discussing IPRs and benefit-sharing in the seed sector has been the reduction of transaction costs. For seeds, the costs of establishing contracts between hundreds or thousands of farmers and breeders, as well as among breeders, often outweigh the cost of limiting the scope of breeders' intellectual property rights. For

countries may be interested in encouraging and investing in science, research and innovative technologies related to these fields to develop new products themselves. This could be helpful for creating business in health research in developing countries, as seen in the international joint research centres in many Asian countries such as China, Malaysia and Vietnam. From the perspective of strengthening domestic science and technology programmes to encourage innovation by domestic inventors, there seems to be no rational reason for minimising, for example, the definition of microorganisms.

In many countries (Japan in particular), patenting of inventions relating to microorganisms is the most frequent among life-science related fields (see Figure 12.1 for the case of Japan), but the mere fact of a great number of patents does not mean that they encroach upon the rights of others to undertake research. Under the Budapest Treaty,[32] the patent applicants of inventions using microorganisms not easily available must deposit the microorganisms at a depository. A third party, to satisfy the enablement requirements for his own invention, can request depositary institutions to furnish deposited microorganisms for study and research. In this field, therefore, the patent system facilitates the disclosure of scientific information probably more than in other fields, without being an obstacle to others' activities.

Patents for basic, post-genomic biotechnologies (receptors, ESTs, etc) are much less numerous, but their scope could be much wider and might involve allegations of infringement if used without the right holder's authorisation. On balance, however, for research activities, the proper functioning of the patent system, which is to disclose the relevant scientific and technological information, is helpful. This depends also on the field of technology. What is also important would be that patentability criteria are clear and consistently applied, to give predictability to the users of the system.

the food or cosmetic industries and the pharmaceutical industry, other considerations are relevant in the search for rules related to benefit-sharing. Owners of biological resources, for example, may be able to relatively easily find commercial players who would act as partners in food or cosmetic industry fields. The relatively strong bargaining power of resource owners in these sectors is made possible by the fact that there are many commercial market players and the technological value added for commercialization abroad may not be so high. The owners may have some idea of the true value of their resources, because their use in food/cosmetics industrial production is relatively similar to the traditional use.

[32] Art 6(2)(viii) of the Budapest Treaty stipulates that the depositary institution must, in its capacity as international depositary authority, 'furnish samples of any deposited microorganism under the conditions and in conformity with the procedure prescribed in the Regulations.' Art 3(1)(a) concerning 'Recognition and Effect of the Deposit of Microorganisms' suggests that samples are deposited on the assumption that they are furnished. This provisions states that: 'Contracting States which allow or require the deposit of microorganisms for the purposes of patent procedure shall recognize, for such purposes, the deposit of a microorganism with any international depositary authority. Such recognition shall include the recognition of the fact and date of the deposit as indicated by the international depositary authority as well as the recognition of the fact that what is furnished as a sample is a sample of the deposited microorganism.'

Figure 12.1: Patent Filings ofmicroorganisms and Enzymes in Japan

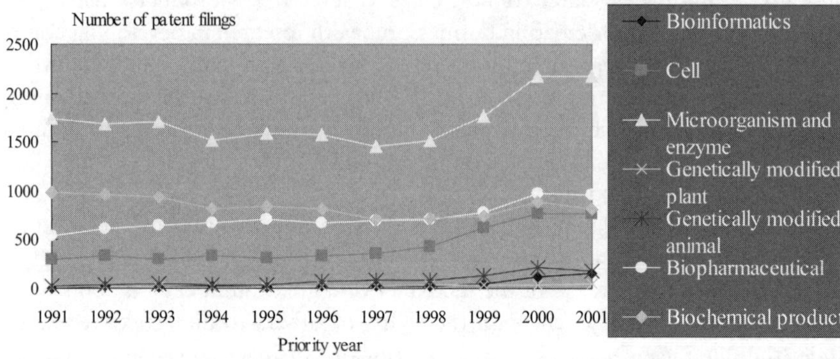

Tamada et al, 'Science linkages in technologies patented in Japan' (2004) RIETI Discussion Paper Series 04-E-034, 12. Many patents are filed by universities and ventures, and increased since 1997 at the same time as patenting in other biomedical technologies.

Although the level of sophistication in the patent examination may broadly depend on the technological levels of a country, this does not mean that less developed countries should always have lower standards of IPR protection. For example, a broad scope and a high level of protection may be suitable for developing countries, including least developed countries (LDCs), to create appropriate investment environments for doing bioscience R&D using microorganisms, which could be a suitable technological field.

The criteria of patentability that are 'most appropriate for the specific level of development'[33] may not be so easy to determine. An 'appropriate' patentability policy ideally would create a 'competitive edge' for a country in light of the globalised research and technological environment and vis-à-vis investors and possible product or licensing markets. How to make such a policy work and produce economic effects over a particular time-span could be a challenging question. Micro-managing different criteria in different technological fields in one country would also be difficult.

In the pharmaceutical and biotech fields, for example, research itself has become a globalised process where the upstream activities are promoted by early leads under the National Institute of Health (NIH) programmes, and downstream research (such as molecular optimisation) is done increasingly in developing countries, by Chinese and Indian researchers in particular.[34] Clinical studies are also increasingly outsourced to these countries, and from the point of view of contract manufacturing organisations (CMO) and contract research and manufacturing services (CRAMS) organisations, strong patent protection

---

[33] *The Resource Book* (n 3) 358.

[34] B Tempest, 'A structural change in the global pharmaceutical marketplace' (2010) 7(2) *Journal of Generic Medicines* 117.

and data exclusivity are lacking in these countries.[35] This conflicts with the view that such protection is not suitable for 'developing countries'.

There are important and inherently more difficult policy and implementation issues than a mere IP policy. For example, merely enlarging or reducing the scope of patentability would be meaningless unless such patent policy is implemented consistently and effectively, in a way linked to positive efforts to raise the scientific and technological levels of the country and to increase the competitiveness of its own industry. Unless universities, research institutes and industry make independent efforts to substantially increase creative R&D, IP policy may not contribute much to local business development. Government efforts to coordinate various domestic efforts would play a crucial role in developing viable business and local industry.

II EVERGREENING, PATENTABILITY REQUIREMENTS AND PUBLIC HEALTH

The above-mentioned WHO-UNCTAD-ICTSD Pharmaceutical Guidelines suggest that the 'flexibilities' contained in Article 27.1 of the TRIPS Agreement be used for public health purposes, by restricting the patentability of certain forms of chemical compounds, in addition to narrowing the scope of patentable inventions, to reduce the scope of claims and to raise the standards of judging 'inventive-steps'. This approach seems to be one of the guiding principles in the evolution of the Indian Patents Act 1970 and its Amendment Act 2005. In the following part of this chapter, the nature of chemical forms of inventions is explored in its relation to 'evergreening' with a view to clarifying this concept, which has increasingly been used globally (and rather pejoratively) in the context of pharmaceutical patenting practice. The prevention of evergreening is the objective of section 3(d) of the Indian Patents (Amendment) Act 2005, legislation which has been considered as a model by several developing countries. The Intellectual Property Appellate Board (IPAB) [36] in *Novartis v Union of India* stated that:

> It appears India has adopted stricter standard[s] of protection with respect to novelty and inventive step taking consideration of its public welfare particularly health concerns permitted by Doha declaration . . .[37]

---

[35] 'China and India tell a tale of two CMO markets', *SCRIP* (30 April 2010) 28.

[36] http://www.ipab.tn.nic.in/. IPAB was created by a Gazette notification of the Ministry of Commerce and Industry on 15 September 2003 to hear appeals against the decisions of the Registrar under the Trade Marks Act 1999 and the Geographical Indications of Goods Act 1999. All the appeals pending before High Courts can be transferred to the IPAB whose headquarters is in Chennai. The IPAB for patents was made fully operational in April 2007 with the appointment of its technical member.

[37] IPAB decision Misc Petition Nos 1–5/2007 in TA/I-5/2007/PT/CH & Misc Petition No 33 of 2008 in TA/1/2007/PT/CH & TA/1–5/2007/PT/CH, 26 June 2009, 156–7.

A TRIPS 27.1 Flexibilities and India

Section 3(d), which provided in the Patents Act 2002, that 'the mere discovery of any new property or new use for a known substance [is not patentable]' was substituted in 2005 to read: 'the mere discovery of *a new form of a known substance which does not result in enhancement of the known efficacy of that substance* or the mere discovery of any new property or new use for a known substance [is not patentable]'. Section 3(d) is accompanied by the following 'explanation', whose relationship to the main provision of 3(d) is not entirely clear:

> For the purposes of this clause, salts, esters, ethers, polymorphs, metabolites, pure form, particle size, isomers, mixtures of isomers, complexes, combinations and other derivatives of known substance shall be considered to be the same substance, unless they differ significantly in properties with regard to efficacy.

In 2007, the Indian government explained at the WTO Trade Policy Review (TPR) of India[38] that the Indian Patents (Amendment) Act 2005, seeks to balance IP protection with public health, national security, and the concerns of public interests.[39] According to the Indian reply to questions at the TPR, the legislative purpose of section 3(d) was to prevent the extension of patent life by evergreening and by 'trivial patents' that block generic entry,[40] elaborated to protect public interest in preventing 'evergreening'.

In *Novartis v Union of India*,[41] the High Court of Madras, quoting the Supreme Court view that the 'ascertainment of legislative intent is a basic rule of statutory construction', stated that:

> If we read the Parliamentary debate on Ordinance 7/2004, it appears that there was a widespread fear in the mind of the members of the House that if Section 3(d) as shown in Ordinance 7/2004 is brought into existence, then, a common man would be denied access to life saving drugs and that there is every possibility of 'evergreening'.[42]

In the 2004 Order in the process of amending the Indian Patents Act 1970,[43] the phrase, 'a mere new use', was used in the text of section 3(d) and, therefore, a new use could be patentable, which was to be reversed in the amendment of 2005

---

[38]   Trade Policy Review: India WT/TPR/M/182/Add 1 (20 July 2007) para 7. 20.

[39]   The Indian reply states that 'Section 64 sets out provisions on revocation of a patent by the Appellate Board. Section 66 stipulates that "Where the Central Government is of opinion that a patent" is "generally prejudicial to the public," "the patent shall be deemed to be revoked." Section 85 allows the Controller to revoke a patent on the ground of non-working. Under Section 117A, an appeal can be filed in any of these cases described in Sections 66 or 85.'

[40]   Trade Policy Review: India (n 38) 195.

[41]   *Novartis AG & Anor v Union of India & Others* (2007) 4 MLJ 1153 (Judgment of the High Court of Judicature at Madras, 6 August 2007) para 8.

[42]   ibid para 12.

[43]   The third amendment to the Patents Act 1970 was introduced through the Patents (Amendment) Ordinance 2004 (effective 1 January 2005). This Ordinance was later replaced by the Patents (Amendment) Act 2005 (Act No 15 of 2005) on 4 April 2005 with retroactive effect from 1 January 2005 (ch 10).

by the deletion of the word 'mere'. According to the Madras High Court in the *Novartis v Union of India* case:

> the Parliamentary debates show that welfare of the people of the country was in the mind of the Parliamentarians when Ordinance 7/2004 was in the House. They also had in mind the International obligations of India arising under "TRIPS" and under "WTO".[44]

In the same case, the Madras High Court noted the scope for national discretion that the TRIPS provisions leave, by Articles 1, 7 and 27. According to the judgment:

> Article 7 of 'TRIPS' provides enough elbow room to a Member country in complying with 'TRIPS' obligations by bringing a law in a manner conducive to social and economic welfare and to a balance of rights and obligations. Article 1 of 'TRIPS' enables [*sic*] a Member country free to determine the appropriate method of implementing the provisions of this agreement within their own legal system and practice. But however [sic], any protection which a Member country provides, which is more extensive in nature than is required under 'TRIPS', shall not contravene 'TRIPS'. Article 27 speaks about patentability.[45]

On the point of Article 27 of the TRIPS Agreement and national patentability criteria, the IPAB decision on the *Novartis* case on appeal endorsed what the Madras High Court had asserted. The IPAB also invoked the Doha Declaration on the TRIPS Agreement and Public Health as follows:

> Since India is having a requirement of higher standard of inventive step by introducing the amended Section 3(d) of the Act, what is patentable in other countries will not be patentable in India . . . As we see, the object of amended Section 3(d) of the Act is nothing but a requirement of higher standard of inventive step in the law particularly for the drug/pharmaceutical substances. This is also one of the different public interest provisions adopted in the patent law at the pre-grant level, which as we see, are also permissible under the TRIPS Agreement and to accommodate the spirit of the Doha Declaration which gives to the WTO Member states including India the right to protect public health and, in particular, to promote access to medicines for all.[46]

Thus, for the Madras High Court, section 3(d) provides 'a higher standard of inventive step'. On the accounts made by the Solicitor General of India and other defendants, the Madras High Court observed that:

> India, being a welfare and a developing country, which is predominantly occupied by people below the poverty line, has a constitutional duty to provide good health care to its citizens by giving them easy access to life saving drugs. In so doing, the Union of India would be right, it is argued, to take into account the various factual aspects prevailing in this big country and prevent evergreening by allowing generic medicine to be available in the market.[47]

---

[44] *Novartis v Union of India* (n 41) para 15.
[45] ibid para 15.
[46] IPAB decision (n 37).
[47] *Novartis v Union of India* (n 41) para 15.

In explaining the examination criteria for section 3(d) of the Indian Patents (Amendment) Act, the Draft Manual of Patent Practice and Procedure 2008 almost reiterates the Explanation in the provision. The Draft Manual states that:

> a known substance in its new form such as amorphous to crystalline or crystalline to amorphous or hygroscopic to dried, one isomer to other isomer, metabolite, complex, combination of plurality of forms, salts, hydrates, polymorphs, esters, ethers, or in new particle size, shall be considered [sic] same as of known substances unless such new forms significantly differ in the properties with regard to efficacy.[48]

Furthermore, the Draft Manual 2008 states that the comparison with regard to properties or enhancement of efficacy is required to be made at the time and date of filing the application or priority date if the application is claiming the priority of any earlier application but not at the stage of subsequent development.[49] The same Manual asserts the meaning of 'efficacy in pharmaceutical products', by reiterating what was decided by the Madras High Court in the *Gleevec* case, namely, that:

> . . . going by the meaning for the word 'efficacy' and 'therapeutic' . . . what the patent applicant is expected to show is, how effective the new discovery made would be in healing a disease/ having a good effect on the body? In other words, the patent applicant is definitely aware as to what is the 'therapeutic effect' of the drug for which he had already got a patent and what is the difference between the therapeutic effect of the patented drug and the drug in respect of which patent is asked for.[50]

Thus, the intention of the Indian Parliament in adopting section 3(d) seems to have been to prevent 'evergreening' as a means to provide good public health policy. However, the meaning of 'evergreening' is not readily understandable. Is it possible to establish a cause-and-effect relationship between the legal provision on patentability in section 3(d) of the Patent Acts on the one hand, and good public health policy results, on the other? There may be a host of intervening factors between the two, and the results may not be a policy or 'public' health. Moreover, it may not be possible, technically, for the patent applicant to explain, at the time of patent filing (ie, before clinical studies are undertaken) the enhanced 'therapeutic' efficacy of the molecule as adequately as the Madras High Court and the Draft Manual 2008 require. Further clarification of the meaning of 'efficacy' in section 3(d) would therefore be necessary for the application of this provision. Such a clarification would be needed all the more if this provision is expected to have a social impact, as was the original legislative intent. However, it may be difficult to predict the social impact of the patentability requirements of chemical forms, for the reasons explained below.

---

[48] Controller General of Patents, Designs & Trade Marks, India, Draft Manual of Patent Practice and Procedure (2008). www.patentoffice.nic.in/ipr/patent/DraftPatent_Manual_2008.pdf para 4.5.1. (New draft Manual is open for public comments as of 4 November 2010).

[49] Draft Manual of Patent Practice and Procedure (2008) (n 48) para 4.5.4.

[50] ibid para 4.5.6.

Crystals, esters, salts or isomers can be easily found and patented at a time not much later than the original substance is patented. After lengthy and costly clinical research efforts, these derived substances may turn out to have increased therapeutic effects, making them valuable medicines. Some of them, on the other hand, may be used as a means to stop generic entry. However, it would be practically impossible for patent examiners to decide at the time of patent examination on such effects in the product market which will be created only after the marketing of the product.

Despite these uncertainties, section 3(d) of the Indian Patents (Amendment) Act 2005, seems to have become a model for developing countries. The Philippines introduced the same provisions as section 22.1 in its Intellectual Property Code.[51] The Maldives, Pakistan, Sri Lanka, Vietnam, Indonesia, Malaysia and Bangladesh were also reported to have been considering adopting provisions similar to section 3(d) of the Indian Patents (Amendment) 2005.[52]

In November 2009, TC James, former Director of Intellectual Property Rights (IPRs) Division, Ministry of Commerce & Industry of India, and today Director of the National Intellectual Property Organization, New Delhi, published a report, 'Patent Protection and Innovation: Section 3(d) of the Patents Act and Indian Pharmaceutical Industry' on behalf of the Indian Pharmaceutical Alliance (IPA).[53] The Report responds to criticisms[54] from the developed country pharmaceutical industry that section 3(d), by prohibiting certain forms of inventions from being patented, does not encourage local incremental innovation. The TC James Report states that: 'Removal of Section 3(d) will result in

---

[51] Universally Accessible Cheaper and Quality Medicines Act of 2008 and Implementing Rules and Regulations of Republic Act 9502. S 1 (Non-Patentable Inventions) and s 2 (Inventive Step) of r 8 (Patent) are almost the same as s 3(d) of the Indian Patents (Amendment) Act 2005. S 22 (non-patentable inventions) of the Philippines Patent Law was amended to read:

'The following shall be excluded from patent protection:

22.1. Discoveries, scientific theories and mathematical methods, and in the case of drugs and medicines, the mere discovery of a new form or new property of a known substance which does not result in the enhancement of the known efficacy of that substance, or the mere discovery of any new property or new use for a known substance, or the mere use of a known process unless such known process results in a new product that employs at least one new reactant.

For the purpose of this clause, salts, esters, ethers, polymorphs, metabolites, pure form, particle size, isomers, mixtures of isomers, complexes, combinations, and other derivatives of a known substance shall be considered to be the same substance, unless they differ significantly in properties with regard to efficacy'.

In the Philippines, s 3(d) of the Indian Patent Act and Art 229-C of the Brazilian Industrial Property Law (which requires the National Health Surveillance Agency (ANVISA), in addition to the Patent Office, to review patent applications claiming pharmaceutical products or processes – see ch 10) were adopted as models in the discussions leading to the amendment of s 22 of the Philippines Patent Law.

[52] 'Copycats popping patent law pill', TNN (New Delhi, 13 August 2007).

[53] TC James, *Patent Protection and Innovation: Section 3(d) of the Patents Act and Indian Pharmaceutical Industry* (Mumbai, Indian Pharmaceutical Alliance (IPA – see ch 11), c/o. Vision Consulting Group, 2009) (TC James Report).

[54] For example, the report by the US–India Business Council, entitled 'The Value of Incremental Innovation: Benefits for Indian Patients and Indian Business', June 2009, is cited.

evergreening and delay in the entry of generics thereby adversely affecting public health', and points out that the '[s]tage of development of a country has to be borne in mind while prescribing patent standards'.[55]

The TC James Report cites the conclusion from the recommendations made by the UK Commission on Intellectual Property (CIPR)[56] and explains that the CIPR 'looked into the issue of integrating development objectives into the making of policy on IPRs world-wide', and 'felt that "developing countries should not feel compelled or indeed be compelled, to adopt developed country standards for IPR regimes."'[57] In this regard, according to TC James:

> [t]he underlying principle should be to aim for strict standards of patentability and narrow scope of allowed claims, with the objective of:
>
> —limiting the scope of subject matter that can be patented
> —applying standards such that only patents which meet strict requirements for patentability are granted and that the breadth of each patent is commensurate with the inventive contribution and the disclosure made
> —facilitating competition by restricting the ability of the patentee to prohibit others from building on or designing around patented inventions
> —providing extensive safeguards to ensure that patent rights are not exploited inappropriately.[58]

While the criteria of patentability enshrined in section 3(d) may not be sufficiently clear for the patent applicant, great expectations seem to have been placed on this provision. According to TC James:

> Patenting becomes one such strategy and many companies seek to increase [the] number of patents on a single product as part of this strategy, mainly to keep off competition. Even without intellectual property protection, originator companies have an advantage over the generic pharma companies as they can bring their products to the market much before the latter and that gives them strong market presence by the time others enter. Generics serve a major public health cause by introducing cheaper drugs compared to the patented ones. Removal of Section 3(d) will result in evergreening and delay in the entry of generics thereby adversely affecting public health.[59]

The TC James Report asserts that IPR standards should depend on the stage of development:

> Patent protection . . . gives a virtual monopoly for a period of 20 years. During this period no competition, including independent invention, is allowed. Therefore, extension of such a monopoly needs to be viewed seriously, particularly where it affects public interest such as public health. In the matter of intellectual property laws, [a] one size fits all approach is neither right nor in the interest of humanity. Stage of development of a country has to be borne in mind while prescribing patent standards.[60]

---

[55] TC James Report (n 53) 24.
[56] CIPR, *Integrating Intellectual Property Rights and Development Policy* (n 19).
[57] TC James cites the CIPR Report (n 19), 49.
[58] TC James Report (n 53) 24.
[59] ibid 7.
[60] TC James Report (n 53) 24.

However, this opinion may be ignoring the actual drug market situation in the sense that several 'me-too' drugs (see below p 438) normally compete in the same product market from the competition law point of view (for example, Tarceva and Iressa). It is therefore not necessarily pro-competitive to prohibit 'me-too' drug patenting. Doing so at the stage of patent filing may be counterproductive in that, at this stage, the future situation of competition in the product market is not foreseeable.

B Patentability of Chemical and Pharmaceutical Inventions

There are different forms of substances in the chemical field, such as new chemical compounds (or new chemical entities (NCE)), new compositions or derivatives. Chemical derivatives have different structures, to which certain properties and sometimes advantages in their usage can be attributed. For example, crystal forms often increase stability against changes in temperature, and polymorphs are easier for synthesis or isolation and could thus reduce manufacturing costs. Medicinal use (therapeutic efficacy) could be considered as contributing to the patentability of a substance. Derivatives of a compound are relatively easily invented, because they are obtained in a relatively conventional way. Solid salts tend to have no inventive step. Advantageous effect sometimes increases the patentability of crystals and other derivatives. As these changes of chemical characteristics may reflect relatively minor innovation, the novelty and inventive step of medicinal use is strictly examined in a rigorous system. Section 3(d) of the Indian Patents Act 2005 emphasises that, for derivatives to be considered 'inventions', they must have sufficiently enhanced 'efficacy' in comparison to the known compound. For example, the polymorphic forms A and B of an organic compound may differ in their solubilities in water and their crystallisation behaviour, but the novelty of such forms may not be recognised, unless they differ significantly in properties with regard to efficacy.[61] The salient characteristic of section 3(d) is that its Explanation emphasises the question of whether a compound must be considered different from a known compound in order for its patentability to be recognised.

The Indian Patent Office (IPO) explains that section 3(d) is a simple clarification adapted to chemical and pharmaceutical inventions.[62] However, Section 3(d) clearly rejects patentability of a new use of a known substance and therefore is not a simple explanation of how the Indian Patents Act recognises novelty, inventive step and industrial applicability. In most countries, the novelty of the

---

[61] Cimetidine (H2 receptor antagonists antihistamine) SmithKline & French obtained a new polymorph patent UK1543238 (filed in 1976) of the cimetidine compound, but its specification did not provide much explanation as to how this polymorph differs from the crystal A form of the substance in UK patent 1397436 (filed in 1972), which only briefly refers to the differences from the B and C crystals in the infrared absorption pattern, and the novelty of crystal B was subsequently denied.

[62] Interview at the IPO, Kolkata on 22 December 2009.

claimed medicinal invention is not denied when it and the cited invention differ in medicinal use; and if an advantageous effect compared with the cited invention cannot be foreseen by a person skilled in the art from the state of the art, the claimed medicinal invention is considered to involve an inventive step (see chapters 1 and 3).

The derivatives may have advantageous effects both in chemical properties (such as stability, better conservation conditions) or therapeutic effects (such as enhanced curative effects, reduced side-effects) or both. Therapeutic effects are proven often as a result of clinical studies which have not yet been effectuated at the time of patent filing. Specific forms of derivatives by themselves do not indicate whether or not they are patentable, and the eligibility of the proposed invention is determined by the proper application of patentability criteria (novel and having inventive step and industrial applicability). Normally, under most patent laws of developed countries, the novelty of the claimed medicinal invention is not denied when the compound, having a specific attribute of the claimed medicinal invention, differs from the compounds of a cited invention.

Many derivatives have predictable properties and their patentability is decided case by case. Among the developed country patent offices, some may have slightly higher criteria of judgment, mainly because of court decisions. For example, the EPO's standards concerning isomers may be slightly higher than those of other jurisdictions.[63] New compounds can be close to the prior art when the new compound is an optically active enantiomer of a compound previously known only in a racemic form.[64] It can therefore be argued that the optically active form cannot be regarded as novel, if the racemate is known.[65] Still, the EPO considered in *Hoechst/Enantiomers* that optical isomers of known racemates are novel per se,[66] and that the patentability of the optical isomers is rather a question of inventive step. Despite some differences in the examination standards among the US, Europe and Japan, the positive attitude towards finding patentability is common, which differs from the perspective that the fewer the patents, the better it is for society.

A metabolite[67] is patentable if novel and inventive. Mevalotin (pravastatin sodium), an antihyperlipidemic agent that acts by inhibiting cholesterol synthesis, is a metabolite whose bio-conversion by streptomyces carbophilus gives fewer side-effects, increased solubility, and cholesterol biosynthesis inhibition several times greater than its previous compound, mevastatin (ML-236B – not commercialised).

---

[63] EPO Guidelines CIV7.5.28, T12/81, T1048, 11048/92, T600/95. www.sipf.se/read/PharmaceuticalPatents.pdf.

[64] PW Grubb, *Patents for Chemicals, Pharmaceuticals and Biotechnology; Fundamentals of Global Law, Practice and Strategy*, 4th edn (Oxford University Press, 2004) 217–18.

[65] ibid.

[66] *Hoechst/Enantiomers* Case T296/87 [1990] OJ 195, as cited in Grubb, *Patents for Chemicals, Pharmaceuticals and Biotechnology; Fundamentals of Global Law, Practice and Strategy* (n 64) 217.

[67] *Merrell Dow Pharmaceuticals Inc v HN Norton & Co Ltd* [1996] RPC 76, HL.

Mevastatin   Pravastatin

However, there are cases where the sales of generic medicines may infringe the patent claiming the active metabolite of the original drug substance. Merrell Dow sold terfenadine, an antihistamine that had been sold world-wide. The patent-holder later obtained a separate patent on the active metabolite of the original compound and sued manufacturers of generic terfenadine in many countries after the patent expiry. In the UK, uninformative prior use cannot invalidate the patent under the Patents Act, 1977. The House of Lords held that the disclosure of the terfenadine patent specification itself, although it did not mention the active metabolite, made available to the public the invention of the acid metabolite because it enabled the public to work the invention by making the active metabolite in their livers, and invalidated the patent.[68] In many other jurisdictions, the metabolite patent of this medicine did not sustain validity.[69]

As long as relevant patents exist, as a general rule, a third party may not manufacture or sell any pharmaceutical products protected by the patents. Under certain conditions, however, testing, such as clinical trials, for approval applications by generic drug manufacturers does not constitute infringement.

For a drug, there are patents such as basic substance patents and its derivative patents (such as compounds and salts, crystals, hydrates, solvates and intermediates), manufacturing method patents, patents for utility and for formulation of other administration methods, and use patents that describe active ingredients in a structural form or a function, or prodrugs.[70] In drug discovery research, there are various types of patents related to the basic product patent, popularly called 'umbrella patents'. These include patents on the manufacturing process and intermediates, various chemical derivatives such as salts, crystals, hydrates, solvates, formulations or methods of administration, and prodrugs, each playing specific

---

[68] Grubb (n 64) 232–33.

[69] eg, in Japan, Tokyo High Court, 10 February 2005, 16 (ke) 233, 12911.

[70] A prodrug is a chemical compound that is administered to the human or animal body in an inactive (or significantly less active) form. Once administered, the prodrug goes through a serious change resulting in a series of metabolites, one or more of which may be active. The use of a prodrug is generally for absorption, distribution, metabolism, and excretion optimisation.

roles in the drug development and marketing strategy. Many of these umbrella patents, variants of the same compound (molecule) could be minor. On the other hand, they may indeed be used as means to stop generic entry.

By comparison, what are popularly called 'me-too' drugs are molecular variants (having different molecular structures, described decades ago as 'molecular roulette'), and should be distinguished from 'evergreening'. Marketing first-of-a-kind products is important in those technological fields where products are outmoded quickly, whereas in medicine, the first-in-class medicines are not necessarily the best-in-class, as newer medicines often improve upon older, in terms of side-effects or modes of administration. These follow-on drugs often compete in the same relevant market (chapters 1 and 9). Both evergreening (umbrella patents) and me-too drugs have been criticised, particularly when there is little or no therapeutic improvement in the variant. However, assumptions about 'me-too' drugs can be completely wrong, in that quite minor changes in the molecule can produce dramatic changes in clinical performance. This was true of beta blockers for the treatment of cardiovascular diseases in the 1960s and 70s (atenolol (Tenormin) was the ninth and then best) and in the 1980s; fluoxetine (Prozac) was a 'me-too' of a Swedish pioneer compound which was not launched on safety grounds. Prozac was the second, not the first-in-class. There are many other examples. In short, minor molecular variations may or may not produce therapeutic advances. At the time of patent application filings, ie, before conducting clinical studies, therapeutic advantages are often difficult to measure.

For pharmaceuticals, the protection afforded by a patent of a single basic substance (or manufacturing process) is extremely important for continuous, long-term R&D efforts (see chapter 1). In addition to the nature of the active ingredient itself, issues such as appropriate formulation technology, elution, absorbability within the body, water solubility, and combined use with other drugs, cannot be ignored. Formulation technologies can be considered patentable inventions if they are novel, having inventive step and industrially applicable. Some examples include taxol (commonly known as paclitaxel, which is a treatment method claim in the US and a formulation claim in Japan) which suppresses side-effects and leuplin (Leuprorelin), which is designed with a special release control for the active pharmaceutical ingredient[71] in dosage forms for intramuscular depot injection every 1, 3 and 4 months, respectively.

The introduction of a new variant of an existing product is called a 'line extension'. Normally, the objective of line extensions is to extend the therapeutic life of the original product by improving its effectiveness, safety or convenience for the patient and not necessarily linked to the preservation of exclusivity. However, line extensions often have that effect in practice if the new line is itself

---

[71] Leuplin (a prostate cancer treatment, commonly known as Leuprorelin) was originally sold as a subcutaneously administered injection formula, but its serum half-life was short and it was excreted, so it was important that through formulation technology, it was made into a release-controlled (Dual Delayed Release™ (DDR)) formulation drug using micro-capsulisation.

patented and is used when the original product loses patent protection (see below p 443).

C The Cost of 'Evergreening'

i Different meanings of 'evergreening'

Patents confer a legal monopoly over the patented technology, but not necessarily an economic monopoly of the products using this technology in the relevant markets (see chapter 1).[72] In fact, most patents do not correspond to a drug on the market and, therefore, the above argument is too general. The development and marketing of pharmaceuticals are supported by a patent strategy that aims to gain a competitive edge through patent life-cycle management. Patenting is normally pro-competitive, but life-cycle management may involve particular anticompetitive behaviour or strategies specifically aimed at eliminating competitors in the relevant product market, depending on the patent or competition laws of a country.

The word 'evergreening' has increasingly been used, but it is not entirely clear what scope of behaviour this word covers, or whether it is a normal behaviour under the patent law or denotes some kind of abuse. The behaviour involves the act of extending exclusivity. The US decision in *Fisons plc v Quigg*[73] stated that '"Evergreening" refers to the use of a series of patents issued at different times to extend the period of exclusivity of a product beyond the 17 years'.

The WHO's Commission on Intellectual Property, Innovation and Public Health (CIPIH) in 2006 defined evergreening as 'a term popularly used to describe patenting strategies that are intended to extend the term on the same compound'.[74] According to this Report, 'evergreening occurs when, in the absence of any apparent additional therapeutic benefits, patent holders use various strategies to extend the length of their exclusivity beyond the 20-year patent term.'[75] However, the scope of 'evergreening' differs widely according to the person who uses the term.

---

[72] To define the relevant market for the purpose of competition analyses, the test of 'Small but Significant and Non-transitory Increase in Price' (SSNIP) is applied. This determines whether a hypothetical monopolist could profit from a price increase of 5% and is an empirical way of testing elasticity of demand. As far as medicines are concerned, however, this method of market definition does not work, due to the fact that it is not the consumer but doctors who prescribe the medication. In this field, therefore, the World Health Organization's Anatomical Therapeutic Classification (ATC) system is used for the definition of relevant product market. The ATC classifies drugs into groups according to the organ or system on which they act and their chemical, pharmacological and therapeutic properties, and normally ATC level 4 together with other pertinent factors such as advertisement are used (for merger analyses, a more general ATC level 3 is used).

[73] *Fisons plc v Quigg* 1988 US Dist 8 USPQ 2D (BNA) 1491, 19.

[74] CIPIH Report http://www.who.int/intellectualproperty/report/en/ at 216. On the CIPIH, see Introductory chapter, n 5.

[75] ibid 131–32.

For many, the word evergreening seems to imply abuse of some kind. According to the European Generic Medicines Association (EGA), it is 'A term which describes techniques employed by pharmaceutical companies to take advantage of loopholes in the patent and regulatory systems to artificially extend the market monopoly of a product beyond its legitimate patent period.'[76] The word 'loopholes' implies that the act is not illegal in the absence of positive law. It further explains that:

> Evergreening, in one common form, occurs when the brand-name manufacturer literally "stockpiles" patent protection by obtaining separate 20-year patents on multiple attributes of a single product. These patents can cover everything from aspects of the manufacturing process to tablet colour, or even a chemical produced by the body when the drug is ingested and metabolised by the patient.

The EGA notes that through patent strategies, the originator manufacturer forces generic manufacturers 'to choose between waiting for all the patents to expire and applying for marketing authorisation anyway, running the risks of litigation and the associated costs and delays'. For the EGA, therefore, 'evergreening' involves not only patenting behaviour, but also a whole range of conducts to delay the entry of generic products:

> . . . originator laboratories no longer wait until the end of a product's patent life to begin the evergreening process. In order to maximise revenues from their products, pharmaceuticals executives begin preparing strategies to extend patents and stifle generic competition at the outset of product life-cycles. To evergreen their products, the originator company will develop what are euphemistically called "life-cycle management plans" composed not only of patent strategies, but an entire range of practices aimed at limiting or delaying the entry of a generic product onto the market.'[77]

For the EGA, 'Though . . . most of these strategies are, in the strictest sense of the word, legal', some represent 'a misuse of pharmaceuticals patents and the regulations governing authorisation'. It states that 'Evergreening is clearly anti-competitive, results in higher expenditure for Europe's financially burdened healthcare systems, and drives up patient co-payments.' According to the EGA, therefore, most 'evergreening' is anti-competitive; it is however not illegal under competition law. The EGA concludes by asserting that these 'questionable practices', which encompass all the conduct aimed at delaying generics, lead to 'higher prices for patients'.

The recent EU Pharmaceutical Sector Inquiry Final Report (EU Report)[78] refers to the word 'evergreening' mostly as it is used by generic companies, their industry associations and consumer associations. For example, the Report cites

[76] www.egagenerics.com/gen-evergrn.htm.

[77] ibid.

[78] European Commission, Competition DG, EU Pharmaceutical Sector Inquiry: Final Report (Staff Working Paper), 8 July 2009; http://ec.europa.eu/competition/sectors/pharmaceuticals/inquiry/index.html. The Public Consultation on the preliminary report (November 2008) is available at: http://ec.europa.eu/competition/consultations/2009_pharma/index.html.

the criticisms of the Bureau Européen de l'Union des Consommateurs (BEUC), which understands evergreening as embracing a wide range of patenting:

> patent strategies can constitute barriers to the entry of new generic medicines into the market. We are very much concerned by the phenomenon of so-called "evergreening", which describes a specific tactic used by originators to extend patents by seeking to obtain as many patents as possible during the development of the product and the marketing phase, and to obtain patent extensions for new manufacturing processes, new coatings and new uses of established products . . . Originators can also slightly change an active ingredient and present an old medicine as a new product and register a new patent.[79]

The EU Report seems to pay particular attention to the use of the term 'evergreening' in explaining the so-called 'follow-on life-cycle strategies':

> Under certain circumstances the patent strategy might also pursue a more specific objective, namely to facilitate the switch to follow-up inventions or second generation products, criticised as "evergreening" by the generics industry, which will be analysed in more detail in Chapter C.2.6. below.[80]

In Chapter C.2.6, the Report describes certain patent life-cycle strategies 'to facilitate the switch to follow-up inventions or second generation products'.[81] According to the EU Report, the effects of 'research for incremental innovation for top-selling products in their portfolio to ensure further development of their products, sometimes lead to "second generation products"', with the result that 'the new products show little or limited innovation but which serve[s] primarily to retain the revenue streams of the first generation product.'[82] Thus, the EU Report calls those patents (variations on the same molecules) 'secondary patents'. On the other hand, the Report rightly distinguishes umbrella patents from 'follow-on product patents', or 'second generation drugs', and considers these practices to be a type of patent life-cycle strategy. Astrazeneca's Losec (omeprazole; Prilosec in the US) case was the European Commission's first abuse of dominance enforcement case[83] in the pharmaceutical sector, in 2005. According

---

[79] Competition DG, EU Pharmaceutical Sector Inquiry: Final Report (n 78) para 1018.

[80] ibid para 480. Chapter C.2.6 of the EU Report deals with 'follow-on life-cycle strategies'.

[81] Competition DG, EU Pharmaceutical Sector Inquiry: Final Report (n 78) para 988.

[82] ibid para 994.

[83] Astrazeneca was fined for abusing its dominant position by misusing the Community rules for the grant of supplementary patent certificates (SPC) and marketing authorisations to delay generic entry of its ulcer treatment drug Losec (omeprazole). Commission Decision on 15 June 2005 (Case COMP/A. 37. 507/F3). On appeal by Astrazeneca, the General Court (GC) issued its judgment on 1 July 2010, in *AstraZeneca AB and AstraZeneca plc v Commission* (Case T-321/05) which largely upheld the European Commission's decision of 15 June 2005. In the proceedings, Astrazeneca submitted that the Commission erred (i) in defining the relevant market as only that of proton pump inhibitors (PPIs) instead of the combined market for PPIs and histamine receptor antagonists (H2 blockers); and (ii) in finding that there had been abuse in the meaning of Art 102 TFEU. The GC affirmed that the Commission correctly assessed the relevant market as consisting only of PPIs (rejecting that H2 blockers were included) and in basing its market definition on the efficacy, differentiated therapeutic use, price indicators as resulted from the regulatory framework in place. On the question of dominance, the GC agreed with the Commission in finding Astrazeneca's position

to the European Commission's Decision on this case, one of the abuses in the meaning of Article 102 of the Treaty on the Functioning of the European Union (TFEU) is the selective deregistration by Astrazeneca (of Losec capsules and/or the launch of Losec tablets) which removed the reference market authorisation on which generic firms and parallel traders arguably needed to rely to enter and/or remain on the market in Denmark, Norway and Sweden.[84]

The EU Pharmaceutical Sector Report further elaborates on the strategies of originator companies in launching the 'second generation drugs' by the use not only of patents and drug regulatory rules[85] but also by the use of doctors' recommendations and promotion of information. The EU Report claims that this makes it difficult for generics to enter:

> generic companies felt that in this manner originator companies could succeed in "evergreening" their blockbuster medicines well beyond the protection period of the patent covering the active ingredient of the previously marketed product.[86]

of dominance, based particularly on high market share (consistently above 60%) and the fact that AZ was able to price its product higher than rival PPIs while maintaining its market share, which suggested it had market power regarding pricing and reimbursement bodies (para 266). Astrazeneca argued that the making of misleading presentations in the course of applications for supplementary protection certificates (SPCs) cannot amount to an abuse of a dominant position unless or until the dishonestly obtained rights are enforced or are capable of being enforced. The GC held that the submission to the public authorities of misleading information which leads to the grant of an exclusive right to which an undertaking is not entitled or to which it is entitled for a shorter period constitutes a practice that falls outside the scope of competition on the merits and may be particularly restrictive of competition. According to the GC, such conduct is characterised by a manifest lack of transparency (para 493) and is not in keeping with the special responsibility of a dominant undertaking not to impair genuine undistorted competition on the market. The Court also held that there was documentary evidence that corroborates the Commission's findings that Astrazeneca had deliberately tried to mislead the patent offices. It was irrelevant whether or not the misleading representations produced any effects. The Court also upheld the Commission's findings that the selective deregistration of the Losec capsule marketing authorisations amounts to abusive conduct under Art 102 to the extent that it restricted access to the market of generic products and parallel imports. The de-registration was not based on the legitimate protection of an investment and was not required by the conversion of AstraZeneca's sales of Losec capsules to Losec MUPS. The Court however found that the Commission had failed to establish to the requisite legal standard that the de-registrations actually prevented parallel imports of Losec in certain Member States. For this reason, the GC reduced the fine imposed by the Commission from €60 million to €52 million.

[84] Under Art 102 of the TFEU, a dominant position of the product in the relevant market must be proven. In this case, the relevant market was considered as comprising national markets for prescription proton pump inhibitors (PPIs) for gastro-intestinal acid related diseases (eg, ulcers). The Commission examined, inter alia, Astrazeneca's market shares and position as incumbent on the PPI market as well as monopsony buyers (ie national health systems), price regulation and held that, over different periods, Astrazeneca held a dominant position on the PPI market in Belgium, the Netherlands, Norway, Sweden, Denmark, the UK and Germany.

[85] In Astrazeneca's case, the original product (Losec) was withdrawn from the market, which prevented generic entry, as such an entry required a reference product being marketed. The Commission considered that Astrazeneca's behaviour was based on a clear anti-competitive strategy to prevent generics from entering the market, and constituted an abuse. The EU Report seems to consider Nexium (esomeprazole) as a typical example of 'follow-on product patents' strategy to extend the monopoly over Losec.

[86] Competition DG, EU Pharmaceutical Sector Inquiry: Final Report (n 78) para 1315.

The EU Report uses the word 'evergreening' to describe the launch of certain second generation products, not solely through patenting behaviour but also by the use of 'information policies':

> The next few sections will look at promotion and information strategies employed by originator companies to present the advantages of their own products (such as sponsoring conferences or providing training for health professionals), strategies involving next-generation products and "evergreening" combined with an information policy pointing out alleged disadvantages of generic products.

However, more than umbrella patents, second generation drugs often bring remarkable improvements in therapy. For example, the second- and third-generation HIV/AIDS medicines such as Viread(tenofovir) and Kaletra are much more effective in combating HIV resistance than patent expired/expiring first generation products. They are indispensable for second-line treatment and, being patent-protected, part of the dispute over access is because of their efficacy.[87]

In the US, strategies promoting 'line extensions' using 'umbrella patents' as well as 'second generation drugs' are collectively called 'product switching' or 'product hopping' without distinction. Seth and Kara argue that product switching strategies come near to the line of antitrust liability, and they propose setting forth guidance on the characteristics of a product switching claim that would likely survive a court motion to dismiss.[88] As typical cases of 'product switching', they analyse *Abbott v Teva (Abbott Labs)*[89] and *Walgreen v Astrazeneca concerning Prilosec/Nexium (Walgreen)*,[90] and they refer to the ongoing FTC cases, *FTC v Warner Chilcott, FTC v Cephalon, FTC v Watson Pharmaceuticals*,[91] as having underlying concerns over product switching strategies.

The *Abbott Labs* case involved line extension by TriCor tablets. The US district court, under a rule of reason, dismissed the case as not having antitrust claims: the new TriCor formulations had significant benefits; the defendants' conduct had not prevented the generic manufacturers from selling fenofibrate and did not foreclose competition. According to the court, the defendants had no duty to aid competitors under the antitrust laws, and thus, were not required to

---

[87] ibid para 930. However, D Schnichels, European Commission, emphasises that the evaluation of second-generation drugs should rely on a proper health technology assessment. Interview with D Schnichels, 1 June 2010.

[88] S Seth and K Kara, 'Product switching in the pharmaceutical industry: Ripe for antitrust scrutiny?' (2010) 7(2) *Journal of Generic Medicines* 119–30(12). According to the authors, monopolisation under the US antitrust laws contains two elements: (1) the possession of monopoly power in the relevant market and (2) the wilful acquisition or maintenance of that power other than through having a superior product, through possessing business acumen, or by historic accident (*US v Grinnell Corp* 384 US 563 (1966). Attempted monopolisation requires: (1) predatory or anti-competitive conduct, together with (2) the specific intent to monopolise and (3) a dangerous probability of achieving monopoly power (*Spectrum Sports v McQuillan* 506 US 447 (1993)).

[89] *Abbott Laboratories v Teva Pharmaceuticals USA, Inc* 432 F Supp 2d 408 (D Del 2006).

[90] *Walgreen Co v AstraZeneca Pharms* 534 F Supp 2d 146 (DDC 2008).

[91] *Complaint, FTC v Watson Pharms* No CV 09-00598 (CD Cal 27 January 2009), *Complaint, FTC v Cephalon, Inc*, No 08-cv-2141-RBS (DDC 13 February 2008), *Complaint, FTC v Warner Chilcott Holdings Co III*, No 1:05-cv-02179-CKK (DDC 7 November 2005).

aid generic manufacturers in free-riding on TriCor. In the *Walgreen* case, where the prior product (Prilosec) remained on the market, the district court found that consumer choice had not been inhibited and dismissed the antitrust claims. The authors cite J Liebowitz, Chairman of the Federal Trade Commission, in concluding that: 'certain strategies used in connection with launching a new [pharmaceutical] product . . . seem to serve no purpose other than to undermine the ability of a generic to compete', and that such conduct may constitute illegal monopolisation or a violation of section 5 of the FTC Act.[92]

In evaluating the cost of 'evergreening', therapeutic effects and regulatory factors such as price regulations (or the absence thereof) should be taken into account. The US and Europe differ about the impact on the original product after patent expiry. Pharmaceutical companies in the US usually allow the price of the original brand to rise when cheap generics come in (thereby briefly maintaining some profit from prescribers and patients who want to stay with the brand), whereas in Europe there is virtually no possibility of obtaining permission to raise prices of the original medicine to public sector healthcare after patent expiry. The longevity of brands in the face of generics depends on other factors which differ from country to country.

ii When does 'evergreening' occur?

Of the world's top-25 brands by sales value in 2008, 23 were single molecules and one of the two exceptions was esomeprazole, which is a proton pump inhibitor and the S-enantiomer of omeprazole. Chemical structures may sometimes lead to improved therapeutic efficacy (in this case, the single enantiomer over the racemic mixture of omeprazole, which could have been difficult to patent and much effort might have been spent on this) but the improvement in efficacy may be due only to the decreased dose from esomeprazole. An alternative benefit may be the reduction in inter-individual variability in efficacy, but this point may not have been tested clinically.

In the context of North American institutions, M Angel described the ways in which the term of patent protection was extended on the same compound through litigations and settlements within the framework of ANDA (see chapter 10, footnote 28), a six-month extension of patent protection for paediatric testing, for slightly modified OTC versions, different formulations, and for changed target syndromes.[93]

In 2007, the Commission on the Future of Health Care in Canada, or Romanow Commission, which was created in April 2001,[94] recommended that

---

[92] J Leibowitz, 'Tales from the crypt episodes '08 and '09: The return of section 5 (Unfair methods of competition in commerce are hereby declared unlawful)', FTC section 5 workshop (17 October 2008), as cited in Seth and Kara, 'Product switching in the pharmaceutical industry' (n 86) 129.

[93] M Angel, *The Truth About the Drug Companies: How They Deceive Us and What to Do about It*, (New York, Random House, 2004) 173–92.

[94] Canada Privy Council, Order in Council PC 2001-569.

the Federal Government review the pharmaceutical industry practices, particularly that of evergreening, which the Commission described as 'manufacturers of brand name drugs mak[ing] variations to existing drugs in order to extend their patent coverage.' This review was recommended to ensure an appropriate balance between the protection of intellectual property and the need to contain costs and provide Canadians with improved access to non-patented prescription drugs.[95] Of particular focus were the regulations under the patent law requiring generic drug manufacturers to demonstrate that their product is not infringing on a patent held by another drug manufacturer; this leads to 'pre-emptory' lawsuits from patented drug manufacturers as a way of delaying the approval of generic drugs.

'Evergreening' is therefore a concept that is not only about patents but can be intricately related to pharmaceutical regulations concerning drug approval. However vague the concept, 'evergreening' has been an important issue also for developed country governments' health policy, for which cost containment is a necessity.

However, what is the exact harm that evergreening causes? By leaving widely open the definition and the criteria of determining in what sense it is abusive, the word could be applied in a wide variety of situations, some of which cause no economic harm.

iii Under what law could 'evergreening' be a problem?

In the US or Canada, where there is a system of 'patent linkage' based on the Orange Book patent registration,[96] the meaning of 'evergreening' could be more precise, because the abuse takes place within a particular legal framework of the Hatch-Waxman Act[97] in the US (see chapter 11 footnote 28), or the Patented Medicines (Notice of Compliance) Regulations (NOC Regulations) in Canada.[98] In fact, section 156(a)(5)(A) of the US Patent Law has been popularly called an 'anti-evergreening' provision, because it restricts permission to the first permitted commercial marketing or use of the product under the provision of law under in which the regulatory review period occurred, if the product was subject to such a review before its commercial marketing or use.

'Patent linkage' is a practice of linking regulatory approval for a generic medicine to the patent status of the originator product. In the US and Canada all the

---

[95] Recommendation 41 of the Report 'Building on Values: The Future of Health Care in Canada, Final Report' (2002) 208–09; www.cbc.ca/healthcare/final_report.pdf. During the Commission's public hearings, it was pointed out that patented medicines are cheaper on average in Canada than in other jurisdictions, particularly the United States (recent reports suggest that this cost advantage is shrinking) and generics more expensive.

[96] US Patent Act 35 USC §§ 1–376. Drugs approved by the FDA are listed in its 'Approved Drug Products with Therapeutic Equivalence' publication, commonly known as the 'Orange Book.' 21 USC § 355(j)(7)(A) (2006).

[97] Drug Price Competition and Patent Restoration Act of 1984, Pub L No 98-417, 98 Stat 1585 55 (2000).

[98] Patented Medicines (Notice of Compliance) Regulations SOR/93-133 (Can).

patents relating to the originator products are registered and made public and regulators take into account the patent status of the product when approving marketing of generics. This regulatory practice, called 'patent linkage'[99] is not undertaken in the EU, where the basic Directive 2001/83[100] does not count among the tasks of drug regulators checking the patent status of the drug for marketing approval. In Japan, regulators take into account the information on the patent status provided by the originators to ensure stability of generic entry (otherwise infringement disputes are likely to arise against approved generic drugs), but the list is not publicly disclosed.

On the question of patent linkage, the EU Pharmaceutical Sector Inquiry Report says that:

> Under EU law, linking the granting of marketing authorisation for a product to the patent status of an originator company's reference product is unlawful. The task of marketing authorisation bodies is to verify whether a medicinal product is safe, effective and of good quality. Their main function is to ensure that the pharmaceutical products reaching the market are not harmful to public health. Other factors, such as the patent status of the product, should therefore not be taken into account when assessing the risk/benefit balance of a medicine. [101]

In *Bayer v Union of India*,[102] the High Court of Delhi cited the EU Pharmaceutical Sector Inquiry Report as saying 'patent-linkage is considered unlawful under Regulation (EC) No 726/2004 and Directive (EC) No 2001/83'[103] and raised the concern that:

> such patent linkage would have the following undesirable results:
>
> (1) It clothes regulatory authorities, which are executive bodies solely concerned with scientific quality, efficacy and safety issues, with completely new powers, and into areas lack in expertise, i.e. patent rights policing.
>
> (2) It transforms patent rights which are private property rights that depend on the owners' promptitude and desire to enforce them, into public rights, whose enforcement is dependent on statutory authorities, who are publicly funded.
>
> (3) Such linkage potentially undermines the 'Bolar/Early Working' exception that encourage quick access to the post patent markets for generic medicines. This is a major public policy consideration in India, which faces a host of public health challenges.

---

[99]   See chs 11 p 408, chs 4, 10 and 13.

[100]   Directive (EC) 2001/83 on the Community code relating to medicinal products for human use [2004] OJ L136.

[101]   EU Pharmaceutical Sector Inquiry Final Report, para 872. Art 81 of Regulation (EC) 726/2004 and Art 126 of Directive (EC) 2001/83 provides that an authorisation to market a medicinal product shall not be refused, suspended or revoked except on the grounds set out in the Regulation and the Directive. Considering that patent status is not included in the grounds set out in the Regulation and the Directive, it cannot be used as an argument to refuse, suspend or revoke a marketing authorisation. The Commission may launch infringement proceedings against any Member State which infringes the Directive.

[102]   *Bayer v Union of India* WP(C) No 7833/2008, 18 August 2009. Subsequently, Bayer appealed to the Supreme Court and a hearing is scheduled for 30 November 2010. 1 December 2010, the Supreme Court of India dismissed the appeal filed by Bayer.

[103]   *Bayer v Union of India* (n 102) 78.

(4) Article 27 of TRIPS requires that patents are made available without discrimination by field of technology. As the patent linkage system is not available outside of the pharmaceutical sector, or in the US, even for biologic products, extending it, as is sought, would potentially violate Article 27, without any debate, or mandate of law.[104]

The reason the EU Pharmaceutical Sector Inquiry Report characterises patent linkage as 'unlawful' is because of the way Article 126 of Directive (EC) 2001/83 was transposed into national law,[105] rather than from the substantive law point of view. The Commission, upon complaint by a stakeholder, started proceedings in 2006 against Slovakia[106] concerning section 22 of the Slovakian Medicinal Law, which provided a system of linkage, but the case was withdrawn after the amendment of this provision in 2008. The case of Portugal is explained in the EU Pharmaceutical Sector Inquiry Report as an example of litigation against the Portuguese authorities' decisions,[107] but the Commission has not taken any action due to its lack of competence to verify infringement, as court decisions are either pending or not consistent.

There have been court decisions in the US and Canada in which judges referred to 'evergreening' as undue extension of the statutory monopoly attached to drug product by means of listing on the patent register multiple patents with obvious or uninventive modifications the patentee prolongs its monopoly beyond what the public has agreed to pay. The Federal Trade Commission (FTC), for its part, prosecuted a case of Taxol, BuSpar and Platinol[108] under section 5 of the FTC Act for improper Orange Book listings of patents and unlawful agreements in restraint of trade. Simply 'building a patent umbrella' around a basic product patent, by contrast, would be legal, unless there is illegal conduct (for example, anticompetitive under competition law) involved in doing so. Normally in the US and Europe, aggressive generic entry is achieved and, therefore, various umbrella patents are economically not harmful for cost containment, unless they are used as a means to extend a monopoly. The economic impact of evergreening would be much more than marginal, if there is 'abuse of dominant position' in the relevant market or extension of monopoly in the sense of competition law by exclusionary behaviour. This points to the fact, first, that 'evergreening' refers to a wide scope of practices for which there is no consensus. Second, these practices individually have different economic effects, which could be negative or positive. Third, there may be instances of 'evergreening' that constitute abuse of IPRs or

---

[104] ibid 79. For *Bolar* exemption, see chs 5 and 7.

[105] Interview with D Schnichels, Competition Directorate, European Commission, in Brussels on 1 June 2010.

[106] Letter 2006/4893.

[107] Examples of litigations in Portugal, Competition DG, EU Pharmaceutical Sector Inquiry: Final Report (n 81) para 917, 330–11.

[108] *In the Matter of Bristol-Myers Squibb Co*, File Nos 0010221 (Taxol), 0110046 (BuSpar), 0210181 (Cisplatin), Consent Agreement, FTC Press Release 7 March 2003. For payment of a would-be generic rival of over $70 million not to bring any competing products to market; and filed baseless patent infringement lawsuits to deter entry by generics.

anticompetitive abuse, but these cases should be examined individually, based on the facts of each case.

Following the above Romanow (Canada) Commission recommendation, RA Bouchard empirically analysed patent/registration/drug development strategies for 95 drugs.[109] There were 40 patents per drug, approximately 5 per cent of which were listed on the patent register, apparently for the purpose of preventing generic entry. The study shows the linkage regime of patenting, patent listing and patent classifications of drugs receiving the Price Review, represents a flexible tool for sophisticated firms to identify rapidly attractive drug targets for legal protection, particularly during the regulatory approval stage, to obtain extended legal protection on drugs at all stages of development, including drugs about to come off patent protection, drugs moving through the regulatory approval stage, and drugs that are currently in development. However, no improper conduct was observed and the authors draw attention rather to the failure of policy incentives intended to induce the desired result. A study was undertaken to examine whether the NOC Regulations are serving their stated goal, which is to stimulate new and innovative drug development and facilitate timely entry of generic products. The study concludes that incentives designed to stimulate innovation in the pharmaceutical industry have had the opposite effect and that shifting to a 'life-cycle' regulatory model is unlikely to alter this scenario absent effort to balance economic incentives for breakthrough and follow-on drug development.

'Evergreening' therefore seems to cover an extremely wide range of questions which cannot be analysed even under several laws. For example, the European Commission's focus on 'second generation' drugs as the main form of evergreening is not really related to patenting, but to how the 'second generation' is clinically more effective than the first blockbuster. If there were anticompetitive behaviour, it might be competition authorities that would be able to determine this, and if the efficacy is the question, it would be doctors and regulatory authorities, not patent offices, who might be able to arrive at the substantive value of 'second generation' drugs or 'secondary patents'.

The EU Pharmaceutical Inquiry Report did not contain any analysis of anticompetitive behaviour under the EU law, nor did it explain what competition criteria are useful in distinguishing abuses from normal exercise of exclusive rights conferred by patents or how to deal with ineffective or unproductive R&D.[110] Concerning the therapeutic value of medicines, it is not only markets which judge the quality and value, but also professional 'detailing' by sales representatives to doctors. With the rapid growth of generics (which are sold on price without promotion to doctors, unless they are 'branded generics'), and the increasing emphasis by health authorities on proof of cost-effectiveness, the growth of

---

[109] RA Bouchard, MD, 'I'm Still Your Baby: Canada's Continuing Support of U.S. Linkage Regulations For Pharmaceuticals' http://works.bepress.com/cgi/viewcontent.cgi?article=1000&context=ron_bouchard.

[110] Public comment by author, http://ec.europa.eu/competition/consultations/2009_pharma/hirokoyamane.pdf.

drugs without much therapeutic value is beginning to falter. Sophisticated evaluation by informed consumers will also be a good judge of 'evergreening'.

The above suggests that the best criteria for judging whether or not a particular instance of 'evergreening' is abusive may not be the patent law. Major 'evergreening' cases seem to be occurring at the later stages of product development or marketing and not at the time of patent filing.

The European Commission's focus of its criticism on the 'second generation' drugs as the main form of evergreening is not really related to patenting but to how the 'second generation' is clinically more effective than the first blockbuster. On the other hand, they may indeed be used as anti-competitive means to stop generic entry, whereas the therapeutic amelioration may not be sufficient. However, it is unlikely that restricting the patentabilitity of new use and derivatives of known compounds necessarily encourages competition in the product market. Patenting can be procompetitive or anticompetitive in the relevant technology market, but does not directly influence competition in the product market. At the time of patent filing, patent examiners would not normally be able to foresee and analyse the competition in the product markets.

D Implementation of Section 3(d)

How has the anti-evergreening provision, section 3(d) of the Patent (Amendment) Acts 2005, been interpreted by Indian courts?

Since 2005, certain high-profile court cases involving pharmaceutical companies have given rise to discussions on the meaning of section 3(d). In the *Novartis v Union of India* case concerning Gleevec, the relationship between section 3(d) and the patentabililty criteria of novelty, inventive step and industrial application, provided in Article 27.1 of the TRIPS Agreement, were discussed, and in the *Roche v Cipla* case concerning Tarceva, the ways in which section 3(d) is relied on by the defendant in the infringement suit. It seems that section 3(d) plays an important role when courts examine the validity of patents.

Together with the more transparent information on patents granted on the Indian Patent Office website today, these court discussions offer a wealth of materials for reflecting on the meaning of TRIPS flexibilities implemented domestically.

i Section 3(d) and the case of Novartis v Union of India

The imatinib mesylate compound (mesylate salt) was filed for patent in Switzerland in 1992.[111] The European patent[112] was granted to imatinib mesylate, free form, and was published in 1993. While the free form of Gleevec was known,[113] its methansulphonic acid addition salt (mesylate), in particular its

---

[111] CH 1083/92.
[112] EP-A-O 564409.
[113] Example 21 of EP 564409.

β-crystal form, was not known in the European patent. Novartis claimed that the β-crystal form of imatinib mesylate shows better properties than the alpha-crystal or amorphous forms, in terms of flow properties, processability, stability and hygroscopic properties. Subsequently, the β crystalline form (polymorph) was filed in 1997 in Switzerland and obtained patents in around 40 countries. In 1998, Novartis filed an application in India for a product patent on the beta-crystalline form of imatinib mesylate (imatinib mesylate) claiming this post-1995 polymorph. As India did not recognise product patents for pharmaceuticals before 1 January 2005, this application was made via the mailbox system, to be examined only after 2005. In 2003, Novartis obtained exclusive marketing rights (EMR; see chapter 5 for Article 70.9 of the TRIPS Agreement) for imatinib mesylate based on this patent application.[114] As there were already several Indian generic companies producing this product, Novartis sued on the strength of the EMR of several Indian generic companies (Ranbaxy, Cipla, Sun Pharmaceuticals, etc) before the High Courts of Madras and Mumbai. The Madras High Court granted an order of injunction, but the court in Mumbai did not.[115] According to Basheer and Reddy, the fact that Novartis offered a free patient access programme for Gleevec was one of the grounds on which the Madras Court upheld the EMR.[116] In the meantime, against Novartis' patent application in India, pre-grant opposition was filed under section 25(1) of the Indian Patents Act by Natco and others[117] and by patient groups. The opposition was based mainly on the grounds that the invention lacks novelty because the 1993 prior art patent ('Gleevec free form patent') discloses and claims pharmaceutically acceptable (acid-addition) salt. The opposition also stated that producing the 1998 β-crystalline form of imatinib mesylate was easy, and therefore lacked an inventive step.

To show the stability of Gleevec mesylate β-crystalline form for industrial production, Novartis submitted to the Opposition Division of the IPO the studies in which Natco found that Gleevec mesylate itself was published in *Nature Medicine* (5 May, 1996) and in US patent 5,521,184. These studies also showed results of experiments conducted by the Indian Institute of Chemical Technology and the Indian Institute of Technology that demonstrated that the salt exists in the β-crystalline form and can be easily obtained. The Opposition Division decided that the claims of Novartis' application were anticipated by prior publication. By the patentability criteria of any country, 'anticipation' destroys novelty, and sometimes inventive step. Importantly, Novartis' application of

---

[114] There was no disclosure of information on which applicants were granted EMR. It is said that the following four pharmaceutical products and one agricultural chemicals were granted EMR: Imatinib mesylate (Novartis), Nadifloxacin (Wockhardt), Cialis (Ely Lilly) and Carbendazin (United Phosphorous).

[115] S Basheer and TP Reddy, 'The "Efficacy" of Indian Patent Law: Ironing out the Creases in Section 3(d)' (2008) 5(2) *Script* 236 fn 17. According to these authors, the fact that Novartis was more expensive than the local products, and that the drug was imported by Novartis, influenced the Court in Mumbai.

[116] ibid 236.

[117] No 1602/MAS/98, 17 July 1998.

Gleevec mesylate β-crystalline form would therefore not have been accepted on the grounds of the lack of novelty and inventive step, regardless of section 3(d).

The IPO Controller's Order in January 2006 rejected Novartis' patent application for the reason, inter alia, that the applicant's invention was only a form of a known substance,[118] which does not satisfy the requirements for patentability unless they differ significantly in properties with regard to efficacy.[119] In other words, the applicant did not indicate that the β-crystalline polymorph 'differs significantly in properties with respect to efficacy' from the other forms of the imatinib mesylate compound, and thus under section 3(d) of the Patents Act, the β-crystalline form of Imatinib mesylate must be considered to be the 'same substance' as the unpatentable generic compound. The IPO had held that the product claimed by Novartis lacked novelty and inventive steps, and also failed to show increased efficacy over the known substance.

Subsequently, Novartis filed multiple challenges in the Madras High Court. It challenged not only the decision of the Patent Office rejecting its application, but also section 3(d) of the Patents Act. Novartis argued that section 3(d) was vague and therefore arbitrarily applied, which is not compatible with section 14 of the Constitution of India concerning equality of rights of citizens before the law. Novartis also argued that section 3(d) was not in compliance with the TRIPS Agreement, because it takes away the right to have an invention patented, which is guaranteed under Article 27 of the Agreement.

According to Novartis, section 3(d) does not refer to an obligation of the applicant to disclose the invention in a manner sufficiently clear and complete for the invention to be carried out[120] and therefore should not be added as a fourth requirement for patentability. Novartis argued also that the expressions 'enhancement of the known efficacy' and 'differ significantly in properties with regard to efficacy' in section 3(d) are ambiguous, leaving 'the Statutory Authority to exercise its power to its whims and fancies'. Novartis claimed that this provision is irrational and does not conform to section 14 of the Indian Constitution. According to Novartis, a considerable number of other applicants have been granted patents for derivatives similar to these. In 2007, the Madras High Court rejected Novartis' challenge to section 3(d) and held that it had no jurisdiction to determine the issue of TRIPS compatibility. In determining the issue of constitutional validity, the Court held that the word 'efficacy' used in section 3(d) had a definite meaning in the pharmaceutical field.[121]

---

[118] The IPO decision was based notably on the argument that the solubility difference between the α and the β forms is insignificant, the α form is not suitable for making solid dosage form and therefore is devoid of utility and therefore not an invention, Novartis' specification mainly focused on the β form and only the negative aspects of the α form and states that the α form is metastable/hygroscopic and hence not suitable for manufacture of solid dosage forms, and no best mode of preparing the claimed invention is provided.

[119] Explanation to s 3(d) of the Patents Act.

[120] Art 29 of the TRIPS Agreement which concerns 'Conditions on Patent Applicants' stipulates in para 1, the requirement of enablement (see ch 5).

[121] In the High Court of Judicature at Madras, 6 August 2007, *Novartis v Union of India* (n 41).

The set of appeals filed by Novartis challenging the Madras Patent Office's decision was transferred from the Madras High Court to the Intellectual Property Appeals Board (IPAB) which was established in July 2002. After hearings conducted before the IPAB in December 2002, the IPAB passed its order in June 2009.[122]

At the hearing, the defendants presented various justifications for section 3(d). The Government of India and some other parties argued against 'evergreening'. The Indian Government justified section 3(d) by saying that the decision was intended to balance patent protection with the public interest.[123] Other defendants invoked not only citizens' access to 'life-saving drugs'[124] but also technical reasons, ie that the intention of the provision is to ensure that 'the technological and scientific research oriented advances already made and likely to be made in the coming future and which may be a continuing process for all time to come' are checked.

The IPAB reversed the findings of the Patent Controller on novelty and inventive step. It held that the imatinib salt is novel and that the β form had surprising results compared with the α form that would not be obvious to a person skilled in the art. It also allowed Novartis to proceed with certain process claims. On the efficacy in the meaning of section 3(d), however, the IPAB stated that the enhanced water solubility of the α crystal form (632 gm/l) compared with the β crystal form (605 gm/l) of about 30 per cent, was insignificant. The IPAB held that Novartis was not entitled to a patent on imatinib mesylate, as its claimed product did not meet the requirements of section 3(d), notably that of 'increased efficacy', which both the Madras High Court and IPAB held to mean 'therapeutic efficacy'. According to the IPAB, section 3(d) of the Indian Patents (Amendment) Act 2005, provides 'a higher standard of inventive step' and a public interest safeguard and that the Novartis invention falls under section 3(d).[125] Novartis appealed to the Supreme Court. While the case was pending, hearings kept being postponed[126] and no judgment had been rendered as of 15 November 2010.

ii Section 3(d) and the case of Roche v Cipla

In *Roche v Cipla*[127] (concerning the Tarceva patent granted by the Indian Patent Office) at the Delhi High Court, the defendant Cipla took on the issue of

---

[122] IPAB Decision *Novartis v Union of India* (n 37).

[123] While generic versions were available for around Rs 8,000 to Rs 12,000 per month, Novartis sold its version at Rs 120,000 per month. However, Novartis continued its donation programmes directly with patients.

[124] 'We have borne in mind the object which the Amending Act wanted to achieve namely, to prevent evergreening; to provide easy access to the citizens of this country to life saving drugs and to discharge their Constitutional obligation of providing good health care to it's citizens'; *Novartis v Union of India* (n 41) para 19.

[125] *Novartis v Union of India* (n 41).

[126] 'Natco & Ranbaxy delay proceedings in the Glivec case before the Supreme Court', Spicy IP (26 July 2010).

[127] *Roche v Cipla, On interlocutory injunction:* in the High Court of Delhi at New Delhi, judgment by a single judge on 19 March 2008 (6442/2008 IN CS(OS) 89/2008) and by the Division Bench on 24 April 2009 (FAO (OS) 188/2008)) On substance: Judgment is pending as of 1 November 2010.

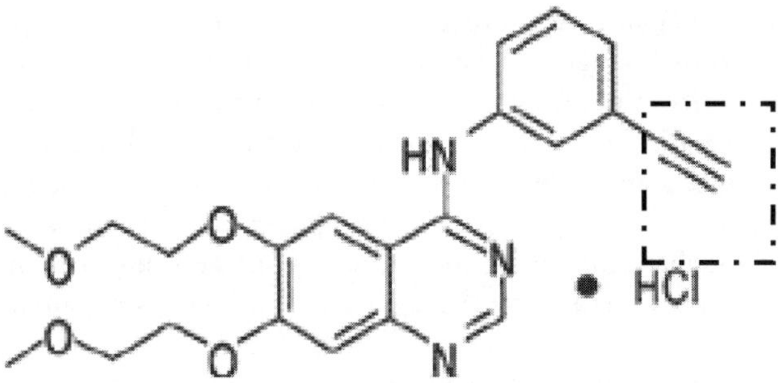

Figure 12.3: Erlotinib structure

'evergreening'. Tarceva (erlotinib) is a small molecule medicine indicated for the treatment of patients with locally advanced or metastatic non-small cell lung cancer after failure of at least one prior chemotherapy regimen (see chapter 9). Cipla contended that erlotinib does not represent an inventive step over gefitinib, although their impact on non-small-cell-lung cancer (NSCLC) is very similar. Erlotinib is probably 'slightly more effective' than gefitinib. In the UK, erlotinib together with gemcitabine is indicated for pancreatic cancer whereas gefitinib (Iressa) is approved only for NSCLC. Erlotinib WO and US patents are in force and generally regarded as valid.

Tarceva is marketed in India by Hoffman-La Roche (Roche), which filed for a patent in India on 13 March 1996 and was granted Indian patent 196774, registered on 13 July 2007. Pre-grant opposition from Natco had been rejected by the Indian Patent Office (IPO) on 4 July 2007.[128] The first HER1/EGFR inhibitor was Iressa (gefitinib), which was approved by the US FDA on 5 June 2003. Astrazeneca applied for a patent for Iressa in India but the IPO denied it on the grounds of prior use. In 2008, after the registration of the Tarceva patent, Cipla started producing Erloticip. Roche sued Cipla at the Delhi High Court for infringing its patent and requested an interlocutory injunction.[129]

Cipla argued that the IPO ought not to have granted a patent for erlotinib, which is a derivative, a mere isostere[130] of known compound gefitinib,[131] and does not satisfy the criteria of being novel and non-obvious. Cipla claimed that in erlotinib, Roche replaced the methyl group at a metha position of a phenyl ring – indicated by the dotted rectangle in Figure 12.3 – by the ethynyl group

---

[128] Natco's pre-grant opposition was filed on 10 April 2007 on the grounds mainly of obviousness and insufficient disclosure.and was rejected by the IPO on 4 July 2007. Natco cited EP 0566226A1, EP 06335507A1, EP 0635498A1, and EP 0520722A1 to support its obviousness arguments. http://patentcircle.blogspot.com/2009/02/minor-modification-structural_19.html.

[129] 2008 (37) PTC 71 (Del).

[130] When two sets of molecules or ions having the identical number of atoms and valence electrons have equivalent chemical activities, they are called isosteres.

[131] Iressa was the first HER/EGFR advanced-stage non-small cell lung cancer drug and was approved by the FDA on 5 June 2003.

of gefitinib. For Cipla, this is 'evergreening', which is contrary to public policy and to the statutory language employed in section 3(d) of the Act. According to Cipla, the Tarceva patent was also against 'national interests in the context of the pharmaceutical industry'.[132] Roche argued that the Tarceva compound is new, which was recognised by the IPO's examination of its patent application as well as by the fact that Natco's pre-grant opposition[133] was rejected by the IPO. Whether or not chemical compounds are the same depends not only on different scientific criteria but also on the legal construction of the patent law, as this case shows.

It is possible to consider the methyl group as a derivative of the ethynyl group. On the other hand, the two molecules of gefitinib and erlotinib appear substantially different according to the Merck Index.[134] In fact, therefore, erlotinib's relation to gefitinib is not 'evergreening', but 'me-too'. Normally, the substitution of similar side chains (methyl and ethynyl) could be regarded as separate inventions' but in a 'me-too' sense. All would depend on therapeutic differences, if any. These seem to exist (modestly) between erlotinib and gefitinib, but probably not much between omeprazole and esomeprazole.

In deciding whether the injunction should be granted to Roche, the single judge applied the *American Cyanamid*[135] principle of the House of Lords. On the basis of this principle, the plaintiff would be entitled to a permanent injunction, taking into consideration the following elements; (i) if there is a serious issue to be tried, (ii) after the court had considered where 'the balance of convenience' lies in the terms of the interlocutory injunction sought, and (iii) where there was a doubt as to the parties' respective remedies in damages being adequate to compensate them for loss occasioned by any restraint imposed on them, it would be prudent to preserve the status quo. The House of Lords in *American Cyanamid* substituted for the above element (i) the consideration of whether 'a prima facie case of infringement had been made', which had to be taken into consideration according to the traditional case law. This was achieved with a view to avoiding lengthy 'mini-trials' on infringement at the stage where only the question of ordering the injunction is to be decided.

The single judge of the Delhi High Court referred to the ongoing discussions regarding *Novartis AG v Union of India*,[136] from which he inferred that in the Indian Patents (Amendment) Act 2005, the test of patentability became more precise and specific than in the past by including not only the requirement of an inventive step but also section 3(d).[137] He also examined under what conditions the validity of granted patents could be presumed under the Indian law, and concluded that the mere granting of a patent does not guarantee its validity if

---

[132]   *Rohe v Cipla* (n 127) para 11.
[133]   Dated 4 July 2007.
[134]   See chemical formulae in Merck Index 14th edn, items 3672 and 4379.
[135]   *American Cyanamid Co v Ethicon Ltd* [1975] All ER 504.
[136]   *Novartis v Union of India* (n 41).
[137]   *Roche v Cipla* (n 127) para 57.

an opposition is filed by the defendant on which his counter-claim is based.[138] The defendant's counter-claim was that erlotinib is a derivative of a known compound and that the plaintiff did not sufficiently describe the inventive step. The defendant alleged that the plaintiff underplayed the presence of the ethynyl substitution, suggested in prior patent EP 0635507 (1995), which the IPO ignored. The IPO, according to the single judge, compared the plaintiff's application only with gefitinib. The judge referred to the *KSR* criteria[139] in examining whether there is an inventive step in the plaintiff's patent and concluded that the defendant's contention appeared plausible,[140] although the judge should refrain from conducting a trial regarding the validity of the patent at the interlocutory stage.

In examining the balance of convenience, the judge examined various factors that the Indian courts have considered, such as non-manufacturing (only importing) the product in India as well as the 'six-year' rule preventing the court from granting an interim injunction.[141] He further cited the US Supreme Court in *eBay v MercExchange*,[142] which said that courts should not issue injunctions automatically but adopt a rule of caution. More concretely, he said the court should consider the traditional four-factor test for the issuance of an injunction: the existence of a prima facie case of infringement, the balance of convenience, irreparable injury and public interest.

It is in this legal context that the judge referred to the situation in India, where about 90,000 men and 79,000 women suffer annually from lung cancer. If an injunction in the case of a life-saving drug were to be granted, he stated, the court would in effect be stifling Article 21 of the Indian Constitution for those who would have or could have access to Erlocip, which is one-third of the price of Tarceva. Such injuries to third parties are uncompensatable. The court therefore refused to grant an interim injunction, stating that:

> between the two competing public interests, that is, the public interest in granting an injunction to affirm a patent during the pendency of an infringement action, as opposed to the public interest in access for the people to a life saving drug, the balance has to be tilted in favour of the latter.[143]

---

[138] *Bilcare v Amartara Pvt Ltd* 2007 (34) PTC 419 (Del).

[139] *KSR International Co v Teleflex Inc* 550 US 398 (2007). In *KSR v Teleflex*, the US Supreme Court corrected the Court of Appeals for the Federal Circuit (CAFC)'s understanding and application criteria of the 'teaching, suggestion or motivation (TSM) test' in evaluating the inventive step. According to the Supreme Court, the question was not whether the combination was obvious to the patentee, but to a person skilled in the art with ordinary creativity, and whether any needs or problem known in the field of endeavour at the time of invention and addressed by the patent must constitute a reason for combining the elements in the manner claimed. In other words, the US Supreme Court accepted the TSM test in principle, but criticised its rigid application, which would make patentable any combination predictable from prior art. According to the Supreme Court, the error committed by the CAFC was in judging from the patentee's point of view and not from that of a person skilled in the art, and imagining a mechanical person skilled in the art led only by the prior art, rather than a person who has ordinary creativity and can grasp the design needs and pressure from the market.

[140] *Roche v Cipla* (n 127) para 78.

[141] ibid paras 62–63.

[142] *eBay v MercExchange* 547 US 338 (2006).

[143] *Roche v Cipla* (n 127) para 86.

Roche and OSI Pharmaceuticals appealed the above judgment of the single judge to the Division Bench of the New Delhi High Court. The defendant continued to argue that the erlotinib patent was 'completely invalid' because it was a derivative of a known patent, 'quinazoline', and simply a derivative of Astrazeneca's gefitinib, for which a patent was refused in India, and whose enhanced efficacy was not proven. Cipla also argued that the pre-conditions for a recently granted patent claim to be protected were not fulfilled, because Tarceva was imported and the patent therefore was not 'worked fully and commercially' In India. Cipla contended that Tarceva was neither easily available nor affordable due to its high pricing.

In examining whether the plaintiffs had a prima facie case for obtaining an injunction, new factors, unexamined by the single judge, were also brought to the attention of the Bench. According to the defendant, Tarceva tablets are wholly a β polymorph of the hydrochloride salt of N-(3-ethynylphenyl)-6, 7 bis(2-methoxyethoxy)-4-quinazolinamine, which corresponds to the pending patent applications and not the granted patent No 196774. Cipla argued that Tarceva is also produced in β polymorph, for which there is no Indian patent and therefore is outside of Roche's patent for Tarceva, because β polymorph is not patented. Cipla contended that the plaintiffs suppressed the material facts to obtain the patent by by-passing the provisions of section 3(d).[144] According to Roche, β polymorph is thermodynamically more stable and helps in providing improved oral dosage in solid form, which is considered an incremental innovation in countries with laws like the US, but unlikely to be patented in India due to section 3(d). The Division Bench found that the defendant had been able to demonstrate prima facie that the plaintiffs did not yet hold a patent for the drug Tarceva, the β polymorph form of a substance for which they did hold a patent. The Bench further concluded that the defendant had raised a credible challenge to the validity of the patent held by the plaintiffs.

The Division Bench of the Delhi High Court held that section 3(d) in 2005 was modified to add significant changes to the Patents Act. According to the Court:

> Not only has the substantive portion of Section 3(d) indicated a change in 2005 but the Explanation which has been added appears to particularly target pharmaceutical products. It discourages evergreening and prevents such derivative or other forms of the already patented product being granted patent unless the derivatives or other forms 'differ significantly in properties in regard to efficacy'.

The Court accepted the defendant's argument that the closest prior art (EP'226) does teach the Tarceva compound. This means it is a derivative of a known substance of which the plaintiff did not demonstrate enhanced efficacy as mandated by section 3(d). In summarising the Single Judge's conclusion, the Division Bench asserted that:

> Section 3(d) of the Patents Act, 1970 was not merely clarificatory of the pre-existing law as contended by the plaintiffs. The Parliament consciously enacted a standard of known

---

[144] *Roche v Cipla* (n 127) para 19.

obviousness as a pre-condition of patentability; it also excluded the derivatives of known substances unless they differed significantly in properties with regard to efficacy.[145]

According to the Division Bench, 'Section 3(d) itself raises several barriers to the grant of a patent particularly in the context of pharmaceutical products. It proceeds on the footing [that] inventions are essentially for public benefit and that non-inventions should not pass off as inventions', and the Tarceva patent should be scrutinised in the light of section 3(d) when a substantial question of validity would be examined at the later stage.[146] The Indian courts seem to emphasise the criteria set out in the Explanation of section 3(d) as specifically for pharmaceutical products. Thus, the Division Bench in *Roche v Cipla* repeated that: 'Not only has the substantive portion of section 3(d) indicated a change in 2005 but the Explanation which has been added appears to particularly target pharmaceutical products.'[147] The Court, therefore, seriously questioned the validity of the patent granted to Tarceva.

In balancing the convenience, the Division Bench also referred to the US Supreme Court decision on *eBay v MercExchange* and held that public interest should be taken into account. The plaintiff argued that not respecting the rights of a patentee would be contrary to the public interest, because it would discourage further research. This would discourage the required disclosure that is inherent in the patent regime, thereby creating a situation where opportunity for further innovation based on fundamental research on an existing patent product/process would be lost or unduly deferred.[148] The Court held that 'whether the public interest in the availability of the drug to the public at large is outweighed by the need to encourage research in the invention, would obviously differ from case to case and depend on a host of factors', but in this case the single judge analysed 'all the relevant factors'. In arriving at the conclusion that the price difference of the products of the plaintiffs and the defendants also could not be ignored, the Court mentioned the general principles applicable to the working of patented inventions which the amendment to the Patent Act 1970 in 2005 introduced: section 83(e) states that patents granted do not in any way prohibit Central Government from taking measures to promote public health, and section 83(g) states that patents are granted to make the benefit of the patented invention available at reasonably affordable prices to the public. The Court further affirmed that section 84 provides that a person may seek compulsory licences, if the patented invention is not available to the public at reasonably affordable price. All these provisions, according to the Court, show that public interest is not alien to the scheme of the Patents Act 1970 (see chapter 10).

The appeal was dismissed and the costs, evaluated at Rs 500,000 were borne by the plaintiffs. Subsequently, Roche filed a special leave petition at the Indian Supreme Court challenging this order passed by the Division Bench of the Delhi

---

[145] ibid para 24.
[146] *Roche v Cipla* (n 127) para 52–55.
[147] ibid para 60.
[148] *Roche v Cipla* (n 127) para 72.

High Court. On 28 August 2009, the Court dismissed the petition, apparently because there was also a trial underway in the generic erlotinib case. It ordered that the ongoing trial at the Delhi High Court be expedited[149].

The above court cases suggest that the provisions in section 3(d) seem to serve the arguments of those defendants in infringement suits in claiming the invalidity of the contested patents. The Indian Patent Office (IPO) used section 3(d) in a few cases where pre-grant or post-grant oppositions were made (see chapter 10). The case of oseltamivir (Tamiflu) was a case in point. In the following part, TRIPS conformity of section 3(d) will be explored by looking into how the IPO has examined patent applications.

E Consistency of Section 3(d) with the TRIPS Agreement

The Indian Patents Act, amended in 2002 and 2005 to conform to the TRIPS Agreement, offers a wealth of suggestions concerning the use of the flexibilities contained in Article 27 of the TRIPS Agreement. Section 3(d) of the Indian Patents (Amendment) Act 2005, in particular, seems to have been adopted by the Indian legislature consciously to limit patentability so that certain market results would be achieved. In the process of amending the Indian Patents Act in the 1990s, there were arguments that minor inventions should be divided into use, selection or analogy inventions, to deny them patentability.[150] This approach, however, was scrutinised and found not to conform to Article 27.1 of the TRIPS Agreement and, as a result of a compromise, the amendment to section 3(d), with an Explanation on the derivatives, was adopted.

i Exclusion of certain forms of inventions?

While the Amendments Bill was still under Parliamentary discussion, issues regarding the definition of 'pharmaceutical substance' to mean only 'a new chemical entity (NCE)' and 'new medical entity (NME)' in draft section (d) and the patentability of microorganisms were raised. The Commerce and Industry Minister then assured the Parliament that he would refer these issues to an Expert Committee for detailed examination and report the matter to the Parliament. Accordingly, a Technical Expert Group (TEG) Committee on Patent Law Issues (often called the Mashelkar Committee, after the Chairperson) was set up by the Ministry of Commerce & Industry, Department of Industrial Policy & Promotion (DIPP) on 4 April 2005.[151] The terms of reference of the Group were: whether it would be TRIPS compatible to limit the grant of patent for a pharmaceutical substance to a new chemical entity or to a new medical entity

---

[149] The judgment on validity by the High Court is pending as of 30 November 2010.

[150] S Chaudhuri, 'TRIPS Agreement and Amendment of Patents Act in India,' *Economic and Political Weekly* (10 August 2002).

[151] OM No 12/14/2005-IPR-III.

involving one or more inventive steps; and whether it would be TRIPS compatible to exclude microorganisms from patenting (see chapter 10 p 459).

The Report of the TEG Committee was published in December 2006 but was the subject of criticism on the grounds, among others, of plagiarism,[152] and was rewritten. The final version of the Report was made public in March 2009 (hereafter 2009 Mashelkar Report)[153]. Certain paragraphs were deleted from the 2006 Report, notably including the following paragraphs from the section of the Report entitled 'National Interest Perspective':

5.9 If the aim of limiting patents to new chemical entities is to prevent a phenomenon loosely referred to as 'evergreening', this can be done by a proper application of patentability criteria as present in the current patent regime.

5.10 It is important to distinguish 'evergreening' from what is commonly referred to as 'incremental innovation'. While 'ever-greening' refers to an extension of a patent monopoly, achieved by executing trivial and insignificant changes to an already existing patented product, 'incremental innovations' are sequential developments that build on the original patented product and may be of tremendous value in a country like India. Therefore, such incremental developments ought to be encouraged by the Indian patent regime.

5.12 In case of patenting of drugs, the protection to various forms of [sic] same substance (salts, esters, ethers, polymorphs, metabolites, pure form, particle size, isomers, mixture, etc.) is often seen as 'evergreening' (extending incremental protection to a subsisting patent) and hence such protection is objected to.

Over 30 new paragraphs were inserted in the 2009 Mashelkar Committee Report, including the following. 'The committee was not mandated to examine the TRIPS compatibility of section 3(d) of the Indian Patents Act or any other existing provision in the same Act and, therefore, the committee has not engaged itself in studying these issues'.[154]The 2009 Report examines section 3(d) from the point of view of TRIPS flexibilities. Thus, new paragraph 5.7 of the Report states that:

Through various submissions that TEG had received, as well as the study of the published literature, TEG found a number of analyses and views on the TRIPS flexibilities. However, from a developing world perspective, it is important to note at this stage the conclusions in a Report by South Centre, which is an 'Intergovernmental Policy Think Tank of Developing Countries'. . . . The Report is authored by a well known international authority on IPR and its role in development, Prof. Carlos Correa, entitled 'Integrating Public Health Concerns into Patent Legislation in Developing Countries'.[155]

---

[152] 'Scrap Mashelkar Report, Demand Scientists, NGOs', *The Hindu* (3 April 2007).
[153] Report of the Technical Expert Group on Patent Law Issues (Revised March 2009) http://www.patentoffice.nic.in/RevisedReport_March2009.doc
[154] Paragraph 5.11 of the 2009 Mashelkar Report.
[155] The following URL is quoted in the Mashelkar Committee 2009 Report: www.who.int/medicinedocs/fr/d/Jh2963e/6.html. According to Business Standard ('Mashelkar report runs into fresh controversy' (New Delhi, 21 August 2009)), Correa 'feels that a WTO member-country has the flexibility to prevent patent protection to incremental innovations in pharmaceuticals that are non-inventive but the result of routine experimentation and known techniques' and that his article was misquoted.

The 2009 Mashelkar Committee Report examines the Declaration on the TRIPS Agreement and Public Health (Doha Declaration), in the light of the analyses in the above Report, ie, compulsory licensing and the interpretative methods according to Articles 7 and 8 of the TRIPS Agreement,[156] and finds that Article 27.1 of TRIPS does not permit exclusion from patentability of medicines in general or, arguably, of specific groups thereof, and that Articles 7 and 8 of TRIPS are not pertinent to determining the possible flexibility before the grant of a patent. The Report suggests that:

> [the] Doha Declaration cannot override the express provisions of the TRIPS provisions, and any flexibilities therein have to be interpreted within the overall confines of TRIPS, which, as has been explained, rules out any 'statutory exclusion' from patentability of [an] entire class of inventions.[157]

At the same time, the 2009 Mashelkar Committee Report stresses the importance of preventing 'evergreening', as follows:

> TEG recommends that every effort must be made to prevent the practice of 'evergreening' often used by some of the pharma companies to unreasonably extend the life of the patent by making claims based sometimes on 'trivial' changes to the original patented product. The Indian patent office has the full authority under law and practice to determine what is patentable and what would constitute only a trivial change with no significant additional improvements or inventive steps involving benefits. Such authority should be used to prevent 'evergreening", rather than to introduce an arguable concept in the light of the foregoing discussion.[158]

The TEG concludes that:

> it would not be TRIPS compliant to limit granting of patents for pharmaceutical substance to New Chemical Entities only, since it prima facie amounts to a 'statutory exclusion of a field of technology'. However, every effort must be made to provide drugs at affordable prices to the people of India. Further, every effort should be made to prevent the grant of frivolous patents and 'evergreening'.[159]

The 2009 Mashelkar Committee Report explicitly stated that the mandate of the Technical Expert Committee was not to examine the TRIPS compatibility of section 3(d), but to see whether it would be TRIPS compatible to limit the grant of patent for pharmaceutical substance to NCEs. The Report responded negatively to the latter question. In the same year, the TC James Report arrived at the conclusion that section 3(d) is TRIPS compatible:

> The criticism that Section 3 (d) is not compatible with TRIPS Agreement is not correct. It has stood the test of time and does not introduce any unreasonable restrictions on patenting. It is a major public health safeguard as it blocks extension of patent period

---

[156] 2009 Mashelkar Report (n 153) subparas 5.8, 5.12–5.29.
[157] Ibid subpara 5.29.
[158] Mashelkar Report (n 153) subpara 5.30.
[159] Mashelkar Report (n 153) subpara 5.38.

through additional patents on insignificant improvements, thus paving way for introduction of generics on expiry of the original patent.[160]

The text of section 3(d) clearly rejects patentability of a new use of a known substance. Would the exclusion of a category of inventions relating to 'a new use of a known substance' which fulfills the criteria of 'novelty, inventive step and industrial applicability' be questioned on the grounds of Article 27.1 of the TRIPS Agreement, which says patents are available to all inventions provided that these three criteria are fulfilled?

The TRIPS Agreement does not say what 'invention'[161] is, and there is no harmonised philosophy, theory or principle concerning what kinds of inventions a country should grant patents for. For example, in Japan, Article 2.1 of the Patent Act says: '"Invention" in this Act means the highly advanced creation of technical ideas utilising the laws of nature'. Many court cases have arisen from instances where the JPO rejected the granting of patents on this basis. Based on this provision, the Japanese Patent Office has not considered certain business models (methods) as 'inventions' for the purpose of the Patent Law. On the other hand, business methods using computers or internet technologies (e-commerce, advertising, etc.) could be considered as inventions for the same reason, and patentable, if other patentability requirements are fulfilled. Article 52(2)(c) of the European Patent Convention provides that methods for doing business are not regarded as inventions within the meaning of paragraph 1 of Article 52 (patentable inventions).[162] However, business methods using computers for solving technical problems could be patented. The US Supreme Court, in contrast, has applied the criteria of 'abstract ideas or not' in recognising the eligibility for patentability, but not those of 'technical or not'.

How a country understands 'invention' could depend in part on its level of science and technology. As a consequence, there is a certain scope for 'flexibility' in interpreting the term 'invention', provided that it is done in good faith, in accordance with the ordinary meaning to be given to the terms of the treaty in their context and in the light of its object and purpose. For deciding whether an invention is worth protection, more than definitions, objectivity and consistency of judgment, and therefore, the criteria for such judgments, seem to be necessary. If scientific and technological progress is the ultimate objective of patent protection, as a Commission in the US, appointed by President T Roosevelt and chaired by CF Kettering, reported in 1941:

> One of the greatest technical weaknesses of the patent system is the lack of a definitive yardstick as to what is invention. To provide such a yardstick and to assure that the various courts of law and the Patent Office shall use the same standards, several

---

[160] TC James Report (n 53) 8.

[161] The Oxford English Dictionary (2nd edn) refers to: '1. the action of coming upon or finding; the action of finding out; discovery (whether accidental, or the result of search and effort).'

[162] Article 52 EPC ('patentable inventions') stipulates in its paragraph (2)(c) that: 'schemes, rules and methods for performing mental acts, playing games or doing business, and programs for computers'.

changes are suggested. It is proposed that Congress shall declare a national standard whereby patentability of an invention shall be determined by the objective test as to its advancement of the arts and sciences.[163]

The TRIPS Agreement in recital 4 of its preamble states that IPRs are private rights, but in recital 5 refers to the 'underlying public policy objectives of national systems for the protection of intellectual property, including developmental and technological objectives'. Article 7 (Objectives) of the same Agreement refers to 'promotion of technological innovation' and Article 8 (Principles), 'technological development'. In such a perspective, a yardstick as to the meaning of 'invention' in the TRIPS Agreement seems to include also the value of objectivity and consistency. Whether or not section 3(d) is TRIPS compatible could be analysed not only by the question that the Mashelkar Report dealt with, ie, whether the exclusion of certain categories of invention is TRIPS compatible but by other criteria.

ii Inconsistent or discriminatory application of patentability criteria?

Article 27.1 of the TRIPS Agreement provides that 'patents shall be available for any inventions' – provided that they are new, involve an inventive step and are capable of industrial application. Is section 3(d) applied consistently?

The TC James Report, cited earlier, gave 86 examples (67 patents for new forms of a known substance which are inventions and 19 combination drugs) of patents granted by India after 2005 for pharmaceutical products which are 'not breakthrough drugs but only minor variations of existing pharmaceuticals'.[164] Notable are patents granted to foreign companies such as: ramipril & atorvastatin compositions, atorvastatin crystalline form, valsartan + amlodipine + HCTZ compositions, olanzapine formulation, compositions, salt, gabapentin compositions, risperidone compositions, formulations and amoxycillin + clavulanic acid modified release.[165] There are also some molecules at an earlier stage of development and not a product.

The list shows that India is not granting patents only to NCEs, but also to what the author calls 'incremental innovations', and therefore TRIPS compliant in the light of the 2009 Mashelkar Report which says: 'it would not be TRIPS compatible to limit the grant of patent for pharmaceuticals to NCEs alone'. From this statement in the Mashelkar Report, TC James draws the conclusion that the Mashelkar Committee is 'supporting the argument for Section 3(d)'.[166]

---

[163] The Commission appointed by President T Roosevelt and chaired by CF Kettering stated in 1941

[164] Data collected by the Indian Pharmaceutical Alliance, TC James Report (n 53) 13–19.

[165] These also cover variants of top sellers by Pfizer (atorvastatin, gabapentin), Novartis (valsartan compositions), Eli Lilly (olanzapine), Johnson & Johnson (risperidone) and GKS's now-ancient Augmentin (co-amoxycla).

[166] TC James Report (n 53) 12.

The list of 67 examples of the patents for new forms of known compounds granted by the Indian Patent Office[167] contains three patents given to Indian companies (Hetero Drugs Ltd, Emcure Pharmaceuticals Ltd and Aurobindo Pharma Ltd). The last one is a novel crystalline form of Cefdinir and the other two are process patents.[168] They seem to have been examined and granted patents on the criteria that new forms (derivatives) of known substances are generally examined in developed countries.

There does not seem to be a pattern of discrimination between domestic and foreign companies or technologies in the grant of these patents as far as the patents on this list.[169] However, no data which would respond to the requirements of section 3(d) (enhanced therapeutic improvements) are included in these patent specifications. It is not clear whether section 3(d) was not taken into consideration by the IPO during examinations, or whether the provision was laxly applied. The end result is that most patents on this list that are accepted in the US and other developed countries are accepted in India.

On the other hand, when pre-grant oppositions are presented, the IPO seems to have consciously applied section 3(d). On 23 March 2009, the IPO rejected Gilead's patent application covering oseltamivir compositions on the grounds of lack of inventive step, failure to comply with section 3(d) and failure to sufficiently disclose the invention claimed. Cipla filed a pre-grant opposition alleging that Tamiflu is only a derivative and consists of pharmaceutically acceptable salts, solvates and derivatives, dissolved enantiomers and purified diastereomers which are not patentable under section 3(d) of the Indian Patents Act. The IPO found also that Gilead failed to provide supportive evidence in the specification in the form of comparative data or examples.[170]

The granted patents relating to new processes or derivatives other than the above 86 show that patents could be granted even to known derivatives of known substances, or without data relating to inventive steps. For example, Cipla's Patent 206564 relates to a known crystal of sertraline, 206139 to a known salt or crystal form of perindopril, No.208501 to a known crystal of finasteride, and 213706, a known amorphous of clopidogrel. In the specifications, it is explained that the new process has led to cost effectiveness (206564) or a higher purity product (206139, 208501) or a more stable product (213706). However, there are no data in the specification to prove the inventive step of the patent invention. Relevant data were probably submitted during the patent examination. In the case of the complex patent of omeprazole and cyclodextrin or the amorphous form of

---

[167] ibid 14–17.

[168] IPO 209657 (Hetero), process for preparation of new crystalline polymorphs of Donepezil compound sufficient information seems to be provided for acquiring process patent rights and IPO 222978 (Emcure), a new enantiomer of Amlodipine.

[169] eg, in comparison to IPO 218230 (Pfizer), a novel (citrate) salt form of Elzasonan with better hygroscopy and solvability. The data normally required for this type of invention are disclosed but those comparing the present invention to prior art are not made available.

[170] 'India says no to Gilead's patent for oseltamivir – Cipla wins its "Pre- Grant Opposition" against Tamiflu', Spicy IP (29 April 2010).

alendronate, Cipla only asserts, but gives no data showing that the complex is stable (219034) or that the amorphous form exhibits better solubility (219022).

Section 3(d) does not seem to be applied to all applicants, as many granted patents do not refer to enhanced efficacy in their specifications. Furthermore, some of them are not even new derivatives of known substances but known derivatives, which makes Novartis' salt form of immatinib mesylate look like a brilliant invention. The reason Novartis' application for Gleevec was rejected may simply because there was pre-grant opposition, if we compare the granted patents.

As a rejection list is not given, it is impossible to compare these patents with those, like immatinib mesylate salt or oseltamivir which have been rejected when there was pre-grant opposition. It seems apparent that section 3(d) becomes extremely important also in court cases where the validity of patents is examined (*Roche v Cipla*, above, for example).

The above observation coincides with a survey undertaken by M Fujii, Committee of Intellectual Property at the Japanese Pharmaceutical Manufacturers' Association, over the state of Indian phameceutical companies' acquisition of patents in India and abroad (USPTO, JPO and EPO) as well as Japanese pharmaceutical companies' state of acquisition (registration/rejection) at the Indian Patent Office (IPO). According to Fujii's survey, Indian companies' incremental innovations (use, salt, polymorph, combination, formulation and others) which are patentable in USPTO, EPO and JPO are patentable also in India, and those patents that the Japanese companies registered in USPTO, EPO and JPO are also patentable in India (see Table 12-5). This means that the actual practice and criteria for patentability at the IPO resemble those of the USPTO, EPO and JPO.

The new draft Manual 2008 (for public comments) does not seem to clarify sufficiently section 3(d) and it is still difficult to discuss this provision in terms of its conformity with the TRIPS Agreement.[171]

iii Discrimination as to the field of technology?

Article 27.1 of the TRIPS Agreement prohibits discrimination as to the field of technology. The Indian courts in the above-mentioned *Novartis v Union of India* and *Roche v Cipla* cases stated that the Explanation in section 3(d) applies only to pharmaceuticals. At the level of examination guidelines, developed countries have specific rules relating to different fields of technology and, therefore, how the application of section 3(d) should be examined whether it is a rational rule pertaining to the specific fields.

---

[171] The Draft Manual (2008) does not seem to provide a clear and predictable guidepost as it only states that: 'A mere discovery of new property of known substance is not considered patentable. For instance, new use of Aspirin for treatment of the cardiovascular disease, which was earlier used for analgesic purpose, is not patentable. However, a new and alternative process for preparing Aspirin is patentable.' Draft Manual of Patent Practice and Procedure (n 48) para 4.5.9.

Table 12-5 State of Patent Application and Acquisition: 12 Japanese Pharmaceutical Companies as of September 2010

1 January 2005–15 July 2010

	India		Total	Japan			US			EU		
	Registration	Rejection		Registration	Rejection	Pending	Registration	Rejection	Pending	Registration	Rejection	Pending
Substance	74	3	77	51	2	22	63	4	7	30	2	42
Use	2	3	5	2	2	1	3	0	0	2	0	2
Salt	3	1	4	1	0	3	4	0	0	1	0	2
Polymorph	6	1	7	5	0	2	5	0	1	1	0	6
Combination	2	0	2	1	0	1	1	0	1	2	0	0
Formulation	19	1	20	15	1	4	12	1	7	10	0	8
Others	27	0	27	17	0	10	26	1	2	17	0	7
Total	133	9	142	92	5	43	114	6	18	63	2	67

The Panel in *Canada–Pharmaceutical Patent Protection* stated that:

> discrimination may arise from explicitly different treatment, sometimes called "*de jure* discrimination", but it may also arise from ostensibly identical treatment which, due to differences in circumstances, produces differentially disadvantageous effects, sometimes called "*de facto* discrimination".[172]

Patent protection of new use of a known compound is particularly important for chemicals and pharmaceuticals and much more so than other fields of technology, such as machinery engineering. Section 3(d) may be considered as de facto discrimination against chemicals and pharmaceuticals, because, for all fields of technology to be treated equally, new use inventions must be protected in these particular fields. Otherwise, it will be particularly difficult to acquire patents in these fields. For these hypotheses to be verified, a more rigorous examination of facts would be necessary.

In India, during 2003–04, the cumulative number of foreign patents in force was only 4331 in all technical fields. The total number of applications during this period, however, increased to 12,613,[173] of which 3218 were Indian (25.5 per cent). Of the foreign applicants, 33.3 per cent were US and 57.5 per cent were German, Japanese, UK and French.[174] The share of patents granted to Indians started to increase from 2000–01 onwards, except for 2002–03.[175] There were 2469 patents granted during 2003–04. Of these, 56.3 per cent were in the names of foreign citizens and 43.7 per cent, Indian. This is a very encouraging evolution for Indian inventors and shows that patent protection in India is gaining legitimacy.

In India, in 2009, there were three times more pharmaceutical patents than in 2005, and there was a greater increase in the number of granted patents. In India, patent examination procedures are not initiated unless formally requested, and there is a time lag between the date of application and the publication of the granted patents. The statistical data concerning the number of applications and that of the patents granted are therefore not readily comparable, except that a rough tendency in the rate of patent applications per acquisition is discernible among different fields of technology. Figures 12.4 and 12.5 show that, in India, it may be easier to obtain patents in the field of mechanics, for example, than in pharmaceuticals. In Japan,[176] for example, the pattern of inter-technology differences[177] differs in that the ratio 'request for examination'/grant is very high, at 73 per cent in biotech medicines[178] and 54 per cent in small molecule medicines,[179]

---

[172] *Canada–Pharmaceutical Patents, (EC)*, Panel Report (adopted 7 April 2000) WT/DS114/R paras 7.94–7.105.

[173] The figure for 2002–03 was 11,466. Research and Development Statistics 2004–05, Government of India at 43. www.nstmis-dst.org/ContentsPage.htm.

[174] ibid 43.

[175] Government of India, Research and Development Statistics (2004–05) 43.

[176] 2002 Examination data in the 76 technological fields (www.jpo.go.jp/cgi/link.cgi?url=/shiryou/toukei/nenpou_toukei_list.htm) for the number of applications and the grants of patents by fields of technology. In Japan, there is also a system of formal requests to the PTO for examination.

[177] www.jpo.go.jp/torikumi/t_torikumi/sinsa_jisseki.htm.

[178] International Patent Classification: C07DHJ, C08B.

[179] IPC: A61C (5/08-5/12, 8/-13/) F(2/-4/,13/-) K,L(9/,15/-)P.

when the average is set at 50 per cent. However, in the absence of sufficient comparative data on India, it is not possible to draw any clear conclusion about the causes of the different grant ratio in different fields of technology in India and across countries.

Figure 12.4: India, Number of Patent Filing Publications by Fields of Technology

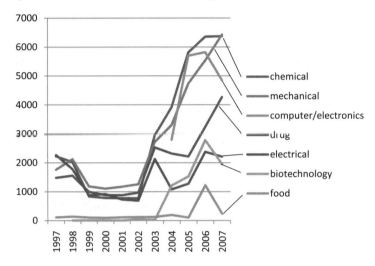

Figure 12.5: India, Number of Patents Granted

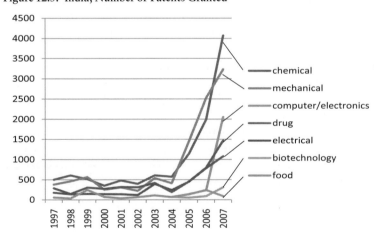

iv Bona fide *differentiation?*

The Panel in *Canada–Pharmaceutical Patent Protection* interpreted the meaning of the word 'discrimination' narrowly to mean pejorative, and distinct from *bona fide* differential treatment. The same Panel also said that the non-discriminatory clause in Article 27.1 of the TRIPS Agreement 'does not prohibit *bona fide* exceptions to deal with problems that may exist only in certain product areas'.[180]

Does section 3(d) *ipso facto* contribute to public health? TC James finds in section 3(d) 'a major public health safeguard'. There seems to be an understanding of the concept of 'evergreening' to mean preventing the entry of generic medicines and therefore to see it as being against the public interest. For example, the Madras High Court's judgment in *Novartis v Union of India* observed that the 'object which the [Patents (Amendment) Act 2005] wanted to achieve [was] to provide easy access to the citizens of this country to life saving drugs and to discharge their Constitutional obligation of providing good health care to its citizens.' The public health effects of those categories of inventions listed in section 3(d) could be better judged at the later stage by health technology assessment and the situation in the product and services market. The public health function of drugs could probably be assessed case by case, depending on the evidence. Section 3(d) then may not be a proportionate means to the declared ends.

In 1997, Cooper-Dreyfuss and Lowenthal, in writing about TRIPS dispute settlements, stated that setting a worldwide IPR standard would reduce flexibility and produce 'a kind of cultural homogenisation that might either induce noncompliance or turn the world into a much less stimulating environment':[181]

> . . . we expect that many complaints will not be so straightforward. . . . Clear cases are unlikely because newcomers to the intellectual property community have little choice but to base their laws on those of developed countries. But literal conformity to the TRIPS Agreement does not tell the entire story: a state intent on preserving access can use the flexibility of the law to strip intellectual property holders of any meaningful protection. These are the cases that we envision, and we expect that they will be difficult to decide.[182]

At the same time, Dreyfuss and Lowenthal advise that the international agreement risks losing effectiveness if the scope of patentability is set out broadly in principle but leaves each Member to fine-tune the scope, which might result in narrowing the scope of actual rights.

In Brazil and India, in particular, it has been argued that the quality of patents could be improved by raising the criteria of judging inventive steps (see chapter 11). Section 3(d) of the Indian Patents (Amendment) Act 2005, has created a 'stimulating environment' for international discussion, but the ways in which it is applied and the effects thereof remain to be verified. How a legal provision is implemented seems to count as much as the text itself.

---

[180] *Canada–Pharmaceutical Patents* (n 174) para 7.92 (see ch 7).

[181] R Cooper-Dreyfuss and AF Lowenfeld, 'Two Achievements of the Uruguay Round: Putting TRIPS and Dispute Settlement Together' (1997) Winter *Virginia Journal of International Law* 307–08.

[182] ibid 283.

13

TRIPS Flexibilities and National Implementation

(2) Protection of Test Data Submitted to Regulatory Authorities

ANOTHER EXAMPLE OF TRIPS flexibilities relates to Article 39.3 concerning the protection of undisclosed test data submitted as a condition for obtaining marketing approvals of pharmaceutical or agricultural chemical products. This chapter examines what kind of policy options the ambiguous wording of Article 39.3 offers.

I FLEXIBILITY WITH RESPECT TO ARTICLE 39.3

A Wording

The TRIPS Agreement contains certain obligations concerning 'undisclosed information' which cover trade secrets (Article 39.2) and test data submitted to regulatory authorities for market authorisation (Article 39.3). Article 39.3 of the TRIPS Agreement reads:

> [WTO] Members, when requiring, as a condition of approving the marketing of pharmaceutical or of agricultural chemical products which utilize new chemical entities, the submission of undisclosed test or other data, the origination of which involves a considerable effort, *shall protect such data against unfair commercial use. In addition, Members shall protect such data against disclosure, except where necessary to protect the public, or unless steps are taken to ensure that the data are protected against unfair commercial use.* (emphasis added)

Normally, test data are submitted to regulatory authorities for proving the safety, efficacy and quality of the chemical products to be marketed. Within this regulatory context, and from the wording of Article 39.3 TRIPS, the reason the data submitted to the regulatory authority must be protected seems to be that the creation of such undisclosed data required 'considerable efforts' to demonstrate that the product 'utilising new chemical entities' is safe, efficacious and of good quality and therefore they have commercial value. Article 39.3 uses the vague term of requiring Member governments to 'protect such data against unfair commercial use'.

Article 10 bis of the Paris Convention (1967), as referred to in Article 39.1[1] of the TRIPS Agreement, provides a context for interpreting the meaning of 'unfair commercial use' in Article 39.3. Article 10 bis of the Paris Convention stipulates a broad principle that *any* act of competition 'contrary to honest practices' constitutes an act of 'unfair competition'.[2] It provides that:

(1) The countries of the Union are bound to assure to nationals of such countries effective protection against unfair competition.
(2) Any act of competition contrary to honest practices in industrial or commercial matters constitutes an act of unfair competition.
(3) The following in particular shall be prohibited:

    (i)   all acts of such a nature as to create confusion by any means whatever with the establishment, the goods, or the industrial or commercial activities, of a competitor;

    (ii) false allegations in the course of trade of such a nature as to discredit the establishment, the goods, or the industrial or commercial activities, of a competitor;

    (iii) indications or allegations the use of which in the course of trade is liable to mislead the public as to the nature, the manufacturing process, the characteristics, the suitability for their purpose, or the quantity, of the goods.

According to Ladas, the law of unfair competition aims at protecting pecuniary interests and business relationships acquired by 'lawful efforts, research, labour, investment or by conducting lawful business'. He further explains that the law of unfair competition 'forms the background and constitutes the general principle of which the laws protecting the various branches of industrial property are only special aspects or particular applications.'[3] The law of unfair competition is applied normally by courts involving civil tort principles, but could be enforced under a special unfair competition law, or under a variety of laws, including penal laws.[4]

Article 39.3, by contrast, clearly requires the government to protect submitted data against unfair commercial use in a regulatory context of authorising marketing pharmaceutical or agricultural chemical products. In concrete terms,

---

[1] Art 39.1 provides that: 'In the course of ensuring effective protection against unfair competition as provided in Article 10bis of the Paris Convention (1967), Members shall protect undisclosed information in accordance with paragraph 2 and data submitted to governments or governmental agencies in accordance with paragraph 3.'

[2] S Ladas, *Patents, Trademarks & Related Rights: National & International Protection* (Cambridge MA, Harvard University Press, 1975) vol III 1686.

[3] Ladas, *Patents, Trademarks & Related Rights* (n 2) 1675–88.

[4] ibid. 1691–1705.

it refers to the government's obligation to prevent leakage of such data from regulatory bodies to competitors, as has been alleged to occur in a number of developing countries.

During the Uruguay Round, the US negotiators seem to have understood that 'protection against unfair commercial use' included the regulators not relying (non-reliance) on the originators' data for examining the second and subsequent applicants for drug approval, for a fixed period of time (ie, market exclusivity- chapter 4). Thus, they agreed to drop the non-reliance language, because they viewed the phrase as no more than 'belt and suspenders'.[5] Contrary to the expectations of the US, however, the wording of Article 39.3 does not imply a 'non-reliance' principle of the regulator. Instead, Article 39.3 left many questions unanswered and allowed a wide scope of flexibilities in interpreting and implementing this provision.

Article 39.3 does not oblige Members to observe data exclusivity in the sense accepted by developed countries (ie, data created by the originator for the purpose of receiving marketing approval are to remain exclusive thereafter for a given period of years). However, Members are required to prevent leakage to competitors of data submitted to the regulatory authorities. Article 39.3 does not limit the term of protection, at least not expressly, and therefore, it is possible to interpret from this provision that authorities are required to protect regulatory data for 'as long as a possibility of unfair commercial use of this data exists'.[6]

As Taubman points out, the Paris conception of 'unfair competition' is more strongly rooted in business ethics and honest practices than the typical IP law aimed at preventing free-riding or unjust enrichment.[7]

From Article 1.2 of the TRIPS Agreement, 'undisclosed information' is part of intellectual property covered under the Agreement, as it says: 'for the purposes of this Agreement, the term intellectual property refers to all categories of intellectual property that are the subject of Sections 1 through 7 of Part II.' This comprises Article 39, the single article within Section 7 of the TRIPS Agreement. According to TRIPS Article 2.1, the Agreement incorporates certain parts of 'intellectual property conventions', including Article 10 *bis* of the Paris Convention (1967).[8] Under the TRIPS Agreement, therefore, that part of data submitted to regulatory authorities, as a condition of marketing approval of pharmaceutical or agricultural chemical products, is treated as a category of intellectual property, if 'considerable efforts' are involved in the creation of data.

---

[5] JJ Gorlin, *An analysis of the Pharmaceutical-related Provisions of the WTO TRIPS (IP) Agreement* (Washington DC, IP Institute, 1999); see ch 4.

[6] M Bronckers and P Ondrusek, 'Protection of Regulatory Data in the EU and WTO Law' (2005) 8(5) *Journal of World Intellectual Property* 594.

[7] A Taubman, 'Unfair competition and the financing of public-knowledge goods: the problem of test data protection' (2008 3(9) *Journal of Intellectual Property Law & Practice* 601.

[8] Art 2.1 of the TRIPS Agreement provides that: 'In respect of PArts II, III and IV of this Agreement, Members shall comply with Articles 1 through 12, and Article 19, of the Paris Convention (1967).'

B National Practices

As a result of the 'constructive ambiguities' achieved over the unbridgeable rift among the Uruguay Round negotiators, however, the general principle of protection underlying Article 39.3, unfortunately, is not readily apparent. Furthermore, national practices diverge radically. In general, developed countries' medicinal law ensures, for drug approval, the safety and efficacy of the drugs to be marketed, and regulates the entry of copy products, safeguarding at the same time the investment and creativity used for the research of the applicant. These laws delineate conditions approving new drugs which are not limited to new chemical entities, and regulate the entry of competitor products equivalent to originator products whose safety and efficacy (generally called 'generic medicines' which is not necessarily a legal concept under medicinal law – see chapter 9) are approved. In these countries, exclusivity of a fixed term is given to originator companies on the basis of public policy grounds, evaluating and balancing the cost of clinical data generation including that of failures, and the social benefit of generic entry. In these countries also, the regulatory authority may rely on the originator's data for reference, only after the period of exclusivity for the originator product.

In the US, section 505[9] of the United States Food, Drug and Cosmetics Act provides protection (market exclusivity) of five years[10] to those drugs of which 'no active ingredient (including any ester or salt of the active ingredient) has been approved in any other application under subsection (b)', unless an action for patent infringement is commenced during the one-year period beginning four years after the date of the approval.[11] Regulatory authorities require first-time applicants to submit a data package to prove the safety, efficacy, and toxicity of medicinal products, for marketing authorisation of pharmaceutical products.

In the EU,[12] the current system of data exclusivity (eight years) and market exclusivity (two years) was introduced under Articles 6 and 10 of Directive 2004/27/EC.[13] In Japan, the application for marketing approval of competitive products is prohibited for eight years on the grounds that the regulatory authorities should, after marketing the original product, re-examine the efficacy, safety and side-effects of the medicines in question during this period of de facto data

---

[9] 21 USC 355(c)(3)(E)(ii). Safety, efficacy, and quality of drugs are regulated by the Food and Drug Administration and the Centers for Disease Control and Prevention.

[10] From the date of the approval of the application under subs (b).

[11] Ester or salt are included here because the data package pertaining to them can be protected when drugs which are inactive derivatives, such as ester or salt, are approved as pro-drugs.

[12] Rules concerning the protection of data submitted to regulatory authorities were in part harmonised at the EC level by Directive 87/21/EEC of December 22, 1986 amending Directive 65/65/EEC on the approximation of provisions laid down by law, regulation or administrative action relating to proprietary medicinal products. Prior to the harmonisation by this Directive, rules relating to the entry of generic medicines had depended on Member States' legislations.

[13] Directive 2004/27/EC of the European Parliament and of the Council of 31 March 2004 amending Directive 2001/83/EC on the Community code relating to medicinal products for human use.

exclusivity. After eight years of exclusivity, the authorities can examine the application of competitive products but cannot authorise their entry for another year. In Japan, therefore, the post-marketing surveillance justifies the non-entry of generic medicines, but, theoretically, such surveillance relating to the drug efficacy, safety and side-effects could be achieved with the existence of corresponding generic medicines on the market.

In the EU, data exclusivity for biosimilars[14] is identical to small molecule medicines. In Japan, the post-marketing surveillance period for biologics, which is identical to that of small molecule medicines, offers protection of exclusivity for the reference products. For the entry of follow-on biologics (generic versions of biotechnology medicines), the US Biologics Price Competition and Innovation Act of 2009[15] provides market exclusivity of 12 years. No application for approval of follow-on biologics can be submitted during the four years from the date on which the original biologics were approved by the FDA.

II INTERPRETING AND IMPLEMENTING TRIPS 39.3

The absence of key explanatory words, the lack of precedents in previous IP treaties, as well as non-converging state practices, would make it difficult to clarify the scope of obligations stipulated in Article 39.3. Under Article 39.3, therefore, Members may adopt different systems for the protection of test data submitted to regulatory authorities as long as relevant TRIPS provisions are interpreted and respected, in accordance with customary rules of international law as has been practiced by the WTO dispute settlement organs. For example, the interpretation of 'new' in the phrase 'products utilizing new chemical entities' in Article 39.3 TRIPS has a wide margin of flexibility. However, in the sense that Article 39.3 is found in the context of the Paris conception of 'unfair competition' and within the legal framework's regulatory and marketing approval processes, it would be difficult to establish an analogy with the concept of 'new' in the patent system.[16]

In China, a data exclusivity period of six years is provided for new drugs, unless the second or subsequent applicant for approval proves that the test data were created by the generic makers who apply for marketing approval (chapter 11).

---

[14] Comparability applied to biosimilars is defined in Regulation EC/726/2004 and amended Directive 2001/83EC. Section 4, Part II, Annex 1 of the latter provides that: 'The provisions of Article 10(1)(a)(iii) [ie for generic medicinal products] may not be sufficient in the case of biological medicinal products. If the information required in the case of essentially similar products (generics) does not permit the demonstration of the similar nature of two biological medicinal products, additional data, in particular, the toxicological and clinical profile shall be provided.'

[15] Patient Protection and Affordable Care Act (HR 3590) Title VII – Improving Access to Innovative Medical Therapies, Subtitle A – Biologics Price Competition. Under s 702, it is provided that the biological product (i) is biosimilar to the reference product; and (ii) can be expected to produce the same clinical result as the reference product in any given patient and that the exclusivity for reference product is 12 years after the date on which the reference product was first licensed under subs (a).

[16] See ch 4 p 138.

In India, the Insecticides Act 1968 deals with agricultural chemicals (insecticides, fungicides and herbicides),[17] and Rule 122-E of the Drugs and Cosmetics Act 1940[18] defines a 'new drug' and the conditions of competitive drug entry.[19] The Drugs and Cosmetics Act also regulates manufacture and marketing approval of drugs and traditional medicines. Both Acts require submission of test data for marketing authorisation, but there is no explicit provision for the protection of test data.[20].

India is presently considering adopting national data protection rules under the TRIPS Agreement both for agricultural and pharmaceutical chemicals.[21] India's government constituted a Consultative Committee in February 2004 for this purpose. This Committee formulated its interpretation of Article 39.3 of the TRIPS Agreement and delineated its recommendations based on various economic and social considerations and facts. A comprehensive report was published by this Committee in May 2007 (Test Data Report).[22]

The Test Data Report examines various forms of data protection that Article 39.3 TRIPS covers and considers the appropriate choices for India. The Report gives separate considerations to data protection requirements for agricultural chemicals, pharmaceuticals and traditional knowledge, and it recommends different measures for these sectors. For agro-chemicals and traditional medicines, the Report recommends that India adopt data exclusivity for three and five years, respectively, based on the non-reliance principle. According to the Report, one of the characteristics of the agricultural chemical sector is that the industry must meet a responsibility toward the toxicity of chemicals for its 'environmental impact to which the pharmaceutical industry is not exposed.'[23] However, the issue of 'spurious' drugs (see chapter 8, note 151) and chemicals are considered as a common concern for all sectors. The Report affirms that:

While spurious drugs have played with the health and lives of patients, spurious pesticides have contributed to crop failure and financial bankruptcy of farmers. Data Protection may be helpful in checking this menace and only those companies which have the resources to produce good quality products should be allowed to market them during the period of protection.[24]

---

[17] The Pesticides Management Bill 2008, which is aimed at replacing the Insecticide Act 1968, contains a proposal to introduce data exclusivity for pesticide chemicals of five years. This Bill was introduced in the Indian Parliament in September 2008 by the Agriculture Minister. 'Parliament misses opportunity to discuss "data exclusivity" for agro-chemicals' Spicy IP, 8 May 2010.

[18] www.cdsco.nic.in/html/Drugs&CosmeticAct.pdf. Amended in June 2005.

[19] 'A new drug shall continue to be considered as new drug for a period of four years from the date of its first approval or its inclusion in the Indian Pharmacopoeia, whichever is earlier.'

[20] For unfair competition, the provisions of common law, law of tort and the Indian Contract Act 1872 could be applied.

[21] 'Govt To Consider Data Protection', *The Economic Times* (29 November 2003).

[22] Ministry of Chemicals & Fertilizers, Report on Steps to be taken by the Government of India in the context of Data Protection Provisions of Article 39.3 of TRIPS Agreement (Test Data Report) (Government of India, 31 May 2007). http://chemicals.nic.in/DPBooklet.pdf.

[23] Test Data Report (n 22) 31–32.

[24] ibid 5–6.

In considering appropriate forms of data protection for pharmaceuticals, the Test Data Report states that their primary consideration is that: 'India has emerged as one of the important producers of generic medicines in the world. There has been a prolonged debate on the likely impact of data protection provisions on the growth of industry and on availability of cost generic medicines.'[25] The Report examines other aspects of pharmaceuticals to be taken into account. One consideration is that data protection may result in the stepping up of R&D by Indian companies.[26] Another consideration for pharmaceuticals is paragraph 4 of the Doha Declaration, which says that TRIPS provisions are to be 'interpreted and implemented in a manner supportive of WTO Members' duty to protect public health and, in particular, to promote access to medicines for all'.[27]

As for pharmaceuticals, the Report reflects on the question of the scope of 'utilising new chemical entities'and states that:

> According to experts like Prof. Carlos Correa, a renowned expert in IPR, a chemical entity is deemed new, if there were no prior application for approval of the same drug or where the same drug was not previously known to commerce. It would, however, not apply to new indications, new dosage forms, new combinations, crystalline forms, isomers etc. of existing drugs since there would be no new chemical entity involved.[28]

The Report evaluates this option as allowing greater competition to take place by not giving monopoly rights to the innovator drug companies on the non-patented new drugs. The Report, however, suggests that this option:

> may have some adverse impact on FDI in pharmaceuticals sector in India since the perception with most international corporates may be that India does not provide adequate IPR protection to new products [and] may slow down the early launch of some of the new drugs in India for lack of adequate protection.[29]

After examining a few options, the Report recommends the following as definitions of 'products which utilize new chemical entities':

- in the case of agro-chemicals, 'an agrochemical product which contains an active ingredient or formulation of such an ingredient that has not been previously approved in India irrespective of whether the product is patentable or not'; and
- in the case of pharmaceutical chemicals, two alternatives with exceptions and safeguards are suggested: (i) a drug as defined within the framework of India's

---

[25] Test Data Report iv.

[26] According to the Report, 'Some of these companies are already working on new molecules which may be introduced in the market in the next few years. Such efforts need to be encouraged and data protection can play a critical role.' The Test Data Report (n 21) 5. For marketing approval of foreign-approved new drugs, for example, the countries which are ICH (ch 8, n 136) members require clinical studies starting from Phase I. In China, India and the Republic of Korea, clinical studies from Phase III are required. In many other developing countries, no clinical study is required for foreign-approved new drugs for which the marketing authorisation is based only on documents.

[27] Test Data Report (n 22) 26.

[28] ibid 31.

[29] Test Data Report (n 22) 32–33.

Drugs and Cosmetics Act 1940[30], ie, a drug, including bulk drug substance, which has not been used in the country to any significant extent under the conditions prescribed, or (ii) 'a drug based on a new chemical entity which had no prior application for approval of the same drug in India or where the same drug or chemical entity was not previously known to commerce', with the exclusion of new indications, new dosage forms, new combinations of two or more drugs, polymorphs/hydrates/solvates/isomers, salts, esters, metabolites, particle sizes, mixtures of isomers, complexes, chelates, mere admixtures or compositions etc of known substances unless they result in the significant enhancement of the known efficacy of that substance.[31]

For data protection for pharmaceuticals, the Report recommends two alternatives, with pros and cons: (i) trade secret form of data protection against unauthorised disclosure and use of proprietary test data (drug Regulator to continue to place reliance on data of first applicant while approving second and subsequent applicants),[32] or (ii) the introduction of data protection for five years in fulfilment of the 'minimum requirements of Article 39.3', ie, only the non-disclosure of test data and the non-acceptance of fraudulently obtained data for pharmaceutical products,[33] to the exclusion of non-reliance. It explains that India is in a 'transition period' which is likely to continue; where drug approvals concern those generic drugs which have already been launched in foreign countries, and, therefore, no reliance rule is necessary.

National laws diverge on the relationship between the chemical forms and the definition of generics even among developed countries. Theoretically, the scope of new chemicals can be designed narrowly to encourage the entry of cheaper competitive medicines without requiring them to undergo the full set of trials.[34] Usually, the scope of chemical forms recognised as generics is included in the overall compromise package. For example, a long period of data exclusivity is compensated by a wide scope of chemical forms allowed as generics in the EU, while in the US, the period of data exclusivity is relatively short and the chemical forms recognised as generics is limited.

In the US and Japan, generic drugs in ester or salt forms are not recognised by regulatory authorities, but in the US, crystal forms which are different from the active ingredients of the initial registered product can be approved as generics. In the European countries, ester, salt, or ether forms can be approved as

---

[30] 122 E of the Drugs and Cosmetics Rules 1945.
[31] Test Data Report (n 22) 49–50.
[32] Test Data Report (n 22) para 6.2.3.
[33] Test Data Report (n 22) para 7.4.3.
[34] In Japan, when the applicant drug is a salt or ester with different crystal forms, each crystal form requires an independent approval procedure for safety reasons. In Japanese patent law, different forms of salt or crystal are considered to be different substances and their novelty can be recognised. Therefore, the categories of chemical entities used for patent applications and those used for obtaining marketing approval could be similar.

generics,[35] in light of the extended term of data protection. The originator companies therefore tend to apply for patents on many kinds of derivatives of known chemical entities, even though they do not necessarily use these substances. The relationship between regulations concerning data protection and those relating to the definition of generics is not easily established and, therefore, narrowing the scope of chemicals which are subject to data protection does not necessarily facilitate the early entry of generics.[36]

III POLICY OPTIONS UNDER ARTICLE 39.3

Research-based pharmaceutical companies seem to prefer data exclusivity to patents in those countries without well-functioning judicial systems, because administrative protection is pre-emptory and more reliable than courts. Be that as it may, enforcement of confidentiality is required by TRIPS, and developing countries should consider this as an immediate and important priority (in India there is no law for that purpose).[37]

As stated earlier, test data protection in developed countries is conceived of not only as a confidentiality rule, but also as a non-reliance obligation on the part of regulatory authorities (ie, data exclusivity). Developing countries are not obliged under Article 39.3 to extend the scope of protection to such a degree.

For most developing countries, data exclusivity has insufficient real attraction, except in relation to contract manufacturing where regulatory control, IPR and data protection all contribute to the business environment. Theoretically, if 'line extension drugs' (new formulations etc) and chemical derivatives (see chapter 12) are not considered as 'products utilising new chemical entities' in the meaning of Article 39.3 TRIPS, the entry of cheaper competitive medicines may be encouraged without requiring them to undergo the full set of trials.

The Uruguay Round discussion on Article 39.3 was not adequate and the resulting compromise was unclear. Only the confidentiality principle, to be respected by regulators, seems to be clear from the wording of Article 39.3. However, this does not mean that less data protection is always better for developing

---

[35] Art 10.1 of Directive 2004/27/EC (n 14). Art 10.2(b) says that 'different salts, esters, ethers, isomers, mixtures of isomers, complexes or derivatives of an active substance shall be considered to be the same active substance, unless they differ significantly in properties with regard to safety and/or efficacy.'

[36] The purposes of granting marketing approval and granting patents differ radically. In Japan, when the applicant drug is a salt or ester with different crystal forms, each crystal form requires an independent approval procedure for safety reasons. In Japanese patent law, different forms of salt or crystal are considered to be different substances and their 'novelty' can be recognised. Therefore, the categories of chemical entities used for patent applications and those used for obtaining marketing approval could be similar. Thus, the criteria for judging a product to be 'new' in the former and 'novelty' in the latter could not be the same in Japan. In the EU however, the categories of chemical forms approved as generics are broad, the handing of substances in patent examination is by and large same in the US and Japan.

[37] 'China and India tell a tale of two CMO markets', *SCRIP* (30 April 2010) 28.

countries, particularly from the point of view of establishing well-functioning regulatory authorities based on clear rules. The difficult task would be to choose the appropriate scope of protection for each country. The size that fits each country best would not necessarily be the least protection, because the regulatory purpose and concern for drug approval procedures cannot be limited to the issue of lowering the price of medicines. India's above-mentioned Test Data Report shows various elements for considering appropriate forms of data protection.

In many developing countries, regulatory authorities tend to acknowledge previous foreign or domestic approvals and rely on the test results of the first applicant for approving competitor products. This practice is often justified by the argument that the cost of generating data is reduced.[38] The actual impact of this practice on the safety and effectiveness of approved drugs in the local conditions has not been examined in detail. Test data exclusivity could serve as a boost to creating a rigorous system of regulation concerning safety, effectiveness and quality of drugs in some of these countries.

In so far as a drug marketing control system is designed to assure safety, efficacy, and quality from the therapeutic point of view, it seems difficult to associate the forms of chemicals directly with the standard by which products can be judged to be new as referred to in Article 39.3 TRIPS. From the investor's point of view, test data protection has another meaning. It can be a substitute for patent protection in particular environments, for example, when the examination leading to drug approval is particularly time-consuming, or when the new drug is a university invention without patent protection, or in countries where the term of patent protection is insufficient or the court system for enforcement is not reliable. Relationships between patent protection and test data protection differ according to the product in question, depending on the institutional environment of each country.

The regulatory purpose of drug approval cannot be limited to lowering the price of medicines. There could be other public policy considerations for the actual functioning of drug regulatory authorities. For example, strengthening the regulatory system and eliminating substandard medicines may matter more to the authorities in developing countries than IPR or data exclusivity.

Data exclusivity may become more acceptable to those developing countries that are able to draw more economic advantage from accepting exclusivity than from resisting it. The incentive to respect and then extend IPR may come also when their own pharmaceutical industries develop to a level where significant IPR is generated locally and/or when attracting foreign R&D-based investment and contract manufacturing for foreign clients becomes a high political priority. For contract manufacturing, China is ahead of India.[39] China is moving towards a compromise on IPR and data protection, both in terms of wanting to attract

---

[38] R Dinca, 'The "Bermuda Triangle" of Pharmaceutical Law: Is Data Protection a Lost Ship?' (2005) 8(4) *Journal of World Intellectual Property* 517–63.

[39] *SCRIP* (n 39)27.

foreign investment for local manufacturing of patented medicines and in competing after patent expiry. Above all, China is ahead of India in biotechnology.[40] The difference of national implementation of the unclear provision in Article 39.3 of the TRIPS Agreement between these two countries can be explained partly by these factors.

For contract manufacturing organisations (CMOs) in developing countries to get overseas contracts, pharmaceutical manufacturing standards and their problems are key issues. Now, patent expiry is gathering pace for many major biologicals (see chapter 3). For Chinese and Indian companies to be able to compete for them without patent restrictions, it is vital that their active ingredients for biogenerics meet the strict quality standards of developed countries. Conversely, data protection is vital for foreign companies when they hand out manufacturing contracts to developing countries. Here, too, China will be more attuned to making concessions on data protection than India. The value of China's exports of active pharmaceutical ingredients (APIs) is currently estimated as roughly three times that of India's.

---

[40] It is predicted that by 2014 half the top-100 drugs will be biologics, up from 11% in 2000. *SCRIP* (n 39) 29.

14

'TRIPS Plus' Provisions in US Free Trade Agreements

THE US BILATERAL Free Trade Agreements (FTAs) restore the standards of intellectual property protection that the US originally expected when concluding the TRIPS Agreement, bring precision to its ambiguous terms, raise the standards above those of TRIPS in certain fields, and introduce standards of protection in response to the situations created by new technologies such as the Internet. Raising the standards of IPR protection above the TRIPS Agreement is allowed under the second sentence of its Article 1.1, which provides that Members may implement more extensive legal protection than is required by the Agreement, provided that such protection does not contravene TRIPS provisions. This is an aspect of the flexibility that the TRIPS Agreement offers to Members. By the same token, these FTA provisions restrict the latitude of US FTA partners from invoking the standard-lowering flexibilities contained in the TRIPS Agreement. Thus, complex layers of TRIPS interpretations have emerged out of the positions taken by different industries and countries vis-à-vis the TRIPS Agreement. This chapter takes stock of US FTA provisions relating to IPRs and compares them with relevant TRIPS provisions. How and when these FTA provisions would impact socio-economic situations would depend on many factors outside the text of the agreements, including how they are implemented. Much, unfortunately, is in the realm of speculation.

I 'TRIPS PLUS' PROVISIONS IN THE US FTAS

A Beyond the Uruguay Round Results

The TRIPS Agreement incorporated many proposals from developed countries, but still insufficiently reflected the US demands both on substantive standards of protection for new technologies and regulated products such as pharmaceuticals as well as on enforcement provisions. We have seen in chapter 4 that, towards the end of the Uruguay Round negotiations, the US pharmaceutical industry was opposing the draft text of what would be the TRIPS Agreement. Their dissatisfaction concerned the 10-year transition periods given before introducing product patent protection to such countries as India, Thailand and Brazil where most copies of drugs were produced at that time, and the fact that the Agreement would not offer protection for drugs in the 'pipeline'.[1] The TRIPS Agreement incorporated many proposals from developed countries, but still insufficiently reflected the US demands both on substantive standards of protection for new technologies and regulated products such as pharmaceuticals as well as on enforcement provisions.

Following the entry into force of the TRIPS Agreement, the built-in agenda discussions within the WTO TRIPS Council on the subject matter of biotech inventions stipulated in TRIPS Article 27.3(b) revealed that it is extremely difficult to modify TRIPS Agreement provisions or to give further discipline in the multilateral rules relating to intellectual property rights (IPRs) within the WTO (see chapters 5 and 12).

The enforcement chapter of the TRIPS Agreement (Part III, Articles 41–61) where new rules concerning domestic enforcement producers and remedies were established for the first time in the history of public international law, did not seem to respond sufficiently to the expectations of US officials and industries who wished for clearer rules and a more effective enforcement system. Watal cites the examples of the language used in Part III of the TRIPS Agreement which disappointed US officials: it merely states that Members 'shall make available to right holders' certain procedures, or that judicial authorities 'shall have the authority to . . .' (chapter 5) [2]

The rift that had existed during the Uruguay Round negotiations between developed countries, such as the US and the EU, and developing countries, such as India and Brazil, about what intellectual property rules should be within the GATT-WTO during the UR negotiations did not change significantly. The TRIPS interpretation instead became a new battleground for the access to medicines debate. The massive support given to the uncertain concept of TRIPS 'flexibilities' introduced further doubts about how reliable the TRIPS Agreement would be. This seems to have given additional reasons for the US to resort to pushing IP provisions in its bilateral agreements for the pursuit of the protection of intellectual property world-wide, relying simultaneously on the TRIPS Agreement and bilateral agreements on IP issues, depending in each case on what suits its agenda. The Panel in *China–Intellectual Property Rights* indicated the limits of Member's discretion,[3] but no Appellate Body Report has yet dealt with the rules concerning the 'flexibilities' that the TRIPS Agreement offers.

Traditionally, it was mainly the European Union (formerly the European Communities (EC)) that most often concluded a nexus of bilateral trade agreements, be it association agreements or other free trade agreements with countries in

[1] H Bale 'Drug, Textile Makers to Fight Trade Pact', *Journal of Commerce* (8 January 1992). See chp 4.

[2] J Watal 'US – China Intellectual Property Dispute – A Comment on the Interpretation of the TRIPS Enforcement Provisions' (2010) 5 *The Journal of World Intellectual Property* 607.

[3] *China–Measures Affecting the Protection and Enforcement of Intellectual Property Rights(China–Intellectual Property Rights)*, Panel Report (adopted 20 March 2009) WT/DS362/R. See ch 7.

neighbouring regions. The agreements in the European region were aimed among other things at political and eventual market integration and at coping with immigration and security problems. In the 1980s, however, when it appeared that the Uruguay Round negotiations were not progressing well, the US started to negotiate bilateral free trade agreements (FTAs), first with Israel and secondly with Canada. The US-Israel FTA entered into effect on 1 September 1985, while the Canada-US Free Trade Agreement (CUSFTA) took effect on 1 January 1989. On 1 January 1994, the CUSFTA was expanded to include Mexico, through the North American Free Trade Agreement (NAFTA). At that time, the US resorted to bilateral relations only with countries with which it had pressing political and security or immigration issues. The US goal may be to create a global rule regarding commerce, but a single multilateral agreement is increasingly difficult to achieve.[4] Bilateral agreements provide a means to supplement various difficulties in strengthening multilateral rules.[5] Thus, there were three negotiating objectives regarding intellectual property stated in the Trade Promotion Authority (TPA).[6] The Bush Administration obtained these objectives from Congress in 2002, and they expired in July 2007. They were:

- to promote adequate and effective protection through various means, including the accelerated and full implementation of the TRIPS Agreement, any multilateral or bilateral trade agreement reflecting a standard of protection similar to that found in US law, responding to new and emerging technologies of transmitting and distributing products embodying IP, preventing or eliminating discrimination with respect to the availability, acquisition, scope, maintenance, use, and enforcement of IPRs, ensuring that standards of protection and enforcement keep pace with technological developments and providing strong enforcement of IPRs;
- to secure fair, equitable, and non-discriminatory market access opportunities for US persons who rely upon IP protection; and
- to respect the Doha Declaration on the TRIPS Agreement and Public Health.

---

[4] With the establishment of a bilateral or regional free trade agreement, trade may be diverted from a more efficient exporter towards a less efficient one. The rise in imports from parties to the agreement may displace either domestic production or imports from other countries. The displacement of domestic production is called trade creation, because it results in a net increase in trade. The displacement of imports from other countries is a trade diversion, since it does not increase trade overall but amounts to a diversion of existing trade.

[5] This view is reflected in the following Congressional Brief: 'Because the proposed free-trade agreements would be of substantial benefit to the economies of small developing countries while having little effect on the US economy (and a beneficial effect at that), they provide a relatively easy way for the United States to help such countries. Economic reasoning alone cannot determine whether FTAs are an advisable path to take to an eventual goal of multilateral free trade. Foreign policy and tactical considerations are also important. Multilateral free trade is the most desirable trade policy from the standpoint of overall U.S. economic productivity and efficiency. FTAs are similarly beneficial, but to a lesser degree, provided that they do not result in too much trade diversion (and, as noted earlier, trade diversion disappears as more countries are covered by such agreements).' B Arnold, CBO Microeconomic and Financial Studies Division, 'The Pros and Cons of Pursuing Free-Trade Agreements' (*Economic and Budget Issue Brief*, A series of issue summaries from the Congressional Budget Office), 31 July, 2003. www.cbo.gov/doc.cfm?index=4458&type=0.

[6] Public Law 107-210, 6 August, 2002, 116 STAT 933 (107th Congress).

B TRIPS and NAFTA provisions relating to IPRs

For the US, approximately the same draft text on IP protection served as the basis for the two parallel negotiations which started in 1986, one for the CUSFTA which entered into force on 1 January 1988, and the other for the TRIPS Agreement. In June 1991, Canada, Mexico and the US started negotiating the North American Free Trade Agreement (NAFTA), which was signed on 17 December 1992 and entered into force on 1 January 1994, one year before the entry into force of the TRIPS Agreement.

The end results of these parallel negotiations differed on several points in relation to TRIPS provisions. NAFTA is less ambiguous and more detailed, because it has fewer Parties with diverging interests. There are some NAFTA provisions which deal with IPRs which do not exist in the TRIPS Agreement, or those which provide tighter limitations to the scope of exceptions than the TRIPS Agreement. These provisions can be called 'TRIPS plus'.

Concerning copyright, for example, NAFTA Chapter XVII contained certain provisions concerning rights which are not within the scope of the TRIPS Agreement, or which extend the protection or limit the scope of exceptions. For instance, Article 1705.6 restricts grounds for compulsory licensing by prohibiting the NAFTA Parties from granting translation and reproduction licences permitted under the Appendix to the Berne Convention,[7] while Article 1707 provides protection of 'encrypted program[s] carrying satellite signals', something which is absent in the TRIPS Agreement.[8]

As for sound recording, Article 14.2 of the TRIPS Agreement provides merely that 'producers of phonograms shall enjoy the right to authorize or prohibit the direct or indirect reproduction of their phonograms.' Article 1706.1 recognises that the producer of a sound recording not only has this right, but also has extended rights over extended modes of distribution, namely, the right to prohibit '(b) the importation of copies of the sound recording made without the producer's authorization, (c) the first public distribution of the original and each copy of the sound recording including by rental, and (d) the commercial rental of the original or a copy of the sound recording, except where expressly otherwise provided in a contract between the producer of the sound recording and the authors of the works fixed therein . . .'

Concerning trademarks, Article 1708.1 of NAFTA includes collective marks among trademarks and states that a Party may include certification marks. Article

---

[7] Where legitimate needs in that party's territory for copies or translations of the work could be met by the right holder's voluntary actions, but for obstacles created by the party's measures.

[8] Art 1707 of NAFTA provides the content of its protection. Encrypted program-carrying satellite signal means a program-carrying satellite signal that is transmitted in a form whereby the aural or visual characteristics, or both, are modified or altered for the purpose of preventing unauthorized reception, by persons without the authorized equipment that is designed to eliminate the effects of such modification or alteration, of a program carried in that signal (Art 1721.2 NAFTA).

1708.2 brings more clarifications to procedures for applying for the registration of trademarks, and Article 1708.6 of NAFTA clarifies the criteria in determining whether a trademark is 'well known', ie, that there is knowledge of the trademark in the relevant sector of the public, including knowledge in the Party's territory obtained as a result of the promotion of the trademark. Article 1708.7 stipulates the term of trademark protection of 10 years, renewable for terms of not less than 10 years when conditions for renewal have been met, which is longer than the seven years stipulated in Article 18 of the TRIPS Agreement. Article 1708.8 of NAFTA provides an uninterrupted period of at least two years for non-use, unless valid reasons based on the existence of obstacles to such use are shown by the trademark owner, and examples are indicated justifying non-use which is independent of the right holder, such as import restrictions on, or other government requirements for, goods or services identified by the trademark. This period is shorter than the three years that is provided by TRIPS Article 19. Article 1708.14 of NAFTA provides what the TRIPS Agreement does not, ie, that 'Each Party shall refuse to register trademarks that consist of or comprise immoral, deceptive or scandalous matter, or matter that may disparage or falsely suggest a connection with persons, living or dead, institutions, beliefs or any Party's national symbols, or bring them into contempt or disrepute.'

Concerning patents, NAFTA introduces a tighter discipline in the grant and enjoyment of patents in Article 1709.8, which provides that a Party may revoke a patent only when: (a) grounds exist that would have justified a refusal to grant the patent; or, (b) the grant of a compulsory license has not remedied the lack of exploitation of the patent, whereas TRIPS Article 32 does not restrict the grounds for revocation or invalidity of patents. NAFTA also limits the scope of certain exceptions to the rights of patent holders. Article 34.1 of the TRIPS Agreement concerns the burden of proof for process patents, in the purposes of civil proceedings in respect of the infringement of the rights of the patent owner (referred to in paragraph 1(b) of Article 28). It states that the judicial authorities shall have the authority to order the defendant to prove that the process to obtain an identical product is different from the patented process and that any identical product when produced without the consent of the patent owner shall, in the absence of proof to the contrary, be deemed to have been obtained by the patented process: (a) if the product obtained by the patented process is new; or, (b) if there is a substantial likelihood that the identical product was made by the process and the owner of the patent has been unable through reasonable efforts to determine the process actually used.[9] Article 1709.11 of NAFTA, by contrast, allows either (a) or (b) above to establish that the allegedly infringing product was made by a process other than the patented process.

---

[9] Art 34.2 provides that: 'Any Member shall be free to provide that the burden of proof indicated in paragraph 1 shall be on the alleged infringer only if the condition referred to in subparagraph (a) is fulfilled or only if the condition referred to in subparagraph (b) is fulfilled.'

Article 1709.3 of NAFTA offers the same options concerning the exceptions to patentable subject matter[10] to the Parties, as do Articles 27.2 and 27.3(a)(b) of the TRIPS Agreement. As for the term of patent protection, however, Article 1709.12 of NAFTA, in the second sentence, provides for patent term extensions due to regulatory delays, which the TRIPS Agreement does not.

Regarding compulsory licensing, NAFTA provisions are similar to those in the TRIPS Agreement, with however, slightly more restrictive conditions with respect to the unauthorised use of the 'first patent' by the holders of second patents, which cannot be exploited without infringing 'the first patent' in Article 1709.10(l).[11] Furthermore, Article 1710 of NAFTA concerning layout designs of semiconductor integrated circuits (in paragraph 5) prohibits compulsory licensing of layout designs of integrated circuits. In contrast, the TRIPS Agreement permits such licensing under the conditions delineated in Article 31. For semiconductor technology, Article 31(c) of the TRIPS Agreement limits the grounds for compulsory licences only for public non-commercial use or to remedy anticompetitive practices determined after judicial or administrative processes. NAFTA has a specific rule for public authorities regarding liability[12] and Article 1715.7 provides for what is not in the TRIPS Agreement, ie, where: 'a Party is sued with respect to an infringement of an intellectual property right as a result of its use of that right or use on its behalf, that Party may limit the remedies available against it to the payment to the right holder of adequate remuneration in the circumstances of each case, taking into account the economic value of the use.'

NAFTA clarifies the definition of trade secret, which in the TRIPS Agreement is referred to as 'undisclosed information'. Article 1711.1 concerning trade secrets states the conditions on which they are protected, namely:

(a) the information is secret in the sense that it is not, as a body or in the precise configuration and assembly of its components, generally known among or readily accessible to persons that normally deal with the kind of information in question;

[10] Art 1709.3 NAFTA stipulates: 'A Party may also exclude from patentability: (a) diagnostic, therapeutic and surgical methods for the treatment of humans or animals; (b) plants and animals other than micro-organisms; and (c) essentially biological processes for the production of plants or animals, other than non-biological and microbiological processes for such production. Notwithstanding subparagraph (b), each Party shall provide for the protection of plant varieties through patents, an effective scheme of sui generis protection, or both.'

[11] Art 31(l) of TRIPS, by comparison, permits compulsory licensing, with the following supplementary conditions in addition to those delineated in Art 31 TRIPS: '(i) the invention claimed in the second patent shall involve an important technical advance of considerable economic significance in relation to the invention claimed in the first patent; (ii) the owner of the first patent shall be entitled to a cross-licence on reasonable terms to use the invention claimed in the second patent; and (iii) the use authorized in respect of the first patent shall be non-assignable except with the assignment of the second patent to permit the exploitation of another patent except as a remedy for an adjudicated violation of domestic laws regarding anticompetitive practices.'

[12] Art 1715 of NAFTA exempts public authorities and officials from liability to appropriate remedial measures where actions are taken or intended in good faith in the course of the administration of such laws.

(b) the information has actual or potential commercial value because it is secret; and

(c) the person lawfully in control of the information has taken reasonable steps under the circumstances to keep it secret.

Article 1711.2 further elaborates on these conditions: 'A Party may require that to qualify for protection a trade secret must be evidenced in documents, electronic or magnetic means, optical discs, microfilms, films or other similar instruments.'

Article 1711.3 explicitly mentions that there is no time limit to the protection of trade secrets.[13] Article 1711.4 provides safeguards against abusive protection of trade secrets, and states: 'No Party may discourage or impede the voluntary licensing of trade secrets by imposing excessive or discriminatory conditions on such licenses or conditions that dilute the value of the trade secrets.'

Concerning regulated pharmaceutical or agricultural chemicals products, NAFTA provides that if product patent protection is unavailable, administrative protection must be available for such products for the unexpired term of the patent (Article 1709.4). Articles 1711.5, 1711.6, and 1711.7 NAFTA concern the protection of test data submitted to regulatory authorities that the TRIPS Agreement refers to vaguely in Article 39.3. Article 39.3, defines the scope of data to be protected, merely as 'undisclosed test or other data, the origination of which involves a considerable effort'. Article 1711.5 of NAFTA explains that the data in question is undisclosed test or other data 'necessary to determine whether the use of such products is safe and effective' and where 'the origination of such data involves considerable effort' except where 'the disclosure is necessary to protect the public or unless steps are taken to ensure that the data is protected against unfair commercial use.' Article 1711.5, together with Article 1711.6 of NAFTA, stipulate the obligation of Parties not only to protect against disclosure of the data of persons making such submissions, but ensure that 'no person other than the person that submitted [the data] may, without the latter's permission, rely on such data in support of an application for product approval during a reasonable period of time after their submission' (ie, 'non-reliance', in the vocabulary of pharmaceutical companies – see chapters 4 and 13). The NAFTA, therefore, provides for the protection of 'data exclusivity'. Further, in the first sentence of Article 1711.7, NAFTA, unlike the TRIPS Agreement, defines the reasonable period of protection to be 'not less than five years from the date on which the Party granted approval to the person that produced the data for approval to market its product, taking account of the nature of the data and the person's efforts and expenditures in producing them.' Article 1711.7 of NAFTA states the starting point from which the protection of data exclusivity, the date of the first marketing approval relied on. Then, in the second sentence of Article 1711.7, NAFTA refers to the compatibility of its own provisions relat-

---

[13] Art 1711.3 NAFTA: 'No Party may limit the duration of protection for trade secrets, so long as the conditions in paragraph 1 exist.'

ing to data exclusivity and the abbreviated generic medicines' entry conditions, on the basis of bioequivalence and bioavailability studies.

Concerning enforcement procedures, NAFTA provides the rules relating to evidence, in Articles 1714 (general provisions), 1715 (specific procedural and remedial aspects of civil and administrative procedures), 1716 (provisional measures), 1717 (criminal procedures and penalties), 1718 (enforcement of intellectual property rights at the border), in more detail than the TRIPS Agreement does. A notable difference between the two treaties is that Article 1716.2(c) of NAFTA enumerates the matters which must be considered by the judicial authorities in determining the kind of provisional measures to be taken.[14]

Thus, most NAFTA provisions are simply clearer or more detailed than the corresponding TRIPS provisions, but some of them set a relatively higher level of IP protection. In the cases where NAFTA provides for TRIPS-minus standards, for the three Members of the NAFTA, the TRIPS provisions prevail. Article 103 of NAFTA refers to the 'existing rights' and obligations with respect to the Parties under the General Agreement on Tariffs and Trade and other agreements to which Parties adhere. Paragraph 2 of the same Article adds that the NAFTA provisions prevail to the extent of the inconsistency, except as otherwise provided in the Agreement, in the event of any inconsistency between NAFTA and such other agreements. In paragraph 1(a) of Annex 1701.3 concerning intellectual property conventions, Mexico is held to make every effort to comply with the substantive provisions of the 1978 or 1991 International Convention for the Protection of New Varieties of Plants (UPOV) as soon as possible, and no later than two years after the date of signature of the NAFTA Agreement.

II 'TRIPS PLUS' PROVISIONS IN THE POST-2000 US FTAS

The United States has 17 FTAs (including multilateral FTAs with a group of countries) [15] as of 30 September 2010. Since 2000, the following FTAs have been negotiated and signed, most of which have entered into force: with Jordan (signed 24 October 2000; entry into force 17 December 2001), Singapore (6 May 2003; 1 January 2004), Chile (6 June 2003; 1 January 2004), Morocco (15 June 2004; 1 July 2005), Australia (18 May 2004; 1 January 2005), the Dominican Republic and Central America (CAFTA-DR, the Central American countries being Costa Rica, El Salvador, Guatemala, Honduras, and Nicaragua) (signed 5 August 2004), Bahrain (14 September 2004; 1 August 2006), Oman (19 January 2006; 1 January 2009), Peru (12 April 2006; 1 February 2009), Colombia (signed 22 November 2006), Panama (signed 28 June 2007), and the Republic of Korea

---

[14] According to NAFTA, the judicial authorities must consider whether 'any delay in the issuance of such measures is likely to cause irreparable harm to the right holder, or there is a demonstrable risk of evidence being destroyed', which is not included in Art 50.3 TRIPS concerning provision measures.

[15] http://www.ustr.gov/trade-agreements/free-trade-agreements.

(KORUS, signed 30 June 2007). In 2004, the US started negotiating FTAs with Thailand and the South African Customs Union (SACU). However, these negotiations stalled. Negotiations to create a Free Trade Areas of the Americas (FTAA), a single free trade area among 34 countries of the Americas, began in December 1994. These have also encountered obstacles.[16]

Among certain US industries, approaches to IPRs have undergone considerable changes since the Uruguay Round. First of all, not all the industries actively involved in the Uruguay Round negotiations maintained their interest in strengthened IPR protection. 'Pro-patent' companies such as IBM, HP and General Electric gradually employed more subtle approaches to the issue, as appropriate (see chapter 1).

The software industry's concern with IPR enforcement against piracy seems to have increased. Business Software Alliance (BSA), for example, requested that Singapore provide administrative protection and the Republic of Korea implement the FTA provisions while the KORUS remains non-ratified.[17] Meanwhile, BSA has intensified campaign activities in Asian countries to promote awareness of copyright protection.[18]

The motion picture and recording industries' keen interest in strengthened global copyright protection occasionally conflicts with the interests of electronics hardware companies, since this could reduce sales of their hardware. Hardware industries also tend to oppose the levy system, which collects royalties from purchasers of recordable media such as CDs and DVDs. The levy system has developed to compensate private copies that are permitted by copyright laws, such as 17 USC § 1008. Since individual collection of royalties from such private use is practically impossible, intermediaries, such as the Alliance of Artists and Recording Companies for featured artists and copyright owners, and Harry Fox Agency for publishers, collect levies and distribute them among the right holders, normally through collecting societies. Whereas industries tend to oppose the levy system,[19] right holders support it.

Research-based pharmaceutical companies and biotech ventures have continued to insist on incorporating, in the IP chapter of the US FTAs, the disciplines for global IPR protection that they did not succeed in including in the TRIPS Agreement, or TRIPS provisions which were not sufficiently detailed or clear.[20]

---

[16] www.ftaa-alca.org/alca_e.asp.

[17] Business Software Alliance, *2008 BSA Year in Review* (Washington DC, BSA, 2009) 10–11.

[18] In 2008 BSA launched 'B4USurf' campaign in Singapore, Taiwan, China, Malaysia, and Philippines, ibid 8.

[19] BSA's position on this issue is available at http://w3.bsa.org/eupolicy/Copyright-and-Intellectual-Property.cfm and www.eabc.org/media/bsa-eabc_position_on_drm_and_levies.html.

[20] The pharmaceutical industry became sensitive to the use of confidential data, seeing a judicial case which supported the registration of a similar product even before the expiration of exclusivity period: *Bayer Inc v Canada (Attorney General)* [1999] 1 FC 553, decided by the Supreme Court of Canada (see ch 4).

A General Provisions

All US FTAs affirm at the outset, in general provisions, that these FTAs are consistent with the disciplines of FTAs in Article XXIV of GATT (1994) and Article V of the General Agreement on Trade in Services (GATS), and that the Parties reaffirm their existing rights and obligations under existing bilateral and multilateral agreements to which both countries are Party, including the WTO Agreement. The IP Chapters of these US FTAs reiterate national treatment[21] and the transparency principle as part of the general provisions.[22] The transparency principle for the IP Chapters of the US FTAs impose, on the Parties, the obligation that all laws, regulations, and procedures concerning the protection or enforcement of IPRs are in writing and published.[23] Article 63.1[24] concerning transparency in Part V (Dispute Prevention and Settlement) of the TRIPS Agreement, in contrast, does not refer to the obligation for these national rules and procedures to be 'written'.

The General Provisions section of US FTAs also enumerates previously enacted treaties,[25] which the Parties should ratify or accede to, including those which the US has not ratified, such as the Patent Law Treaty of 2000.[26]

---

[21] In the US FTAs, the meaning of national treatment is, as in the TRIPS Agreement, a 'treatment no less favourable than it accords to its own nationals with regard to the protection and enjoyment of such intellectual property rights and any benefits derived from such rights.' With respect to secondary uses of phonograms by means of analogue communications and free-to-air radio broadcasting, however, US FTAs provide that a Party may limit the rights of the performers and producers of the other Party to the rights its persons are accorded in the territory of the other Party, based on the principle of reciprocity.

[22] eg, Singapore Art 19.3.1, Chile Art 17.1.12, Morocco Art 15.11.1, CAFTA-DR Art 15.1.14 and Bahrain Art 14.1.11.

[23] eg, according to Art 17.1.12 of the US-Singapore FTA, 'with the object of making its protection and enforcement of intellectual property rights as transparent as possible, each Party shall ensure that all laws, regulations, and procedures concerning the protection or enforcement of intellectual property rights shall be in writing and shall be published, or where such publication is not practicable, made publicly available, in a national language in such a manner as to enable governments and right holders to become acquainted with them.'

[24] Art 63.1 of the TRIPS Agreement on transparency provides that: 'laws and regulations, and final judicial decisions and administrative rulings of general application, made effective by a Member pertaining to the subject matter of this Agreement (the availability, scope, acquisition, enforcement and prevention of the abuse of intellectual property rights) shall be published, or where such publication is not practicable made publicly available, in a national language, in such a manner as to enable governments and right holders to become acquainted with them. Agreements concerning the subject matter of this Agreement which are in force between the government or a governmental agency of a Member and the government or a governmental agency of another Member shall also be published.'

[25] Examples include the Patent Cooperation Treaty (1970), the Budapest Treaty on the International Recognition of the Deposit of Micro-organisms for the Purposes of Patent Procedure (1980), the Convention Relating to the Distribution of Programme-Carrying Signals Transmitted by Satellite (1974), the Trademark Law Treaty (1994) and the International Convention for the Protection of New Varieties of Plants (UPOV, 1991).

[26] US FTAs refer also to those WIPO Recommendations adopted after 1995, including the Joint Recommendation Concerning Provisions on the Protection of Well-Known Marks (1999 see ch 5); Jordan Art 4.1(a), Singapore Art 16.1.2(b), Chile Art 17.2.9.

B Trademarks

The Chile-US FTA (Article 17.2.1) and CAFTA-DR FTA (Article 15.2.1) integrate sound marks as a mandatory subject matter, and scent as an optional one. Many US FTAs prohibit the denial of trademark registration solely on the grounds that the sign of which it is composed is a sound or a scent.[27] Protection of well-known marks is also provided for in all US FTAs.[28]

Internet-related IP referred to in the US FTAs includes domain names.[29] In order to address the problems of trademark cyber-piracy, the US FTAs require that a Party's country-code top level domain (ccTLD) provide a dispute procedure based on the uniform domain-name policy (UDP), and online public access to a database of contact information (see Singapore FTA Article 16.3(2); Chile Article 17.3.2; Morocco Article 15.4.2; Australia Article 17.3.2; CAFTA-DR Article 15.4.2; Bahrain Article 14.3.2; Oman Article 15.3.2; Peru Article 16.4.2; Colombia Article 16.4.2; Panama Article 15.4.2; and KORUS Article 18.3.2, except US-Jordan FTA).[30]

C Copyright and Related Rights

All the US FTAs (except US-Jordan FTA) prolong the term of protection for a literary and artistic work (including a photographic work), performance or phonogram,[31] by the specified method to calculate the term.

[27] Morocco Art 15.2.1, Australia Art 17.2.2, Bahrain Art 14.2.1, Oman Art 15.2.1, Colombia Art 16.2.1 and KORUS Art 18.2.1.

[28] Jordan Art 4.8, Singapore Art 16.2.4, Chile Art 17.2.6, Morocco Art 15.2.6, Australia Art 17.2.6, CAFTA-DR Art 15.2.5, Bahrain Art 14.2.6, Oman Art 15.2.6, Peru Art 16.2.6, Colombia Art 16.2.6, Panama Art 15.2.4, and KORUS Art 18.2.7. Referral to the Recommendation on the protection of well-known trademarks (1999) also obliges Chile, Jordan and Singapore to protect such trademarks.

[29] Although not currently classified as a form of intellectual property, intellectual property issues relating to the Internet domain name system (DNS) are generally treated as trademark, rather than copyright issues. According to WIPO, '. . . domain names as identifiers function in a manner similar to trademarks, and recent developments in the DNS and in connection with the Internet Corporation for Assigned Names and Numbers (ICANN), established to coordinate the DNS, raise significant issues for the intellectual property system.' (WIPO, 'Intellectual Property on the Internet: A Survey of Issues' (2002). http://www.wipo.int/copyright/en/ecommerce/ip_survey/chap3.html#3c

[30] eg, US-Bahrain FTA, Art 14.3.1 stipulates: '1. Each Party shall require that the management of its country-code top-level domain (ccTLD) provide an appropriate procedure for the settlement of disputes, based on the principles established in the Uniform Domain-Name Dispute-Resolution Policy (UDRP), in order to address the problem of trademark cyber-piracy.'

[31] If calculated on the basis of the life of a natural person, the term shall be not less than the life of the author and 70 years after the author's death; and on a basis other than the life of a natural person, the term shall be not less than 70 years from the end of the calendar year of the first authorised publication of the work, performance, or phonogram or, failing such authorised publication within 50 years from the creation of the work, performance, or phonogram, not less than 70 years from the end of the calendar year of the creation of the work. The TRIPS Agreement, by contrast, stipulates a minimum term of 50 years calculated on the life of a natural person and refers to Art 9.1 TRIPS, referring to Arts 7 and 7 *bis* of the Berne Convention (for other than a photographic work or a work of applied art, no less than 25 years). Art 12 TRIPS stipulates a term of protection of no less than 50 years of a work (other than a photographic work or a work of applied art), if calculated on a basis

In addition to those rights and enforcement means that are found in NAFTA or TRIPS, US FTAs introduce the obligations and responsibilities for a series of new or extended subjects of protection, restrain the scope of exceptions and strengthen enforcement measures, particularly in regard to Internet-related copyright or 'related rights'. These probably reflect ongoing technological changes, but since agreement was reached in the US-Bahrain FTA in 2004, these enforcement measures have been either significantly extensive, or more detailed, particularly in US-Australia.

US FTAs, with the exception of the US-Jordan FTA, include provisions relating to the protection of encrypted satellite signals. The US FTAs with Singapore (Article 16.1.1), Morocco (Article 15.8.1), Bahrain (Article 14.7.1), Oman (Article 15.7.1) and Peru (Article 16.8.1) made it a criminal offence to manufacture and trade in these tools and to 'receive or further distribute' such signals. The Chile-US FTA (Article 17.8.1(b)) defines all these acts in terms of either civil or criminal liability and states that the right holder or person holding an interest in the encrypted signal must prove that the act was done wilfully, to subject the offender to civil liability.

Those US FTAs concluded after the year 2000 reflect the US software and copyright industries' particular concerns about Internet piracy.[32] These FTAs create liability and provide specific remedies for those who circumvent the technological measure[33] that controls access to a protected work, performance, phonogram, or other subject matter, as well as for those who manufacture, provide, or sell devices, products, or components to do so (Jordan Article 4.13; Singapore, Article 16.4(7)(c); Chile, Article 17.7(5); Morocco Article 15.5.8(a); Australia Article 17.4.7(a); CAFTA-DR Article 15.5.7(a); Bahrain Article 14.4.7(a); Oman Article 15.4.7(a); Peru Article 16.7.4(ii); Panama Article 15.5.7(ii); and KORUS Article 18.4.7(a)).

The US attaches importance to anti-circumvention obligations which are incorporated in both the 1996 WIPO Copyright Treaty (WCT)[34] and the

---

other than the life of a natural person, 'from the end of the calendar year of authorized publication, or, failing such authorized publication within 50 years from the making of the work, 50 years from the end of the calendar year of making'. On the protection of performers, producers of phonograms and broadcasting organisations, Art 14.5 TRIPS accords no less than 50 years computed from the end of the calendar year in which the fixation was made or the performance took place. The term of protection for broadcasting organisations is at least 20 years from the end of the calendar year in which the broadcast took place.

[32] See eg, countries' PC software piracy rates found in BSA (n 19) 5.

[33] eg, US-Singapore FTA Art 16.4(7)(b) defines 'effective technological measure' as 'any technology, device, or component that, in the normal course of its operation, controls access to a protected work, performance, phonogram, or other protected subject matter, or protects any copyright.'

[34] Art 11 of the WCT (ch 2 n 12), entitled 'Obligations concerning Technological Measures', establishes a general principle that 'Contracting Parties shall provide adequate legal protection and effective legal remedies against the circumvention of effective technological measures that are used by authors in connection with the exercise of their rights under this Treaty or the Berne Convention and that restrict acts, in respect of their w orks, which are not authorized by the authors concerned or permitted by law.'

Performances and Phonograms Treaties (WPPT).[35] However, the obligation is expressed in general language, and protection details are left to be dealt with through national law. These obligations were enacted in the US in the 1998 Digital Millennium Copyright Act (DMCA).[36] In the US FTA, the act of knowingly[37] circumventing, without authorisation of the right holder or law, through any effective technological measure that controls access to a protected work, performance, or phonogram, is civilly liable and, in certain circumstances criminal. There is, however, a variation according to the specific partner country of each FTA on the elements constituting the act of anti-circumvention, for example, whether or not the act is wilful. The prohibition of technological circumvention is not without limits in US domestic case law. Non-DMCA public interests are considered by US courts.[38]

Civil remedies and criminal liabilities for the infringement of protection of rights management information are also mandated in Singapore (Article 16.4.8), Chile (Article 17.7.6), Morocco (Article 15.5.9), Australia (Article 17.4.8), CAFTA (Article 15.5.8), Bahrain (Article 14.4.8), Oman (Article 15.4.8), Peru (Article 16.7.5), Colombia (Article 16.7.5), Panama (Article 15.5.8) and KORUS (Article 18.4.8), but not found in the US-Jordan FTA.

US FTAs also prohibit the re-transmission of television signals (whether terrestrial, cable, or satellite) on the Internet without the authorisation of the right holder of the content of the signal (see for example, Article 16.4.2 (b) of the US-Singapore FTA). This occurs except for traditional, free-to-air (ie, non-interactive) broadcasting and other limitations to this right for such broadcasting activity, as a result of each Party's national laws.

Aside from agreeing on these provisions aimed at adapting IP protection to the era of digital technologies, the US FTAs oblige the Parties to accede to the WIPO Copyright Treaty (1996) and WIPO Performances and Phonographs Treaty (1996). The US FTAs also enumerate those earlier treaties,[39] which the

---

[35] Art 18 of the WPPT (ch 2 n 10), entitled 'Obligations concerning Technological Measures', provides that: 'Contracting Parties shall provide adequate legal protection and effective legal remedies against the circumvention of effective technological measures that are used by performers or producers of phonograms in connection with the exercise of their rights under this Treaty and that restrict acts, in respect of their performances or phonograms, which are not authorized by the performers or the producers of phonograms concerned or permitted by law.' The US ratified the WCT and the WPPT on 14 September 1999.

[36] Enacted on 20 October 1998 and signed into law on 28 October 1998 as Public Law 105-304. Chapter 12 relates to Copyright Protection and Management Systems and provides in s 1201 for circumvention of copyright protection systems; s 1202, integrity of copyright management information; s 1203, civil remedies; s 1204, criminal offences and penalties; and s 1205, a savings clause.

[37] According to the US-Chile FTA in fn 23 of Art 17.8, 'knowledge may be demonstrated through reasonable evidence taking into account the facts and circumstances surrounding the alleged illegal act.'

[38] The Chamberlain Group, Inc v Skylink Technologies, Inc 381 F 3d 1178 (Fed Cir 2004), August 31, 2004 decided; Lexmark International, Inc v Static Control Components, Inc 387 F 3d 522 (6th Cir 2004), 26 October 2004.

[39] Examples include the Patent Cooperation Treaty (1970), the Budapest Treaty on the International Recognition of the Deposit of Micro-organisms for the Purposes of Patent Procedure (1980), the Convention Relating to the Distribution of Programme-Carrying Signals Transmitted by Satellite

Parties should ratify or accede to, including those which the US has not ratified, such as the Patent Law Treaty of 2000.[40]

D 'Certain Regulated Products'

The US FTAs contain those provisions relating specifically to patent protection and regulatory approval processes for the safety and efficacy of pharmaceutical or agricultural chemical products.

As does NAFTA, US FTAs (with the exception of the US-Jordan FTA) mandate the extension of patent terms, equal to delays caused by regulatory approval processes of up to five years. The US FTAs with Singapore, Morocco and Bahrain delimit the scope of experimental manufacturing and sales, and establish the 'linkage' between patent status and drug approval. They also link the status of patents and marketing approval in the original country to marketing approval in the FTA partner country where the drug approval is requested, and oblige regulatory authorities to make available to the patent-owner, the identity of any third party requesting marketing approval during the term of the patent (Jordan Article 4.23, Singapore Article 16.8.4, Chile Article 17.10.2, Morocco Article 15.10.4, Australia Article 17.10.4, CAFTA-DR Article 15.10.2, Bahrain Article 14.9.4, Oman Article 15.9.4, Peru Article 16.10.4, Colombia Article 16.10.4, Panama Article 15.10.4 and KORUS Article 18.9.5).

In Article 39.3 of TRIPS, as we have seen in chapters 4, 5 and 13, it can be interpreted to mean that: (i) the data submitted to regulatory authorities may not be considered as intellectual property over which the owner has exclusive rights; (ii) the obligation imposed on regulatory authorities to protect data against unfair commercial use may concern a narrow scope of data; and (iii) there is no obligation on the regulator not to rely on the originator's data on efficacy and safety for examining the later third party submission of the same data for marketing approval of the same medicines. Against this interpretation of Article 39.3 of TRIPS, US FTAs clarify that the data in this context means 'undisclosed test or other data necessary to determine whether the use of such products is safe and effective'; the origination of which involves considerable effort except where 'the disclosure is necessary to protect the public or unless steps are taken to ensure that the data is protected against unfair commercial use'. In all US FTAs, the Parties have the obligation of non-disclosure as well as 'non-reliance' for a period of five years from the date of the marketing approval for pharmaceutical products, and

---

(1974), the Trademark Law Treaty (1994) and the International Convention for the Protection of New Varieties of Plants (UPOV, 1991).

[40] US FTAs refer also to the Recommendations adopted after 1995, including: the provisions on the protection of well-known trademarks (1999); trademarks licences (2000); and provisions on the protection of marks and other industrial property rights in signs on the Internet (2001). Negotiation processes initiated after 1995 include Substantive Patent Law Treaty and reform of the Patent Cooperation Treaty.

10 years for agricultural chemical products. The US seems to have attempted to overhaul the ambiguities and omissions of Article 39.3 of the TRIPS Agreement by re-instituting its own model of data exclusivity in its FTAs. Alternatively, some governments and academics argue that the requirements of Article 39.3 should be interpreted in a way that reduces the cost of medicines in developing countries.[41]

In mandating data exclusivity protection, the US FTAs define the term 'new product' from the point of view of the regulatory authorities that approve drugs, which is not the same as the 'novelty' requirement for patentability. The IPR Group of the Industry Trade Advisory Committee (ITAC-15)[42] explains that the US interprets the term 'new chemical entity' in TRIPS Article 39.3 based on the regulatory definition of a 'new product', ie, a product that does not contain a chemical entity that had been previously approved in the country for use in a pharmaceutical or agricultural chemical product. Thus, for the US, the FTA provisions on data exclusivity only clarify the intent of the US negotiations during the Uruguay Round, and do not impose any additional obligations beyond those contained in TRIPS Article 39.3.

The US FTAs with Australia, Bahrain and CAFTA-DR stipulate that data exclusivity of at least three years is given to the data submitted for medicines which are considered 'new' due to the new use or formulation of known medicines which do not contain new active pharmaceutical ingredients (API). The data exclusivity period commences from the date of marketing approval by regulatory authorities, either from the third country or the Party's territory, whichever is later. Furthermore, when drug approval is requested on the basis of the test data used for obtaining approval of the same or similar drug in another country, the Party shall defer the date of any such approval to third Parties not having the consent of the Party providing the information in the other country, for at least five years from the date of approval for a pharmaceutical product, and 10 years from the date of approval for an agricultural chemical product. In addition to the obligation of 'non reliance', the US FTA with Colombia imposes a second set of obligations on the Parties to restrict terminating the data protection period with the expiration of the underlying patent (Article 16.10.2). It obliges Colombia to issue a new regulation to govern such data, and excludes concepts like 'undisclosed' data, 'considerable effort,' or 'unfair commercial use' which are found in Article 39.3 of the TRIPS Agreement. The US seems to have tried to overhaul the unintended outcome of the Uruguay Round negotiations to link the protection of clinical test data to unfair competition law in Article 39.3 TRIPS. For example, Article 15.10(1)(a) of the CAFTA-DR stipulates that the originator company, in order to prevent third parties from relying on its data,

---

[41]   See chs 4 and 13.

[42]   The Industry Trade Advisory Committees (ITACs) is one of the 28 advisory committees jointly administered by the Department of Commerce and the United States Trade Representative (USTR). The advisory committee system was established by the US Congress in 1974; www.ustr.gov/about-us/intergovernmental-affairs/advisory-committees. ITAC's composition has been criticised by civil society groups for the lack of representation of citizens' groups.

does not have to prove unfair commercial practices on the part of the third party. In CAFTA-DR, the rigour of the rules concerning data exclusivity is somewhat toned down. In this case, exclusivity is given from the date of approval only in the country of the Party, and not in another country. CAFTA-DR also qualifies that it is the obligation of Parties to protect the test data against disclosure, 'except where necessary to protect the public'.

E Enforcement

The enforcement provisions of the US FTAs relating to copyright and related rights (piracy) and trademark (counterfeit) are designed to provide effective deterrents against IPR infringement. For example, US FTAs: add penalties in those situations where neither the infringer nor the right holder is identified; require the imposition of fines irrespective of the injury suffered by the right holder; specify the conditions under which the authorities order that the prevailing right holder shall be paid the court costs or fees and reasonable attorney's fees by the infringing Party, setting the methods of calculating damages; and supplement the conditions of seizure and destruction of infringing goods, which are not necessarily clear in the TRIPS Agreement. The burden of proof for copyright infringement is placed on the defending Party, ie, the defendant has the obligation to show that works in question are in the public domain (Jordan Article 4.27, Singapore Article 16.9.6, Chile Article 17.11.6, Morocco Article 15.11.4, Australia Article 17.11.4, CAFTA-DR Article 15.11.5, Bahrain Article 14.10.4, Oman Article 15.10.4, Peru Article 16.11.5, Colombia Article 16.11.5, Panama Article 15.11.5 and KORUS Article 18.10.3).

US FTAs have provisions relating to the remedies for the enforcement of intellectual property during civil judicial procedures. For example, the judicial authority to order damages adequate to compensate for the right holder's injury and, at least in copyright or related rights and trademark cases, profits of the infringer. Injury must be calculated based on the suggested retail price, or other equivalent or legitimate measure of value (Jordan Article 4.24, Singapore Article 16.9.8, Chile Article 17.11.8, Morocco Article 15.11.6, Australia Article 17.11.6, CAFTA-DR Article 15.11.7, Bahrain Article 14.10.6, Oman Article 15.10.6, Peru Article 16.11.7, Colombia Article 16.11.7, Panama Article 15.11.7, and KORUS Article 18.10.5). Damages, therefore, do not necessarily have to be based on the entire market value (EMV), but only compensatory.[43]

Whether the EMVs should be used in calculating the 'reasonable royalty' has been discussed heavily in the US. Recent US case law sometimes requires that damages be limited to the proven number of instances of actual infringement.[44] However, case law is mixed, and certain high-tech and financial industries, such as the Coalition for Patent Fairness (CPF), support the recent Bill (S 515 and

[43] *Lucent Techs Inc v Gateway Inc* 580 F Supp 2d 1016 (SD Cal 2008).
[44] *Dynacore Holdings Corp v US Philips Corp* 363 F 3d 1263 (2004), also referred by *Lucent Techs*.

HR.1260) which limits the EMV rule. On the other hand, biotech and pharmaceutical industries, such as the Coalition for 21st Century Patent Reform, supports the EMV rule.

Statutory 'pre-established' damages are provided for civil judicial cases involving copyright or related rights and trademarks under US FTAs (Singapore Article 16.9.9, Chile Article 17.11.9, Morocco Article 15.11.7, Australia Article 17.11.7, CAFTA-DR Article 15.11.8, Bahrain Article 14.10.7, Oman Article 15.10.7, Peru Article 16.11.8, Colombia Article 16.11.8, Panama Article 15.11.8, and KORUS Article 18.10.6), although these are not found in the US-Jordan FTA. Under US case law, statutory damages serve as a sanction to deter future infringement, and are not duplicative of the compensatory damages award.[45]

US FTAs, except the US-Jordan FTA, mandate the judiciary to have the authority to order the infringer to provide information regarding the third Party involved in the infringement (Singapore Article 16.9.13, Chile Article 17.11.13, Morocco Article 15.11.11, Australia Article 17.11.11, CAFTA-DR Article 15.11.12, Bahrain Article 14.10.11, Oman Article 15.10.11, Peru Article 16.11.12, Colombia Article 16.11.13, Panama Article 15.11.12, and KORUS Article 18.10.10). Rules concerning the penalties to be imposed on third party infringement are not mandated by US FTAs, but are instead left to national law. In the US itself, case law is not yet clear on the conditions and the scope of the so-called contributory infringement.[46]The FTA provisions attempt, rather, to consolidate the information infrastructure enabling the right holder to enforce their rights against such third parties.

The US FTAs which were concluded after 2000 provide a clearer meaning for the standards set out in the TRIPS Agreement. For example, Article 61 of TRIPS concerning criminal procedures and penalties is 'brief and flexible', according to the WTO Panel Report in *China–Intellectual Property Rights* (see chapter 7). In Article 61, the acts subject to criminal procedures and penalties should cover at least those 'cases of wilful trademark counterfeiting or copyright piracy on a commercial scale'. US FTAs provide a definition of 'wilful copyright piracy on a commercial scale' that includes infringing acts that do not have 'a profit-motive or commercial purpose but which cause damage', such as the act of posting infringing material on the Internet. According to the US-Australia FTA in Article 17.1.26(a), and the US-Singapore FTA in Article 16.9.21, criminal procedures and penalties are applied to: (i) significant wilful infringements of copyright that have no direct or indirect motivation of financial gain; and

---

[45] *St Luke's Cataract and Laser Institute, PA v Sanderson* 573 F 3d 1186 (11th Cir 2009).

[46] The Supreme Court (*Metro-Goldwyn-Mayer Studios Inc v Grokster Ltd* 125 US 2764) unanimously expressed the view that 'One who distributes a device with the object of promoting its use to infringe copyright . . . going beyond a mere distribution with the knowledge of the third-party action, is liable . . . for the resulting acts of infringement by the third parties using the device, regardless of the device's lawful uses.' However, two judges out of the five denied the contributory infringement in this case, because of 'a significant future market for noninfringing uses.' These judges based their judgment on the *Betamax* case, where the contributory infringement was denied due to the 'significant noninfringing use': *Sony Corp of America v Universal City Studio Inc* 464 US 417 (1984). The scope of the *Betamax* case and its relation to the above case is not clear-cut.

(ii) wilful infringements for the purposes of 'commercial advantage or financial gain'. The US-Bahrain FTA (Article 14.10.28), CAFTA-DR (Article 15.26(a)(b)), Peru (Article 16.11.28), and KORUS (Article 18.10.26, 27(a)–(f), 28) broaden the scope of application, even to cases of absent wilful trademark counterfeiting or copyright piracy to include: (a) the knowing trafficking in counterfeit labels affixed or designed to be affixed to a phonogram, to a copy of a computer program or to documentation or packaging for a computer program, or to a copy of a motion picture or other audiovisual work; and (b) the knowing trafficking in counterfeit documentation or packaging for a computer program. The ITAC[47] to the USTR and the Department of Commerce explains that this concept of piracy is critical and that this provision seeks to reach one of 'the most serious problems for right holders globally – the failure of judges or other enforcement authorities to actually impose penalties at a level that effectively deters further infringements'.[48] The US-CAFTA-DR and US-Morocco, US-Bahrain and US-Oman FTAs refer to the obligation of the FTA Parties to create 'policies and guidelines' (including sentencing guidelines) that encourage the imposition of deterrent penalties.

Against circumvention of technical devises to protect copyrighted works, the US FTAs provide extensive civil remedies such as provisional measures that sustain the burden of proving that such an entity was not aware and had no reason to believe that its acts constituted a prohibited activity (Morocco Article 15.11.14, CAFTA-DR Article 15.11.14, Bahrain Article 14.10.14, Oman Article 15.10.14, KORUS Article 18.10.13). However, this does not apply in the cases of non-profit libraries, archives, educational institutions and public non-commercial broadcasting entities).

Further, US FTAs establish the liability of those who, for the circumvention of technological devices against unauthorised use or who provide such devices, as well as the obligations of service providers to cooperate with right holders, concerning the unauthorised storage and transmission of copyrighted materials.[49] US FTAs have also introduced active regulations concerning government acquisition, management and use of computer software, which should only be authorised by the right holder (Jordan Article 4.15, Singapore Article 16.4.9, Chile Article 17.7.4, Morocco Article 15.5.10, Australia Article 17.4.9, CAFTA Article 15.5.9, Bahrain Article 14.4.9, Oman Article 15.4.9, Peru Article 16.7.6, Colombia Article 16.7.6, Panama Article 15.5.9, and KORUS Article 18.4.9).

---

[47] See n 42.

[48] Advisory Committee Report to the President, the Congress and the United States Trade Representative on the U.S.-Colombia Trade Promotion Agreement Prepared by the Industry Trade Advisory Committee on Intellectual Property Rights (ITAC-15); www.ustr.gov/sites/default/files/uploads/agreements/fta/colombia/asset_upload_file605_9835.pdf.

[49] At the same time delineating limitations on the scope of remedies available against service providers for copyright infringements that they do not control, initiate or direct (Singapore Art 16.9.22, Chile Art 17.11.23, Morocco Art 15.11.28, Australia Art 17.11.29, CAFTA-DR Art 15.11.27, Bahrain Art 14.10. 29, Oman Art 15.10.29, Peru Art 16.11.29, Colombia Art 16.11.29, Panama Art 15.11.27, and KORUS Art 18.10.30).

F Patents

All US FTAs, like Article 27.1 of the TRIPS Agreement, stipulate that each Party 'shall make patents available for any invention, whether a product or a process, in all fields of technology, provided that the invention is new, involves an inventive step, and is capable of industrial application.' Articles 1709.2 and 1709.3 of NAFTA allow Parties to exclude from the patentable subject matter what is provided for in Articles 27.2 and 27.3 (a) and (b) of the TRIPS Agreement. Those US FTAs which were concluded after NAFTA, by contrast, extend the scope of patentable subject matter by limiting possible exclusions. For example, the US-Singapore FTA stipulates in Article 16.7.1 that 'Each Party may exclude inventions from patentability only as defined in Articles 27.2 and 27.3(a) of the TRIPS Agreement ie, (i) 'inventions, the prevention within their territory of the commercial exploitation of which is necessary to protect *ordre public* or morality, including to protect human, animal, or plant life or health or to avoid serious prejudice to the environment, provided that such exclusion is not made merely because the exploitation is prohibited by law'; and (ii) 'diagnostic, therapeutic, and surgical methods for the treatment of humans and animals'. The option of excluding from the patentable subject matter (i) plants and animals (other than microorganisms) and (ii) essentially biological processes for the production of plants or animals (as opposed to non-biological and microbiological processes for such production), provided for in Article 27.3 (b) of the TRIPS Agreement or in Articles 1709.2 and 1709.3 of NAFTA, is not included in Article 16.7.1 of the US-Singapore FTA. Exceptionally, however, this type of biotech exclusion limitation is not stipulated in the US FTA with Jordan. Likewise, the US FTA with Chile provides for plants to be excluded from patentability, subject to future development.[50]

Like NAFTA, later US FTAs provide for the adjustment of the term of a patent to compensate for unreasonable delays that occur in granting the patent.[51] The extension of the term of protection includes a delay in the issuance of the patent of more than four years (Bahrain, KORUS, Morocco, Singapore, Oman, and Australia) and five years (Chile and CAFTA) from the date of filing of the application in the Party country, or three years after a request for examination of the application has been made, whichever is later.

As in Article 1709.8 of NAFTA, the US FTAs (except the US-Jordan FTA) limit revocation of patents to the cases when grounds exist that would have justified a refusal to grant the patent, for example, 'fraud in obtaining a patent may con-

---

[50] US-Chile FTA, Art 17.9. 2: 'Each Party will undertake reasonable efforts, through a transparent and participatory process, to develop and propose legislation within 4 years from the entry into force of this Agreement that makes available patent protection for plants that are new, involve an inventive step, and are capable of industrial application.'

[51] Singapore Art 16.7.7, Chile Art 17.9.6, Morocco Art 15.9.7, Australia Art 17.9.8, CAFTA-DR Art 15.9.6, Bahrain Art 14.8.6, Oman Art 15.8.6, Peru Art 16.9.6, Colombia Art 16.9.6, Panama Art 15.9.6 and KORUS Art 18.8.6.

stitute grounds for revocation or cancellation'(Chile Article 17.9.5, footnote 24). It is sometimes explicitly provided in the treaty (for example in Article 15.9.4 of the US-CAFTA-DR FTA) that fraud, misrepresentation, or inequitable conduct may be the basis for revoking, cancelling, or holding a patent unenforceable.

Article 6 of the TRIPS Agreement excludes the question of the exhaustion of rights from dispute settlement, except provisions of Articles 3 and 4 (chapter 5). The Doha Declaration on the TRIPS Agreement and Public Health, by contrast, largely reformulated Article 6 and stated that 'The effect of the provisions in the TRIPS Agreement that are relevant to the exhaustion of intellectual property rights is to leave each member free to establish its own regime for such exhaustion without challenge, subject to the MFN and national treatment provisions of Articles 3 and 4', whatever the legal nature of this Declaration (chapter 9).[52] The US FTAs with Jordan, Singapore and Australia, but not with Chile, prohibit international exhaustion for patents, if the patentee has proven its intention to restrict its sales outside the territory. For example, according to the US-Australia FTA (Article 17.9.4), 'Each Party shall provide that the exclusive right of the patent owner to prevent importation of a patented product, or a product that results from a patented process, without the consent of the patent owner shall not be limited by the sale or distribution of that product outside its territory, at least where the patentee has placed restrictions on importation by contract or other means.'

Further, the US FTAs narrow the scope of exceptions allowed to the rights conferred to the right holder, or to the effects of the patent. Thus, in the US-Jordan (Article 4.20), US-Australia (Article 17.9.7) and US-Singapore (Article 16.7.6) FTAs, but not the US-Chile FTA, the grounds on which to permit 'the use of the subject matter of a patent without the authorisation of the right holder' (compulsory licence) are restricted, except (a) to remedy a practice determined after judicial or administrative process to be anticompetitive under the Party's laws relating to prevention of anti-competitive practices, or (b) in cases of public non-commercial use, or of national emergency, or other circumstances of extreme urgency. Additionally, the US-Singapore and US-Australia (although not US-Jordan) FTAs stipulate three conditions for public non-commercial use and compulsory licensing for national emergency/urgency. One of these conditions is that the Party may not require the patent-owner to provide undisclosed information or technical know-how related to a patented invention that has been authorised for such use.

G TRIPS/GATT Rules Applicable to TRIPS-plus Provisions

According to the first sentence of Article 1.1 of the TRIPS Agreement, Members are required to comply with the minimum standards for the protection of IPRs. The second sentence of Article 1.1 provides that Members may choose to

---

[52] The Doha Declaration on the TRIPS Agreement and Public Health (WT/MIN(01)/DEC/2, 20 November 2001) para 5(d).

implement laws which give 'more extensive protection' than is required in the agreement, 'provided the additional protection does not contravene the provisions of the Agreement' (chapter 5).

In general, 'more extensive protection' refers to the extended term or scope of protection or narrower exceptions. For example, the period of patent protection may be extended or the scope of patentable subject matter enlarged. 'More extensive protection' may also mean extending the rights conferred to the right holders of the categories of IP covered by TRIPS through laws, regulations, final judicial decisions and administrative rules of general application relating to availability, scope, acquisition or enforcement. 'Extended protection' would also include procedural rules and various administrative and judicial measures facilitating the examination/grant process and maintaining the validity of IPRs, as well as civil, administrative and criminal procedures strengthening the defence of right holders. Qualifications such as 'more' or 'less', however, could be subjective. They are based on the TRIPS standards which, in turn, depend on the interpretation of TRIPS provisions which diverge widely, even if the same method of interpretation based on the customary rules of international law, as practiced by the WTO dispute settlement organs, is applied. Furthermore, higher or lower standards by themselves do not imply any value judgment as to whether or not their content is appropriate. The TRIPS standards have the merit of having been accepted by all WTO Members, but their interpretations differ and the appropriateness of the standards has been disputed, as we have seen in this book. The concept of 'flexibilities' originates mainly from these discussions and is often meant to reduce the TRIPS requirements by interpretation (unlike the use of the concept by the WTO dispute settlement organs). The discussions using the criteria of TRIPS 'plus' or 'minus' may not bear fruit,, if there is no common understanding or rules about the base-line, the limits of 'flexibilities' that treaty interpretation allows, or the criteria for judging their values.

Article 1.2 provides that: 'for the purpose of this Agreement, the term "intellectual property" refers to all categories of intellectual property that are the subject of Sections 1 through 7 of Part II', which includes copyright and related rights, trademarks, trade names,[53] geographic indication, industrial design, patent, integrated circuits and undisclosed information. Members are therefore not likely to violate the TRIPS provisions by creating new rights not covered by the TRIPS (although they could be scrutinised under other WTO Agreements). One example of such rights may be domain names.

The TRIPS Agreement does not cover certain new technological fields such as internet-related copyright protection, technical protection measures, internet service provider liability, etc, although the WIPO Internet Treaties were concluded in 1996.[54] With the evolution of digital technology, copyright industry had to respond to the infringements of digital versions of their content, and so

---

[53] *United States–Section 211 Omnibus Appropriations Act of 1998*, Appellate Body Report (adopted 1 February 2002) WT/DS176/AB/R paras 336–41.

[54] See above nn 34 and 35.

does the public. As we have seen, the TRIPS Agreement is silent or only implicit regarding reverse engineering, because reverse engineering is allowed generally under patent laws (unless software patents are involved) and treated divergently under national laws relating to trade secrets (chapters 4 and 5). Hence, there is interest in and the need for a rule concerning the access to and uses of digital forms of copyright at different levels. It is another matter whether the DMCA[55] rule is proportionate, rational and optimum given its objectives and its various impacts. Samuelson and Scotchmer consider that the DMCA gives no incentive for content providers to moderate their prices and little incentive to employ effective technical measures.[56] Better rules could have probably have been proposed but this would not justify rejecting anti-circumvention measures merely because they are 'TRIPS plus'. The substance of 'TRIPS plus' provisions should be evaluated its their own right and with facts.

If a WTO Member accords 'more extensive protection' bilaterally to another Member regarding those IPRs covered by the TRIPS Agreement, the additional protection must not contravene the provisions of the Agreement. Within the GATT, there is a particular discipline for customs unions and free trade agreements in Article XXIV. However, the TRIPS Agreement does not contain such a discipline and, as TRIPS is not a *lex specialis* of the GATT 1994, this GATT provision does not seem to apply to IPR provisions in FTAs.

Article 4 of the TRIPS Agreement, on the other hand, delineates the principle of most favoured-nation treatment (MFN). Article 4 TRIPS provides that: 'With regard to the protection of intellectual property, any advantage, favour, privilege or immunity granted by a Member to the nationals of any other country shall be accorded immediately and unconditionally to the nationals of all other Members.' Unlike the GATT, this TRIPS provision concerns nationality-based measures relating to the protection of IPRs. The Appellate Body held that sections 211(a)(2) and 211(b) of the US law violated the MFN obligations under the TRIPS Agreement because, under the definition of 'designated national' in the US regulations, an 'original owner' who is Cuban is subject to the measures at issue, whereas a non-Cuban 'original owner' is not.[57] The MFN principle of the TRIPS Agreement contains a grandfathering clause in Article 4(d) and therefore does not apply to the IPR provisions of the agreements entered into force prior to the entry into force of the WTO Agreement, provided that such agreements are notified to the Council for TRIPS and do not constitute an arbitrary or unjustifiable discrimination against nationals of other Members. The IPR provisions in the NAFTA Agreement, for example, seem to fall under the grandfathering exception of Article 4(d). The meaning of 'any advantage, favour, privilege or immunity' may not always be clear. For example, a requirement to use both the mother language and English for patent application will not be an advantage to

---

[55] See above n 36.

[56] P Samuelson and S Scotchmer, 'The Law and Economics of Reverse Engineering' (2002) 111(7) *Yale Law Journal* 1639–49.

[57] *US–Section 211 Appropriation Act* Appellate Body Report (n 53) para 319.

certain other Members. In fact, some 'TRIPS plus' provisions in the IPR provision in the FTAs fall under Article 4 TRIPS whereas others do not, depending on the wording and the content of the provision.

On the other hand, certain ways and means of IPR enforcement in the provisions at higher protection standards may conflict with relevant TRIPS provisions. There may also be other provisions of WTO-covered agreements, as well as intellectual property treaty provisions incorporated in the TRIPS Agreement which may be of relevance to WTO Members' 'TRIPS plus' standards of IPR protection. For example, such measures may violate GATT provisions if they are not justified by Article XX(d). In *EU and a Member State–Seizure of Generic Drugs in Transit*,[58] Brazil and India requested consultations over the conformity of the European Communities Council Regulation 1383/2003 (and other measures) to the provisions stipulated in Part III of the TRIPS Agreement, entitled 'Enforcement of Intellectual Property Rights', as well as to Articles V and X of the GATT 1994. Article V of the GATT requires WTO Members not to hinder traffic in transit by imposing unnecessary delays or restrictions or by imposing unreasonable charges.

EU Regulation 1383/2003 delineates rules for customs actions against goods suspected of infringing IPRs, including patent rights,[59] such as the seizure of these goods including goods in transit. Article 51 requires that WTO Members adopt procedures allowing trademark and copyright owners to prevent counterfeit trademark and pirated copyright goods from entering the markets through the seizure of such goods at the border. Footnote 13 of Article 51 indicates that there is no obligation for Members to establish such border procedures for parallel traded goods or goods in transit. This implies, however, that WTO Members are allowed to apply certain border measures in certain ways to goods in transit, including goods suspected of infringing patents.[60] Part III of the TRIPS Agreement relating to enforcement stipulates certain principles of procedural rules against IPR enforcement constituting 'barriers to legitimate trade' and 'abuse of IPR enforcement'. For example, Article 41(1) provides that enforcement procedures should be applied 'in such a manner as to avoid the creation of

---

[58] *EU and a Member State–Seizure of Generic Drugs in Transit*, Request for consultations by India (19 May 2010) WT/DS408/1; Request for consultations by Brazil (19 May 2010) WT/DS409/1.

[59] By virtue of Council Reg (EC) 2913/92 of 12 October 1992 establishing the Community Customs Code, the procedures delineated in Reg 1381/2003 apply to goods in transit and to goods suspected of infringing the following IPRs: (i) a patent under that Member State's law; (ii) a supplementary protection certificate of the kind provided for in Council Reg (EEC) 1768/92(1) or Reg (EC) 1610/96 of the European Parliament and of the Council (2); (iii) a national plant variety right under the law of that Member State or a Community plant variety right of the kind provided for in Council Reg (EC) 2100/94(3); (iv) designations of origin or geographical indications under the law of that Member State or Council Regs (EEC) 2081/92(4) and (EC) 1493/1999(5); and, (v) geographical designations of the kind provided for in Council Reg (EEC) 1576/89(6).

[60] On the question of the principle of territoriality of patent rights, goods in transit and Art 5-*ter* of the Paris Convention (limited exception to infringements of patented devices forming part of vessels, aircraft, or land vehicles), see N Pires de Carvalho, *The TRIPS Regime of Patent Rights* (3rd edn) (Alphen aan den Rijn, Kluwer Law International, 2010) 80–83.

barriers to legitimate trade and to provide for safeguards against their abuse'. Article 41(2) refers also to the principle of 'fair and equitable' procedures and states that enforcement procedures should not be 'unnecessarily complicated or costly, or entail unreasonable time-limits or unwarranted delays'. The meaning of 'legitimate trade' and 'abuse', which were important concepts in the Uruguay Round negotiations (chapter 4), is not defined in the TRIPS Agreement or in the GATT and would therefore require thorough analyses of the relevant agreements. Whether and to what extent the EU measures in question constituted barriers to the trade of goods lawfully placed on and circulating in the market would be evaluated against the facts of the case.

The extent to which measures strengthening IPRs beyond the TRIPS level may or may not be subject to non-violation complaints, in the sense of Article XXIII(b) of GATT 1949, will depend on the decision of the Ministerial Conference relating to the scope and modalities for non-violation complaints based on Article 64(3) of the TRIPS Agreement.

III. MASSIVE CRITICISMS

'TRIPS plus' provisions in the US FTAs, described above, have provoked extensive criticism not only among civil society groups and academics both in and outside the US, but also among US policy-makers, as self-interested pursuit of US industries. The impacts of the TRIPS Agreement on access to medicines had been discussed intensely from 1999 through to 2003, before agreement was reached at the WTO on the paragraph 6 system (see chapter 9) on 30 August 2003. Parallel to these discussions, criticisms against the IP provisions in the US FTAs mounted, particularly against those FTA provisions which regulate the entry of generic medicines. They are, notably, the extended protection of patent rights, the 'non-reliance' principle and the cross-border effects of market exclusivity based on the test data submitted to drug approval authorities, the linkage between the market approval of medicines by regulatory authorities and the patent status of the medicines concerned, and the coordination of marketing approval with foreign approval of medicines.

Several members of the US Congress actively questioned the IP provisions of the US FTAs. For example, on 15 July 2004, SS Levin and some other members of Congress addressed a letter to the USTR, to which the latter and the Moroccan Ambassador to the US replied in detail.[61] On 7 June 2005, Representative HA

[61] The letter by R Zoellick, the US Trade Representative at that time, on 19 July 2004 includes the argument that the US-Morocco FTA is consistent with the Doha Declaration which does not prohibit limiting parallel imports. According to the letter, the US FTA adopts the law of the party concerning exhaustion. Thus, Morocco prohibited international exhaustion before the signing of the FTA, whereas Chile and Bahrain did not. The US FTAs with Chile and Bahrain, therefore, do not limit parallel imports. Data protection has the potential of facilitating and accelerating access to medicines. The Moroccan law does not approve generic versions of medicines based on approvals in other countries and therefore their entry is predicated upon the approval of the original medicines.

Waxman released a report entitled 'Trade Agreements and Access to Medications under the Bush Administration'.[62] These criticisms related to the idea that US trade agreements, by delaying approval of affordable generic drugs, impede the rights of developing countries to acquire essential medicines at affordable prices and by imposing strict conditions on compulsory licensing and parallel imports. US negotiations on extended IPR protections in the FTAs went side-by-side with the worldwide debate on the access to medicines which led to the Doha Declaration on the TRIPS Agreement and Public Health. Criticisms of IP provisions in the US FTAs emphasised that they amount to restricting the 'flexibilities' which exist in the TRIPS Agreement.

US civil society groups urged US policy-makers to take into account a wider range of views than just the narrow industry view, particularly in the Industry Trade Advisory Committee on Intellectual Property Rights (ITAC-15) which the USTR is required by Congress to call on.[63]

In 2002, the UK Commission on Intellectual Property Rights adopted a Report which[64] examined the 'TRIPS plus' provisions in the US FTA agreements, and warned that:

> it would be unwise to let IP policy be influenced principally by domestic industrial and commercial interest groups in developed countries, whose view of what is appropriate for developing countries is very much coloured by their perception of their own interest. Governments from developed countries need to form their own view, in the light of all the evidence, as to how the interests of development in developing countries and their own commercial interests can best be reconciled.[65]

Some foreign governments were critical. France, for its part, seems to have been displeased by the US agreement with Morroco. At the 15th International AIDS Conference in Bangkok in 2004, France's representative read this message from President Chirac:

> Let's avoid any unnecessary competition between multilateral and bilateral donors by acknowledging that it is the countries concerned that are primarily responsible for coordinating and leading the fight against AIDS, based on the three-unities rule: unity of national action, unity of approach and unity of assessment. Let's implement the generic

---

Data exclusivity thus provides an incentive for the originator to enter the market which may in turn expand the potential universe of generic drugs in Morocco. This development is observed in Jordan. The Ambassador on the same date replied that the Moroccan Government signed the Agreement in consideration of further economic developments in the country, and that the Agreement did not prevent compulsory licensing or parallel trade in emergencies or exporting generics under the para 6 system.

[62] www.twnside.org.sg/title2/FTAs/Intellectual_Property/IP_and_Access_to_Medicines/TradeAgreementsandAccesstoMedicationsUnderTheBushAdmini.pdf.

[63] 'USTR's Advisory Committee on Intellectual Property Rights: Public Interest Groups Still Calling for a Voice', IP Watch (4 November 2004).

[64] 'Integrating Intellectual Property Rights and Development Policy' (Report of the Commission on Intellectual Property Rights), DFID (September 2002).

[65] Report of the Commission on Intellectual Property Rights, (2002) 163. www.iprcommission.org/graphic/documents/final_report.htm.

drug agreement to consolidate price reductions. Making certain countries drop these measures in favour of bilateral trade negotiations would be immoral blackmail. . .[66]

Development NGO Oxfam urged[67] the US to refrain from imposing TRIPS-plus standards in bilateral and regional trade agreements with developing countries, called on the EU and other 'rich countries and developing countries to collectively call for an end to this practice at international forums such as the WTO and WHO', and appealed to developing countries to refuse to negotiate IP standards in FTAs.

Opposition to 'TRIPS plus' provisions took an increasingly political tone, first of all, because the IPR standards in these FTAs reflected the US intention to impose their own preferred IP protection system. Critics also asserted that these FTAs had immediate and inherently adverse effects on developing countries.

It is difficult to assess the value of these FTAs without knowing what benefits the counterparts were receiving in return for agreeing to the US demands on IPRs. Related economic effects, either positive or negative, are not easily discernible either, due to the time required for IPR provisions to take effect, particularly when they are often not enforced. Patent rights, for example, take years to be established once they are filed, and, in small countries, they may not even be filed. The implementation of these agreements and the modernisation of administrations and courts may take a long time, delaying enforcement mechanisms. It is also difficult to identify cause and effect relationships; for example, the impact of the FTA provisions on the prices of specific products is unclear. The US negotiation attitudes which may not be considerate of local situations in small, developing countries may not be difficult to establish, but the social and economic impacts of these FTAs may take longer to demonstrate.

It is in this complex context that various parties have expressed concern over access to medicines. It is certain that the US FTAs allow compulsory licensing only on limited grounds, such as for emergencies and to combat anti-competitive behaviour. This clearly restricts the provisions in Article 31 of the TRIPS Agreement, which does not restrict the grounds on which Members may issue compulsory licences.

In 2004, responding to these concerns, the USTR agreed with the FTA Parties on a 'side letter' (ie, additional agreement) on public health. The letter affirms, for each FTA, that the obligations contained in FTA IP chapters do not (i) affect the ability of either Party to take necessary measures to protect public health by promoting access to medicines for all, in particular concerning cases such as HIV/AIDS, tuberculosis, malaria, and other epidemics as well as in circumstances of extreme urgency or national emergency, or (ii) prevent the utilisation of the TRIPS/health solution, namely, the paragraph 6 system established by

---

[66] Message from M Jacques Chirac, President of the Republic, read by M Xavier Darcos, Minister Delegate for Cooperation, Development and Francophony, to the participants of the fifteenth International AIDS Conference, Bangkok, 13 July 2004. On the French position, interview, Ministry of Overseas Cooperation, Paris, 6 June 2004.

[67] 'Undermining access to medicines: Comparison of five US FTA's: A technical note', June 2004.

the Decision of the General Council of 30 August 2003 (Morocco,[68] Bahrain,[69] CAFTA-DR[70]).[71]

On 10 May 2007, the USTR obtained agreement from the Congressional leadership for the US FTA negotiations.[72] However, consideration for the Doha Declaration became increasingly an important condition for the USTR in obtaining understanding and approval from the US legislature. For the FTAs to integrate, within IP chapters, recognition that nothing in these chapters prevents FTA partners from taking 'necessary measures to protect public health by promoting access to medicines for all' and a statement affirming mutual commitment to the 2001 Doha Declaration on the TRIPS Agreement and Public Health. Given the fact that the legal status of the Doha Declaration is unclear and that there are divergent interpretations of how the Declaration is related to the provisions of the TRIPS Agreement (chapter 9), the US could have made clearer its views on how the Declaration is related to its FTA provisions. The US could also have clarified its policy relating to the public health problems of its FTA partner countries.

At any rate, domestic interest in, and support for, pushing a strong overall level of IPR protection in the US has waned considerably since then. The purpose of concluding high-standards FTAs with small developing countries was unclear from the beginning, but increasingly, diverse elements came to be taken into consideration, which could be a way of integrating these FTAs in local realities. Significantly, the US took into account the concerns of Peru and Colombia regarding biodiversity protection in the context of the US FTAs with these countries. Thus, the US-Peru FTA, which entered into force on 1 February 2009, is accompanied by the 'Understanding regarding biodiversity and traditional knowledge,' which was agreed upon on 12 April 2006.[73]

---

[68] 15 June 2004.

[69] 14 September 2004.

[70] 5 August 2004.

[71] The side letters add that, if an amendment of the TRIPS Agreement enters into force with respect to the parties and a party's application of a measure in conformity with that amendment violates this Chapter, the parties shall immediately consult in order to adapt this Chapter as appropriate in the light of the amendment. This understanding is integrated in Art 18.11, parags 1 and 2, of KORUS. www.ustr.gov/assets/Trade_Agreements/Bilateral/Republic_of_Korea_FTA/Draft_Text/asset_upload_file273_12717.pdf. In the KORUS there are other side letters relating to medicines. www.mofat.go.kr/mofat/fta/eng_0707/2E66(e).pdf.

[72] http://waysandmeans.house.gov/Media/pdf/110/05%2014%2007/05%2014%2007.pdf.

[73] According to the Understanding with Peru (http://www.ustr.gov/sites/default/files/uploads/agreements/fta/peru/asset_upload_file719_9535.pdf) and Colombia (http://www.ustr.gov/sites/default/files/uploads/agreements/fta/colombia/asset_upload_file953_10182.pdf), the Parties recognize the importance of: traditional knowledge and biodiversity, as well as the potential contribution of traditional knowledge and biodiversity to cultural, economic, and social development; obtaining informed consent from the appropriate authority prior to accessing genetic resources under the control of such authority; equitably sharing the benefits arising from the use of traditional knowledge and genetic resources; and promoting quality patent examination to ensure the conditions of patentability are satisfied. The Parties endeavor to seek ways to share information that may have a bearing on the patentability of inventions based on traditional knowledge or genetic resources by providing: publicly accessible databases that contain relevant information; and an opportunity to cite, in writing, to the appropriate examining authority prior art that may have a bearing on patentability.

The same Understanding was concluded with Colombia, on 22 November 2006.[74]

It is not entirely comprehensible, from the effectiveness point of view, why the US seeks to impose very high standards on extremely small markets through its FTAs. It may be because these small countries could play an important trading role at the borders of important producer countries in stopping counterfeit and pirated goods. Bilateral solutions have been sought to maintain the standards which were originally expected when concluding the TRIPS Agreement in order to respond to new needs arising from advanced technologies and even to strengthen the level of IP protection.

Most likely, the US was preparing a multilateral regime for the very distant future instead of looking into the individual situation of each country. The global need for IPR protection does not necessarily depend on the level of development of each country. The US may have started to negotiate its FTA and the TRIPS Agreement to apply the same standards to all countries without taking into account local realities.

If developed countries aim to establish a global system of IPR protection, they should normally be explaining why, despite the diversity of economic and technological situations, it would be better to have a global system and what kind of global system would be globally optimal, and be helping low-income developing countries to work towards such a system. It seems that the US and probably other developed countries are not sufficiently explaining or assisting these categories of less-developed countries in building the scientific and technological bases which would make IPR protection meaningful for these countries. Developed countries may not have even conscious of the impacts of a global IPR system for developing countries. This may be a weakness in the global endeavour.

In today's controversial discussions on IPR protection, all actors need to prove, more factually, how strengthening or weakening IPR protection could be beneficial in developing countries in extremely divergent situations. However, in the situation where political and public opinion believe that the weakness of the Doha Declaration is its insufficient implementation, and that it is necessary to further enlarge the scope of exceptions to intellectual property, there may be little incentive for any party to clarify these issues. If anything, further discussions may lead to further arguments for weakening of IPRs. In this particular context, developed countries have no choice but to use the flexibilities offered by Article 1.1, which says that countries are free to have a higher standard of IPR protection.

Roffe and Vivas point out that:

Even though [FTAs] consolidate important market access opportunities in developed countries, experts and civil society groups have expressed concern that the TRIPS plus

---

[74] D Vivas-Eugui and M J Oliva, 'Biodiversity Related Intellectual Property Provisions in Free Trade Agreements', ICTSD, Issue Paper No.4, 2010) 6.

provisions in these agreements raise many implementation challenges in terms of policy coherence and ultimately reduce opportunities to use the flexibilities built into the TRIPS.[75]

Thus, TRIPS plus provisions narrow the options which the TRIPS Agreement and its 'flexibilities' offer for reducing the level or the scope of IPR protection. Setting aside the fact that agreed-upon FTA provisions are presumably policy options chosen by the parties, the evaluation of those 'TRIPS plus' provisions in bilateral agreements becomes complex. In the absence of clear rules defining and interpreting the scope of 'TRIPS flexibilities', standard-lowering flexibilities are pitted against standard-raising ones that the US and other developed countries are using, faced with level- or scope-reducing TRIPS flexibilities. Whereas these flexibilities of developed countries are heavily criticised, these developing countries are also proposing TRIPS plus measures to modify the TRIPS Agreement, such as the proposed Article 29*bis* concerning the disclosure of the origin of biological resources and/or associated traditional knowledge about biological material.[76] Some developing country national laws also have TRIPS plus provisions. For example, China's IPR border measures administrative order allows the right holders to apply for an injunction when he or she discovers goods suspected of infringing his or her IP rights and the court can order a preliminary injunction or other property preservation measures relating to all categories of IPR and prohibit the import or export of goods in violation of those rights.[77] These TRIPS plus measures are considered good for these countries. Today, complex structures and layers of TRIPS interpretations seem to have developed around TRIPS flexibilities, which differ for each party. They may also differ from the 'flexibility' of TRIPS provisions as the dispute settlement body would understand them. Would each party understand which flexibility is being referred to by other parties? For example, according to an NGO source, the proposed bilateral Economic Partnership Agreement between India and Japan includes the following Article:

---

[75] P Roffe and D Vivas, 'A Case Study on IP Technical Assistance in FTA', April 2007, ICTSD Issue Paper No 19, 2.

[76] 'Doha Work Programme – The Outstanding Implementation Issue on The Relationship between the TRIPS Agreement and the Convention on Biological Diversity', Communication from Brazil, China, Colombia, Cuba, India, Pakistan, Peru, Thailand and Tanzania, (5 July 2006) Revision WT/GC/W/564/Rev 2, TN/C/W/41/Rev 2, IP/C/W/474. According to this proposal, WTO Members must require that: patent applicants disclose the country providing the resources and/or associated traditional knowledge, from whom they were obtained, and, after reasonable inquiry, the country of origin; applicants provide information including evidence of compliance with the applicable legal requirements in the providing country for prior informed consent for access and fair and equitable benefit-sharing arising from the commercial or other utilisation of such resources and/or associated traditional knowledge. Members are also required to set up effective enforcement procedures so as to ensure compliance with these obligations; empower administrative and/or judicial authorities to prevent the further processing of an application or the grant of a patent and to revoke or render unenforceable a patent when the applicant has, knowingly or with reasonable grounds to know, failed to comply with the above obligations or provided false or fraudulent information.

[77] Article 12 of the IPR Border Measures Administrative Order (adopted on 24 March 2010, entered into force on 1 April 2010).

The Parties shall grant and ensure adequate, effective and non-discriminatory protection of intellectual property, promote efficiency and transparency in the administration of their respective intellectual property protection systems and provide for measures for adequate and effective enforcement of intellectual property rights against infringement, counterfeiting and piracy, in accordance with the provisions of this Chapter and the international agreements to which both Parties are parties.

This is exactly the same as Article 107 of the Switzerland-Japan EPA.[78] Between Switzerland and Japan, there will not be as much difference in interpreting TRIPS as between Japan and India. This is due to their fairly common understanding of the overall objectives for intellectual property protection. However, there may not be certainties as to the scope of flexibilities and the margin of discretion that the above paragraph allows to India and Japan in interpreting their agreement. During the negotiations, the phrase 'international agreements to which both Parties are parties' was replaced by the words 'the TRIPS Agreement'. This was probably done to limit vast uncertainties in interpreting IPR provisions by excluding those international agreements whose subject matter may have only remote cause-and- effect relations with IPRs.

---

[78] Agreement on Free Trade and Economic Partnership between Japan and the Swiss Confederation (February 2009).

Part VI

Interpreting TRIPS for Innovation

15

Recasting the Debate on Intellectual Property Rights

THE DOHA DECLARATION on the TRIPS Agreement and Public Health was a symbolic and powerful statement reflecting the popular world-wide movement for access to medicines. The movement showed that patent rights do not justify denial of access and that pharmaceutical companies should not consider developing countries merely from a marketing point of view. The health-care world has become globalised, and a balance between ensuring strong patent protection and safeguarding patient access to patented medicines has become difficult to strike.

The Doha approach to intellectual property came to lead subsequent discussions among various international organisations on other issues, such as development and transfer of technology and, more recently, within the United Nations Framework Convention on Climate Change (UNFCCC).[1] For the access to climate change mitigation and adaptation technologies, TRIPS 'flexibilities' (particularly those relating to compulsory licensing, limitations and exceptions to patent rights and exclusion from patentability), have been sought on behalf of

---

[1] The United Nations Conference on Environment and Development (UNCED), known as the Earth Summit, was held in Rio de Janeiro from 3 to 14 June 1992. The Summit promoted the text of the UNFCCC, elaborated by the Intergovernmental Negotiating Committee and opened for signature on 9 May 1992. The UNFCCC entered into force on 21 March 1994 and as of 1 November 2010, has 192 parties. Its principal update, to assess progress in dealing with climate change, the Kyoto Protocol (184 parties), was agreed upon in 1997 at the Conferences of the Parties (COP) 3 which established legally binding obligations for developed countries to reduce their greenhouse gas emissions (GHG) and rules for national inventories and removals of GHG emissions, which were used to create the 1990 benchmark levels for accession of Annex I countries to the Kyoto Protocol. The Secretariat (UNFCCC in Bonn) is supported by the Intergovernmental Panel on Climate Change (IPCC) and aims to gain consensus through meetings and the discussion of various strategies. On 3 and 15 December 2007, in Bali, an agreement on a timeline and structured negotiation on the post-2012 framework (the end of the first commitment period of the Kyoto Protocol) was achieved with the adoption of the Bali Action Plan (Decision 1/CP.13) and the Ad Hoc Working Group on Long-term Cooperative Action under the Convention (AWG-LCA) was established. In the discussions leading to the Action Plan, IPR rules concerning climate change adaptation technologies were discussed and certain proposals such as flexibilities in international rules concerning IPRs, were made in the subsequent non-papers (such as No 36 of 2 November 2009 and No 47 of 6 November 2009) as means to facilitate the transfer of technology by certain developing countries such as Brazil, Bolivia, China, Indonesia and Tanzania. For proposals, see http://unfccc.int/documentation/items/2643.php. On the present state of discussion, see the Report of the AWG-LCA to COP 15 (FCCC/AWGLCA/2009/14).

developing countries. Most of the solutions proposed for the access to medicines problems have been similar to those proposed to increase access to different types of technologies. This has been done on the assumption that IPRs prevent access, technology transfer and research. Why the same assumption is made and the standardised solution has been followed is not entirely clear. It seems meaningful therefore to summarise the implications from 15 years of debate over IPRs and access to medicines for future considerations in the discussions on global rules relating to IPRs.

I LONG-TERM RESEARCH AND DEVELOPMENT (R&D)

A Balance

In the discussions leading up to the Doha Declaration, the idea that affordability is possible only by limiting intellectual property rights was accepted as given, while other options were not discussed. The idea of dynamic welfare through innovation was made subordinate to arguments that patents only hinder access to technologies.

The interest of long-term R&D has been left out in these discussions. The concept of 'innovation' has come to be often understood to equate with the short-term goal of producing goods cheaply. While this in itself contributes to welfare, little attention has been paid to the question of how long-term technological innovation could be achieved and accelerated globally.

Nor has much attention been paid to the actual obstacles to long-term R&D in developing countries.[2] Lack of expertise, insufficient institutional framework and lack of support for undertaking and funding biotechnology research for clinical studies are frequent obstacles, as well as insufficient information on the existing research technologies. Few companies in emerging economies would forgo short-term profits for long-term research. It is probably for this reason that the Chinese Government is re-centralising long-term R&D activities. Strengthening the legitimacy of IPR protection and eliminating barriers to entry for new local technologies and human resources would also help build local R&D infrastructure. Creating R&D infrastructure for clinical testing adapted to local needs will improve the availability of new technologies and contribute to access to medicines.

Encouraging local innovation realistically (and not simply subsidising those domestic companies close to the government) may have a real impact on develop-

---

[2] In the Asian Dialogue on Technology Transfer for Local Manufacturing Capacity of Drugs and Vaccines, organised by the UNCTAD-ICTSD with the support of the WHO and the European Union (29–30 April 2010, Kuala Lumpur), an opinion was expressed that developing countries are not interested so much on the long-term R&D for drug development, involving various phases. On the other hand, some Asian governments, including Malaysia, explained that their programmes were to strengthen science and technology education, with a view to encouraging long-term drug R&D projects.

ing-country efforts to build local businesses (chapter 11). Developing countries successful in clinical research should play a key role in regional cooperation in such research fields.

Concerns have been expressed by developing countries about the lack of R&D on the medicines for treatment of neglected diseases. The following figure shows that there are ongoing research projects. For developing drugs for HIV/AIDS, malaria and tuberculosis, 'Big Pharma'[3] is relatively active, but for other truly neglected diseases, unknown, unexpected researchers are more active. Their main difficulty is a lack of funds to undertake clinical studies and information, particularly on available research tools such as animal models for a particular virus. The WHO Expert Working Group on Research and Development Financing recently published a report entitled 'Research and Development – Coordination and Financing', emphasising the importance of coordination among researchers.[4] This solution seems to be a little removed from the realities of R&D, and from the obstacles that researchers actually face.

Table 15.1: PCT Patent Filing Publication References to Neglected Diseases (Database: MICROPAT (IPC-A61K, 1991–2000, 51,267 cases)

	Total	Big Pharma 10
HIV/AIDS	3263	573
Tuberculosis	419	33
Malaria	533	108
Leishmania	146	6
Onchocerciasis	3	0
Chagas Disease	50	1
Leprosy	155	2
Schistosomiasis	31	4
Lymphatic Filariasis	2	0
African Tripanosomiasis	38	1
Dengue	83	9

Source: H Yamane, *Globalisation of Intellectual Property Protection* (Tokyo, Iwanami, 2008, in Japanese) 401.

II POLITICS CONTINUE

[3] The 'Big Pharma' 10 at the time of the search (2005) were: Pfizer, GSK, Merck, Astrazeneca, Aventis, Bristol-Myers Squibb, Novartis (including Sandoz and Ciba-Geigy), Eli Lilly, Hoffmann-La Roche, Abbott.

[4] www.who.int/phi/documents/RDFinancingwithISBN.pdf.

In the developed world, more and accelerated innovation is necessary, and the need for clear and well-functioning IP protection in emerging economies is increasingly expected. A balanced, factual analysis convincing projections should persuade emerging economies not only to improve their public health situations but also to engage in long-term, effective R&D with appropriate protection of IPRs.

B Tempest, former CEO of Ranbaxy, predicts that there will be two systems of IPR protection and two systems of pricing medicines in the next decade: one for developed (OECD) and one for developing countries.[5] Some differential pricing is already in place, although whether it is sufficient or based on the right principle are different questions. Two systems of IPR protection for developed and developing countries may be what many emerging economy countries are presently working toward, probably with the understanding that emerging economies are to be considered 'developing countries' in the bifurcated system of IPR protection. Based on this vision of 'two systems', a new coalition is opposing the so-called 'TRIPS plus standards' that developed countries are said to be imposing on the developing world, through a network of bilateral treaties and the Anti-Counterfeiting Trade Agreement (ACTA),[6] the text of which was finalised in November 2010. The ACTA aims to establish a plurilateral framework to strengthen domestic enforcement provisions to combat global proliferation of commercial-scale counterfeiting and piracy.

Reality, on the other hand, seems to be much more complex. This book has attempted to describe only a small fraction of these complexities. Most developing countries aspire to build knowledge and technology-based economies, and there have been local innovations. On the other hand, there are also countries where laws are not applied consistently, or enforcement is difficult. Often, the system of IPR protection is not integrated in the overall efforts of the country for scientific and technological progress. In fact, the globalised world perhaps is not bifurcated, but fragmented into countries with varying degrees of administrative and judicial capabilities to ensure that R&D efforts are more or less rewarded by some kind of effective incentive systems, such as IPR protection.

Meanwhile, new drug discovery has become more expensive, less certain[7] and riskier, due probably to ineffective R&D. Patents on many hitherto best-selling blockbusters have been expiring during the past decade and will continue to do so after 2010, often without counterbalancing launches of improved patentable

---

[5] B Tempest, 'A structural change in the global pharmaceutical marketplace' (2010) 7(2) *Journal of Generic Medicines* 115.

[6] Participants in the negotiations included: Australia, Canada, the European Union (EU, represented by the European Commission and the EU Presidency (Belgium) and the EU Member States), Japan, Korea, Mexico, Morocco, New Zealand, Singapore, Switzerland and the US.

[7] According to Grabowski and Wang, the 'number of novel medicines reaching the market' is not necessarily a measure of innovation. This number depends on regulatory criteria, and many novel medicines, unfortunately, are 'not sufficiently innovative'. Drug innovation could be measured by the number of 'high-quality' global and first-in-class new chemical entities (NCEs). HG Grabowski and YR Wang 'The quantity and quality of worldwide new drug introductions, 1982–2003' (2006) 25(2) *Health Affairs*.

second or third generation drugs.[8]

The pace of pharmaceutical innovation in emerging economies is not fast enough to save their own patients and those in poorer developing countries. Conflicts over IPRs and the opposition of views over the ways in which global rules should be conceived and enforced are likely to continue between the pro-IPR developed countries/industries and those emerging economies where the legitimacy of patent protection as innovation incentive has not yet been established for pharmaceuticals.

For developed countries, strengthening their entire system of R&D and maintaining market-based incentives for innovation will continue to be important, and, for this reason, they consider global IPR protection to be a matter of global interest. This seems to be essential for pharmaceutical R&D, because copying chemical and even biotech substances is simply too easy and other means to recoup R&D investment costs, such as 'time to market', trade secrets or know-how, do not offer protection, as they do to other sectors of technology, such as engineering, electronics etc.

The research-based pharmaceutical industry is clearly one of the major beneficiaries of patent systems that provide strong protection for patented inventions. Thus it seems important for the industry to show its commitment to serving the 'public interest' by clarifying the criteria it uses to evaluate its own patenting practices and pricing policies in countries at different levels of economic development. Research-based pharmaceutical companies have become willing to adapt their pricing policies to the needs of the poorest countries, and they should certainly do more.[9] To respond to those who want to improve infrastructure for healthcare and for pharmaceutical R&D, the industry could establish a voluntary fund for providing technical assistance for developing countries. Such a fund would have to be of real help where that help is most needed, and respond to the situations particularly where emergency or humanitarian assistance is required. Such a fund should ensure the transfer of know-how to help build medicines distribution systems or strengthen the foundations of clinical R&D, to improve access where drug prices are unaffordable. Such know how transfer (especially for R&D) could gradually persuade some countries to recognise the connection between R&D and IPRs.

The conflicts over IPRs in emerging economies may not disappear, however, as these economies will become richer during the patent life of recent and prospective new medicines.

In this politicised situation, all countries claim their system to be TRIPS consistent, and the notion of TRIPS flexibilities makes it possible to support such

---

[8] Areas where this is generally reckoned to be the outlook include hypolipidaemics like statins, anti-ulcer medicines, and antidepressants, where R&D expenditure is actually being cut by Big Pharma companies because generics represent satisfactory therapy and are not yet obsolescent; therefore new patented medicines cannot get the high market shares at premium prices that would be needed to achieve an adequate return on R&D investment.

[9] Provided there is no reflux trading into their developed markets.

claims. More factual analysis with balanced understanding and convincing projections may be needed for better international cooperation. The text of the TRIPS Agreement provides inherent flexibilities and, therefore, a certain margin of discretion to Members in interpreting TRIPS provisions within the existing legal standards of the Agreement. However, better legal security and certainty are also needed for investing in long-term research where there is a high risk of failure. In any case, the scope of flexibilities is not wider than the text of the TRIPS Agreement allows. A monolithic, super-flexibilities, ie, 'one-size-fits-all developing countries' type of flexibilities should not lead to illusory notions.

Flexibilities of the TRIPS Agreement (and the Agreement itself, for that matter) do not by themselves solve socio-economic problems, because other conditions are necessary for any IPR to have any effect on the situation on the ground. Arguing about TRIPS flexibilities and TRIPS-plus, in a new Tower of Babel, may become an excuse for not making real efforts to ensure that new technologies are developed.

III EVOLVING SITUATION SURROUNDING THE TRIPS AGREEMENT

International IPR protection, which started in nineteenth century Europe as a form of inter-governmental cooperation, evolved along with technological changes and across different economies and cultures. In the second half of the twentieth century, IPRs were used as one of the major instruments of competition among companies. The TRIPS Agreement was adopted in the context of the late twentieth century, when IPR concerns were much more important for developed countries' sustained investment in new technologies than tariff concessions, which had already been considerably achieved within the GATT. Since then, the pace of R&D was accelerated, which made possible present-day speed and volume of information over the world.

In the meantime, however, for certain industries, other incentives such as 'time to market' and trade secrets became more important for the success of innovative products than IPR exclusivity, in the technological context of the twenty-first century. For these industries, numerous IPRs held by others became a heavy burden, and the value of their own IPRs became relatively insignificant. Inventing on paper for the purpose of staging infringement law suits against manufacturers became commonplace. 'Pools' of depreciated IPRs came into existence, to sell manufactured goods for outlet markets. Thus, industry views on IPRs are diversified today, and pharmaceutical and biotech industries remain attached to IPR protection as incentives for investing in R&D.

In the climate change related technologies and pharmaceutical fields, there are significant differences in the pace of and incentives for innovation, the ease of entry and the role of patents. In the former engineering fields, other IPRs such as know-how and trade secrets are very important and appropriate forms of international cooperation differ as a consequence. Despite these differences, ready-made proposals for IPRs, derived from the access to medicines debate, have been made in the current debate on climate change mitigation and adaptation technologies. Proposals to limit the exclusive rights conferred by IPRs which have been made in the debate over access to medicines may have been standardised and become a mere negotiating tool for a wide range of technologies. This is not an encouraging sign, because facts were lacking in the first place in the debate over IPRs and access to medicines.

The TRIPS Agreement was negotiated explicitly to protect the rights of IPR holders and, at that time, there was not much discussion about the economic benefits to developing countries of developed countries' innovations (see chapter 1). Today, on the other hand, it is assumed that weaker IPR will, ipso facto, benefit developing countries' economies.

In 1942, JA Schumpeter pointed out that innovations by entrepreneurship, more than just inventions, cause old inventories, ideas, technologies, skills, and equipment to become obsolete, by introducing new means of production, new products, and new forms of organisation.[10] Even today, much more than mere invention is needed for innovation. Furthermore, for Schumpeter, competition was important, but not 'perfect competition', where all firms in an industry produce the same good, sell it for the same price, and have access to the same technology. What counts, he said, was 'competition from the new commodity, the new technology, the new source of supply, the new type of organisation . . . competition which . . . strikes not at the margins of the profits and the outputs of the existing firms but at their foundations and their very lives'. A degree of monopoly, which enables 'ever-present threat', that 'disciplines before it attacks', therefore was preferable to perfect competition.

Over-emphasising the role of IPR alone, either as a key promoter of innovation or a main obstacle to economic development, seems to lack the proper perspective.

As examined in chapter 12, a mere patentability policy is meaningless unless such a policy is implemented consistently, in a way linked to positive efforts of researchers and industry to raise their scientific and technological skills. Such investment and efforts constitute an important part of the 'absorption capacity' of a country for technology transfer. Simply manipulating the scope and level of IP protection as a policy tool, without a solid linkage with other policies to increase creative research activities and investment in human resources, may result in a waste of resources.

It seems from our exploration into the discussions on TRIPS interpretation that developing countries are seeking guaranteed results from IP protection, rather than entrepreneurship that requires investment and risk-taking in scientific and technological endeavours. This amounts to dependency on developed countries' investment and goodwill which has consistently been repudiated by developing

---

[10] JA Schumpeter, *Capitalism, Socialism and Democracy* (London, Routledge, 1994; originally published by Allen & Unwin, 1942).

countries themselves. Emerging, technologically advanced countries are able to invest in their independent, risk-taking, research-oriented efforts and establish long-term policies based on market principles. What seems to be lacking, as we have observed, is the determination to consistently implement coordinated policies that are set up, without developing countries' resources being drained to unintended places.

It is time to recast the debate to view IPR protection as an element within a larger effort to encourage knowledge creation and technological innovation through integrated national policies and international cooperation.

Index